Student Survival & Solutions Manual

SECOND EDITION
Calculus

Gerald L. Bradley ▪ Karl J. Smith

PRENTICE HALL, Upper Saddle River, NJ 07458

Executive Editor: George Lobell
Editorial Assistant: Gale A. Epps
Special Projects Manager: Barbara A. Murray
Production Editor: James Buckley
Supplement Cover Manager: Paul Gourhan
Supplement Cover Designer: Liz Nemeth
Manufacturing Buyer: Alan Fischer

 © 1999 by Prentice-Hall, Inc.
Simon & Schuster / A Viacom Company
Upper Saddle River, NJ 07458

Printed in the United States of America

10 9 8 7 6 5 4 3 2 1

ISBN   0-13-081953-0

Prentice-Hall International (UK) Limited, *London*
Prentice-Hall of Australia Pty. Limited, *Sydney*
Prentice-Hall Canada, Inc., *London*
Prentice-Hall Hispanoamericana, S.A., *Mexico*
Prentice-Hall of India Private Limited, *New Delhi*
Prentice-Hall of Japan, Inc., *Tokyo*
Simon & Schuster Asia Pte. Ltd., *Singapore*
Editora Prentice-Hall do Brazil, Ltda., *Rio de Janeiro*

CONTENTS

PREFACE

This manual was designed to help you bridge the gap between the textbook and a working knowledge of calculus. It has been said that "Mathematics is not a Spectator Sport" and this means you cannot learn calculus by simply attending class, but instead you must build a body of information that will enable you to do problem solving in the real world. I decided to entitle this supplement, *Student Survival and Solutions Manual* because I want it to be more than a Student Solution's Manual. Thirty years of teaching experience have given me the ability to anticipate the types of errors and difficulties you may have while taking this course. Here I will show you some of the steps that are left out of the text, and most all of these steps in the included problems.

There are at several things you must do if you wish to be successful with calculus:

- Attend every class.

- Read the book.
  Regardless of how clear and lucid your professor's lecture on a particular topic may be, do not attempt to do the problems without first reading the text and studying the examples. It will serve to reinforce and clarify the concepts and procedures.

- ## Problems, Problems, Problems, problems...
  You must work problems every day; work the assigned problems; work **Think Tank** problems. Look over the entire problem set (even those problems which are not assigned).

- Ask questions when you are stuck (and you will get stuck — that is part of the process).

- Keep asking questions until you receive answers that are understandable to you.

- Todays calculators and computers are good at obtaining answers, and if all that is desired is an answer, then you have relegated yourself to the level of a machine. Do not work problems to obtain answers. It is the *concepts* that are important. Even though a solutions manual is basically a "how to" document, always ask *why* a particular approach was used, and understand the concept the problem is illustrating.

The problems I have chosen to include in this manual are those problems which are typical of the problems included in the book. These problems are designated in the text by a colored problem number. I did not include **WHAT THIS SAYS**, **Think Tank**, discussion or research problems.

There are several places in this manual where we used computer software. Even though such software is, of course, optional, it can help us through much of the tedium. The output shown is from *Converge* 4.0 available from JEMware, The Kawaiahao Plaza Executive Center, 567 South King Street, Suite 178, Honolulu, Hawaii 96813. Phone: 808-523-9911.

CHAPTER 1

Functions and Graphs

SURVIVAL HINT: If your instructor does not begin with Chapter 1, you might wish to take some time looking over this chapter anyway. As you look through this first chapter you will notice that we cover calculator graphing, absolute value, trigonometry, lines, exponentials, and logarithms. Pay particular attention to the definition of a function in Section 1.3, as well as functional notation. In order to succeed in this course, you will need to be thoroughly familiar with the meaning and use of the notation $y = f(x)$. The name of this function is f and the value of f at a value x is denoted by $f(x)$. Even though all of the material of this chapter was covered in precalculus classes, you will notice that calculus is probably the first course that you take which **actually assumes** that you remember the content and ideas of previous courses.

If you purchased the textbook new, you should have found a **free** supplement entitled *Mathematics Handbook*. This book not only reviews geometry, algebra, trigonometry, curve sketching, and the conic sections, it also summarizes the ideas you will study in this course; namely limits, derivatives, integrals, and series. Finally, it contains a complete integration table. If you purchased the textbook used, you may find this supplement is missing. You can ask your bookstore to order you a copy, or you can check Amazon.com to order a copy.

Find out from your instructor what is expected of you. You will probably need a copy of this textbook, engineering paper, a straight-edge, and calculator. (By the way, the cover for your calculator makes a good straight-edge.) Put your name and phone number inside the cover of your calculator, so if you lose it, it is, at least, possible that it be returned.

As you begin on your calculus journey, Bon Voyage!

1.1 Preliminaries, Pages 12-14

SURVIVAL HINT: *Interval notation is very compact and we will use it frequently in the book. Problems 1-4 are designed to see if you are familiar with this notation.*

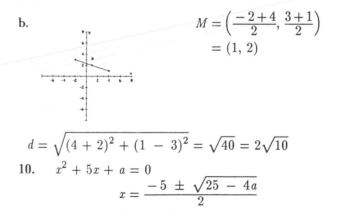

5. a.

$$M = \left(\frac{2-2}{2}, \frac{5+3}{2}\right)$$
$$= (0, 4)$$
$$d = \sqrt{(-2-2)^2 + (5-3)^2}$$
$$= \sqrt{20} = 2\sqrt{5}$$

b.

$$M = \left(\frac{-2+4}{2}, \frac{3+1}{2}\right)$$
$$= (1, 2)$$
$$d = \sqrt{(4+2)^2 + (1-3)^2} = \sqrt{40} = 2\sqrt{10}$$

10. $x^2 + 5x + a = 0$

$$x = \frac{-5 \pm \sqrt{25 - 4a}}{2}$$

Note: A calculator solution such as

$$x = \frac{-\sqrt{-(4a - 25)} - 5}{2} \text{ and}$$

$$x = \frac{\sqrt{-(4a - 25)} - 5}{2} \text{ is not considered}$$

simplified.

11. Obtain a zero on one side, and then use the quadratic formula.

$$3x^2 - bx = c$$
$$3x^2 - bx - c = 0$$
$$x = \frac{-(-b) \pm \sqrt{b^2 - 4(3)(-c)}}{2(3)}$$
$$= \frac{b \pm \sqrt{b^2 + 12c}}{6}$$

SURVIVAL HINT: *Is* $- a$ *positive or negative? Without further information we do not know. It might be neither. Be comfortable with the definition of absolute value. Especially the fact that* $- a$ *is positive when* $a < 0$.

15. $3 - 2w = 7$ or $-(3 - 2w) = 7$

$$2w = -4 \quad \text{or} \quad 2w = 10$$

$$w = -2, 5$$

You could have started with $3 - 2w = 7$ or $3 - 2w = -7$, and then proceeded as shown above.

17. $\emptyset$; (The empty set; an absolute value can never be equal to a negative number.)

Note: The TI-92 returns the answer: FALSE To see why this is correct, recall the three types of equations you studied in algebra, namely, true, false, and open. An equation

such as $5 = 5$ is true, regardless of the values of the variable; an equation such as $5 = 4$ is false, no matter what the replacement for the variable, there is no value that will make $5 = 4$; finally, an equation such as $x = 5$ is true for the replacement of 5 and false for the replacement of 4.

SURVIVAL HINT: *Most students need some review of solving trigonometric equations. Notice the logo in the text that looks like*

$$\boxed{\text{S}^\text{M}_\text{H}}$$

The techniques for solving trigonometric equations are reviewed in the handbook, and Problems 7-24 review this skill.

23.
$$\cot x + \sqrt{3} = \csc x$$
$$\cot^2 x + 2\sqrt{3} \cot x + 3 = \csc^2 x$$
$$\cot^2 x - \csc^2 x + 2\sqrt{3} \cot x + 3 = 0$$
$$-1 + 2\sqrt{3} \cot x + 3 = 0$$
$$\cot x = -\frac{\sqrt{3}}{3}$$
$$x = \frac{2\pi}{3}, \frac{5\pi}{3}$$

A check is necessary because we squared both sides: $x = 5\pi/3$ is extraneous, so the solution is: $x = \frac{2\pi}{3}$

SURVIVAL HINT: *Be careful to pay attention to the endpoints of intervals. Is the interval open, closed, or half-open? On most problems later in the text, the interval is not specified, but may be implied by the given function. For example, if*

$$f(x) = \sqrt{4 - x^2}$$

the endpoints are included, but on

$$f(x) = \frac{1}{\sqrt{4 - x^2}}$$

the endpoints are not included.

26. $5(3 - x) > 3x - 1$

$15 - 5x > 3x - 1$

$-8x > -16$

$x < 2$ Answer: $(-\infty, 2)$

29. $3 \leq -y < 8$

$-3 \geq y > -8$ *Reverse inequality*

$-8 < y \leq -3$ *Restore proper order*

Answer: $(-8, -3]$

31. $t^2 - 2t \leq 3$

$t^2 - 2t - 3 \leq 0$

$(t + 1)(t - 3) \leq 0$

Consider the factors, one at a time;

plot the critical values

determine where each factor

is positive and where it is negative.

We illustrate the procedure:

$t + 1:$
$t - 3:$

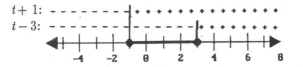

We wish the product to be negative (≤ 0), so
the part that is darkened is the part where
the product of the factors is negative.

Answer: $[-1, 3]$.

33. Read this problem as a distance function: The
distance between x and 8 is less than or equal
to 0.001. The interval is $[7.999, 8.001]$.

SURVIVAL HINT: *Problems 35-38 require that you
you remember the equation of a circle. It is assumed
that you have mastered the algebraic skill of
completing the square. If not, do some review (see
Section 2.4 of the Mathematics Handbook, for
example).*

42. $2x^2 + 2y^2 + 2x - 6y - 9 = 0$

$x^2 + x + y^2 - 3y = \frac{9}{2}$

$(x^2 + x + \frac{1}{4}) + (y^2 - 3y + \frac{9}{4}) = \frac{9}{2} + \frac{1}{4} + \frac{9}{4}$

$(x + \frac{1}{2})^2 + (y - \frac{3}{2})^2 = 7$

Circle with center $(-\frac{1}{2}, \frac{3}{2})$ and $r = \sqrt{7}$

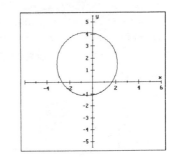

44. $\cos(\frac{7\pi}{12}) = \cos(\frac{\pi}{4} + \frac{\pi}{3})$

$= \cos\frac{\pi}{4}\cos\frac{\pi}{3} - \sin\frac{\pi}{4}\sin\frac{\pi}{3}$

$= \frac{\sqrt{2} - \sqrt{6}}{4} \approx -0.2588$

51. a. period 2π, amp 1

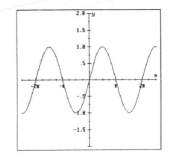

b. period 2π, amp 1

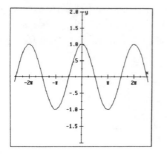

SURVIVAL HINT: *Note that the sine and cosine functions have the same shape, but are "out of phase" by $\pi/2$. Also note that in calculus work is done in radian measure. Set your calculator to radian mode and change to degree mode only when you see the degree symbol.*

c. period π

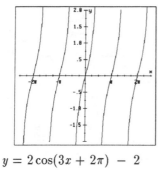

54.
$$y = 2\cos(3x + 2\pi) - 2$$
$$= 2\cos 3(x + \tfrac{2\pi}{3}) - 2$$

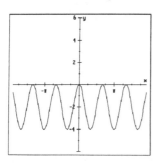

The period is $2\pi/3$.

57. Plot the given points:

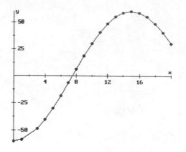

Answers vary; it looks like $(h, k) = (7.5, 0)$, $a = 60$ and the period is found by solving $30 = 2\pi/b$ so that $b = \pi/15$. A possible equation is $y = 60\sin\frac{\pi}{15}(x - 7.5)$.
$A = 0$, $B = 60$, $C = \frac{\pi}{15}$, and $D = 7.5$

1.2 Lines in the Plane, Pages 21-23

SURVIVAL HINT: *Many mistakes are made by good students, when doing material with which they are quite competent, because they try to do too much in their heads. Get into the habit NOW of showing work on all problems which could be handed in to your instructor. It is not a waste of your time to be neat and well organized and write a sufficient number of steps so that someone else could follow your work. In a job situation this will be required. Your boss will not want to see a page of scrap-work with an answer circled at the bottom!*

1. If the equation does not contain y, solve for x and draw the vertical line $x = c$. Otherwise, solve for $y = mx + b$. Plot the y-intercept $(0, b)$ and then count out the slope, m. Draw the line passing through the y-intercept and the slope point.

SURVIVAL HINT: *Generally we will not show answers to **WHAT DOES THIS SAY?** problems in* *this manual. The reason we show the answer to this one is to make sure you realize that plotting points is not the best way to be graphing lines.*

15. $x - 4y + 5 = 0$ has $m = \frac{1}{4}$ so our line must have $m = -4$. Solve the two given equations simultaneously to find their intersection at $(-1, 1)$. Now use the point and slope to find the line:

$$y - 1 = -4(x + 1)$$

$$4x + y + 3 = 0$$

22. $2x - 3y - 2,550 = 0$

$$y = \frac{2}{3}x - 850$$

$m = 2/3$

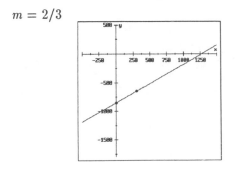

For the y-intercept, set $x = 0$: $y = -850$;

for the x-intercept, set $y = 0$: $x = 1,275$

Intercepts: $(1,275, 0)$, $(0, -850)$.

29. vertical line; no slope

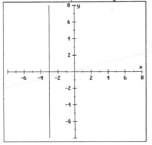

intercept: $(-3, 0)$

30.

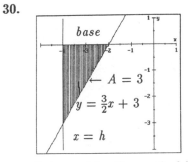

Let $x = h$ be the vertical line. The height of the triangle at $x = h$ is

$$y = \frac{3}{2}(h + 2)$$

and the area of the triangle is

$$A = \frac{1}{2}(\text{base})(\text{height})$$

$$= \frac{1}{2}(h + 2)\frac{3}{2}(h + 2)$$

Thus, when $A = 3$,

$$3 = \frac{3}{4}(h + 2)^2$$

$$4 = (h + 2)^2$$

$$h + 2 = \pm 2$$

$$h = 0, -4$$

There are two such vertical lines:

$$x = 0, \text{ and } x = -4.$$

34. $(2, 4)$

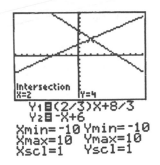

45. $(-1.9, 3.4), (-1.9, -3.4)$

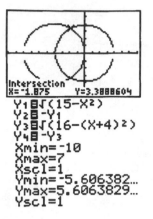

The exact solution is

$$\left(-\frac{15}{8}, \frac{7\sqrt{15}}{8}\right), \left(-\frac{15}{8}, -\frac{7\sqrt{15}}{8}\right)$$

51. Let t denote the age in years of the machinery and V be a linear function of t. At the time of purchase, $t = 0$ and $V(0) = 200,000$. Ten years later, $t = 10$ and $V(10) = 10,000$. The slope of the line through $(0, 200\,000)$ and $(10, 1000)$ is

$$m = \frac{10,000 - 200,000}{10 - 0}$$

$$= -19,000$$

Thus, $V(t) = -19,000t + 200,000$.

In particular,

$$V(4) = -19,000(4) + 200,000$$

$$= 124,000$$

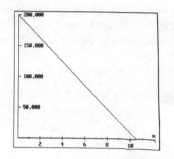

The value in 4 years is $124,000.

54. $A(1, 3), B(-1, 2)$. Let d_1 and d_2 be the distances from $P(x, y)$ to A and B, respectively. Then

$$d_1{}^2 = d_2{}^2$$

$$(x - 1)^2 + (y - 3)^2 = (x + 1)^2 + (y - 2)^2$$

$$-2x + 1 - 6y + 9 = 2x + 1 - 4y + 4$$

$$4x + 2y - 5 = 0$$

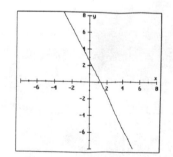

58. Let x denote the number of days since the reduced rate went into effect and $N(x)$ the corresponding number of vehicles qualifying for the reduced rate. Since the number of qualifying vehicles is increasing at a constant rate, N is a linear function of x. Since

$N(0) = 157$ and $N(30) = 247$, we have

$$m = \frac{247 - 157}{30 - 0} = 3$$

$N(x) = 3x + 157$ for $x \geq 0$. In 14 days,

$N(44) = 3(44) + 157 = 289$;

289 vehicles would qualify.

1.3 Functions, Pages 32-34

Let D represent the domain in Problems 1-12.

1. $D =$ all reals or $D = \mathbb{R}$ or $D = (-\infty, \infty)$

$$f(-2) = 2(-2) + 3$$
$$= -1$$
$$f(1) = 2(1) + 3$$
$$= 5$$
$$f(0) = 2(0) + 3$$
$$= 3$$

6. $D = (\frac{1}{2}, \infty)$

$$f(1) = [2(1) - 1]^{-3/2}$$
$$= 1$$
$$f(\tfrac{1}{2}) = [2(\tfrac{1}{2}) - 1]^{-3/2} \text{ is undefined}$$
$$f(13) = [2(13) - 1]^{-3/2}$$
$$= 25^{-3/2}$$
$$= \frac{1}{125}$$

10. $D = (-\infty, \infty)$

$$f(0) = \sin 0 - \cos 0$$
$$= -1$$
$$f(-\tfrac{\pi}{2}) = \sin(-\tfrac{\pi}{2}) - \cos(-\tfrac{\pi}{2})$$
$$= -1$$

$$f(\pi) = \sin \pi - \cos \pi$$
$$= 1$$

11. $D = (-\infty, \infty)$

$$f(3) = 3 + 1$$
$$= 4$$
$$f(1) = -2(1) + 4$$
$$= 2$$
$$f(0) = -2(0) + 4$$
$$= 4$$

SURVIVAL HINT: *Problems 13-20 involve a calculation that is required when using the definition of derivative in Chapter 2.*

15. $$\frac{f(x+h) - f(x)}{h} = \frac{5(x+h)^2 - 5x^2}{h}$$
$$= \frac{5x^2 + 10xh + 5h^2 - 5x^2}{2}$$
$$= \frac{10xh + 5h^2}{h}$$
$$= 10x + 5h$$

17. $f(x) = |x| = -x$ since $x < 0$;

$$\frac{f(x+h) - f(x)}{h} = \frac{-x - h - (-x)}{h}$$
$$= \frac{-h}{h} = -1$$

SURVIVAL HINT: *Spend some time with Problem 17. It illustrates important skills about how to deal with an absolute value. In Chapter 2 we will also calculate slopes of secant lines as a prelude to understanding the meaning of a line tangent to a curve at a given point. Problems 21-26 deal with finding the slope of a line passing through two points of a given curve.*

24. $f(1) = -5$; point is $(1, -5)$

$f(1.01) = -5.0702$; point is $(1.01, -5.0702)$

$$m = \frac{-5.0702 - (-5)}{1.01 - 1}$$

$$= -7.02$$

31. $f(x) = \dfrac{3x^2 - 5x - 2}{x - 2}$

$$= \frac{(3x + 1)(x - 2)}{x - 2}$$

$$= 3x + 1, \ x \neq 2$$

$f \neq g$ since the domains are not the same.

38. $\quad (f \circ g)(x) = f(\tan x)$

$$= \frac{1}{\tan x}$$

$$= \cot x$$

$$(g \circ f)(x) = g(\tfrac{1}{x})$$

$$= \tan \tfrac{1}{x}$$

SURVIVAL HINT: *Pay close attention to these answers. Remember,*

$$\frac{1}{\tan x} \neq \tan \frac{1}{x}$$

43. $u(x) = \tan x; \ g(u) = u^2$

48. $u(x) = \dfrac{2x}{1 - x}; \ g(u) = \tan u$

SURVIVAL HINT: *Most useful functions are compositions, and most in the text are compositions. If you are not really comfortable with these problems, spend a little extra time on them now and it will save you time later.*

53. **a.** $\quad C(25t) = (25t)^2 + (25t) + 900$

$$= 625t^2 + 25t + 900$$

b. $\quad C(75) = 75^2 + 75 + 900 = \$6,600.$

c. $\quad 11,000 = 625t^2 + 25t + 900$

$$0 = 625t^2 + 25t - 10,100$$

$$0 = 25t^2 + t - 404$$

$$0 = (25t + 101)(t - 4)$$

$$t = -\tfrac{101}{25}, \ 4$$

Negative values of time are not in the domain so $t = 4$ hours.

SURVIVAL HINT: *Notice that the technology problems 54-59 define the slope of a function as the slope of a secant line for a very small number δ. In the next chapter we will see this secant line approximates what will be defined to be a line tangent to the curve at the target value $x = 3$.*

1.4 Functions and Graphs, Pages 41-43

5. $f_5(-x) = \dfrac{1}{[(-x)^3 + 3]^2}$

$$= \frac{1}{(-x^3 + 3)^2}$$

neither

6. $f_6(-x) = \dfrac{1}{[(-x)^3 + (-x)]^2}$

$$= \frac{1}{(-x^3 - x)^2}$$

$$= \frac{1}{(x^3 + x)^2}$$

$$= f_6(x)$$

even

SURVIVAL HINT: *Compare the solutions to problems 19 and 20, and note the effect the parentheses have on the answer, and on the graphs.*

19. Compare the given equation with the equation $y - k = a \cos b(x - h)$ to find $(h, k) = (1, 0)$, $a = 1$, $b = 1$ and the period is $2\pi/1 = 2\pi$.

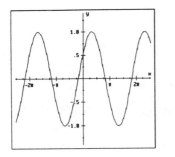

20. $(h, k) = (0, -1)$, $a = 1$, $b = 1$, and the period is 2π.

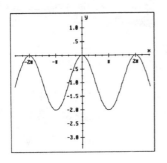

26. $R(a, g(a))$; $S(x_0, g(x_0))$

SURVIVAL HINT: *This may seem like an easy problem, but the identification of points such as R and S is an important skill that you will use many times in this course.*

33.
$$5x^3 - 3x^2 + 2x = 0$$
$$x(5x^2 - 3x + 2) = 0$$
$$x = 0$$

(The other solutions are not real numbers.)

43. The technology you use may, of course, vary. Begin by entering the function:

Next, set a scale. You may need to make several attempts before you find a window which shows the graph. Find the root finder on your calculator:

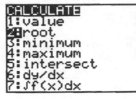

Finally, look at the calculator output to find approximate values for the roots:

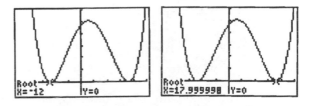

The roots seem to be -12.00, 18.00.

50. **a.** $s(0) = 16(0)^2 + 96(0) + 144 = 144$

The height of the cliff is 144 ft.

b. $s(t) = 0$ if
$$-16t^2 + 96t + 144 = 0$$
$$t^2 - 6t - 9 = 0$$

$$t = \frac{6 \pm \sqrt{36 - 4(-9)}}{2}$$
$$= 3 \pm 3\sqrt{2}$$

The ball hits the ground when

$$t = 3 + 3\sqrt{2}$$
$$\approx 7.24 \quad \text{(reject the negative } t\text{)}$$

The ball hits the ground in 7.24 seconds.

c. The maximum height occurs at the vertex
of the parabola $s = -16t^2 + 96t + 144$.

$$s - 144 = -16(t^2 - 6t)$$
$$s - 144 + (-16)(9) = -16(t^2 - 6t + 9)$$
$$s - 288 = -16(t - 3)^2$$

It takes 3 seconds for the ball to reach its
highest point. The maximum height is

$$s(3) = 288 \text{ ft}$$

52.

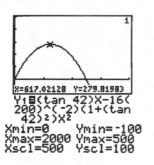

The maximum height of the cannonball is
approximately 280 ft.

57.

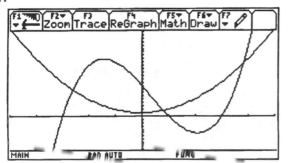

Rough crossings at $x \approx -2.6, 0.8, 3.8$. You
could use a solve utility on a calculator or a
computer to find a better estimate of the
solution:

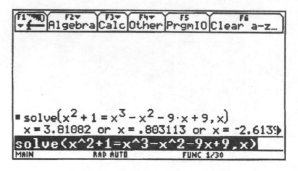

$x \approx -2.6139, 0.8031, 3.8108$

**1.5 Inverse Functions; Inverse Trigonometric
Functions, Pages 52-53**

5. $f[g(x)] = \frac{4}{5}(\frac{5}{4}x + 3) + 4 = x + \frac{12}{5} + 4 \neq x$

These are not inverse functions.

10. Interchanging components yields $\{(9, 3),$
$(9, -3), (16, 4), (16, -4)\}$ which is not a
function because $(9, 3)$ and $(9, -3)$ have the
same first component but different second
components. Thus, g has no inverse.

13. Given $y = x^2 - 5$, $x \geq 0$; inverse is

$$x = y^2 - 5, \ y \geq 0$$

or

$$y = \sqrt{x + 5}$$

(positive value since $y \geq 0$).

26. Let $\theta = \cos^{-1}\frac{1}{\sqrt{2}}$

so

$$\cos \theta = \frac{1}{\sqrt{2}};$$

$$\sin^2\theta = 1 - \cos^2\theta$$

$$= 1 - \frac{1}{2}$$

$$= \frac{1}{2}$$

Thus, $\sin \theta = \frac{\sqrt{2}}{2}$.

29. Let $\alpha = \sin^{-1}\frac{1}{5}$ and $\beta = \cos^{-1}\frac{1}{5}$

Then $\sin \alpha = \frac{1}{5}$, $\cos \beta = \frac{1}{5}$ and using reference

triangles we find $\cos \alpha = \sin \beta = \frac{2\sqrt{6}}{5}$

$$\cos(\sin^{-1}\tfrac{1}{5} + 2\cos^{-1}\tfrac{1}{5}) = \cos(\alpha + 2\beta)$$

$$= \cos \alpha \cos 2\beta - \sin \alpha \sin 2\beta$$

$$= \cos\alpha(\cos^2\beta - \sin^2\beta) - \sin\alpha(2\cos\beta \sin\beta)$$

$$= \frac{2\sqrt{6}}{5}\left[\frac{1}{25} - \frac{24}{25}\right] - \frac{1}{5}\left[2\cdot\frac{1}{5}\cdot\frac{2\sqrt{6}}{5}\right]$$

$$= \frac{2\sqrt{6}}{5}\left[-\frac{23}{25} - \frac{2}{25}\right]$$

$$= -\frac{2\sqrt{6}}{5}$$

$$\approx -0.9798$$

35.

The inverse exists, since it passes the

horizontal line test. Plot points to find the inverse function.

37.

$f(x) = \sqrt{1 - x^2}$ does not have an inverse because it is not a one-to-one function.

45. In any right triangle, the sum of the acute angles is $\frac{\pi}{2}$, so for $|x| < 1$, we know

$\sin^{-1}x + \cos^{-1}x = \frac{\pi}{2}$, so

$\sin(\sin^{-1}x + \cos^{-1}x) = \sin\frac{\pi}{2} = 1$

47. Consider a reference triangle as shown.

a. $\cot \alpha = \frac{x}{1}$ so $\cot^{-1}x = \alpha$

$\tan \beta = \frac{x}{1}$ so $\tan^{-1}x = \beta$

Also, since the triangle is a right triangle,

$$\alpha + \beta = \frac{\pi}{2}$$

$$\cot^{-1}x + \tan^{-1}x = \frac{\pi}{2}$$

$$\cot^{-1}x = \frac{\pi}{2} - \tan^{-1}x$$

b. $\sec \beta = x$, so $\beta = \sec^{-1}x$

$\cos \beta = \frac{1}{x}$, so $\beta = \cos^{-1}\left(\frac{1}{x}\right)$

Thus,

$$\sec^{-1}x = \cos^{-1}\left(\frac{1}{x}\right)$$

c. $\sin \alpha = \frac{1}{x}$, so $\alpha = \sin^{-1}\left(\frac{1}{x}\right)$

$\csc \alpha = x$, so $\alpha = \csc^{-1} x$

Thus, $\csc^{-1} x = \sin^{-1}\left(\frac{1}{x}\right)$

50. Let the angles θ and α be drawn as shown in the figure.

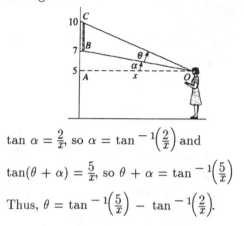

$\tan \alpha = \frac{2}{x}$, so $\alpha = \tan^{-1}\left(\frac{2}{x}\right)$ and

$\tan(\theta + \alpha) = \frac{5}{x}$, so $\theta + \alpha = \tan^{-1}\left(\frac{5}{x}\right)$

Thus, $\theta = \tan^{-1}\left(\frac{5}{x}\right) - \tan^{-1}\left(\frac{2}{x}\right)$.

1.6 Exponential and Logarithm Functions, Pages 65-67

SURVIVAL HINT: *You need to be comfortable with logarithms as inverses of exponentials. $y = e^x$ has inverse $x = e^y$, where y is described as $\ln x$, i.e. the exponent of e that gives x. Logarithms are exponents. $\ln 5$ is the exponent of e that gives 5. $e^{\ln 3} = 3$ because e to the exponent e that gives 3 will, of course be 3. If you are not really comfortable with these concepts, it might be a good idea to review the sections on logarithms and inverses in a trigonometry or precalculus text. For applications involving the way the world and inverse is built, the two most important numbers are π and e.*

14. $2^{\log_2 3 - \log_2 5} = 2^{\log_2 3}/2^{\log_2 5}$

$= \frac{3}{5}$

17. $\left(3^{\log_7 1}\right)\left(\log_5 0.04\right) = 3^0(\log_5 \frac{1}{25})$

$= -2$

21. $\exp(\ln 3 - \ln 10) = \exp(\ln \frac{3}{10}) = \frac{3}{10}$

SURVIVAL HINT: *Study the steps of this problem until you understand each one. Remember exponential and natural logarithm are inverses.*

23. Use the definition of logarithm: $x^2 = 16$; $x = 4$

24. $x = 10^{5.1} \approx 125{,}892.5412$

35. $(\sqrt[3]{2})^{x+10} = 2^{x^2}$

$2^{x/3+10/3} = 2^{x^2}$

$\frac{x}{3} + \frac{10}{3} = x^2$

$3x^2 - x - 10 = 0$

$(x - 2)(3x + 5) = 0$

$x = 2, \ -\frac{5}{3}$

39. $\log_3 x + \log_3(2x + 1) = 1$

$\log_3 x(2x +1) = 1$

$x(2x + 1) = 3$

$2x^2 + x - 3 = 0$

$(x - 1)(2x + 3) = 0$

$x = 1, \ -\frac{3}{2}$

(Reject the negative value since logarithms of negative numbers are not defined.)

43. $\log_{\sqrt{b}} 106 = 2$, so $b = 106$; Thus,

$$\sqrt{b - 25} = \sqrt{106 - 25}$$
$$= 9$$

57. Compare A_1 and A_2 for a fixed P where $t > 0$.

$$A_1 = (1 + \frac{0.07}{12})^{12t}$$
$$\approx (1.07229)^t$$

and

$$A_2 = e^{0.0695t}$$
$$\approx (1.07197)^t$$

Since

$$1.07229 > 1.07197$$

and

$$t > 0$$

it follows that $A_1 > A_2$ for all t. First National offers the better deal.

61. For a rock concert at 110 decibels,

$I_r = I_0 10^{110/10}$ and for normal conversation,

$I_n = I_0 10^{50/10}$. The difference in loudness

between the concert and normal conversation

is

$$D = 10 \log \frac{10^{11}}{10^5}$$
$$= 10 \log 10^6$$
$$= 60$$

Thus, the concert is 60 times as loud as normal conversation.

$$\frac{I_r}{I_n} = \frac{10^{11}}{10^5}$$
$$= 10^6$$

The rock concert is one million times as intense as normal conversation.

64. a.

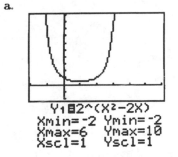

```
Y₁▆2^(X²-2X)
Xmin=-2  Ymin=-2
Xmax=6   Ymax=10
Xscl=1   Yscl=1
```

b. It crosses the y-axis at $(0, 1)$.

As $x \to +\infty$, $y \to +\infty$.

As $x \to -\infty$, $y \to +\infty$.

c. The smallest value of $y = E$ is $E = 0.5$.

67. a. $m = \dfrac{10,000(\frac{0.12}{12})}{1 - (1 + \frac{0.12}{12})^{-48}}$

$$\approx 263.34$$

b. $m = \dfrac{210,000(0.80)(\frac{0.08}{12})}{1 - (1 + \frac{0.08}{12})^{-360}}$

$$\approx 1,232.72$$

69. We are given $A = 10$, $B = 98.6$, and

$T = 40$. Therefore, we have

$$40 = 10 + (98.6 - 10)e^{-0.03t}$$

Solving for t, we find

$$30 = 88.6e^{-0.03t}$$

$$\frac{30}{88.6} = e^{-0.03t}$$

$$-0.03t = \ln\left(\frac{30}{88.6}\right)$$

$$t = -\frac{100}{3}\ln\left(\frac{30}{88.6}\right)$$

$$\approx 36.09781586$$

Thus, the body had been in the freezer for about 36 hr, so Siggy had been put into the freezer on Wednesday morning at about 1:00 AM. Coldfinger was in the slammer, so Scélérat must have done it.

CHAPTER 1 REVIEW

Proficiency Examination, Page 68

SURVIVAL HINT: *The concept problems of each Proficiency Examination are designed to remind you what was covered in the chapter. It is a worthwhile activity to **hand write** the answers to each of these questions onto your own paper. If you concentrate as you are doing this, some good things will happen. Here we show one possible answer for each question, but remember you will benefit only if you use the following list as a check after you answer the question.*

1. $\mathbb{N} = \{1, 2, 3, \cdots\}$;

    $\mathbb{W} = \{0, 1, 2, 3, \cdots\}$;

    $\mathbb{J} = \{\cdots, -3, -2, -1, 0, 1, 2, 3, \cdots\}$;

    $\mathbb{Q} = \{p/q$ so that p is an integer and q is a

         nonzero integer$\}$;

    $\overline{\mathbb{Q}} = \{$nonrepeating or nonterminating

         decimals$\}$;

    $\mathbb{R} = \mathbb{Q} \cup \overline{\mathbb{Q}}$

2. $|a| = a$ if $a \geq 0$; $|a| = -a$ if $a < 0$

3. $|x + y| \leq |x| + |y|$

4. $d = \sqrt{(x_2 - x_1)^2 + (y_2 - y_1)^2}$

5. $m = \tan \theta$ where θ is the angle of inclination

6. **a.** $Ax + By + C = 0$

    b. $y = mx + b$

    c. $y - k = m(x - h)$

    d. $y = k$

    e. $x = h$

7. Lines are parallel if they have the same slope, and perpendicular if their slopes are negative reciprocals of one another.

8. A function is a rule that assigns to each element x of the domain D a unique element of the range R.

9. $(f \circ g) = f[g(x)]$

10. The graph of a function f consists of all points (x, y) such that $y = f(x)$ for x in the domain of f.

11. **a.**   **b.**

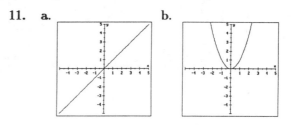

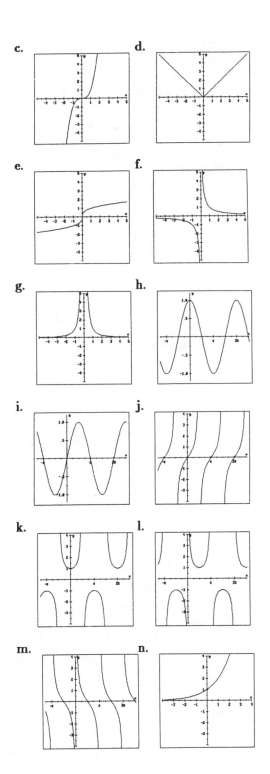

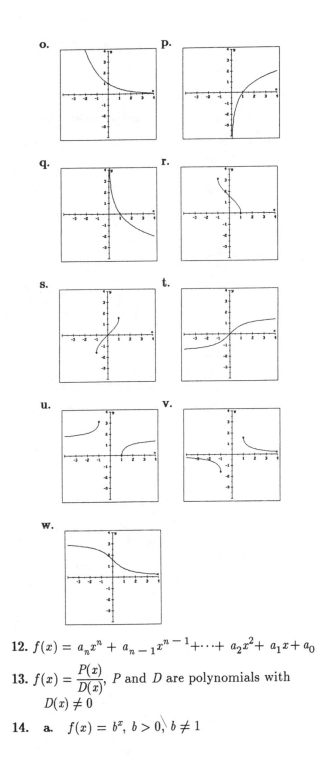

12. $f(x) = a_n x^n + a_{n-1} x^{n-1} + \cdots + a_2 x^2 + a_1 x + a_0$

13. $f(x) = \dfrac{P(x)}{D(x)}$, P and D are polynomials with $D(x) \neq 0$

14. **a.** $f(x) = b^x$, $b > 0$, $b \neq 1$

b. They are inverse functions. If $y = b^x$, the inverse is $x = b^y$, where $y = \log_b x$.

15. a. $f(x) = \log_b x$, $b > 0$, $b \neq 1$

b. A common logarithm, written $\log x$, is a logarithm to the base 10; that is, $\log x = \log_{10} x$.

c. A natural logarithm, written $\ln x$, is a logarithm to the base e; that is, $\ln x = \log_e x$.

16. a. Let f be a function with domain D and range R. Then the function f^{-1} with domain R and range D is the inverse of f if

$f^{-1}[f(x)] = x$ for all x in D and

$f[f^{-1}(y)] = y$ for all y in R

b. Reflect the graph of $y = f(x)$ in the line $y = x$.

17. The horizontal line test says that a function f has an inverse f^{-1} if and only if no horizontal line meets the graph of f in more than one point (that is, f is a one-to-one function).

18. $\log_a x = \dfrac{\log_b x}{\log_b a}$; the useful form for natural logarithms is a special case: $\log_a x = \dfrac{\ln x}{\ln a}$

19. $\sin(\sin^{-1} x) = x$ for $-1 \leq x \leq 1$

$\sin^{-1}(\sin y) = y$ for $-\dfrac{\pi}{2} \leq y \leq \dfrac{\pi}{2}$

$\tan(\tan^{-1} x) = x$ for all x

$\tan^{-1}(\tan y) = y$ for $-\dfrac{\pi}{2} < y < \dfrac{\pi}{2}$

20. $\cot^{-1} x = \begin{cases} \tan^{-1} \dfrac{1}{x} & \text{if } x \text{ is positive} \\ \tan^{-1} \dfrac{1}{x} + \pi & \text{if } x \text{ is negative} \\ \dfrac{\pi}{2} & \text{if } x = 0 \end{cases}$

$\sec^{-1} x = \cos^{-1} \dfrac{1}{x}$ if $|x| \geq 1$

$\csc^{-1} x = \sin^{-1} \dfrac{1}{x}$ if $|x| \geq 1$

21. a. $\quad y - 5 = -\dfrac{3}{4}[x - (-\dfrac{1}{2})]$

$\quad 6x + 8y - 37 = 0$

b. $m = \dfrac{2 - 5}{7 + 3} = \dfrac{-3}{10}$

$\quad y - 5 = -\dfrac{3}{10}[x - (-3)]$

$\quad 3x + 10y - 41 = 0$

c. $\quad \dfrac{x}{4} + \dfrac{y}{-\frac{3}{7}} = 1$

$\quad 3x - 28y - 12 = 0$

d. Writing the given equation in slope-intercept form, $y = -\dfrac{2}{5}x + \dfrac{11}{5}$, we see that the slope is $-2/5$. A parallel line must have the same slope. Now use the point-slope form.

$\quad y - 5 = -\dfrac{2}{5}(x + \dfrac{1}{2})$

$\quad 2x + 5y - 24 = 0$

e. Find the slope of $\overline{PQ}$. A perpendicular line will have a slope which is the negative reciprocal. Find the midpoint of $\overline{PQ}$. Then use the point-slope form for the equation of the line. The slope of $\overline{PQ}$ is $-3/4$. The midpoint of $\overline{PQ}$ is $(1, 4)$.

$\quad y - 4 = \dfrac{4}{3}(x - 1)$

$\quad 4x - 3y + 8 = 0$

24. $y - 3 = -2(x - 1)^2$

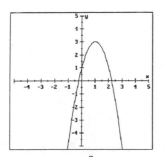

27. $y + 1 = \tan 2(x + \frac{3}{2})$

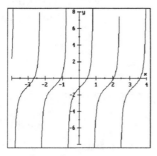

30. $y = e^{-x} + e^x$

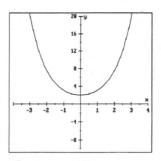

33. $y = e^x - \ln x + 15$

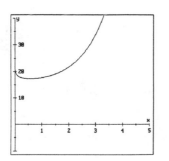

36. $f \circ g = \sin (\sqrt{1 - x^2})$
$g \circ f = \sqrt{1 - \sin^2 x} = |\cos x|$

39. Let the base of the box be x and the height z.

Then, $V = x^2 z$, so

sides: xz with a cost of $\$3xz$

bottom: x^2 with a cost of $\$8x^2$

Then

$$96 = 4(3xz) + 8x^2$$

$$24 = 2x^2 + 3xz$$

$$z = \frac{24 - 2x^2}{3x}$$

$$V = x^2\left(\frac{24 - 2x^2}{3x}\right) = \frac{2}{3}x(12 - x^2)$$

SURVIVAL HINT: *There is a large set of supplementary problems at the end of each chapter. You can use these problems for a variety of different uses. They are presented in random order, some routine, and some challenging. The answers to the odd numbered supplementary problems are given at the back of the textbook. You might try some of these problems to practice for examinations.*

CHAPTER 2

Limits and Continuity

SURVIVAL HINT: If your instructor does not begin with Chapter 1, you might wish to take some time looking over that chapter anyway. Look at the survival hint on page 1 for some information about the **free** supplement that accompanies this book.

If your instructor does not assign the **"What Does This Say?"** problems, take a few minutes to think about these problems anyway. These problems involve the *concepts* of the section. Could you explain the concept to classmate or another student? If not, it needs more work. Working with another student or a small group is highly recommended! Be bold and introduce yourself to a classmate.

2.1 What Is Calculus?, Pages 81-84

SURVIVAL HINT: *This section gives you a preview about the nature of a calculus course. The important ideas of calculus, namely **limit, derivative**, and **integral**, are introduced informally. In answering the questions of this section, you are not expected to have formal methods, but rather to conjecture and guess and boldly go where you have not gone before!*

1. A mathematical model is a mathematical framework whose results parallel the real world situation. It involves abstraction, predictions, and then interpretations and comparisons with real world events. An excellent example of real world modeling from *Scientific American* (March 1991) is mentioned in the margin on page 79.

SURVIVAL HINT: *Problems 5-12 ask you to guess the limit of a sequence. Later we will develop some formal methods to answer questions such as these, but for these problems just guess. A calculator might help.*

9. $0.2, 0.27, 0.272, 0.2727, \cdots$ The limit appears to be $0.272727\cdots$. We can write this as a fraction by letting $x = 0.272727\cdots$ so that

$$100x = 27.2727\cdots$$
$$x = \ \ 0.2727\cdots$$
$$99x = 27 \qquad \text{By subtraction}$$
$$x = \frac{27}{99}$$
$$= \frac{3}{11}$$

SURVIVAL HINT: *For Problems 13-16, begin by tracing the curves given in the book onto your own paper.*

17. $\lim\limits_{n \to \infty} \dfrac{2n}{n+4}$; Suppose n is very large, then adding the finite number 4 is negligible. For the sake of approximating, the denominator can be treated as n since $n + 4 \approx n$ for large n, so we might guess the limit to be 2.

Another possible solution is to notice for

$n = 1, 10, 100, 1{,}000;$ $L = \frac{2}{5}, \frac{20}{14}, \frac{200}{104}, \frac{2{,}000}{1{,}004}.$

It appears that $L = 2$. Finally, notice that as n gets very large the 4 becomes negligible, and the numerator is always twice the denominator. Mathematically, we might present the following argument:

$$\lim_{n \to \infty} \frac{2n}{n+4} = \lim_{n \to \infty} \frac{2n}{n+4} \cdot \frac{1/n}{1/n}$$

$$= \lim_{n \to \infty} \frac{2}{1 + 4/n}$$

$$= 2$$

22.
$$\lim_{n \to \infty} \frac{3n^2 + 1}{2n^2 - 1} = \lim_{n \to \infty} \frac{3n^2 + 1}{2n^2 - 1} \cdot \frac{1/n^2}{1/n^2}$$

$$= \lim_{n \to \infty} \frac{3 + \frac{1}{n^2}}{2 - \frac{1}{n^2}} = \frac{3}{2}$$

29. a.

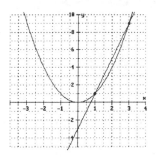

The slope of the secant line is $m = 4$.

b.

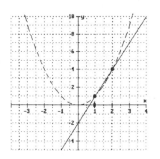

The slope of the secant line is $m = 3$.

c.

n	x_n	point	slope
1	3	(3, 9)	$m = 4$
2	2	(2, 4)	$m = 3$
3	1.5	(1.5, 2.25)	$m = 2.5$
4	1.1	(1.1, 1.21)	$m = 2.1$

d.

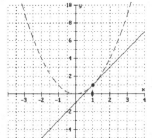

The slope of the tangent line is $m = 2$.

SURVIVAL HINT: *In Problems 31-36, you are not expected to use a formula, simply estimate.*

It is common to gather data points and then hypotheses a model which fits given data points. Problems 37-46 are designed to get you started with this process.

37. quadratic model

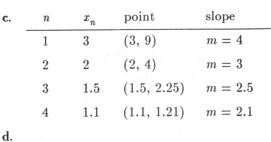

SURVIVAL HINT: Historical Quest problems are designed to get you thinking about some of the famous persons who contributed to calculus. With these problems we have attempted to give you an *accessible problem from these mathematician's notebooks.*

47. Using modern notation, we see $A = (4.5)^2\pi$ for the area of the circle and $A = 8^2$ for the area of the square. If we accept Ahmes' assumption, then $(4.5)^2\pi = 8^2$ which implies that $\pi \approx 3.16$. This is a remarkably good approximation for π.

49. A_3 is an inscribed equilateral triangle. Connect the center with each vertex on the circle; since it is a unit circle, each of these lengths is 1. Three triangles are formed, each with central angle $2\pi/3$. Draw a perpendicular from the center of the circle to a side of the triangle, thus forming 6 triangles. If θ is the central angle for this small right triangle, $\theta = \pi/3$. The total area of A_3 is the area of the 6 triangles:

$$A_3 = 6[\tfrac{1}{2}(\cos\tfrac{\pi}{3})(\sin\tfrac{\pi}{3})] \approx 1.2990$$

A_4 is an inscribed square. Connect the center with each vertex on the circle; since it is a unit circle, each of these lengths is 1. Four triangles are formed, each with central angle $2\pi/4 = \pi/2$. Draw a perpendicular from the center of the circle to a side of the square, thus forming 8 triangles. If θ is the central angle for this small triangle, $\theta = \pi/4$. The total area of A_4 is the area of the 8 triangles:

$$A_4 = 8[\tfrac{1}{2}(\cos\tfrac{\pi}{4})(\sin\tfrac{\pi}{4})] = 2$$

Continue the same process for A_5, A_6, $\cdots$ to obtain:

$$A_5 = 10[\tfrac{1}{2}(\cos\tfrac{\pi}{5})(\sin\tfrac{\pi}{5})] \approx 2.3776$$

$$A_6 = 12[\tfrac{1}{2}(\cos\tfrac{\pi}{6})(\sin\tfrac{\pi}{6})] \approx 2.5981$$

$$A_7 = 14[\tfrac{1}{2}(\cos\tfrac{\pi}{7})(\sin\tfrac{\pi}{7})] \approx 2.7364$$

$$\vdots$$

$$A_{100} = 200[\tfrac{1}{2}(\cos\tfrac{\pi}{100})(\sin\tfrac{\pi}{100})] \approx 3.1395$$

Later in the book, we will find

$$\text{AREA OF CIRCLE} = \pi(1)^2 = \lim_{n\to\infty}\frac{n}{2}\sin\frac{2\pi}{n}$$

52. There are 16 rectangles, each with a width of $\frac{1}{16}$ and a height of the square of the right endpoint of the rectangle.

$$A = \tfrac{1}{16}[(\tfrac{1}{16})^2 + (\tfrac{2}{16})^2 + (\tfrac{3}{16})^2 + \cdots + (\tfrac{16}{16})^2]$$

$$= \tfrac{1}{16^3}(1^2 + 2^2 + 3^2 + \cdots + 16^2) \approx 0.3652$$

57. a. Cost = cost of base + cost of top
+ 4(cost of each side) + cost of assembly
If C is the cost, x is the length of a side of the base, and y is the height, then
$$V = x^2 y = 231, \text{ so that } y = 231x^{-2}$$
$$\begin{aligned}C &= a(x^2) + a(x^2) + 4(axy) + 8bx + 4by\\ &= 2ax^2 + 8bx + 4ax(231x^{-2})\\ &\quad + 4b(231x^{-2})\\ &= 2ax^2 + 8bx + 924ax^{-1} + 924bx^{-2}\end{aligned}$$

b.

Length of base	Cost of the box
1	$1,858
2	$717
3	$452.67
4	$352.75
5	$311.76
6	$299.67
7	$304.86
8	$321.94
9	$348.07
10	$381.64

The cost is minimized if the base is 6 in. and the height is 6.42 in. Later in the book we will be able to find an exact solution for the base (namely, $x = 6.136$ in.).

c. Answers vary, but in each case, the cost is minimized if the base is 6 in. and the height is 6.42 in.

d. The minimum cost is independent of the cost of materials and assembly.

2.2 The Limit of a Function, Pages 95–97

SURVIVAL HINT: *The limit is the basic concept underlying both the derivative and the definite integral. Your intuitive concept of limit is correct, but you will find it essential to develop the ability to use the formal definition and learn some evaluation techniques. It is a spiral type concept, in that you will come back to it time and time again; each time at a higher level and with more understanding and greater perspective.*

6. Look at Figure 2.19

a. Find the graph named t, and look to see what happens as x approaches 2 from the left. It looks like y approaches 4.

b. Contrast this with part **a**. As x approaches 2 from the right, it looks like y approaches 2.

c. Since the left and right limits (parts **a** and **b**) are not the same, we say this limit is not defined. If the left and right hand limits are the same, then that value is called the limit.

9. You will use a calculator for this problem.

x	1	1.9	1.99	1.999
$f(x)$	7	9.7	9.97	9.997

x	3	2.5	2.1	2.001
$f(x)$	13	11.5	10.3	10.003

$\lim_{x \to 2} h(x)$ appears to be 10.

13. Look at the graph; when x is close to 4, we see that the graph is close to 2; thus, $\lim_{x \to 4} h(x) = 2$

24. Does not exist because as $x \to 3$ (from either the left or the right), the value of the denominator is getting closer and closer to zero (but does not equal 0). As 1 is divided by these smaller and smaller numbers the quotient becomes large without limit.

SURVIVAL HINT: *When using your calculator to evaluate trigonometric functions in calculus, be sure the mode is set to radian measure. All angles in calculus are in radians, unless specifically stated otherwise.*

28. a. Use a table of values (with a calculator).

The graph is useful in checking your table values, but not accurate enough to *find* this limits, which is approximately 0.24.

b. Use a table of value (with a calculator) or use the graph to guess hypothesize that the limit is 0.00.

29. a. From the graph it looks like the limit is 0.00.

b. Use a table of values (with a calculator), to find the limit to be approximately 0.64. The graph is useful in checking your table values.

30. a. A graph (with TRACE) works well to find the limit of 8.00.

b. This limit does not exist because as x approaches 3, the quotient becomes large without limit.

37. Use a table of values to find that the limit is approximately 0.25.

42. Use a table of values to find the limit is approximately 3.00.

SURVIVAL HINT: *Do not forget to set your calculator to radian mode.*

SURVIVAL HINT: *Without the limiting idea, there is no such thing as "instantaneous velocity" or "instantaneous rate of change." In an instant, both time and motion are frozen. The concept of limit allows us to define what we mean by these terms.*

51. a. $v(t) = \lim\limits_{x \to t} \dfrac{s(x) - s(t)}{x - t}$

$$= \lim\limits_{x \to t} \frac{(-16x^2 + 40x + 24) - (-16t^2 + 40t + 24)}{x - t}$$

$$= \lim\limits_{x \to t} (-16x - 16t + 40) = -32t + 40$$

b. $v(0) = \lim\limits_{x \to 0}(-32x + 40)$

$$= 40 \text{ ft/s}$$

c. $s(t) = 0$ if $-16t^2 + 40t + 24 = 0$ or if

$$2t^2 - 5t - 3 = 0$$

$$(t - 3)(2t + 1) = 0$$

$$t = 3, \ -\tfrac{1}{2}$$

Reject the negative solution. Impact velocity is

$$v(3) = -32(3) + 40$$
$$= -56 \text{ ft/s}$$

d. At the highest point on the trajectory, the ball has stopped moving upward and has not yet started on its downward fall. This occurs at $-32t + 40 = 0$ or

$t = 1.25$ seconds.

58. $\left| f(x) - L \right| = \left| (x + 3) - 5 \right|$

$$= |x - 2|$$

$$< \delta$$

Choose $\delta = \epsilon$.

59. $\left| f(x) - L \right| = \left| (3t - 1) - 0 \right|$

$$< |3t - 1|$$

This statement is false. Choose $\epsilon = 0.3$ and it is not possible to find a delta.

2.3 Properties of Limits, Pages 105-106

SURVIVAL HINT: *If the limit of a rational expression has the form 0/0 then it may have any value, L. But if it has the form a/0, then we note that as the denominator of a fraction decreases, the quotient increases. We sometimes write that the limit is $+\infty$ or $-\infty$ to symbolize this idea.*

3. $\lim\limits_{x \to 3} (x + 5)(2x - 7) = (3 + 5)(2 \cdot 3 - 7)$

$$= -8$$

SURVIVAL HINT: *When finding the limit of a polynomial (such as in Problem 1-3), you can evaluate the limits by substitution.*

9. $\lim\limits_{x \to 1/3} \dfrac{x \sin \pi x}{1 + \cos \pi x} = \dfrac{\frac{1}{3} \sin \frac{\pi}{3}}{1 + \cos \frac{\pi}{3}}$

$$= \dfrac{\sqrt{3}/6}{3/2}$$

$$= \dfrac{\sqrt{3}}{9}$$

SURVIVAL HINT: *If your finding a limiting value of a trigonometric function which is defined at the limiting value, then you can evaluate the limit by substitution.*

13. $\lim\limits_{x \to 1} \dfrac{\frac{1}{x} - 1}{x - 1} = \lim\limits_{x \to 1} \dfrac{\frac{1 - x}{x}}{x - 1}$

$$= \lim\limits_{x \to 1} \dfrac{-1}{x}$$

$$= -1$$

15. $\lim\limits_{x \to 1} \left(\dfrac{(x - 2)(x - 1)}{(x + 2)(x - 1)} \right)^2 = \lim\limits_{x \to 1} \dfrac{(x - 2)^2}{(x + 2)^2}$

$$= \dfrac{\lim\limits_{x \to 1} (x - 2)^2}{\lim\limits_{x \to 1} (x + 2)^2}$$

$$= \dfrac{1}{9}$$

SURVIVAL HINT: *When working limit problems, use proper form and notation to avoid errors and to make each statement value. Write $\lim\limits_{x \to 1}$ for each transformed expression until you actually evaluate the limit. Do not be lazy in your notation.*

18. $\lim\limits_{y \to 2} \dfrac{\sqrt{y + 2} - 2}{y - 2}$

$$= \lim\limits_{y \to 2} \dfrac{(\sqrt{y + 2} - 2)(\sqrt{y + 2} + 2)}{(y - 2)(\sqrt{y + 2} + 2)}$$

$$= \lim\limits_{y \to 2} \dfrac{y + 2 - 4}{(y - 2)(\sqrt{y + 2} + 2)}$$

$$= \lim\limits_{y \to 2} \dfrac{1}{\sqrt{y + 2} + 2} = \dfrac{1}{\sqrt{2 + 2} + 2}$$

$$= \dfrac{1}{4}$$

21. $\lim\limits_{t \to 0} \dfrac{\tan 5t}{\tan 2t} = \lim\limits_{t \to 0} \left(\dfrac{\sin 5t}{\cos 5t} \dfrac{\cos 2t}{\sin 2t} \right)$

$$= \lim\limits_{t \to 0} \dfrac{\sin 5t}{5t} \lim\limits_{t \to 0} \dfrac{5}{\cos 5t} \lim\limits_{t \to 0} \dfrac{2t}{\sin 2t} \lim\limits_{t \to 0} \dfrac{\cos 2t}{2}$$

$$= (1)\left(\dfrac{5}{1}\right)(1)\left(\dfrac{1}{2}\right)$$

$$= \dfrac{5}{2}$$

SURVIVAL HINT: *Problem 21 illustrates a general technique which you will frequently use when evaluating limits of the type illustrated by this problem.*

30. $\lim\limits_{x \to \pi/4} \dfrac{1 - \tan x}{\sin x - \cos x}$

$$= \lim\limits_{x \to \pi/4} \dfrac{1 - \frac{\sin x}{\cos x}}{\sin x - \cos x}$$

$$= \lim\limits_{x \to \pi/4} \dfrac{\cos x - \sin x}{\cos x(\sin x - \cos x)}$$

$$= \lim\limits_{x \to \pi/4} \dfrac{-1}{\cos x}$$

$$= -\sqrt{2}$$

36. $\lim\limits_{x \to 2^{-}} (x^2 - 2x) = 2^2 - 2(2)$

$$= 0$$

40. $\lim\limits_{x \to 0^{-}} \frac{|x|}{x} = \lim\limits_{x \to 0^{-}} \frac{-x}{x}$

$$= -1$$

and

$$\lim\limits_{x \to 0^{+}} \frac{|x|}{x} = \lim\limits_{x \to 0^{+}} \frac{x}{x}$$

$$= 1$$

Thus, the limit does not exist because the left- and right-hand limits are not equal.

44. As $x \to 1$, the denominator $(x - 1)$ is approaching 0, the result of dividing a constant (1 in this case) by a quantity approaching zero, becomes infinite.

47. $\lim\limits_{x \to 3} \frac{x^2 + 4x + 3}{x - 3} = \lim\limits_{x \to 3} \frac{(x + 3)(x + 1)}{x - 3}$

As $x \to 3$, the numerator is approaching $(6)(4) = 24$ and the denominator $(x - 3)$ is approaching 0, the result of dividing a number close to 24 by a quantity approaching zero, becomes infinite.

59. $\lim\limits_{x \to 3} f(x) = 8$ since the left and right limits both equal to 8.

62. $\lim\limits_{x \to 0} \frac{\cos x - 1}{x} = \lim\limits_{x \to 0} \left(\frac{\cos x - 1}{x} \cdot \frac{\cos x + 1}{\cos x + 1} \right)$

$$= \lim\limits_{x \to 0} \frac{\cos^2 x - 1}{x(\cos x + 1)}$$

$$= \lim\limits_{x \to 0} \frac{-\sin^2 x}{x(\cos x + 1)}$$

$$= (-1) \lim\limits_{x \to 0} \left[\left(\frac{\sin x}{x} \right)\left(\frac{\sin x}{\cos x + 1} \right) \right]$$

$$= (-1) \lim\limits_{x \to 0} \left(\frac{\sin x}{x} \right) \lim\limits_{x \to 0} \left(\frac{\sin x}{\cos x + 1} \right)$$

$$= (-1)(1)(0) = 0$$

2.4 Continuity, Pages 115-117

SURVIVAL HINT: *Once again, your intuitive notion of continuity will help. Think about all the possible situations that could make a function discontinuous. The formal definition takes care of all of these. Do not just memorize the definition, **understand the concept.***

9. The denominator factors to $x(x - 1)$, so suspicious points would be $x = 0, 1$. There will be a hole discontinuity at $x = 0$ and a pole discontinuity at $x = 1$.

13. $x = 1$ is a suspicious point; there are no points of discontinuity.

19. For continuity, $f(2)$ must equal

$$\lim\limits_{x \to 2} f(x) = \lim\limits_{x \to 2} \frac{(x - 2)(x + 1)}{x - 2}$$

$$= \lim\limits_{x \to 2} (x + 1)$$

$$= 3$$

SURVIVAL HINT: *A common error is to apply a theorem when it really is not applicable. Theorems are if-then statement, and the conclusion is not justified unless the hypotheses is met. When learning a theorem, pay careful attention to the "if" part, and make sure the hypotheses are met.*

25. a. No suspicious points on $[1, 2]$; continuous

b. Suspicious point $x = 0$. Discontinuous on $[0, 1]$ since the pole $x = 0$ is in the domain. If the interval had been $(0, 1]$, the function would be continuous on the interval.

28. No suspicious points; $y = x$ and $y = \sin x$ are continuous on the reals, so $f(x) = x \sin x$ will be continuous on $(0, \pi)$.

31. $f(x) = \sqrt[3]{x} - x^2 - 2x + 1$ is continuous on $[0, 1]$ and $f(0) = 1$, $f(1) = -1$ so the hypotheses of the intermediate value theorem are met, and we are guaranteed that there is at least one number c on $[0, 1]$ such that $f(c) = 0$.

39.
$$\lim_{x \to 2^-} f(x) = 2 + 1$$
$$= 3$$
$$= f(2)$$
$$\lim_{x \to 2^+} f(x) = 2^2$$
$$= 4$$
$$\neq f(2)$$

47. Must have $a = 1$ or $\lim_{x \to 1} f(x)$ does not exist. With $a = 1$,
$$\lim_{x \to 1} \frac{\sqrt{x} - 1}{x - 1} = \lim_{x \to 1} \frac{1}{\sqrt{x} + 1}$$
$$= \frac{1}{2}$$

Since $f(1) = b$, we must have $b = \frac{1}{2}$, so $a = 1$ and $b = \frac{1}{2}$

55. a. Suppose f is a continuous function on the closed interval $[a, b]$ with, for example, $f(a) > 0$ and $f(b) < 0$. Then, by the intermediate value theorem, the equation $f(x) = 0$ has a root somewhere between $x = a$ and $x = b$. To estimate the location of this root with more precision, evaluate f at the midpoint $x_1 = (a + b)/2$ of the interval $[a, b]$. There are three possibilities, as shown below.

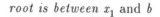

root is between x_1 and b

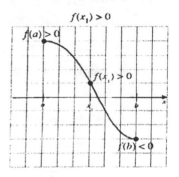

x_1 is the root you seek

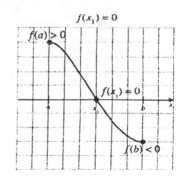

root is between a and x_1

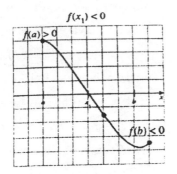

$f(x_1) < 0$

$f(a) > 0$

$f(b) < 0$

Either x_1 is the root or you have found a new interval that is only half as wide as the original interval and must contain the desired root. If there is more than one root in the interval, then you can use this method to find the first root, and then take a subinterval to find the other roots.

b. Repeat the steps outlined in part **a.** The approximations x_1, x_2, ... generated by the bisection method converge on the true value of the desired root. However, the rate of this convergence is often fairly slow when compared to other methods. The graph is shown below.

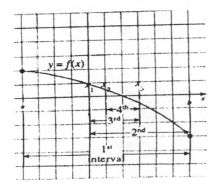

$y = f(x)$

4th

3rd

2nd

1st

interval

c. $f(x) = x^3 + x - 1 = 0$ on $[0, 1]$

Left: $x_{l_0} = 0$ and right: $x_{r_0} = 1$ so that

$f(x_{l_0}) = -1$, $f(x_{r_0}) = 1$

$x_1 = \frac{0+1}{2} = \frac{1}{2}$; $f(x_1) = -0.375$, so

$x_{l_1} = \frac{1}{2}$ and $x_{r_1} = 1$

$x_2 = \frac{\frac{1}{2}+1}{2} = \frac{3}{4}$; $f(x_2) = 0.171875$, so

$x_{l_2} = \frac{1}{2}$ and $x_{r_2} = \frac{3}{4}$

$x_3 = \frac{\frac{1}{2}+\frac{3}{4}}{2} = \frac{5}{8}$; $f(x_3) \approx -0.1309$ so

$x_{l_3} = \frac{5}{8}$ and $x_{r_3} = \frac{3}{4} = 0.75$

$x_4 = \frac{\frac{5}{8}+\frac{3}{4}}{2} = \frac{11}{16} = 0.6875$

Continue with a calculator to find $0.68232 < x < 0.68233$.

57. Answers vary:

$$f(x) = \begin{cases} \dfrac{1}{x-1} & \text{if } x \neq 1 \\ -2 & \text{if } x = 1 \end{cases}$$

and

$$g(x) = \begin{cases} x^2 - 1 & \text{if } x \neq 1 \\ -1 & \text{if } x = 1 \end{cases}$$

f is discontinuous at $x = 1$, but

$$f(x)g(x) = \begin{cases} x + 1 & \text{if } x \neq 1 \\ 2 & \text{if } x = 1 \end{cases}$$

CHAPTER 2 REVIEW

Proficiency Examination, Pages 117-118

SURVIVAL HINT: *Since your class may have skipped Chapter 1, we will repeat the hint we gave in the proficiency examination for Chapter 1. The concept problems of each Proficiency Examination are designed to remind you what was covered in the chapter. It is a worthwhile activity to* **hand write** *the answers to each of these questions onto your own paper. If you concentrate as you are doing this, some good things will happen.*

1. limit, derivative, and integral; answers vary

2. Answers vary; choosing appropriate mathematics to analyze a problem that has not previously been solved. In this book, it is a process of abstraction, deriving results, and then comparing and interpreting the result in terms of a real-world problem.

3. $\lim_{x \to c} f(x) = L$ means that the function values $f(x)$ can be made arbitrarily close to L by choosing x sufficiently close to c.

4. $\lim_{x \to c} f(x) = L$ means that for each $\epsilon > 0$ there exists a number $\delta > 0$ such that $\big|f(x) - L\big| < \epsilon$ whenever $0 < |x - c| < \delta$

5. a. $\lim_{x \to c} k = k$ for any constant k

    b. $\lim_{x \to c}[sf(x)] = s \lim_{x \to c} f(x)$

    c. $\lim_{x \to c}[f(x) + g(x)] = \lim_{x \to c} f(x) + \lim_{x \to c} g(x)$

    d. $\lim_{x \to c}[f(x) - g(x)] = \lim_{x \to c} f(x) - \lim_{x \to c} g(x)$

    e. $\lim_{x \to c}[f(x)g(x)] = [\lim_{x \to c} f(x)][\lim_{x \to c} g(x)]$

    f. $\lim_{x \to c} \dfrac{f(x)}{g(x)} = \dfrac{\lim_{x \to c} f(x)}{\lim_{x \to c} g(x)}$ if $\lim_{x \to c} g(x) \neq 0$

    g. $\lim_{x \to c}[f(x)]^n = \Big[\lim_{x \to c} f(x)\Big]^n$ n is a rational number and the limit on the right exists.

    h. If P is a polynomial function, then
    $$\lim_{x \to c} P(x) = P(c)$$

    i. If Q is a rational function defined by
    $$Q(x) = \frac{P(x)}{D(x)}, \text{ then } \lim_{x \to c} Q(x) = \frac{P(c)}{D(c)}$$
    provided $\lim_{x \to c} D(x) \neq 0$.

    j. If T is a trigonometric, exponential, or a natural logarithmic function, defined at $x = c$, then $\lim_{x \to c} T(x) = T(c)$.

6. If $g(x) \leq f(x) \leq h(x)$ for all x on an open interval containing c, and if
    $$\lim_{x \to c} g(x) = \lim_{x \to c} h(x) = L$$
    then $\lim_{x \to c} f(x) = L$.

7. a. $\lim_{x \to 0} \frac{\sin x}{x} = 1$ b. $\lim_{x \to 0} \frac{\cos x - 1}{x} = 0$

8. A function f is continuous at a point $x = c$ if
    (1) $f(c)$ is defined
    (2) $\lim_{x \to c} f(x)$ exists
    (3) $\lim_{x \to c} f(x) = f(c)$

9. If f is a polynomial, rational, power, or trigonometric, logarithmic exponential, or inverse trigonometric function, then f is continuous at any number $x = c$ for which $f(c)$ is defined.

10. If f is a continuous function on the closed interval $[a, b]$ and L is some number strictly

between $f(a)$ and $f(b)$, then there exists at least one number c on the open interval (a, b) such that $f(c) = L$.

12. $\lim\limits_{x \to 4} \dfrac{\sqrt{x} - 2}{x - 4} \cdot \dfrac{\sqrt{x} + 2}{\sqrt{x} + 2}$

$= \lim\limits_{x \to 4} \dfrac{x - 4}{(x - 4)(\sqrt{x} + 2)}$

$= \lim\limits_{x \to 4} \dfrac{1}{\sqrt{x} + 2}$

$= \dfrac{1}{4}$

15. $\lim\limits_{x \to 0} \dfrac{\sin 9x}{\sin 5x} = \lim\limits_{x \to 0} \dfrac{9x}{9x}(\sin 9x) \cdot \dfrac{5x}{5x}\left(\dfrac{1}{\sin 5x}\right)$

$= \lim\limits_{x \to 0} \dfrac{9x}{5x}\left(\dfrac{\sin 9x}{9x}\right) \cdot \left(\dfrac{5x}{\sin 5x}\right)$

$= \dfrac{9}{5}(1)(1)$

$= \dfrac{9}{5}$

18. Suspicious points $x = -2$ and $x = 1$ are also points of discontinuity (since the denominator is 0)

CHAPTER 3

Differentiation

3.1 An Introduction to the Derivative: Tangents, Pages 139–142

SURVIVAL HINT: *Derivative is one of the great ideas of calculus. Spending some extra time with this idea now will pay dividends throughout the book. It would be a good idea to memorize the definition of derivative given on page 132 of the text.*

Recognize the concept of slope as the change in y divided by the change in x. In calculus, we symbolize this by $\Delta y/\Delta x$. Think of Δx as a single symbol for "change in x" and Δy as a single symbol for "change in y."

3. Answers vary; continuity does not imply differentiability, but differentiability implies continuity.

SURVIVAL HINT: *Look at the answer to Problem 3 even if your instructor did not assign this problem. This is an important principle that you should remember.*

8. When the derivative is positive the graph of the function is increasing and when the derivative is negative, the graph of the function is decreasing. When the derivative is zero, the function may change from increasing to decreasing or from decreasing to increasing.

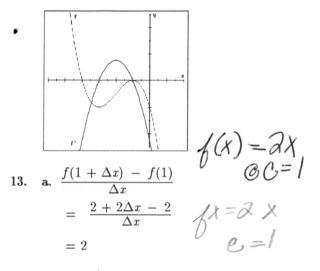

$f(x) = 2x$

@ $c = 1$

$fx = 2x$

$c = 1$

13. a. $\dfrac{f(1 + \Delta x) - f(1)}{\Delta x}$

$= \dfrac{2 + 2\Delta x - 2}{\Delta x}$

$= 2$

b. $f'(1) = \lim\limits_{\Delta x \to 0} 2$

$= 2$

19. $f'(x) = \lim\limits_{\Delta x \to 0} \dfrac{f(x + \Delta x) - f(x)}{\Delta x}$

$= \lim\limits_{\Delta x \to 0} \dfrac{[3(x + \Delta x) - 7] - [3x - 7]}{\Delta x}$

$= \lim\limits_{\Delta x \to 0} 3$

$= 3$

Differentiable for all x.

28. $f'(x) = \lim\limits_{\Delta x \to 0} \dfrac{f(x + \Delta x) - f(x)}{\Delta x}$

$= \lim\limits_{\Delta x \to 0} \dfrac{\sqrt{x + \Delta x + 1} - \sqrt{x + 1}}{\Delta x}$

$$= \lim_{\Delta x \to 0} \frac{\sqrt{x+\Delta x+1} - \sqrt{x+1}}{\Delta x} \left[\frac{\sqrt{x+\Delta x+1}+\sqrt{x+1}}{\sqrt{x+\Delta x+1}+\sqrt{x+1}} \right]$$

$$= \lim_{\Delta x \to 0} \frac{x + \Delta x + 1 - x - 1}{\Delta x(\sqrt{x + \Delta x + 1} + \sqrt{x + 1})}$$

$$= \lim_{\Delta x \to 0} \frac{1}{\sqrt{x + \Delta x + 1} + \sqrt{x + 1}}$$

$$= \frac{1}{2\sqrt{x + 1}}$$

Differentiable for $x > -1$.

33. $f'(x) = \lim_{\Delta x \to 0} \frac{f(x + \Delta x) - f(x)}{\Delta x}$

$\dfrac{1}{x+3}$

Ⓐ

$x = 2$

$$= \lim_{\Delta x \to 0} \frac{1}{\Delta x}\left(\frac{1}{x + \Delta x + 3} - \frac{1}{x + 3} \right)$$

$$= \lim_{\Delta x \to 0} \frac{1}{\Delta x}\left[\frac{x + 3 - x - \Delta x - 3}{(x + 3)(x + \Delta x + 3)} \right]$$

$$= \lim_{\Delta x \to 0} \frac{-1}{(x + 3)(x + \Delta x + 3)} = \frac{-1}{(x + 3)^2}$$

$$f'(2) = \frac{-1}{25} = m; \quad f(2) = \frac{1}{2 + 3} = \frac{1}{5}$$

$$y - \frac{1}{5} = \frac{-1}{25}(x - 2)$$

$$x + 25y - 7 = 0$$

35. From Problem 19, $f'(3) = 3$; so the normal line has slope $m = -\frac{1}{3}$. Since it passes through $(3, 2)$, the equation is

$$y - 2 = -\frac{1}{3}(x - 3) + 2$$

$$x + 3y - 9 = 0$$

42. $\dfrac{dy}{dx} = \lim_{\Delta x \to 0} \dfrac{f(x + \Delta x) - f(x)}{\Delta x}$

$$= \lim_{\Delta x \to 0} \frac{1}{\Delta x}\left(\frac{4}{x + \Delta x} - \frac{4}{x} \right)$$

$$= \lim_{\Delta x \to 0} \frac{4(x - x - \Delta x)}{x\Delta x(x + \Delta x)}$$

$$= \lim_{\Delta x \to 0} \frac{-4}{x(x + \Delta x)}$$

$$= \frac{-4}{x^2}$$

$$\frac{dy}{dx}\bigg|_{x=1} = -4$$

SURVIVAL HINT: *Do not confuse zero slope with no slope. Zero slope is a horizontal line, no slope may mean the function is discontinuous at the given value, is continuous but has a cusp, or that it is a vertical line.*

43. **a.** $f(-2) = 4$ and $f(-1.9) = 3.61$

$$m_{\text{sec}} = \frac{4 - 3.61}{-2 + 1.9} = -3.9$$

b. $f'(x) = \lim_{\Delta x \to 0} \dfrac{(x + \Delta x)^2 - x^2}{\Delta x}$

$$= \lim_{\Delta x \to 0} \frac{x^2 + 2x\Delta x + (\Delta x)^2 - x^2}{\Delta x}$$

$$= \lim_{\Delta x \to 0} (2x + \Delta x) = 2x$$

$$m_{\text{tan}} = f'(-2) = 2(-2) = -4$$

46. **a.** $f(x) = x^2 - 3x$

$$f'(x) = \lim_{\Delta x \to 0} \frac{f(x + \Delta x) - f(x)}{\Delta x}$$

$$= \lim_{\Delta x \to 0} \frac{[(x + \Delta x)^2 - 3(x + \Delta x)] - [x^2 - 3x]}{\Delta x}$$

$$= \lim_{\Delta x \to 0} \frac{x^2 + 2x\Delta x + (\Delta x)^2 - 3x - 3\Delta x - x^2 + 3x}{\Delta x}$$

$$= \lim_{\Delta x \to 0} (2x + \Delta x - 3)$$

$$= 2x - 3$$

b. The derivative is 0 when $x = \frac{3}{2}$; $f\left(\frac{3}{2}\right) = -\frac{9}{4}$, so there is a horizontal tangent line through $(\frac{3}{2}, -\frac{9}{4})$. This tangent line is $4y + 9 = 0$.

c. Two lines are parallel if their slopes are the same. For the given line, $y = -3x + 11$ or $m = -3$. The tangent line to $y = x^2 - 3x$ at (x_0, y_0) has slope $f'(x_0) = 2x_0 - 3$ which is -3 if $x_0 = 0$. Then $y_0 = 0^2 - 3(0) = 0$ and the point is $(0, 0)$.

d.

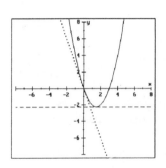

52. $f(x) = |x - 5|$ is continuous on $(-\infty, \infty)$, but not differentiable at $x = 5$ (because of the corner point; see Example 7).

53. Let $\Delta x = 0.1$, $c = 1$, $f(x) = (2x - 1)^2$

$$f'(x) \approx \frac{f(x + \Delta x) - f(x)}{\Delta x}$$
$$= \frac{f(1.1) - f(1)}{0.1}$$
$$= \frac{1.44 - 1}{0.1}$$
$$= 4.4$$

Let $\Delta x = 0.01$

$$f'(x) \approx \frac{f(x + \Delta x) - f(x)}{\Delta x}$$

$$= \frac{f(1.01) - f(1)}{0.01}$$
$$= \frac{1.0404 - 1}{0.01}$$
$$= 4.04$$

It appears that $f'(x) = 4$.

54. We could proceed as shown in the solution for Problem 53, but here we present data which could be generated using a graphing calculator, spreadsheet, or a computer program.

$f(x) = \dfrac{1}{x + 1}$, $c = 2$

Δx	$c + \Delta x$	$\dfrac{f(c + \Delta x) - f(c)}{\Delta x}$
0.5	2.5	-0.0952
0.125	2.125	-0.1067
0.03125	2.0313	-0.1100
0.00781	2.0078	-0.1108
0.00195	2.0012	-0.1111
0.00049	2.0005	-0.1110

We might guess that the derivative is

$$f'(2) = -\frac{1}{9} \approx 0.1111$$

3.2 Techniques of Differentiation, Pages 150-151

SURVIVAL HINT: *This section is a powerhouse section, and the power rule, product rule, and quotient rules must be thoroughly mastered. Since addition is commutative, the product rule can be used as*

$$(fg)' = fg' + gf'$$

or $gf' + fg'$. To help you remember the product rule, the following rhyme might help:

f-g prime is one-two prime plus two prime one

f-g prime is two prime one plus one-two prime

You will remember this rule when your remember this rhyme.

On the other hand, since subtraction is **not** commutative, you must always begin with the denominator times the derivative of the numerator.

The quotient rule is: $\left(\dfrac{f}{g}\right)' = \dfrac{gf' - fg'}{g^2}$

Quotient rule help rhyme:

"To find the derivative of high-low prime, all you need is this stupid little rhyme,

low dee high minus high dee low, over the square of the denominator must go."

5.   **a.** $f'(x) = 3(4)x^3 - 0 = 12x^3$

     b. $g'(x) = 0 - 1 = -1$

SURVIVAL HINT: *Pay special attention to the differences between parts **a** and **b**. You do not apply the power rule to a constant. Look at Problem 6b, and remember that π^3 is a constant.*

8.   **a.** $10(-t^{-2}) = -10t^{-2}$

     b. $g(t) = 7t^{-1}; \; g'(t) = -7t^{-2}$

SURVIVAL HINT: *If you can write a quotient as a sum, you will often simply reduce the amount of work you need to do. In Problems 9-14 you will write each expression as a sum **before** you attempt to find the derivative.*

14. $f(x) = 2x^2 - 3x^{-1} + 11x^{-3}$

     $f'(x) = 4x + 3x^{-2} - 33x^{-4}$

15. $f(x) = (2x + 1)(1 - 4x^3)$

$= 2x - 8x^4 + 1 - 4x^3$

$f'(x) = -32x^3 - 12x^2 + 2$

SURVIVAL HINT: *Compare Problems 17-18 with Problems 9-14. You should use the quotient rule for these problems.*

18. $f'(x) = \dfrac{(x^2 + 5)(2x) - (x^2 + 3)(2x)}{(x^2 + 5)^2}$

$\qquad = \dfrac{2x(x^2 + 5 - x^2 - 3)}{(x^2 + 5)^2}$

$\qquad = \dfrac{4x}{(x^2 + 5)^2}$

23. $f(x) = -2x^{-2};$

     $f'(x) = 4x^{-3};$

     $f''(x) = -12x^{-4};$

     $f'''(x) = 48x^{-5};$

     $f^{(4)}(x) = -240x^{-6}$

26. $y = (x^2 + 4)(1 - 3x^3) = -3x^5 - 12x^3 + x^2 + 4$

     $\dfrac{dy}{dx} = -15x^4 - 36x^2 + 2x$

     $\dfrac{d^2y}{dx^2} = -60x^3 - 72x + 2$

31. $f(x) = \dfrac{x^2 + 5}{x + 5}; \; f(1) = 1,$ so the point of

tangency is $(1, 1)$.

$f'(x) = \dfrac{(x + 5)(2x) - (x^2 + 5)(1)}{(x + 5)^2}$

$\qquad = \dfrac{x^2 + 10x - 5}{(x + 5)^2},$

and $f'(1) = \dfrac{1}{6} = m_{\tan}$

Using the point-slope formula:

$$y - 1 = \tfrac{1}{6}(x - 1)$$

$$x - 6y + 5 = 0$$

33. $f'(x) = 6x^2 - 14x + 8$; solve

$$6x^2 - 14x + 8 = 0$$

$$2(3x - 4)(x - 1) = 0$$

$$x = \tfrac{4}{3}, 1$$

$f(\tfrac{4}{3}) = -\tfrac{1}{27}$ and $f(1) = 0$; the points are $(1, 0)$ and $(\tfrac{4}{3}, -\tfrac{1}{27})$.

41. a. $\quad f'(x) = \dfrac{x^3(2) - (2x - 3)(3x^2)}{x^6}$

$$= \dfrac{-4x + 9}{x^4}$$

b. $\quad f'(x) = x^{-3}(2) + (-3x^{-4})(2x - 3)$

$$= 2x^{-3} - 6x^{-3} + 9x^{-4}$$

$$= -4x^{-3} + 9x^{-4}$$

c. $\quad f'(x) = 2(-2)x^{-3} - 3(-3)x^{-4}$

$$= -4x^{-3} + 9x^{-4}$$

d. $\quad \dfrac{-4x + 9}{x^4} = -4x^{-3} + 9x^{-4}$

52. $f'(x) = 4x + 1$; $f''(x) = 4$; $f'''(x) = 0$

$$y''' + y'' + y' = 4x + 1 + 4 + 0$$

$$= 4x + 5$$

The equation is not satisfied.

56. $F(x) = f(x) + g(x)$

$$F'(x) = \lim_{\Delta x \to 0} \dfrac{F(x + \Delta x) - F(x)}{\Delta x}$$

$$= \lim_{\Delta x \to 0} \frac{f(x+\Delta x) + g(x+\Delta x) - [f(x) + g(x)]}{\Delta x}$$

$$= \lim_{\Delta x \to 0} \frac{f(x+\Delta x) - f(x)}{\Delta x} + \lim_{\Delta x \to 0} \frac{g(x+\Delta x) - g(x)}{\Delta x}$$

$$= f'(x) + g'(x)$$

59. $\left(\dfrac{f}{g}\right)' = \lim_{\Delta x \to 0} \dfrac{1}{\Delta x}\left[\dfrac{f(x+\Delta x)}{g(x+\Delta x)} - \dfrac{f(x)}{g(x)}\right]$

$$= \lim_{\Delta x \to 0} \frac{f(x+\Delta x)g(x) - \mathbf{f(x)g(x)} - f(x)g(x+\Delta x) + \mathbf{f(x)g(x)}}{\Delta x g(x)g(x+\Delta x)}$$

$$= \lim_{\Delta x \to 0} \frac{g(x)[f(x+\Delta x) - f(x)] - f(x)[g(x+\Delta x) - g(x)]}{\Delta x g(x)g(x+\Delta x)}$$

$$= g(x) \lim_{\Delta x \to 0}\left[\frac{f(x+\Delta x) - f(x)}{\Delta x}\right]\left[\frac{1}{g(x)g(x+\Delta x)}\right] - f(x) \lim_{\Delta x \to 0}\left[\frac{g(x+\Delta x) - g(x)}{\Delta x}\right]\left[\frac{1}{g(x)g(x+\Delta x)}\right]$$

$$= g(x)f'(x)\left[\frac{1}{g^2(x)}\right] - f(x)g'(x)\left[\frac{1}{g^2(x)}\right]$$

3.3 Derivatives of the Trigonometric, Exponential, and Logarithmic Functions, Pages 158-159

SURVIVAL HINT: *If your precalculus is rusty, it will save you time in the long run to do some serious review right now. About the second or third time you must look up a graph, exact value, or trigonometric identity, add it to your list of formulas, definitions, or facts to remember.*

3. $g'(t) = 2t - \sin t$

5. Write $f(t) = (\sin t)(\sin t)$

$f'(x) = (\sin t)(\cos t) + (\cos t)(\sin t)$

$$= 2 \sin t \cos t$$

$$= \sin 2t$$

7. $f'(x) = \sqrt{x}\,(-\sin x) + (\cos x)\tfrac{1}{2}\,x^{-1/2}$

$$+ \; x(-\csc^2 x) + (\cot x)(1)$$

$$= -\sqrt{x}\,\sin x + \tfrac{1}{2}\,x^{-1/2}\cos x$$

$$- \; x\csc^2 x + \cot x$$

17. $h'(x) = e^x(-\sin x + \cos x) + e^x(\cos x + \sin x)$

$$= -e^x\sin x + e^x\cos x + e^x\cos x + e^x\sin x$$

$$= 2\,e^x\cos x$$

20. Write $g(x) = \dfrac{x\cos x}{e^x}$ and use the quotient rule.

$$g'(x) = \frac{e^x[\cos x + x(-\sin x)] - e^x(x\cos x)}{(e^x)^2}$$

$$= \frac{\cos x - x\sin x - x\cos x}{e^x}$$

28. $g'(x) = \dfrac{(1 + \cos x)(-\sin x) - (\cos x)(-\sin x)}{(1 + \cos x)^2}$

$$= \frac{-\sin x - \cos x \sin x + \cos x \sin x}{(1 + \cos x)^2}$$

$$= \frac{-\sin x}{(1 + \cos x)^2}$$

43. $h'(t) = \sqrt{t}\left(\dfrac{1}{t}\right) + \tfrac{1}{2}t^{-1/2}\ln t$

$$= \tfrac{1}{2}t^{-1/2}(2 + \ln t)$$

$$h''(t) = \tfrac{1}{2}t^{-1/2}\left(\tfrac{1}{t}\right) + \tfrac{1}{2}\left(-\tfrac{1}{2}t^{-3/2}\right)(2 + \ln t)$$

$$= \tfrac{1}{4}t^{-3/2}(2 - 2 - \ln t)$$

$$= -\tfrac{1}{4}t^{-3/2}\ln t$$

49. $f(x) = \sin x;$

$$f\left(\tfrac{\pi}{6}\right) = \tfrac{1}{2};$$

$$f'(x) = \cos x;$$

$$f'\left(\tfrac{\pi}{6}\right) = \frac{\sqrt{3}}{2}$$

The equation of the tangent line is

$$y - \tfrac{1}{2} = \frac{\sqrt{3}}{2}\left(x - \tfrac{\pi}{6}\right)$$

$$\sqrt{3}x - 2y + \left(1 - \frac{\sqrt{3}\pi}{6}\right) = 0$$

56. $\quad y' = -A\sin x + B\cos x$

$$y'' = -A\cos x - B\sin x$$

$$y'' + 2y' + 3y = 2\sin x$$

$$-A\cos x - B\sin x + 2(-A\sin x + B\cos x)$$
$$+ 3(A\cos x + B\sin x) = 2\sin x$$

$$(-A + 2B + 3A)\cos x + (-B - 2A + 3B)\sin x$$
$$= 2\sin x$$

Equating like coefficients leads to:

$$-A + 2B + 3A = 2(A + B) = 0$$

and

$$-B - 2A + 3B = 2(-A + B) = 2$$

Thus, $-A = B$, $B = \tfrac{1}{2}$, $A = -\tfrac{1}{2}$, and

$$y = -\tfrac{1}{2}\cos x + \tfrac{1}{2}\sin x$$

58. Let $f(x) = \begin{cases} x^2\sin\tfrac{1}{x} & \text{if } x > 0 \\ 0 & \text{if } x \leq 0 \end{cases}$

Then the derivative is

$$f'(x) = \begin{cases} 2x\sin\tfrac{1}{x} - \cos\tfrac{1}{x} & \text{if } x > 0 \\ 0 & \text{if } x \leq 0 \end{cases}$$

which is not continuous at the origin.

63. $\dfrac{d}{dx}(\tan x) = \lim\limits_{\Delta x \to 0} \dfrac{\tan(x + \Delta x) - \tan x}{\Delta x}$

$$= \lim_{\Delta x \to 0} \frac{1}{\Delta x}\left[\frac{\sin(x + \Delta x)}{\cos(x + \Delta x)} - \frac{\sin x}{\cos x}\right]$$

$$= \lim_{\Delta x \to 0} \frac{\sin(x + \Delta x)\cos x - \sin x \cos(x + \Delta x)}{\Delta x \cos x \cos(x + \Delta x)}$$

$$= \lim_{\Delta x \to 0} \frac{\sin \Delta x}{\Delta x} \lim_{\Delta x \to 0} \frac{\cos^2 x + \sin^2 x}{\cos x \cos(x + \Delta x)}$$

$$= (1)\left(\frac{1}{\cos^2 x}\right) = \sec^2 x$$

3.4 Rates of Change: Rectilinear Motion, Pages 166-169

3. $f'(x) = -4x + 1$; $f'(1) = -4 + 1 = -3$

9. $f'(x) = \ln\sqrt{x} + \frac{1}{2}$; $f'(1) = \frac{1}{2}$

13. Write $f(x) = \left(x - \frac{2}{x}\right)\left(x - \frac{2}{x}\right)$; then use the product rule:

$$f'(x) = \left(x - \frac{2}{x}\right)\left(1 + \frac{2}{x^2}\right) + \left(x - \frac{2}{x}\right)\left(1 + \frac{2}{x^2}\right)$$

$$= 2\left(\frac{x^2 - 2}{x}\right)\left(\frac{x^2 + 2}{x^2}\right)$$

$$= \frac{2(x^4 - 4)}{x^3};$$

$$f'(1) = -6$$

15. **a.** $s'(t) = v(t) = 2t - 2$

    b. $s''(t) = a(t) = 2$

    c. Object begins at $s(0) = 6$ and ends at $s(2) = 6$; $s'(t) = 0$ when $2t - 2 = 0$ or when $t = 1$. On $[0, 1)$ object retreats to $s(1) = 5$; on $(1, 2]$ object advances. Distance covered:

$$\left| s(2) - s(1) \right| + \left| s(1) - s(0) \right| = 2$$

    d. Because $a(t) > 0$, the object is continuously accelerating.

21. **a.** $s'(t) = v(t) = -3 \sin t$

    b. $s''(t) = a(t) = -3 \cos t$

    c. Object begins at $s(0) = 3$ and ends at $s(2\pi) = 3$; $s'(t) = 0$ when

$$-3 \sin t = 0$$

On $[0, 2\pi]$: $t = 0, \pi, 2\pi$

On $[0, \pi)$ object retreats to $s(\pi) = -3$; on $(\pi, 2\pi]$ object advances to $s(2\pi) = 3$. Distance covered:

$$\left| s(\pi) - s(0) \right| + \left| s(2\pi) - s(\pi) \right|$$
$$= \left| -3 - 3 \right| + \left| 3 - (-3) \right|$$
$$= 6 + 6$$
$$= 12$$

    d. $s''(t) = 0$ when $-3 \cos t = 0$

On $[0, 2\pi]$: $t = \frac{\pi}{2}, \frac{3\pi}{2}$

On $[0, \frac{\pi}{2})$ the object is decelerating, on $(\frac{\pi}{2}, \frac{3\pi}{2})$ the object is accelerating, and on $(\frac{3\pi}{2}, 2\pi]$ it is decelerating again.

25. $v(t) = x'(t) = 3t^2 - 18t + 24 = 0$ at $t = 2, 4$, so $x(t)$ is advancing on $[0, 2)$ and $(4, 8]$ and retreating on $(2, 4)$. Thus, the total distance traveled is

$$\left| x(2) - x(0) \right| + \left| x(4) - x(2) \right| + \left| x(8) - x(4) \right|$$
$$= \left| 40 - 20 \right| + \left| 36 - 40 \right| + \left| 148 - 36 \right|$$
$$= 20 + 4 + 112$$
$$= 136 \text{ units}$$

29. $s(t) = -16t^2 + v_0 t + s_0$

    a. The maximum height when $v(t) = -32t + v_0 = 0$ or when $v_0 = 64$ The initial velocity is 64 ft/sec.

    b. The rock hits the ground when $s(t) = 0$. The occurs when $t = 7$; so $-16(7)^2 + 64(7) + s_0 = 0$ when $s_0 = 336$ The cliff is 336 ft high.

c. $s'(t) = -32t + 64$ ft/sec

d. $s'(7) = -32(7) + 64$

$= -160$ ft/sec

The negative sign indicated downward motion, since upward is positive.

36. $s(t) = 88t - 8t^2$;

$v(t) = s'(t) = 88 - 16t = 0$ at the instant t_1 the car stops. Thus,

$8(11 - 2t_1) = 0$ or $t_1 = 5.5$ s

The distance required to stop is

$s(5.5) = 8[(11)(5.5) - (5.5)^2]$

$= 242$ ft

44. a. Because your starting salary is \$30,000 and you obtain a raise of \$3,000 per yr, your salary x yr from now will be $S(x) = 30,000 + 3,000x$ dollars. The percentage rate of change of this salary x years from now is

$$100\left[\frac{S'(x)}{S(x)}\right] = 100\left[\frac{3,000}{30,000 + 3,000x}\right]$$

$$= \frac{100}{10 + x}$$

percent per year.

b. The percentage rate of change after one year is $100/11 = 9.09\%$ per year.

c. In the long run, $100/(10 + x) \to 0$. That is, the percentage rate of change of your salary approaches zero (even though your salary will continue to increase at a constant rate).

51. $s(t) = -\frac{g}{2}t^2 + v_0 t$. It hits when $t = 5$, so

$-\frac{g}{2}(5)^2 + v_0(5) = 0$

$v_0 = \frac{5}{2}g$

The maximum height is reached when $v(t) = 0$:

$v(t) = -gt + \frac{5}{2}g = 0$

$t = \frac{5}{2}$

and

$-\frac{1}{2}g(\frac{5}{2})^2 + \frac{5}{2}g(\frac{5}{2}) = 37.5$

$g = \frac{(37.5)(8)}{25}$

$= 12$

Our friendly Spy finds himself on Mars.

3.5 The Chain Rule, Pages 174-176

SURVIVAL HINT: *The chain rule is probably the most used of all the differentiation rules. Most interesting and/or useful functions are compositions, and their derivatives require the chain rule. When you are finding $f'[u(x)]$, identify the u function, and remember to include the du/dx. Write out intermediate steps; many mistakes are made by trying to do too much "in your head."*

5. $\dfrac{dy}{dx} = \dfrac{dy}{du}\dfrac{du}{dx}$

$= \left(\dfrac{-4}{u^3}\right)(2x)$

$= \dfrac{-8x}{(x^2 - 9)^3}$

11. a. $g'(u) = 3u^2$

b. $u'(x) = 2x$

c. $f'(x) = 3(x^2 + 1)^2(2x)$

$$= 6x(x^2 + 1)^2$$

14. **a.** $f'(x) = (2\sin x \cos x)\cos x + \sin^2 x(-\sin x)$

$$= 2\sin x \cos^2 x - \sin^3 x$$

b. $g'(x) = -\sin^2\theta(\sin x)$

16. **a.** $f'(x) = \frac{1}{2}(\sin x^2)^{-1/2}(\cos x^2)(2x)$

$$= \frac{x\cos x^2}{\sqrt{\sin x^2}}$$

b. $g'(x) = 2\sin\sqrt{x}\,\cos\sqrt{x}\,(\frac{1}{2}x^{-1/2})$

$$= \frac{\sin 2\sqrt{x}}{2\sqrt{x}}$$

18. Since $c(\theta) = \cos(5 - 3\theta)$; think of

$u(\theta) = 5 - 3\theta$ so that

$c'(\theta) = 3\sin(5 - 3\theta)$

23. Use the product rule (as well as the chain rule):

$$f'(x) = (2x^2 + 1)^4(5)(x^2 - 2)^4(2x)$$

$$+ (x^2 - 2)^5(4)(2x^2 + 1)^3(4x)$$

$$= x(2x^2+1)^3(x^2 - 2)^4[10(2x^2+1)+16(x^2 - 2)]$$

$$= 2x(2x^2 + 1)^3(x^2 - 2)^4(18x^2 - 11)$$

29. $f'(t) = (2t + 1)\exp(t^2 + t + 5)$

35. $f'(x) = x^2(2)(x - 1)(1) + 2x(x - 1)^2$

$$= 2x(x - 1)(x + x - 1)$$

$$= 2x(x - 1)(2x - 1)$$

$f'(\frac{1}{2}) = 0; \; f(\frac{1}{2}) = \frac{1}{16}$

Using the point-slope formula:

$$y - \frac{1}{16} = 0$$

41. $q'(x) = \dfrac{(x+2)^3 2(x-1) - (x-1)^2 3(x+2)^2(1)}{(x + 2)^6}$

$$= \frac{(x - 1)(-x + 7)}{(x + 2)^4}$$

$q'(x) = 0$ and therefore has a horizontal tangent when $x = 1, 7$

46. **a.** $V = \frac{4}{3}\pi r^3; \; \frac{dr}{dt} = -\frac{10}{2} = -5$ cm/hr

$$\frac{dV}{dt} = 4\pi r^2 \frac{dr}{dt} = 4\pi(5^2)(-5)$$

$$= -500\pi \text{ cm}^3/\text{hr}$$

b. Since the surface area is $S = 4\pi r^2$,

$$\frac{dS}{dt} = 8\pi r \frac{dr}{dt} = (8\pi)(5)(-5)$$

$$= -200\pi \text{ cm}^2/\text{hr}$$

54. **a.** From Figure 3.26, $\tan\theta = \dfrac{s(t)}{2}$, but

$\theta = 6\pi t$, so $s(t) = 2\tan 6\pi t$.

b. When $|LP| = 4$ km,

$|OP| = \sqrt{4^2 - 2^2} = \sqrt{12}$ km. To find the

time when the light is at P_1, we set

$$\sqrt{12} = 2\tan 6\pi t$$

$$t = \frac{\tan^{-1}\sqrt{3}}{6\pi}$$

$$= \frac{1}{18} \text{ min}$$

$$s'(t) = 2(\sec^2 6\pi t)(6\pi)$$

$$= 12\pi \sec^2 6\pi t$$

We can now find $s'(t) = 12\pi \sec^2 6\pi t$

$$s'(\tfrac{1}{18}) = 12\pi \sec^2 \tfrac{\pi}{3}$$

$$= 12\pi(4)$$

$$= 48\pi$$

$$\approx 150.8 \text{ km/min}$$

57. a. $f'(u) = \dfrac{1}{u^2 + 1}$;

let $g(x) = f[u(x)]$ so

$$g'(x) = \frac{d}{du} f(u) \frac{du}{dx}$$

$$u(x) = 3x - 1;$$

$$g'(x) = \frac{3}{u^2 + 1}$$

$$= \frac{3}{(3x - 1)^2 + 1}$$

b. Let $h(x) = f[u(x)]$; $u(x) = x^{-1}$

$$h'(x) = \frac{1}{x^{-2} + 1}(-x^{-2})$$

$$= \frac{-1}{x^2 + 1}$$

3.6 Implicit Differentiation, Pages 186-189

SURVIVAL HINT: *Since y is assumed to be a function of x, implicit differentiation can be thought of as applying the chain rule with y = u(x).*

1. $2x + 2y\dfrac{dy}{dx} \doteq 0$

$$\frac{dy}{dx} = -\frac{x}{y}$$

5. $2x + 3(x\dfrac{dy}{dx} + y) + 2y\dfrac{dy}{dx} = 0$

$$(3x + 2y)\frac{dy}{dx} = -2x - 3y$$

$$\frac{dy}{dx} = \frac{-(2x + 3y)}{3x + 2y}$$

11. $(-\sin xy)\dfrac{d}{dx}(xy) = -2x$

$$(-\sin xy)(x\frac{dy}{dx} + y) = -2x$$

$$(-x \sin xy)\frac{dy}{dx} = y \sin xy - 2x$$

$$\frac{dy}{dx} = \frac{2x - y \sin xy}{x \sin xy}$$

17. a. $1 - \dfrac{1}{y^2}\dfrac{dy}{dx} = 0$

$$\frac{dy}{dx} = y^2$$

b. $xy + 1 = 5y$

$$(x - 5)y = -1$$

$$y = \frac{-1}{x - 5}$$

$$\frac{dy}{dx} = -\frac{-1}{(x - 5)^2}$$

$$= \frac{1}{(x - 5)^2}$$

19. $\dfrac{dy}{dx} = \dfrac{1}{\sqrt{1 - (2x + 1)^2}}(2)$

$$= \frac{2}{\sqrt{-4x^2 - 4x}}$$

$$= \frac{1}{\sqrt{-x^2 - x}}$$

SURVIVAL HINT: *The functions in Problems 19-32 are inverse function, not reciprocal functions. Remember, $\sin^{-1} x$ is an inverse sine, whereas $(\sin x)^{-1}$ is the reciprocal of a sine function.*

31. $\quad x\dfrac{1}{\sqrt{1-y^2}}\,y' + \sin^{-1}y + y\dfrac{1}{1+x^2}$

$$+ \, y'(\tan^{-1}x) = 1$$

$$y'\left(\dfrac{x}{\sqrt{1-y^2}} + \tan^{-1}x\right)$$

$$= 1 - \sin^{-1}y - \dfrac{y}{1+x^2}$$

$$y' = \dfrac{1 - \sin^{-1}y - \dfrac{y}{1+x^2}}{\dfrac{x}{\sqrt{1-y^2}} + \tan^{-1}x}$$

34. $\quad 3x^2 + 3y^2 y' = y'$

$$3x^2 = y'(1 - 3y^2)$$

$$y' = \dfrac{3x^2}{1 - 3y^2}$$

$$y'(3, -2) = -\dfrac{27}{11}$$

The equation of the tangent line is

$$y + 2 = -\dfrac{27}{11}(x - 3)$$

$$11y + 22 = -27x + 81$$

$$27x + 11y - 59 = 0$$

41. $\quad 3x^2 + 3y^2 y' - \dfrac{9}{2}[xy' + y] = 0$

$$y' = \dfrac{3y - 2x^2}{2y^2 - 3x}$$

At $(2, 1)$: $y' = \dfrac{3-8}{2-6}$

$$= \dfrac{5}{4}$$

45. $\quad 7x + 5y^2 = 1$

$$7 + 10yy' = 0$$

$$y' = -\dfrac{7}{10y}.$$

For y'' we again differentiate:

$$\dfrac{d}{dx}(y') = \dfrac{d}{dx}\left(-\dfrac{7}{10y}\right)$$

$$y'' = \dfrac{7}{10y^2}\,y'$$

$$= \left(\dfrac{7}{10y^2}\right)\left(-\dfrac{7}{10y}\right)$$

$$= -\dfrac{49}{100y^3}$$

52. $\quad y = \dfrac{e^{2x}}{(x^2 - 3)^2 \ln\sqrt{x}}$

$$\ln y = 2x - 2\ln(x^2 - 3) - \ln(\ln\sqrt{x})$$

$$\dfrac{1}{y}\dfrac{dy}{dx} = 2 - 2(2x)(x^2 - 3)^{-1} - \left[\dfrac{\frac{1}{2}(\frac{1}{x})}{\frac{1}{2}\ln x}\right]$$

$$\dfrac{dy}{dx} = y\left[2 - \dfrac{4x}{x^2 - 3} - \dfrac{1}{x\ln x}\right]$$

56. **a.** $\quad b^2 u^2 + a^2 v^2 = a^2 b^2$

$$b^2 u u' + a^2 v = 0$$

$$u' = -\dfrac{a^2 v}{b^2 u}$$

b. $\quad b^2 u + a^2 v v' = 0$

$$v' = -\dfrac{b^2 u}{a^2 v}$$

61. **a.** $\quad 2x + 2y\dfrac{dy}{dx} = 6\dfrac{dy}{dx}$

$$(2y - 6)\dfrac{dy}{dx} = -2x$$

$$\dfrac{dy}{dx} = \dfrac{-2x}{2y - 6}$$

$$= \dfrac{x}{3 - y}$$

b. $\quad x^2 + y^2 = 6y - 10$

$$x^2 + (y - 3)^2 = -1$$

This is impossible since the sum of two

squares is not negative (in the real number system).

c. The derivative does not exist.

63. $\frac{3}{2}(x^2 + y^2)^{1/2}(2x + 2yy')$

$= \frac{1}{2}(x^2 + y^2)^{-1/2}(2x + 2yy') + 1$

$\left[3y(x^2 + y^2)^{1/2} - y(x^2 + y^2)^{-1/2}\right]y'$

$= x(x^2 + y^2)^{-1/2} - 3x(x^2 + y^2)^{1/2} + 1$

$y' = \dfrac{x(x^2 + y^2)^{-1/2} - 3x(x^2 + y^2)^{1/2} + 1}{3y(x^2 + y^2)^{1/2} - y(x^2 + y^2)^{-1/2}}.$

Multiplying numerator and denominator by

$(x^2 + y^2)^{1/2}$ we obtain:

$y' = \dfrac{x - 3x(x^2 + y^2) + (x^2 + y^2)^{1/2}}{3y(x^2 + y^2) - y}$

$= \dfrac{x(1 - 3x^2 - 3y^2) + (x^2 + y^2)^{1/2}}{y(3x^2 + 3y^2 - 1)}$

Now the denominator, $y(3x^2 + 3y^2 - 1) = 0$, when $y = 0$, or $3x^2 + 3y^2 - 1 = 0$.

To find the x-coordinate of the point let $y = 0$ in the equation of the cardioid:

At $y = 0$, $\quad x^3 = |x| + x$.

For $x < 0$, $\quad x^3 = 0$, $\quad x = 0$.

For $x > 0$. $\quad x^3 = 2x$, $\quad x = 0, \pm\sqrt{2}$

At $(0, 0)$ the derivative is undefined. At $(-\sqrt{2}, 0)$ the function is undefined. So this factor of the denominator gives one vertical tangent at $(\sqrt{2}, 0)$. Now consider the other

factor:

$$3x^2 + 3y^2 - 1 = 0$$
$$x^2 + y^2 = \frac{1}{3}$$

is a circle with radius of $\sqrt{3}/3$. We need to find the points where it intersects the cardioid. Substituting $x^2 + y^2 = 1/3$ into the cardioid equation:

$$\left(\frac{1}{3}\right)^{3/2} = \left(\frac{1}{3}\right)^{1/2} + x$$
$$x = -\frac{2\sqrt{3}}{9}$$

Using the circle to find y at this point:

$$\left(-\frac{2\sqrt{3}}{9}\right)^2 + y^2 = \frac{1}{3}$$
$$y^2 = \frac{5}{27}$$
$$y = \pm\frac{\sqrt{15}}{9}$$

There are two additional vertical tangents, at $\left(-\frac{2\sqrt{3}}{9}, \frac{\sqrt{15}}{9}\right)$ and $\left(-\frac{2\sqrt{3}}{9}, -\frac{\sqrt{15}}{9}\right)$.

3.7 Related Rates and Applications, Pages 194-197

SURVIVAL HINT: *The common error when working related rate problems is to use constants in place of variables. For instance: if a 12 ft ladder is sliding down a wall and we wish to know how fast the top is descending when the bottom is 4 ft from the wall, **do not** put the 4 ft on your figure. The 12 ft is a constant and belongs on the figure. The vertical and horizontal distances are in motion, and should be given variable names. The 4 ft is a point at which* you wish to evaluate your solved equation. *Draw a careful figure, label constant and variables, then set up the **general situation**. Then, find a specific equation by substituting the given values to set up the **specific situation**.*

3.
$$10x\frac{dx}{dt} - \frac{dy}{dt} = 0$$

When $x = 10$, $y = 400$, and $\frac{dx}{dt} = 10$

$$10(10)(10) - \frac{dy}{dt} = 0$$

$$\frac{dy}{dt} = 1,000$$

9.
$$2x\frac{dx}{dt} + x\frac{dy}{dt} + \frac{dx}{dt}y - 2y\frac{dy}{dt} = 0$$

When $x = 4$,

$$16 + 4y - y^2 = 11$$

$$y^2 - 4y - 5 = 0$$

$$(y + 1)(y - 5) = 0$$

$$y = -1 \text{ (discard)}, 5$$

When $x = 4$, $y = 5$ and $\frac{dy}{dt} = 5$,

$$2(4)\frac{dx}{dt} + (4)(5) + \frac{dx}{dt}(5) - 2(5)(5) = 0$$

$$\frac{dx}{dt} = \frac{30}{13}$$

11. $\frac{d}{dt}F(x) = -12\frac{dx}{dt} = -12(\frac{1}{4}) = -3$

Notice that since F is a linear function of x, the change in F is a constant, and does not depend upon the value of x. (See Problems 10 and 11.)

15. The area of the ripple is $A = \pi r^2$ in.^{2}

$$\frac{dA}{dt} = 2\pi r\frac{dr}{dt} \text{ or } 4 = 2\pi(1)\frac{dr}{dt} \text{ so that}$$

$$\frac{dr}{dt} = \frac{2}{\pi}$$

$$\approx 0.637 \text{ ft/s}$$

27. Let x be the horizontal distance from the boat to the pier and D the length of the rope; D is the hypotenuse of a right triangle with legs 12 and x.

$$12^2 + x^2 = D^2$$

$$0 + 2x\frac{dx}{dt} = (2D)\frac{dD}{dt}$$

We are given that $dD/dt = -6$ and find that $D = 20$ when $x = 16$. At this instant, we have

$$2(16)\frac{dx}{dt} = 2(20)(-6)$$

$$\frac{dx}{dt} = -\frac{240}{32}$$

$$= -7.5$$

The negative value means the distance is decreasing at the rate of 7.5 ft/min.

29. $H(t) = -16t^2 + 160$ is the height of the ball at time t. The distance from the tip of the shadow to a point directly under the ball on the ground is x. $H(t)$ and x form a right triangle. The lamp is at 160 ft above the ground and at a horizontal distance $x + 10$ from the shadow of the ball. The line through the lamp, ball, and shadow is the hypotenuse of a right triangle similar to the one discussed above.

$$H = -16t^2 + 160 = \frac{160x}{x + 10}$$

Now,

$$-32t = 160\left[\frac{10}{(x+10)^2}\right]\frac{dx}{dt}$$

When $t = 1$, $H = 144$ and

$$144 = \frac{160x}{x+10} \text{ so that } x = 90$$

Thus,

$$-32(1) = 160\left[\frac{10}{(90+10)^2}\right]\frac{dx}{dt}$$

$$-200 = \frac{dx}{dt}$$

Thus, the shadow is moving at 200 ft/s.

32. Assume the ice is in the shape of a sphere of radius r.

$$V = \tfrac{4}{3}\pi r^3$$

$$\frac{dV}{dt} = 4\pi r^2 \frac{dr}{dt}$$

With $r = 4$ and $\frac{dV}{dt} = -5$,

$$-5 = 4\pi(4)^2 \frac{dr}{dt}$$

$$\frac{dr}{dt} = -\frac{5}{64\pi}$$

$$\approx -0.025$$

The radius is decreasing at the rate of 0.025 in./min. The surface area is given by

$$S = 4\pi r^2$$

$$\frac{dS}{dt} = 8\pi r \frac{dr}{dt}$$

With $r = 4$ and $\frac{dr}{dt} = \frac{-5}{64\pi}$,

$$\frac{dS}{dt} = 8\pi(4)\left(-\frac{5}{64\pi}\right)$$

$$= -2.5 \text{ in.}^2/\text{min.}$$

The surface area is decreasing at the rate of 2.5 in.^{2}/min.

37. At noon, the car is at the origin, while the truck is at $(250, 0)$. At time t, the truck is at position $(250 - x, 0)$, while the car is at $(0, y)$. Let H be the distance between them. Also, we are given $dx/dt = 25$, $dy/dt = 50$, $x = 25t$ and $y = 50t$.

$$H^2 = (250 - x)^2 + y^2$$

$$H^2 = (250 - 25t)^2 + 50^2 t^2$$

$$H^2 = 3{,}125t^2 - 12{,}500t + 62{,}500$$

a. $$2H\frac{dH}{dt} = 6{,}250t - 12{,}500$$

$$\frac{dH}{dt} = \frac{3{,}125t - 6{,}250}{\sqrt{3{,}125t^2 - 12{,}500t + 62{,}500}}$$

b. $dH/dt = 0$ when $3{,}125t - 6{,}250 = 0$ or when $t = 2$.

c. $$H^2 = 3{,}125(2)^2 - 12{,}500(2) + 62{,}500$$

$$= 50{,}000$$

$$H = 100\sqrt{5}$$

$$\approx 224 \text{ mi} \quad (\text{reject negative})$$

39. Let x denote the horizontal distance (in miles) between the plane and the observer. Let t denote the time (in hours), and draw a diagram representing the situation so that the angle is labeled θ and the distance is labeled D. It is given $dx/dt = -500$ mi/h. We are asked to find $d\theta/dt$ at the instant when $x = 4$

and $dx/dt = -500$.

$$\tan \theta = \tfrac{3}{x}.$$

$$(\sec^2\theta)\,\frac{d\theta}{dt} = -\frac{3}{x^2}\frac{dx}{dt}$$

We note that $D = 5$ when $x = 4$ so we have

$$(\tfrac{5}{4})^2\,\frac{d\theta}{dt} = -\frac{3}{4^2}(-500)$$

$$\frac{d\theta}{dt} = 60 \text{ rad/hr}$$

$$= 1 \text{ rad/min}$$

43. Draw a figure using the variables of A for the distance traveled by the first ship, B for the distance traveled by the second ship, D for the distance between them, and the constant angle of 60°. We are asked to find dD/dt at $t = 2$ and $t = 5$. As the hint suggests, these variables are all generally related by the law of cosines:

$$D^2 = A^2 + B^2 - 2AB\cos\theta.$$

$$2D\frac{dD}{dt} = 2A\frac{dA}{dt} + 2B\frac{dB}{dt} - \left(A\frac{dB}{dt} + B\frac{dA}{dt}\right)$$

(Note that $\cos\theta = \tfrac{1}{2}$ is a constant.)

At $t = 2$ $A = 16$, $B = 12$, $\frac{dA}{dt} = 8$, $\frac{dB}{dt} = 12$,

$$D^2 = 16^2 + 12^2 - 2(16)(12)(\tfrac{1}{2})$$

$$D = \sqrt{208}$$

$$2\sqrt{208}\,\frac{dD}{dt} = 2(16)(8) + 2(12)(12)$$

$$- [16(12) + 12(8)]$$

$$\frac{dD}{dt} = \frac{128}{\sqrt{208}}$$

$$= \frac{32\sqrt{13}}{13}$$

$$\approx 8.875 \text{ knots}$$

At $t = 5$, $A = 40$, $B = 48$, $\frac{dA}{dt} = 8$, $\frac{dB}{dt} = 12$,

$$D^2 = 40^2 + 48^2 - 2(40)(48)(\tfrac{1}{2})$$

$$D = \sqrt{1984}$$

$$2\sqrt{1984}\,\frac{dD}{dt} = 2(40)(8) + 2(48)(12)$$

$$- [40(12) + 48(8)]$$

$$\frac{dD}{dt} = \frac{464}{\sqrt{1984}}$$

$$= \frac{58\sqrt{31}}{31}$$

$$\approx 10.417 \text{ knots}$$

3.8 Linear Approximations and Differentials, Pages 206–209

SURVIVAL HINT: *The differential can be though of as the change in f along the tangent. If Δx is "small" and the function is reasonably "well behaved," then the difference between the actual value of f and the corresponding value of the tangent will be relatively small. It is most useful when extrapolating data, that is, when we really do know how the function will behave beyond a given point, and our best bet is the tangent at that point.*

1. $d(2x^3) = 6x^2\,dx$

7. $d\left(\dfrac{\tan 3x}{2x}\right) = \dfrac{x(3\sec^2 3x) - (\tan 3x)(1)}{2x^2}\,dx$

$$= \frac{3x\sec^2 3x - \tan 3x}{2x^2}\,dx$$

11. $d(e^x\ln x) = \left[e^x \cdot \dfrac{1}{x} + e^x\ln x\right]dx$

$$= \frac{e^x}{x}(1 + x\ln x)\,dx$$

15. $d\left(\dfrac{x-5}{\sqrt{x+4}}\right)$

$$= \dfrac{\sqrt{x+4}(1) - (x-5)(\frac{1}{2})(x+4)^{-1/2}}{x+4}\, dx$$

$$= \dfrac{2x+8 - x + 5}{2(x+4)^{3/2}}\, dx$$

$$= \dfrac{x+13}{2(x+4)^{3/2}}\, dx$$

21. Let $f(x) = x^5 - 2x^3 + 3x^2 - 2$;

$f'(x) = 5x^4 - 6x^2 + 6x$;

$x_0 = 3$ and $\Delta x = dx = 0.01$.

Now, $f(x_0 + \Delta x) \approx f(x_0) + f'(x_0)dx$, so

$$f(3.01) \approx f(3) + f'(3)dx$$
$$= [(3)^5 - 2(3)^3 + 3(3)^2 - 2]$$
$$+ [5(3)^4 - 6(3)^2 + 6(3)](0.01)$$
$$= 214 + 3.69$$
$$= 217.69$$

Comparing this to a calculator value of

$$f(3.01) = 217.7155882$$

we see an error of approximately 0.0255882.

28. Because the cost is

$$C(q) = 0.1q^3 - 0.5q^2 + 500q + 200$$

the change in cost resulting from a decrease in production from 4 units to 3.9 units $(\Delta q = -0.1)$ is

$$\Delta C = C(3.9) - C(4) \approx C'(4)(-0.1)$$

Since $C'(q) = 0.3q^2 - q + 500$ and $C'(4) = 500.80$, it follows that

$$\Delta C = 500.80(-0.1) = -50.08$$

That is, the cost will decrease by approximately \$50.08.

31. $V = \frac{4}{3}\pi r^3$ and $dV = 4\pi r^2 dr$

When $r = 8.5/2$ and $\Delta r = dr = 1/8$, we have

$$dV = 4\pi(4.25)^2(\tfrac{1}{8})$$

$$\approx 28.37 \text{ in.}^3$$

32. Let x be the length of an edge of the cube.

The the total cost (in cents) is

$$C(x) = \underbrace{2(4x^2)}_{\text{sides}} + \underbrace{3x^2}_{\text{bottom}} + \underbrace{4x^2}_{\text{top}} = 15x^2$$

$$\Delta C \approx C'(x)\Delta x = 30x\Delta x$$

When $x = 20$, $\Delta x = 1$,

$$\Delta C \approx 30(20)(1) = 600 \text{ cents}$$

The actual change is

$$C(21) - C(20) = 615 \text{ cents}$$

The actual increase is 615 cents = \$6.15.

35. Let $S(R)$ be the speed of the blood.

$$S(R) = cR^2$$

$$S'(R) = 2cR$$

We have

$$\dfrac{\Delta S}{S} \approx \dfrac{S'(R)\Delta R}{S}$$

$$= \dfrac{2cR\Delta R}{cR^2}$$

$$= 2\dfrac{\Delta R}{R}$$

A 1% error in R means $\Delta R/R = 0.01$ and the propagated error in S is

$$\frac{\Delta S}{S} \approx 2(0.01)$$
$$= 0.02$$

The error in S is approximately $\pm 2\%$.

SURVIVAL HINT: *Anytime you see the adjective "marginal" in an economics application, you can translate it as derivative. It designates a rate of change.*

44. **a.** Let $C(x)$ be the total cost of producing x units and $p(x)$ the selling price; the marginal cost is $C'(x) = \frac{2}{7}x + 4$.

b. If $10 = \frac{2}{7}x + 4$, then $x = 21$ and
$$p(21) = \frac{1}{4}(80 - 21) = 14.75$$

c. The cost of producing the eleventh unit is approximately
$$C'(10) = \frac{20}{7} + 4 = 6.86$$

d. The actual cost of producing the 11th unit is
$$C(11) - C(10) = \frac{11^2 - 10^2}{7} + 4(11 - 10)$$
$$= 7$$

46. $f(x) = x^6 - x^5 + x^3 - 3$;
$f'(x) = 6x^5 - 5x^4 + 3x^2$;
$f(0) = -3, f(1) = -2,$
and $f(2) = 37$, so there is a root on $[1, 2]$.

$x_0 = 1.4$; $\quad f(1.4) \approx 1.895$;
$$f'(1.4) \approx 18.9, \text{ so}$$

$$x_1 = 1.4 - \frac{1.895}{18.9} \approx 1.2997$$

$$f(1.2997) \approx 0.307; f'(1.2997) \approx 13.1;$$

$$x_2 = 1.2997 - \frac{0.307}{13.1}$$

$$\approx 1.2763$$

$$f(1.2763) \approx 0.0147;$$

$$f'(1.2763) \approx 11.9;$$

$$x_3 = 1.2763 - \frac{0.0147}{11.9}$$

$$\approx 1.2751;$$

$$x_4 \approx 1.2751$$

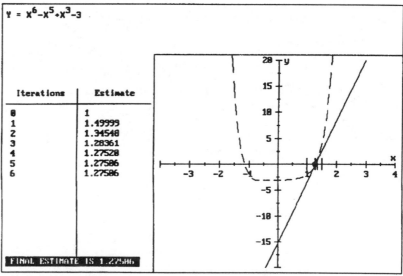

Note: there is another real root, as shown below. $x_3 = -1.16137$

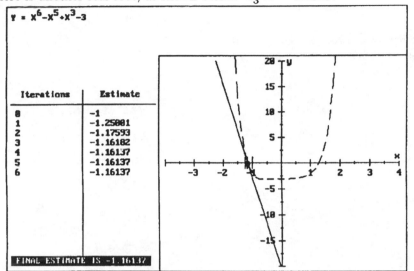

The approximate roots are 1.27506, $-$ 1.16137.

55. $f(x) = \sqrt{x}$ and $f'(x) = \dfrac{1}{2x^{1/2}}$; $\Delta x = -3$

$f(97) = f(100 - 3) = f(100) + f'(100)(-3)$

$= 10 - \dfrac{3}{2\sqrt{100}} = 9.85$

Calculator check: $\sqrt{97} \approx 9.848857802$

If $\Delta x = 16$,

$f(97) = f(81 + 16)$

$= f(81) + f'(81)(16)$

$= 9 + \dfrac{16}{2\sqrt{81}}$

≈ 9.89

57. a. Let $P(x)$ be the profit when producing x units at a total cost of $C(x)$ and revenue of $R(x)$.

$$P(x) = R(x) - C(x)$$

$$P'(x) = R'(x) - C'(x)$$

$$P'(x) = 0 \text{ if } C'(x) = R'(x).$$

b. $A'(x) = \dfrac{xC'(x) - C(x)}{x^2}$

$= \dfrac{1}{x}\left[C'(x) - \dfrac{C(x)}{x}\right]$

$A'(x) = 0$ if $C'(x) = A(x)$.

CHAPTER 3 REVIEW

Proficiency Examination, Pages 209-210

SURVIVAL HINT: *To help you review the concepts of this chapter, **hand write** the answers to each of these questions onto your own paper.*

1. $m_{\text{sec}} = \dfrac{\Delta y}{\Delta x} = \dfrac{f(x + \Delta x) - f(x)}{\Delta x}$

    $m_{\text{tan}} = \lim\limits_{\Delta x \to 0} \dfrac{f(x + \Delta x) - f(x)}{\Delta x}$

2. If $y = f(x)$, then

    $\dfrac{dy}{dx} = \lim\limits_{\Delta x \to 0} \dfrac{f(x + \Delta x) - f(x)}{\Delta x}$,

    provided this limit exists.

3. A normal line is perpendicular to the tangent line at a point on the graph of a function.

4. If a function is differentiable at $x = c$, then it must be continuous at that point. The converse is not true: If a function is continuous at $x = c$, then it may or may not be differentiable at that point. Finally, if a function is discontinuous at $x = c$, then it cannot possibly have a derivative at that point.

5. Answers should include $f'(x)$, $\dfrac{dy}{dx}$ and y'.

6. **a.** $(cf)' = cf'$

    b. $(f + g)' = f' + g'$

    c. $(f - g)' = f' - g'$

    d. $(af + bg)' = af' + bg'$

    e. $(fg)' = fg' + f'g$

    f. $\left(\dfrac{f}{g}\right)' = \dfrac{gf' - fg'}{g^2}$

    g. $d(cf) = c\,df$

    $d(f + g) = df + dg$

    $d(f - g) = df - dg$

    $d(af + bg) = a\,df + b\,dg$

    $d(fg) = f\,dg + g\,df$

    $d\left(\dfrac{f}{g}\right) = \dfrac{g\,df - f\,dg}{g^2} \quad (g \neq 0)$

7. **a.** $\dfrac{d}{dx}(k) = 0$

    b. $\dfrac{d}{dx}(x^n) = nx^{n-1}$

    c. $\dfrac{d}{dx}\sin x = \cos x;\ \dfrac{d}{dx}\cos x = -\sin x$

    $\dfrac{d}{dx}\tan x = \sec^2 x;\ \dfrac{d}{dx}\cot x = -\csc^2 x$

    $\dfrac{d}{dx}\sec x = \sec x \tan x;$

    $\dfrac{d}{dx}\csc x = -\csc x \cot x$

    d. $\dfrac{d}{dx}e^x = e^x$

    e. $\dfrac{d}{dx}\ln x = \dfrac{1}{x}$

    f. $\dfrac{d}{dx}\left(\sin^{-1}x\right) = \dfrac{1}{\sqrt{1 - x^2}};$

    $\dfrac{d}{dx}\left(\cos^{-1}x\right) = \dfrac{-1}{\sqrt{1 - x^2}};$

    $\dfrac{d}{dx}\left(\tan^{-1}x\right) = \dfrac{1}{1 + x^2};$

    $\dfrac{d}{dx}\left(\cot^{-1}x\right) = \dfrac{-1}{1 + x^2};$

    $\dfrac{d}{dx}\left(\sec^{-1}x\right) = \dfrac{1}{|x|\sqrt{x^2 - 1}};$

$$\frac{d}{dx}\left(\csc^{-1}x\right) = \frac{-1}{|x|\sqrt{x^2 - 1}}$$

8. A higher derivative is a derivative of a derivative.

$$y''; \; y'''; \; y^{(4)}; \; \cdots ; \; \frac{d^2y}{dx^2}; \; \frac{d^3y}{dx^3}; \; \frac{d^4y}{dx^4}; \; \cdots$$

9. Rate of change refers to both average and instantaneous rates of change. The average rate of change for a function f is

$$\frac{f(x + \Delta x) - f(x)}{\Delta x}$$

The instantaneous rate of change is

$$\lim_{\Delta x \to 0} \frac{f(x + \Delta x) - f(x)}{\Delta x} = f'(x)$$

10. The relative rate of change of $y = f(x)$ with respect to x is given by the ratio $f'(x)/f(x)$.

11. $v(t) = s'(t); \; a(t) = v'(t) = s''(t)$

12. $\dfrac{dy}{dx} = \dfrac{dy}{du}\dfrac{du}{dx}$ or $f(u(x))]' = f'[u(x)]u'(x)$

13. Logarithmic differentiation is a procedure in which logarithms are used to trade the task of differentiating products and quotients for that of differentiating sums and differences. It is especially valuable as a means for handling complicated product or quotient functions and power functions where variables appear in both the base and the exponent.

14. Apply all the rules of differentiation, treating y as a function of x and remembering the chain rule.

15. (1) Draw a figure.

    (2) Relate the variables through a formula or equation.

    (3) Differentiate the equations (formulas).

    (4) Substitute numerical values and solve algebraically for the required rate in terms of known rates.

16. $f(b) \approx f(a) + f'(a)(b - a)$

17. $dx = \Delta x; \; dy = f'(x)dx$

See Figure 3.51, page 199 of text.

18. The propagated error is the difference between $f(x + \Delta x)$ and $f(x)$ and is defined by

$$\Delta f = f(x + \Delta x) - f(x)$$

The relative error is $\Delta f/f$, and the percentage error is $100|\Delta f/f|$.

19. Marginal analysis is the use of the derivative to approximate a change in a function produced by a unit change in the variable. It is especially useful in economics, where the function is cost, revenue, or profit.

20. The Newton-Raphson method approximates a root of a function by locating a point near a root, and then finding where the tangent line at this point intersects the x-axis. That is,

$$x_{n+1} = x_n - \frac{f(x_n)}{f'(x_n)}$$

Repetition of this technique usually closes in on the root.

21. $y = x^3 + x^{3/2} + \cos 2x$

$\dfrac{dy}{dx} = 3x^2 + \dfrac{3}{2} x^{1/2} - 2 \sin 2x$

24. $x \dfrac{dy}{dx} + y + 3y^2 \dfrac{dy}{dx} = 0$

$(x + 3y^2)\dfrac{dy}{dx} = -y$

$\dfrac{dy}{dx} = \dfrac{-y}{x + 3y^2}$

27. $y' = \dfrac{3}{\sqrt{1 - (3x + 2)^2}}$

30. $\ln y = \ln \dfrac{\ln (x^2 - 1)}{\sqrt[3]{x} \,(1 - 3x)^3}$

$= \ln[\ln(x^2 - 1)] - \dfrac{1}{3} \ln x - 3 \ln(1 - 3x)$

$\dfrac{1}{y} y' = \dfrac{1}{\ln (x^2-1)} \dfrac{1}{x^2 - 1}(2x) - \dfrac{1}{3x} - \dfrac{3}{1-3x}(-3)$

$= \dfrac{2x}{(x^2 - 1)\ln (x^2 - 1)} - \dfrac{1}{3x} - \dfrac{9}{3x - 1}$

$y' = y\left[\dfrac{2x}{(x^2 - 1)\ln(x^2 - 1)} - \dfrac{1}{3x} - \dfrac{9}{3x - 1}\right]$

33. When $x = 1$, $y = 8$, so the point in $(1, 8)$;

$\dfrac{dy}{dx} = (x^2 + 3x - 2)(-3) + (7 - 3x)(2x + 3)$

At $x = 1$, $\dfrac{dy}{dx} = 14$

$y - 8 = 14(x - 1)$

$14x - y - 6 = 0$

CHAPTER 4

Additional Applications of the Derivative

SURVIVAL HINT: *It is likely that you have had a test covering Chapter 3. The concepts of limit and derivative, and skill in finding derivatives accurately and quickly, are essential to success in the remainder of the course. It is essential that your examination not be filed away until you have mastered the material of Chapter 3! Analyze your mistakes. They are usually one of three types: you did not understand the concept, you made a computational or algebraic error, you did not have time to finish the exam. For the first type, ask the instructor, a tutor, or another student to explain the concept to you. It is a good idea to form a small group of 3 to 5 students to do a "post mortem" on each examination. For the second type of error, attempt to organize your work better. Put more steps on paper and do less in your head. Stay composed during the examination, and do not rush. It is usually better to do fewer problems and get them right, than to turn in more completed problems full of errors. The solution for the third type of difficulty, assuming most other students completed the examination, is to practice. The more problems you solve, the faster you become. Do all of the chapter review problems, and some of the supplementary problems before the next examination. This takes **time**, but the standard rule-of-thumb is two to three hours of time for every hour of classroom time.*

4.1 Extreme Values of a Continuous Function, Pages 226–227

SURVIVAL HINT: *Remember that the **candidates** for extrema are the endpoints, and points where the derivative is either zero or does not exist.*

3. $f(-1) = -4; f(3) = 0;$

$f'(x) = 3x^2 - 6x$

$3x^2 - 6x = 0$

$3x(x - 2) = 0$

$x = 0, 2$

$f(0) = 0; f(2) = -4;$ maximum value is 0 and the minimum value is -4.

11. $f(-1) = 1; f(1) = 1;$

$f'(x)$ is not defined at $x = 0; f(0) = 0$
Maximum value is 1 and the minimum value is 0.

16. The calculator does not seem to take the derivative at $x = 0$ and $x < 0$ into account. The derivative is not defined at $x = 0$, but it certainly is defined for $x < 0$. If you enter $(x^2)\hat{\ }(1/3)(5 - 2x)$ you will obtain the correct graph.

17. $f(1) = 0; f(-1) = 0;$

$f'(u) = -\frac{2}{3}u^{-1/3}$ which is not defined at

$u = 0$. $f(0) = 1$. The maximum value is 1 and the minimum value is 0.

20. $g(-4) = 76; g(4) = 12$

$$g'(x) = 3x^2 + 6x - 24$$

$$3x^2 + 6x - 24 = 0$$

$$3(x + 4)(x - 2) = 0$$

$$x = -4, 2$$

$g(2) = -32$

The maximum value is 76 and the minimum value is -32.

SURVIVAL HINT: *If the function has a discontinuity on the specified interval, there may be additional "endpoint" to consider.*

23. $h'(x) = \sec^2 x + \sec x \tan x$

$$= \sec x(\sec x + \tan x);$$

$h'(x) = 0$ when $\sec x = 0$ (never), or when

$\sec x + \tan x = 0$:

$$\sec x + \tan x = 0$$
$$\frac{1 + \sin x}{\cos x} = 0$$
$$\sin x = -1$$
$$x = \frac{3\pi}{2} \text{ on } [0, 2\pi]$$

We need also consider points where $h'(x)$ is undefined, namely $\frac{\pi}{2} + k\pi$. But $h(x)$ is also undefined for these values. Our only candidates are the endpoints: $h(0) = 1$, $h(2\pi) = 1$ but h is not continuous. There is no maximum and no minimum value.

28. $f(-1) = 11; f(4) = -4; f(2) = 2$

$f'(x) = -3$ if $x < 2$; $f'(x) = -2x + 3$

for $x \geq 2$; $f'(x) = 0$ when $x = \frac{3}{2}$, but $\frac{3}{2} < 2$.

The maximum value is 11 and the minimum value is -4.

31. $g(1) = 7; g(9) = 7; g'(x) = -9x^{-2} + 1$

which is equal to 0 when $x = 3$ (-3 is not in the domain). $g(3) = 3$. The smallest value is 3.

35. $g(2) = \dfrac{\ln 2}{\cos 2}$

$$\approx -1.6656;$$

$$g(3) = \frac{\ln 3}{\cos 3}$$

$$\approx -1.1097$$

$$g'(x) = \frac{\cos x \left(\frac{1}{x}\right) - \ln x(-\sin x)}{\cos^2 x}$$

$$\frac{\cos x + x(\ln x)(\sin x)}{x \cos^2 x} = 0$$

$$x \ln x = -\cot x$$

$$x \approx 2.8098445$$

$g(2.8098445) \approx -1.0927$

the largest value of g on $[2, 3]$ is approximately -1.1 at $x \approx 2.81$.

40. $f(0) = 0; f(4) = -2$

$$f'(w) = \frac{1}{2}w^{-1/2}(w - 5)^{1/3} + \frac{1}{3}w^{1/2}(w - 5)^{-2/3}$$

$$= \frac{1}{6}w^{-1/2}(w - 5)^{-2/3}[3(w - 5) + 2w]$$

$$= \frac{1}{6}w^{-1/2}(w - 5)^{-2/3}(5w - 15)$$

$$= \tfrac{5}{6}w^{-1/2}(w-5)^{-2/3}(w-3)$$

$f'(w) = 0$ when $w = 3$, and does not exist when $w = 0$, $w = 5$.

$$f(3) = \sqrt{3}(3-5)^{1/3}$$
$$= -\sqrt[6]{108}$$
$$\approx -2.1822$$

The maximum value is 0 and the minimum value is $-\sqrt[6]{108} \approx -2.1822$.

47. **a.** No such function can be found because of the extreme value theorem (theorem 3.1).

b. No such function can be found because of the extreme value theorem.

c. $f(x) = \sin x$ for $[0, 2\pi]$.

d. No such function can be found because of the extreme value theorem.

52. Let x and y be the numbers we are seeking on $[0, 8]$. Then $x + y = 8$ and $P = x^2(8-x)^2$.

$$P'(x) = x^2(2)(8-x)(-1) + 2x(8-x)^2$$
$$= 2x(8-x)(8-2x)$$

$P'(x) = 0$ when $x = 0$, 8, and 4.

$P(0) = P(8) = 0$; $P(4) = 256$.

The largest product occurs when $x = y = 4$.

59. $A(x) = \dfrac{C(x)}{x}$

$$= 0.125x + \frac{20,000}{x}$$
$$A'(x) = 0.125 - \frac{20,000}{x^2}$$

$= 0$ when

$$x^2 = 160,000$$
$$x = 400$$

Now consider $A(x) = C'(x)$:

$$0.125x + \frac{20,000}{x} = 0.25x$$
$$0.125x^2 = 20,000$$
$$x = 400$$

4.2 The Mean Value Theorem, Pages 233–235

SURVIVAL HINT: *Never use a theorem until you have verified that the hypotheses are met.*

5. Polynomials are everywhere continuous and differentiable, so the hypotheses of MVT are met. $f'(x) = 3x^2 + 1$, so there exists a c on the interval $[1, 2]$ such that

$$f'(c) = \frac{f(2) - f(1)}{2 - 1}$$
$$3c^2 + 1 = \frac{10 - 2}{1}$$
$$3c^2 = 7$$
$$c = \pm\sqrt{\frac{7}{3}}$$

The number $c = \sqrt{\frac{7}{3}} \approx 1.5275$ is on the interval $[1, 2]$.

11. f is continuous and differentiable everywhere on $[0, 2]$, so the hypotheses of MVT are met.

$f'(x) = -\dfrac{1}{(x+1)^2}$, so there exists a c on the interval $[0, 2]$ such that

$$f'(c) = \frac{f(2) - f(0)}{2 - 0}$$

$$-\frac{1}{(c+1)^2} = \frac{\frac{1}{3} - 1}{2},$$

$$\frac{2}{3}(c+1)^2 = 2$$

$$c + 1 = \pm\sqrt{3}$$

$$c = -1 \pm \sqrt{3}$$

Note that only $c = -1 + \sqrt{3} \approx 0.73$ lies in the specified interval.

18. f is continuous and differentiable everywhere on $[1, 3]$, so the hypotheses of MVT are met.
$f'(x) = \dfrac{1 - \ln x}{2x^2}$, so that

$$f'(c) = \frac{f(3) - f(1)}{3 - 1}$$

$$\frac{1 - \ln c}{2c^2} = \frac{1}{2}\left[\frac{\ln\sqrt{3}}{3} - \frac{\ln\sqrt{1}}{1}\right]$$

$$= \frac{1}{12}\ln 3$$

Solve graphically or using a solving utility to find $c \approx 1.65$ which is on the interval $[1, 3]$.

23. Rolle's theorem is applicable since $f(x) = \sin x$ is continuous on $[0, 2\pi]$ and differentiable on $(0, 2\pi)$.

29. f is continuous everywhere, and
$f'(x) = 2\sin x \cos x = \sin 2x$ so
$f(x)$ is differentiable everywhere, in particular on $[-\frac{\pi}{2}, \frac{\pi}{2}]$.

$$f(-\tfrac{\pi}{2}) = f(\tfrac{\pi}{2}) = 1$$

Rolle's theorem applies.

32. By the constant difference theorem
$f(x) = \sqrt{x^2 + 5} + K$, for some constant K.

$$f(2) = \sqrt{2^2 + 5} + K = 1$$

$$3 + K = 1$$

$$K = -2$$

Thus, $f(x) = \sqrt{x^2 + 5} - 2$

33. $f(x) - g(x) = \dfrac{x + 4}{5 - x} - \dfrac{-9}{x - 5}$

$$= -1$$

The constant difference theorem does not apply because f and g are not continuous at $x = 5$. If the interval does not contain 5, then the theorem applies.

$$f'(x) = \frac{9}{(x - 5)^2}; \quad g'(x) = \frac{9}{(x - 5)^2};$$

$$f'(x) = g'(x), \quad x \neq 5.$$

42. $f(x) = \cos x$ is continuous on $[x, y]$ and differentiable on (x, y). Also, $f'(x) = -\sin x$, so by the MVT we have

$$\frac{\cos x - \cos y}{x - y} = -\sin c \leq 1$$

Thus,

$$|\cos x - \cos y| \leq |x - y|$$

45. **a.** Let $f(x) = \cos x - 1$ on $[0, x]$. The hypotheses of the MVT apply, so there exists a w on the interval such that

$$f'(w) = \frac{f(x) - f(0)}{x - 0}$$

$$-\sin w = \frac{(\cos x - 1) - 0}{x}$$

b. Since w is on the interval $[0, x]$, as x approaches 0, w must approach 0 also. So

$$\lim_{x \to 0} \frac{\cos x - 1}{x} = \lim_{w \to 0} \frac{\cos w - 1}{w}$$
$$= \lim_{w \to 0} (-\sin w) = 0$$

50. Let $s(t)$ be the distance traveled during time t. Then

$$\frac{s(5) - s(0)}{5 - 0} = s'(t) = v(t)$$

Now, $v(t) = \frac{6 \text{ mi}}{5 \text{ min}} \cdot \frac{60 \text{ min}}{\text{hr}} = 72 \text{ mi/hr}$; the sports car exceeded the speed limit.

54. Let $f(x) = \frac{1}{2x + 1}$ which is continuous and differentiable on $[0, 2]$; $f'(x) = -\frac{2}{(2x + 1)^2}$

$f(2) = \frac{1}{5}$; With $x < c < 2$, we have from the MVT,

$$\frac{\frac{1}{2x+1} - \frac{1}{5}}{x - 2} = -\frac{2}{(2c + 1)^2}$$

$$\frac{1}{2x+1} - \frac{1}{5} = \frac{2(2 - x)}{(2c + 1)^2}$$

Since $c < 2$, we have

$$\frac{1}{(2c+1)^2} > \frac{1}{25}$$

$$\frac{1}{2x+1} > \frac{1}{5} + \frac{2(2 - x)}{25}$$

4.3 First-Derivative Test, Pages 244-246

3. Notice that each function has a value of 0 when the other has a horizontal tangent. So this does not tell us which is which. Next consider that when f is increasing f' must be positive. This identifies which graph is f and

which is f'. The black curve is the function and the blue one is the derivative.

7. The graph is the function, and on $(-\infty, 2)$ the slope is -1, and on $(2, +\infty)$ the slope is $+1$, so the derivative function is constant on each of these integrals.

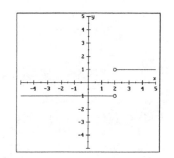

9. The graph is the derivative, so the the function is falling where the derivative is negative; on $(-\infty, 1)$. The function is rising where the derivative is positive; on $(1, +\infty)$. The minimum value occurs where the graph of the derivative crosses the x-axis. The function must be parabolic in shape.

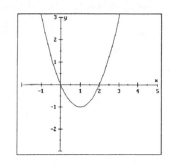

15. a. $f'(x) = 3x^2 + 70x - 125$
critical numbers: $x = \frac{5}{3}$, $x = -25$

b. increasing on $(-\infty, -25) \cup (\frac{5}{3}, +\infty)$

decreasing on $(-25, \frac{5}{3})$

c. critical points: $(\frac{5}{3}, -9{,}481)$, relative minimum; $(-25, 0)$, relative maximum

d.

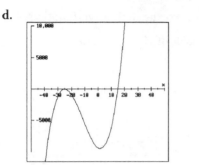

22. a. $f'(t) = (2t-1)^2(2t) + 2(2t-1)(2)(t^2 - 9)$

$= 2(2t - 1)[t(2t-1) + 2t^2 - 18]$

$= 2(2t - 1)(4t^2 - t - 18)$

$= 2(2t - 1)(t + 2)(4t - 9)$

critical numbers: $t = \frac{1}{2}, -2, \frac{9}{4}$

b. increasing on $(-2, \frac{1}{2}) \cup (\frac{9}{4}, +\infty)$;

decreasing on $(-\infty, -2) \cup (\frac{1}{2}, \frac{9}{4})$

c. critical points: $(-2, -125)$, relative minimum; $(\frac{1}{2}, 0)$ relative maximum; $(\frac{9}{4}, -48.2)$, relative minimum

d.

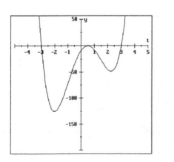

27. a. $g'(x) = x^{2/3}(2) + \frac{2}{3}x^{-1/3}(2x - 5)$

$= \frac{10}{3}(x - 1)x^{-1/3}$

critical numbers: $x = 1$ and $f'(x)$ is undefined at $x = 0$

b. increasing on $(-\infty, 0) \cup (1, +\infty)$

decreasing on $(0, 1)$

c. critical points: $(1, -3)$, relative minimum; $(0, 0)$, relative maximum

d.

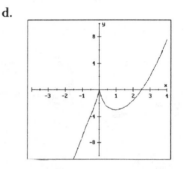

32. a. $f'(x) = -9 \sin x + 8 \cos x \sin x$

$= (-\sin x)(9 - 8 \cos x)$

critical numbers: $x = 0$, $x = \pi$; note: no solution for $\cos x = \frac{9}{8}$

b. decreasing on $(0, \pi)$

c. critical point $(0, 5)$, relative maximum; $(\pi, -13)$, relative minimum

d.

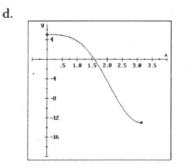

42.
$$f'(x) = (x^2 - 4)^4(3)(x^2 - 1)^2(2x)$$
$$+ (x^2 - 1)^3(4)(x^2 - 4)^3(2x)$$
$$= (x^2 - 4)^3(x^2 - 1)^2(2x)(3x^2 - 12 + 4x^2 - 4)$$
$$= (x^2 - 4)^3(x^2 - 1)^2(2x)(7x^2 - 16)$$

At $x = 1$ (check left and right sides), neither; at $x = 2$, relative minimum.

44. $f'(x) = (x - 1)^2(x - 2)(x - 4)(x + 5)^4$ has

critical numbers of $x = 1, 2, 4,$ and -5
At $x = 1$, $\uparrow\uparrow$ pattern, so it is neither a relative maximum nor a relative minimum; At $x = 2$, $\uparrow\downarrow$ pattern, so it is a relative maximum; At $x = 4$, $\downarrow\uparrow$ pattern, so it is a relative minimum; At $x = -5$, $\uparrow\uparrow$ pattern, neither a maximum nor a relative minimum

49. This is a system of three variables for which we have three pieces of information. $(5, 12)$ is on the curve so: $12 = 25a + 5b + c$.

$(0, 3)$ is on the curve so $3 = c$.

$f'(x) = 2ax + b = 0$ when x is 5, so:

$0 = 10a + b$. Substituting the second and third equations into the first:

$$12 = 25a - 50a + 3$$
$$a = -\frac{9}{25}$$

$b = \frac{18}{5}$, $c = 3$;

Therefore,

$$f(x) = -\frac{9}{25}x^2 + \frac{18}{5}x + 3$$

51.
$$f(x) = (x - p)(x - q) = x^2 - (p + q)x + pq$$
$$f'(x) = 2x - (p + q) = 0, \text{ so } x_1 = \frac{p + q}{2}$$

which is midway between $(0, p)$ and $(0, q)$

57. $f(x) = \left(Ax^{5/3} + Bx^{2/3}\right)^{1/2}$

$$f'(x) = \frac{1}{2}\left(Ax^{5/3} + Bx^{2/3}\right)^{-1/2}\left(\frac{5}{3}Ax^{2/3} + \frac{2}{3}Bx^{-1/3}\right)$$
$$= \frac{1}{6}\left(Ax^{5/3} + Bx^{2/3}\right)^{-1/2}\left(5Ax^{2/3} + 2Bx^{-1/3}\right)$$
$$= \frac{1}{6}x^{-1/3}\left(Ax^{5/3} + Bx^{2/3}\right)^{-1/2}\left(5Ax + 2B\right)$$

$f'(x) = 0$ when $5Ax + 2B = 0$; that is, $x = -2B/5A$; this exhibits an $\downarrow\uparrow$ pattern, and therefore is a relative minimum. We also have a critical number when $x = 0$, as the denominator will be 0. This exhibits the $\uparrow\uparrow$ pattern, and consequently is neither.

4.4 Concavity and the Second-Derivative Test, Pages 256-259

SURVIVAL HINT: $f''(x) =$ gives **candidates** for inflection points. Even though the second derivative is zero, there may not be a change in concavity. They must be tested.

9. $f'(x) = 2 - 18x^{-2}$; $f''(x) = 36x^{-3}$

critical points:

$(-3, -11)$, relative maximum;

$(3, 13)$, relative minimum;

increasing on $(-\infty, -3) \cup (3, +\infty)$

decreasing on $(-3, 0) \cup (0, 3)$;

concave up on $(0, +\infty)$;

concave down on $(-\infty, 0)$

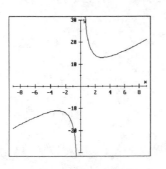

14. $f'(t) = 3(t^3 + 3t^2)^2(3t^2 + 6t)$

$$= 9t(t^3 + 3t^2)^2(t + 2)$$

$$= 9t^5(t + 3)^2(t + 2)$$

$f''(t) = 18t^4(2t + 3)(2t + 5)(t + 3)$

critical points:

$\quad$ (0, 0), relative minimum;

$\quad$ $(-2, 64)$, relative maximum;

points of inflection:

$\quad$ $(-3, 0), (-2.5, 30.5), (-1.5, 38.44)$

increasing on

$(-\infty, -3) \cup (-3, -2) \cup (0, +\infty)$

decreasing on $(-2, 0)$

concave up on $(-3, -2.5) \cup (-1.5, +\infty)$

concave down on $(-\infty, -3) \cup (-2.5, -1.5)$

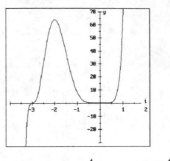

23. $f'(x) = \dfrac{4}{(e^x + e^{-x})^2} = \dfrac{4e^{2x}}{(e^{2x} + 1)^2}$

$f''(x) = \dfrac{-8(e^x - e^{-x})}{(e^x + e^{-x})^3} = \dfrac{-8e^{2x}(e^{2x} - 1)}{(e^{2x} + 1)^3}$

critical point (0, 0), point of inflection

increasing on $(-\infty, +\infty)$

concave up for $(-\infty, 0)$

concave down for $(0, +\infty)$

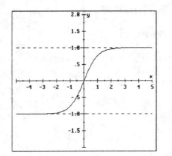

34. $f'(x) = (x + 1)(x^2 + 1)^{-1} + \tan^{-1}x$

Using a solve utility, we find $f'(x) = 0$ when

$x \approx -0.467339$, so a critical point is

$(-0.47, -0.23)$, relative minimum

$f''(x) = (x^2+1)^{-1}+(x+1)[-(x^2+1)^{-2}(2x)]$

$$+ (x^2 + 1)^{-1}$$

$$= 2(x^2+1)^{-1}+(x+1)(-2x)(x^2+1)^{-2}$$

$$= (x^2 + 1)^{-2}(2 - 2x)$$

$$= -2(x - 1)(x^2 + 1)^{-2}$$

$f''(x) = 0$ when $x = 1$; $f(1) = \frac{\pi}{2}$, so the point of inflection is $(1, \frac{\pi}{2})$.

decreasing on $(-1.57, -0.47)$

increasing on $(-0.47, 1.57)$

concave up on $(-1.57, 1)$

concave down on $(1, 1.57)$

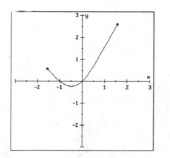

SURVIVAL HINT: *Think Tank Problems 39-42 make excellent test questions to determine if you are understanding the concepts. You should be able to visualize if you are understanding the concepts. You should be able to visualize the graph of any of the 27 combinations $f(x)$, $f'(x)$, and $f''(x)$ positive, negative, or zero.*

40.

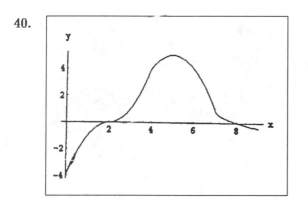

45. $f(x) = Ax^3 + Bx^2 + C$

$$f'(x) = 3Ax^2 + 2Bx$$

$$f''(x) = 6Ax + 2B$$

$E(2, 11)$ is an extremum, so

$$f'(2) = 12A + 4B = 0 \text{ or } B = -3A$$

$I(1, 5)$ is a point of inflection, so

$$f''(1) = 6A + 2B = 0 \text{ or } B = -3A$$

Since the points E and I are on the curve, their coordinates must satisfy its equation. Thus,

$$f(2) = 8A + 4B + C = 8A - 12A + C = 11$$
$$f(1) = A + B + C = A - 3A + C = 5$$

Solving these equations simultaneously, we find $A = -3$, $B = 9$, and $C = -1$. Thus,

$$f(x) = -3x^3 + 9x^2 - 1$$

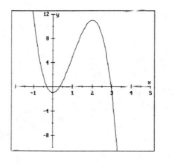

47. a. $S'(x) = \frac{1}{2}(e^x - (-1)e^{-x}) = C(x)$
$C'(x) = \frac{1}{2}(e^x + (-1)e^{-x}) = S(x)$

b. $y = \cosh x$

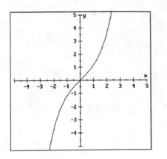

$y = \sinh x$

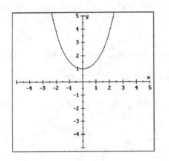

49. a. $D'(t)$

$$= \frac{1}{\sqrt{2\pi}\sigma} \exp\left[-\frac{1}{2}\left(\frac{t-m}{\sigma}\right)^2\right]\left(-\frac{1}{2\sigma^2}\right)(2)(t-m)$$

$= 0$ when $t = m$;

$$D(m) = \frac{1}{\sqrt{2\pi}\sigma}$$

b. $\lim\limits_{t \to \pm\infty} D(t) = 0$

c.   We graph $y = D(x)$ where $\sigma = 1$, $m = 0$

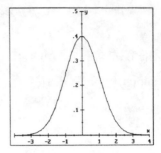

52. $D(x) = \frac{9}{4}x^4 - 7\ell x^3 + 5\ell^2 x^2$ on $[0, \ell]$

$D'(x) = 9x^3 - 21\ell x^2 + 10\ell^2 x$

$\qquad = x(9x^2 - 21\ell x + 10\ell^2)$

$\qquad = x(3x - 5\ell)(3x - 2\ell)$

$D'(x) = 0$ when $x = 0, \frac{2}{3}\ell$

$\qquad\qquad$ ($\frac{5}{3}\ell$ is not in domain)

$D''(x) = 27x^2 - 42\ell x + 10\ell^2$

$D''(\frac{2}{3}\ell) < 0$, so $\frac{2}{3}\ell$ is a maximum.

Maximum deflection at $x = \frac{2\ell}{3}$

56. a. $\left(P + \frac{a}{V^2}\right)(V - b) = nRT_C$

$\qquad\qquad P + \frac{a}{V^2} = \frac{nRT_C}{V - b}$

$\qquad\qquad\qquad P = \frac{nRT_C}{V - b} - \frac{a}{V^2}$

$\qquad\quad \frac{dP}{dV} = \frac{-nRT_C}{(V - b)^2} + \frac{2a}{V^3}$

$\qquad\quad \frac{d^2P}{dV^2} = \frac{2nRT_C}{(V - b)^3} - \frac{6a}{V^4}$

b. $P'(V_C) = 0$ when $\dfrac{-nRT_C}{(V_C - b)^2} + \dfrac{2a}{V_C{}^3} = 0$

and $P''(V_C) = 0$ when

$$\frac{2nRT_C}{(V_C - b)^3} - \frac{6a}{V_C{}^4} = 0$$

Solve these equations simultaneously to

find $V_C = 3b$. This is the critical volume.

c. Solve $P'(V_C) = 0$ for T_C to find

$$T_C = \frac{1}{nR}\left[\frac{2a}{V_C{}^3}(V_C - b)^2\right], \text{ so that when}$$

$V_C = 3b$, we have $T_C = \frac{8a}{27nbR}$. Finally,

$$P_C = P(V_C) = \frac{nRT_C}{V_C - b} - \frac{a}{V_C{}^2} \text{ and since}$$

$V_C = 3b$, and $T_C = \frac{8a}{27nbR}$, we have

$$P_C = \frac{a}{27b^2}$$

d.

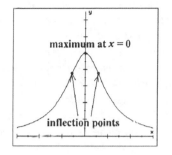

maximum at $x = 0$

inflection points

59. $y = a^3(x^2 + a^2)^{-1}$

$$y' = -2a^3x(x^2 + a^2)^{-2}$$

Critical value at $x = 0$

$$y'' = -2a^3(x^2 + a^2)^{-2} + 8a^3x^2(x^2 + a^2)^{-3}$$

When $x = 0$, $y'' < 0$ so it is a relative maximum. Point of inflection when $x = \pm\frac{\sqrt{3}}{3}a$. Here is the graph.

4.5 Curve Sketching: Limits Involving Infinity and Asymptotes, Pages 270–272

SURVIVAL HINT: *Do not define an asymptote as a line that is approached, but not reached. A function f may cross the asymptotes. For instance, $y = \sin x/x$ has $y = 0$ as a horizontal asymptote, and it is crossed an infinite number of times.*

7. $\displaystyle\lim_{x\to+\infty} \frac{3 + \frac{5}{x}}{1 - \frac{2}{x}} = \frac{3 + 0}{1 - 0}$

$$= 3$$

10. $\displaystyle\lim_{x\to-\infty} \frac{(2 + \frac{5}{x})(1 - \frac{3}{x})}{(7 - \frac{2}{x})(4 + \frac{1}{x})} = \frac{(2)(1)}{(7)(4)}$

$$= \frac{1}{14}$$

11. $\displaystyle\lim_{x\to+\infty} \frac{x}{\sqrt{x^2 + 1{,}000}} = \lim_{x\to+\infty} \frac{1}{\sqrt{1 + \frac{1{,}000}{x^2}}}$

$$= \frac{1}{\sqrt{1 + 0}}$$

$$= 1$$

13. $\sqrt{35} > 5.916$, so the denominator is growing faster than the numerator, and $\displaystyle\lim_{x\to+\infty} f(x) = 0$

SURVIVAL HINT: *Values for which the denominator of a rational expression are zero are* **candidates** *for vertical asymptotes If the numerator is also zero for that value, then you have a hole in the graph, and not an asymptote. The steps listed on page 269 a powerful set of analytic tools. You need not use every tool in your toolbox on each problem. Skill in knowing which tool to use comes with practice. Often you have some idea about the general shape of the graph, and calculators that help with the process are common.*

25. $f'(x) = \dfrac{26}{(7-x)^2}$; $f''(x) = \dfrac{52}{(7-x)^3}$

asymptotes: $x = 7$, $y = -3$;

graph rising on $(-\infty, 7) \cup (7, +\infty)$;

concave up on $(-\infty, 7)$;

concave down on $(7, +\infty)$;

no critical points;

no points of inflection

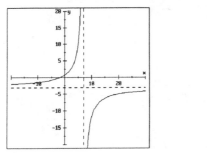

29. $f'(x) = -\dfrac{27x^2}{(x^3-8)^2}$; $f''(x) = \dfrac{108x(x^3+4)}{(x^3-8)^3}$

asymptotes: $x = 2$, $y = 1$

graph falling on $(-\infty, 2) \cup (2, +\infty)$

concave up on $(-\sqrt[3]{4}, 0)$ or $(2, +\infty)$

concave down on $(-\infty, -\sqrt[3]{4})$ or $(0, 2)$

critical point is $(0, -\frac{1}{8})$

points of inflection $(0, -\frac{1}{8})$, $(-\sqrt[3]{4}, \frac{1}{4})$

38. $f'(u) = \dfrac{5u - 14}{3u^{1/3}}$

$f''(u) = \dfrac{2(5u + 7)}{9u^{4/3}}$

no asymptotes

graph rising on $(-\infty, 0) \cup (\frac{14}{5}, +\infty)$

graph falling on $(0, \frac{14}{5})$

concave down on $(-\infty, -\frac{7}{5})$

concave up on $(-\frac{7}{5}, 0) \cup (0, +\infty)$

critical points are $(0, 0)$, relative maximum;

approximately $(2.8, -8.3)$, relative minimum

point of inflection is approximately

$(-1.4, -10.5)$

42. $f'(x) = 1 - 2\cos 2x$

$f''(x) = 4\sin 2x$

no asymptotes

graph rising on $(\frac{\pi}{6}, \frac{5\pi}{6})$

graph falling on $(0, \frac{\pi}{6})$ or $(\frac{5\pi}{6}, 0)$

concave up on $(0, \frac{\pi}{2})$

concave down on $(\frac{\pi}{2}, \pi)$

critical points are $\left(\frac{\pi}{6}, \frac{\pi}{6} - \frac{\sqrt{3}}{2}\right)$, relative

minimum; $\left(\frac{5\pi}{6}, \frac{5\pi}{6} + \frac{\sqrt{3}}{2}\right)$, relative maximum

Chapter 4, Additional Applications of the Derivative

points of inflection $(\frac{\pi}{2}, \frac{\pi}{2})$

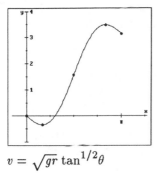

45. $v = \sqrt{gr}\ \tan^{1/2}\theta$

$$v' = \frac{\sqrt{gr}}{2}\left(\frac{\sec^2\theta}{\sqrt{\tan\theta}}\right)$$

This is not defined at $\theta = 0$ and $\frac{\pi}{2}$

$$v'' = \frac{\sqrt{gr}}{2}\left(\frac{\sqrt{\tan\theta}(2)\sec^2\theta\ \tan\theta}{\tan\theta}\right)$$

$$-\ \frac{\sqrt{gr}}{2}\left(\frac{\sec^2\theta(\frac{1}{2})\tan^{-1/2}\theta\ \sec^2\theta}{\tan\theta}\right)$$

$$=\ \frac{\sqrt{gr}}{4}\left[\frac{\sec^2\theta(4\tan^2\theta\ -\ \sec^2\theta)}{(\tan\theta)^{3/2}}\right]$$

In terms of sines and cosines,

$$v'' = \frac{\sqrt{gr}}{4}\left[\frac{4\sin^2 x\ -\ 1}{\sin^{3/2} x\ \cos^{5/2} x}\right]$$

$v'' = 0$ if

$$\sec^2\theta(4\tan^2\theta\ -\ \sec^2\theta) = 0$$

$$4\tan^2\theta\ -\ \sec^2\theta = 0$$

$$(2\tan\theta\ -\ \sec\theta)(2\tan\theta\ +\ \sec\theta) = 0$$

$$2\tan\theta = \pm\sec\theta$$

$$\frac{2\sin\theta}{\cos\theta} = \pm\frac{1}{\cos\theta}$$

$$\sin\theta = \pm\frac{1}{2}$$

On $[0, \frac{\pi}{2}]$ the solution is $\theta = \frac{\pi}{6}$

Point of inflection at $(0.52, 0.76\sqrt{gr})$

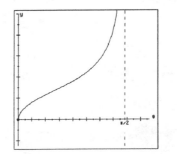

47.

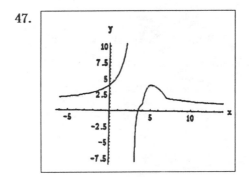

49. Frank is not correct.

$$\lim_{x\to 0^+}\left(\frac{1}{x^2} - \frac{1}{x}\right) = \lim_{x\to 0^+}\frac{1-x}{x^2} = +\infty$$

55. $x^2 = 1 + \frac{2}{3}y^2$ implies $y = \pm\frac{1}{2}\sqrt{6(x^2-1)}$

$$\lim_{x\to+\infty}\frac{1}{2}\sqrt{6(x^2-1)} = +\infty$$

4.6 Optimization in the Physical Sciences and Engineering, Pages 280-285

SURVIVAL HINT: *If the hypotheses of the extreme value theorem apply to a particular problem, you can sometimes avoid testing a candidate to see if it is a maximum or a minimum. Suppose you have three* *candidates and two are minimums — then the third* **must** *be a maximum.*

6. Let x be the side $\overline{CD}$ and y the other dimension of the rectangle. The cost of the fence is

$$C = 3\left(2y + \tfrac{3x}{2}\right)$$

Since the area is 1,200 m^2, $xy = 1,200$ or $y = \dfrac{1,200}{x}$. Thus,

$$C(x) = 3\left(\frac{2,400}{x} + \frac{3x}{2}\right) = 7,200x^{-1} + 4.5x$$

$$C'(x) = -7,200x^{-2} + 4.5$$

$C'(x) = 0$ if $x = 40$. $C(40) = 360$ is a minimum since $C''(40) > 0$. The minimum amount that Jones must pay is \$360.

11. A vertex of the inner square subdivides a side of the outer square into line segments x and y $(0 \le x \le L)$. The given outer square has side $x + y$. Thus, $x^2 + y^2 = L^2$. The area of the outer square is

$$A(x) = (x + y)^2 = (x + \sqrt{L^2 - x^2})^2$$

$$A'(x) = 2(x + \sqrt{L^2 - x^2})\left(1 + \frac{-2x}{2\sqrt{L^2 - x^2}}\right)$$

$A'(x) = 0$ if $x = \sqrt{L^2 - x^2}$ or $x_c = \dfrac{L}{\sqrt{2}} = y_c$

Thus, a circumscribed square of side

$$s = \frac{L}{\sqrt{2}} + \frac{L}{\sqrt{2}} = \sqrt{2}\,L$$

yields a maximum area.

12. Draw the figure and label the dimensions of the cylinder r and h. Maximize the volume of the cylinder: $V = \pi r^2 h$. By similar triangles:

$$\frac{h}{R - r} = \frac{H}{R}$$

Substituting:

$$V = \pi r^2\left[\frac{H}{R}(R - r)\right]$$

$$= \pi\left(Hr^2 - \frac{H}{R}r^3\right).$$

$$V' = \pi\left(2Hr - \frac{3H}{R}r^2\right)$$

$V' = 0$ when

$$2Hr - \frac{3H}{R}r^2 = 0$$

$$\frac{H}{R}r(2R - 3r) = 0$$

$$r = 0 \text{ or } \tfrac{2}{3}R$$

The extreme value theorem applies, so the maximum volume of the cylinder occurs when its radius is $\tfrac{2}{3}$ of the radius of the cone. Its height will be

$$\frac{H}{R}\left(R - \tfrac{2}{3}R\right) = \tfrac{1}{3}H$$

that is; $\tfrac{1}{3}$ the height of the cone.

16. Maximize $V = x^2 y$ subject to

$$C(x) = 5(x^2) + 1[x^2 + 4xy] = 72$$

Solving,

$$y = \frac{72 - 6x^2}{4x}$$

and

$$V = \left[\frac{72 - 6x^2}{4x}\right]x^2 = \tfrac{1}{4}(72x - 6x^3)$$

$$V' = 18 - \tfrac{9}{2}x^2$$

$V' = 0$ when $x = \pm 2$. The extreme value theorem applies, the end points and $x = -2$ are not reasonable, so the maximum volume with the given restrictions occurs when $x = 2$ ft and $y = 6$ ft.

18. Let the horizontal distance from the camera to the wall be x, and name the resulting angles as indicated:

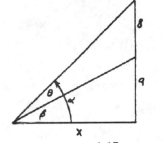

$$\theta = \alpha - \beta = \tan^{-1}\frac{17}{x} - \tan^{-1}\frac{9}{x}$$

Maximize with derivatives:

$$\frac{d\theta}{dx} = \frac{1}{1 + (\frac{17}{x})^2}\left(-\frac{17}{x^2}\right) - \frac{1}{1 + (\frac{9}{x})^2}\left(-\frac{9}{x^2}\right)$$

$$= -\frac{17}{x^2 + 289} + \frac{9}{x^2 + 81}$$

$$= \frac{1224 - 8x^2}{(x^2 + 289)(x^2 + 81)}$$

$\frac{d\theta}{dx} = 0$ when $8(x^2 - 153) = 0$, $x = \sqrt{153}$
Since the endpoint $x = 0$ is obviously a minimum, we have the maximum angle when $x = \sqrt{153} = 3\sqrt{17} \approx 12.4$ ft.

23. Draw a figure; pick a point x km down the road (toward the power plant) from the nearest point on the paved road and have the jeep head toward that point. The distance traveled by the jeep on the sand is $\sqrt{x^2 + 32^2}$ and the distance on the paved road is $16 - x$ (assuming $x < 16$). The total time traveled (in hours) is

$$t = \frac{\sqrt{32^2 + x^2}}{48} + \frac{16 - x}{80}$$

$$t' = \frac{1}{48}(\tfrac{1}{2})(32^2 + x^2)^{-1/2}(2x) - \frac{1}{80}$$

$t' = 0$ when

$$\frac{1}{48}(\tfrac{1}{2})(32^2 + x^2)^{-1/2}(2x) - \frac{1}{80} = 0$$

$$\frac{x}{48(32^2 + x^2)^{1/2}} = \frac{1}{80}$$

$$80x = 48(32^2 + x^2)^{1/2}$$

$$5x = 3(32^2 + x^2)^{1/2}$$

$$25x^2 = 9(32^2 + x^2)$$

$$16x^2 = 9 \cdot 32^2$$

$$x = \frac{3 \cdot 32}{4} = 24$$

This distance is further than the power plant. The minimum time corresponds to heading for the power plant on the sand. The time is

$$t = \frac{\sqrt{32^2 + 16^2}}{48} + 0 = \frac{\sqrt{5}}{3} \approx 0.745$$

This is 44 minutes 43 seconds; so he has about 5 minutes 17 seconds to diffuse the bomb.

26. Let x be the dimension of one side of the equilateral triangle, which is also the dimension of the base of the rectangle. Let y be the height of the rectangle. The perimeter of the window is $3x + 2y = 20$ giving

$$y = \frac{20 - 3x}{2} \text{ with } 0 \le x < \frac{20}{3}$$

We need to find h, the height of the equilateral triangle. With x as the hypotenuse of one-half the equilateral triangle,

$$h = x \sin \frac{\pi}{3} = \frac{\sqrt{3}}{2} x$$

The base of the right triangle is $x/2$. Thus, the area of the entire equilateral triangle is

$$A_t = \frac{\sqrt{3}}{4} x^2$$

The area of the rectangle is

$$A_r = xy = \frac{x(20 - 3x)}{2}$$

Since twice as much light passes through the rectangle as through the stained glass equilateral triangle, then

$$L = k\left[\frac{\sqrt{3}}{4} x^2 + (2)\frac{x(20 - 3x)}{2}\right]$$

$$= k\left[\left(\frac{\sqrt{3}}{4} - 3\right)x^2 + 20x\right]$$

$$L' = k\left[\left(\frac{\sqrt{3}}{2} - 6\right)x + 20\right]$$

$L' = 0$ when $x = \dfrac{20}{6 - \dfrac{\sqrt{3}}{2}} \approx 3.8956 \approx 4$ ft

Then $y = (\frac{1}{2})(20 - 11.6868) \approx 4.1566 \approx 4$ ft;

$L'' < 0$ which signifies that the window that admits the most light is when $x = 4$ and $y = 4$. This means that one side of the equilateral triangles is equal to the height of the rectangle and this length is 4 ft.

32. $I(h) = \dfrac{k \sin\phi}{d^2}$ where $\sin \phi = \dfrac{h}{d}$ and

$$d = \sqrt{h^2 + 16}.$$

$$I(h) = \frac{kh}{d^3}$$

$$I'(h) = \frac{kd^3 - 3khd^2d'}{d^6}$$

$$= \frac{kd - 3khd'}{d^4}$$

$I'(h) = 0$ when

$$k(d - 3hd') = 0$$

Substitute:

$$\sqrt{h^2 + 16} = 3h\left(\frac{h}{\sqrt{h^2 + 16}}\right)$$

$$h^2 + 16 = 3h^2$$

$$h^2 = 8$$

$$h = 2\sqrt{2} \approx 2.8 \text{ ft.}$$

This answer is the same as the one in Problem 31.

33. $T(x) = N(k + \frac{c}{x})p^{-x}$

a. We use logarithmic differentiation.

$$\ln T(x) = \ln N(k + \tfrac{c}{x}) - x \ln p$$

$$\frac{1}{T} T'(x) = \frac{-cx^{-2}}{k + c/x} - \ln p$$

$$T'(x) = -T\left[\frac{c}{(kx + c)x} + \ln p\right]$$

Note: if you use technology to find this derivative, you may find a different form. For example, you might obtain

$$T'(x) = \frac{-Np^{-x}[(kx^2 + cx)\ln p + c]}{x^2}$$

You can show these forms are equivalent.

b. Solve

$$-T\left[\frac{c}{(kx + c)x} + \ln p\right] = 0$$

$$(kx^2 + cx)\ln p + c = 0$$

$$x = \frac{-c\ln p + \sqrt{c^2(\ln p)^2 - 4kc\ln p}}{2k\ln p}$$

(Reject the negative root since x must be positive.)

c.

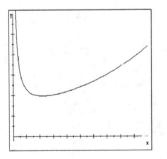

43. Refer to Figure 4.69. Let s be the side of the square base with $0 \le s \le 10\sqrt{2}$. Consider a plane that passes through the vertex of the

pyramid (is perpendicular to the base) and is parallel to two sides in the base. The slanted sides of the pyramid intersect this plane in a length ℓ. If one-half of the pyramid is unfolded, we obtain half of our original sheet of paper. The hypotenuse is

$$20\sqrt{2} = 2\ell + s$$

$$\ell = \frac{20\sqrt{2} - s}{2}$$

Return to the pyramid and the vertical cutting plane. Half of this intersection consists of a right plane with altitude h (the height of the pyramid), base $s/2$, and hypotenuse ℓ.

$$h = \sqrt{\ell^2 - \frac{s^2}{4}}$$

$$= \sqrt{\frac{(20\sqrt{2} - s)^2 - s^2}{4}}$$

$$= \frac{1}{2}\sqrt{800 - 40\sqrt{2}\, s}$$

$$= \sqrt{200 - 10\sqrt{2}\, s}$$

The volume of the pyramid is

$$V = \frac{1}{3}s^2 h = \frac{1}{3}s^2\sqrt{200 - 10\sqrt{2}\, s}$$

with $0 \le s \le 10\sqrt{2}$.

$$V' = \frac{1}{3}\left[s^2 \frac{-10\sqrt{2}}{2\sqrt{200 - 10\sqrt{2}\, s}} + 2s\sqrt{200 - 10\sqrt{2}\, s}\right]$$

$$= \frac{1}{3}\left[\frac{-5\sqrt{2}\, s^2 + 2s(200 - 10\sqrt{2}\, s)}{\sqrt{200 - 10\sqrt{2}\, s}}\right]$$

$$= \frac{1}{3}\frac{-25\sqrt{2}\, s^2 + 400s}{\sqrt{200 - 10\sqrt{2}\, s}}$$

$V' = 0$ if

$$-25\sqrt{2}\, s^2 + 400s = 0$$

$$-25s(\sqrt{2}\, s - 16) = 0$$

$$s = 0,\ 8\sqrt{2}$$

If $s = 0$ we obtain a minimum, and if $s = 8\sqrt{2}$ we obtain a maximum.

$$V = \frac{1}{3}s^2\sqrt{200 - 10\sqrt{2}\, s}$$

$$= \frac{128}{3}\sqrt{200 - 10\sqrt{2}(8\sqrt{2})}$$

$$= \frac{128}{3}\sqrt{200 - 160}$$

$$= \frac{256}{3}\sqrt{10}$$

$$\approx 270 \text{ in.}^3$$

4.7 Optimization in Business, Economics, and the Life Sciences, Pages 295-300

3. The profit is maximized when the marginal revenue equals the marginal cost.

$C'(x) = \frac{1}{5}$

$R(x) = xp$

$$= \frac{70x - x^2}{x + 30}$$

$$R'(x) = \frac{(x + 30)(70 - 2x) - (70x - x^2)}{(x + 30)^2}$$

$$R'(x) = C'(x)$$

$$\frac{(x + 30)(70 - 2x) - (70x - x^2)}{(x + 30)^2} = \frac{1}{5}$$

$$(x + 30)(70 - 2x) - (70x - x^2) = \frac{1}{5}(x + 30)^2$$

$$5(-x^2 - 60x + 2{,}100) = x^2 + 60x + 900$$

$$6x^2 + 360x - 9{,}600 = 0$$

$$x^2 + 60x - 1{,}600 = 0$$

$$(x + 80)(x - 20) = 0$$

$x = 20$ (-80 is not in the domain). To maximize profit produce 20 items.

7. **a.** Total cost, $C(x)$, is the average cost, $A(x)$, times the number of items produced, x.

$$C(x) = x\left(5 + \frac{x}{50}\right)$$

$$= 5x + \frac{x^2}{50}$$

$$R(x) = x\left(\frac{380 - x}{20}\right)$$

$$P(x) = R(x) - C(x)$$

$$= \frac{380x - x^2}{20} - \frac{250x + x^2}{50}$$

$$= \frac{-7x^2 + 1{,}400x}{100}$$

$$= -0.07x^2 + 14x$$

b. The maximum profit occurs when

$$R'(x) = C'(x).$$

$$19 - \frac{x}{10} = 5 + \frac{x}{25}$$

$$14 = \frac{7}{50}x$$

$$x = 100$$

This gives a price per item,

$$p = \frac{380 - x}{20} = \$14 \text{ per item.}$$

The maximum profit is

$$P(x) = \frac{(-7x + 1{,}400)x}{100}$$

$$= \frac{(-700 + 1{,}400)100}{100}$$

$$= \$700$$

10. a. $Q(t) = 20{,}000e^{-0.4t};$

$$Q'(t) = -8{,}000e^{-0.4t};$$

$$Q'(5) = -8{,}000e^{-2}$$

$$\approx -1{,}082.68$$

The value of the machine is decreasing by $1,082.68/yr.

b. The rate is $\dfrac{-8{,}000\,e^{-0.4t}}{20{,}000e^{-0.4t}} = -0.40;$

that is the percentage rate is 40%.

12. $g'(t) = t(\frac{1}{t}) + (\ln t)(1) = 1 + \ln t$

$g'(t) = 0$ when $\ln t = -1$, $t = \frac{1}{e}.$

Candidates: $\{0, \frac{1}{e}, 4\}$. Using the second derivative test on the critical point:

$g''(t) = \frac{1}{t}$, $g''(\frac{1}{e}) = e > 0$, so there is a relative minimum at $(\frac{1}{e}, 1 - \frac{1}{e}).$

$g(0) = 1$, $g(4) = 4 \ln 4 + 1 \approx 6.545.$

So $(\frac{1}{e}, 1 - \frac{1}{e}) = (0.3679, 0.6321)$ is an absolute minimum and $(4, 6.545)$ is an absolute maximum.

15. Let x denote the number of cases of connectors in each shipment, and $C(x)$ the corresponding (variable) cost. Then,

$$C(x) = \text{STORAGE COST} + \text{ORDERING COST}$$
$$= \frac{4.5x}{2} + 20\left(\frac{18{,}000}{x}\right)$$
$$= 2.25x + 360{,}000x^{-1} \text{ on } [0, 18{,}000]$$

$$C'(x) = 2.25 - 360{,}000x^{-2}$$

$C'(x) = 0$ when $x = 400$. Since this is the only critical point in the interval, and since $C''(x) = 720{,}000x^{-3} > 0$ when $x = 400$, C is minimized when $x = 400$. The number of shipments should be $18{,}000/400 = 45$ times per year.

22. Let x be the distance from the 60 ppm plant. Then emission at this distance is $60/x$. For the 240 ppm plant, the emission is $240/(10 - x)$. The total pollution is

$$p = \frac{60}{x} + \frac{240}{10 - x} \quad 1 \le x \le 9$$

$$p' = 60\left[-\frac{1}{x^2} + \frac{4}{(10 - x)^2}\right]$$

$$= \frac{-60}{x^2(10 - x)^2}[(10 - x)^2 - 4x^2]$$

$p' = 0$ if $x = \frac{10}{3}$ ($x = -10$ is not in the domain). Since

$$p(1) \approx 86.67,$$

$p(\frac{10}{3}) = 54,$

$p(9) \approx 246.67$

we see the minimum pollution is 54 ppm at

$x = \frac{10}{3}$ and the maximum is 246.67 at $x = 9$.

23. Let x be the number of people above the 100

level ($0 \le x \le 50$). Then, the number of

travelers is $100 + x$. The fare per traveler is

$2,000 - 10x$. The revenue is

$R(x) = (100 + x)(2,000 - 10x)$

and the profit is

$P(x) = (100 + x)(2,000 - 10x)$

$\qquad - 125,000 - 500(x + 100)$

$\qquad = -10x^2 + 500x + 25,000$

$P'(x) = -20x + 500 = 0$ at $x = 25$

Thus, lower the fare by $10(25) = \$250$.

28. Let x be the number of groups of 50 people

above the 600 passenger level. Then the

number of passengers is $600 + 50x$. The fare

is $500 - 25x$ (in cents). The revenue is

$R(x) = (600 + 50x)(500 - 25x)$

$\qquad = 1,250(12 + x)(20 - x)$

$\qquad = 1,250(240 + 8x - x^2)$

The domain is $0 \le x \le 20$.

$R'(x) = 1,250(8 - 2x) = 0$ if $x = 4$

$R(0) = 3,000; \; R(4) = 3,200; \; R(20) = 0$

Revenue is maximized at the

$600 + 50(4) = 800$

passenger group level and the fare is

$5.00 - 1.00 = \$4.00$.

32. Let E be the amount of energy. Since it

requires twice as much energy over water than

over land, let us double the distance ℓ over

the water. Let x be the distance along the

shore where the pigeon is crossing the

shoreline.

$E = 2\ell + 10 - x$

$\quad = 2\sqrt{9 + x^2} + 10 - x$

$\dfrac{dE}{dx} = \dfrac{2x}{\sqrt{9 + x^2}} - 1 = 0$ if $x = \sqrt{3}$

If $\tan \theta = \dfrac{\sqrt{3}}{3}$, then $\theta = \dfrac{\pi}{6}$.

38. The total cost of production is the cost of

setting up the machines plus the cost of

supervising machine operation. Let $x =$ the

number of machines used. The number of

hours the machines must run is 8,000 divided

by 50 times the number of machines working.

Supervision is $35 for each of these hours.

a. $\qquad C(x) = 800x + \dfrac{8,000}{50x}(35)$

$\qquad\qquad = 800x + \dfrac{5,600}{x}$

$\qquad C'(x) = 800 - \dfrac{5,600}{x^2} = 0$

when $x^2 = 7$, $x \approx 2.65$.

Since this is a discrete rather than a

continuous function, we need to test the

nearest integer values. $C(2) = 4,400$,

$C(3) \approx 4{,}267$. So if we set up and run 3 machines, the number of operational hours will be $\dfrac{8000}{3(50)} \approx 53.3$ h.

b. The supervisor will earn approximately $(53.3)(35) \approx \$1{,}866.67$

39. a.

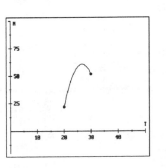

$N'(t) = -1.7T + 45.45;\ N'(T) = 0$ when $T \approx 26.74$

largest survival percentage is 60.56% for $T \approx 26.74$ and smallest survival percentage is 22% for T = 20

b. $S'(T) = -(-0.06T + 1.67)(-0.03T^2 + 1.67T - 13.67)^{-2}$

$S'(T) = 0$ when $T = \frac{167}{6} \approx 27.83$

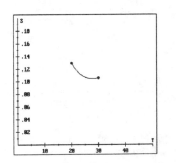

c.

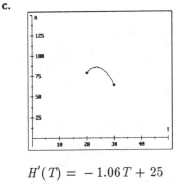

$H'(T) = -1.06T + 25$

$H'(T) = 0$ when $T \approx 23.58$

largest hatching occurs when $T \approx 25.58$ and the smallest when $T = 30$.

43. The epidemic is spreading most rapidly when the rate of change $R(t)$ is a maximum, that is, when $R'(t) = f''(t) = 0$.

$f'(t) = A(-1)(1 + Ce^{-kt})^{-2}(-Cke^{-kt})$

$\qquad = kACe^{-kt}(1 + Ce^{-kt})^{-2}$

$f''(t) = kAC(1 + Ce^{-kt})^{-4}[(1$

$+ Ce^{-kt})^2(-ke^{-kt}) - (e^{-kt})(2)(1$

$+ Ce^{-kt})(-Cke^{-kt})]$

$= \dfrac{k^2ACe^{-kt}(Ce^{-kt} - 1)}{(1 + Ce^{-kt})^3} = 0$ if $Ce^{-kt} = 1$

or $t = k^{-1}\ln C$. Substituting in the original equation leads to

$f(k^{-1}\ln C) = A(1 + Ce^{-\ln C})^{-1} = \frac{1}{2}A$

This means half of the total number of susceptible residents. $R'(t) < 0$ when

$t > (\ln C)k^{-1}$ (the graph of the curve is decreasing) and $R'(t) > 0$ when $t < (\ln C)k^{-1}$ (the graph of the curve is increasing).

4.8 l'Hôpital's Rule, Pages 307-308

SURVIVAL HINT: *Do not attempt to apply l'Hôpital's rule unless you have verified that the limit has the form 0/0 or ∞/∞. It is good practice to evaluate the limit and indicate which form you have.*

4. The limit is not an indeterminate form.

$$\lim_{x \to 2} \frac{x^3 - 27}{x^2 - 9} = \frac{8 - 27}{4 - 9}$$

$$= \frac{19}{5}$$

9. $\lim_{x \to \pi} \dfrac{\cos \frac{x}{2}}{\pi - x} = \lim_{x \to \pi} \dfrac{-\frac{1}{2} \sin \frac{x}{2}}{-1}$

$$= \frac{1}{2}$$

15. $\lim_{t \to \pi/2} \dfrac{3 \sec t}{2 + \tan t} = 3 \lim_{t \to \pi/2} \dfrac{\sec t \tan t}{\sec^2 t}$

$$= 3 \lim_{t \to \pi/2} \sin t$$

$$= 3$$

17. $\lim_{x \to 0} \dfrac{\sin 3x \sin 2x}{x \sin 4x}$

$$= \lim_{x \to 0} \dfrac{6\left(\frac{\sin 3x}{3x}\right)\left(\frac{\sin 2x}{2x}\right)}{4\left(\frac{\sin 4x}{4x}\right)}$$

$$= \frac{6(1)(1)}{4}$$

$$= \frac{3}{2}$$

21. $\lim_{x \to +\infty} x^{3/2} \sin \frac{1}{x}$; Let $u = \frac{1}{x}$;

$$\lim_{u \to 0^+} \frac{\sin u}{u} \cdot u^{-1/2} = \lim_{u \to 0^+} \frac{\sin u}{u} \lim_{u \to 0^+} \frac{1}{\sqrt{u}}$$

$$= (1)(+\infty) = +\infty$$

26. $\lim_{x \to (\pi/2)^-} \sec 3x \cos 9x$ is not in the proper form to apply l'Hôpital's rule;

$$\lim_{x \to (\pi/2)^-} \frac{\cos 9x}{\cos 3x} = \lim_{x \to (\pi/2)^-} \frac{-9 \sin 9x}{-3 \sin 3x}$$

$$= \frac{-9(1)}{-3(-1)}$$

$$= -3$$

30. $\lim_{x \to 0^+} (\sin x)(\ln x) = \lim_{x \to 0^+} \dfrac{\ln x}{\csc x}$

$$= \lim_{x \to 0^+} \frac{\frac{1}{x}}{-\csc x \cot x}$$

$$= \lim_{x \to 0^+} \frac{-\sin^2 x}{x \cos x}$$

$$= \left(\lim_{x \to 0^+} \frac{\sin x}{x}\right)\left(\lim_{x \to 0^+} \frac{-\sin x}{\cos x}\right)$$

$$= (1)(0)$$

$$= 0$$

40. $\lim_{x \to +\infty} (\sqrt{x^2 - x} - x)$

$$= \lim_{x \to +\infty} \left[\frac{(\sqrt{x^2 - x} - x)(\sqrt{x^2 - x} + x)}{\sqrt{x^2 - x} + x}\right]$$

$$= \lim_{x \to +\infty} \left[\frac{(x^2 - x) - x^2}{\sqrt{x^2 - x} + x}\right]$$

$$= \lim_{x \to +\infty} \frac{-1}{\sqrt{1 - \frac{1}{x}} + 1}$$

$$= -\frac{1}{2}$$

43. Since

$$\lim_{x \to 0^+} x^2 \ln\sqrt{x} = \lim_{x \to 0^+} \frac{\ln\sqrt{x}}{1/x^2}$$

$$= \lim_{x \to 0^+} \frac{1/(2x)}{-2/x^3}$$

$$= \lim_{x \to 0^+} \frac{x^2}{-4} = 0$$

we see

$$\lim_{x \to 0^+} \left(\frac{1}{x^2} - \ln\sqrt{x} \right) = \lim_{x \to 0^+} \left(\frac{1 - x^2 \ln\sqrt{x}}{x^2} \right)$$

$$= +\infty$$

53. Let $u = \frac{1}{x}$

$$\lim_{x \to +\infty} x^5 \left[\sin(\tfrac{1}{x}) - \tfrac{1}{x} + \frac{1}{6x^3} \right]$$

$$= \lim_{u \to 0} \frac{\sin u - u + \frac{1}{6}u^3}{u^5} \qquad Form \ \tfrac{0}{0}$$

$$= \lim_{u \to 0} \frac{\cos u - 1 + \frac{1}{2}u^2}{5u^4} \qquad Form \ \tfrac{0}{0}$$

$$= \lim_{u \to 0} \frac{-\sin u + u}{20u^3} \qquad Form \ \tfrac{0}{0}$$

$$= \lim_{u \to 0} \frac{-\cos u + 1}{60u^2} \qquad Form \ \tfrac{0}{0}$$

$$= \lim_{u \to 0} \frac{\sin u}{120u} = \frac{1}{120}$$

57. a.

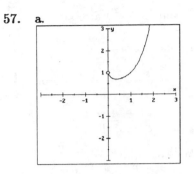

It looks like the limit is 1.

b. $\displaystyle \lim_{x \to 0^+} x^x = \lim_{x \to 0^+} \exp(\ln x^x)$

$$= \lim_{x \to 0^+} \exp(x \ln x)$$

$$= \lim_{x \to 0^+} \exp\left(\frac{\ln x}{x^{-1}} \right)$$

$$= \lim_{x \to 0^+} \exp\left(\frac{x^{-1}}{-x^{-2}} \right)$$

$$= \lim_{x \to 0^+} \exp(-x) = 1$$

c. Answers vary, depending on the software.
The answer 1.

62. The conditions for f and g are

$$f(a) = g(a) = 0.$$

$$\frac{f(a + dx)}{g(a + dx)} = \frac{f(a) + f'(a)\ dx}{g(a) + g'(a)\ dx}$$

Linearization of f and g

$$= \frac{f'(a)\ dx}{g'(a)\ dx} \qquad Since \ f(a) = g(a) = 0$$

$$= \frac{f'(a)}{g'(a)} \qquad \frac{dx}{dx} = 1$$

66. **a.** L_1 (1^∞) and L_2 (∞^0) are both

indeterminate forms.

$$\ln L_1 = \lim_{x \to 0} \frac{B\ln(e^x + Ax)}{x} \qquad \text{Form } \frac{0}{0}$$

$$= \lim_{x \to 0} B\left[\frac{e^x + A}{e^x + Ax}\right] = B(1 + A)$$

$$L_1 = e^{B(1 + A)}$$

Also,

$$\ln L_2 = \lim_{x \to +\infty} \frac{B\ln(e^x + Ax)}{x}$$

$$= \lim_{x \to +\infty} B\left[\frac{e^x + A}{e^x + Ax}\right]$$

$$= \lim_{x \to +\infty} B\left[\frac{e^x}{e^x + A}\right] = B$$

$$L_2 = e^B$$

b. $$Be^B = e^{B(1 + A)}$$

$$Be^B = e^B e^{AB}$$

$$B = e^{AB}$$

$$A = \frac{\ln B}{B}$$

To maximize A, we differentiate

$$f(B) = \frac{\ln B}{B} \text{ and set } f'(B) = 0:$$

$$f'(B) = \frac{1 - \ln B}{B^2}$$

$$f'(B) = 0 \text{ when } B = e; \ A = \frac{\ln e}{e} = \frac{1}{e}$$

When $A = e^{-1}$, $B = e$, we have

$$L_1 = e^{e(1 + 1/e)} = e^{e+1} \approx 41.19$$

$$L_2 = e^e \approx 15.15$$

Thus, $L_1 = eL_2$.

Chapter 4 Review

Proficiency Examination, Page 309

SURVIVAL HINT: *To help you review the concepts of this chapter, **hand write** the answers to each of these questions onto your own paper.*

1. A relative extremum is an extremum only in the neighborhood of the point of interest. An absolute extremum is largest (or smallest) for all values in the domain.

2. A continuous function f on a closed interval $[a, b]$ has an absolute maximum and an absolute minimum.

3. A critical number of a function is a value of the independent variable at which the derivative of the function is zero or is not defined. A critical point $(c, f(c))$ is the point on $y = f(x)$ that corresponds to the critical number c.

4. Find critical numbers, evaluate the function at these values and at the endpoints of the closed interval. Finally, determine the absolute extrema by selecting the largest and smallest of the evaluated functional values.

5. If f is continuous on the closed interval $[a, b]$ and differentiable on the open interval (a, b),

then there exists at least one number c such that

$$\frac{f(b) - f(a)}{b - a} = f'(c) \text{ for } a < c < b$$

Rolle's theorem is a special case where $f(a) = f(b)$ (so $f'(c) = 0$).

6. Given $f(x)$, find c such that $f'(c) = 0$ or $f'(c)$ is not defined (that is, c is a critical number). If $f'(x) < 0$ for $x < c$ and $f'(x) > 0$ for $x > c$ (what we have been calling the $\downarrow\uparrow$ pattern), there is a relative minimum at $x = c$. If $f'(x) > 0$ for $x < c$ and $f'(x) < 0$ for $x > c$ (the $\uparrow\downarrow$ pattern), there is a relative minimum at $x = c$.

7. Given $f(x)$ and c such that $f'(c) = 0$. If $f''(x) > 0$ there is a relative minimum at $x = c$ (concave up). If $f''(c) < 0$, there is a relative maximum at $x = c$ (concave down).

8. For a plane curve, an asymptote is a line which has the property that the distance from a point P on the curve to the line approaches zero as the distance from P to the origin increases without bound and P is on a suitable portion of the curve.

9. $\lim_{x \to +\infty} f(x) = L$, given an $\epsilon > 0$, there exists a number N_1 such that $|f(x) - L| < \epsilon$ whenever $x > N_1$ for x in the domain of f. $\lim_{x \to c} f(x) = +\infty$ if for any number $N > 0$, it is possible to find a number $\delta > 0$ such that

$f(x) > N$ whenever $0 < |x - c| < \delta$.

10. Find the domain and range of a function, locate intercepts, if any. Investigate symmetry, asymptotes, and find extrema and/or points of inflection, if any. Determine where the graph is rising, where it is falling, and determine the concavity. (See Table 4.2).

11. An optimization problem involves finding the largest, or smallest value of a function. Procedure:

    (1) Understand the question;

    (2) Choose the variables; let Q be the quantity to be maximized or minimized.

    (3) Express Q in terms of the defined variables.

    (4) Determine the domain;

    (5) Find the extrema;

    (6) Answer the question that was asked.

12. Let f and g be functions that are differentiable on an open interval containing c (except possibly at c itself). If $\lim_{x \to c} \dfrac{f(x)}{g(x)}$ produces an indeterminate form $\dfrac{0}{0}$ or $\dfrac{\infty}{\infty}$, and $\lim_{x \to c} \dfrac{f'(x)}{g'(x)}$ exists, then

$$\lim_{x \to c} \frac{f(x)}{g(x)} = \lim_{x \to c} \frac{f'(x)}{g'(x)}$$

15. $\lim\limits_{x \to +\infty} \left(\dfrac{1}{x} - \dfrac{1}{\sqrt{x}} \right) = \lim\limits_{x \to +\infty} \dfrac{1 - \sqrt{x}}{x}$

$= \lim\limits_{x \to +\infty} \dfrac{-\frac{1}{2} x^{-1/2}}{1} = \dfrac{1}{\infty} = 0$

18. $f(x) = 27x^{1/3} - x^{4/3}$

$f'(x) = 9x^{-2/3} - \frac{4}{3}x^{1/3} = 0$ when

$\dfrac{9}{x^{2/3}} = \dfrac{4x^{1/3}}{3}$

$x = \dfrac{27}{4}$ (not defined at $x = 0$)

$f''(x) = -6x^{-5/3} - \frac{4}{9}x^{-2/3} = 0$ when

$x = -\frac{27}{2}.$ $f''(-\frac{27}{2}^-) > 0,$ $f''(-\frac{27}{2}^+) < 0,$

so there are inflection points at approximately

$(-\frac{27}{2}, -96.43)$ and $(0, 0).$ Relative

maximum at $(\frac{27}{4}, 38.27)$

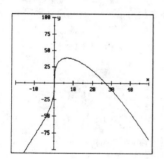

21. $f'(x) = 1 + (1 + x^2)^{-1} > 0;$ the curve is rising for all x.

$f''(x) = -2x(1 + x^2)^{-2} = 0$ when $x = 0;$ $(0, 0)$ is a point of infection. The graph is concave up for $x < 0$ and down for $x > 0$.

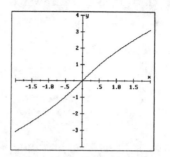

24. We are asked to minimize the amount of material, $S = x^2 + 4xh$, with the restriction that $V = x^2h = 2$. We can use the volume formula to find $h = 2/x^2$ to express S as a function of x.

$S = x^2 + 4x\left(\dfrac{2}{x^2}\right) = x^2 + \dfrac{8}{x};$

$S' = 2x - \dfrac{8}{x^2} = 0$ when $x^3 = 4,$ $x = \sqrt[3]{4};$

$h = \dfrac{2}{x^2} = \dfrac{2}{\sqrt[3]{4^2}}$

The dimensions of the box are approximately 1.587 by 1.587 by .794 ft, or to the nearest inch: 19 in. × 19 in. × 10 in.

CHAPTER 5

Integration

5.1 Antidifferentiation, Pages 327-328

SURVIVAL HINT: *Antiderivatives constitute a parametric family of curves. There is an infinite set of "parallel" curves that all have the same slope at any given value of x. Any curve that is an antiderivative can be translated vertically by C units and still be a solution.* **Always** *remember the $+C$.*

3. $\displaystyle \int (2x + 3)\, dx = x^2 + 3x + C$

11. $\displaystyle \int \sec^2\theta\, d\theta = \tan\theta + C$

17. $\displaystyle \int (u^{3/2} - u^{1/2} + u^{-10})\, du$

$\displaystyle = \frac{u^{5/2}}{\frac{5}{2}} - \frac{u^{3/2}}{\frac{3}{2}} + \frac{u^{-9}}{-9} + C$

$\displaystyle = \frac{2}{5} u^{5/2} - \frac{2}{3} u^{3/2} - \frac{1}{9} u^{-9} + C$

21. $\displaystyle \int (t^{-2} - t^{-3} + t^{-4})\, dt$

$\displaystyle = -t^{-1} + \frac{1}{2}t^{-2} - \frac{1}{3}t^{-3} + C$

25. $\displaystyle \int \left(\frac{x^2 + 3x - 1}{x^4} \right) dx$

$\displaystyle = \int (x^{-2} + 3x^{-3} - x^{-4})\, dx$

$\displaystyle = -x^{-1} - \frac{3}{2}x^{-2} + \frac{1}{3}x^{-3} + C$

28. $\displaystyle \int (1 + x^{-1})(1 - 4x^{-2})\, dx$

$\displaystyle = \int (1 - 4x^{-2} + x^{-1} - 4x^{-3})\, dx$

$\displaystyle = x + 4x^{-1} + \ln|x| + x^{-4} + C$

30. $\displaystyle \int \frac{x^2}{x^2 + 1}\, dx = \int \left[1 - \frac{1}{x^2 + 1} \right] dx$

$\displaystyle = x - \tan^{-1}x + C$

33. $\displaystyle F(x) = \int (2x - 1)^2\, dx = \int (4x^2 - 4x + 1)\, dx$

$\displaystyle = \frac{4}{3}x^3 - 2x^2 + x + C;$

$\displaystyle F(1) = \frac{4}{3}(1)^3 - 2(1)^2 + 1 + C = 3,$ so

$\displaystyle C = \frac{8}{3};\ F(x) = \frac{4}{3}x^3 - 2x^2 + x + \frac{8}{3}$

39. **a.** $F(x) = \int (x^{-1/2} - 4)\, dx = 2x^{1/2} - 4x + C$

$F(1) = 2 - 4 + C = 0$, so $C = 2$;

$F(x) = 2\sqrt{x} - 4x + 2$

b.

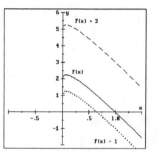

c. $G(x) = F(x) + C_0$;

$G'(x) = F'(x) = \dfrac{1}{\sqrt{x}} - 4 = 0$

At $x = \frac{1}{16}$ (note the original integrand),

$G(\frac{1}{16}) = 2(\frac{1}{4}) - 4(\frac{1}{16}) + 2 + C_0 = 0$, so

$$C_0 = -\tfrac{9}{4}$$

45. $a(t) = k,\quad v(t) = \displaystyle\int a(t)\, dt = \int k\, dt = kt + C$

But $v(0) = 0$, so $C = 0$

$s(t) = \displaystyle\int v(t)\, dt = \int kt\, dt = \dfrac{kt^2}{2} + C$

We know that $s(0) = C$ and $s(6) = 18k + C$

and are given

$s(6) - s(0) = 18k = 360$

Thus, $k = 20$ ft/s^2.

48. With $a(t) = k$, $v(t) = kt + C_1$; the initial

speed of the car is $v_0 = 88$ so $v(0) = C_1 = 88$

and the distance is $s(t) = kt^2/2 + 88t + C_2$.

For convenience, measure the distance from

the point where the car begins moving so

$s(0) = 0$ so $C_2 = 0$. Let t_1

be the time required for stopping.

$s(t_1) = \dfrac{kt_1^{\,2}}{2} + 88t_1 = 121$ and $v(t_1) = 0$

or $t_1 = -\dfrac{88}{k}$. Substituting into the distance

formula leads to

$$\dfrac{88^2 k}{2k^2} - \dfrac{88^2}{k} - 121 = 0, \text{ or}$$

$$k = -\dfrac{88^2}{242} = -32 \text{ ft/s}^2$$

50. $\dfrac{dv}{dt} = -28;\ \dfrac{ds}{dt} = v = -28t + 88$ so that

$$s = -14t^2 + 88t$$

where s is the distance from the point where
the brakes are applied. Before the brakes are
applied, he travels

$$s_1 = (88)(0.7)$$

$$= 61.6 \text{ ft}$$

After the brakes are applied, he travels until
$v = 0$; that is $t = 88/28 = 22/7$ sec. The
distance traveled after the brakes are applied
is

$$s_2 = -14(\tfrac{22}{7})^2 + 88(\tfrac{22}{7})$$

$$\approx 138.3$$

Thus, the total stopping distance is

$$s_1 + s_2 = 61.6 + 138.3$$

$$= 199.9 \text{ ft}$$

The camel is toast! However, if you want to have some fun with this solution, you might argue that if the camel is standing so that the car is positioned between the camel's front and rear legs, and if the hood of the car is more than 0.9 ft $\approx$ 10.8 in. in length, the camel will escape undamaged. Here, of course, it is assumed that the camel's stomach is above the car's hood ornament.

56.
$$F(x) = \int \frac{x+1}{x}\, dx$$
$$= \int (1 + x^{-1})\, dx$$
$$= x + \ln|x| + C$$
$$F(2) - F(1) = [2 + \ln 2 + C] - [1 + 0 + C]$$
$$= 1 + \ln 2$$

5.2 Area As the Limit of a Sum, Pages 335–337

SURVIVAL HINT: *In order to evaluate sums, you will need to use the summation formulas on page 334. If the sum does not look like one of those four formulas, then you should rewrite the sum to match one of those forms.*

3.
$$\sum_{k=1}^{15} k = \frac{(15)(16)}{2}$$
$$= 120$$

6.
$$\sum_{k=1}^{7} k^2 = \frac{(7)(8)(15)}{6}$$
$$= 140$$

9.
$$\lim_{n \to +\infty} \sum_{k=1}^{n} \frac{k}{n^2} = \lim_{n \to +\infty} \frac{1}{n^2} \sum_{k=1}^{n} k$$
$$= \lim_{n \to +\infty} \frac{1}{n^2}\left[\frac{n(n+1)}{2}\right]$$
$$= \lim_{n \to +\infty} (1)(\tfrac{1}{2})\left(1 + \tfrac{1}{n}\right)$$
$$= \tfrac{1}{2}$$

12.
$$\lim_{n \to +\infty} \sum_{k=1}^{n} \left(1 + \frac{2k}{n}\right)^2\left(\frac{2}{n}\right)$$
$$= \lim_{n \to +\infty} \left(\frac{2}{n}\right)\left(\sum_{k=1}^{n} 1 + \frac{4}{n} \sum_{k=1}^{n} k + \frac{4}{n^2} \sum_{k=1}^{n} k^2\right)$$
$$= \lim_{n \to +\infty} \left(\frac{2}{n}\right)\left(n + \frac{4}{n}\frac{n(n+1)}{2} + \frac{4}{n^2}\frac{n(n+1)(2n+1)}{6}\right)$$
$$= \lim_{n \to +\infty} \left[2 + 4(1)\left(1 + \tfrac{1}{n}\right) + \tfrac{4}{3}(1)\left(1 + \tfrac{1}{n}\right)\left(2 + \tfrac{1}{n}\right)\right]$$
$$= 2 + 4 + \tfrac{8}{3} = \tfrac{26}{3} \approx 8.67$$

15. a.

$$n = 4,\ \Delta x = 0.25,\ f(a + k\Delta x) = \left(1 + \frac{k}{4}\right)^2;$$

$$S \approx [f(1.25) + f(1.50) + f(1.75) + f(2.00)](0.25)$$
$$= [1.25^2 + 1.50^2 + 1.75^2 + 2.00^2](0.25)$$
$$= [10.875](0.25)$$
$$= 2.71875$$

b.

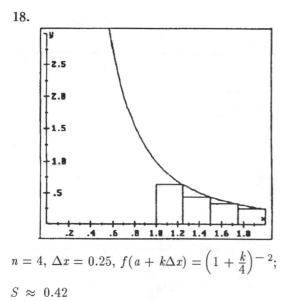

$n = 6$, $\Delta x = \frac{1}{6}$, $f(a + k\Delta x) = \left(1 + \frac{k}{6}\right)^2$;

$S \approx 2.58796$

18.

$n = 4$, $\Delta x = 0.25$, $f(a + k\Delta x) = \left(1 + \frac{k}{4}\right)^{-2}$;

$S \approx 0.42$

24. $\Delta x = \dfrac{b - a}{n} = \dfrac{3 - 0}{n} = \dfrac{3}{n}$

$$A = \lim_{n \to +\infty} \sum_{k=1}^{n} f\left(\frac{3k}{n}\right) \Delta x$$

$$= \lim_{n \to +\infty} \sum_{k=1}^{n} \left[6\left(\frac{3k}{n}\right)^2 + 2\left(\frac{3k}{n}\right) + 4\right]\left(\frac{3}{n}\right)$$

$$= \lim_{n \to +\infty} \sum_{k=1}^{n} \left(\frac{54k^2}{n^2} + \frac{6k}{n} + 4\right)\left(\frac{3}{n}\right)$$

$$= \lim_{n \to +\infty} \left[\frac{162}{n^3} \sum_{k=1}^{n} k^2 + \frac{18}{n^2} \sum_{k=1}^{n} k + \frac{12}{n} \sum_{k=1}^{n} 1\right]$$

$$= \lim_{n \to +\infty} \left[\frac{162}{n^3} \frac{n(n+1)(2n+1)}{6} + \frac{18}{n^2} \frac{n(n+1)}{2} + \frac{12n}{n}\right]$$

$$= \frac{162}{3} + 9 + 12 = 75$$

30.   The statement is true. Consider the trapezoid of base $(b - a)$ and parallel sides of lengths a^2 and b^2. The area is

$$A = \tfrac{1}{2}(b - a)(b^2 + a^2)$$

The area under the parabola is less than the area of the trapezoid.

34. $f(x) = x^3$ on $[0, 1]$; $\Delta x = \frac{1}{n}$;

$$f(a + kx) = f\left(\frac{k}{n}\right) = \frac{k^3}{n^3}.$$

$$A = \lim_{n \to +\infty} \frac{1}{n^4} \sum_{k=1}^{n} k^3$$

$$= \lim_{n \to +\infty} \frac{1}{n^4} \frac{n^2(n+1)^2}{4} = \frac{1}{4}$$

37.   **a.** $f(x) = 2x^2$; $\Delta x = \frac{1}{n}$;

$$f(a + kx) = 2\left(1 + \frac{k}{n}\right)^2$$

$$A = \lim_{n \to +\infty} \sum_{k=1}^{n} \left[2\left(1 + \tfrac{k}{n}\right)^2 \left(\tfrac{1}{n}\right) \right]$$

$$= \lim_{n \to +\infty} \left[\frac{2n}{n} + \frac{4}{n^2} \sum_{k=1}^{n} k + \frac{2}{n^3} \sum_{k=1}^{n} k^2 \right]$$

$$= \lim_{n \to +\infty} \left[2 + \frac{4n(n+1)}{2n^2} + \frac{2n(n+1)(2n+1)}{6n^3} \right]$$

$$= 2 + 2 + \frac{2}{3} = \frac{14}{3}$$

b. If $g(x) = \frac{2}{3}x^3$; $g'(x) = 2x^2$;

$$g(2) - g(1) = \frac{16}{3} - \frac{2}{3} = \frac{14}{3} = A$$

c. If $h(x) = \frac{2}{3}x^3 + C$; $h'(x) = 2x^2$;

$$h(2) - h(1) = \frac{16}{3} + C - \frac{2}{3} - C$$

$$= \frac{14}{3}$$

$$= A$$

regardless of C. The statement is true.

42.

# OF TERMS	RIEMANN SUM OVER [0, 3]
4	4.297237
8	3.844611
16	3.623472
32	3.51422
64	3.459924
128	3.432858
256	3.419345
512	3.412594
1024	3.40922
THIS IS THE FINAL ESTIMATE	

(Network points are right endpoints.)

The area seems to be 3.40922.

45. a.

# OF TERMS	RIEMANN SUM OVER [0, π/2]
4	1.974232
8	1.99357
16	1.998393
32	1.999598
64	1.9999
128	1.999975
256	1.999994
512	1.999998
1024	2
THIS IS THE FINAL ESTIMATE	

(Network points are right endpoints.)

The area seems to be 2.

b. With $g(x) = -\cos x + \sin x$;

$$g'(x) = \sin x + \cos x = f(x)$$

$$g\left(\tfrac{\pi}{2}\right) = -0 + 1 = 1;$$

$$g(0) = -1 + 0 = -1, \text{ and}$$

$$g\left(\tfrac{\pi}{2}\right) - g(0) = 1 - (-1) = 2 = A$$

c. With $h(x) = -\cos x + \sin x + C$;

$$h'(x) = \sin x + \cos x = f(x).$$

$$h\left(\tfrac{\pi}{2}\right) = -0 + 1 + C = 1 + C;$$

$$h(0) = -1 + 0 + C = -1 + C, \text{ and}$$

$$h\left(\tfrac{\pi}{2}\right) - h(0) = 1 + C - (-1) - C = 2 = A$$

The statement is true.

5.3 Riemann Sums and the Definite Integral, Pages 348–349

SURVIVAL HINT: *Thoroughly understand the significance of each symbol in the limit of a Riemann sum as given on page 338. This concept of an infinite sum of infinitely small parts will be used repeatedly throughout the text. Any successful calculus student should be able to state and explain the definitions of limit, derivative, and definite integral.*

3. $f(x) = x^2;\ a = 1;\ \Delta x = \frac{1}{2}$

$$f(a + k\Delta x) = f(1 + \tfrac{k}{2}) = \left(1 + \tfrac{k}{2}\right)^2$$

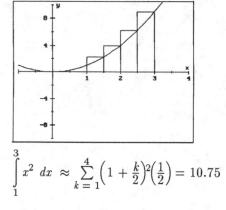

$$\int_1^3 x^2\ dx \approx \sum_{k=1}^4 \left(1 + \tfrac{k}{2}\right)^2\left(\tfrac{1}{2}\right) = 10.75$$

6. $f(x) = x^2 - x^3;\ a = 1;\ \Delta x = \frac{1}{2}$

$$f(a + k\Delta x) = f(1 + \tfrac{k}{2})$$
$$= \left(1 + \tfrac{k}{2}\right)^2 - \left(1 + \tfrac{k}{2}\right)^3$$

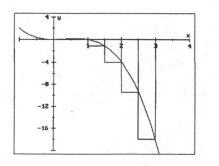

$$\int_1^3 (x^2 - x^3)\ dx \approx \sum_{k=1}^4 \left[\left(1 + \tfrac{k}{2}\right)^2 - \left(1 + \tfrac{k}{2}\right)^3\right]\left(\tfrac{1}{2}\right)$$

$$= -16.25$$

11. $v(t) = 3t + 1;\ a = 1;\ \Delta t = \frac{3}{4};$

$$v(a + k\Delta t) = v(1 + \tfrac{3k}{4}) = 3\left(1 + \tfrac{3k}{4}\right) + 1$$

$$S_4 = \sum_{k=1}^4 \left(4 + \tfrac{3k}{4}\right)\left(\tfrac{3}{4}\right)$$

$$= \frac{231}{8}$$

$$= 28.875$$

14. $v(t) = \cos t;\ a = 0;\ \Delta t = \frac{\pi}{8}$

$$v(a + k\Delta t) = v(\tfrac{k\pi}{8}) = \cos \tfrac{k\pi}{8}$$

$$S_4 = \sum_{k=1}^4 \cos \tfrac{k\pi}{8}\left(\tfrac{\pi}{8}\right)$$

$$\approx 0.791$$

19. $\displaystyle \int_{-1}^2 (2x^2 - 3x)\ dx = 2\int_{-1}^2 x^2\ dx - 3\int_{-1}^2 x\ dx$

$$= 2(3) - 3(\tfrac{3}{2})$$

$$= \frac{3}{2}$$

22. $\displaystyle \int_{-1}^0 (3x^2 - 5x)\ dx = 3\int_{-1}^0 x^2\ dx - 5\int_{-1}^0 x\ dx$

$$= 3(\tfrac{1}{3}) - 5(-\tfrac{1}{2})$$

$$= 1 + \frac{5}{2} = \frac{7}{2}$$

23. On $[0, 1]$ $x^3 \leq x$, so $\displaystyle\int_0^1 x^3 \, dx \leq \int_0^1 x \, dx = \frac{1}{2}$

26. **a.** Let $F = \displaystyle\int_0^2 f(x)dx = 3;\ G = \int_0^2 g(x)dx = -1$

and $H = \displaystyle\int_0^2 h(x) \, dx = 3$. Then

$\displaystyle\int_0^2 [2f(x) + 5g(x) - 7h(x)] \, dx$

$= 2F + 5G - 7H$

$= 2(3) + 5(-1) - 7(3)$

$= -20$

b. $\displaystyle\int_0^2 [5f(x) + sg(x) - 6h(x)] \, dx$

$= 5F + sG - 6H$

$= 5(3) + (-1)s - 6(3)$

$= -s - 3$

$= 0$

which implies $s = -3$

30. In the 18th century, in the German town of Königsberg (now a Russian city), a popular pastime was to walk along the bank of the Pregel River and cross over some of the seven bridges that connected two islands, as shown below.

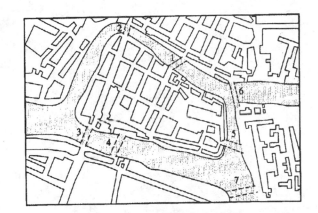

One day a native asked a neighbor this question, "How can you take a walk so that you cross each of our seven bridges once and only once?" The problem intrigued the neighbor, and soon caught the interest of many other people of Königsberg as well. Whenever people tried it, they ended up either not crossing a bridge at all or else crossing one bridge twice. This problem was brought to the attention of the Swiss mathematician Leonhard Euler, who was serving at the court of the Russian empress Catherine the Great in St. Petersburg. The method of solution developed by Euler led to the development of two major topics in geometry, networks, and topology. The solution concludes that it is impossible to cross all of the bridges exactly once.

33. $f(x) = x^2$ and $\Delta x = \dfrac{b - a}{n}$; $x_k = a + \dfrac{b - a}{n}k$;

$$S_n = \sum_{k=1}^{n}\left[a + \frac{b - a}{n}k\right]^2\left(\frac{b - a}{n}\right)$$

$$= \sum_{k=1}^{n}\frac{b-a}{n}\left[a^2 + \frac{2(b-a)}{n}ak + \frac{(b-a)^2}{n^2}k^2\right]$$

$$= \frac{b-a}{n}\left(a^2\sum_{k=1}^{n}1 + \frac{2(b-a)}{n}a\sum_{k=1}^{n}k\right.$$

$$\left. + \frac{(b-a)^2}{n^2}\sum_{k=1}^{n}k^2\right)$$

$$= \frac{b-a}{n}\left(a^2 n + \frac{2(b-a)}{n}\frac{an(n+1)}{2}\right.$$

$$\left. + \frac{(b-a)^2}{n^2}\frac{n(n+1)(2n+1)}{6}\right)$$

$$\int_{a}^{b} x^2 dx = \lim_{n\to+\infty}S_n$$

$$= \lim_{n\to+\infty}\frac{b-a}{n}\left(a^2 n + \frac{2(b-a)}{n}\frac{an(n+1)}{2}\right.$$

$$\left. + \frac{(b-a)^2}{n^2}\frac{n(n+1)(2n+1)}{6}\right)$$

$$= \left(a^2 + ab - a^2 + \frac{(b-a)^2}{3}\right)(b - a)$$

$$= \left(\frac{b-a}{3}\right)(3a^2 + 3ab - 3a^2 + b^2 - 2ab + a^2)$$

$$= \tfrac{1}{3}(b - a)(b^2 + ab + a^2) = \tfrac{1}{3}(b^3 - a^3)$$

35. $f(x) = 4 - 5x$

k:	1	2	3	4	5
x_k^*:	-0.5	0.8	1	1.3	1.8
$f(x_k^*)$:	6.5	0	-1	-2.5	-5
Δx_k:	0.8	1.1	0.4	0.4	0.3

$$R_5 = \sum_{1}^{5}f(x_k)\Delta x_k$$

$$= 6.5(0.8) + 0 + (-1)(0.4)$$

$$+ (-2.5)(0.4) + (-5)(0.3)$$

$$= 2.3$$

5.4 The Fundamental Theorems of Calculus; Pages 355-357

SURVIVAL HINT: *The **fundamental theorem of calculus** sounds really important — and it is. However, most calculus students seem not to appreciate its significance upon first exposure. It will become more meaningful as you encounter it in more advanced contexts, when your have a greater perspective. For now, see that it relates the two major concepts of elementary calculus — the derivative and the Riemann sum. Try to see that the increase in the area under a curve, as x is incremented, depends upon the slope of the curve.*

1.
$$\int_{-10}^{10} 7\,dx = 7x\Big|_{-10}^{10}$$

$$= 7[10 - (-10)] = 140$$

6. $\displaystyle\int_{-1}^{1} (x^3 + bx^2)\,dx = (\tfrac{1}{4}x^4 + \tfrac{1}{3}bx^3)\Big|_{-1}^{1}$

$$= \tfrac{1}{4} + \tfrac{1}{3}b - (\tfrac{1}{4} - \tfrac{1}{3}b)$$

$$= \tfrac{2}{3}b$$

11. $\displaystyle\int_{0}^{1} (5u^7 + \pi^2)\,du = (\tfrac{5}{8}u^8 + \pi^2 u)\Big|_{0}^{1}$

$$= \tfrac{5}{8} + \pi^2$$

17. $\displaystyle\int_{0}^{4} \sqrt{x}(x + 1)\,dx = \int_{0}^{4} (x^{3/2} + x^{1/2})\,dx$

$$= \left[\tfrac{2}{5}x^{5/2} + \tfrac{2}{3}x^{3/2}\right]\Big|_{0}^{4}$$

$$= \tfrac{272}{15}$$

21. $\displaystyle 6a\int_{1}^{\sqrt{3}} \frac{dx}{1 + x^2} = 6a\tan^{-1}x\Big|_{1}^{\sqrt{3}}$

$$= 6a(\tfrac{\pi}{3} - \tfrac{\pi}{4})$$

$$= \tfrac{a\pi}{2}$$

24. **SURVIVAL HINT:** *Note the use of a trigonometric identity **before** integration. Simplify expressions whenever possible.*

$$\int_{0}^{\pi/4} (\sec^2 x - \tan^2 x)\,dx = \int_{0}^{\pi/4} dx$$

$$= x\Big|_{0}^{\pi/4} = \tfrac{\pi}{4}$$

29. $\displaystyle\int_{-1}^{0} (x - x)\,dx + \int_{0}^{2} (x + x)\,dx = \frac{2x^2}{2}\Big|_{0}^{2}$

$$= 4$$

34. $f(x) = \sin x + \cos x$ is continuous on $[0, \tfrac{\pi}{2}]$ and $f(x) \geq 0$ on the interval, we have

$$\int_{0}^{\pi/2} (\sin x + \cos x)\,dx = (-\cos x + \sin x)\Big|_{0}^{\pi/2}$$

$$= 2$$

37. $f(x) = \dfrac{x^2 - 2x + 3}{x}$ is continuous on $[1, 2]$ and $f(x) \geq 0$ on the interval, we have

$$\int_{1}^{2} (x - 2 + 3x^{-1})\,dx = \left(\frac{x^2}{2} - 2x + 3\ln|x|\right)\Big|_{1}^{2}$$

$$= 3\ln 2 - \tfrac{1}{2}$$

43. From the second fundamental theorem of calculus, we have

$$F'(x) = \frac{-1}{\sqrt{1 + 3x^2}}$$

45. $\dfrac{d}{du}\left(\dfrac{u}{2} + \dfrac{\sin 2au}{4a} + C\right) = \tfrac{1}{2} + \tfrac{2a}{4a}\cos 2uu + 0$

$$= \tfrac{1}{2} + \tfrac{1}{2}\cos 2au$$

$$= \tfrac{1}{2} + \tfrac{1}{2}(2\cos^2 au - 1)$$

$$= \cos^2 au$$

50. $\dfrac{d}{du}[u(\ln|u|)^2 - 2u\ln|u| + 2u + C]$

$= (\ln|u|)^2 + 2u(\ln|u|)\cdot\dfrac{1}{u} - 2\ln|u| - 2u\cdot\dfrac{1}{u} + 2$

$= (\ln|u|)^2$

54. $\displaystyle\int_0^2 f(x)\,dx = \int_0^1 f(x)\,dx + \int_1^2 f(x)\,dx$

$\displaystyle = \int_0^1 x^3\,dx + \int_1^2 x^4\,dx$

$= \dfrac{1}{4}x^4\Big|_0^1 + \dfrac{1}{5}x^5\Big|_1^2$

$= 6.45$

57. **a.** It is a relative minimum since the derivative (function f) shows the $\downarrow\uparrow$ pattern.

b. It looks like f has a point of inflection at $x = 1$, so we estimate $g(1) = 0$

c. It has a relative maximum where f crosses the x-axis, about $x = 0.75$.

d.

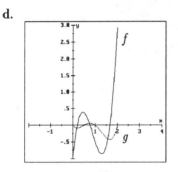

62. Let $G(x) = \displaystyle\int_1^x \dfrac{2t+1}{t+2}\,dt$.

Then, $F(x) = G(u(x))$ where $u(x) = \sqrt{x}$ and

$F'(x) = G'(u)u'(x)$

$= \left[\dfrac{2u+1}{u+2}\right]\left(\dfrac{1}{2}\dfrac{1}{\sqrt{x}}\right)$

$= \dfrac{2\sqrt{x}+1}{2\sqrt{x}(\sqrt{x}+2)}$

$F(1) = 0$ and $F'(1) = \frac{1}{2}$, so the equation of the tangent line at P is

$y = \dfrac{1}{2}(x-1)$

5.5 Integration by Substitution, Pages 362-363

2. **a.** $\displaystyle\int_0^{\pi/2} \sin\theta\,d\theta = -\cos\theta\Big|_0^{\pi/2}$

$= 1$

b. $\displaystyle\int_0^{\pi/2} \sin 2\theta\,d\theta = \int_0^{\pi} \sin u\left(\tfrac{1}{2}\,du\right)$

$u = 2\theta;\ du = 2\,d\theta;$

if $\theta = 0,\ u = 0;$ if $\theta = \frac{\pi}{2},\ u = \pi$

$= -\dfrac{1}{2}\cos u\Big|_0^{\pi}$

$= 1$

5. **a.** $\displaystyle\int_0^{16} \sqrt[4]{x}\,dx = \dfrac{4}{5}x^{5/4}\Big|_0^{16}$

$$= \frac{128}{5}$$

$$= \tfrac{1}{4}(\tfrac{2}{3})\,u^{3/2} + C$$

$$= \tfrac{1}{6}(2x^2 + 1)^{3/2} + C$$

b. $\displaystyle \int_{-16}^{0} \sqrt[4]{-x}\,dx = -\int_{16}^{0} u^{1/4}\,du$

28. $\displaystyle \int x^3(x^2 + 4)^{1/2}\,dx$

> $u = -x,\ du = -\,dx;$

> if $x = -16,\ u = 16;\ x = 0,\ u = 0$

> Let $u = x^2 + 4;\ du = 2x\,dx$
> and $x^2 = u - 4$

$$= -\tfrac{4}{5} u^{5/4}\Big|_{16}^{0}$$

$$= \frac{128}{5}$$

$$= \tfrac{1}{2}\int (u^{3/2} - 4u^{1/2})\,du$$

SURVIVAL HINT: *Do not try to do any but the simplest u substitutions in your head. You will have fewer errors, and save time in the long run, if for each problem you write down:* $\boxed{u = \dots \text{ and } du = \dots}$. *Most errors in u substitutions come from a failure to property introduce constants to "set-up the du."*

$$= \tfrac{1}{2}(\tfrac{2}{5} u^{5/2} - \tfrac{8}{3} u^{3/2}) + C$$

$$= \tfrac{1}{5}(x^2 + 4)^{5/2} - \tfrac{4}{3}(x^2 + 4)^{3/2} + C$$

$$= \tfrac{1}{15}(x^2 + 4)^{3/2}(3x^2 - 8) + C$$

9. $u = 2x + 3;$

$$\int (2x + 3)^4\,dx = \tfrac{1}{2}\int u^4\,du$$

35. $\displaystyle \int_{0}^{1} \frac{5x^2\,dx}{2x^3 + 1} = \tfrac{5}{6}\int_{0}^{1} \frac{6x^2\,dx}{2x^3 + 1}$

$$= \tfrac{1}{2}\cdot\tfrac{1}{5} u^5 + C$$

> Let $u = 2x^3 + 1;\ du = 6x^2\,dx$
> $x = 0,\ u = 1;\ x = 1,\ u = 3$

$$= \tfrac{1}{10}(2x + 3)^5 + C$$

18. $u = x^2 - 3x + 5;$

$$= \tfrac{5}{6}\int_{1}^{3} \frac{du}{u}$$

$$\int \frac{(6x - 9)\,dx}{(x^2 - 3x + 5)^3} = 3\int u^{-3}\,du$$

$$= \tfrac{5}{6}(\ln 3 - \ln 1)$$

$$= -\tfrac{3}{2}(x^2 - 3x + 5)^{-2} + C$$

$$= \tfrac{5}{6}\ln 3$$

23. $u = 2x^2 + 1;$

$$\int x\sqrt{2x^2 + 1}\,dx = \tfrac{1}{4}\int u^{1/2}\,du$$

41. $\displaystyle\int_0^{\pi/6} \tan 2x\, dx$

$$u = \cos 2x;\ du = -2\sin 2x\, dx;$$
$$x = 0,\ u = 1;\ x = \pi/6,\ u = 1/2$$

$$= -\frac{1}{2}\int_0^{1/2} \frac{du}{u}$$

$$= -\frac{1}{2}\ln|u|\,\Big|_1^{1/2}$$

$$= \frac{1}{2}\ln 2$$

48. $f(x) = x(x-1)^{1/3}$ is continuous and positive on $[2, 9]$.

$$\int_2^9 x(x-1)^{1/3}\, dx = \int_1^8 (u+1)u^{1/3}\, du$$

$$u = x - 1;\ du = dx$$
$$x = 2,\ \text{then}\ u = 1;$$
$$x = 9,\ \text{then}\ u = 8$$

$$= \int_1^8 (u^{4/3} + u^{1/3})\, du$$

$$= \left(\frac{3}{7}u^{7/3} + \frac{3}{4}u^{4/3}\right)\Big|_1^8$$

$$= \frac{1,839}{28}$$

$$\approx 65.6786$$

52. $\displaystyle\int_{-\pi/2}^{\pi/2} \cos x\, dx = 2\int_0^{\pi/2} \cos x\, dx = 2$

since $\cos x$ is even.

57. $\dfrac{dy}{dx} = \dfrac{2x}{1 - 3x^2}$

$$F(x) = \int \frac{2x}{1 - 3x^2}\, dx$$

$$u = 1 - 3x^2;\ du = -6x\, dx$$

$$= -\frac{1}{3}\int \frac{du}{u} = -\frac{1}{3}\ln|u| + C$$

$$= -\frac{1}{3}\ln|1 - 3x^2| + C$$

$F(0) = -\frac{1}{3}\ln|1| + C = 5$ implies $C = 5$, so

$$F(x) = -\frac{1}{3}\ln|1 - 3x^2| + 5$$

59. Water flows into the tank at the rate of

$$R(t) = v'(t) = t(3t^2 + 1)^{-1/2}\ \text{ft}^3/\text{s}$$

The volume at time t is

$$v(t) = \frac{1}{6}\int (3t^2 + 1)^{-1/2}(6t\, dt)$$

$$= \frac{1}{3}\sqrt{3t^2 + 1} + C$$

The tank is empty to start, so

$$v(0) = 0 = \frac{1}{3} + C,\ \text{so}\ C = -\frac{1}{3}$$

Thus,

$$v(t) = \frac{1}{3}(\sqrt{3t^2 + 1} - 1)$$

$$v(4) = \frac{1}{3}(\sqrt{49} - 1) = 2\ \text{ft}^3$$

The amount of water at 4 seconds is $2\ \text{ft}^3$.

The height h is given by the equation

$$100h = 2, \text{ so } h = \frac{1}{50} \text{ ft or } \frac{12}{50} = 0.24 \text{ in.}$$

The depth at that time is about $\frac{1}{4}$ in.

5.6 Introduction to Differential Equations, Pages 374-377

SURVIVAL HINT: *The solution to a differential equation, like the process of antidifferentiation, has an infinite set of functions (all translated vertically). Technology, if available, will draw a direction field of the solution, and can be used to sketch a particular member of that infinite set. Unless you are given initial values that will specify one particular function from this set, you must remember to include "+ C" in the general solution.*

3.
$$xy = C$$

$$x\frac{dy}{dx} + y = 0$$

$$\frac{dy}{dx} = -\frac{y}{x}$$

6. $\frac{dy}{dx} = \frac{x^3}{5} + \frac{A}{x^2}; \frac{d^2y}{dx^2} - \frac{3x^2}{5} - \frac{2A}{x^3}$

Thus,

$$x\frac{d^2y}{dx^2} + 2\frac{dy}{dx} = x\left(\frac{3x^2}{5} - \frac{2A}{x^3}\right) + 2\left(\frac{x^3}{5} + \frac{A}{x^2}\right)$$

$$= \frac{3x^3}{5} - \frac{2A}{x^2} + \frac{2x^3}{5} + \frac{2A}{x^2}$$

$$= x^3$$

9.
$$\frac{dy}{dx} = -\frac{x}{y}$$

$$y \, dy = -x \, dx$$

$$\int y \, dy = -\int x \, dx$$

$$\frac{y^2}{2} = -\frac{x^2}{2} + C_1$$

$$x^2 + y^2 = C$$

Passes through $(2, 2)$, so $4 + 4 = C$;

$$x^2 + y^2 = 8$$

15. First plot the given point, namely $(0, 1)$. Next, sketch the curve (using a pencil) from point to point using adjacent slope marks to move from point to point.

23.
$$\frac{dy}{dx} = \frac{x}{y}\sqrt{1 - x^2}$$

$$y \, dy = x\sqrt{1 - x^2} \, dx$$

$$\int y \, dy = \int x\sqrt{1 - x^2} \, dx$$

Let $u = (1 - x^2);$ $du = -2x \, dx$

$$\int y \, dy = \int (-\tfrac{1}{2})u^{1/2} du$$

$$\frac{y^2}{2} = -\frac{1}{2}\frac{(1-x^2)^{3/2}}{\frac{3}{2}} + C_1$$

$$\frac{(1-x^2)^{3/2}}{3} + \frac{y^2}{2} = C_1$$

$$2(1-x^2)^{3/2} + 3y^2 = C$$

27.
$$\frac{dy}{dx} = \frac{\sin x}{\cos y}$$

$$\cos y \, dy = \sin x \, dx$$

$$\int \cos y \, dy = \int \sin x \, dx$$

$$\sin y = -\cos x + C$$

$$\cos x + \sin y = C$$

31. Write $y \, dx = x \, dy$ as $\dfrac{x \, dy - y \, dx}{x^2} = 0$;

$\dfrac{d}{dx}\left(\dfrac{y}{x}\right) = 0$, so $\dfrac{y}{x} = C$ or $y = Cx$

33. Family of curves: $2x - 3y = C$;
differentiating with respect to x leads to the
slope of the tangent lines $dy/dx = 2/3$. For
the orthogonal trajectories, the slope is the
negative reciprocal, or $dY/dX = -3/2$.
Integrating leads to the orthogonal
trajectories: $2Y + 3X = K$

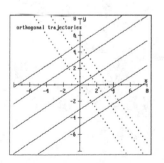

36. Family of curves: $y = x^4 + C$; differentiating
with respect to x leads to the slope of the
tangent lines $dy/dx = 4x^3$. For the
orthogonal trajectories, the slope is the
negative reciprocal, or $dY/dX = -X^{-3}/4$.
Integrating leads to $4Y = \frac{1}{2}X^{-2} + K_1$ or
$Y = \frac{1}{8}X^{-2} + K$.

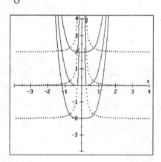

42. Let Q denote the number of bacteria. Then,
dQ/dt is the rate of change of Q, and since
this rate of change is proportional to Q, it
follows that

$$\frac{dQ}{dt} = kQ$$

where k is a positive constant of
proportionality.

45. Let Q denote the number of facts recalled and
N the total number of relevant facts in the
person's memory. Then dQ/dt is the rate of
change of Q, and $(N - Q)$ is the number of
relevant facts not recalled. Since the rate of
change is proportional to $N - Q$,
it follows that

$$\frac{dQ}{dt} = k(N - Q)$$

where k is a positive constant of proportionality.

52. For carbon dating $k = \ln(1/2)/5,730$;

$$\frac{Q}{Q_0} = e^{kt}$$

$0.907 = e^{kt}$ *k is the known value given above*

$$t = \frac{\ln 0.907}{k} \approx 807$$

This dates the Shroud at around $1988 - 807 \approx 1200$ AD.

56. a. $v^2 = \frac{2gR^2}{s} + v_0{}^2 - 2gR$

$$= \frac{2(32)(3,956)^2(5,280)^2}{(3,956)(5,280) + 200}$$

$$+ 150^2 - 2(32)(3,956)(5,280)$$

$$= 9,700 \text{ or } v$$

$$\approx 98.5 \text{ ft/s}$$

b. The velocity at the maximum height is 0:

$$0 = \frac{2gR^2}{s} + v_0{}^2 - 2gR \text{ so}$$

$R/s = 1 - v_0{}^2/(2gR) \approx 0.9999831689$; thus,

$s \approx 3,956.067$. We now find $h \approx 0.067$ mi

≈ 352 ft.

60.
$$\frac{dP}{dt} = k\sqrt{P}$$

$$\int P^{-1/2} \, dP = \int k \, dt.$$

$$2\sqrt{P} = kt + C$$

$P(0) = 9,000$, so $C = 60\sqrt{10}$, and

$P(-10) = 4,000$, so

$$2\sqrt{4,000} = -10k + 60\sqrt{10}$$

$$k = 2\sqrt{10}$$

We now have the equation:

$$2\sqrt{P} = 2\sqrt{10}t + 60\sqrt{10}$$

$$\sqrt{P} = \sqrt{10}t + 30\sqrt{10}$$

To find t for $P = 16,000$,

$$\sqrt{16,000} = \sqrt{10}t + 30\sqrt{10}$$

$$t = 10$$

The population will be 16,000 10 years from now.

62. Differentiating $V = 9\pi h^3$ leads to

$$\frac{dV}{dt} = 9\pi\left(3h^2 \frac{dh}{dt}\right) = -4.8A_0\sqrt{h}$$

from Toricelli's law. Since the area of the hole (in ft^2) is $A_0 = \pi\left(\frac{1}{12}\right)^2 = \frac{\pi}{144}$

$$27\pi h^2 \frac{dh}{dt} = (-4.8)(\frac{\pi}{144})\sqrt{h}$$

$$\int h^{3/2} \, dh = -\int \frac{4.8\pi}{144(27\pi)} \, dt$$

$$\frac{2}{5}h^{5/2} = -\frac{1}{810}t + C$$

If $t = 0$, then $h = 4$, so that $C = \frac{64}{5}$. The height is zero when

$$0 = -\frac{1}{810}t + \frac{64}{5}$$

$$10{,}368 = t$$

10,368 sec is about 173 min or 2 hr and

53 min.

5.7 The Mean Value Theorem for Integrals; Average Value, Pages 381-383

1. $f(x)$ is continuous on $[1, 2]$, so the MVT

guarantees the existence of a c such that:

$$\int_{1}^{2} 4x^3 \, dx = f(c)(2 - 1)$$

$$15 = f(c)$$

$$15 = 4c^3$$

$$c^3 = \frac{15}{4}$$

$$c = \frac{\sqrt[3]{30}}{2} \approx 1.55$$

1.55 is on the interval $[1, 2]$

SURVIVAL HINT: *Remember, that the MVT is a theorem and as such, has a hypotheses that must be verified before the theorem is valid. Know the hypotheses, and understand why they are necessary, for every theorem you learn.*

5. The mean value theorem does not apply

because $f(x) = \csc x$ is discontinuous at

$x = 0$.

12. $A = \int_{0}^{3} x^2 \, dx = \frac{1}{3}x^3 \Big|_{0}^{3} = 9$

$$f(c)(b - a) = c^2(3) = 9$$

so $c = \sqrt{3}$ ($-\sqrt{3}$ is not in the domain)

and $f(\sqrt{3}) = 3$

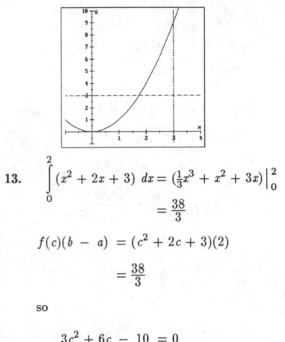

13. $\int_{0}^{2} (x^2 + 2x + 3) \, dx = (\frac{1}{3}x^3 + x^2 + 3x) \Big|_{0}^{2}$

$$= \frac{38}{3}$$

$$f(c)(b - a) = (c^2 + 2c + 3)(2)$$

$$= \frac{38}{3}$$

so

$$3c^2 + 6c - 10 = 0$$

$$c \approx 1.08$$

(negative is not in the domain)

$$f(1.08) \approx 6.33$$

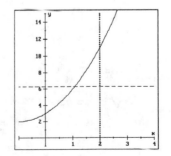

20. $\dfrac{1}{1-0}\displaystyle\int_0^1 \dfrac{x}{2x+3}\,dx = \int_0^1 \left[\dfrac{1}{2} - \dfrac{3}{2}\cdot\dfrac{1}{2x+3}\right]dx$

Use long division.

$= \left[\dfrac{1}{2}x - \dfrac{3}{4}\ln|2x+3|\right]\Big|_0^1$

$= \dfrac{1}{2} - \dfrac{3}{4}\ln\dfrac{5}{3}$

≈ 0.1169

21. $\dfrac{1}{\frac{\pi}{4}-0}\displaystyle\int_0^{\pi/4}\sin x\,dx = -\dfrac{4}{\pi}\cos x\,\Big|_0^{\pi/4}$

$= -\dfrac{4}{\pi}\left(\cos\dfrac{\pi}{4} - 1\right)$

≈ 0.3729

27. $\dfrac{1}{1-(-2)}\displaystyle\int_{-2}^1 x(x^2+1)^3\,dx = \dfrac{1}{6}\dfrac{(x^2+1)^4}{4}\Big|_{-2}^1$

$= -\dfrac{609}{24}$

$= -25.375$

30. $\dfrac{1}{2-0}\displaystyle\int_0^2 \sqrt{2x-x^2}\,dx$

$= \dfrac{1}{2}(\text{area of a half-circle with } r = 1)$

$= \dfrac{\pi}{4}$

≈ 0.785

34. a. $\dfrac{1}{3-0}\displaystyle\int_0^3 te^{-0.01t^2}\,dt$

$= \dfrac{1}{3}\left[\dfrac{e^{-0.01t^2}}{-0.02}\right]_0^3$

≈ 1.43

b. We need to solve the equation

$1.43 = te^{-0.01t^2}$, and to do so we use a

solve utility (or look for the intersection

of the graphs of $y_1 = 1.43$ and

$y_2 = te^{-0.01t^2}$) to find

$t_1 \approx 1.47$ years (a little less than 1 yr, 6

months) more than 3 years

$t_2 \approx 15.41$ years (a little less than 15

yr, 5 months)

5.8 Numerical Integration: The Trapezoidal Rule and Simpson's Rule, Pages 388-391

SURVIVAL HINT: *Successful use of the trapezoidal rule and Simpson's rule is highly dependent upon your careful organization of the data. To simultaneously compute and keep a running total of values in your calculator takes considerable skill. Make a table of x_n values, $f(x_n)$, and $f(x_n)$ times the appropriate multiplier. It will save you time in the long run. Graphing calculators or computer software can often help with this process.*

1. $\Delta x = \dfrac{2-1}{4} = \dfrac{1}{4}$

$x_0 = 1 \qquad f(x_0) = 1$

$x_1 = 1.25 \quad f(x_1) = 1.5625$

$x_2 = 1.5 \quad f(x_2) = 2.25$

$x_3 = 1.75 \quad f(x_3) = 3.0625$

$x_4 = 2 \qquad f(x_4) = 4$

Trapezoidal rule:

$A \approx \frac{1}{2}[1 + 2(1.5625) + 2(2.25) + 2(3.0625) + 4](\frac{1}{4})$

$= \frac{1}{8}(18.75)$

$= 2.34375$

Simpson's rule:

$A \approx \frac{1}{3}[1 + 4(1.5625) + 2(2.25) + 4(3.0625) + 4](\frac{1}{4})$

$= \frac{1}{12}(28)$

≈ 2.33333

Check with exact value:

$A = \int_{1}^{2} x^2 \, dx$

$= \frac{x^3}{3} \Big|_{1}^{2}$

$= \frac{8}{3} - \frac{1}{3}$

$= \frac{7}{3}$

4. $\Delta x = \frac{0 - (-1)}{4} = \frac{1}{4}$

$x_0 = -1 \qquad f(x_0) = 1.414$

$x_1 = -0.75 \qquad f(x_1) = 1.250$

$x_2 = -0.5 \qquad f(x_2) = 1.118$

$x_3 = -0.25 \qquad f(x_3) = 1.031$

$x_4 = 0 \qquad f(x_4) = 1.000$

a. Trapezoidal rule:

$A \approx \frac{1}{2}[1(1.414) + 2(1.250) + 2(1.118)$

$+ 2(1.031) + 1(1.000)](\frac{1}{4})$

$= \frac{1}{8}(9.212)$

$= 1.1515$

b. Simpson's rule:

$A \approx \frac{1}{3}[1(1.414) + 4(1.250) + 2(1.118)$

$+ 4(1.031) + 1(1.000)](\frac{1}{4})$

$= \frac{1}{12}(13.774)$

≈ 1.1478

14. $f'(x) = -x^{-2};$

$f''(x) = 2x^{-3};$

$f'''(x) = -6x^{-4};$

$f^{(4)}(x) = 24x^{-5}$

The maximum value of $\left| f^{(4)}(x) \right|$ on $[1, 2]$ is 24 on $[1, 2]$. For Simpson's rule

$\frac{1^5(24)}{180n^4} < 0.0005$

$n^4 > 267$

$n \geq 4.04$

from which we will pick $n = 6$ (n must be even).

$\Delta x = \frac{2 - 1}{6} = \frac{1}{6}$

$x_0 = 1.000 \qquad f(x_0) = 1.000$

$x_1 = 1.167 \qquad f(x_1) = 0.857$

$x_2 = 1.333 \qquad f(x_2) = 0.750$

$x_3 = 1.500 \qquad f(x_3) = 0.667$

$x_4 = 1.667 \qquad f(x_4) = 0.600$

$x_5 = 1.833 \qquad f(x_5) = 0.545$

$x_6 = 2.000 \qquad f(x_6) = 0.500$

$A \approx 0.693$; the exact answer is between

$0.693 - 0.0005$ and $0.693 + 0.0005$.

19. $f'(x) = -x^{-2}; f''(x) = 2x^{-3};$

$f'''(x) = -6x^{-4}; f^{(4)}(x) = 24x^{-5}$

a. $\dfrac{2^3(2)}{12n^2} \leq 0.00005$ or $n \approx 163.3$;

pick $n = 164$

b. $\dfrac{2^5(24)}{180n^4} \leq 0.00005$ or $n \approx 17.09$

pick $n = 18$

28. The distance traveled is $s = \displaystyle\int_0^{60} v(t)\, dt$ since

$v(t) \geq 0$ for $0 \leq t \leq 60$. By the

trapezoidal rule (using $\Delta t = 1/12$ hr):

$s \approx \frac{1}{2}[54 + 2(57) + 2(50) + \cdots$

$+ 2(42) + 2(48) + 53](\frac{1}{12})$

≈ 50.38 miles

32. a. Trapezoidal approximation

no./intervals:	10	20	40	80
I (est)	1.9835235	1.9958860	1.9989718	1.9997430
E_n	0.0164765	0.0041140	0.0010282	0.0002570
$E_n \cdot n$	0.164765	0.08228	0.41128	0.02056
$E_n \cdot n^2$	1.64765	1.6456	1.6451	1.6445
$E_n \cdot n^3$	16.4765	32.912	65.8041	131.598
$E_n \cdot n^4$	164.765	658.24	2,632.165	10,527.85

Based on these results, it seems that the trapezoidal approximation has order of convergence n^2 (since the n^2 row is essentially a constant 1.645).

b. Simpson's rule

no./intervals:	10	20	40	80
I (est)	2.0001095	2.0000068	2.0000004	2.0000000
E_n	0.0001095	0.0000068	0.0000004	0.0000000
$E_n \cdot n$	0.001095	0.000136	0.000017	0.0000000
$E_n \cdot n^2$	0.01095	0.00271	0.00068	0.0000000
$E_n \cdot n^3$	0.1095	0.0543	0.0271	0.0000000
$E_n \cdot n^4$	1.095	1.086	1.083	0.0000000

The last approximation has no error, but the others seem to indicate that Simpson's approximation has order of convergence n^4.

c. Rectangular approximation

no./intervals:	10	20	40	80
I (est)	1.9835235	1.9958860	1.9989718	1.9997430
E_n	0.0164765	0.0041140	0.0010282	0.0002570
$E_n \cdot n$	0.164765	0.08228	0.041128	0.02056
$E_n \cdot n^2$	1.64765	1.6456	1.64512	1.645
$E_n \cdot n^3$	16.4765	32.912	65.8041	131.598
$E_n \cdot n^4$	164.765	658.24	2,632.165	10,527.85

Again, it seems the order of convergence is n^2. In numerical analysis, it is shown that trapezoidal approximations generally converge about twice as fast as rectangular approximations.

36.

Type of estimate	Estimate
Left endpoint	2.08415012194
Trapezoid	2.55254228659
Simpson	2.59973141073

Newton-Cotes:

$\frac{3}{8}(\tan^{-1}0 + 3\tan^{-1}1 + 3\tan^{-1}2$
$\quad + \tan^{-1}3)(1) \approx 2.597507406$

Answers vary.

5.9 An Alternative Approach: The Logarithm as an Integral, Pages 395-396

SURVIVAL HINT
The material of this section may seem confusing because you already "know" too much about logarithms and exponents. In precalculus you were introduced to $y := b^x$ without any proof that it was continuous for irrational values. The approach here is really better because the area function used is continuous to begin with, so the other functions derived from it, e^x, b^x, and $\log_b x$ will also be continuous. Try to read the section as if you were seeing $\ln x$ for the first time.

1. Let $L(x) = \int_1^x \frac{dt}{t}$. Then we have

$$L(xy) = L(x) + L(y) \text{ and } L(x^r) = rL(x)$$

in particular,

$$L(2^{-N}) = -NL(2) < 0$$

since

$$L(2) = \int_1^2 \frac{dt}{t} > 0$$

As $N \to +\infty$, $2^{-N} \to 0$ and $L(2^{-N}) \to -\infty$.

Thus, $\lim_{x \to 0^+} \ln x = -\infty$.

2. $\Delta x = \frac{3-1}{8} = \frac{1}{4} = 0.25$

$x_0 = 1.00$	$f(x_0) = 1.00$
$x_1 = 1.25$	$f(x_1) = 0.80$
$x_2 = 1.50$	$f(x_2) = 0.67$
$x_3 = 1.75$	$f(x_3) = 0.57$
$x_4 = 2.00$	$f(x_4) = 0.50$
$x_5 = 2.25$	$f(x_5) = 0.44$
$x_6 = 2.50$	$f(x_6) = 0.40$
$x_7 = 2.75$	$f(x_7) = 0.36$
$x_8 = 3.00$	$f(x_8) = 0.33$

Simpson's rule:

$$A \approx \tfrac{1}{3}[1(1.00)+4(0.80)+2(0.67)$$

$$+4(0.57)+2(0.50)$$

$$+4(0.44)+2(0.40)$$

$$+4(0.36)+1(0.33)](\tfrac{1}{4})$$

$$\approx \tfrac{1}{12}(13.15) \approx 1.0958$$

The calculator value is 1.098612289.

7. **a.** $f(xy) = f(x) + f(y)$ leads to

$f(1) = f(1) + f(1)$ when $x = y = 1$.

Thus, $f(1) = 2f(1)$ holds only when

$f(1) = 0$.

b. $f(1) = f(-1) + f(-1)$ when

$x = y = -1$. Thus, $0 = f(1) = 2f(-1)$

holds when $f(-1) = 0$

c. $f(-x) = f(-1) + f(x)$ so

$f(-x) = 0 + f(x)$ or $f(-x) = f(x)$

d. Hold x fixed in the equation

$$f(xy) = f(x) + f(y)$$

and differentiate with respect to y

by the chain rule.

$$xf'(xy) = 0 + f'(y)$$

In particular, when $y = 1$:

$$f'(x) = \frac{f'(1)}{x}$$

so

$$f(x) = \int_1^x \frac{f'(1)}{t}\, dt = f'(1)\int_1^x \frac{dt}{t}$$

e. From part **d**, it can be seen that f' is
continuous and hence integrable on any
closed interval $[a, b]$ not including the
origin. By the fundamental theorem of
calculus,

$$f(x) - f(c) = \int_c^x f'(t)\, dt = f'(1)\int_c^x \frac{dt}{t}$$

for $x > 0$ if $c > 0$ and $x < 0$ if $c < 0$. Since
$f(1) = 0$, we can use $c = 1$ to obtain

$$f(x) = f'(1)\int_1^x \frac{dt}{t} \quad \text{if } x > 0$$

If $x < 0$, then $-x > 0$ and since $f(x) = f(-x)$, we obtain

$$f(x) = f'(1)\int_1^{-x} \frac{dt}{t} \quad \text{if } x < 0$$

Combining these two formulas:

$$f(x) = f'(1)\int_1^{|x|} \frac{dt}{t} \quad \text{if } x \neq 0$$

Finally, if $f'(1) \neq 0$ (that is, f is not
identically zero), we can let

$$F(x) = \frac{f(x)}{f'(1)} = \int_1^{|x|} \frac{dt}{t}$$

It is easy to show that if

$$f(xy) = f(x) + g(x), \text{ then}$$

$$F(xy) = F(x) + F(y)$$

All solutions of $f(xy) = f(x) + f(y)$

can be obtained as multiples of $F(x)$

CHAPTER 5 REVIEW

Proficiency Examination, Pages 396-397

SURVIVAL HINT: *To help you review the concepts of this chapter,* **hand write** *the answers to each of these questions onto your own paper.*

1. An antiderivative of a function f is a function F that satisfies $F' = f$.

2. $\displaystyle\int u^n \, du = \begin{cases} \dfrac{u^{n+1}}{n+1} + C; & n \neq -1 \\ \ln|u| + C; & n = -1 \end{cases}$

3. $\displaystyle\int e^u \, du = e^u + C$

4. $\displaystyle\int \sin u \, du = -\cos u + C$

   $\displaystyle\int \cos u \, du = \sin u + C$

   $\displaystyle\int \sec^2 u \, du = \tan u + C$

   $\displaystyle\int \sec u \tan u \, du = \sec u + C$

   $\displaystyle\int \csc u \cot u \, du = -\csc u + C$

   $\displaystyle\int \csc^2 u \, du = -\cot u + C$

5. $\displaystyle\int \frac{du}{\sqrt{1 - u^2}} = \sin^{-1} u + C$

   $\displaystyle\int \frac{du}{1 + u^2} = \tan^{-1} u + C$

   $\displaystyle\int \frac{du}{|u|\sqrt{u^2 - 1}} = \sec^{-1} u + C$

6. The *area function*, $A(t)$, as the area of the region bounded by the curve $y = f(x)$, the x-axis, and the vertical lines $x = a$, $x = t$.

   If f is a continuous function such that $f(x) \geq 0$ for all x on the closed interval $[a, b]$ for its integral to represent area.

7. Suppose f is continuous and $f(x) \geq 0$ throughout the interval $[a, b]$. Then the *area* of the region under the curve $y = f(x)$ over this interval is given by

   $$A = \lim_{n \to +\infty} \sum_{k=1}^{n} f(a + k\Delta x)\Delta x$$

   where $\Delta x = \dfrac{b - a}{n}$.

8. $f(\overset{*}{x}_2)\Delta x_2 + \ldots + f(\overset{*}{x}_n)\Delta x_n = \displaystyle\sum_{k=1}^{n} f(\overset{*}{x}_k)\Delta x_k$

9. If f is defined on the closed interval $[a, b]$ we say f is integrable on $[a, b]$ if

   $$I = \lim_{\|P\| \to 0} \sum_{k=1}^{n} f(\overset{*}{x}_k)\Delta x_k$$

   exists. This limit is called the definite integral of f from a to b. The definite integral is denoted by

$$I = \int_a^b f(x)\,dx \quad \text{or} \quad I = \int_{x=a}^{x=b} f(x)\,dx$$

on $[a, b]$.

10. **a.** $\displaystyle\int_a^a f(x)\,dx = 0$

b. $\displaystyle\int_a^b f(x)\,dx = -\int_b^a f(x)\,dx$

11. The total distance traveled by an object with continuous velocity $v(t)$ along a straight line from time $t = a$ to $t = b$ is

$$S = \int_a^b \left| v(t) \right|\,dt$$

12. If f is continuous on the interval $[a, b]$ and F is any function that satisfies $F'(x) = f(x)$ throughout this interval, then

$$\int_a^b f(x)\,dx = F(b) - F(a)$$

13. Let $f(t)$ be continuous on the interval $[a, b]$ and define the function G by the integral equation

$$G(x) = \int_a^x f(t)\,dt$$

for $a \le x \le b$. Then G is an antiderivative of f on $[a, b]$; that is,

$$G'(x) = \frac{d}{dx}\left[\int_a^x f(t)\,dt \right] = f(x)$$

14. Define a new variable of integration, $u = g(x)$. Find dx as a function of du and transform the limits. Make sure that new integrand involves only the new variables.

15. A differential equation is an equation that contains derivatives.

16. A separable differential equation can be rewritten with one variable in the left side of the equation and the other variable in the right side. Each side of the equation is now integrated (if possible).

17. The growth/decay equation is

$$Q(t) = Q_0 e^{kt}$$

where $Q(t)$ is the amount of the substance present at time t, Q_0 is the initial amount of the substance, and k is a constant. The sign of k depends on the substance: growth if $k > 0$ and decay if $k < 0$. For carbon dating, $k = \ln 0.5/5{,}730$.

18. An orthogonal trajectory of a given family of curves is any curve that cuts all curves in the family at right angles.

19. If f is continuous on the interval $[a, b]$, there is at least one number c between a and b such that

$$\int_a^b f(x)\, dx = f(c)(b - a)$$

20. If f is continuous on the interval $[a, b]$, the average value of f on this interval is given by the integral

$$\frac{1}{b - a} \int_a^b f(x)\, dx$$

21. a. Divide the interval $[a, b]$ into n subintervals, each of width $\Delta x = \frac{b - a}{n}$, and let $\overset{*}{x}_k$ denote the right endpoint of the kth subinterval. The base of the kth rectangle is the kth subinterval, and its height is $f(\overset{*}{x}_k)$. Hence, the area of the kth rectangle is $f(\overset{*}{x}_k)\Delta x$. The sum of the areas of all n rectangles is an approximation for the area under the curve and hence an approximation for the corresponding definite integral. Thus,

$$\int_a^b f(x)\, dx \approx \sum_{k=1}^n f(\overset{*}{x}_k)\Delta x$$

b. Let f be continuous on $[a, b]$. The trapezoidal rule is

$$\int_a^b f(x)\, dx \approx \tfrac{1}{2}[f(x_0) + 2f(x_1)$$
$$+ 2f(x_2) + \cdots + 2f(x_{n-1}) + f(x_n)]\Delta x$$

where $\Delta x = \frac{b - a}{n}$ and, for the kth

subinterval, $x_k = a + k\Delta x$.

c. Let f be continuous on $[a, b]$. Simpson's rule is

$$\int_a^b f(x)\, dx \approx \tfrac{1}{3}[f(x_0) + 4f(x_1) + 2f(x_2)$$
$$+ \cdots + 4f(x_{n-1}) + f(x_n)]\Delta x$$

where $\Delta x = \frac{b - a}{n}$, $x_k = a + k\Delta x$, k an integer and n an even integer. Moreover, the larger the value for n, the better the approximation.

24. $\displaystyle\int \frac{dx}{1 + 4x^2} = \tfrac{1}{2}\int \frac{du}{1 + u^2} = \tfrac{1}{2}\tan^{-1}(2x) + C$

$u = 2x;\ du = 2\, dx$

27. $\displaystyle\int_0^1 (2x - 6)(x^2 - 6x + 2)^2\, dx$

Let $u = x^2 - 6x + 2;\ du = 2x - 6,$

If $x = 1$, then $u = -3$; if $x = 0$, $u = 2.$

$$= \int_2^{-3} u^2\, du = \left.\frac{u^3}{3}\right|_2^{-3} = -\frac{35}{3}$$

30. $\displaystyle A = \int_{-1}^3 (3x^2 + 2)\, dx = x^3 + 2x\Big|_{-1}^3$

$$= 27 + 6 + 1 + 2 = 36$$

33. The half life for ^{14}C is 5,730 so when using the decay formula

$$Q(t) = Q_0 e^{-kt}$$

To compute the percent of amount originally
present, we find

$$e^{-(\ln 2/5730)(3,500,000)}$$

This is approximately 1.33×10^{-184} which
exceeds the accuracy of most calculators and
measuring devices. Other dating methods
were used to date this artifact.

36.

$$\frac{dy}{y^2} = \sin 3x \, dx$$

$$\int y^{-2} \, dy = \frac{1}{3} \int \sin 3x \, (3 \, dx)$$

$$-\frac{1}{y} = -\frac{1}{3} \cos 3x + C_1$$

$$y = \frac{3}{\cos 3x + C}$$

CHAPTER 6

Additional Applications of the Integral

SURVIVAL HINT: In this chapter we move, for the first time, from two dimensions to three dimensions. We refer to two dimensions as $\mathbb{R}^2$ and three dimensions as $\mathbb{R}^3$. Throughout the book we provide several drawing lessons because visualization in $\mathbb{R}^3$ requires nurturing and practice. Today, many software packages and calculators are available to help this visualization. What we draw on our papers is often a two-dimensional cross-section or some boundary conditions. Spend some time with the drawing lessons, the first of which is found on page 418 of the textbook.

6.1 Area Between Two Curves, Pages 413–415

SURVIVAL HINT: *When finding area between curves, you should be neat, organized, and follow these steps:*

- *Draw a careful sketch, finding the coordinates of the points of intersection.*
- *Decide whether horizontal or vertical strips will be most efficient. Draw the strip.*
- *Be careful about which is the leading curve, and express it properly; y as a function of x, or x as a function of y.*
- *Sum the strips between the appropriate values; x values for vertical strips, and y values for horizontal strips.*

3.
$$y^2 - 5y = 0$$
$$y(y - 5) = 0$$
$$y = 0, 5$$

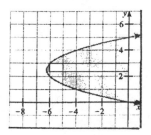

$$\int_0^5 [0 - (y^2 - 5y)] \, dy = \int_0^5 (5y - y^2)dy$$
$$= \left[\frac{5y^2}{2} - \frac{y^3}{3} \right] \Bigg|_0^5$$
$$= \frac{125}{6}$$

4.
$$x^2 - 8x = 0$$
$$x(x - 8) = 0$$
$$x = 0, 8$$

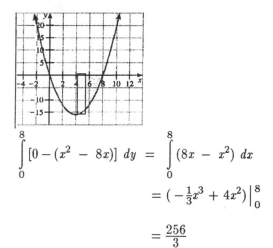

$$\int_0^8 [0 - (x^2 - 8x)] \, dy = \int_0^8 (8x - x^2) \, dx$$
$$= \left(-\tfrac{1}{3}x^3 + 4x^2 \right) \Big|_0^8$$
$$= \frac{256}{3}$$

6.

$$(x - 1)^3 = x - 1$$
$$(x - 1)^3 - (x - 1) = 0$$
$$(x - 1)[(x - 1)^2 - 1] = 0$$
$$(x - 1)(x - 1 - 1)(x - 1 + 1) = 0$$
$$x = 0, 1, 2$$

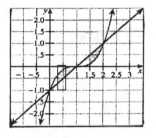

$$\int_0^1 [(x - 1)^3 - (x - 1)]\,dx + \int_1^2 [(x - 1) - (x - 1)^3]\,dx$$

$$[\tfrac{1}{4}(x - 1)^4 - \tfrac{1}{2}(x - 1)^2]\Big|_0^1 + [\tfrac{1}{2}(x - 1)^2 - \tfrac{1}{4}(x - 1)^4]\Big|_1^2 = \tfrac{1}{2}$$

10.

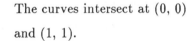

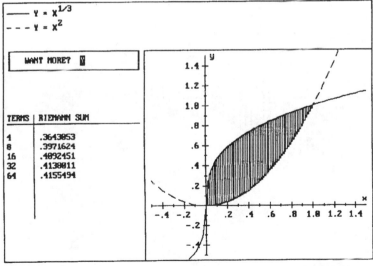

TERMS	RIEMANN SUM
4	.3643853
8	.3971624
16	.4092451
32	.4138011
64	.4155494

The curves intersect at $(0, 0)$ and $(1, 1)$.

$$A = \int_0^1 (x^{1/3} - x^2)\,dx$$

$$= (\tfrac{3}{4}x^{4/3} - \tfrac{1}{3}x^3)\Big|_0^1$$

$$= \frac{5}{12}$$

12.

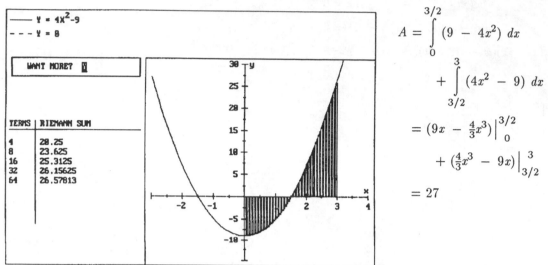

The curves intersect at $\left(\frac{3}{2}, 0\right)$.

$$A = \int_0^{3/2} (9 - 4x^2)\, dx$$

$$+ \int_{3/2}^3 (4x^2 - 9)\, dx$$

$$= \left(9x - \tfrac{4}{3}x^3\right)\Big|_0^{3/2}$$

$$+ \left(\tfrac{4}{3}x^3 - 9x\right)\Big|_{3/2}^3$$

$$= 27$$

15.

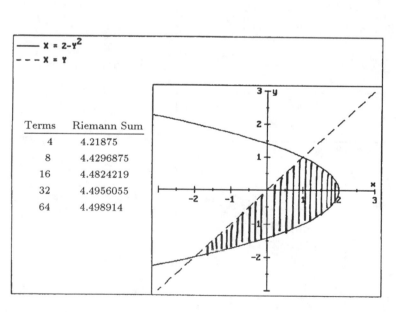

The curves intersect at $(1, 1)$ and $(-2, -2)$.

$$A = \int_{-2}^1 (2 - y^2 - y)\, dy$$

$$= \left(2y - \tfrac{1}{3}y^3 - \tfrac{1}{2}y^2\right)\Big|_{-2}^1$$

$$= \frac{9}{2}$$

18.

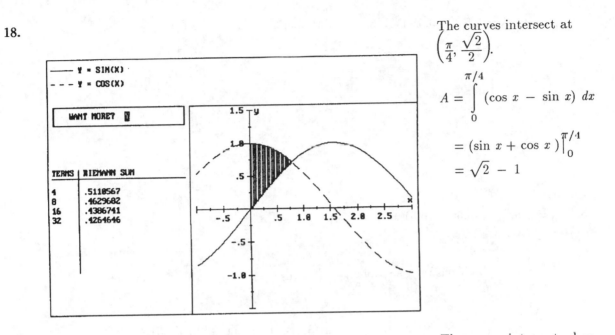

The curves intersect at $\left(\dfrac{\pi}{4}, \dfrac{\sqrt{2}}{2}\right)$.

$$A = \int_0^{\pi/4} (\cos x - \sin x)\, dx$$

$$= (\sin x + \cos x)\Big|_0^{\pi/4}$$

$$= \sqrt{2} - 1$$

19.

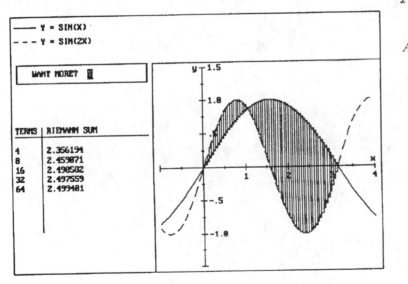

The curves intersect when $x = 0$, $\pi/3$, and π.

$$A = \int_0^{\pi/3} (\sin 2x - \sin x)\, dx$$

$$+ \int_{\pi/3}^{\pi} (\sin x - \sin 2x)\, dx$$

$$= \left(-\tfrac{1}{2}\cos 2x + \cos x\right)\Big|_0^{\pi/3}$$

$$+ \left(-\cos x + \tfrac{1}{2}\cos 2x\right)\Big|_{\pi/3}^{\pi}$$

$$= \frac{5}{2}$$

26. **a.** $q_0 = 1$, $p_0 = 3.5 - (0.5)(1) = 3$;   Consumer's surplus $= \displaystyle\int_0^{q_0} D(q)\, dq - p_0 q_0$

$$= \int_0^1 (3.5 - 0.5q)\, dq - 3$$

$$= \left(3.5q - \tfrac{1}{4}q^2\right)\Big|_0^1 - 3$$

$$= 3.25 - 3$$

$$= 0.25$$

b. $q_0 = 1.5$, $p_0 = 3.5 - (0.5)(1.5) = 2.75$;

$$\text{Consumer's surplus} = \int_0^{q_0} D(q)\, dq - p_0 q_0$$

$$= \int_0^{1.5} (3.5 - 0.5q)\, dq - 2.75(1.5)$$

$$= \left(3.5q - \tfrac{1}{4}q^2\right)\Big|_0^{1.5} - 4.125$$

$$= 0.5625$$

32. Equilibrium occurs when $D(q) = S(q)$.

$$14 - q^2 = 2q^2 + 2$$

$$3q^2 = 12$$

$$q = 2 \quad (-2 \text{ is meaningless here.})$$

$p = D(2) = 10$

Consumer surplus is:

$$\int_0^2 (14 - q^2)\, dq - 2(10) = \left[14q - \frac{q^3}{3}\right]\Big|_0^2 - 20$$

$$\approx \$5.33$$

37.

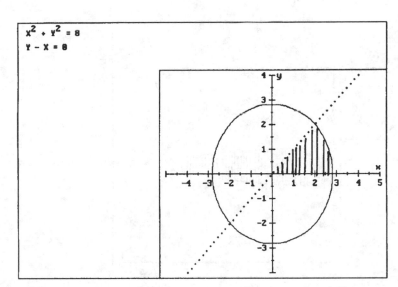

This is one-eighth of a circle with radius $\sqrt{8}$. $A = \frac{1}{8}\pi(\sqrt{8})^2 = \pi$

39. **a.** The use of the machine will be profitable as long as $P(x) > 0$; that is, $R(x) \geq C(x)$. This means that the machine is profitable until $R(x) = C(x)$.

$$6{,}025 - 10x^2 = 4{,}000 + 15x^2$$

$$25x^2 = 2{,}025$$

$$x^2 = 81$$

$$x = \pm 9$$

The machine will be profitable for 9 years.

b. The difference $R(x) - C(x)$ represents the net earnings (profit) of the machine at time x. Using integration to "add up" the net earnings over the period of profitability ($0 \leq x \leq 9$), we obtain

$$\int_0^9 [R(x) - C(x)]\, dx = \int_0^9 [(6{,}025 - 10x^2) - (4{,}000 + 15x^2)]\, dx$$

$$= \int_0^9 (2{,}025 - 25x^2)\, dx = (2{,}025x - \tfrac{25}{3}x^3)\Big|_0^9 = 12{,}150$$

In geometric terms, the net earnings is represented by the area of the region between the curves $y = R(x)$ and $y = C(x)$ from $x = 0$ to $x = 9$.

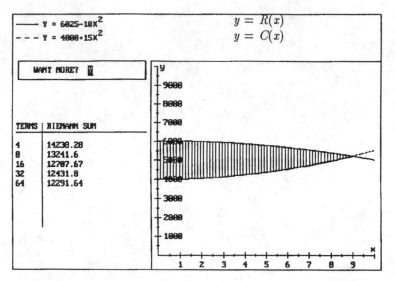

42. **a.** $P(x) = xp(x) - C(x) = (110 - x)x - (x^3 - 25x^2 + 2x + 30) = -x^3 + 24x^2 + 108x - 30$

$P'(x) = -3x^2 + 48x + 108 = -3(x - 18)(x + 2)$

$P'(x) = 0$ when $x = 18$ (disregard negative root);

$P''(x) = -6x + 48 < 0$ when $x = 18$, so $x = 18$ is a maximum.

b. Consumer's surplus $= \int\limits_{0}^{18} (110 - x)\,dx - 18(92) = (110x - \tfrac{1}{2}x^2)\Big|_0^{18} - 1{,}656 = 162$

6.2 Volume by Disks and Washers, Pages 423–425

SURVIVAL HINT: *In order to use the method of slices, each must use the same formula for its area. Write the **general** formula for the cross-sectional area, and then substitute the appropriate functional values. Finally, sum over the given values.*

3.

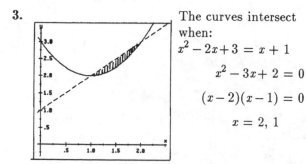

The curves intersect when:

$x^2 - 2x + 3 = x + 1$

$x^2 - 3x + 2 = 0$

$(x - 2)(x - 1) = 0$

$x = 2, 1$

$V = \int\limits_{1}^{2} [(x + 1) - (x^2 - 2x + 3)]^2\,dx$

$= \int\limits_{1}^{2} (x^4 - 6x^3 + 13x^2 - 12x + 4)\,dx$

$= (\tfrac{1}{5}x^5 - \tfrac{3}{2}x^4 + \tfrac{13}{3}x^3 - 6x^2 + 4x)\Big|_1^2$

$= \tfrac{1}{30}$

In Problems 7-12, we note that an equilateral triangle of side a has area $\frac{1}{4}\sqrt{3}\,a^2$.

9.

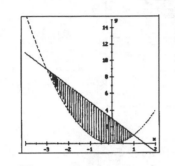

The curves intersect when

$$x^2 = -2x + 3$$

$$x^2 + 2x - 3 = 0$$

$$(x + 3)(x - 1) = 0$$

$$x = -3,\ 1$$

$$V = \frac{\sqrt{3}}{4}\int_{-3}^{1}(x^2 + 2x - 3)^2\,dx$$

$$= \frac{\sqrt{3}}{4}\int_{-3}^{1}(x^4 + 4x^2 + 9 + 4x^3 - 6x^2 - 12x)\,dx$$

$$= \frac{\sqrt{3}}{4}\int_{-3}^{1}(x^4 + 4x^3 - 2x^2 - 12x + 9)\,dx$$

$$= \frac{\sqrt{3}}{4}\left(\tfrac{1}{5}x^5 + x^4 - \tfrac{2}{3}x^3 - 6x^2 + 9x\right)\Big|_{-3}^{1}$$

$$= \frac{128\sqrt{3}}{15}$$

14. The curves intersect where

$$y = \tfrac{1}{3}x = \tfrac{1}{3}y^2$$

$$y^2 - 3y = 0$$

$$y = 0,\ 3$$

a. By washers: $V = \pi\displaystyle\int_{0}^{9}\left[(\sqrt{x})^2 - \left(\tfrac{x}{3}\right)^2\right]dx$

b. By washers: $V = \pi\displaystyle\int_{0}^{3}\left[(3y)^2 - (y^2)^2\right]dy$

21. The cross section is a square of side $2y$ and area $4y^2$.

$$V = \int_{-3}^{3}4(9 - x^2)\,dx$$

$$= 8\int_{0}^{3}(9 - x^2)\,dx$$

$$= 8\left(9x - \frac{x^3}{3}\right)\Big|_{0}^{3} = 144 \text{ cubic units}$$

27. The curves intersect at $(-1, 0)$ and $(2, 3)$. The cross section is a rectangle of side $x + 1 - (x^2 - 1)$ and area $(-x^2 + x + 2)$.

$$V = \int_{-1}^{2}(-x^2 + x + 2)\,dx$$

$$= \left(-\tfrac{1}{3}x^3 + \tfrac{1}{2}x^2 + 2x\right)\Big|_{-1}^{2}$$

$$= \tfrac{9}{2} \text{ cubic units}$$

32.

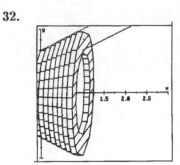

Use washers;

$$V = \pi \int_0^1 [(x+2)^2 - (x+1)^2] \, dx$$

$$= \pi(x^2 + 3x)\Big|_0^1$$

$$= 4\pi \text{ cubic units}$$

33.

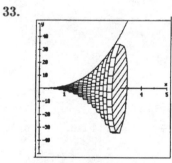

Use disks;

$$V = \pi \int_0^\pi (x^2 + x^3)^2 \, dx$$

$$= \pi \int_0^\pi (x^4 + 2x^5 + x^6) \, dx$$

$$= \frac{\pi^8}{7} + \frac{\pi^7}{3} + \frac{\pi^6}{5}$$

$$\approx 2{,}555 \text{ cubic units}$$

40.

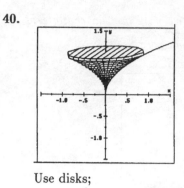

Use disks;

$$V = \pi \int_0^1 (y^2)^2 \, dy = \frac{\pi}{5} y^5 \Big|_0^1$$

$$= \frac{\pi}{5} \text{ cubic units}$$

41.

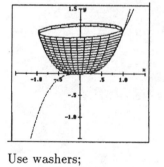

Use washers;

$$V = \pi \int_0^1 \left[\left(y^{1/3}\right)^2 - \left(y^{1/2}\right)^2 \right] dy$$

$$= \frac{\pi}{10} \text{ cubic units}$$

47.

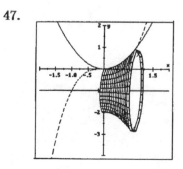

The curves intersect at $(0, 0)$ and $(1, 1)$. Use washers;

$$V = \pi \int_0^1 [(x^2 + 1)^2 - (x^3 + 1)^2] \, dx$$

$$= \pi \int_0^1 (-x^6 + x^4 - 2x^3 + 2x^2) \, dx$$

$$= \frac{47\pi}{210} \text{ cubic units}$$

53. The base of the right triangle has its legs on the coordinate axes with a vertex at the origin. The equation of the line passing through the hypotenuse is $y = -x + 4$. The diameter of a typical semicircular cross section of the solid is y, and the area is $\frac{1}{2}\pi(\frac{1}{2}y)^2 = \frac{1}{8}\pi y^2$.

$$V = \frac{\pi}{8} \int_0^4 (4 - x)^2 \, dx = -\frac{1}{24}\pi(4 - x)^3 \Big|_0^4$$

$$= \frac{8\pi}{3}$$

59. $V \approx \frac{1}{3}[1(1.12)+4(1.09)+2(1.05)+4(1.03)$

$$+2(0.99)+4(1.01)+2(0.98)+4(0.99)$$

$$+2(0.96)+4(0.93)+1(0.91)](2.0)$$

$$= \frac{2}{3}(30.19) \approx 20.13$$

The volume is approximately 20.13 m^3.

61. Let B be the top vertex of a rectangular tetrahedron of side a. The y-axis is vertical and contains B. The x-axis passes through a vertex A in the base. $|\overline{AB}| = a$. The origin

O is the projection of B onto the base. Draw the perpendicular $\overline{OC}$ from O to a side containing A in the base. $|\overline{AC}| = \frac{\sqrt{2}}{2} a$. The height of the tetrahedron is H. By the Pythagorean theorem,

$$H^2 + \frac{1}{3}a^2 = a^2 \text{ or } H = \sqrt{\frac{2}{3}} \, a$$

Let (x, y) be a point on $\overline{AB}$. Then, by similar triangles,

$$\frac{\sqrt{\frac{2}{3}}a - y}{\sqrt{\frac{2}{3}} \, a} = \frac{x}{\frac{1}{\sqrt{3}} a}$$

$$x = \frac{1}{\sqrt{2}}\left(\frac{\sqrt{2}}{\sqrt{3}} a - y\right)$$

Consider a horizontal element of area with cross section an equilateral triangle at altitude y. In this triangle, x corresponds to $\overline{OA} = (1/\sqrt{3})a$ in the base, so the side of the elemental equilateral triangle is $\sqrt{3}x$. The element of volume is

$$dV = \frac{1}{4}\sqrt{3}(\sqrt{3}x)^2 \, dy = \frac{3\sqrt{3}}{4}x^2 \, dy$$

$$= \frac{3\sqrt{3}}{4}(\frac{1}{2})\left(\frac{\sqrt{2}}{\sqrt{3}} a - y\right)^2 dy$$

Thus,

$$V = \frac{3\sqrt{3}}{8} \int_0^{\sqrt{2/3}\,a} \left(\frac{\sqrt{2}}{\sqrt{3}} a - y\right)^2 dy$$

$$= -\frac{3\sqrt{3}}{8}(\tfrac{1}{3})\left(\frac{\sqrt{2}}{\sqrt{3}}a - y\right)^3\Bigg|_{\;0}^{\;\sqrt{2/3}\,a}$$

$$= \frac{\sqrt{2}}{12}\,a^3 \text{ cubic units}$$

6.3 Volume by Shells, Pages 431–433

SURVIVAL HINT: *Success in finding volumes by slices is highly dependent upon good visualization in $\mathbb{R}^3$ (called spatial perception). Practice drawing a good sketch for each problem. Draw the slice in $\mathbb{R}^2$ and write the appropriate **general formula**: πr^2 for disks, $\pi(R^2 - r^2)$ for washers, and $2\pi rh$ for shells. **Then** substitute the functional values for r, R, and h, and sum over the correct limits.*

The given volumes are all in cubic units.

3.   **a.** shell: $2\pi \displaystyle\int_0^2 y\sqrt{4 - y^2}\, dy$

    b. disk: $\pi \displaystyle\int_0^2 (4 - y^2)\, dy$

    c. shell: $2\pi \displaystyle\int_0^2 (y + 1)\sqrt{4 - y^2}\, dy$

    d. washer: $\pi \displaystyle\int_0^2 [(x + 2)^2 - 2^2]\, dy$

$$= \pi \int_0^2 [4 - y^2 + 4\sqrt{4 - y^2}]\, dy$$

11.

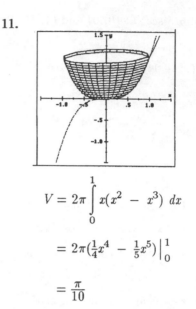

$$V = 2\pi \int_0^1 x(x^2 - x^3)\, dx$$

$$= 2\pi(\tfrac{1}{4}x^4 - \tfrac{1}{5}x^5)\Big|_0^1$$

$$= \frac{\pi}{10}$$

16.

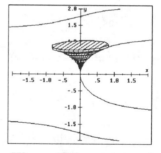

We use disks:

$$V = \pi \int_0^{\sqrt{\pi}/2} (\tan y^2)^2\, dy$$

$$\approx 0.447148$$

(Use numerical integration.)

19. $V = 2\pi \int_{1/4}^{1/2} x\left[\dfrac{1}{x\sqrt{1-x^2}}\right] dx$

$= 2\pi \sin^{-1}x \Big|_{1/4}^{1/2}$

≈ 1.7022

24. $V = 2\pi \int_{1/2}^{1} \dfrac{\sqrt{x^{-2}-1}}{x^3} dx$

$\text{Let } u = \frac{1}{x}, \text{ so } du = \dfrac{-1}{x^2} dx$

$= 2\pi \int_{2}^{1} -u\sqrt{u^2-1}\, du$

$= -\frac{2}{3}\pi(u^2-1)^{3/2}\Big|_{2}^{1}$

$= 2\sqrt{3}\,\pi \approx 10.8828$

29. To find the limits of integration, set $y = 2$:

$2(x-3)^2 = 6$, so $x = 3 \pm \sqrt{3}$. Then,

$y = 2 \pm \sqrt{2 - \frac{2}{3}(x-3)^2}$

and the height of the vertical strip at x is

$h = (2 + \sqrt{2 - \frac{2}{3}(x-3)^2})$

$\qquad - (2 - \sqrt{2 - \frac{2}{3}(x-3)^2})$

$= 2\sqrt{2 - \frac{2}{3}(x-3)^2}$

Thus, using the shell method

$V = 2\pi \int_{3-\sqrt{3}}^{3+\sqrt{3}} x\left[2\sqrt{2}\sqrt{1 - \frac{1}{3}(x-3)^2}\right] dx$

$= 6\sqrt{6}\,\pi^2$

≈ 146.0530

33. Let $A(1, 1)$, $B(2, 5)$, and $C(4, 1)$;

$m_{AB} = 4$ so $\overline{AB}$ is $y - 1 = 4(x - 1)$

$m_{BC} = -2$, so $\overline{BC}$ is $y - 1 = -2(x - 4)$

The element of area is parallel to the x-axis.

Use shells;

$V = 2\pi \int_{1}^{5} [\frac{1}{2}(9 - y) - \frac{1}{4}(y + 3)]y\, dy$

$= \frac{3}{2}\pi \int_{1}^{5} (5y - y^2)\, dy$

$= \frac{3}{2}\pi(\frac{5}{2}y^2 - \frac{1}{3}y^3)\Big|_{1}^{5}$

$= 28\pi$

≈ 87.9646

35. a. Use disks; $\quad V = \pi \int_{1}^{4} (x^{-1/2})^2\, dx$

$= \pi \ln|x|\Big|_{1}^{4}$

$= \pi \ln 4$

b. Use shells; $\quad V = 2\pi \int_{0}^{4} x^{1/2}\, dx$

$= 2\pi(\frac{2}{3})x^{3/2}\Big|_{1}^{4}$

$= \dfrac{28\pi}{3}$

c. Use washers;

$$dV = \pi[(y+2)^2 - 2^2]\,dx$$

$$= \pi[(x^{-1/2} + 2)^2 - 4]\,dx$$

$$V = \pi \int_1^4 [x^{-1} + 4x^{-1/2} + 4 - 4]\,dx$$

$$= \pi(\ln|x| + 8\sqrt{x})\Big|_1^4$$

$$= \pi(8 + \ln 4)$$

39. Use washers with strips perpendicular to the y-axis rotated about the y-axis. The element of volume is

$$dV = \pi[(b + \sqrt{a^2 - y^2})^2$$

$$- (b - \sqrt{a^2 - y^2})^2]\,dy$$

$$V = 2\pi \int_0^a [(b^2 + 2b\sqrt{a^2 - y^2} + a^2 - y^2)$$

$$- (b^2 - 2b\sqrt{a^2 - y^2} + a^2 - y^2)]\,dy$$

$$= 8b\pi \int_0^a \sqrt{a^2 - y^2}\,dy = 8\pi b(\tfrac{1}{4})A$$

$$= 2\pi^2 a^2 b \qquad (A = \pi a^2; \text{ area of circle})$$

43. Let volume V_1 be the base of the gem and V_2 the top of the gem.

$$V_1 = \pi \int_0^{h_1} x^2\,dy$$

$$= \pi \int_0^{h_1} \left[\frac{\sqrt{R^2 - h_1^2}\,y}{h_1}\right]^2 dy$$

$$= \pi\left(\frac{R^2 - h_1^2}{h_1^2}\right)\left[\frac{y^3}{3}\right]\Big|_0^{h_1}$$

$$= \frac{\pi}{3}\left(\frac{R^2 - h_1^2}{h_1^2}\right)h_1^3$$

$$= \frac{\pi}{3}(R^2 - h_1^2)h_1$$

Note: this integration is not really necessary because V_1 is just the volume of a cone of radius $\sqrt{R^2 - h_1^2}$ and height h_1.

$$V_2 = \pi \int_{h_1}^{h_2} x^2\,dy$$

$$= \pi \int_{h_1}^{h_2} (R^2 - y^2)\,dy$$

$$= \pi\left[R^2 y - \frac{y^3}{3}\right]\Big|_{h_1}^{h_2}$$

$$= \pi[(R^2 h_2 - \tfrac{1}{3}h_2^3) - (R^2 h_1 - \tfrac{1}{3}h_1^3)]$$

Total volume

$$V = V_1 + V_2$$

$$= \pi[R^2 h_2 - \tfrac{1}{3}(2R^2 h_1 + h_2^3)]$$

6.4 Arc Length and Surface Area, Pages 439–441

SURVIVAL HINT: *Formulas do not need to be "memorized" if you understand the concept. The length of the arc is the sum (integral) of a collection of oblique line segments — each of which can be considered as the hypotenuse of a right triangle with* base 1 and height equal to the slope of the line, namely $f'(x)$. *This hypotenuse has length found by the Pythagorean theorem, namely* $\sqrt{1 + [f'(x)]^2}$.

3. $\sqrt{1 + [f'(x)]^2}\; dx = \sqrt{1 + (-2)^2}$

$$= \sqrt{5}$$

$$s = \int_{1}^{3} \sqrt{5}\; dx$$

$$= 2\sqrt{5}$$

9. $\sqrt{1 + [f'(x)]^2} = \sqrt{1 + (x^3 - \frac{1}{4}x^{-3})^2}$

$$= \sqrt{1 + x^6 - \frac{1}{2} + \frac{1}{16}x^{-6}}$$

$$= \sqrt{(x^3 + \frac{1}{4}x^{-3})^2}$$

$$s = \int_{1}^{2} (x^3 + \frac{1}{4}x^{-3})\; dx$$

$$= (\frac{1}{4}x^4 - \frac{1}{8}x^{-2})\Big|_{1}^{2}$$

$$= \frac{123}{32}$$

13.

Y = SIN(X)

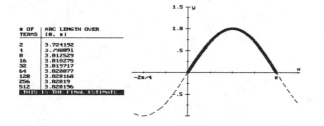

# OF TERMS	ARC LENGTH OVER [0, π]
2	3.724192
4	3.798091
8	3.812529
16	3.818275
32	3.819717
64	3.820077
128	3.820168
256	3.82019
512	3.820196
THIS IS THE FINAL ESTIMATE

It appears the arc length is approximately 3.82.

16. $f'(x) = y^{2/3} - \frac{1}{4}y^{-2/3}$;

$$ds = \sqrt{1 + (y^{2/3} - \frac{1}{4}y^{-2/3})^2}\; dy$$

$$= \sqrt{1 + (y^{2/3})^2 - \frac{1}{2} + (\frac{1}{4}y^{-2/3})^2}\; dy$$

$$= \sqrt{(y^{2/3} + \frac{1}{4}y^{-2/3})^2}\; dy$$

$$= y^{2/3} + \frac{1}{4}y^{-2/3}\; dy$$

a. About the y-axis, distance is $-x$;

$$S = 2\pi \int_{0}^{1} (-1)\left(\frac{3}{5}y^{5/3} - \frac{3}{4}y^{1/3}\right)\left(y^{2/3} + \frac{1}{4}y^{-2/3}\right) dy$$

$$= -2\pi \int_{0}^{1} (\frac{3}{5}y^{7/3} - \frac{3}{5}y - \frac{3}{16}y^{-1/3}) dy$$

$$= -2\pi(\frac{9}{50}y^{10/3} - \frac{3}{10}y^2 - \frac{9}{32}y^{2/3})\Big|_{0}^{1}$$

$$= -2\pi(-\frac{321}{800}) = \frac{321\pi}{400}$$

$$\approx 2.5211$$

b. About the x-axis, distance is y;

$$S = 2\pi \int_0^1 y(y^{2/3} + \tfrac{1}{4}y^{-2/3})\, dy$$

$$= 2\pi \int_0^1 (y^{5/3} + \tfrac{1}{4}y^{1/3})\, dy$$

$$= 2\pi(\tfrac{3}{8}y^{8/3} + \tfrac{3}{16}y^{4/3})\Big|_0^1$$

$$= \frac{9\pi}{8}$$

$$\approx 3.5343$$

c. About the line $y = -1$, distance is $y + 1$;

$$S = 2\pi \int_0^1 (y+1)(y^{2/3} + \tfrac{1}{4}y^{-2/3})\, dy$$

$$= 2\pi \int_0^1 [y^{5/3} + y^{2/3} + \tfrac{1}{4}y^{1/3} + \tfrac{1}{4}y^{-2/3}]\, dy$$

$$= 2\pi(\tfrac{3}{8}y^{8/3} + \tfrac{3}{5}y^{5/3} + \tfrac{1}{4}\cdot\tfrac{3}{4}y^{4/3} + \tfrac{1}{4}\cdot\tfrac{3}{1}y^{1/3})\Big|_0^1$$

$$= \frac{153\pi}{40}$$

$$\approx 12.0166$$

18. $S = 2\pi \displaystyle\int_2^6 (\sqrt{x})(1 + \tfrac{1}{4}x^{-1})^{1/2}\, dx$

$$= 2\pi \int_2^6 (x + \tfrac{1}{4})^{1/2}\, dx$$

$$= \tfrac{4}{3}\pi(x + \tfrac{1}{4})^{3/2}\Big|_2^6$$

$$= \frac{49\pi}{3}$$

23. $dy = (\tfrac{1}{2}x^{-1/2} - \tfrac{1}{2}x^{1/2})\, dx$

$$ds = \sqrt{1 + (\tfrac{1}{2}x^{-1/2} - \tfrac{1}{2}x^{1/2})^2}\, dx$$

$$= (\tfrac{1}{2}x^{-1/2} + \tfrac{1}{2}x^{1/2})\, dx$$

$$S = 2\pi \int_1^3 x(\tfrac{1}{2}x^{-1/2} + \tfrac{1}{2}x^{1/2})\, dx$$

$$= \pi \int_1^3 (x^{1/2} + x^{3/2})\, dx$$

$$= \pi(\tfrac{2}{3}x^{3/2} + \tfrac{2}{5}x^{5/2})\Big|_1^3$$

$$= \pi\left(\frac{28\sqrt{3}}{5} - \frac{16}{15}\right)$$

$$\approx 27.12$$

25. $f(x) = (1 - x^{2/3})^{3/2}$;

$$f'(x) = \tfrac{3}{2}(1 - x^{2/3})^{1/2}(-\tfrac{2}{3}x^{-1/3})$$

$$= -x^{-1/3}(1 - x^{2/3})^{1/2}$$

$$ds = \sqrt{1 + x^{-2/3}(1 - x^{2/3})}\, dx$$

$$= x^{-1/3}\, dx$$

$$s = 4\int_0^1 x^{-1/3}\, dx$$

$$= 6x^{2/3}\Big|_0^1$$

$$= 6$$

28. $L = \displaystyle\int_0^3 \sqrt{1 + (y')^2}\, dx$

x_k	$f'(x_k)$	$\sqrt{1 + [f'(x)]^2}$
0.0	3.7	3.8328
0.3	3.9	4.0262
0.6	4.1	4.2202
0.9	4.1	4.2202
1.2	4.2	4.3174
1.5	4.4	4.5122
1.8	4.6	4.7074
2.1	4.9	5.0010
2.4	5.2	5.2953
2.7	5.5	5.5902
3.0	6.0	6.0828

$$L \approx \tfrac{1}{2}[3.8328 + 2(4.0262) + \cdots + 2(5.5902)$$
$$+ 6.0828](0.3)$$
$$\approx 14.0543$$

30. Double the area obtained by rotating the quarter circle defined by the equation $x^2 + y^2 = r^2$ with $x \geq 0$, $y \geq 0$ rotated about the y-axis. Thus,

$$y = \sqrt{r^2 - x^2} \text{ so } y' = -x(r^2 - x^2)^{-1/2}$$

$$S = 2 \cdot 2\pi \int_0^r x\sqrt{1 + [f'(x)]^2}\, dx$$

$$= 2 \cdot 2\pi \int_0^r x\sqrt{1 + [-x(r^2 - x^2)^{-1/2}]^2}\, dx$$

$$= 4\pi \int_0^r x\sqrt{1 + x^2(r^2 - x^2)^{-1}}\, dx$$

$$= -4\pi r\sqrt{r^2 - x^2}\,\Big|_0^r = 4\pi r^2$$

37. $y = Cx^{2n} + Dx^{2(1-n)}$

$$y' = 2nCx^{2n-1} + 2(1-n)Dx^{1-2n}$$

$$1 + (y')^2 = 1 + [2nCx^{2n-1} + 2(1-n)Dx^{1-2n}]^2$$

$$= 1 + 4n^2C^2x^{2(2n-1)} - 8n(n-1)CD$$

$$+ 4(1-n)^2D^2x^{2(1-2n)}$$

$$= 4n^2C^2x^{2(2n-1)} + \tfrac{1}{2}$$

$$+ 4(1-n)^2D^2x^{2(1-2n)}$$

$$Since\ 8n(n-1)CD = \tfrac{1}{2}$$

$$= [2nCx^{2n-1} + 2(n-1)Dx^{1-2n}]^2$$

Thus, the arc length is

$$L = \int_a^b [2nCx^{2n-1} + 2(n-1)Dx^{1-2n}]\, dx$$

$$= [Cx^{2n} - Dx^{2(1-n)}]\,\Big|_a^b$$

$$= C[b^{2n} - a^{2n}] - D[b^{2(1-n)} - a^{2(1-n)}]$$

6.5 Physical Applications: Work, Liquid Force, and Centroids, Pages 451–454

5. $W = (850)(15) = 12{,}750 \text{ ft} \cdot \text{lb}$

7. $F(x) = kx;\ F(\tfrac{3}{4}) = 5,$ so $k = \tfrac{20}{3}$

$$W = \tfrac{20}{3} \int_0^1 x\, dx$$

$$= \tfrac{20}{3} \cdot \tfrac{1}{2}\, x^2\,\Big|_0^1$$

$$= \frac{10}{3} \text{ ft} \cdot \text{lb}$$

11. The cable weighs 20/50 lb/ft. Let x be the length of cable hanging over the cliff. It is raised a distance x. $dF = \frac{2}{5}x \, dx$

$$W = \frac{2}{5} \int_0^{50} x \, dx$$

$$= \frac{1}{5}x^2 \Big|_0^{50}$$

$$= 500$$

The work done by the ball is

$$W = (30)(50)$$

$$= 1,500$$

Thus, the total work is

$$500 + 1,500 = 2,000 \text{ ft} \cdot \text{lb}$$

17.

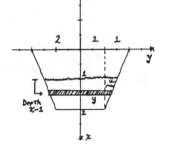

$$\Delta F = 51.2(x - 1)(2y)\Delta x$$

where $y = 1 + u$ and $\dfrac{u}{1} = \dfrac{2 - x}{2}$

$$F = 51.2 \int_1^2 2(x - 1)\left[1 + \left(\frac{2 - x}{2}\right)\right] dx$$

$$= 51.2\left[\frac{5x^2}{2} - 4x - \frac{x^3}{3}\right]\Big|_1^2$$

$$\approx 59.7$$

The force is 59.7 lb.

19.

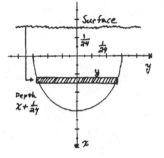

$$\Delta F = 64.5(x + \tfrac{1}{24})(2y)\Delta x \text{ where}$$

where $y = \sqrt{\left(\frac{1}{24}\right)^2 - x^2} \, dx$

$$F = 64.5 \int_0^{1/24} 2\left(x + \frac{1}{24}\right)\sqrt{\left(\frac{1}{24}\right)^2 - x^2} \, dx$$

SURVIVAL HINT: *To find $\overline{x}$ you use the moment about the y-axis, and to find $\overline{y}$ you use M_x. You will not confuse the formulas if you remember that the moment about the y-axis can be found by placing all the mass at $\overline{x}$: $M_y = m\overline{x}$, and the moment about the x-axis is found by replacing all the mass at $\overline{y}$: $M_x = m\overline{y}$.*

26. The curves intersect where

$$x^{-1} = \tfrac{1}{2}(5 - 2x)$$

$$2 = 5x - 2x^2$$

$$2x^2 - 5x + 2 = 0$$

$$(2x - 1)(x - 2) = 0$$

$$x = \tfrac{1}{2}, 2$$

$$m = \int_{1/2}^{2} (\tfrac{5}{2} - x - x^{-1})\,dx$$

$$= (\tfrac{5}{2}x - \tfrac{1}{2}x^2 - \ln|x|)\Big|_{1/2}^{2}$$

$$= \tfrac{15}{8} - 2\ln 2$$

$$\approx 0.4887$$

$$M_y = \int_{1/2}^{2} x(\tfrac{5}{2} - x - x^{-1})\,dx$$

$$= (\tfrac{5}{4}x^2 - \tfrac{1}{3}x^3 - x)\Big|_{1/2}^{2}$$

$$= \tfrac{9}{16}$$

$$= 0.5625$$

$$M_x = \int_{1/2}^{2} \tfrac{1}{2}[\tfrac{1}{4}(5 - 2x)^2 - x^{-2}]\,dx$$

$$= \tfrac{1}{2}[-\tfrac{1}{24}(5 - 2x)^3 + x^{-1}]\Big|_{1/2}^{2}$$

$$= \tfrac{9}{16}$$

$$(\overline{x}, \overline{y}) \approx \left(\frac{0.5625}{0.4887}, \frac{0.5625}{0.4887}\right) \approx (1.15, 1.15)$$

29. $A = \tfrac{1}{2}(5)(5) = \tfrac{25}{2}$

The centroid of a triangle is located where the three medians meet, at the point $(\overline{x}, \overline{y})$ located $\tfrac{2}{3}$ of the distance from each vertex to the midpoint of the opposite side. The midpoint of the side with vertices $(-3, 0)$, and $(2, 0)$ is $(-\tfrac{1}{2}, 0)$, so

$$(\overline{x}, \overline{y}) = (0, 5) + \tfrac{2}{3}(-\tfrac{1}{2} - 0, 0 - 5)$$

$$= (-\tfrac{1}{3}, \tfrac{5}{3})$$

the distance from $(\overline{x}, \overline{y})$ to the line $y = -1$ is $s_1 = \tfrac{5}{3} + 1 = \tfrac{8}{3}$, so the volume of the solid formed by revolving the triangle about $y = -1$ is

$$V_1 = 2\pi s_1 A = 2\pi(\tfrac{8}{3})(\tfrac{25}{2}) = \tfrac{200\pi}{3}$$

When the triangle is revolved about $x = 3$, the radius is $s_2 = 3 - (-\tfrac{1}{3}) = \tfrac{10}{3}$, and the volume of revolution is

$$V_2 = 2\pi s_2 A = 2\pi(\tfrac{10}{3})(\tfrac{25}{2}) = \tfrac{250\pi}{3}$$

Using calculus to find $\overline{y}$ is considerably more difficult, as there are two different curves for the upper bound.

$$m = \int_{-3}^{0} \tfrac{5}{3}(x + 3)\,dx + \int_{0}^{2} -\tfrac{5}{2}(x - 2)\,dx$$

$$= \tfrac{5}{3}\left(\tfrac{x^2}{2} + 3x\right)\Big|_{-3}^{0} - \tfrac{5}{2}\left(\tfrac{x^2}{2} - 2x\right)\Big|_{0}^{2}$$

$$= \tfrac{25}{2}$$

$$M_x = \tfrac{1}{2}\int_{-3}^{0} \left[\tfrac{5}{3}(x + 3)\right]^2 dx + \tfrac{1}{2}\int_{0}^{2} \left[-\tfrac{5}{2}(x - 2)\right]^2 dx$$

$$= \tfrac{25}{18}\left(\tfrac{x^3}{3} + 3x^2 + 9x\right)\Big|_{-3}^{0} + \tfrac{25}{8}\left(\tfrac{x^3}{3} - 2x^2 + 4x\right)\Big|_{0}^{2}$$

$$= \frac{125}{6};$$

$$\overline{y} = \frac{M_x}{M} = \frac{\frac{125}{6}}{\frac{25}{2}} = \frac{5}{3}$$

$$V = 2\pi\left(\frac{5}{3} + 1\right)\left(\frac{25}{2}\right) = \frac{200\pi}{3} \quad \text{(as before)}$$

31. $A = \frac{1}{2}\pi(2)^2 = 2\pi$

$$\overline{x} = \frac{1}{2\pi}\int_{-2}^{2} \frac{1}{2}\left[\sqrt{4 - y^2}\right]^2 dy$$

$$= \frac{1}{2\pi}\left[\frac{1}{2}(4y - \frac{y^3}{3})\right]\Big|_{-2}^{2}$$

$$= \frac{8}{3\pi}$$

$$V = (2\pi)\left[2\pi\left(\frac{8}{3\pi} + 2\right)\right]$$

$$= \frac{8\pi}{3}(4 + 3\pi)$$

34.

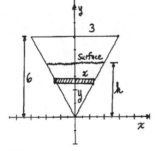

When the tank is full, its volume is

$$\frac{1}{3}\pi(3)^2(6) = 18\pi$$

Let h and r be the height of water and the corresponding radius when the tank is half full. Then,

$$\frac{h}{6} = \frac{r}{3} \text{ and } \frac{1}{3}\pi r^2 h = 9\pi,$$

so

$$h = \sqrt[3]{108} \approx 4.7622$$

To compute the work W required to pump all the water over the top of the tank, we proceed as in Example 3. Since the radius x of the disk of water satisfies

$$\frac{x}{3} = \frac{y}{6}$$

and the distance moved by the disk is $6 - y$, we have

$$\Delta W = \underbrace{62.4\pi x^2 \Delta y}_{weight} \underbrace{(6 - y)}_{distance}$$

$$= 62.4\pi(\frac{1}{2}y)^2(6 - y)\Delta y$$

and

$$W = 62.4\pi\int_{0}^{4.7622} \left(\frac{1}{2}y\right)^2(6 - y) \, dy$$

$$\approx 4{,}284$$

The amount of work is approximately 4,284 ft-lb.

41.   The horizontal force is 9 ft below the surface, so the force on this face is

$$F_1 = 62.4(1)^2(9) = 561.6 \text{ lb}$$

The force on each of the four vertical faces is

$$F_2 = 62.4 \int_9^{10} x(1)\ dx$$

$$= 592.8\ \text{lb}$$

Thus, the total force on the five exposed sides is

$$F = F_1 + 4F_2$$

$$= 2{,}932.8\ \text{lb}$$

42. Let a Cartesian coordinate system pass through the center of the circular base of the log at the bottom of the pool. The equation of the circle is

$$x^2 + (y - 1)^2 = 1 \text{ or } x = \sqrt{1 - (y - 1)^2}$$

$$F = 62.4(2) \int_0^2 (10 - y)\sqrt{1 - (y - 1)^2}\ dy$$

$$= 124.8 \int_0^2 (10 - y)\sqrt{2y - y^2}\ dy$$

$$= \frac{2{,}808\pi}{5}$$

$$\approx 1{,}764.32\text{lb}$$

We use a calculator (or numerical integration) to evaluate this integral.

47. The force on the bottom of the flat shallow end is

$$F_1 = 62.4(3)[(4)(12)] = 8{,}985.6\ \text{lb}$$

To find the force on the inclined plane part of the bottom, put the x-axis along one edge of the bottom as shown:

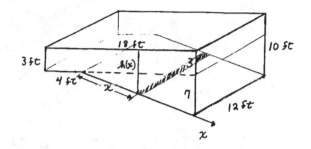

Note that the length of the incline is

$$\sqrt{14^2 + 7^2} = 7\sqrt{5}$$

If $h(x)$ is the depth of the water above point x on the bottom edge, then by similar triangles,

$$\frac{h(x) - 3}{7} = \frac{x}{7\sqrt{5}} \text{ or } h(x) = \frac{1}{\sqrt{5}}x + 3$$

Thus, the fluid force on the inclined plane part of the bottom is

$$F_2 = 62.4 \int_0^{7\sqrt{5}} \left(\frac{1}{\sqrt{5}}x + 3\right)(12)\ dx \approx 76{,}183.7$$

$$F = F_1 + F_2$$

$$\approx 8{,}985.6 + 76{,}183.7$$

$$= 85{,}169.3$$

The total force of the bottom is about 85,169 lb.

48.

depth, x_k	width L_k	$x_k L_k$
1.0	0.0	0.00
1.2	3.3	3.96
1.4	3.6	5.04
1.6	3.7	5.92
1.8	3.7	6.66
2.0	3.6	7.20
2.2	3.4	7.48
2.4	2.9	6.96
2.6	0.0	0.00

The fluid force on the plate is given by

$$F = \int_1^{2.6} 62.4x\, L(x)\ dx$$

$$\approx \tfrac{1}{3}[0.00 + 4(3.96) + 2(5.04) + \cdots$$

$$+ \ 4(6.96) + 0.00](0.2)$$

$$\approx 8.97$$

and

$$F \ \approx \ (62.4)(8.97)$$

$$\approx \ 559.7; \text{ thus, the fluid}$$

force on the plate is approximately 560 lb.

57. Assume the region is under a curve $y = f(x) > 0$ over $[0, a_2]$. Then,

$$\overline{x} = \frac{\displaystyle\int_0^{a_2} xy\, dx}{\displaystyle\int_0^{a_2} y\, dx} = \frac{\displaystyle\int_0^{a_1} xy\, dx + \int_{a_1}^{a_2} xy\, dx}{\displaystyle\int_0^{a_1} y\, dx + \int_{a_1}^{a_2} y\, dx}$$

$$= \frac{1}{A_1 + A_2}\left[A_1 \frac{\displaystyle\int_0^{a_1} xy\, dx}{A_1} + A_2 \frac{\displaystyle\int_{a_1}^{a_2} xy\, dx}{A_2} \right]$$

$$= \frac{1}{A_1 + A_2}\left[A_1 \frac{\displaystyle\int_0^{a_1} xy\, dx}{\displaystyle\int_0^{a_1} y\, dx} + A_2 \frac{\displaystyle\int_{a_1}^{a_2} xy\, dx}{\displaystyle\int_{a_1}^{a_2} y\, dx} \right]$$

$$= \frac{A_1\overline{x}_1 + A_2\overline{x}_2}{A_1 + A_2}$$

Similarly, $\overline{y} = \dfrac{A_1\overline{y}_1 + A_2\overline{y}_2}{A_1 + A_2}$. Any region can be subdivided into subregions whose sum and/or differences are under a curve $y = f(x)$ over some interval $[0, a_2]$.

CHAPTER 6 REVIEW

Proficiency Examination, Page 454

SURVIVAL HINT: *To help you review the concepts of this chapter,* **hand write** *the answers to each of these questions onto your own paper.*

1. If f and g are continuous and satisfy $f(x) \geq g(x)$ on the closed interval $[a, b]$, then the area between the two curves $y = f(x)$ and $y = g(x)$ is given by

$$A = \int_a^b [f(x) \ - \ g(x)]\ dx$$

2. Take cross-sections perpendicular to a convenient line — say the x-axis. If $A(x)$ is the area of the cross-section at x and the base region extends from $x = a$ to $x = b$, the volume is given by

$$V = \int_a^b A(x)\ dx$$

3. Use disks or washers when the approximating strip is perpendicular to the axis of revolution. Use shells when the strip is parallel to the axis.

4. Let f be a function whose derivative f' is continuous on the interval $[a, b]$. Then the arc length, s, of the graph of $y = f(x)$ between $x = a$ to $x = b$ is given by the integral

$$s = \int_a^b \sqrt{1 + [f'(x)]^2}\ dx$$

Similarly, for the graph of $x = g(y)$, where g' is continuous on the interval $[c, d]$, the arc length from $y = c$ to $y = d$ is

$$s = \int_c^d \sqrt{1 + [g'(y)]^2}\ dy$$

5. Suppose f' is continuous on the interval $[a, b]$. Then the surface generated by revolving about the x-axis the arc of the curve

$y = f(x)$ on $[a, b]$ has surface area

$$S = 2\pi \int_a^b f(x)\sqrt{1 + [f'(x)]^2}\ dx$$

6. The work done by the variable force $F(x)$ as an object moves along the x-axis from $x = a$ to $x = b$ is given by

$$W = \int_a^b F(x)\ dx$$

7. Suppose a flat surface (a plate) is submerged vertically in a fluid of weight density ρ (lb/ft^3) and that the submerged portion of the plate extends from $x = a$ to $x = b$ on a vertical axis. Then the total force, F exerted by the fluid is given by

$$F = \int_a^b \rho\, h(x) L(x)\ dx$$

where $h(x)$ is the depth at x and $L(x)$ is the corresponding length of a typical horizontal approximating strip.

8. Let f and g be continuous and satisfy $f(x) \geq g(x)$ on the interval $[a, b]$, and consider a thin plate (lamina) of uniform density ρ that covers the region R between the graphs of $y = f(x)$ and $y = g(x)$ on the interval $[a, b]$. Then
The mass of R is: $\quad m = \rho \int_a^b [f(x) - g(x)]\ dx$

The centroid of R is the point $(\overline{x}, \overline{y})$ such that

$$\overline{x} = \frac{M_y}{m} = \frac{\rho \displaystyle\int_a^b x[f(x) - g(x)]\, dx}{\rho \displaystyle\int_a^b [f(x) - g(x)]\, dx} \quad \text{and}$$

$$\overline{y} = \frac{M_x}{m} = \frac{\frac{1}{2}\rho \displaystyle\int_a^b \{[f(x)]^2 - [g(x)]^2\}\, dx}{\rho \displaystyle\int_a^b [f(x) - g(x)]\, dx}$$

9. The solid generated by revolving a region R about a line outside its boundary (but in the same plane) has volume $V = As$, where A is the area of R and s is the distance traveled by the centroid of R.

10. Hooke's law states that when a spring is pulled x units past its equilibrium (rest) position, there is a restoring force $F(x) = kx$ that pulls the spring back toward equilibrium.

11. Pascal's principle states that fluid pressure is the same in all directions.

12.-18. *The definite integrals could represent the following:*

A. Disks revolved about the y-axis.

B. Disks revolved about the x-axis.

C. Slices taken perpendicular to the x-axis.

D. Slices taken perpendicular to the y-axis.

E. Mass of a lamina with density π.

F. Washers taken along the x-axis.

G. Washers taken along the y-axis.

12. All but E are formulas for volumes of solids.

15. C, D

18. $$A = \int_{-1}^{3} (3x^2 + 2)\, dx$$

$$= (x^3 + 2x)\Big|_{-1}^{3}$$

$$= 36$$

21. a.

$$A = 2\int_0^2 [4 - (x - 2)^2]\, dx$$

$$= 2\int_0^2 (4x - x^2)\, dx$$

$$= 2\Big(2x^2 - \frac{x^3}{3}\Big)\Big|_0^2$$

$$= \frac{32}{3}$$

$$= \left[x^2 - \frac{x^3}{3} - \frac{x^4}{4} \right] \Big|_0^1$$

b. $V = 2\pi \int_0^2 [R^2 - r^2] \, dx$

$$= \frac{5}{12}$$

$$= 2\pi \int_0^2 [4^2 - (x-2)^4] \, dx$$

$$M_y = \int_0^1 x(2x - x^2 - x^3) \, dx$$

$$= 2\pi \int_0^2 (-x^4 + 8x^3 - 24x^2 + 32x) \, dx$$

$$= \int_0^1 (2x^2 - x^3 - x^4) \, dx$$

$$= 2\pi \left(-\frac{x^5}{5} + 2x^4 - 8x^3 + 16x^2 \right) \Big|_0^2$$

$$= \frac{2x^3}{3} - \frac{x^4}{4} - \frac{x^5}{5} \Big|_0^1$$

$$= \frac{256\pi}{5}$$

$$= \frac{13}{60}$$

c. $V = \int_0^4 2\pi r h \, dx$

$$= 2\pi \int_0^4 x[4 - (x-2)^2] \, dx$$

$$M_x = \frac{1}{2} \int_0^1 [(x - x^3)^2 - (x^2 - x)^2] \, dx$$

$$= 2\pi \int_0^4 x(4x - x^2) \, dx$$

$$= \frac{1}{2} \int_0^1 (x^6 - 3x^4 + 2x^3) \, dx$$

$$= 2\pi \int_0^4 (4x^2 - x^3) \, dx$$

$$= \frac{1}{2} \left(\frac{x^7}{7} - \frac{3x^5}{5} + \frac{x^4}{2} \right) \Big|_0^1$$

$$= 2\pi \left(\frac{4x^3}{3} - \frac{x^4}{4} \right) \Big|_0^4$$

$$= \frac{3}{140}$$

$$= \frac{128\pi}{3}$$

$$\bar{x} = \frac{M_y}{M} = \frac{\frac{13}{60}}{\frac{5}{12}} = \frac{13}{25} \; ;$$

24. $M = \int_0^1 [(x - x^3) - (x^2 - x)] \, dx$

$$\bar{y} = \frac{M_x}{M} = \frac{\frac{3}{140}}{\frac{5}{12}} = \frac{9}{175}$$

$$= \int_0^1 (2x - x^2 - x^3) \, dx$$

The centroid is $\left(\frac{13}{25}, \frac{9}{175} \right)$.

**Cumulative Review for Chapters 1-6,
Pages 463-464**

SURVIVAL HINT: *The Cumulative Review for Chapters 1-6 can be very valuable to refresh some of the skills and concepts that you may not have been using too often. It is also a variable tool to prepare for a final exam. If you do not have time to actually do all of the problems, try looking at each one to see if recall the concept involved and how to proceed with the solution. If you are confident about your ability to solve the problem, do not spend the time. If you feel a little uncertain about the problem, refer back to the appropriate section, review the concepts, look in your old homework for a similar problem, and then see if you can work it. Be more concerned about understanding the concept than about getting the "right answer." Do not spend a lot of your time looking for algebra and arithmetic errors.*

As with the other reviews, we suggest that you **hand write** *the answers to the questions about definitions and important results.*

1. Formally, the limit statement $\lim_{x \to c} f(x) = L$ means that for each $\epsilon > 0$, there corresponds a number $\delta > 0$ with the property that
$$|f(x) - L| < \epsilon$$
whenever $0 < |x - c| < \delta$. The notation $\lim_{x \to c} f(x) = L$ is read "the limit of $f(x)$ as x approaches c is L" and means that the functional values $f(x)$ can be made arbitrarily close to L by choosing x sufficiently close to c (but not equal to c).

2. The derivative of f at x is given by
$$f'(x) = \lim_{\Delta x \to 0} \frac{f(x + \Delta x) - f(x)}{\Delta x}$$
provided this limit exists. This is the slope of the tangent line to the curve at the point $(x, f(x))$.

3. If f is defined on the closed interval $[a, b]$ we say f is integrable on $[a, b]$ if
$$I = \lim_{\|P\| \to 0} \sum_{k=1}^{n} f(x_k^*)\Delta x_k$$
exists. This limit is called the definite integral of f from a to b. The definite integral is denoted by
$$I = \int_a^b f(x)\, dx$$

4. A differential equation is an equation involving derivatives (or differentials). The differential equation is *separable* if it can be rewritten so that all the terms containing the independent variable appear on one side of the equation and all terms involving the dependent variable appear on the other side.

6. $\lim_{x \to +\infty} \frac{3x^2 + 7x + 2}{5x^2 - 3x + 3} = \lim_{x \to +\infty} \frac{3 + \frac{7}{x} + \frac{2}{x^2}}{5 - \frac{3}{x} + \frac{3}{x^2}}$
$$= \frac{3}{5}$$

9. $\lim_{x \to 0} \frac{x \sin x}{x + \sin^2 x} = \lim_{x \to 0} \frac{x}{\frac{x}{\sin x} + \sin x}$
$$= 0$$

12. $\lim_{x \to 0} \frac{\ln(x^2 + 50)}{2x}$ is not defined

15. $y = (x^2 + 1)^3(3x - 4)^2$
$$y' = (x^2 + 1)^3(2)(3x - 4)(3)$$
$$+ 3(x^2 + 1)^2(2x)(3x - 4)^2$$
$$= 6(x^2 + 1)^2(3x - 4)[x^2 + 1 + 3x^2 - 4x]$$
$$= 6(2x - 1)^2(x^2 + 1)^2(3x - 4)$$

18.

$$x^2 + 3xy + y^2 = 0$$

$$2x + 3xy' + 3y + 2yy' = 0$$

$$(3x + 2y)y' = -(2x + 3y)$$

$$y' = -\frac{2x + 3y}{3x + 2y}$$

21. $y = \ln(5x^2 + 3x - 2)$

$$y' = \frac{10x + 3}{5x^2 + 3x - 2}$$

24.

$$\int_{-1}^{1} 50(2x - 5)^3 \, dx = 25 \int_{-1}^{1} (2x - 5)^3 \, (2 \, dx)$$

$$= \frac{25}{4}(2x - 5)^4 \Big|_{-1}^{1}$$

$$= -14,500$$

27. $\int \frac{e^x \, dx}{e^x + 2} = \ln\left| e^x + 2 \right| + C$

$$= \ln(e^x + 2) + C$$

30. $y = x^3 - 5x^2 + 2x + 8$

$$y' = 3x^2 - 10x + 2$$

$$y' = 0 \text{ when } x = \frac{5 \pm \sqrt{19}}{3}$$

$$y'' = 6x - 10$$

$$y'' = 0 \text{ when } x = \frac{5}{3}$$

(0.214, 8.209) is a relative maximum;

(3.120, −4.061) is a relative minimum;

(1.67, 2.05) is a point of inflection

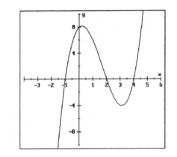

33. The curve crosses the x-axis at $(0, 0)$.

$$A = \int_{-2}^{0} [0 - x(x^2 + 8)^{1/2}] \, dx$$

$$+ \int_{0}^{1} [x(x^2 + 8)^{1/2} - 0] \, dx$$

$$= -\frac{1}{3}(x^2 + 8)^{3/2} \Big|_{-2}^{0} + \frac{1}{3}(x^2 + 8)^{3/2} \Big|_{0}^{1}$$

$$= \frac{1}{3}[24\sqrt{3} - 32\sqrt{2} + 27]$$

$$\approx 7.77146$$

36.

$$\frac{dy}{dx} = x^2 y^2 \sqrt{4 - x^3}$$

$$\int y^{-2} \, dy = \int x^2 (4 - x^3)^{1/2} \, dx$$

$$-y^{-1} = -\frac{2}{9}[(4 - x^3)^{3/2} + C]$$

$$y = \frac{9}{2(4 - x^3)^{3/2} + C}$$

39.

$$\frac{dy}{dx} = e^y \sin x$$

$$\int e^{-y} \, dy = \int \sin x \, dx$$

$$-e^{-y} = -\cos x - C$$

$$e^{-y} = \cos x + C$$

Since $y = 5$ when $x = 0$, $C = e^{-5} - 1$;
Thus,

$$e^{-y} = e^{-5} - 1 + \cos x$$

$$y = -\ln|\cos x + e^{-5} - 1|$$

42.
$$V = \pi \int_1^2 [2(3x - 2)^{-1/2}]^2 \, dx$$

$$= \pi \int_1^4 4u^{-1} \frac{du}{3} = \frac{4\pi}{3} \ln|u| \Big|_1^4$$

$$= \frac{4\pi}{3} \ln 4$$

$$\approx 5.8069$$

45. **a.** $x = \int v(t) \, dt = 2t^3 - t^2 - 4t + C$

$x(2) = 2 \cdot 8 - 4 - 8 + C = 4 + C$, so $C = 2$

$x(t) = 2t^3 - t^2 - 4t + 2$

b. AVERAGE VELOCITY $= \dfrac{x(3) - x(0)}{3 - 0}$

$$= \frac{35 - 2}{3}$$

$$= 11$$

$$6t^2 - 2t - 4 = 11$$

$$6t^2 - 2t - 15 = 0$$

$$t = \frac{2 + \sqrt{4 - 4(6)(-15)}}{2(6)}$$

$$\approx 1.75657$$

c. DISTANCE $= \displaystyle\int_0^3 |v(t)| \, dt$

$$= \int_0^1 |6t^2 - 2t - 4| \, dt + \int_1^3 |6t^2 - 2t - 4| \, dt$$

$$= 3 + 36$$

$$= 39$$

48. **a.** $f(x) = x^3 - 6x^2 + k$

$f'(x) = 3x^2 - 12x$;

$f'(x) = 0$ when $x = 0, 4$

$f''(x) = 6x - 12$;

$f''(0) = -12$,

relative maximum at $x = 0$

$f''(4) = 12$, relative minimum at $x = 4$

$f(0) = k$, so relative maximum at $(0, k)$;

$f(4) = k - 32$,

relative minimum at $(4, k - 32)$

b. $f(x)$ has three distinct real roots when
$k > 0$ and $k - 32 < 0$, so $0 < k < 32$.

c. AVERAGE VALUE

$$= \frac{1}{2 - (-1)} \int_{-1}^2 (x^3 - 6x^2 + k) \, dx$$

We now find the value of k for which the average value is 2:

$$\frac{1}{3}\left[3k - \frac{57}{4}\right] = 2, \text{ so } k = \frac{27}{4}$$

CHAPTER 7

Methods of Integration

7.1 Review of Substitution and Integration by Table, Pages 473-475

SURVIVAL HINT: *You will make fewer errors with substitution if you take the time to write down* $u = \cdots$, $du = \cdots$ *each time, and then carefully make the substitutions. In this manual, we show this information enclosed in boxes. On definite integrals, do not forget to change the limits when you make a u-substitution.*

1.
$$\int \frac{2x + 5}{\sqrt{x^2 + 5x}}\, dx = \int u^{-1/2}\, du$$

$$\boxed{\text{Let } u = x^2 + 5x;\ du = (2x + 5)\, dx}$$

$$= \frac{u^{1/2}}{\frac{1}{2}} + C$$

$$= 2(x^2 + 5x)^{1/2} + C$$

SURVIVAL HINT: *When making a u-substitution (as shown here with Problem 1, we often carry out the actual substitution steps mentally, which means that many will work Problem 1 as follows:*

$$\int \frac{2x + 5}{\sqrt{x^2 + 5x}}\, dx = \int (x^2 + 5x)^{-1/2}[(2x + 5)\, dx]$$

$$= 2(x^2 + 5x)^{1/2} + C$$

6. $\displaystyle\int \frac{t^2\, dt}{9 + t^6}$ $\boxed{u = \frac{1}{3}t^3}$

$$= \frac{1}{3}\int \frac{3t^2\, dt}{9 + (t^3)^2}$$

$$= (\tfrac{1}{3})^2 \tan^{-1}\tfrac{1}{3}t^3 + C$$

$$= \frac{1}{9} \tan^{-1}\frac{t^3}{3} + C$$

SURVIVAL HINT: *Note the work shown above for Problem 6. The box tells you the u-substitution that works. It leads you to mentally think through the following **mental** steps:*

$$\int \frac{t^2\, dt}{9 + t^6} = \int \frac{t^2\, \frac{du}{t^2}}{9 + 9u^2}$$

$$\boxed{\text{Let } u = \tfrac{1}{3}t^3,\ du = t^2\, dt,\ \text{so } dt = \frac{du}{t^2}}$$

$$= \int \frac{du}{9 + (9u^2)}$$

$$= \frac{1}{9}\int \frac{du}{1 + u^2}$$

$$= \frac{1}{9}\tan^{-1} u + C$$

$$= \frac{1}{9}\tan^{-1}\frac{t^3}{3} + C$$

12. $\displaystyle\int \frac{2x - 1}{(4x^2 - 4x)^2}\, dx \;=\; \int \frac{(2x - 1)\, dx}{16(x^2 - x)^2}$

$\boxed{\text{Let } u = x^2 - x;\; du = (2x - 1)\, dx}$

$$= \frac{1}{16} \int u^{-2}\, du$$

$$= -\frac{1}{16}\, u^{-1} + C$$

$$= -\frac{1}{16}(x^2 - x)^{-1} + C$$

13. $\displaystyle\int \frac{dx}{x^2 \sqrt{x^2 - a^2}} = \frac{\sqrt{x^2 - a^2}}{a^2 x} + C$

$\boxed{\text{Formula 201}}$

15. $\displaystyle\int x \ln x\, dx = \frac{1}{2}x^2\!\left(\ln x - \frac{1}{2}\right) + C$

$\boxed{\text{Formula 502}}$

21. $\displaystyle\int \frac{x\, dx}{\sqrt{4x^2 + 1}} = \frac{1}{4}\sqrt{4x^2 + 1} + C$

$\boxed{\text{Formula 173};\; u = 2x}$

32. $\displaystyle\int \ln^3 x\, dx \qquad\qquad \boxed{\text{Formula 501}}$

$= x(\ln x)^3 - 3\displaystyle\int (\ln x)^2 dx \quad \boxed{\text{Formula 500}}$

$= x(\ln x)^3 - 3[x(\ln x)^2 - 2x \ln x + 2x] + C$

$= x \ln^3 x - 3x \ln^2 x + 6x \ln x - 6x + C$

33. $\displaystyle\int \frac{x^3\, dx}{\sqrt{4x^4 + 1}} \;=\; \frac{1}{16}\int u^{-1/2}\, du \;\;\boxed{u = 4x^4 + 1}$

$$= \tfrac{1}{8}(4x^4 + 1)^{1/2} + C$$

39. $\displaystyle\int \frac{\sin^2 x}{\cos x}\, dx \qquad \boxed{\text{Formula 382 or let } u = \cos x}$

$$= -\sin x + \ln\left|\tan\!\left(\frac{x}{2} + \frac{\pi}{4}\right)\right| + C$$

40. $\displaystyle\int \sin^2 x\, dx \;=\; \int \frac{1 - \cos 2x}{2}\, dx$

$$= \tfrac{1}{2}x - \tfrac{1}{2}\frac{\sin 2x}{2} + C$$

$$= \tfrac{1}{2}x - \tfrac{1}{4}\sin 2x + C$$

SURVIVAL HINT: *It is common to integrate either a* $\sin^2 x$ *or* $\cos^2 x$ *and Problems 40 and 41 give these forms. You should remember or otherwise mark these problems for future use. They are found as Formulas 317 and 348 in the table of integrals.*

43. $\boxed{\text{Let } u = \cos x,\;\; du = -\sin x\, dx}$

$\displaystyle\int \sin^3 x \cos^4 x\, dx \;=\; \int \sin^2 x \cos^4 x\, (\sin x\, dx)$

$$= \int (1 - u^2)u^4(-du)$$

$$= \int (u^6 - u^4)\, du$$

$$= \frac{u^7}{7} - \frac{u^5}{5} + C$$

$$= \tfrac{1}{7}\cos^7 x - \tfrac{1}{5}\cos^5 x + C$$

SURVIVAL HINT: *The procedure shown in Problem 43 is common when working with powers of sines and cosines. It anticipates a method which is presented formally in Section 7.3.*

49. $\int \dfrac{4\,dx}{x^{1/3} + 2x^{1/2}}$ $\boxed{\text{Let } x = u^6;\ dx = 6u^5\,du}$

$$= \int \dfrac{4(6u^5\,du)}{u^2 + 2u^3}$$

$$= 24 \int \dfrac{u^5\,du}{u^2 + 2u^3}$$

$$= 24 \int \dfrac{u^3\,du}{2u + 1}$$

SURVIVAL HINT: *We could use Formula 44, but since the degree of the numerator is greater than the degree of the denominator, do long division to obtain:*

$$24 \int \left(\tfrac{1}{2}u^2 - \tfrac{1}{4}u + \tfrac{1}{8} - \dfrac{\tfrac{1}{8}}{2u + 1} \right) du$$

$$= 24\left(\dfrac{u^3}{6} - \dfrac{u^2}{8} + \dfrac{u}{8} - \tfrac{1}{16} \ln|2u + 1| \right) + C$$

$$= 4x^{1/2} - 3x^{1/3} + 3x^{1/6} - \tfrac{3}{2}\ln(2x^{1/6} + 1) + C$$

55. $V = \pi \displaystyle\int_0^9 \left(\dfrac{x^{3/2}}{\sqrt{x^2 + 9}} \right)^2 dx$

$$= \pi \int_0^9 \dfrac{x^3}{x^2 + 9}\,dx$$

SURVIVAL HINT: *When the degree of the numerator is greater than the degree of the denominator, consider long division:*

$$\dfrac{x^3}{x^2 + 9} = x - \dfrac{9x}{x^2 + 9}$$

$$\pi \int_0^9 \dfrac{x^3}{x^2 + 9}\,dx = \pi \left[\int_0^9 x\,dx - \int_0^9 \dfrac{9x}{x^2 + 9}\,dx \right]$$

$$\boxed{\text{Let } u = x^2 + 9,\ du = 2x\,dx}$$
$$\boxed{\text{If } x = 0, \text{ then } u = 0 \text{ and if } x = 9, \text{ then } u = 90}$$

$$= \pi \dfrac{x^2}{2}\Big|_0^9 - \pi \int_0^{90} \dfrac{9x\left(\frac{du}{2x} \right)}{u}$$

$$= \tfrac{81}{2}\pi - \tfrac{9}{2}\pi \ln u \Big|_9^{90}$$

$$= \tfrac{81}{2}\pi - \tfrac{9}{2}\pi (\ln 90 - \ln 9)$$

$$= \tfrac{81}{2}\pi - \tfrac{9}{2}\pi \ln 10$$

$$\approx 94.68 \text{ cubic units}$$

58. $xy' = \sqrt{(\ln x)^2 - x^2}$

$$y' = \tfrac{1}{x}\sqrt{(\ln x)^2 - x^2}$$

$$= \sqrt{\dfrac{(\ln x)^2 - x^2}{x^2}}$$

$$s = \int_{1/4}^{1/2} \sqrt{1 + \dfrac{(\ln x)^2}{x^2} - 1}$$

$$\boxed{u = \ln x;\ du = \tfrac{1}{x}\,dx \text{ or a calculator}}$$

$$= -\int_{1/4}^{1/2} \dfrac{\ln x}{x}\,dx$$

$$= -\tfrac{1}{2}\ln^2 x \Big|_{1/4}^{1/2} = \tfrac{3}{2}\ln^2 2$$

$$\approx 0.7207$$

61. $ds = \sqrt{1 + 4x^2}\ dx;\ dS = 2\pi y\ ds$

$$S = 2\pi \int_0^1 x^2\sqrt{1+4x^2}\ dx$$

$$\boxed{\text{Formula 170; } u = 2x}$$

$$= 2\pi \int_0^2 \frac{u^2}{4}\sqrt{1+u^2}\ \left(\frac{du}{2}\right)$$

$$= \frac{\pi}{4}\Bigg(\frac{u(u^2+1)^{3/2}}{4} - \frac{u(u^2+1)^{1/2}}{8}$$

$$\left. - \frac{1}{8}\ln\left|u + (u^2 + 1^2)^{1/2}\right|\right)\Bigg)\Bigg|_0^2$$

$$= \frac{9\sqrt{5}\pi}{16} - \frac{\pi\ln(\sqrt{5}+2)}{32}$$

$$\approx 3.8097$$

65. Let $u = \pi - x$, $du = -\ dx$. Then $\sin x = \sin u$

$$\int_0^\pi xf(\sin x)\ dx = \int_\pi^0 (\pi - u)f(\sin u)(-\ du)$$

$$= \int_0^\pi (\pi - u)\ f(\sin u)du$$

$$= \int_0^\pi \pi\ f(\sin u)\ du - \int_0^\pi u\ f(\sin u)\ du$$

The value of the integral is independent of the variable used so

$$= \pi \int_0^\pi f(\sin x)\ dx - \int_0^\pi x\ f(\sin x)\ dx$$

Add the second integral to both sides and divide by 2 to obtain the desired result.

7.2 Integration by Parts, Pages 480–481

SURVIVAL HINT: *Along with substitution, integration by parts is the most common technique of integration. When using parts, when selecting u and dv, a necessary criteria is the integrability of dv, a desirable, but not necessary criteria is that the derivative of u be simpler.*

Remember: $\int u\ dv = uv - \int v\ du$

3. $\quad \int x\ln x\ dx = (\ln x)(\tfrac{1}{2}x^2) - \int (\tfrac{1}{2}x^2)(\tfrac{1}{x}\ dx)$

$$\boxed{u = \ln x;\ dv = x\ dx}$$
$$\boxed{du = \tfrac{1}{x}\ dx;\ v = \tfrac{1}{2}x^2}$$

$$= \tfrac{1}{2}x^2\ln x - \tfrac{1}{2}\int x\ dx$$

$$= \tfrac{1}{2}x^2\ln x - \tfrac{1}{4}x^2 + C$$

4. $\quad \int x\tan^{-1}x\ dx \quad \boxed{u = \tan^{-1}x;\ dv = x\ dx}$

$$= \tfrac{1}{2}x^2\tan^{-1}x - \tfrac{1}{2}\int \frac{x^2\ dx}{x^2+1}$$

$$= \tfrac{1}{2}x^2\tan^{-1}x - \tfrac{1}{2}\int \left[1 + \frac{-1}{x^2+1}\right]dx$$

$$= \tfrac{1}{2}x^2\tan^{-1}x - \tfrac{1}{2}[x - \tan^{-1}x] + C$$

SURVIVAL HINT: *Problem 8 illustrates the common variation of integration by parts illustrated by Example 4. You will use this technique when integration by parts gives a form which is a multiple of the original integral.*

8. $I = \int e^{2x} \sin 3x \, dx$ $\boxed{u = e^{2x}; \; dv = \sin 3x \, dx}$

$$= -\tfrac{1}{3}e^{2x}\cos 3x + \tfrac{2}{3}\int e^{2x}\cos 3x \, dx$$

$$\boxed{u = e^{2x}; \; dv = \cos 3x \, dx}$$

$$= -\tfrac{1}{3}e^{2x}\cos 3x + \tfrac{2}{3}(\tfrac{1}{3}e^{2x}\sin 3x$$

$$-\tfrac{2}{3}\int e^{2x}\sin 3x \, dx)$$

$$= -\tfrac{1}{3}e^{2x}\cos 3x + \tfrac{2}{9}e^{2x}\sin 3x - \tfrac{4}{9}I + C_1$$

$$\tfrac{13}{9}I = -\tfrac{1}{3}e^{2x}\cos 3x + \tfrac{2}{9}e^{2x}\sin 3x + C_1$$

$$I = -\tfrac{3}{13}e^{2x}\cos 3x + \tfrac{2}{13}e^{2x}\sin 3x + C$$

13. $\displaystyle\int_{1}^{4} \sqrt{x} \, \ln x \, dx$ $\boxed{u = \ln x; \; dv = \sqrt{x} \, dx}$

$$= \tfrac{2}{3}x^{3/2}\ln x \Big|_{1}^{4} - \tfrac{2}{3}\int_{1}^{4} x^{1/2} \, dx$$

$$= \tfrac{16}{3}\ln 4 - \tfrac{4}{9}x^{3/2}\Big|_{1}^{4}$$

$$= \tfrac{32}{3}\ln 2 - \tfrac{28}{9} \approx 4.28246$$

21. $\displaystyle\int [\sin 2x \ln(\cos x)]\, dx = \int 2\sin x\cos x \ln(\cos x)\, dx$

$$\boxed{t = \cos x; \; dt = -\sin x \, dx}$$

$$= -2\int t \ln t \, dt \quad \boxed{u = \ln t; \; dv = t \, dt}$$

$$= -2\left[\tfrac{1}{2}t^2\ln t - \tfrac{1}{2}\int t \, dt\right]$$

$$= -t^2\ln t + \tfrac{1}{2}t^2 + C$$

$$= \tfrac{1}{2}\cos^2 x - (\cos^2 x)\ln(\cos x) + C$$

25. $I = \displaystyle\int \cos^2 x \, dx$ $\boxed{u = \cos x; \; dv = \cos x \, dx}$

$$= \sin x \cos x + \int \sin^2 x \, dx$$

$$= \sin x \cos x + \int (1 - \cos^2 x)\, dx$$

$$= \sin x \cos x + x - \int \cos^2 x \, dx$$

$$2I = \sin x \cos x + x + C_1$$

$$I = \tfrac{1}{2}(x + \sin x \cos x) + C$$

$$= \tfrac{x}{2} + \tfrac{1}{2}\sin x \cos x + C$$

$$= \tfrac{x}{2} + \tfrac{1}{4}\sin 2x + C$$

27. $\displaystyle\int x \cos^2 x \, dx$ $\boxed{u = x; \; dv = \cos^2 x \, dx}$

$$\boxed{du = dx; \; v = \tfrac{x}{2} + \tfrac{\sin 2x}{4} \text{ from Problem 25}}$$

$$= x(\tfrac{x}{2} + \tfrac{\sin 2x}{4}) - \int (\tfrac{x}{2} + \tfrac{\sin 2x}{4})\, dx$$

$$= \tfrac{1}{2}x^2 + \tfrac{1}{4}x\sin 2x - \tfrac{1}{4}x^2 + \tfrac{1}{8}\cos 2x + C$$

$$= \tfrac{1}{4}x^2 + \tfrac{1}{4}x\sin 2x + \tfrac{1}{8}\cos 2x + C$$

31. Let $Q(t)$ be the number of units produced.

$$\frac{dQ}{dt} = 100te^{-0.5t}$$

$$Q(t) = \int_0^3 100te^{-0.5t}dt \quad \boxed{u = t;\ dv = e^{-0.5t}\ dt}$$

$$= -200\ te^{-0.5t}\Big|_0^3$$

$$\qquad - 400 \int_0^3 e^{-0.5t}\left(-\tfrac{1}{2}\right)dt$$

$$= [-200\ te^{-0.5t} - 400\ e^{-0.5t}]\Big|_0^3$$

$$= -200\ e^{-0.5t}(t + 2)\Big|_0^3$$

$$= -1000\ e^{-1.5} + 400 \approx 177\ \text{units}$$

35. a. $\quad V = \pi \int_1^e (\ln x)^2 dx \quad \boxed{u = (\ln x)^2;\ dv = dx}$

$$= \pi \int_1^e (\ln x)^2 dx$$

$$= \pi x(\ln x)^2\Big|_1^e - 2\pi \int_1^e x \ln x \left(\frac{dx}{x}\right)$$

$$= \pi x(\ln x)^2 - 2\pi(x \ln x - x)\Big|_1^e$$

$$= \pi(e - 2e + 2e - 2)$$

$$= \pi(e - 2)$$

b. $\quad V = 2\pi \int_1^e x \ln x\ dx = 2\pi \left[\frac{x^2}{4}(2 \ln x - 1)\right]\Big|_1^e$

(See Problem 3)

$$= 2\pi[\tfrac{e^2}{4} + \tfrac{1}{4}]$$

$$= \tfrac{\pi}{2}(e^2 + 1)$$

37. The curves intersect when $x = 0$. Assume the density is 1.

$$A = \int_0^1 (e^x - e^{-x})\ dx$$

$$= (e^x + e^{-x})\Big|_0^1 \approx 1.0862$$

$$M_x = \frac{1}{2}\int_0^1 (e^x - e^{-x})(e^x + e^{-x})\ dx$$

$$= \frac{1}{2}\int_0^1 (e^{2x} - e^{-2x})\ dx$$

$$= \frac{1}{4}(e^{2x} + e^{-2x})\Big|_0^1$$

$$\approx 1.3811$$

$$M_y = \int_0^1 x(e^x - e^{-x})\ dx$$

$$\boxed{u = x;\ dv = (e^x - e^{-x})\ dx}$$

$$= x(e^x + e^{-x})\Big|_0^1 - \int_0^1 (e^x + e^{-x})\ dx$$

$$= [x(e^x + e^{-x}) - (e^x - e^{-x})]\Big|_0^1$$

$$= \tfrac{2}{e}$$

$$\approx 0.7358$$

$$(\bar{x}, \bar{y}) \approx \left(\frac{0.7358}{1.0862}, \frac{1.3811}{1.0862}\right) \approx (0.68, 1.27)$$

39. $\quad \dfrac{dy}{dx} = \sqrt{xy}\ \ln x$

$$\int y^{-1/2}\ dy = \int x^{1/2} \ln x\ dx$$

$$\boxed{\text{Use parts or Formula 503}}$$

$$2y^{1/2} = \tfrac{2}{3}x^{3/2}\ln x - \tfrac{2}{3}\int x^{1/2} \, dx$$

$$2y^{1/2} = \tfrac{2}{3}x^{3/2}(\ln x - \tfrac{2}{3}) + C$$

42. $\displaystyle\int_0^\pi [f(x) + f''(x)] \sin x \, dx$

$$= \int_0^\pi f(x) \sin x \, dx + \int_0^\pi f''(x) \sin x \, dx$$

$\boxed{u = f(x); \; dv = \sin x \, dx}$ $\boxed{u = \sin x; \; dv = f''(x) \, dx}$

$$= -\cos x f(x)\Big|_0^\pi + \int_0^\pi f'(x) \cos x \; dx$$

$$+ \sin x \, f'(x) \Big|_0^\pi - \int_0^\pi f'(x) \cos x \, dx$$

$$= -\cos \pi \, f(\pi) + \cos 0 f(0)$$

This is 0, so that $f(\pi) = -f(0) = -3$.

47. $\displaystyle \text{AV} = \frac{1}{9V_1}\int_{V_1}^{10V_1} nRT \ln \frac{V}{V_1} \, dV$

$$= \frac{nRT}{9V_1}\int_{V_1}^{10V_1} (\ln V - \ln V_1) dV.$$

$\boxed{\text{Formula 499}}$

$$= \frac{nRT}{9V_1}(V\ln V - V - V\ln V_1)\Big|_{V_1}^{10V_1}$$

$$= \frac{nRT}{9} (10 \ln 10 - 9)$$

$$\approx 1.558nRT$$

7.3 Trigonometric Methods, Pages 487–488

7. $\displaystyle\int \sin^2 x \cos^3 \, dx = \int \sin^2 x \cos^2 x \, (\cos x \, dx)$

$$= \int (\sin^2 x - \sin^4 x)(\cos x \, dx)$$

$$= \int (u^2 - u^4) \, du \quad \boxed{u = \sin x}$$

$$= \tfrac{1}{3}u^3 - \tfrac{1}{5}u^5 + C$$

$$= \tfrac{1}{3}\sin^3 x - \tfrac{1}{5}\sin^5 x + C$$

SURVIVAL HINT: *You might wish to compare Problem 7 with Problem 43, Section 7.1. Notice that Problem 7 is nothing more than a variation of substitution, in which you "peel off" one of the factors of the odd power.*

13. $\displaystyle\int \sin^2 x \cos^2 x \, dx = \int \left[\frac{1-\cos 2x}{2}\right]\left[\frac{1+\cos 2x}{2}\right] dx$

$$= \tfrac{1}{4}\int (1 - \cos^2 2x) \, dx$$

$$= \tfrac{1}{4}x - \tfrac{1}{4}\int \left[\frac{1+\cos 4x}{2}\right] dx$$

$$= \tfrac{1}{4}x - \tfrac{1}{8}x - \tfrac{1}{8}\left[\frac{\sin 4x}{4}\right] + C$$

$$= \tfrac{1}{8}x - \tfrac{1}{32}\sin 4x + C$$

18. $\displaystyle\int \sec^5 x \tan x \, dx = \int \sec^4 x (\sec x \tan x \, dx)$

$$= \tfrac{1}{5}\sec^5 x + C \quad \boxed{u = \sec x}$$

26. $\int x\sec^2 x\, dx = x\tan x + \ln|\cos x| + C$

$\boxed{\text{By parts, } u = x,\ dv = \sec^2 x\, dx \text{ or Formula 433}}$

31. $\int \csc^2 x \cos x\, dx = \int \dfrac{\cos x\, dx}{\sin^2 x} \quad \boxed{u = \sin x}$

$\qquad\qquad = -(\sin x)^{-1} + C$

$\qquad\qquad = -\csc x + C$

34. $\int \dfrac{dx}{\sqrt{9 - x^2}} \quad \boxed{\text{Formula 22}}$

$\qquad = \sin^{-1}\dfrac{x}{3} + C$

By trigonometric substitution: let

$x = 3\sin\theta.$ Then $dx = 3\cos\theta\, d\theta,$ and

$\sqrt{9 - x^2} = \sqrt{9 - 9\sin^2\theta} = 3\cos\theta;$

$\int \dfrac{dx}{\sqrt{9 - x^2}} = \int \dfrac{3\cos\theta}{3\cos\theta}\, d\theta$

$\qquad = \theta + C$

$\qquad = \sin^{-1}\left(\dfrac{x}{3}\right) + C$

38. $\int \dfrac{dx}{5 + 2x^2} = \int \dfrac{1}{2}\left(\dfrac{1}{\frac{5}{2} + x^2}\right) dx$

$\qquad = \dfrac{1}{5}\sqrt{\dfrac{5}{2}}\tan^{-1}\left(\sqrt{\dfrac{2}{5}}x\right) + C$

42. $\int \dfrac{dx}{x\sqrt{x^2 + 9}} \quad \boxed{x = 3\tan\theta \text{ or Formula 176}}$

$\qquad = \int \dfrac{3\sec^2\theta\, d\theta}{3\tan\theta\sqrt{9\tan^2\theta + 9}}$

$\qquad = \int \dfrac{\sec\theta}{3\tan\theta}\, d\theta$

$\qquad = \dfrac{1}{3}\int \csc\theta\, d\theta$

$= -\dfrac{1}{3}\ln|\csc\theta + \cot\theta| + C$

$= -\dfrac{1}{3}\ln\left|\dfrac{3 + \sqrt{x^2 + 9}}{x}\right| + C$

45. $\int \dfrac{dx}{9 - (x + 1)^2}$

$\boxed{\text{Let } x + 1 = 3\sin\theta \text{ or Formula 93}}$

$= \int \dfrac{3\cos\theta\, d\theta}{9 - 9\sin^2\theta}$

$= \dfrac{1}{3}\int \dfrac{d\theta}{\cos\theta}$

$= \dfrac{1}{3}\ln|\sec\theta + \tan\theta| + C$

$= \dfrac{1}{3}\ln\left|\dfrac{3}{\sqrt{9 - (x+1)^2}} + \dfrac{x + 1}{\sqrt{9 - (x+1)^2}}\right| + C$

By Formula 93, we obtain:

$\dfrac{1}{6}\ln\left|\dfrac{3 + (x+1)}{3 - (x+1)}\right| + C = \dfrac{1}{6}\ln\left|\dfrac{4 + x}{2 - x}\right| + C$

47. $\int \dfrac{dx}{\sqrt{x^2 - 2x + 6}} = \int \dfrac{dx}{\sqrt{(x - 1)^2 + 5}}$

$= \int \dfrac{\sqrt{5}\sec^2\theta\, d\theta}{\sqrt{5\tan^2\theta + 5}}$

$\boxed{\text{Let } x - 1 = \sqrt{5}\tan\theta}$

$= \int \sec\theta\, d\theta$

$= \ln|\sec\theta + \tan\theta| + C$

$= \ln\left|\dfrac{\sqrt{x^2 - 2x + 6}}{\sqrt{5}} + \dfrac{x - 1}{\sqrt{5}}\right| + C$

This can be written $\ln\left|\sqrt{x^2 - 2x + 6} + x - 1\right| + C$

50. $\displaystyle\int \frac{\sec^2 x\, dx}{\tan^2 x + \sec^2 x} = \int \frac{(\sec^2 x\, dx)}{2\tan^2 x + 1}$

$\displaystyle = \int \frac{du}{2u^2 + 1} \quad \boxed{u = \tan x}$

$\displaystyle = \frac{1}{\sqrt{2}}\tan^{-1}(\sqrt{2}\, u) + C$

$\displaystyle = \frac{1}{\sqrt{2}}\tan^{-1}(\sqrt{2}\tan x) + C$

56. $a(t) = \sin^2 t$

$\displaystyle v(t) = \int \sin^2 t\, dt = \tfrac{1}{2}t - \tfrac{1}{4}\sin 2t + C$

$v(0) = \tfrac{1}{2}(0) - \tfrac{1}{4}\sin 0 + C = 2,\; C = 2$

$\displaystyle s(t) = \int_0^\pi \left|\tfrac{1}{2}t - \tfrac{1}{4}\sin 2t + 2\right| dt$

$\displaystyle = \frac{\pi^2}{4} + 2\pi$

≈ 8.75

63. $f'' = -\tfrac{1}{2}(\tan x)f'$

$\displaystyle \int \frac{f''}{f'}\, dx = \int -\tfrac{1}{2}(\tan x)\, dx$

$\ln f' = \tfrac{1}{2}\ln|\cos x| + C_1$

$f' = C\sqrt{\cos x}$

$f'(0) = 1 = C,\; \text{so } f' = \sqrt{\cos x}$

$\displaystyle s = \int_{\pi/4}^{\pi/3} \sqrt{1 + (\sqrt{\cos x})^2}\, dx$

$\displaystyle = \int_{\pi/4}^{\pi/3} \sqrt{2\cos^2 \tfrac{x}{2}}\, dx$

$\displaystyle = \sqrt{2} - \sqrt{4 - \sqrt{2}}$

≈ 0.3318

7.4 The Method of Partial Fractions,
Pages 497-499

2. $\displaystyle \frac{3x - 1}{x^2 - 1} = \frac{A_1}{x + 1} + \frac{A_2}{x - 1}$

$3x - 1 = A_1(x - 1) + A_2(x + 1)$

If $x = 1$, then $A_2 = 1$; if $x = -1$, then $A_1 = 2$

Thus,

$\displaystyle \frac{3x - 1}{x^2 - 1} = \frac{2}{x + 1} + \frac{1}{x - 1}$

7. $\displaystyle F = \frac{4x^3 + 4x^2 + x - 1}{x^2(x + 1)^2}$

$\displaystyle = \frac{A_1}{x} + \frac{A_2}{x^2} + \frac{A_3}{x + 1} + \frac{A_4}{(x + 1)^2}$

$4x^3 + 4x^2 + x - 1 = A_1 x(x^2 + 2x + 1)$

$\qquad + A_2(x^2 + 2x + 1) + A_3(x^3 + x^2) + A_4 x^2$

If $x = 0$, then $A_2 = -1$; if $x = -1$, then $A_4 = -2$; finally equate the coefficient of x^3 and those of x to find $4 = A_1 + A_3$ and

$1 = A_1 + 2A_2$, so $A_1 = 3$, and $A_3 = 1$

$$F = \frac{3}{x} + \frac{-1}{x^2} + \frac{1}{x+1} + \frac{-2}{(x+1)^2}$$

15. $\displaystyle\int \frac{3x^2 + 2x - 1}{x(x+1)}\, dx = 3\int dx - \int \frac{1}{x}\, dx$

$$= 3x - \ln|x| + C$$

21. $\displaystyle \frac{x^2 + 1}{x^2 + x - 2} = 1 + \frac{-x + 3}{x^2 + x - 2}$

$$= 1 + \frac{-x + 3}{(x-1)(x+2)}$$

$$= 1 + \frac{A_1}{x-1} + \frac{A_2}{x+2}$$

Partial fraction decomposition gives

$A_1 = \frac{2}{3}$, $A_2 = -\frac{5}{3}$.

$$\int \frac{x^2 + 1}{x^2 + x - 2}\, dx$$

$$= \int dx - \frac{5}{3}\int \frac{dx}{x+2} + \frac{2}{3}\int \frac{dx}{x-1}$$

$$= x - \frac{5}{3}\ln|x+2| + \frac{2}{3}\ln|x-1| + C$$

27. $\displaystyle \frac{1}{x(x+1)(x-2)} = \frac{A_1}{x} + \frac{A_2}{x+1} + \frac{A_3}{x-2}$

Partial fraction decomposition gives

$A_1 = -\frac{1}{2}$, $A_2 = \frac{1}{3}$, $A_3 = \frac{1}{6}$.

$$\int \frac{dx}{x(x+1)(x-2)}$$

$$= -\frac{1}{2}\int \frac{dx}{x} + \frac{1}{3}\int \frac{dx}{x+1} + \frac{1}{6}\int \frac{dx}{x-2}$$

$$= -\frac{1}{2}\ln|x| + \frac{1}{3}\ln|x+1| + \frac{1}{6}\ln|x-2| + C$$

33. $\displaystyle\int \frac{3x^2 - 2x + 4}{x^3 - x^2 + 4x - 4}\, dx$

$$\boxed{u = x^3 - x^2 + 4x - 4}$$

$$= \ln|x^3 - x^2 + 4x - 4| + C$$

36. $\displaystyle\int \frac{\cos x\, dx}{\sin^2 x - \sin x - 2}$ $\boxed{u = \sin x;\ du = \cos x\, dx}$

$$= \int \frac{du}{u^2 - u - 2}$$

$$= \int \frac{du}{(u-2)(u+1)}$$

Now, $\displaystyle \frac{1}{(u-2)(u+1)} = \frac{A_1}{u-2} + \frac{A_2}{u+1}$

Partial fraction decomposition gives $A_1 = \frac{1}{3}$, $A_2 = -\frac{1}{3}$.

$$\int \frac{du}{(u-2)(u+1)}$$

$$= \frac{1}{3}\int \frac{du}{u-2} - \frac{1}{3}\int \frac{du}{u+1}$$

$$= \frac{1}{3}\ln|u-2| - \frac{1}{3}\ln|u+1| + C$$

$$= \frac{1}{3}\ln|\sin x - 2| - \frac{1}{3}\ln|\sin x + 1| + C$$

43. $\displaystyle\int \frac{dx}{x^{2/3} - x^{1/2}}$ $\boxed{x = u^6;\ dx = 6u^5\, du}$

$$= \int \frac{6u^5\, du}{u^4 - u^3} = \int \frac{6u^2\, du}{u-1}$$

$$= 6\int \left[u + 1 + \frac{1}{u-1} \right] du$$

$$= 6\left[\frac{u^2}{2} + u + \ln|u - 1|\right] + C$$

$$= 3x^{1/3} + 6x^{1/6} + 6\ln|x^{1/6} - 1| + C$$

SURVIVAL HINT: *Check with your instructor concerning Weierstrass substitutions. Find out if you need to memorize them or if you will have access to them on exams.*

46. $\int \dfrac{dx}{5 \sin x + 4}$ $\boxed{\text{Weierstrass substitution}}$

$$= \int \frac{\dfrac{2\,du}{1 + u^2}}{5\left(\dfrac{2u}{1 + u^2}\right) + 4}$$

$$= \int \frac{2\,du}{10u + 4(1 + u^2)}$$

$$= \int \frac{du}{2u^2 + 5u + 2}$$

$$= \int \frac{du}{(u + 2)(2u + 1)}$$

Now, $\dfrac{1}{(u + 2)(2u + 1)} = \dfrac{A_1}{u + 2} + \dfrac{A_2}{2u + 1}$

Partial fractions decomposition gives

$A_1 = -\frac{1}{3}, A_2 = \frac{2}{3}.$

$$\int \frac{du}{(u + 2)(2u + 1)} = -\frac{1}{3}\int \frac{du}{u + 2} + \frac{1}{3}\int \frac{2\,du}{2u + 1}$$

$$= -\frac{1}{3}\ln|u + 2| + \frac{1}{3}\ln|2u + 1| + C$$

$$= -\frac{1}{3}\ln\left|\tan\frac{x}{2} + 2\right| + \frac{1}{3}\ln\left|2\tan\frac{x}{2} + 1\right| + C$$

52. $\int \dfrac{dx}{2\csc x - \cot x + 2} = \int \dfrac{\sin x\,dx}{2 - \cos x + 2\sin x}$

$\boxed{\text{Weierstrass substitution}}$

$$= \int \frac{\left(\dfrac{2u}{1 + u^2}\right)\left(\dfrac{2\,du}{1 + u^2}\right)}{2 - \left(\dfrac{1 - u^2}{1 + u^2}\right) + 2\left(\dfrac{2u}{1 + u^2}\right)}$$

$$= \int \frac{4\,u\,du}{(1 + u^2)(3u^2 + 4u + 1)}$$

$$= \int \left[\frac{-\frac{2}{5}u + \frac{4}{5}}{u^2 + 1} - \frac{\frac{9}{5}}{3u + 1} + \frac{1}{u + 1}\right] du$$

$$= \frac{4}{5}\tan^{-1}u - \frac{1}{5}\ln|u^2 + 1| - \frac{3}{5}\ln|3u + 1|$$
$$+ \ln|u + 1| + C$$

$$= \frac{4}{10}x - \frac{1}{5}\ln\left|\tan^2\frac{x}{2} + 1\right|$$
$$- \frac{3}{5}\ln\left|3\tan\frac{x}{2} + 1\right| + \ln\left|\tan\frac{x}{2} + 1\right| + C$$

56. a. $V = \displaystyle\int_0^1 \frac{2\pi x\,dx}{x^2 + 5x + 4}$

$$\approx 0.4177$$

b. $V = \pi\displaystyle\int_0^1 (x^2 + 5x + 4)^{-2}\,dx$

$$\approx 0.0826$$

c. $V = \displaystyle\int_0^1 \frac{2\pi(x + 1)}{x^2 + 5x + 4}\,dx$

$$\approx 1.4021$$

58. $V = \pi \displaystyle\int_0^4 y^2 \, dx$

$= \pi \displaystyle\int_0^4 \dfrac{x^2(4 - x)}{4 + x} \, dx.$

$= \pi \displaystyle\int_0^4 \left(- x^2 + 8x - 32 + \dfrac{128}{x + 4}\right) dx$

$= \pi \left[- \dfrac{x^3}{3} + 4x^2 - 32x + 128 \ln(x + 4)\right]\Bigg|_0^4$

$= \pi \left(- \dfrac{256}{3} + 128 \ln 2\right) \approx 10.648$

60. Substitution:

$\displaystyle\int \dfrac{x \, dx}{x^2 - 9} \qquad \boxed{u = x^2 - 9}$

$= \dfrac{1}{2} \displaystyle\int \dfrac{du}{u}$

$= \dfrac{1}{2} \ln\left| x^2 - 9 \right| + C$

Partial fractions:

$\displaystyle\int \dfrac{x \, dx}{x^2 - 9} = \displaystyle\int \dfrac{dx}{2(x - 3)} + \displaystyle\int \dfrac{dx}{2(x + 3)}$

$= \dfrac{1}{2} \ln\left| x - 3 \right| + \dfrac{1}{2} \ln\left| x + 3 \right| + C$

$= \dfrac{1}{2} \ln\left| x^2 - 9 \right| + C$

Trigonometric substitution:

$\displaystyle\int \dfrac{x \, dx}{x^2 - 9} \qquad \boxed{x = 3 \sin \theta}$

$= \displaystyle\int \dfrac{3 \sin \theta \, (3 \cos \theta \, d\theta)}{9 \sin^2\theta - 9}$

$= - \displaystyle\int \dfrac{\sin \theta}{\cos \theta} \, d\theta$

$= - \displaystyle\int \tan \theta \, d\theta$

$= \ln\left| \cos \theta \right| + C$

$= \ln\sqrt{9 - x^2} + C$

$= \dfrac{1}{2} \ln\left| x^2 - 9 \right| + C$

66. $\displaystyle\int \csc x \, dx = \displaystyle\int \dfrac{dx}{\sin x}$

$\boxed{\text{Weierstrass substitution}}$

$= \displaystyle\int \dfrac{\dfrac{2 \, du}{1 + u^2}}{\dfrac{2u}{1 + u^2}} \, du$

$= \displaystyle\int \dfrac{2 \, du}{2u} = \ln\left| u \right| + C = \ln\left| \tan \dfrac{x}{2} \right| + C$

$= \ln\left| \dfrac{\sin \dfrac{x}{2}}{\cos \dfrac{x}{2}} \right| + C$

$= \ln\left| \dfrac{\cos \dfrac{x}{2} \sin \dfrac{x}{2}}{\cos^2 \dfrac{x}{2}} \right| + C$

$= \ln\left| \dfrac{2 \sin \dfrac{x}{2} \cos \dfrac{x}{2}}{2 \cos^2 \dfrac{x}{2}} \right| + C$

$= \ln \dfrac{\left| \sin x \right|}{\left| 1 + \cos x \right|} + C$

$= - \ln\left| \dfrac{1}{\sin x} + \dfrac{\cos x}{\sin x} \right| + C$

$= - \ln\left| \csc x + \cot x \right| + C$

7.5 Summary of Integration Techniques, Pages 502–503

SURVIVAL HINT: *It would take an unreasonable amount of time to do all the problems in this problem set. However, it would be an excellent use of time for you, or a small study group, to look at each problem and decide **how** to proceed. Identify one or more techniques that look promising.*

5. $\int (e^x \cot e^x)\, dx$ $\boxed{u = e^x;\ du = e^x\, dx}$

$$-\int \cot u\, du$$

$$= \ln|\sin e^x| \ + \ C$$

10. $\int \dfrac{2 + \cos x}{\sin x}\, dx$

$$= 2\int \csc x\, dx + \int \frac{\cos x}{\sin x}\, dx$$

$$= -2\ln|\csc x + \cot x| + \ln|\sin x| + C$$

15. $\int \dfrac{1 + e^x}{1 - e^x}\, dx$

$$= \int \left[-1 + \frac{2}{1 - e^x}\right] dx$$

$$= \int \left[-1 + \frac{2e^{-x}}{e^{-x} - 1}\right] dx \ \boxed{\text{Let } u = e^{-x} - 1}$$

$$= -x + 2\int \frac{-du}{u}$$

$$= -x - 2\ln|e^{-x} - 1| + C$$

20. $\int \dfrac{dx}{4 - e^{-x}} = \dfrac{1}{4}\int \dfrac{4e^x\, dx}{4e^x - 1}$

$$\boxed{u = 4e^x - 1;\ du = 4e^x\, dx}$$

$$= \frac{1}{4}\int \frac{du}{u} = \frac{1}{4}\ln|u| + C$$

$$= \frac{1}{4}\ln|4e^x - 1| + C$$

25. $\int \tan^{-1}x\, dx$ $\boxed{\text{Formula 457}}$

$$= x\tan^{-1}x - \frac{1}{2}\ln(x^2 + 1) + C$$

30. $\int \sin^{-1}2x\, dx$ $\boxed{\text{Parts or Formula 451}}$

$$= x\sin^{-1}2x + \sqrt{\frac{1}{4} - x^2} + C$$

$$= x\sin^{-1}2x + \frac{1}{2}\sqrt{1 - 4x^2} + C$$

35. $\int \sin^2 x \cos^4 x\, dx$

$$= \frac{1}{8}\int (1 - \cos 2x)(1 + \cos 2x)^2\, dx$$

$$= \frac{1}{8}\int (1 - \cos^2 2x)(1 + \cos 2x)\, dx$$

$$= \frac{1}{8}\int \sin^2 2x(1 + \cos 2x)\, dx$$

$$= \frac{1}{8}\int \sin^2 2x\, dx + \frac{1}{8}\int \sin^2 2x\, (\cos 2x)\, dx$$

$$= \frac{1}{16}\left[x - \frac{1}{4}\sin 4x\right] + \frac{1}{16}\cdot\frac{1}{3}\sin^3 2x + C$$

$$= \frac{1}{16}x - \frac{1}{64}\sin 4x + \frac{1}{48}\sin^3 2x + C$$

40. $\displaystyle\int \tan^4 x \sec^4 x \; dx$

$\displaystyle = \int \tan^4 x (\tan^2 x + 1) \sec^2 x \; dx$

$\displaystyle = \int \tan^6 x \sec^2 x \; dx + \int \tan^4 x \sec^2 x \; dx$

$\displaystyle = \tfrac{1}{7} \tan^7 x + \tfrac{1}{5} \tan^5 x + C$

45. $\displaystyle\int \frac{dx}{x\sqrt{x^2 + 1}}$ $\boxed{\text{Formula 176; } x = \tan\theta}$

$\displaystyle = -\ln\left|\frac{1 + \sqrt{x^2 + 1}}{x}\right| + C$

$\displaystyle = \ln|x| - \ln\left|1 + \sqrt{x^2 + 1}\right| + C$

50. $\displaystyle\int \frac{\sec^2 x \; dx}{\sqrt{\sec^2 x - 2}} = \int \frac{\sec^2 x \; dx}{\sqrt{1 + \tan^2 x - 2}}$

$\boxed{u = \tan x; \; du = \sec^2 x \; dx}$

$\displaystyle = \int \frac{du}{\sqrt{u^2 - 1}}$ $\boxed{\text{Formula 196}}$

$\displaystyle = \ln\left|u + \sqrt{u^2 - 1}\right| + C$

$\displaystyle = \ln\left|\tan x + \sqrt{\tan^2 x - 1}\right| + C$

55. $\displaystyle\int_1^2 \frac{dx}{x^4\sqrt{x^2 + 3}} = \int_{x=1}^{x=2} \frac{\sqrt{3}\,\sec^2\theta \; d\theta}{9\tan^4\theta \;\sqrt{3}\,\sec\theta}$

$\boxed{x = \sqrt{3}\tan\theta, \; dx = \sqrt{3}\sec^2\theta \; d\theta}$

$\displaystyle = \frac{1}{9} \int_{x=1}^{x=2} \frac{(1 - \sin^2\theta)(\cos\theta \; d\theta)}{\sin^4\theta}$

$\displaystyle = \tfrac{1}{9}\left[-\tfrac{1}{3}\csc^3\theta + \csc\theta\right]\Big|_{x=1}^{x=2}$

$\displaystyle = \tfrac{1}{9}\left(\frac{\sqrt{3 + x^2}}{x}\right)\left[-\tfrac{1}{3}\frac{3 + x^2}{x^2} + 1\right]\Big|_1^2$

$\displaystyle = \tfrac{1}{9}\left[\frac{\sqrt{7}}{2}\left(-\tfrac{1}{3}\tfrac{7}{4} + 1\right) - 2\left(-\tfrac{1}{3}\cdot 4 + 1\right)\right]$

$\displaystyle = \tfrac{1}{27}(\tfrac{5}{8}\sqrt{7} + 2)$

60. $\displaystyle\int_1^4 \frac{\sqrt{x^2 + 9}}{x^3} \; dx$ $\boxed{\text{Formula 181 or } x = 3\tan\theta}$

$\displaystyle = -\frac{\sqrt{x^2 + 9}}{2x^2} - \frac{1}{2(3)} \ln\left|\frac{3 + \sqrt{x^2 + 9}}{x}\right|\Big|_1^4$

$\displaystyle = -\frac{5}{32} + \frac{\sqrt{10}}{2} + \tfrac{1}{6}\left[\ln(3 + \sqrt{10}) - \ln 2\right]$

≈ 1.61243

65. $\displaystyle\int \frac{e^x \; dx}{\sqrt{1 + e^{2x}}}$ $\boxed{u = e^x; \; du = e^x dx}$

$\displaystyle\int \frac{du}{\sqrt{1 + u^2}} = \ln\left(\sqrt{1 + e^{2x}} + e^x\right) + C$

70. $\displaystyle\int \frac{-3x^2 + 9x + 21}{(x + 2)^2(2x + 1)} \; dx$

$\displaystyle \frac{-3x^2 + 9x + 21}{(x+2)^2(2x+1)} = \frac{A_1}{x + 2} + \frac{A_2}{(x + 2)^2} + \frac{A_3}{2x + 1}$

Partial fraction decomposition gives

$A_1 = -5, A_2 = 3, A_3 = 7.$

$$\int \frac{-3x^2 + 9x + 21}{(x+2)^2(2x+1)}\, dx$$

$$= -5\int \frac{dx}{x+2} + 3\int \frac{dx}{(x+2)^2} + 7\int \frac{dx}{2x+1}$$

$$= -5\ln|x+2| - 3(x+2)^{-1} + \tfrac{7}{2}\ln|2x+1| + C$$

75. $\displaystyle\int \frac{dx}{5\cos x - 12 \sin x}$ $\boxed{\text{Weierstrass substitution}}$

$$= \int \frac{2\, du}{5(1-u^2) - 24u}$$

$$= \int \frac{-2\, du}{5u^2 + 24u - 5}$$

$$\frac{-2}{(u+5)(5u-1)} = \frac{A_1}{u+5} + \frac{A_2}{5u-1}$$

Partial fraction decomposition gives
$A_1 = \tfrac{1}{13},\ A_2 = -\tfrac{5}{13}.$

$$\int \frac{-2\, du}{(u+5)(5u-1)} = \frac{1}{13}\int \frac{du}{u+5} - \frac{5}{13}\int \frac{du}{5u-1}$$

$$= \tfrac{1}{13}\big(\ln|u+5| - \ln|5u-1|\big) + C$$

$$= \tfrac{1}{13}\ln\left|\frac{u+5}{5u-1}\right| + C$$

$$= \tfrac{1}{13}\ln\left|\frac{\tan\frac{x}{2}+5}{5\tan\frac{x}{2}-1}\right| + C$$

80. $\displaystyle V = \pi \int_0^{\pi/2} \cos^2 x\, dx = \pi\left[\frac{x}{2} + \frac14 \sin 2x\right]\Big|_0^{\pi/2}$

$$= \frac{\pi^2}{4}$$

85. $\displaystyle V = \pi \int_0^3 \left(x\sqrt{9-x^2}\right)^2 dx$

$$= \pi \int_0^3 (9x^2 - x^4)\, dx$$

$$= \pi\left[3x^3 - \frac{x^5}{5}\right]\Big|_0^3$$

$$= \frac{162\pi}{5}$$

$$\approx 101.7876$$

90. $\displaystyle\int x^m(\ln x)^n\, dx$ $\boxed{u = (\ln x)^n;\ dv = x^m\, dx}$

$$= \frac{x^{m+1}(\ln x)^n}{m+1} - \frac{n}{m+1}\int x^m(\ln x)^{n-1}\, dx$$

For example,

$$\int x^2(\ln x)^3\, dx = \frac{x^3(\ln x)^3}{3} - \frac33\int x^2(\ln x)^2\, dx$$

$$= \frac{x^3}{3}(\ln x)^3 - \left[\frac{x^3}{3}(\ln x)^2 - \frac23\int x^2\ln x\, dx\right]$$

$$= \frac{x^3}{3}(\ln x)^3 - \frac{x^3}{3}(\ln x)^2 + \frac23\left[\frac{x^3}{3}\ln x - \frac13\int x^2\, dx\right]$$

$$= \frac{x^3}{3}(\ln x)^3 - \frac{x^3}{3}(\ln x)^2 + \frac{2x^3}{9}(\ln x) - \frac{2x^3}{27} + C$$

7.6 First-Order Differential Equations, Pages 512–515

1. $P(x) = \frac{3}{x};\ Q(x) = x;$

$$I(x) = e^{\int \frac{3}{x}\, dx} = e^{3\ln x} = e^{\ln x^3} = x^3$$

$$y = \frac{1}{x^3}\left(\int x(x^3)\ dx + C\right)$$

$$= \frac{1}{x^3}\left(\frac{x^5}{5} + C\right)$$

$$= \frac{1}{5}x^2 + Cx^{-3}$$

5. Divide both sides by x: $\dfrac{dy}{dx} + \dfrac{2}{x}y = e^{x^3}$

$$P(x) = \frac{2}{x};\ Q(x) = e^{x^3};$$

$$I(x) = e^{\int \frac{2}{x}\ dx} = e^{2\ln x} = x^2$$

$$y = \frac{1}{x^2}\left[\int x^2(e^{x^3})\ dx + C\right]$$

$$= \frac{1}{x^2}\left[\frac{1}{3}e^{x^3} + C\right]$$

$$= \frac{1}{3}x^{-2}e^{x^3} + Cx^{-2}$$

11. $P(x) = \dfrac{x}{1+x};\ Q(x) = x(1+x);$

$$I(x) = e^{\int \frac{x}{1+x}\ dx} = e^{x-\ln(x+1)} = \frac{e^x}{x+1}$$

$$y = \frac{x+1}{e^x}\left[\int x(1+x)\cdot\frac{e^x}{1+x}\ dx + C\right]$$

$$= \frac{x+1}{e^x}\left[e^x(x-1) + C\right]$$

$$= x^2 - 1 + C\left(\frac{x+1}{e^x}\right)$$

Since $y = -1$, when $x = 0$, $C = 0$; thus,

$$y = x^2 - 1$$

15.
$$y^2 = 4kx$$

$$2yy' = 4k$$

$$y' = \frac{2k}{y}$$

$$= \frac{2\dfrac{y^2}{4x}}{y}$$

$$= \frac{y}{2x}$$

The slope of the orthogonal trajectory is the negative reciprocal:

$$\frac{dY}{dX} = -\frac{2X}{Y}$$

$$\int Y\ dY = \int -2X\ dX$$

$$\frac{1}{2}Y^2 = -X^2 + K$$

$$2X^2 + Y^2 = C$$

20. Assume the growth rate for the period 1980 to 1992 remained at 2.5%.

$$Q(t) = 1{,}481e^{0.025t}$$

$$Q(12) = 1{,}481e^{12(0.025)}$$

$$\approx 1{,}999.14$$

The predicted GDP is about $2,000 billion. *The 1992 World Almanac and Book of Facts* reports a GNP of $5,465.1 billion. One possible reason for the great discrepancy is that the data in this problem is in 1972 dollars, and the 1992 may be using a different year as a basis.

23. a. Let $Q(t)$ be the amount of salt in the solution at time t (minutes). Then

$$\frac{dQ}{dt} = \underbrace{(1)(2)}_{\text{inflow}} - \underbrace{\frac{Q}{30}(2)}_{\text{outflow}}$$

$$\frac{dQ}{dt} + \frac{Q}{15} = 2$$

Integrating factor is $\exp\left[\int e^{1/15} dt\right] = e^{t/15}$

$$Q(t) = e^{-t/15}\left[\int 2e^{t/15} dt + C\right]$$

$$= e^{-t/15}\left[2\frac{e^{t/15}}{\frac{1}{15}} + C\right] = 30 + Ce^{-t/15}$$

$Q(0) = 10 = 30 + Ce^0$ or $C = -20$

$Q(t) = 30 - 20e^{-t/15}$

b. When $Q = 15$, we have

$$15 = 30 - 20e^{-t/15}$$

$$-\frac{t}{15} = \ln\frac{15}{20}$$

$$t = -15\ln\frac{3}{4} \approx 4.31523 \text{ min}$$

This is about 4 minutes, 19 seconds.

29.
$$\frac{dM}{dt} = r\left(\frac{k}{r} - M\right)$$

$$\frac{dM}{\frac{k}{r} - M} = r\,dt$$

$$-\ln\left|\frac{k}{r} - M\right| = rt + K$$

$$\frac{k}{r} - M = e^{-rt}e^{-K} = Ce^{-rt}$$

$$M(t) = \frac{k}{r} - Ce^{-rt}$$

$M(0) = 0 = \frac{k}{r} - C$, so $C = \frac{k}{r}$

Thus, $M(t) = \frac{k}{r}(1 - e^{-rt})$

31.
$$V = 5h$$

$$\frac{dV}{dt} = 5\frac{dh}{dt}$$

$$-4.8(0.07)\sqrt{h} = 5\frac{dh}{dt} \qquad by \ Toricelli's \ law$$

$$-0.0672\,dt = \frac{1}{\sqrt{h}}\,dh$$

$$2h^{1/2} + C = -0.0672\,t$$

When $t = 0$, $h = 4$, so $4 + C = 0$ or $C = -4$.

$$2h^{1/2} - 4 = -0.0672t$$

When $h = 0$, $t \approx 59.5$.

It will take about an hour to drain.

33. a. We have $y^{iv} = -k$ with $y(0) = y(L) = 0$ and $y''(0) = y''(L) = 0$.

$$y^{iv} = -k$$

$$y''' = -kx + C_1$$

$$y'' = -\frac{k}{2}x^2 + C_1x + C_2$$

$$y' = -\frac{k}{6}x^3 + \frac{C_1}{2}x^2 + C_2x + C_3$$

$$y = -\frac{k}{24}x^4 + \frac{C_1}{6}x^3 + \frac{C_2}{2}x^2 + C_3x + C_4$$

Since $y(0) = 0$, and $y''(0) = 0$, we have $C_4 = 0$ and $C_2 = 0$, and the conditions $y(L) = 0$ and $y''(L) = 0$ tell us that

$$-\frac{kL^4}{24} + \frac{C_1 L^3}{6} + C_3 L = 0$$

$$-\frac{kL^2}{2} + C_1 L = 0$$

$$C_1 = \frac{kL}{2}$$

Thus, $C_3 = -\frac{kL^3}{24}$, so

$$y = -\frac{k}{24}(x^4 - 2Lx^3 + L^3 x)$$

b. Maximum deflection occurs where $y' = 0$. Solve

$$y' = -\frac{k}{24}[4x^3 - 6Lx^2 + L^3] = 0$$

to obtain $x = L/2$; reject $(1 \pm \sqrt{3})L/2$ because these points lie outside the interval $[0, L]$. This maximum deflection since y is minimized at $x = L/2$; note $y''(L/2) = kL^2/8 > 0$. The maximum deflection is

$$y_m = y(L/2) = -\frac{k}{24}\left[\frac{L^4}{16} - 2L\left(\frac{L^3}{8}\right) + L^3\left(\frac{L}{2}\right)\right]$$

$$\approx -0.0130kL^4$$

c. For a cantilevered beam, we have

$$y = -\frac{k}{24}x^4 + \frac{C_1}{6}x^3 + \frac{C_2}{2}x^2 + C_3 x + C_4$$

with boundary conditions $y(0) = y(L) = 0$ and $y''(0) = y'(L) = 0$. The conditions $y(0) = 0$ and $y''(0) = 0$ imply

$$C_2 = C_4 = 0,$$

and the other two conditions yield

$C_1 = \frac{3}{8}kL$ and $C_3 = -\frac{1}{48}kL^3$.

Thus,

$$y = -\frac{k}{48}(2x^4 - 3Lx^3 + L^3 x)$$

To find where maximum deflection occurs, we find

$$y' = -\frac{k}{48}(8x^3 - 9Lx^2 + L^3)$$

$y' = 0$ when $x = L, \left(\dfrac{1 \pm \sqrt{33}}{16}\right)L$

Checking, we find that the maximum deflection occurs at

$$x = \left(\frac{1 + \sqrt{33}}{16}\right)L \approx 0.4215L$$

and the maximum deflection is

$$y_m = y(0.4215L) \approx -0.0054kL^4$$

The maximum deflection in the cantilevered case is less than that in part **b.**

38. **a.** We start with $U(0) = U_0$ of uranium and $T(0) = 0$ of thorium. Then,

$$\frac{dU}{dt} = -k_1 U$$

$$U(t) = U_0 e^{-k_1 t}$$

Now

$$\frac{dT}{dt} = -k_2 T + k_1 U_0 e^{-k_1 t}$$

$$\frac{dT}{dt} + k_2 T = k_1 U_0 e^{-k_1 t}$$

The integrating factor is

$$I(t) = e^{\int k_2 \, dt} = e^{k_2 t}$$

so

$$T = e^{-k_2 t} \left[\int e^{k_2 t}(k_1 U_0 e^{-k_1 t}) \, dt + C \right]$$

$$= e^{-k_2 t} \left[\frac{k_1 U_0}{k_2 - k_1} e^{(k_2 - k_1)t} + C \right]$$

$$= \frac{k_1 U_0}{k_2 - k_1} e^{-k_1 t} + C e^{-k_2 t}$$

Since $T(0) = 0$, we have

$$0 = \frac{k_1 U_0}{k_2 - k_1} + C; \; C = \frac{-k_1 U_0}{k_2 - k_1}$$

and

$$T(t) = \frac{k_1 U_0}{k_2 - k_1} \left(e^{-k_1 t} - e^{-k_2 t} \right)$$

b. $U_0 = 100$ and since the half-lives of the uranium and thorium are 2.48×10^5 and $80,000$, respectively, we have

$$k_1 = \frac{-\ln \frac{1}{2}}{2.48 \times 10^5}$$

$$\approx 2.79 \times 10^{-6}$$

$$k_2 = \frac{-\ln \frac{1}{2}}{80,000}$$

$$\approx 8.66 \times 10^{-6}$$

After $t = 5,000$ years

$$T(5,000) \approx 1.3557 \text{ g}$$

43. Let $Q(t)$ be the amount of pollutant in the lake at time t. Then

$$\frac{dQ}{dt} = (0.0006)(350) - \frac{Q}{6,000}(350)$$

where units are in millions of ft^3. Thus, $\frac{dQ}{dt} + 0.0583 Q = 0.21$. The integrating factor is

$$I(t) = e^{\int 0.0583 \, dt} = e^{0.0583 t}$$

so

$$Q(t) = e^{-0.0583 t} \left[\int e^{0.0583 t}(0.21) \, dt + C \right]$$

$$= 3.602 + C e^{-0.0583 t}$$

Since the lake initially contains $Q(0) \approx 13.2$ million cubic feet of pollutant, we find $C \approx 9.598$, so

$$Q(t) = 3.602 + 9.598 e^{-0.0583 t}$$

The lake will contain 0.15% pollutant when

$$0.0015(6,000) = 3.602 + 9.598 e^{-0.0583 t}$$

Solving this equation, we obtain $t \approx 9.872$ days.

46.

$$\frac{dS}{dt} = -pS + \left(\frac{S}{N} \right) \frac{dN}{dt} + \frac{pS^2}{mN}$$

Let $y = \frac{S}{N}$, so $S = yN$ and the differential equation becomes

$$\frac{dS}{dt} = -pS + y \frac{dN}{dt} + \frac{pS}{m} \left(\frac{S}{N} \right)$$

$$\frac{d(yN)}{dt} = -pS + y \frac{dN}{dt} + \frac{pS}{m} \left(\frac{S}{N} \right)$$

$$y \frac{dN}{dt} + N \frac{dy}{dt} = -pS + y \frac{dN}{dt} + \frac{pS}{m} \left(\frac{S}{N} \right)$$

$$N \frac{dy}{dt} = -pS + \frac{pS}{m} y$$

$$\frac{dy}{dt} = -py + \frac{p}{m} y \left(\frac{S}{N} \right)$$

$$\frac{dy}{dt} + py = \frac{p}{m} y^2$$

This is a Bernoulli equation (see Problem 44).

Let $u = y^{1-2} = y^{-1}$. Then

$$y = \frac{1}{u} \text{ and } \frac{dy}{dt} = \frac{-1}{u^2} \frac{du}{dt}$$

and the differential equation is

$$-\frac{1}{u^2} \frac{du}{dt} + p\left(\frac{1}{u}\right) = \frac{p}{m}\left(\frac{1}{u}\right)^2$$

$$\frac{du}{dt} - pu = \frac{-p}{m}$$

The integrating factor is

$$I(t) = e^{\int -p \, dt} = e^{-pt}$$

so $\quad u = e^{pt}\left[\int \left(\frac{-p}{m}\right)e^{-pt} \, dt + C\right]$

$$= \frac{1}{m} + Ce^{pt}$$

and since $u = \frac{1}{y} = \frac{N}{S}$, we have

$$\frac{N}{S} = \frac{1}{m} + Ce^{pt}$$

$$N = \left(\frac{1}{m} + Ce^{pt}\right)S$$

7.7 Improper Integrals, Pages 524-525

5. $\displaystyle\int_{1}^{+\infty} \frac{dx}{x^{0.99}} = \lim_{N \to +\infty} \int_{1}^{N} \frac{dx}{x^{0.99}}$

$$= 100 \lim_{N \to +\infty} x^{0.01}\Big|_{1}^{N}$$

$$= 100 \lim_{N \to +\infty} (N^{0.01} - 1)$$

$$= +\infty; \text{ diverges}$$

10. $\displaystyle\int_{3}^{+\infty} \frac{dx}{\sqrt[3]{2x-1}} = \frac{1}{2} \lim_{N \to +\infty} \int_{3}^{N} (2x-1)^{-1/3}(2 \, dx)$

$$= \frac{3}{4} \lim_{N \to +\infty} (2x - 1)^{2/3}\Big|_{3}^{N}$$

$$= +\infty; \text{ diverges}$$

15. $\displaystyle\int_{1}^{+\infty} \frac{x^2 \, dx}{(x^3 + 2)^2} = \frac{1}{3} \lim_{N \to +\infty} \int_{1}^{N} \frac{3x^2 \, dx}{(x^3 + 2)^2}$

$$= \lim_{N \to +\infty} \frac{1}{3}\left(-\frac{1}{x^3 + 2}\right)\Big|_{1}^{N}$$

$$= \lim_{N \to \infty} \left(-\frac{1}{3N^3 + 6} + \frac{1}{9}\right)$$

$$= \frac{1}{9}$$

20. $\displaystyle\int_{0}^{+\infty} xe^{-x} \, dx \quad \boxed{u = x; \; dv = e^{-x} \, dx}$

$$= \lim_{N \to +\infty}\left[-xe^{-x} - e^{-x}\Big|_{0}^{N}\right]$$

$$= \lim_{N \to +\infty} (-e^{-x})\Big|_{0}^{N}$$

$$= 1$$

Note: $\displaystyle\lim_{x \to +\infty} \frac{x}{e^x} = \lim_{x \to +\infty} \frac{1}{e^x} = 0$

by l'Hôpital's rule.

25. $\displaystyle\int_0^{+\infty} x^2 e^{-x}\,dx$ $\boxed{\text{Parts or Formula 485}}$

$\displaystyle = \lim_{N\to+\infty} \frac{e^{-x}}{-1}\left(x^2 - \frac{2x}{-1} + \frac{2}{1}\right)\Big|_0^N$

$\displaystyle = \lim_{N\to+\infty}\left[2 - e^{-N}(N^2 + 2N + 2)\right]$

$= 2$

30. $\displaystyle\int_{-\infty}^4 \frac{dx}{(5-x)^2} = \lim_{t\to-\infty}\int_t^4 (5-x)^{-2}\,dx$

$\displaystyle = \lim_{t\to-\infty} \frac{1}{5-x}\Big|_t^4$

$= 1$

35. $\displaystyle\int_0^1 \frac{dx}{(1-x)^{1/2}} = \lim_{N\to1^-}\int_0^N (1-x)^{-1/2}\,dx$

$\displaystyle = -2\lim_{N\to1^-}\sqrt{1-x}\,\Big|_0^N$

$\displaystyle = \lim_{N\to1^-} -2(\sqrt{1-N} - 1)$

$= 2$

40. $\displaystyle\int_0^1 \frac{x\,dx}{1-x^2} = -\frac{1}{2}\lim_{t\to1^-}\ln|1-x^2|\,\Big|_0^t$

$= +\infty;\ \text{diverges}$

45. $\displaystyle A = \lim_{T\to+\infty}\int_0^T 200e^{-0.002t}\,dt$

$\displaystyle = -100{,}000 \lim_{T\to+\infty} e^{-0.002t}\Big|_0^T$

$= 100{,}000$

There will be 100,000 millirads.

50. $\displaystyle I = \int_0^{1/2} \frac{dx}{x(\ln x)^p}$

$\displaystyle = \lim_{t\to0^+}\int_t^{1/2} (\ln x)^{-p}\,\frac{dx}{x}$

$\displaystyle = \lim_{t\to0^+} \frac{(\ln x)^{-p+1}}{1-p}\Big|_t^{1/2}$

$\displaystyle = \lim_{t\to0^+} \frac{1}{(1-p)(\ln x)^{p-1}}\Big|_t^{1/2}$

$\displaystyle = (1-p)^{-1}(-\ln 2)^{1-p}$

converges if $p > 1$, and diverges if $p \le 1$.

If $0 \le x < 1$, then p must be an integer for $\ln x < 0$.

54. $\displaystyle \mathcal{L}\{f(x)\} = \lim_{N\to+\infty}\int_0^N e^{-st}f(t)\,dt$

a. $\displaystyle \mathcal{L}\{e^{at}\} = \lim_{N\to+\infty}\int_0^N e^{(a-s)t}\,dt$

$\displaystyle = \frac{1}{a-s}\lim_{N\to+\infty} e^{(a-s)t}\,dt\Big|_0^N$

$\displaystyle = -\frac{1}{a-s}$

$\displaystyle = \frac{1}{s-a}\ \text{since}\ s - a > 0$

b. $\displaystyle \mathcal{L}\{a\} = \lim_{N\to+\infty} -\frac{a}{s}\int_0^N e^{-st}(-s\,dt)$

$$= \lim_{N \to +\infty} -\frac{a}{s} e^{-st} \Big|_0^N$$

$$= \frac{a}{s}$$

c. $\quad \mathcal{L}\{t\} = \lim_{N \to +\infty} \int_0^N t e^{-st} \, dt$

$$= \lim_{N \to +\infty} \left[\frac{-st - 1}{s^2} e^{-t} \right] \Big|_0^N$$

$$= \lim_{N \to +\infty} \left[\frac{-sN - 1}{s^2} e^{-N} + \frac{1}{s^2} \right]$$

$$= \frac{1}{s^2}$$

d. $\quad \mathcal{L}\{t^n\} = \lim_{N \to +\infty} \int_0^N t^n e^{-st} \, dt$

$$= \lim_{N \to +\infty} \left[\frac{-e^{-st} t^n}{s} \right] \Big|_0^N$$

$$+ \frac{n}{s} \int_0^{+\infty} t^{n-1} e^{-st} \, dt$$

$$= 0 + \frac{n}{s} \mathcal{L}\{t^{n-1}\} \qquad \begin{array}{l} L'H\widehat{o}pital's \\ rule \ used \ n \\ times \end{array}$$

Continuing in this fashion, we obtain

$$\mathcal{L}\{t^n\} = \left(\frac{n}{s}\right)\left(\frac{n-1}{s}\right) \cdots \left(\frac{1}{s}\right) \mathcal{L}\{1\}$$

$$= \frac{n!\, 1}{s^n}\left(\frac{1}{s}\right)$$

$$= \frac{n!}{s^{n+1}}$$

e. $\quad \mathcal{L}\{\cos at\} = \int_0^{+\infty} e^{-st} \cos at \, dt$

$$= \lim_{N \to +\infty} \frac{(-s \cos at + a \sin at) e^{-st}}{s^2 + a^2} \Big|_0^N$$

$$= \lim_{N \to +\infty} \frac{(-s \cos aN + a \sin aN) e^{-sN}}{s^2 + a^2}$$

$$- \frac{-s}{s^2 + a^2} = \frac{s}{s^2 + a^2}$$

f. $\quad \mathcal{L}\{\sin at\} = \int_0^{+\infty} e^{-st} \sin at \, dt$

$$= \lim_{N \to +\infty} \frac{(-s \sin at - a \cos at) e^{-st}}{s^2 + a^2} \Big|_0^N$$

$$= \lim_{N \to +\infty} \frac{(-s \sin aN - a \cos aN) e^{-sN}}{s^2 + a^2}$$

$$- \frac{-a}{s^2 + a^2}$$

$$= \frac{a}{s^2 + a^2}$$

7.8 The Hyperbolic and Inverse Hyperbolic Functions, Pages 532-533

SURVIVAL HINT: *The hyperbolic functions are good news and bad news. The good news is that the identities, derivatives, and integrals are **almost** the same as the trigonometric functions. The bad news is the **almost**. Try to learn these function definitions by concentrating on which one are different by a sign.*

3. $\tan 2 = \dfrac{e^2 - e^{-2}}{e^2 + e^{-2}}$

$$\approx -0.7616$$

11. $\text{sech } 1 = \dfrac{2}{e^1 + e^{-1}}$

≈ 0.6481

15. $y' = (4x + 3)\sinh(2x^2 + 3x)$

20. $y' = \tanh^{-1}(3x) + x\left(\dfrac{3}{1 - 9x^2}\right)$

$= \tanh^{-1}(3x) + \dfrac{3x}{1 - 9x^2}$

SURVIVAL HINT: *We will not provide alternate solutions, but we provided one for this problem to illustrate answers you might obtain if you use a CAS programs.*

Alternately, $y = x\tanh^{-1}(3x) = \dfrac{x}{2}\ln\dfrac{1 + 3x}{1 - 3x}$

$y' = \dfrac{1}{2}\left[\ln\dfrac{1 + 3x}{1 - 3x}\right] + \dfrac{x}{2}\left[\dfrac{3}{1 + 3x} - \dfrac{-3}{1 - 3x}\right]$

$= \dfrac{1}{2}\ln\dfrac{1 + 3x}{1 - 3x} + \dfrac{3x}{1 - 9x^2}$

24. $y' = \text{sech}\left[\dfrac{1 - x}{1 + x}\right]\tanh\left[\dfrac{1 - x}{1 + x}\right]\left(\dfrac{-(1 + x) - (1 - x)}{(1 + x)^2}\right)$

$= \dfrac{-2}{(1 + x)^2}\,\text{sech}\left[\dfrac{1 - x}{1 + x}\right]\tanh\left[\dfrac{1 - x}{1 + x}\right]$

28. $\qquad x\cosh y = y\sinh x + 5$

$x(\sinh y)y' + \cosh y = y\cosh x + (\sinh x)y'$

$(x\sinh y - \sinh x)y' = y\cosh x - \cosh y$

$y' = \dfrac{y\cosh x - \cosh y}{x\sinh y - \sinh x}$

31. $\displaystyle\int\dfrac{\sinh\frac{1}{x}\,dx}{x^2} = -\int\sinh(x^{-1})(-x^{-2}\,dx)$

$= -\cosh x^{-1} + C$

36. $\displaystyle\int\dfrac{dt}{36 - 16t^2} = \dfrac{1}{36}\int\dfrac{dt}{1 - \left(\frac{4t}{6}\right)^2}$

$= \dfrac{3}{2(36)}\int\dfrac{\left(\frac{2\,dt}{3}\right)}{1 - \left(\frac{2t}{3}\right)^2}$

$= \dfrac{1}{24}\tanh^{-1}\dfrac{2t}{3} + C$

45. $\displaystyle\int_0^1 x\,\text{sech}^2 x^2\,dx = \dfrac{1}{2}\int_0^1 \text{sech}^2 x^2\,(2x\,dx)$

$= \dfrac{1}{2}\tanh x^2\Big|_0^1$

$= \dfrac{1}{2}\tanh 1$

≈ 0.3808

55. $s = \displaystyle\int_{-a}^{a}\sqrt{1 + (y')^2}\,dx$

$= 2\displaystyle\int_0^a\sqrt{1 + \sinh^2\dfrac{x}{a}}\,dx$

$= 2a\displaystyle\int_0^a\cosh\dfrac{x}{a}\left(\dfrac{1}{a}\,dx\right)$

$= 2a\sinh\dfrac{x}{a}\Big|_0^a$

$= 2a(\sinh 1 - \sinh 0)$

$= (e - e^{-1})a \approx 2.3504a$

61. **a.** $y = \cosh^{-1} x$, so $x = \cosh y = \dfrac{e^y + e^{-y}}{2}$

$$x = \frac{e^y + e^{-y}}{2}$$

$$2x = e^y + e^{-y}$$

$$e^{2y} - 2xe^y + 1 = 0$$

$$e^y = \frac{2x \pm \sqrt{4x^2 - 4}}{2}$$

Reject negative choice since it corresponds to the second branch of solution $y = \cosh^{-1} x$. Thus,

$$y = \ln(x + \sqrt{x^2 - 1})$$

b. $$x = \tanh y$$

$$x = \frac{e^y - e^{-y}}{e^y + e^{-y}}$$

$$xe^y + xe^{-y} = e^y - e^{-y}$$

$$e^y(x - 1) = -e^{-y}(x + 1)$$

$$e^{2y} = \frac{1 + x}{1 - x}$$

$$2y = \ln \frac{1 + x}{1 - x}$$

$$y = \tfrac{1}{2} \ln \frac{1 + x}{1 - x}$$

Thus $\tan^{-1} x = \tfrac{1}{2} \ln \dfrac{1 + x}{1 - x}$

CHAPTER 7 REVIEW

Proficiency Examination, Page 533

SURVIVAL HINT: *To help you review the concepts of this chapter,* **hand write** *the answers to each of these questions onto your own paper.*

1. Let u replace a more complicated expression in the variable of integration, say x. Obtain all forms of x in terms of u. Substitute, integrate, return form of answers from u back to x. In the case of a definite integral transform the limits of x into limits for u and evaluate using the fundamental theorem.

2. $\displaystyle\int u \, dv = uv - \int v \, du$

3. A reduction integration formula expresses an integral involving a power of a particular function in terms of an integral involving a lower power of the same function. By using the formula repeatedly, the given integral can be reduced to one that is more manageable.

4. **a.** A trigonometric substitution may be handy when the integrand contains one of the following forms:

$$\sqrt{x^2 + a^2}$$

$$\sqrt{x^2 - a^2}$$

$$\sqrt{a^2 - x^2}$$

b. The Weierstrass substitutions are:
$u = \tan \frac{x}{2}$, $\sin x = \dfrac{2u}{1 + u^2}$;

$\cos x = \dfrac{1 - u^2}{1 + u^2}$, and $dx = \dfrac{2 \, du}{1 + u^2}$.

5. The method of partial fractions may be handy when integrating a rational function.

6. Sec Pages 499-500:

Step 1: simplify

Step 2: use basic formulas (check table)

Step 3: substitute

Step 4: classify; parts, trig powers,

Weierstrass substitution, trig

substitutions, or partial fractions

Step 5: try again

7. Equations that can be expressed in the form

$$\frac{dy}{dx} + P(x)y = Q(x)$$

are called first-order linear differential equations. The general solution is given by

$$y = \frac{1}{I(x)}\left[\int Q(x)I(x)\ dx + C\right]$$

where $I(x) = e^{\int P(x)dx}$.

8. An improper integral is one in which a limit of integration is infinite and/or at least one value in the interval of integration leads to an undefined integrand.

9. $\sinh x = \frac{1}{2}(e^x - e^{-x})$;

$\cosh x = \frac{1}{2}(e^x + e^{-x})$;

$\tanh x = \dfrac{e^x - e^{-x}}{e^x + e^{-x}}$

10. Let u be a differentiable function of x. Then:

$$\frac{d}{dx}(\sinh u) = \cosh u \frac{du}{dx}$$

$$\frac{d}{dx}(\cosh u) = \sinh u \frac{du}{dx}$$

$$\frac{d}{dx}(\tanh u) = \text{sech}^2 u \frac{du}{dx}$$

$$\frac{d}{dx}(\coth u) = -\text{csch}^2 u \frac{du}{dx}$$

$$\frac{d}{dx}(\text{sech } u) = -\text{sech } u \tanh u \frac{du}{dx}$$

$$\frac{d}{dx}(\text{csch } u) = -\text{csch } u \coth u \frac{du}{dx}$$

$$\int \sinh x\ dx = \cosh x + C$$

$$\int \cosh x\ dx = \sinh x + C$$

$$\int \text{sech}^2 x\ dx = \tanh x + C$$

$$\int \text{csch}^2 x\ dx = -\coth x + C$$

$$\int \text{sech } x \tanh x\ dx = -\text{sech } x + C$$

$$\int \text{csch } x \coth x\ dx = -\text{csch } x + C$$

11. $\sinh^{-1}x = \ln(x + \sqrt{x^2 + 1})$, all x

$$\text{csch}^{-1}x = \ln\left(\frac{1}{x} + \frac{\sqrt{1 + x^2}}{|x|}\right),\ x \neq 0$$

$$\cosh^{-1}x = \ln(x + \sqrt{x^2 - 1}),\ x \geq 1$$

$$\text{sech}^{-1}x = \ln\left(\frac{1 + \sqrt{1 - x^2}}{x}\right),\ 0 < x \leq 1$$

$$\tanh^{-1}x = \frac{1}{2}\ln\frac{1 + x}{1 - x},\ |x| < 1$$

$$\coth^{-1} x = \tfrac{1}{2} \ln \frac{x+1}{x-1}, \ |x| > 1$$

12. $\dfrac{d}{dx}(\sinh^{-1} u) = \dfrac{1}{\sqrt{1+u^2}} \dfrac{du}{dx}$

$\dfrac{d}{dx}(\cosh^{-1} u) = \dfrac{1}{\sqrt{u^2-1}} \dfrac{du}{dx}$

$\dfrac{d}{dx}(\tanh^{-1} u) = \dfrac{1}{1-u^2} \dfrac{du}{dx}$

$\dfrac{d}{dx}(\operatorname{csch}^{-1} u) = \dfrac{-1}{|u|\sqrt{1+u^2}}$

$\dfrac{d}{dx}(\operatorname{sech}^{-1} u) = \dfrac{-1}{u\sqrt{1-u^2}} \dfrac{du}{dx}$

$\dfrac{d}{dx}(\coth^{-1} u) = \dfrac{1}{1-u^2} \dfrac{du}{dx}$

$\displaystyle\int \dfrac{du}{\sqrt{1+u^2}} = \sinh^{-1} u + C$

$\displaystyle\int \dfrac{du}{\sqrt{u^2-1}} = \cosh^{-1} u + C$

$\displaystyle\int \dfrac{du}{1-u^2} = \tanh^{-1} u + C$

$\displaystyle\int \dfrac{du}{u\sqrt{1+u^2}} = -\operatorname{csch}^{-1}|u| + C$

$\displaystyle\int \dfrac{du}{u\sqrt{1-u^2}} = -\operatorname{sech}^{-1}|u| + C$

$\displaystyle\int \dfrac{du}{1-u^2} = \coth^{-1} u + C$

15. $\displaystyle\int x \sin 2x \, dx \quad \boxed{u = x; \ dv = \sin 2x \, dx}$

$$= -\tfrac{x}{2} \cos 2x - \int -\tfrac{1}{2} \cos 2x \, dx$$

$$= -\tfrac{x}{2} \cos 2x + \tfrac{1}{4} \sin 2x + C$$

18. $\dfrac{x^2}{(x^2+1)(x-1)} = \dfrac{A_1 x + B_1}{x^2+1} + \dfrac{A_2}{x-1}$

Partial fraction decomposition gives

$A_1 = \tfrac{1}{2}, \ A_2 = \tfrac{1}{2}, \ B_1 = \tfrac{1}{2}.$

$\displaystyle\int \dfrac{x^2 \, dx}{(x^2+1)(x-1)} = \tfrac{1}{2}\int \dfrac{x+1}{x^2+1}\, dx + \tfrac{1}{2}\int \dfrac{dx}{x-1}$

$= \tfrac{1}{4}\displaystyle\int \dfrac{2x\, dx}{x^2+1} + \tfrac{1}{2}\int \dfrac{dx}{x^2+1} + \tfrac{1}{2}\int \dfrac{dx}{x-1}$

$= \tfrac{1}{4}\ln(x^2+1) + \tfrac{1}{2}\tan^{-1} x + \tfrac{1}{2}\ln|x-1| + C$

21. $\dfrac{1}{(x-1)^2(x+2)} = \dfrac{A_1}{(x-1)^2} + \dfrac{A_2}{x-1} + \dfrac{A_3}{x+2}$

Partial fraction decomposition gives

$A_1 = \tfrac{1}{3}, \ A_2 = -\tfrac{1}{9}, \ A_3 = \tfrac{1}{9}$

$\displaystyle\int_2^3 \dfrac{dx}{(x-1)^2(x+2)}$

$= \tfrac{1}{9}\displaystyle\int_2^3 \left(\dfrac{3}{(x-1)^2} - \dfrac{1}{x-1} + \dfrac{1}{x+2} \right) dx$

$= \tfrac{1}{9}\left[-\dfrac{3}{x-1} - \ln(x-1) + \ln(x+2) \right]\Big|_2^3$

$= \tfrac{1}{9}\left(\ln \tfrac{5}{8} + \tfrac{3}{2} \right) \approx 0.1144$

24. $\lim\limits_{t\to+\infty} \int\limits_0^t x e^{-2x}\,dx$ $\boxed{\text{use parts or Formula 484}}$

$$= \lim_{t\to+\infty} -\frac{x}{2}\,e^{-2x} - \frac{1}{4}\,e^{-2x}\Big|_0^t$$

$$= \lim_{t\to+\infty}\left[-\frac{1}{4}\,e^{-2t}(2t+1) + \frac{1}{4}\right]$$

$$= \frac{1}{4}$$

27. $\int\limits_0^{+\infty} e^{-x}\sin x\,dx = \lim\limits_{t\to+\infty} \int\limits_0^t e^{-x}\sin x\,dx$

$\boxed{\text{Formula 492}}$

$$= \lim_{t\to+\infty}\left[\frac{e^{-x}(-\sin x - \cos x)}{2}\Big|_0^t\right]$$

$$= \lim_{t\to+\infty}\left[\frac{e^{-t}(-\sin t - \cos t)}{2} + \frac{1}{2}\right]$$

$$= \frac{1}{2}$$

30. $\dfrac{dy}{dx} + \left(\dfrac{x}{x+1}\right)y = e^{-x}$

$$P(x) = \frac{x}{x+1};\ Q(x) = e^{-x}$$

$$I(x) = e^{\int x/(x+1)\,dx} = \frac{e^x}{x+1}$$

$$y = \frac{x+1}{e^x}\left[\int \frac{e^x}{x+1}(e^{-x})\,dx + C\right]$$

$$= \left(\frac{x+1}{e^x}\right)\!\left[\ln|x+1| + C\right]$$

Since $y = 1$ when $x = 0$, $C = 1$; thus,

$$y = \frac{x+1}{e^x}(\ln|x+1| + 1)$$

CHAPTER 8

Infinite Series

8.1 Sequences and Their Limits, Pages 550-551

3. We use the general term $1 + (-1)^n$ as a formula:

If $n = 1$: $\quad 1 + (-1)^1 = 0$

$n = 2$: $\quad 1 + (-1)^2 = 2$

$n = 3$: $\quad 1 + (-1)^3 = 0$

$n = 4$: $\quad 1 + (-1)^4 = 2$

$n = 5$: $\quad 1 + (-1)^5 = 0$

The sequence is $0, 2, 0, 2, 0, \cdots$

7. Use the formula $\dfrac{3n + 1}{n + 2}$:

if $n = 1$: $\quad \dfrac{3(1) + 1}{1 + 2} = \dfrac{4}{3}$

$n = 2$: $\quad \dfrac{3(2) + 1}{2 + 2} = \dfrac{7}{4}$

$n = 3$: $\quad \dfrac{3(3) + 1}{3 + 2} = \dfrac{10}{5} = 2$

$n = 4$: $\quad \dfrac{3(4) + 1}{4 + 2} = \dfrac{13}{6}$

$n = 5$: $\quad \dfrac{3(5) + 1}{5 + 2} = \dfrac{16}{7}$

The sequence is $\frac{4}{3}, \frac{7}{4}, 2, \frac{13}{6}, \frac{16}{7}, \cdots$

11. Use the formula $a_n = a_{n-1}^2 + a_{n-1} + 1$

if $n = 1$, $a_1 = 1$ is given

if $n = 2$: $a_2 = 1^2 + 1 + 1 = 3$ for $a_1 = 1$

$n = 3$: $a_3 = 3^2 + 3 + 1 = 13$ for $a_2 = 3$

$n = 4$: $a_4 = 13^2 + 13 + 1 = 183$ for $a_3 = 13$

$n = 5$: $a_5 = 183^2 + 183 + 1 = 33{,}673$

The sequence is $1, 3, 13, 183, 33{,}673, \cdots$

SURVIVAL HINT: *Many limits (such as those in Problems 12-19) can be evaluated by multiplying by 1, written as*

where k is the largest power of n in the expression. For example, in Problem 16 (shown below) we multiply by 1 written as

16. $\lim\limits_{n\to\infty} \dfrac{8n^2 + 800n + 5{,}000}{2n^2 - 1{,}000n + 2}$

$$= \lim\limits_{n\to\infty} \dfrac{8 + \dfrac{800}{n} + \dfrac{5{,}000}{n^2}}{2 - \dfrac{1{,}000}{n} + \dfrac{2}{n^2}}$$

$$= \dfrac{8}{2}$$

$$= 4$$

SURVIVAL HINT: *L'Hôpital's rule can be used as an alternate method for Problem 16:*

$$\lim\limits_{n\to\infty} \dfrac{8n^2 + 800n + 5{,}000}{2n^2 - 1{,}000n + 2} = \lim\limits_{n\to\infty} \dfrac{16n + 800}{4n - 1{,}000}$$

$$= \lim\limits_{n\to\infty} \dfrac{16}{4} = 4$$

Never use l'Hôpital's rule without first verifying that the limit has the form 0/0 or ∞/∞.

23. l'Hôpital's rule:

$$\lim\limits_{n\to\infty} \dfrac{\ln n}{n^2} = \lim\limits_{n\to\infty} \dfrac{\dfrac{1}{n}}{2n}$$

$$= \lim\limits_{n\to\infty} \dfrac{1}{2n^2}$$

$$= 0$$

26. $\lim\limits_{n\to\infty} \left(1 + \dfrac{3}{n}\right)^n$

$$= \left[\lim\limits_{n\to\infty}\left(1 + \dfrac{3}{n}\right)^{n/3}\right]^3 \quad \text{Let } \dfrac{1}{t} = \dfrac{3}{n}$$

$$= \left[\lim\limits_{t\to\infty}\left(1 + \dfrac{1}{t}\right)^t\right]^3$$

$$= e^3$$

Alternatively you can let $L = \lim\limits_{n\to\infty} \left(1 + \dfrac{3}{n}\right)^n$

and find $\ln L = 3$, so $L = e^3$.

27. l'Hôpital's rule is used:

Let $L = \lim\limits_{n\to\infty} (n + 4)^{1/n}$

$$\ln L = \lim\limits_{n\to\infty} \dfrac{\ln(n + 4)}{n}$$

$$= \lim\limits_{n\to\infty} \dfrac{\dfrac{1}{n+4}}{1}$$

$$= 0$$

$$L = e^0 = 1$$

30. $\lim\limits_{n\to\infty} \displaystyle\int_0^\infty e^{-nx}\, dx$

$$= \lim\limits_{n\to\infty}\left[\lim\limits_{t\to\infty}\int_0^t e^{-nx}\, dx\right]$$

$$= \lim\limits_{n\to\infty}\left[\lim\limits_{t\to\infty}\left(\dfrac{e^{-nt}}{-n} + \dfrac{1}{n}\right)\right]$$

$$= \lim\limits_{n\to\infty}\left[0 + \dfrac{1}{n}\right]$$

$$= 0$$

31. $\lim\limits_{n\to\infty} \left(\sqrt{n^2 + n} - n\right)$

$$= \lim\limits_{n\to\infty} \dfrac{(\sqrt{n^2 + n} - n)(\sqrt{n^2 + n} + n)}{\sqrt{n^2 + n} + n}$$

$$= \lim\limits_{n\to\infty} \dfrac{n^2 + n - n^2}{\sqrt{n^2 + n} + n}$$

$$= \lim_{n \to \infty} \frac{n}{\sqrt{n^2 + n} + n}$$

$$= \lim_{n \to \infty} \frac{1}{\sqrt{1 + \frac{1}{n}} + 1}$$

$$= \frac{1}{2}$$

37. The elements of $\{a_n\} = \left\{ \ln\left(\frac{n+1}{n}\right) \right\}$

lie on the curve $f(x) = \ln(x+1) - \ln x$.

$f'(x) = (x+1)^{-1} - x^{-1} < 0$. Thus, $f(x)$

and $\{a_n\}$ are both decreasing. $M = 0$ is a

lower bound of the sequence (the elements are

positive since $\ln(n+1) > \ln n$), so $\{a_n\}$

converges.

41. The elements of $\{a_n\} = \{ \sqrt[n]{n} \}$ lie on the

curve

$$f(x) = \sqrt[x]{x} = \exp[\ln x^{1/x}]$$

$$= \exp[x^{-1} \ln x].$$

$f'(x) = \exp[\frac{\ln x}{x}](x^{-2} - x^{-2} \ln x) < 0$ (when

$e < x$). Note: if you use technology for the

derivative you may obtain the following

equivalent form: $f'(x) = x^{(1-2x)/x}(1 - \ln x)$

Thus, $f(x)$ and $\{a_n\}$ are both decreasing. M

$= 0$ is a lower bound of the sequence since

$n^{1/n} > 0$ for all n, so $\{a_n\}$ converges.

43. The elements $\{a_n\} = \{\cos n\pi\}$

alternate between -1 and 1, so the sequence

diverges by oscillation.

44. The sequence $\{a_n\} = \left\{ \frac{n^3 - 7n + 5}{100n^2 + 219} \right\}$

diverges because $\lim_{n \to \infty} a_n = \infty$.

48. a. $a_1 = 1;\ a_2 = 1;\ a_3 = 2;\ a_3 = 3;\ a_4 = 5;\ \cdots$

Each new element is found by adding

together the number of pairs of rabbits

alive the previous two months; that is

$$a_{n+1} = a_n + a_{n-1}$$

b. $r_1 = 1,\ r_2 = 2,\ r_3 = \frac{3}{2},\ r_4 = \frac{5}{3} \approx 1.67,$

$r_5 = \frac{8}{5} = 1.6,\ r_6 = \frac{13}{8} \approx 1.63,$

$r_7 = \frac{21}{13} \approx 1.62,\ r_8 = \frac{34}{21} \approx 1.62,$

$r_9 = \frac{55}{34} \approx 1.618,\ r_{10} = \frac{89}{55} \approx 1.618$

c. $\quad \frac{a_{n+1}}{a_n} = 1 + \frac{a_{n-1}}{a_n}$

$$L = \lim_{n \to \infty} \frac{a_{n+1}}{a_n}$$

$$= \lim_{n \to \infty} \left(1 + \frac{a_{n-1}}{a_n} \right)$$

$$= \lim_{n \to \infty} \left(1 + \frac{1}{\frac{a_n}{a_{n-1}}} \right)$$

$$= 1 + \frac{1}{L}$$

Solving $\quad\quad L = 1 + L^{-1}$

$$L^2 = L + 1$$

$$L^2 - L - 1 = 0$$

$$L = \tfrac{1}{2}(1 \pm \sqrt{5}) \approx 1.618034$$

(for the positive root)

49.
$$\left|\frac{n}{n+1} - 1\right| < 0.01$$

$$\left|\frac{n - n - 1}{n + 1}\right| < 0.01$$

$$n + 1 > 100$$

$$n > 99$$

Choose $N = 100$.

54. **a.** Let A be the least upper bound of the nondecreasing sequence $\{a_n\}$. Since $\epsilon > 0$, it follows that $A - \epsilon < A$ and

$$A - \epsilon < a_N < A$$

for some integer N. If $n > N$, then $a_n \geq a_N$ since the sequence is nondecreasing, and

$$A - \epsilon < a_N \leq a_n \leq A$$

c. The inequality $A - \epsilon < a_n \leq A$ from part **a** can be written as

$$\left| a_n - A \right| < \epsilon$$

for all $n > N$. Thus $\lim\limits_{n \to \infty} a_n = A$.

8.2 Introduction to Infinite Series: Geometric Series, Pages 558-561

SURVIVAL HINT: *The last section dealt with sequences (range values of a function whose domain is the set of natural numbers). and this section deals with series (the sum of the terms of a sequence). A sequence may converge, while its related series diverges. An example of this situation is given on page 558.*

5. $S = \sum\limits_{k=0}^{\infty} \frac{2}{3^k} = \frac{2}{1 - \frac{1}{3}} = 3$

7. $S = \sum\limits_{k=1}^{\infty} \left(\frac{3}{2}\right)^k$; this is a geometric series with

$r = \frac{3}{2} > 1$, so it diverges.

11. The sequence $e^{-0.2}$, $e^{-0.4}$, $e^{-0.6}$, $\cdots$ is a geometric sequence with first term $e^{-0.2}$ and common ratio $e^{-0.2}$.

$$S = \sum\limits_{k=1}^{\infty} e^{-0.2k}$$

$$= e^{-0.2}(1 - e^{-0.2})^{-1}$$

$$\approx 4.51665$$

19. The sequence 2, $\sqrt{2}$, 1, $\cdots$ is a geometric sequence with first term 2 and common ratio $1/\sqrt{2}$. It is easier to calculate the sum if we first factor out a common factor of 2:

$$S = 2 + \sqrt{2} + 1 + \cdots$$

$$= 2\left[1 + \frac{1}{\sqrt{2}} + \left(\frac{1}{\sqrt{2}}\right)^2 + \left(\frac{1}{\sqrt{2}}\right)^3 + \cdots\right]$$

$$= 2\left(\frac{1}{1 - 1/\sqrt{2}}\right) \quad \textit{First term 1, } r = \frac{1}{\sqrt{2}}$$

$$= 2(2 + \sqrt{2})$$

21. $S = (1 + \sqrt{2}) + 1 + (-1 + \sqrt{2}) + \ldots$

$$= (1 + \sqrt{2})\left[1 + \left(\frac{1}{1 + \sqrt{2}}\right) + \left(\frac{1}{1 + \sqrt{2}}\right)^2 + \cdots\right]$$

$$= (1 + \sqrt{2})\left[\frac{1}{1 - \frac{1}{1 + \sqrt{2}}}\right] \quad \textit{First term 1, } r = \frac{1}{1 + \sqrt{2}}$$

$$= \frac{(1 + \sqrt{2})^2}{\sqrt{2}}$$

$$= \tfrac{1}{2}(4 + 3\sqrt{2})$$

24. $S_n = \displaystyle\sum_{k=1}^{n}\left[\frac{1}{2k+1} - \frac{1}{2k+3}\right]$

$$= \left(\frac{1}{3} - \frac{1}{5}\right) + \left(\frac{1}{5} - \frac{1}{7}\right) \quad \textit{Telescoping series}$$

$$+ \cdots + \left(\frac{1}{2n+1} - \frac{1}{2n+3}\right)$$

$$= \frac{1}{3} - \frac{1}{2n+3}$$

$$S = \lim_{n\to\infty} S_n$$

$$= \lim_{n\to\infty} \sum_{k=1}^{\infty}\left[\frac{1}{2k+1} - \frac{1}{2k+3}\right]$$

$$= \lim_{n\to\infty}\left(\frac{1}{3} - \frac{1}{2n+3}\right)$$

$$= \frac{1}{3}$$

The series converges to $\frac{1}{3}$.

29. $S_n = \displaystyle\sum_{k=1}^{n} \frac{2k+1}{k^2(k+1)^2}$

$$= \sum_{k=1}^{n}\left[\frac{1}{k^2} - \frac{1}{(k+1)^2}\right]$$

(Use partial fraction decomposition — we did not show the steps.)

$$S_n = (1 - \tfrac{1}{4}) + (\tfrac{1}{4} - \tfrac{1}{9}) + \cdots$$

$$+ [n^{-2} - (n+1)^{-2}]$$

$$\textit{Telescoping series}$$

$$= 1 - (n+1)^{-2}$$

$$S = \lim_{n\to\infty} S_n$$

$$= 1$$

The series converges to 1.

32. $2.2311111\cdots$

$$= 2.23 + 0.001[1 + \tfrac{1}{10} + (\tfrac{1}{10})^2 + \cdots]$$

is a geometric series with $r = \frac{1}{10}$.

$$S = \frac{223}{100} + \frac{\frac{1}{1,000}}{1 - \frac{1}{10}}$$

$$= \frac{223}{100} + \frac{1}{900}$$

$$= \frac{502}{225}$$

SURVIVAL HINT: *The procedure shown in Problem 32 illustrates a procedure for changing any repeating decimal into fractional form.*

37. $\dfrac{\ln\left[\frac{n^{n+1}}{(n+1)^n}\right]}{n(n+1)} = \dfrac{1}{n(n+1)}[(n+1)\ln n - n\ln(n+1)]$

$$S_N = \sum_{k=1}^{N}\left[\frac{\ln k}{k} - \frac{\ln(k+1)}{k+1}\right]$$

$$= \left(\frac{\ln 1}{1} - \frac{\ln 2}{2}\right) + \left(\frac{\ln 2}{2} - \frac{\ln 3}{3}\right)$$

$$+ \left(\frac{\ln N}{N} - \frac{\ln(N+1)}{N+1}\right)$$

$$= \frac{-\ln(N+1)}{N+1}$$

$$S = \lim_{N\to\infty}\left[\frac{-\ln(N+1)}{N+1}\right]$$

$$= 0$$

SURVIVAL HINT: *The solution to Problem 37 uses properties of logarithms. You might wish to review these properties in Theorem 1.7 on Page 58 of the text.*

43.
$$S_n = \sum_{k=0}^{n}\frac{1}{(a+k)(a+k+1)}$$

$$= \sum_{k=0}^{n}\left(\frac{1}{a+k} - \frac{1}{a+k+1}\right)$$

Partial fractions

$$= \left(\frac{1}{a+0} - \frac{1}{a+1}\right) + \left(\frac{1}{a+1} - \frac{1}{a+2}\right)$$

$$+ \cdots + \left(\frac{1}{a+n} - \frac{1}{a+n+1}\right)$$

$$= \frac{1}{a} - \frac{1}{a+n+1}$$

$$S = \lim_{n\to\infty} S_n = \frac{1}{a}$$

49.
$$D = h + 2(0.75)(h) + 2(0.75)^2(h) + \cdots$$

$$= h + 0.75(2h)[1 + 0.75 + 0.75^2 + \cdots]$$

$$= h + 0.75(2h)\left(\frac{1}{1 - 0.75}\right)$$

$$= h + 0.75(2h)(4) = 7h$$

If $7h = 21$, then $h = 3$ ft.

56.
$$P = 2{,}000e^{-0.15} + 2{,}000(e^{-0.15})^2$$

$$+ 2{,}000(e^{-0.15})^3 + \cdots$$

$$= 2{,}000(e^{-0.15})(1 - e^{-0.15})^{-1}$$

$$\approx 12{,}358.32$$

Need to invest \$12,358.32.

57. Let T be the time it takes to run the first half of the course. The total time is

$$T + \tfrac{1}{2}T + \tfrac{1}{4}T + \tfrac{1}{8}T + \cdots = T(1 + \tfrac{1}{2} + \tfrac{1}{4} + \cdots)$$

$$= T\left(\frac{1}{1 - \tfrac{1}{2}}\right) = 2T$$

SURVIVAL HINT: *Problem 57 is one of those little problems that are part of the history of mathematics with which every literate mathematics student should have some contact. Even if your instructor does not assign this problem, you might want to at least read the problem and its solution.*

65. Let s_k be the length of one of the legs of the right triangle shaded in the kth set of the process and let A_k be the area of the triangle. Then $s_1 = \frac{1}{2}$, $s_2 = \frac{1}{2}\sqrt{\left(\frac{1}{2}\right)^2 + \left(\frac{1}{2}\right)^2} = \frac{1}{4}\sqrt{2}$, and in general,

$$s_{n+1} = \tfrac{1}{2}\sqrt{s_n^2 + s_n^2} = \frac{\sqrt{2}}{2}s_n$$

$$A_{n+1} = \left(\frac{\sqrt{2}}{2}s_n\right)^2 = \tfrac{1}{2}A_n$$

Thus, the total shaded area is

$$A = \sum_{k=1}^{\infty} A_k$$

$$= \tfrac{1}{2}\left(\tfrac{1}{2}\right)^2 + \tfrac{1}{2}\left(\tfrac{1}{2}\right)\left(\tfrac{1}{2}\right)^2 + \left(\tfrac{1}{2}\right)^5 + \cdots$$

$$= \frac{1}{8} + \frac{1}{16} + \frac{1}{32} + \cdots$$

$$= \tfrac{1}{8}\left(1 + \tfrac{1}{2} + \tfrac{1}{4} + \cdots\right)$$

$$= \tfrac{1}{8}\left(\frac{1}{1 - \tfrac{1}{2}}\right) = \tfrac{1}{4}$$

8.3 The Integral Test: *p*-series, Pages 567-568

SURVIVAL HINT: *The convergence of the **sequence** a_n to 0 is a necessary, but not sufficient, condition for the convergence of a **series**. If the sequence does not converge to 0, then the series **must diverge**. However, if the sequence does converge to 0 the series may either converge or diverge. Developing tests to decide the question of convergence or divergence is one of the main objectives of this chapter.*

*Study the **p-series test** and remember that* $\displaystyle\sum_{k=1}^{\infty} \frac{1}{k^p}$ *converges if* ***p > 1*** *and diverges if* ***p ≤ 1***. *We show the solutions to Problem 5, but you should look at 3-6 and check out that the answers are found by identifying a p-series.*

5. $p = \frac{1}{3}$; diverges

7. $S = \displaystyle\sum_{k=1}^{\infty} \frac{1}{(2 + 3k)^2}$

$f > 0$, continuous on $[1, \infty)$, and decreasing.

$$I = \int_{1}^{\infty} \frac{dx}{(2 + 3x)^2}$$

$$= \lim_{b \to \infty} \int_{1}^{b} (2 + 3x)^{-2} dx$$

$$= -\frac{1}{3} \lim_{b \to \infty} (2 + 3x)^{-1} \Big|_{1}^{b}$$

$$= \frac{1}{15}$$

I converges, so *S* converges.

12. $S = \displaystyle\sum_{k=1}^{\infty} ke^{-k^2}$

$f > 0$, continuous on $[1, \infty)$, and decreasing.

$$I = \int_{1}^{\infty} xe^{-x^2} dx$$

$$= -\frac{1}{2} \lim_{b \to \infty} \int_{1}^{b} e^{-x^2}(-2x \, dx)$$

$$= -\frac{1}{2} \lim_{b \to \infty} e^{-x^2} \Big|_{1}^{b}$$

$$= \frac{1}{2e}$$

I converges, so *S* converges.

17. $S = \displaystyle\sum_{k=1}^{\infty} \frac{1}{k^4}$; this is a *p*-series where

$p = 4 > 1$, so *S* converges.

23. $S = \displaystyle\sum_{k=1}^{\infty} \frac{k^2}{\sqrt{k^3 + 2}}$

$$I = \lim_{n \to \infty} \int_{1}^{n} \frac{x^2 \, dx}{\sqrt{x^3 + 2}}$$

$$= \lim_{n \to \infty} \frac{2}{3} \sqrt{x^3 + 2} \Big|_{1}^{n}$$

$$= \infty$$

The series diverges.

29. $S = \displaystyle\sum_{k=1}^{\infty} \frac{k}{e^k}$

$$I = \lim_{n \to \infty} \int_{1}^{n} \frac{x}{e^x} \, dx \quad \boxed{u = x; \; dv = e^{-x} \, dx}$$

$$= \lim_{n \to \infty} \left[-\frac{x}{e^x} \Big|_{1}^{n} + \int_{1}^{n} e^{-x} dx \right]$$

$$= \lim_{n \to \infty} - \frac{1}{e^x}(x+1) \Big|_1^n$$

$$= \lim_{n \to \infty} \left(-\frac{n}{e^n} - \frac{1}{e^n} + \frac{2}{e} \right)$$

$$= \frac{2}{e}$$

The series converges.

33. $S = \sum_{k=1}^{\infty} \frac{1}{e^k + e^{-k}}$

$$I = \lim_{n \to \infty} \int_1^n \frac{dx}{e^x + e^{-x}}$$

$$= \lim_{n \to \infty} \tan^{-1} e^x \Big|_1^n$$

$$= \lim_{n \to \infty} [\tan^{-1} e^n - \tan^{-1} e]$$

$$= \frac{\pi}{2} - \tan^{-1} e$$

The series converges.

34. $S = \sum_{k=1}^{\infty} 3e^{-2k}$

S is a convergent geometric series because $r = 1/e^2 < 1$.

39. $S = \sum_{k=1}^{\infty} \frac{1}{k^2}$

This is a p-series with $p = 2 > 1$, so S converges.

40. $S = \sum_{k=1}^{\infty} \frac{-k^5 + k^2 + 1}{k^5 + 2}$

$$\lim_{k \to \infty} \frac{-k^5 + k^2 + 1}{k^5 + 2} = -1 \neq 0$$

The necessary condition for convergence is not satisfied, so S diverges.

41. $S = \sum_{n=1}^{\infty} \frac{n^{\sqrt{3}} + 1}{n^{2.7321}}$

$$= \sum_{n=1}^{\infty} \left[\frac{1}{n^{2.7321 - \sqrt{3}}} + \frac{1}{n^{2.7321}} \right]$$

Both of these are p-series with $|p| > 1$, so the series converges.

SURVIVAL HINT: *Compare and contrast Problems 42 and 42. The issue here is not one of calculator accuracy, but of recognizing when $|p| > 1$. Note in Problem 41, $2.7321 > \sqrt{3}$, and in Problem 42, $2.236 < \sqrt{5}$.*

47. $S = \sum_{k=2}^{\infty} \frac{k}{(k^2 - 1)^p}$

$$I = \lim_{n \to \infty} \frac{1}{2} \int_2^n (x^2 - 1)^{-p} (2x \, dx)$$

$$= \lim_{n \to \infty} \frac{1}{2} \frac{(x^2 - 1)^{-p+1}}{-p+1} \Big|_2^n$$

$$= \frac{1}{2(1-p)} \lim_{n \to \infty} \left[(n^2 - 1)^{1-p} - 3^{1-p} \right]$$

The improper integral converges if $p > 1$, so the series also converges.

54. a. $\lim_{b \to \infty} \int_N^b \frac{1}{x^3} = -\frac{1}{2} \lim_{b \to \infty} \frac{1}{x^2} \Big|_N^b$

$$= \frac{1}{2N^2}$$

$$\frac{1}{2N^2} \leq 0.0005$$

$$N^2 \geq 1,000$$

$$N \geq 32$$

b. Using computer software,

$$S_{32} = \sum_{k=1}^{32} \frac{1}{k^3}$$

$$\approx 1.20158$$

and

$$S_{64} = \sum_{k=1}^{64} \frac{1}{k^3}$$
$$\approx 1.20194$$

These answers differ by 0.00035, so

$N \geq 32$ appears to be a good choice.

8.4   Comparison Tests, Pages 573-574

SURVIVAL HINT: *Pay attention to Problems 1 and 2. These are both series you need to remember.*

1.   The geometric series converges when $|r| < 1$.

2.   The p-series converges when $p > 1$.

4. $S = \sum_{k=0}^{\infty} 0.5^k$ is a convergent geometric series with $r = 0.5 < 1$.

5. $S = \sum_{k=0}^{\infty} 1.5^k$ is a divergent geometric series with $r = 1.5 > 1$.

8. $S = \sum_{k=1}^{\infty} \frac{1}{k^{0.5}}$ is a divergent p-series since $p = 0.5 \leq 1$.

SURVIVAL HINT: *In order to use the comparison tests, you need to know some convergent and divergent series with which to compare. It is a good idea to keep a list of series for that purpose. In addition to the p, geometric, and harmonic series, add other general types as you determine their convergence or divergence.*

14. $S = \sum_{k=1}^{\infty} \frac{1}{k^2 + 3k + 2}$ is dominated by the convergent p-series $\sum_{k=1}^{\infty} \frac{1}{k^2}$, so S converges.

20. $S = \sum_{k=1}^{\infty} \frac{1}{\sqrt{k^2 + 1}}$ behaves like the divergent p-series $\sum_{k=1}^{\infty} \frac{1}{k}$.

26. $S = \sum_{k=1}^{\infty} \frac{3k^2 + 2}{k^2 + 3k + 2}$

$\lim\limits_{k \to \infty} \frac{3k^2 + 2}{k^2 + 3k + 2} = 3 \neq 0$, so the necessary condition for convergence is not satisfied; S diverges.

32. $S = \sum_{k=1}^{\infty} \frac{1,000}{\sqrt{k}\, 3^k}$ is dominated by $\sum_{k=1}^{\infty} \frac{1,000}{3^{k+1}}$

which converges (geometric series with $r = \frac{1}{3} < 1$). Thus, S also converges.

38. $S = \sum_{k=1}^{\infty} \frac{\ln k}{\sqrt{2k + 3}}$;

since $\lim\limits_{k \to \infty} \dfrac{\frac{\ln k}{\sqrt{2k + 3}}}{\frac{1}{\sqrt{k}}} = \infty$, and $\Sigma(1/\sqrt{k})$ diverges (p-series with $p = \frac{1}{2} < 1$), it follows from the zero-infinity comparison test that S also diverges.

43. $S = \sum_{k=1}^{\infty} \frac{\sqrt[6]{k}}{\sqrt[4]{k^3 + 2}\,\sqrt[8]{k}}$

$= \sum_{k=1}^{\infty} \frac{k^{4/24}}{(k^3 + 2)^{6/24} k^{3/24}}$

$= \sum_{k=1}^{\infty} \frac{k^{1/24}}{(k^3 + 2)^{6/24}}$ behaves like the divergent p-series $\sum_{k=1}^{\infty} \frac{1}{k^{17/24}}$.

49. $S = \sum\limits_{k=2}^{\infty} \dfrac{1}{(k+3)(\ln k)^{1.1}}$ behaves like

$\sum\limits_{k=1}^{\infty} \dfrac{1}{k(\ln k)^{1.1}}$ which converges by the integral

test since

$$\int\limits_{2}^{\infty} \frac{dx}{x(\ln x)^{1.1}} \approx 10.37$$

Thus, S converges.

50. $S = \sum\limits_{k=2}^{\infty} \dfrac{1}{(k+3)(\ln k)^{0.9}}$ behaves like

$\sum\limits_{k=1}^{\infty} \dfrac{1}{k(\ln k)^{0.9}}$ which diverges by the integral

test since

$$\int\limits_{2}^{\infty} \frac{dx}{x(\ln x)^{0.9}} = \infty$$

Thus, S diverges.

53. $S = \sum\limits_{k=1}^{\infty} \dfrac{k^2}{(k+3)!}$ compare with the

convergent series $\sum\limits_{k=1}^{\infty} \dfrac{1}{(k+1)!}$

(see Example 3). Since

$$\lim_{k\to\infty} \frac{\dfrac{k^2}{(k+3)!}}{\dfrac{1}{(k+1)!}} = \lim_{k\to\infty} \frac{k^2(k+1)!}{(k+3)(k+2)(k+1)!}$$

$$= 1$$

we see S also converges by the limit

comparison test.

8.5 The Ratio Test and the Root Test, Pages 581-582

SURVIVAL HINT: *Look at the summaries on Pages 579-580. Study this summary and make sure you understand what is being said. Do not move quickly past these pages.*

3. $a_k = \dfrac{1}{k!}$; use the ratio test.

$$\lim_{k\to\infty} \frac{\dfrac{1}{(k+1)!}}{\dfrac{1}{k!}} = \lim_{k\to\infty} \frac{k!}{(k+1)!}$$

$$= \lim_{k\to\infty} \frac{1}{k+1}$$

$$= 0 < 1$$

The series converges.

11. $a_k = k(\tfrac{4}{3})^k$; diverges since

$$\lim_{k\to\infty} k\frac{4^k}{3^k} = \infty \neq 0.$$

Following the directions, we use the ratio test:

$$\lim_{k\to\infty} \frac{(k+1)4^{k+1}3^k}{3^{k+1}k4^k} = \frac{4}{3} > 1$$

The series diverges.

14. $a_k = \dfrac{k^{10}2^k}{k!}$; use the ratio test.

$$\lim_{k\to\infty} \frac{k!(k+1)^{10}2^{k+1}}{k^{10}2^k(k+1)!} = 2\lim_{k\to\infty} \frac{(k+1)^{10}}{k^{10}(k+1)}$$

$$= 0 < 1$$

The series converges.

17. $a_k = \left(\dfrac{k}{3k+1}\right)^k$; use the root test.

$$\lim_{k \to \infty} \sqrt[k]{\left(\frac{k}{3k+1}\right)^k} = \lim_{k \to \infty} \frac{k}{3k+1}$$

$$= \frac{1}{3} < 1$$

The series converges.

27. $S = \sum_{k=1}^{\infty} \frac{1,000}{k}$; directly compare with the

divergent p-series $T = \sum_{k=1}^{\infty} \frac{1}{k}$, so S diverges.

33. $S = \sum_{k=1}^{\infty} \frac{2^k k!}{k^k}$; use the ratio test.

$$\lim_{k \to \infty} \frac{2^{k+1}(k+1)! k^k}{(k+1)^{k+1} 2^k k!} = 2 \lim_{k \to \infty} \frac{k^k}{(k+1)^k}$$

$$= 2 \lim_{k \to \infty} \frac{1}{\left(1 + \frac{1}{k}\right)^k}$$

$$= \frac{2}{e} < 1$$

S converges

36. $S = \sum_{k=1}^{\infty} \frac{1}{k^k}$; use the root test.

$$\lim_{k \to \infty} \sqrt[k]{\frac{1}{k^k}} = \lim_{k \to \infty} \frac{1}{k}$$

$$= 0 < 1$$

S converges

37. $S = \sum_{k=1}^{\infty} \frac{k!}{(k+1)!}$

$$= \sum_{k=1}^{\infty} \frac{1}{k+1}$$

Directly compare with harmonic series to see that S diverges. (Integral test also works.)

45. $S = \sum_{k=1}^{\infty} k^2 x^k$; use the ratio test.

$$\lim_{k \to \infty} \frac{(k+1)^2 x^{k+1}}{k^2 x^k} = x$$

By the ratio test, S converges when $x < 1$. Since the ratio test fails when the ratio equals 1, investigate

$$S = \sum_{k=1}^{\infty} k^2$$

separately to see that S diverges at $x = 1$. Thus, S converges for $0 \le x < 1$.

48. $S = \sum_{k=1}^{\infty} \frac{(3x - 0.4)^k}{k^2}$; use the ratio test.

$$\lim_{k \to \infty} \frac{(3x - 0.4)^{k+1} k^2}{(k+1)^2 (3x - 0.4)^k}$$

$$= (3x - 0.4) \lim_{k \to \infty} \frac{k^2}{(k+1)^2}$$

$$= 3x - 0.4$$

By the ratio test, S converges when

$$3x - 0.4 < 1$$

$$x < \frac{7}{15}$$

Since the ratio test fails when the ratio equals 1, investigate

$$S = \sum_{k=1}^{\infty} \frac{1}{k^2}$$

separately to see that this p-series converges at $x = \frac{7}{15}$. Thus, S converges for $0 \le x \le \frac{7}{15}$.

54. a. $S = \sum_{k=1}^{\infty} 2^{-k+(-1)^k}$; use the ratio test.

$$\lim_{k \to \infty} \frac{2^{-k-1+(-1)^{k+1}}}{2^{-k+(-1)^k}}$$

$$= \lim_{k \to \infty} 2^{-k-1+(-1)^{k+1}+k-(-1)^k}$$

$$= \lim_{k \to \infty} 2^{-1-2(-1)^k} = \begin{cases} 2^{-3} \text{ for even } k \\ 2 \text{ for odd } k \end{cases}$$

Since these are not the same, there is no limit. Ratio test does not give a limit.

b. $S = \sum\limits_{k=1}^{\infty} 2^{-k+(-1)^k}$; use the root test.

$$\lim_{k \to \infty} \sqrt[k]{2^{-k+(-1)^k}} = \lim_{k \to \infty} 2^{-1+(-1)^k/k}$$

$$= 2^{-1}$$

S converges since $2^{-1} < 1$.

8.6 Alternating Series; Absolute and Conditional Convergence, Pages 590–592

SURVIVAL HINT: *When using the alternating series test, it does not matter whether the first term is positive or negative. However, when writing a particular series in sigma notation, take care to use* $(-1)^k$ *or* $(-1)^{k+1}$, *whichever gives the first term the correct sign.*

Study the guidelines for determining convergence of series on page 589.

4. $S = \sum\limits_{k=1}^{\infty} \dfrac{(-1)^{k+1}k}{k^2 + 1}$ does not converge

absolutely since $\sum\limits_{k=1}^{\infty} \dfrac{k}{k^2 + 1}$ behaves like the

divergent p-series $\Sigma(1/k)$. To apply the alternating series test, first note that $\left\{\dfrac{k}{k^2 + 1}\right\}$ is a decreasing sequence since

$$\frac{d}{dx}\left(\frac{x}{x^2 + 1}\right) = \frac{-(x^2 - 1)}{(x^2 + 1)^2} < 0 \text{ for } x > 1$$

Since $\lim\limits_{k \to \infty} \dfrac{k}{k^2 + 1} = 0$ (l'Hôpital's rule), it follows that S converges conditionally.

6. $S = \sum\limits_{k=1}^{\infty} \dfrac{(-1)^{k+1}k}{2k + 1}$ diverges because

$$\lim_{k \to \infty} \frac{k}{2k + 1} = \frac{1}{2} \neq 0$$

10. $S = \sum\limits_{k=1}^{\infty} (-1)^{k+1}\dfrac{k^2}{e^k}$

Apply the ratio test to the series of absolute values:

$$\lim_{k \to \infty} = \frac{(k + 1)^2 e^k}{k^2 e^{k+1}} = \frac{1}{e} < 1$$

S is absolutely convergent.

20. $S = \sum\limits_{k=1}^{\infty} \dfrac{(-1)^{k+1}k}{(k + 1)(k + 2)}$ does not converge

absolutely since $\sum\limits_{k=1}^{\infty} \dfrac{k}{(k + 1)(k + 2)}$ behaves

like the divergent p-series $\Sigma(1/k)$. To apply the alternating series test, note that

$\left\{\dfrac{k}{(k + 1)(k + 2)}\right\}$ is decreasing because

$$\frac{k + 1}{(k + 2)(k + 3)} \leq \frac{k}{(k + 1)(k + 2)}$$

and $\lim\limits_{k \to \infty} \dfrac{k}{(k + 1)(k + 2)} = 0$; thus S

converges conditionally.

22. $S = \sum\limits_{k=2}^{\infty} \dfrac{(-1)^{k+1}}{\ln(\ln k)}$ does not converge

absolutely since $\sum\limits_{k=2}^{\infty} \dfrac{1}{\ln(\ln k)}$ diverges. To

see this, use the integral test:

$$\int_2^\infty \frac{dx}{\ln(\ln x)} > \int_2^\infty \frac{dx}{x \ln x} = \infty$$

Since the sequence $\left\{\dfrac{1}{\ln(\ln k)}\right\}$ is decreasing because

$$\frac{d}{dx}\left[\frac{1}{\ln(\ln x)}\right] = \frac{-1}{x \ln x(\ln(\ln x))^2} < 0$$

and $\lim\limits_{k\to\infty} \dfrac{1}{\ln(\ln k)} = 0$; thus S converges conditionally.

30. $S = \sum\limits_{k=1}^{\infty} (-1)^{k+1}\left(\dfrac{1}{k}\right)^{1/k}$

$$\lim_{k\to\infty} \frac{1}{k^{1/k}} = \lim_{k\to\infty} \exp[\ln k^{-1/k}]$$

$$= \lim_{k\to\infty} \exp\left[-\frac{\ln k}{k}\right]$$

$$= \lim_{k\to\infty} e^{-1/k}$$

$$= 1 \neq 0$$

S diverges because the necessary condition for convergence is not satisfied.

32. $S = \sum\limits_{k=1}^{\infty} \dfrac{(-1)^{k+1}}{2^{2k-2}}$

a. $S_4 = 1 - \dfrac{1}{4} + \dfrac{1}{16} - \dfrac{1}{64}$

$$= \frac{51}{64}$$

$\left|S - S_4\right| < a_5 = \dfrac{1}{256} \approx 0.0039$

b. $$\frac{1}{2^{2n-2}} < 0.0005$$

$$2^{2n-2} > 2{,}000$$

$$2n - 2 > \log_2 2{,}000$$

$$n > 6.48$$

Choose $n = 7$; $S_7 = \dfrac{3{,}277}{4{,}096} \approx 0.800$

39. $S = \sum\limits_{k=1}^{\infty} \dfrac{x^k}{\sqrt{k}}$; use generalized ratio test.

$$\lim_{k\to\infty}\left|\frac{x^{k+1}\sqrt{k}}{\sqrt{k+1}x^k}\right| = |x| < 1$$

For $x = 1$, $S = \sum\limits_{k=1}^{\infty} \dfrac{1}{k^{1/2}}$ diverges.

For $x = -1$, $S = \sum\limits_{k=1}^{\infty} \dfrac{(-1)^{k+1}}{\sqrt{k}}$ converges.

The interval of convergence is $[-1, 1)$.

40. $S = \sum\limits_{k=1}^{\infty} \dfrac{2^k x^k}{k!}$; use generalized ratio test.

$$\lim_{k\to\infty}\left|\frac{2^{k+1}x^{k+1}k!}{(k+1)!2^k x^k}\right| = \lim_{k\to\infty} \frac{2|x|}{(k+1)}$$

$$= 0 < 1$$

Converges for all x. You can also answer by saying the interval of convergence is $(-\infty, \infty)$.

48. $S = \sum\limits_{k=2}^{\infty} \dfrac{(-1)^{k+1}}{k(\ln k)^p}$ converges absolutely for $p > 1$ since by the integral test.

$$I = \int_2^\infty \frac{dx}{x(\ln x)^p}$$

$$= \lim_{b \to \infty} \left. \frac{1}{(1-p)(\ln x)^{p-1}} \right|_2^b$$

which converges when $p > 1$. Testing for conditional convergence, we note that for all p,

$$\frac{d}{dx}\left[\frac{1}{x(\ln x)^p}\right] = \frac{-(p + \ln x)}{x^2(\ln x)^{p+1}} < 0$$

and $\displaystyle\lim_{k \to \infty} \frac{1}{k(\ln k)^p} = 0$ (l'Hôpital's rule is

needed for $p < 0$). To summarize, S converges absolutely for $p > 1$ and conditionally for $p \leq 1$.

51. Consider the alternating series

$$S = \sum_{n=1}^\infty (-1)^{n+1} a_n,$$

where

$$a_1 = 1,$$

$$a_2 = \int_1^2 \frac{dx}{x},$$

$$a_3 = \frac{1}{2},$$

$$a_4 = \int_2^3 \frac{dx}{x}, \cdots$$

The $(2n - 1)$st partial sum of the series is

$$S_{2n-1} = 1 - \int_1^2 \frac{dx}{x} + \frac{1}{2} - \int_2^3 \frac{dx}{x} + \cdots$$

$$+ \frac{1}{n-1} - \int_{n-1}^n \frac{dx}{x} + \frac{1}{n}$$

$$= 1 + \frac{1}{2} + \cdots + \frac{1}{n} - \int_1^n \frac{dx}{x}$$

$$= 1 + \frac{1}{2} + \cdots + \frac{1}{n} - \ln n$$

Since $\dfrac{1}{k+1} < \displaystyle\int_k^{k+1} \frac{dx}{x} \leq \frac{1}{k}$, the sequence $\{a_n\}$ is

decreasing and clearly $\displaystyle\lim_{n \to \infty} a_n = 0$. Thus, S converges and we have

$$S = \lim_{n \to \infty} S_{2n-1}$$

$$= \lim_{n \to \infty}\left(1 + \frac{1}{2} + \cdots + \frac{1}{n} - \ln n\right)$$

The limit S is called the *Euler constant* and has the approximate value $S \approx 0.577216\cdots$.)

SURVIVAL HINT: *Problem 52 is another of those problems that introduces a new number, known as **Euler's constant**. Not of earthshaking importance, but these ideas help to broaden your mathematical background.*

8.7 Power Series, Pages 600–602

SURVIVAL HINT: *Power series and their associated intervals of convergence are the basis for the development of Taylor series in the next section. Taylor series are a powerful tool for the computation of values for various transcendental functions. To gain a better perspective about our interest in power* series and their convergence it might be a good idea to read the next section at this point. It is always a good idea to take a quick look at the material in the next section before it is presented by your professor. This process increases your understanding and allows you to ask perceptive questions.

3. $L = \lim\limits_{k \to \infty} \left| \dfrac{(k+1)(k+2)^2}{(k+3)(k+1)(k)} \right|$

$= 1$

The interval of absolute convergence is $(-1, 1)$.

At both endpoints, $\sum\limits_{k=1}^{\infty} \dfrac{k(k+1)}{k+2}$ diverges

because $\lim\limits_{k \to \infty} \dfrac{k(k+1)}{k+2} \neq 0$

The convergence set is $(-1, 1)$.

SURVIVAL HINT: *The interval of convergence may be open, closed, or half-open. Always remember to test both endpoints.*

6. $L = \lim\limits_{k \to \infty} \left| \dfrac{(k+1)^2 3^k}{k^2 3^{k+1}} \right|$

$= \dfrac{1}{3}$

so $R = 3$. The interval of absolute convergence is $|x - 2| < 3$, or $(-1, 5)$.

At $x = -1$, $\sum\limits_{k=1}^{\infty} (-1)^k k^2$ diverges since

$$\lim\limits_{k \to \infty} k^2 \neq 0.$$

At $x = 5$, $\sum\limits_{k=1}^{\infty} k^2$ diverges.

The convergence set is $(-1, 5)$.

9. $L = \lim\limits_{k \to \infty} \left| \dfrac{(k+1)!5^k}{5^{k+1}k!} \right| = \infty$, so $R = 0$.

This series converges only at $x = 1$ when all the terms vanish.

16. $L = \lim\limits_{k \to \infty} \left| \dfrac{(2k+2)!(3k)!}{(3k+3)!(2k)!} \right|$

$= \lim\limits_{k \to \infty} \left[\dfrac{(2k+2)(2k+1)}{(3k+3)(3k+2)(3k+1)} \right] = 0,$

so the radius of convergence is $R = \infty$ and the interval of absolute convergence is $(-\infty, \infty)$.

19. $L = \lim\limits_{k \to \infty} \left| \dfrac{k(\ln k)^2}{(k+1)[\ln(k+1)]^2} \right| = 1$, so

$R = 1$. The interval of absolute convergence is $(-1, 1)$.

At both $x = -1$, and $x = 1$, the series

$\sum\limits_{k=2}^{\infty} \dfrac{(-1)^k x^k}{k(\ln k)^2}$ converges absolutely by the

integral test:

$$\lim\limits_{b \to \infty} \int\limits_{2}^{b} (\ln x)^{-2} \dfrac{1}{x}\, dx = \lim\limits_{b \to \infty} \left[-(\ln x)^{-1} \right]\Big|_{2}^{b}$$

$$= \dfrac{1}{\ln 2}$$

so it converges. The convergence set is $[-1, 1]$.

22. $L = \lim\limits_{k \to \infty} \left| \dfrac{3^k}{3^{k+1}} \right|$

$= \dfrac{1}{3}$

so $R = 3$. Interval of absolute convergence is

$(x + 2)^2 < 3$ or

$$-\sqrt{3} < x + 2 < \sqrt{3}$$
$$-2 - \sqrt{3} < x < -2 + \sqrt{3}$$

or $(-2 - \sqrt{3}, -2 + \sqrt{3})$.

At both $x = -2 - \sqrt{3}$, and $-2 + \sqrt{3}$, the series becomes $\sum\limits_{k=1}^{\infty} 1$ which diverges. The convergence set is $(-2 - \sqrt{3}, -2 + \sqrt{3})$.

27. $\lim\limits_{k \to \infty} \left| \dfrac{k\sqrt{k}}{(k+1)\sqrt{k+1}} \right| = 1$, so $R = 1$ and the

interval of absolute convergence is $(-1, 1)$.

At both endpoints, the series

$\sum\limits_{k=1}^{\infty} \dfrac{x^k}{k\sqrt{k}}$ converges absolutely (p-series with

$p = \dfrac{3}{2} > 1$). The convergence set is $[-1, 1]$.

30. $\lim\limits_{k \to \infty} \left| \dfrac{2^{\sqrt{k+1}}(x-1)^{k+1}}{2^{\sqrt{k}}(x-1)^k} \right| = |x - 1| < 1$

since $\lim\limits_{k \to \infty} 2^{\sqrt{k+1} - \sqrt{k}} = \lim\limits_{k \to \infty} 2^u = 1$

where $u = \dfrac{1}{\sqrt{k+1} + \sqrt{k}}$. Thus, $R = 1$.

33. $\lim\limits_{k \to \infty} \left| \dfrac{(k+1)(ax)^{k+1}}{k(ax)^k} \right| = |ax| < 1$

when $|x| < \dfrac{1}{|a|}$. Thus, $R = \dfrac{1}{|a|}$.

35. $f(x) = 1 + \dfrac{x}{2} + \dfrac{x^2}{4} + \dfrac{x^3}{8} + \dfrac{x^4}{16} + \cdots$

$f'(x) = (1)\dfrac{1}{2} + (2)\dfrac{x}{4} + (3)\dfrac{x^2}{8} + (4)\dfrac{x^3}{16} + \cdots$

$= \sum\limits_{k=1}^{\infty} \dfrac{kx^{k-1}}{2^k}$

39. $f(x) = 1 + \dfrac{x}{2} + \dfrac{x^2}{4} + \dfrac{x^3}{8} + \dfrac{x^4}{16} + \cdots$

$F(x) = \int\limits_0^u f(u) \, du$

$= x + \dfrac{x^2}{2(2)} + \dfrac{x^3}{3(2)^2} + \dfrac{x^4}{4(2)^3} + \cdots$

$= \sum\limits_{k=1}^{\infty} \dfrac{x^k}{k(2)^{k-1}}$

Alternatively, we can write $f(x) - \sum\limits_{k=0}^{\infty} \left(\dfrac{x}{2}\right)^k$

$F(x) = \sum\limits_{k=0}^{\infty} \int\limits_0^x \dfrac{x^k}{2^k} \, dx$

$= \sum\limits_{k=0}^{\infty} \dfrac{x^{k+1}}{(k+1)2^k}$

45. Let $S = \sum\limits_{k=1}^{\infty} a_k x^{kp}$; by the ratio test

$\lim\limits_{k \to \infty} \left| \dfrac{a_{k+1} x^{kp+p}}{a_k x^{kp}} \right| - |x|^p \lim\limits_{k \to \infty} \left| \dfrac{a_{k+1}}{a_k} \right|$

$= |x|^p \left(\dfrac{1}{R}\right) < 1$

if $|x|^p < R$ or $|x| < R^{1/p}$. Thus, S has radius of convergence $R^{1/p}$.

8.8 Taylor and Maclaurin Series, Pages 616–619

SURVIVAL HINT: *The power and utility of the Taylor series is well illustrated by the list of functions on Page 615.*

5. $e^{x^2} = 1 + x^2 + \frac{1}{2!}(x^2)^2 + \cdots + \frac{1}{k!}(x^2)^k + \cdots$

$$= \sum_{k=0}^{\infty} \frac{x^{2k}}{k!}$$

8. $\sin^2 x = \frac{1}{2}(1 - \cos 2x)$

$$= \frac{1}{2}\left[1 - 1 + \frac{1}{2!}(2x)^2 - \frac{1}{4!}(2x)^4 + \cdots\right]$$

$$= \frac{1}{2}\sum_{k=1}^{\infty} \frac{(-1)^{k+1}(2x)^{2k}}{(2k)!}$$

12. $\cos x^3 = 1 - \frac{1}{2!}(x^3)^2 + \frac{1}{4!}(x^3)^4 + \cdots$

$$= \sum_{k=0}^{\infty} \frac{(-1)^k (x^3)^{2k}}{(2k)!}$$

20. $\sin x + \cos x$

$$= \left[x - \frac{x^3}{3!} + \frac{x^5}{5!} - \cdots\right] + \left[1 - \frac{x^2}{2!} + \frac{x^4}{4!} - \cdots\right]$$

$$= 1 + x - \frac{x^2}{2!} - \frac{x^3}{3!} + \frac{x^4}{4!} + \frac{x^5}{5!} - \frac{x^6}{6!} - \frac{x^7}{7!} + \cdots$$

25. $\ln(3 + x) = \ln 3(1 + \frac{x}{3})$

$$= \ln 3 + \ln(1 + \frac{x}{3})$$

$$= \ln 3 + \frac{1}{3}x - \frac{1}{2(3^2)}x^2 + \frac{1}{3(3^3)}x^3 - \frac{1}{4(3^4)}x^4 + \cdots$$

$$= \ln 3 + \sum_{k=0}^{\infty} \frac{(-1)^k x^{k+1}}{(k+1)3^{k+1}}$$

35. $f(x) = \tan x;\ f(0) = 0$

$f'(x) = \sec^2 x;\ f'(0) = 1$

$f''(x) = 2\sec^2 x \tan x;\ f''(0) = 0$

$f'''(x) = 6\sec^4 x - 4\sec^2 x;\ f'''(0) = 2$

$\tan x \approx 0 + 1 \cdot x + \frac{0x^2}{2!} + \frac{2x^3}{3!}$

Note: you could use the *Mathematics Handbook*, Formula 35, page 179.

39. $f(x) = (2 - x)^{-1};\ f(5) = -\frac{1}{3}$

$f'(x) = (2 - x)^{-2};\ f'(5) = \frac{1}{9}$

$f''(x) = 2(2 - x)^{-3};\ f''(5) = -\frac{2}{27}$

$f'''(x) = 6(2 - x)^{-4};\ f'''(5) = \frac{6}{81}$

$f(x) \approx -\frac{1}{3} + \frac{1}{9}(x - 5) - \frac{1}{27}(x - 5)^2 + \frac{1}{81}(x - 5)^3$

40. We show an alternative method of solution from the method shown in Problem 39.

$$f(x) = \frac{1}{4 - x}$$

$$= \frac{1}{6 - (x + 2)}$$

$$= \frac{1}{6}\left[\frac{1}{1 - \frac{x + 2}{6}}\right]$$

$$= \frac{1}{6}\left[1 + \frac{x + 2}{6} + \left(\frac{x + 2}{6}\right)^2 + \left(\frac{x + 2}{6}\right)^3 + \cdots\right]$$

$$\approx \frac{1}{6} + \frac{1}{6^2}(x + 2) + \frac{1}{6^3}(x + 2)^2 + \frac{1}{6^4}(x + 2)^3$$

47. $f(x) = x(1 - x^2)^{-1/2}$

$$= x\Big[1 - (-\tfrac{1}{2})x^2 + \frac{(-\tfrac{1}{2})(-\tfrac{3}{2})x^4}{2!}$$
$$- \frac{(-\tfrac{1}{2})(-\tfrac{3}{2})(-\tfrac{5}{2})x^6}{3!} + \cdots\Big]$$
$$= x + \tfrac{1}{2}x^3 + \tfrac{3}{8}x^5 + \tfrac{5}{16}x^7 + \cdots$$

Interval of absolute convergence is $(-1, 1)$.

53. $R_n(\tfrac{1}{3}) \le \dfrac{e^{z_n}}{(n+1)!}\big(\tfrac{1}{3}\big)^{n+1}$ for $0 < z_n < \tfrac{1}{3} < 1$

$$\frac{e^{z_n}}{(n+1)!\,3^{n+1}} < \frac{3}{3^{n+1}(n+1)!} < 0.0005$$

Thus, $3^{n+1}(n+1)! > 6{,}000$ or choose $n = 4$.

59. $f(x) = \dfrac{-x^2}{(2+x)(1-x^2)}$

$$= \frac{\tfrac{4}{3}}{2(1+\tfrac{x}{2})} + \frac{-\tfrac{1}{6}}{1-x} + \frac{-\tfrac{1}{2}}{1+x}$$

$$= \frac{2}{3}\sum_{k=0}^{\infty}\big(-\tfrac{x}{2}\big)^k - \frac{1}{6}\sum_{k=0}^{\infty}x^k - \frac{1}{2}\sum_{k=0}^{\infty}(-x)^k$$

$$= \sum_{k=0}^{\infty}\Big[\tfrac{2}{3}(-\tfrac{1}{2})^k - \tfrac{1}{6} - \tfrac{1}{2}(-1)^k\Big]x^k$$

66. $f(x) = x + \sin x$

$$= x + \Big(x - \frac{x^3}{3!} + \frac{x^5}{5!} - \cdots\Big) \text{ and }$$

$$\lim_{x\to 0}\frac{x + \sin x}{x} = \lim_{x\to 0}\Big[2 - \frac{x^2}{3!} + \frac{x^4}{5!} - \cdots\Big]$$

$$= 2$$

70. Let $f(x) = \ln(x + 1)$. Then

$$f^{(n+1)}(x) = \frac{(-1)^n(n)!}{(x+1)^{n+1}} \text{ and }$$

$$|R_n(x)| = \left|\frac{f^{(n+1)}(c)}{(n+1)!}x^{n+1}\right| \text{ for } 0 < c < x < 1$$

$$= \left|\frac{(-1)^n n! x^{n+1}}{(c+1)^{n+1}(n+1)!}\right|$$

$$\le \frac{|x|^{n+1}}{n+1}$$

since $(c+1)^{n+1} \ge 1$.

CHAPTER 8 REVIEW

Proficiency Examination, Pages 619-620

SURVIVAL HINT: *To help you review the concepts of this chapter,* **hand write** *the answers to each of these questions onto your own paper.*

1. A sequence is a succession of numbers that are listed according to a given prescription or rule.

2. If the terms of the sequence approach the number L as n increases without bound, we say that the sequence *converges to the limit L* and write $L = \lim_{n\to\infty} a_n$.

3. A sequence converges if the limit of the nth element is finite (and unique). If not, it diverges.

4. **a.** The elements of a bounded sequence lie

within a finite range.

b. A sequence $\{a_n\}$ is nonincreasing if

$$a_1 \geq a_2 \geq \cdots \geq a_{k-1} \geq a_k \geq \cdots$$

c. A sequence is monotonic if it is nondecreasing or nonincreasing.

d. A sequence is strictly monotonic if it is increasing or decreasing.

5. A monotonic sequence $\{a_n\}$ converges if it is bounded and diverges otherwise.

6. An infinite series is a sum of infinitely many terms.

7. A sequence $\{a_n\}$ converges if $\lim\limits_{n \to \infty} a_n = L$ is finite (and unique). A series $\sum\limits_{k=0}^{\infty} a_k$ converges if the sequence $\{S_n\}$ of partial sums

$$S_n = \sum_{k=1}^{n} a_k \text{ converges.}$$

8. The middle terms of a telescoping series vanish (by addition and subtraction of the same numbers). Specifically, the series $S = \Sigma a_k$ telescopes if $a_k = b_k - b_{k-1}$.

9. The harmonic series is a p-series with $p = 1$. It diverges, but the alternating harmonic series converges.

10. The ratio of consecutive terms of a geometric series is a constant, r. That is, a geometric series is one of the form Σar^k. It diverges if $|r| \geq 1$ and converges to $S = a/(1 - r)$ if $|r| < 1$.

11. $S = \sum\limits_{k=0}^{\infty} a_k$ diverges if $\lim\limits_{k \to \infty} a_n \neq 0$.

12. If $a_k = f(k)$ for $k = 1, 2, \ldots$, where f is a positive, continuous, and decreasing function of x for $x \geq 1$, then

$$\sum_{k=1}^{\infty} a_k \quad \text{and} \quad \int_{1}^{\infty} f(x)\, dx$$

either both converge or both diverge.

13. $\sum\limits_{k=1}^{\infty} \dfrac{1}{k^p}$ is a convergent p-series if $p > 1$. It diverges when $p \leq 1$.

14. Let $0 \leq a_k \leq c_k$ for all k. If $\sum\limits_{k=1}^{\infty} c_k$ converges, then $\sum\limits_{k=1}^{\infty} a_k$ also converges.

Let $0 \leq d_k \leq a_k$ for all k.

If $\sum\limits_{k=1}^{\infty} d_k$ diverges, then $\sum\limits_{k=1}^{\infty} a_k$ also diverges.

15. Suppose $a_k > 0$ and $b_k > 0$ for all sufficiently large k and that

$$\lim_{k \to \infty} \frac{a_k}{b_k} = L$$

where L is finite and positive $(0 < L < \infty)$. Then Σa_k and Σb_k either both converge or both diverge.

16. Suppose $a_k > 0$ and $b_k > 0$ for all sufficiently large k. Then,

If $\lim\limits_{k \to \infty} \dfrac{a_k}{b_k} = 0$ and Σb_k converges,

the series Σa_k converges.

If $\lim\limits_{k \to \infty} \dfrac{a_k}{b_k} = \infty$ and Σb_k diverges, the series Σa_k diverges.

17. Given the series Σa_k with $a_k > 0$, suppose

    that $\lim\limits_{k \to \infty} \dfrac{a_{k+1}}{a_k} = L$. The ratio test states

    the following:

    If $L < 1$, then Σa_k converges.

    If $L > 1$ or if L is infinite, then Σa_k diverges.

    If $L = 1$, the test is inconclusive.

18. Given the series Σa_k with $a_k \geq 0$, suppose

    that $\lim\limits_{k \to \infty} \sqrt[k]{a_k} = L$. The root test states the

    following:

    If $L < 1$, then Σa_k converges.

    If $L > 1$ or if L is infinite, then Σa_k diverges.

    If $L = 1$, the root test is inconclusive.

19. If $a_k > 0$, then an alternating series

    $$\sum_{k=1}^{\infty} (-1)^k a_k \quad \text{or} \quad \sum_{k=1}^{\infty} (-1)^{k+1} a_k$$

    converges if both of the following two

    conditions are satisfied:

    1. $\lim\limits_{k \to \infty} a_k = 0$

    2. $\{a_k\}$ is a decreasing sequence; that is,

        $a_{k+1} < a_k$ for all k.

20. Suppose an alternating series

    $$\sum_{k=1}^{\infty} (-1)^k a_k \quad \text{or} \quad \sum_{k=1}^{\infty} (-1)^{k+1} a_k$$

    satisfies the conditions of the alternating

    series test; namely, $\lim\limits_{k \to \infty} a_k = 0$ and $\{a_k\}$ is a

    decreasing sequence $(a_{k+1} < a_k)$. If the series

    has sum S, then $\left| S - S_n \right| < a_{n+1}$, where S_n

is the nth partial sum of the series.

21. A series of real numbers Σa_k must converge if

    the related absolute value series $\Sigma |a_k|$

    converges.

22. The series Σa_k is absolutely convergent if the

    related series $\Sigma |a_k|$ converges. The series Σa_k

    is conditionally convergent if it converges but

    $\Sigma |a_k|$ diverges.

23. For the series Σa_k, suppose $a_k \neq 0$ for $k \geq 1$

    and that

    $$\lim_{k \to \infty} \left| \frac{a_{k+1}}{a_k} \right| = L$$

    where L is a real number or ∞. Then:

    If $L < 1$, the series Σa_k converges absolutely

        and hence converges.

    If $L > 1$ or if L is infinite, the series Σa_k

        diverges.

    If $L = 1$, the test is inconclusive.

24. An infinite series of the form

    $$\sum_{k=0}^{\infty} a_k (x - c)^k$$
    $$= a_0 + a_1(x - c) + a_2(x - c)^2 + \dots$$

    is called a power series in $(x - c)$.

25. Let $\Sigma a_k u^k$ be a power series, and consider

    $$L = \lim_{k \to \infty} \left| \frac{a_{k+1}}{a_k} \right|$$

    Then: If $L = \infty$, the power series converges

    only at $u = 0$. If $L = 0$, the power series

    converges for all real u. If $0 < L < \infty$, let

$R = 1/L$. Then the power series *converges absolutely* for $|u| < R$ (or $-R < u < R$) and *diverges* for $|u| > R$. This is called the *interval of absolute convergence*. Finally, check for convergence at the endpoints $u = -R$ and $u = R$. The resulting set (with convergent endpoints) is the *convergence set*.

26. The interval of convergence of a power series consists of those values of x for which the series converges. If the interval is $-R < x < R$, then R is the radius of convergence.

27. $P_n(x) = \sum_{k=1}^{\infty} a_k(x - c)^k$ is a Taylor polynomial if $a_k = \dfrac{f^{(k)}(c)}{k!}$.

28. If f and all its derivatives exist in an open interval I containing c, then for each x in I
$$f(x) = f(c) + \frac{f'(c)}{1!}(x - c) + \frac{f''(c)}{2!}(x - c)^2 + \ldots + \frac{f^{(n)}(c)}{n!}(x - c)^n + R_n(x)$$
where the remainder function $R_n(x)$ is given by
$$R_n(x) = \frac{f^{(n+1)}(z_n)}{(n + 1)!}(x - c)^{n+1}$$
for some z_n that depends on x and lies between c and x.

29. The Taylor series is $T = \sum_{k=1}^{\infty} a_k(x - c)^k$ and is a Maclaurin series if $c = 0$.

30. The binomial function $(1 + x)^p$ is represented by its Maclaurin series

$$(1 + x)^p = 1 + px + \frac{p(p - 1)}{2!}x^2 + \frac{p(p - 1)(p - 2)}{3!}x^3 + \ldots + \frac{p(p - 1)\cdots(p - k + 1)}{k!}x^k + \ldots$$

$-1 < x < 1$ if $p \le -1$;
$-1 < x \le 1$ if $-1 < p < 0$;
$-1 \le x \le 1$ if $p > 0$, p not an integer;
all x if p is a nonnegative integer.

31. This is the definition of e.

33. $S = \sum_{k=2}^{\infty} \dfrac{1}{k \ln k}$; Use the integral test.
$$= \lim_{b \to \infty} \int_2^b (\ln x)^{-1} \frac{dx}{x} = \lim_{b \to \infty} \ln|\ln x| \Big|_2^b = \infty$$
S diverges.

36. $S = \sum_{k=1}^{n} \dfrac{3k^2 - k + 1}{(1 - 2k)k}$; check the necessary condition: $\lim_{k \to \infty} \dfrac{3k^2 - k + 1}{(1 - 2k)k} = -\dfrac{3}{2} \ne 0$
S diverges

39. $\sin x = \sum_{k=0}^{\infty} \dfrac{(-1)^k x^{2k+1}}{(2k + 1)!}$
$\sin 2x = \sum_{k=0}^{\infty} \dfrac{(-1)^k (2x)^{2k+1}}{(2k + 1)!}$

CHAPTER 9

Polar Coordinates and Parametric Forms

9.1 The Polar Coordinate System, Pages 630-631

SURVIVAL HINT: *When a problem asks for exact values, rather than calculator approximations, use those values in Table 1.2 (page 10). The sides of triangles involving exact values are usual sides of a 45°-45°-90° triangle or a 30°-60°-90° triangle. The sides are in the ratio of 1, 1, $\sqrt{2}$ or 1, 2, $\sqrt{3}$, respectively. Proper placement of the triangle on a coordinate system often leads to an exact value.*

5. $x = 5 \cos \frac{2\pi}{3} = 5(-\frac{1}{2}) = -\frac{5}{2}$

$y = 5 \sin \frac{2\pi}{3} = 5(\frac{\sqrt{3}}{2}) = \frac{5}{2}\sqrt{3}$

rectangular point: $(-\frac{5}{2}, \frac{5}{2}\sqrt{3})$

11. polar: $(0, -3)$ and $(0, \theta)$ for any number θ;

rectangular: $(0, 0)$

SURVIVAL HINT: *You should remember the conversion formulas on page 627. Some calculators automatically do this conversions, but if you remember the formulas it is often easier to use them directly than to use the calculator conversion.*

12. $r = \sqrt{5^2 + 5^2} = 5\sqrt{2}$; $(5, 5)$ is in Quadrant I,

and $\tan \overline{\theta} = \frac{5}{5} = 1$, so $\theta = \overline{\theta} = \frac{\pi}{4}$

polar point: $(5\sqrt{2}, \frac{\pi}{4})$

17. $r = \sqrt{3^2 + 7^2} = \sqrt{58}$; $(3, 7)$ is in Quadrant I,

and $\tan \overline{\theta} = \frac{7}{3}$, so $\theta = \overline{\theta} = \tan^{-1}\frac{17}{3}$

polar point: $(\sqrt{58}, \tan^{-1}\frac{17}{3}) \approx (7.6, 1.2)$,

23. $r = 4 \sin \theta$

$r^2 = 4r \sin \theta$

$x^2 + y^2 = 4y$

$x^2 + (y - 2)^2 = 4$

28. $r = 4 \tan \theta$

$r \cos \theta = 4 \sin \theta$

$r \cos \theta = \frac{4r \sin \theta}{r}$

$x = \frac{4y}{\sqrt{x^2 + y^2}}$

$x\sqrt{x^2 + y^2} = 4y$

$x^2(x^2 + y^2) = 16y^2$

34. $r = 4$ is a circle; center $(0, 0)$, radius 4.

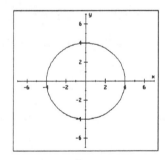

35. $\theta = 1$ is a line passing through $(0, 0)$ with slope $\tan 1 \approx 1.56$ (that is, the angle of inclination is 1)

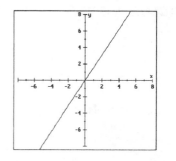

SURVIVAL HINT: *Look at some of the problems and form some conclusions; for example, compare Problems 34-35. If r is a constant the curve is a circle, and if θ is a constant the curve is a line. Also, contrast Problems 35-37; Problem 35 illustrates a line (both positive and negative r), Problem 36 illustrates a ray (r is non-negative) with endpoint (0, 0) included; and Problem 37 is a ray (r is negative) with end point (0, 0) excluded.*

39. Substitute $(10, \frac{\pi}{6})$ into the given equation:

$$10 = \frac{5}{1 - \sin \frac{\pi}{6}} = \frac{5}{1 - \frac{1}{2}}$$

Since this is a true equation, we conclude that

$(10, \frac{\pi}{6})$ is a point on the curve.

41. Substitute $(-10, \frac{5\pi}{6})$ into the given equation:

$$-10 = \frac{5}{1 - \sin(\frac{5\pi}{6})} = \frac{5}{1 - \frac{1}{2}}$$

This is not a true equation, but we cannot conclude that $(-10, \frac{5\pi}{6})$ is not on the curve. We need to try another representation, namely $(10, \frac{11\pi}{6})$:

$$10 = \frac{5}{1 - \sin(\frac{11\pi}{6})} = \frac{5}{1 + \frac{1}{2}}$$

This is also not a true equation, so the given point is not on the curve.

45. Substitute $(1, \frac{\pi}{3})$ into the given equation:

$$1 = 2(1 - \cos \frac{\pi}{3}) = = 2(1 - \frac{1}{2})$$

Since this is a true equation, we conclude that $(1, \frac{\pi}{3})$ is a point on the curve.

53. Answers vary; $(3, 0)$, $(-3, \pi)$, $(3, \pi)$, $(-3, 0)$, $(0, \frac{\pi}{2})$

9.2 Graphing in Polar Coordinates, Pages 640-641

SURVIVAL HINT: *The answers for many of Problems 1-6 are given in the back of the book, so they are not given here, but it would be worthwhile to work all of these problems, even it not assigned by your instructor.*

11. Recognize this as a spiral.

17. Recognize this as a three-leaved rose

19. lemniscate

22. four-leaved rose

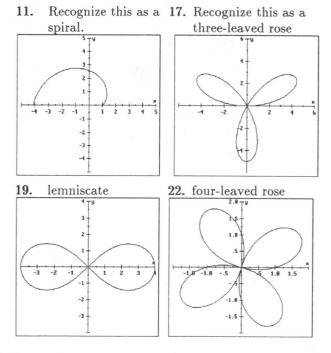

29. limaçon

32. cardioid

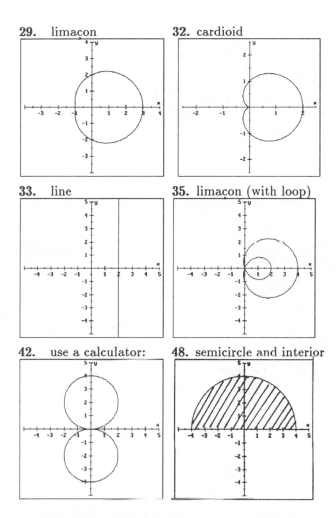

33. line

35. limaçon (with loop)

42. use a calculator:

48. semicircle and interior

SURVIVAL HINT: *Study Page 639 until you can identify a circle, limaçon, cardioid, rose curve, and lemniscate from its equation. Once the general shape is identified, a decent sketch can usually be drawn by plotting the four intercepts (if they exist). Using the polar mode on your calculator, you can sketch most of these using a calculator.*

55.

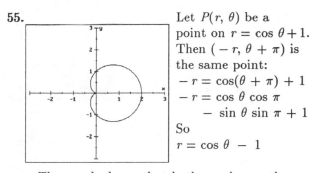

Let $P(r, \theta)$ be a point on $r = \cos\theta + 1$. Then $(-r, \theta + \pi)$ is the same point:
$$-r = \cos(\theta + \pi) + 1$$
$$-r = \cos\theta\cos\pi$$
$$\quad - \sin\theta\sin\pi + 1$$
So
$$r = \cos\theta - 1$$

The graph shows that both graphs are the same.

56. a.

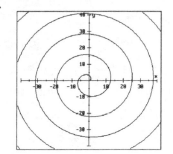

b.

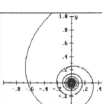

c.

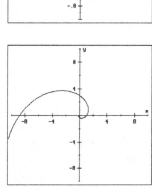

61.

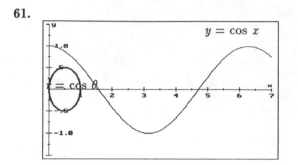

71. Converting $r = \dfrac{\theta}{\cos\theta}$ to Cartesian coordinates, we obtain

$$r\cos\theta = \theta$$

$$x = \tan^{-1}\frac{y}{x} \quad 0 \le x < \frac{\pi}{2}$$

$$y' = \tan x + x\sec^2 x$$

$y' \ge 0$ for all $0 \le x < \frac{\pi}{2}$. Thus, the graph is always rising and $y \to +\infty$ as $x \to \left(\frac{\pi}{2}\right)^-$, so there is a vertical asymptote at $x = \frac{\pi}{2}$.

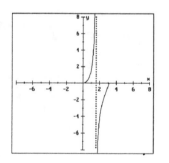

9.3 Area and Tangent Lines in Polar Coordinates, Page 649-650

SURVIVAL HINT: *Graphing in polar coordinates is not a strict one-to-one correspondence, as it is in Cartesian graphs. Any value θ for which $r = 0$ designates the pole. Remember to treat the pole as a singleton point. If r can be zero for any real value of θ, the pole is a point of graph.*

7. The pole is not a point of intersection.

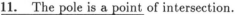

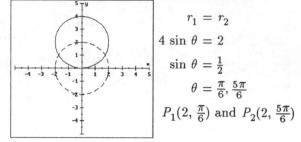

$$r_1 = r_2$$

$$4\sin\theta = 2$$

$$\sin\theta = \tfrac{1}{2}$$

$$\theta = \tfrac{\pi}{6}, \tfrac{5\pi}{6}$$

$$P_1(2, \tfrac{\pi}{6}) \text{ and } P_2(2, \tfrac{5\pi}{6})$$

11. The pole is a point of intersection.

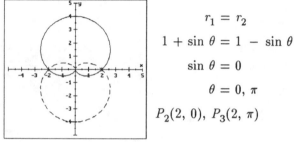

$$r_1 = r_2$$

$$1 + \sin\theta = 1 - \sin\theta$$

$$\sin\theta = 0$$

$$\theta = 0, \pi$$

$$P_2(2, 0), P_3(2, \pi)$$

17. The pole is a point of intersection.

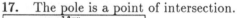

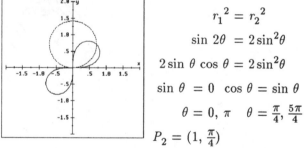

$$r_1{}^2 = r_2{}^2$$

$$\sin 2\theta = 2\sin^2\theta$$

$$2\sin\theta\cos\theta = 2\sin^2\theta$$

$$\sin\theta = 0 \quad \cos\theta = \sin\theta$$

$$\theta = 0, \pi \quad \theta = \tfrac{\pi}{4}, \tfrac{5\pi}{4}$$

$$P_2 = (1, \tfrac{\pi}{4})$$

18. The pole is a point of intersection.

$$r_1 = r_2$$

$$2(1 - \cos\theta) = 4\sin\theta$$

$$1 - \cos\theta = 2\sin\theta$$

$$1 - 2\cos\theta + \cos^2\theta = 4\sin^2\theta$$

$$1 - 2\cos\theta + \cos^2\theta = 4(1 - \cos^2\theta)$$

$$5\cos^2\theta - 2\cos\theta - 3 = 0$$

$$(5\cos\theta + 3)(\cos\theta - 1) = 0$$

$$\cos \theta = 1, \ -\frac{3}{5}$$

$$\cos \theta = 1 \qquad \cos \theta = -\frac{3}{5}$$

$$\theta = 0 \ \text{(pole)} \qquad \theta = \cos^{-1}\left(-\frac{3}{5}\right) \approx 2.214$$

$$P_2(3.2, \ 2.2)$$

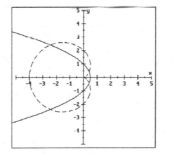

26. The pole is not a point of intersection.

$$r_1 = r_2$$

$$\frac{1}{1 + \cos \theta} = 2(1 - \cos \theta)$$

$$2(1 - \cos^2\theta) = 1$$

$$2 \sin^2\theta = 1$$

$$\sin \theta = \pm\frac{1}{\sqrt{2}}$$

$$\theta = \frac{\pi}{4}, \frac{3\pi}{4}, \frac{5\pi}{4}, \frac{7\pi}{4}$$

$$P_1\left(0.59, \frac{\pi}{4}\right), \ P_2\left(0.59, \frac{7\pi}{4}\right), \ P_3\left(3.41, \frac{5\pi}{4}\right), \ P_4\left(3.41, \frac{7\pi}{4}\right)$$

31. $\quad A = \frac{1}{2}\displaystyle\int_0^{\pi/6} \cos^2\theta \ d\theta$

$$= \frac{1}{4}\left(\theta + \frac{1}{2}\sin 2\theta\right)\Big|_0^{\pi/6}$$

$$= \frac{\pi}{24} + \frac{\sqrt{3}}{16}$$

$$\approx 0.2392$$

38. $f'(\theta) = \sin \theta; \ f'\left(\frac{\pi}{4}\right) = \frac{\sqrt{2}}{2}$

$$m = \frac{\dfrac{2 - \sqrt{2}}{2}\dfrac{\sqrt{2}}{2} + \dfrac{\sqrt{2}}{2}\dfrac{\sqrt{2}}{2}}{-\dfrac{2 - \sqrt{2}}{2}\dfrac{\sqrt{2}}{2} + \dfrac{\sqrt{2}}{2}\dfrac{\sqrt{2}}{2}}$$

$$= 1 + \sqrt{2}$$

40. At the pole, $0 = \sqrt{\cos 2\theta}$ or $\theta = \frac{\pi}{4}, \frac{3\pi}{4}$

$$f\left(\frac{\pi}{4}\right) = f\left(\frac{3\pi}{4}\right) = 0$$

As noted in the text, the formula used in the solution to Problems 38 and 39 is not easy to remember. Instead, you might find it easier to use $dy/dx = (dy/d\theta)/(dx/d\theta)$

$$x = \sqrt{\cos 2\theta} \ \cos \theta$$

$$\frac{dx}{d\theta} = \sqrt{\cos 2\theta}(-\sin \theta) - \frac{\cos \theta \sin 2\theta}{\sqrt{\cos 2\theta}}$$

$$= \frac{-\cos 2\theta \sin \theta - \cos \theta \sin 2\theta}{\sqrt{\cos 2\theta}}$$

$$= \frac{-\sin 3\theta}{\sqrt{\cos 2\theta}};$$

$$y = \sqrt{\cos 2\theta} \ \sin \theta$$

$$\frac{dy}{d\theta} = \sqrt{\cos 2\theta} \ \cos \theta - \frac{\sin \theta \sin 2\theta}{\sqrt{\cos 2\theta}}$$

$$= \frac{\cos 2\theta \cos \theta - \sin \theta \sin 2\theta}{\sqrt{\cos 2\theta}}$$

$$= \frac{\cos 3\theta}{\sqrt{\cos 2\theta}}$$

$$m = -\frac{\cos 3\theta}{\sin 3\theta} = -\cot 3\theta$$

At $\theta = \frac{\pi}{4}$, $m = 1$; at $\theta = \frac{3\pi}{4}$, $m = -1$

48. $y = \sin\theta + \sin^2\theta$; $\frac{dy}{d\theta} = \cos\theta + 2\sin\theta\cos\theta$

$\frac{dy}{d\theta} = 0$ if $\cos\theta(1 + 2\sin\theta) = 0$ when

$$\theta = \frac{\pi}{2}, \frac{3\pi}{2}, \frac{7\pi}{6}, \frac{11\pi}{6}$$

There is a cusp at the pole (where $\theta = \frac{3\pi}{2}$)

and horizontal tangents where $\theta = \frac{\pi}{2}, \frac{7\pi}{6}, \frac{11\pi}{6}$

since

$$f(\tfrac{\pi}{2}) = 2;$$

$$f(\tfrac{7\pi}{6}) = f(\tfrac{11\pi}{6}) = \tfrac{1}{2};$$

the points of tangency are:

$$P_1(2, \tfrac{\pi}{2}),\ P_2(\tfrac{1}{2}, \tfrac{7\pi}{6}),\ P_3(\tfrac{1}{2}, \tfrac{11\pi}{6})$$

53. We will find the area from $\theta = 0$ to $\theta = \frac{\pi}{3}$ and multiply by 3.

$$A = (3)\frac{1}{2}\int_0^{\pi/3} a^2 \sin^2 3\theta\ d\theta$$

$$= \frac{3}{2}a^2 \int_0^{\pi/3} \left(\frac{1 - \cos 6\theta}{2}\right) d\theta$$

$$= \frac{3a^2}{4}\left(\theta - \frac{1}{6}\sin 6\theta\right)\Big|_0^{\pi/3}$$

$$= \frac{\pi a^2}{4}$$

59. The inner loop is scanned out for $\pi/6 \leq \theta \leq 5\pi/6$ and the outer loop for $5\pi/6 \leq \theta \leq 13\pi/6$. Thus, the area between the loops is

$$A = \int_{5\pi/6}^{13\pi/6} \frac{1}{2}(2 - 4\sin\theta)^2\ d\theta$$

$$- \int_{\pi/6}^{5\pi/6} \frac{1}{2}(2 - 4\sin\theta)^2\ d\theta$$

$$= \left[6\theta + 8\cos\theta - 2\sin 2\theta\right]\Big|_{5\pi/6}^{13\pi/6}$$

$$- \left[6\theta + 8\cos\theta - 2\sin 2\theta\right]\Big|_{\pi/6}^{5\pi/6}$$

$$= (8\pi + 6\sqrt{3}) - (4\pi - 6\sqrt{3})$$

$$= 4\pi + 12\sqrt{3}$$

$$\approx 33.3510$$

62. The given point has polar form $P_1(\tfrac{1}{3}, \tfrac{1}{6})$.

a. On the spiral $r = 2\theta$, we have

$$x = 2\theta\cos\theta \text{ and } y = 2\theta\sin\theta$$

so P_1 has Cartesian form

$$P_1\left[2\left(\tfrac{1}{6}\right)\cos\tfrac{1}{6},\ 2\left(\tfrac{1}{6}\right)\sin\tfrac{1}{6}\right] \approx (0.3287, 0.0553)$$

The slope to $r = 2\theta$ at $\theta = \frac{1}{6}$ is

$$\frac{y'(\tfrac{1}{6})}{x'(\tfrac{1}{6})} = \frac{2\sin\tfrac{1}{6} + 2\left(\tfrac{1}{6}\right)\cos\tfrac{1}{6}}{2\cos\tfrac{1}{6} - 2\left(\tfrac{1}{6}\right)\sin\tfrac{1}{6}}$$

$$\approx 0.3446$$

If the tangent line to $r = 2\theta$ at P_1 intersects the curve again at $P_2(r_2, \theta_2)$ for

$\pi < \theta_2 < 2\pi$, the slope between P_1 and P_2 must be

$m \approx 0.3446$. Thus,

$$\frac{2\theta_2 \sin \theta_2 - 0.0553}{2\theta_2 \cos \theta_2 - 0.3287} \approx 0.3446$$

$$\theta_2 \approx 3.4813$$

and P_2 in polar form $P_2(6.9626, 3.4813)$.

b. The slope to $r = 2\theta$ at the point P_2 where

$\theta_2 \approx 3.4813$ is

$$m = \frac{y'(\theta_2)}{x'(\theta_2)}$$

$$= \frac{2 \sin \theta_2 + 2\theta_2 \cos \theta_2}{2 \cos \theta_2 - 2\theta_2 \sin \theta_2}$$

$$\approx -16.65$$

c. The area bounded by the spiral $r = 2\theta$

between $\theta_1 = \frac{1}{6}$ and $\theta_2 \approx 3.4813$ is

$$\int_{1/6}^{3.4813} \frac{1}{2}(2\theta)^2 \, d\theta \approx 28.1245$$

9.4 Parametric Representation of Curves, Pages 659–661

SURVIVAL HINT: *Parametric representation of a graph is an extremely important new idea, one which is essential to future study of calculus. Parametric graphing is particularly easy when using a calculator.*

*In Problems 3–30, the domain of t is given, but beyond these problems the domain of the parameter is frequently not given. When you eliminate the parameter to obtain an explicit equation, it may not have the same domain as the original parametric equations. Always use the domain of the **original** equations; for instance see the solution to Problem 21 below.*

5. $t = \frac{x}{60}$

$$y = \frac{80x}{60} - \frac{16x^2}{60^2}$$

$$= \frac{4}{3}x - \frac{1}{225}x^2$$

$$0 \leq x \leq 180$$

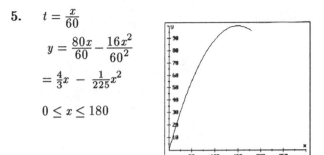

11. $t = x^{1/3}$

$$x^{1/3} = y^{1/2}$$

$$y = x^{2/3}, \quad x \geq 0$$

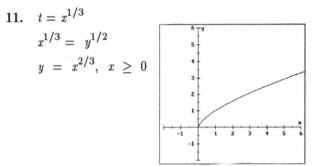

13. $\frac{x}{3} = \cos \theta;$

$$\frac{y}{3} = \sin \theta$$

$$x^2 + y^2 = 9$$

$$-3 \leq x \leq 3$$

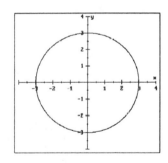

17. $\frac{x}{4} = \tan 2t$

$$\frac{y}{3} = \sec 2t$$

$$\frac{x^2}{16} + 1 = \frac{y^2}{9}$$

$$\frac{y^2}{9} - \frac{x^2}{16} = 1$$

$$-\infty \leq x \leq \infty$$

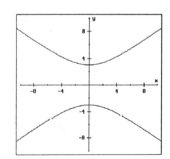

21. Given $x = e^t$, $y = e^{t+1}$

We find,

$$y = e^{t+1} = e^t e$$

$$= x(e)$$

$$= ex$$

$x \geq 1$ since $x = e^t$

27. $\dfrac{dy}{dt} = 2 \cos 2t$; $\dfrac{dx}{dt} = 4e^{4t}$; $\dfrac{dy}{dx} = \dfrac{\cos 2t}{2e^{4t}}$;

$$\frac{d}{dt}(y') = \frac{-\sin 2t - 2\cos 2t}{e^{4t}}$$

$$\frac{d^2 y}{dx^2} = \left(\frac{-\sin 2t - 2\cos 2t}{e^{4t}}\right)\left(\frac{1}{4e^{4t}}\right)$$

33. $\dfrac{dx}{dt} = e^{-t}$; $\dfrac{dy}{dt} = e^t$;

$$\frac{dy}{dx} = e^{2t}$$

$$= (y - 1)^2$$

$$= \frac{1}{(1 - x)^2}$$

39. $A = \displaystyle\int_0^1 u^3\left(\dfrac{du}{1 + u^2}\right)$

$$= \int_0^1 \left(u - \frac{u}{u^2 + 1}\right) du$$

$$= \left(\frac{u^2}{2} - \frac{1}{2}\ln(u^2 + 1)\right)\Big|_0^1$$

$$= \frac{1}{2}(1 - \ln 2)$$

$$\approx 0.1534$$

45. $\dfrac{dx}{dt} = \dfrac{2}{\sqrt{1 - t^2}}$; $\dfrac{dy}{dt} = \dfrac{-2t}{1 - t^2}$

$$\frac{ds}{dt} = \sqrt{\left(\frac{dx}{dt}\right)^2 + \left(\frac{dy}{dt}\right)^2}$$

$$= \frac{2}{1 - t^2}\sqrt{(1 - t^2) + t^2}$$

$$= \frac{2}{1 - t^2}$$

$$s = \int_0^{\sqrt{3}/2} \frac{2\,dt}{1 - t^2}$$

$$= \int_0^{\sqrt{3}/2} \left[\frac{1}{1 + t} + \frac{1}{1 - t}\right] dt$$

$$= (\ln|1 + t| - \ln|1 - t|)\Big|_0^{\sqrt{3}/2}$$

$$= \ln \frac{1 + \sqrt{3}/2}{1 - \sqrt{3}/2}$$

$$= \ln(7 + 4\sqrt{3})$$

$$\approx 2.6339$$

49. $\dfrac{dx}{dt} = -6\cos^2 t \sin t$; $\dfrac{dy}{dt} = 6\sin^2 t \cos t$

$$\frac{ds}{dt} = \sqrt{\left(\frac{dx}{dt}\right)^2 + \left(\frac{dy}{dt}\right)^2}$$

$$= 6 \sin t \cos t$$

$$= 3 \sin 2t$$

By symmetry, the total length of the curve is 4 times the part in the first quadrant.

$$s = 4 \int_0^{\pi/2} (3 \sin 2t)\,dt$$

$$= 6(-\cos 2t)\Big|_0^{\pi/2}$$

$$= 12$$

51. $r = f(\theta) = 2\cos\theta, f'(\theta) = -2\sin\theta$

$$ds = \sqrt{[f(\theta)]^2 + [f'(\theta)]^2}\, d\theta$$

$$= 2\sqrt{\cos^2\theta + \sin^2\theta}\, d\theta$$

$$s = \int_0^{\pi/3} 2\, d\theta$$

$$= \frac{2\pi}{3}$$

CHAPTER 9 REVIEW

Proficiency Examination, Page 661

SURVIVAL HINT: *To help you review the concepts of this chapter,* **hand write** *the answers to each of these questions onto your own paper.*

1. $x = r\cos\theta, y = r\sin\theta$

2. $r = \sqrt{x^2 + y^2}; \overline{\theta} = \tan^{-1}\left|\frac{y}{x}\right|$

3. A cardioid is heart-shaped (see Table 9.1, Page 639); $r = a(1 \pm \sin\theta), r = a(1 \pm \cos\theta)$

4. $r = f(\theta - \theta_0)$, where the graph is rotated through an angle θ_0.

5. Let $P(r, \theta)$ be a point on the graph. If the following forms of the point also satisfy the equation $r = f(\theta)$, then the graph has the indicated symmetry.

Symmetry with respect to the x-axis:

$P(r, -\theta)$ or $P(-r, \pi - \theta)$

Symmetry with respect to the y-axis:

$P(-r, -\theta)$ or $P(r, \pi - \theta)$

Symmetry with respect to the origin:

$P(-r, \theta)$ or $P(r, \theta + \pi)$

6. A limaçon looks like a heart with a loop or dent (see Table 9.1, Page 639);

$r = b \pm a\cos\theta$ or $r = b \pm a\sin\theta$.

If $a = b$, it is a cardioid; if $|a| > |b|$, an inner loop exists.

7. A rose curve looks like a flower (see Table 9.1, Page 639); $r = a\cos n\theta$ or $r = a\sin n\theta$, where n is an integer. If n is odd, the curve has n leaves; if n is even, the curve has $2n$ leaves.

8. A lemniscate is a figure-eight curve (see Table 9.1, Page 639); $r^2 = a^2\cos 2\theta$ or $r^2 = a^2\sin 2\theta$.

9. If $f(\theta)$ is a differentiable function of θ, then the slope of the tangent line to the polar curve $r = f(\theta)$ at the point $P(r_0, \theta_0)$ is given by

$$m = \frac{f(\theta_0)\cos\theta_0 + f'(\theta_0)\sin\theta_0}{-f(\theta_0)\sin\theta_0 + f'(\theta_0)\cos\theta_0}$$

whenever the denominator is not zero.

10. Step 1. Find the simultaneous solution of the given system of equations. Step 2. Determine whether the pole lies on the two graphs. Step 3. Graph the curves to look for other points of intersection. Some may require the alternate representation for (r, θ); namely,

$(-r, \theta + \pi)$.

11. Let $r = f(\theta)$ define a polar curve, where f is continuous and $f(\theta) \geq 0$ on the closed interval $0 \leq \alpha \leq \theta \leq \beta \leq 2\pi$. Then the region bounded by the curve $r = f(\theta)$ and the rays $\theta = \alpha$ and $\theta = \beta$ has area

$$A = \frac{1}{2}\int_{\alpha}^{\beta} r^2 \, d\theta = \frac{1}{2}\int_{\alpha}^{\beta} [f(\theta)]^2 \, d\theta$$

12. Parametric equations for a curve in the plane represent each point $P(x, y)$ on the curve in terms of one or more auxiliary variables, called parameters.

13. A trochoid is the path described by a point attached to a fixed radius on a moving wheel. The cycloid is the special case of the point being on the rim of the wheel. If it rolls *inside* the circle then the trace is called a *hypocycloid*, and if it rolls around the *outside*, the trace is called an *epicycloid*.

14. $\dfrac{dy}{dx} = \dfrac{dy/dt}{dx/dt}$

15. $s = \displaystyle\int_{a}^{b} \sqrt{\left(\dfrac{dx}{dt}\right)^2 + \left(\dfrac{dy}{dt}\right)^2} \, dt$

16. $A = \displaystyle\int_{t_1}^{t_2} y(t)\, \dfrac{dx}{dt} \, dt$

18. cardioid

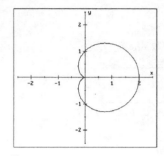

21. limaçon

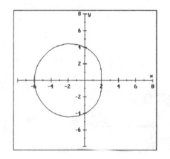

24. The curve $x = 2t^2 + 1$; $y = t - 1$ has slope

$$\frac{dy}{dx} = \frac{y'(t)}{x'(t)} = \frac{1}{4t}$$

Since the tangent line is to pass through $(7, 1)$, we must have

$$\frac{(t - 1) - 1}{(2t^2 + 1) - 7} = \frac{1}{4t}$$

$$4t(t - 2) = 2t^2 - 6$$

$$t = 1, 3$$

For these values of t, we have

$t = 1$: $x = 2(1)^2 + 1 = 3$, $y = 1 - 1 = 0$

$t = 3$: $x = 2(3)^2 + 1 = 19$, $y = 3 - 1 = 2$

Thus, the points are $(3, 0)$ and $(19, 2)$.

CHAPTER 10

Vectors in the Plane and in Space

10.1 Introduction to Vectors, Pages 674-676

11. $PQ = (0 + 4)i + (-1 + 3)j = 4i + 2j$

$\|PQ\| = \sqrt{(0 + 4)^2 + (-1 + 3)^2} = 2\sqrt{5}$

16. Let $v = -4i + 7j$; $\|v\| = \sqrt{(-4)^2 + 7^2} = \sqrt{65}$

$u = \dfrac{v}{\|v\|} = \dfrac{1}{\sqrt{65}}(-4i + 7j) = -\dfrac{4}{\sqrt{65}}i + \dfrac{7}{\sqrt{65}}j$

17. $su + tv = \langle -3s + t, 4s - t \rangle$ so that

$-3s + t = 6$ and $4s - t = 0$; solving

simultaneously, we have $s = 6$ and $t = 24$.

21. $2u + 3v - w = 2(3i - 4j) + 3(4i - 3j) - (i + j)$

$= 6i - 8j + 12i - 9j - i - j$

$= (6 + 12 - 1)i + (-8 - 9 - 1)j$

$= 17i - 18j$

26. Equate the corresponding components:

$x = 5 - 3y$ and $-4y^2 = 10 - 7x$; solving

simultaneously, we have the system:

$\begin{cases} x + 3y = 5 \\ 7x - 4y^2 = 10 \end{cases}$

$\begin{cases} 7x + 21y = 35 \\ -7x + 4y^2 = -10 \end{cases}$

$4y^2 + 21y - 25 = 0$

$(y - 1)(4y + 25) = 0$

$y = 1, -\dfrac{25}{4}$

The solutions are $(2, 1)$ and $(\frac{95}{4}, -\frac{25}{4})$

28. Equate the corresponding components:

$y - 1 = \log x$ and $y = \log 2 + \log(x + 4)$;

Solve this system by substituting the value for

y from the first equation into the second

equation:

$\log x + 1 = \log 2 + \log(x + 4)$

$\log 2 + \log(x + 4) - \log x = 1$

$\log \dfrac{2(x + 4)}{x} = 1$

$\dfrac{2(x + 4)}{x} = 10$

$2x + 8 = 10x$

$x = 1$

If $x = 1$, then $y = 1$, so the solution is $(1, 1)$.

29. $i = \cos 30°$, $j = \sin 30°$; $\dfrac{\sqrt{3}}{2}i + \dfrac{1}{2}j$

34. $u - 2v + 2w = -4i + 3j$;

The desired vector is $-\dfrac{12}{5}i + \dfrac{9}{5}j$.

43. a. $\|u - u_0\| = \sqrt{(x - x_0)^2 + (y - y_0)^2} = 1$

This is the set of points on the circle with

center (x_0, y_0) and radius 1.

b. $\|\mathbf{u} - \mathbf{u}_0\| \leq 2$ is the set of points on or interior to the circle with center (x_0, y_0) and radius 2.

47. Let $\mathbf{F}_3 = a\mathbf{i} + b\mathbf{j}$. We want

$$\mathbf{F}_1 + \mathbf{F}_2 + \mathbf{F}_3 = 0$$

Thus, $3\mathbf{i} + 4\mathbf{j} + 3\mathbf{i} - 7\mathbf{j} + a\mathbf{i} + b\mathbf{j} = 0\mathbf{i} + 0\mathbf{j}$

so that $a = -6$ and $b = 3$; $\mathbf{F}_3 = -6\mathbf{i} + 3\mathbf{j}$

50. $\mathbf{F}_1 = \langle 10 \cos \frac{\pi}{6}, 10 \sin \frac{\pi}{6} \rangle$

$= \langle 5\sqrt{3}, 5 \rangle$

$\mathbf{F}_2 = \langle 0, 8 \rangle$;

$\mathbf{F}_3 = \langle 5 \cos \frac{4\pi}{3}, 10 \sin \frac{4\pi}{3} \rangle$

$= \langle -\frac{5}{2}, -5\sqrt{3} \rangle$

$\mathbf{F}_4 = -(\mathbf{F}_1 + \mathbf{F}_2 + \mathbf{F}_3)$

$= -[(5\sqrt{3} + 0 - \frac{5}{2})\mathbf{i} + (5 + 8 - 5\sqrt{3})\mathbf{j}]$

$= (\frac{5}{2} - 5\sqrt{3})\mathbf{i} - (13 - 5\sqrt{3})\mathbf{j}$

10.2 Quadric Surfaces and Graphing in Three Dimensions, Page 684-686

SURVIVAL HINT: *The solutions for Problems 1-4 are not given here, because you can easily check your answers with those given at the back of the book. We might note, however, that when using the distance formula, it is immaterial as to which point you consider the first or the second, since*

$$(x_2 - x_1)^2 = (x_1 - x_2)^2$$

It is usually easiest to think in terms of the change Δx, form one point to the other:

$$d = \sqrt{(\Delta x)^2 + (\Delta y)^2 + (\Delta z)^2}$$

7. $(x - 0)^2 + (y - 4)^2 + (z + 5)^2 = 9$

$x^2 + (y - 4)^2 + (z + 5)^2 = 9$

11. $x^2 + y^2 + z^2 - 6x + 2y - 2z + 10 = 0$

$(x^2 - 6x + 3^2) + (y^2 + 2y + 1^2) + (z^2 - 2z + 1^2)$

$= -10 + 9 + 1 + 1$

$(x - 3)^2 + (y + 1)^2 + (z - 1)^2 = 1$

$C(3, -1, 1); \; r = 1$

23. $\|\mathbf{AB}\|^2 = 16 + 4 + 16 = 36$

$\|\mathbf{AC}\|^2 = 4 + 16 + 16 = 36$

$\|\mathbf{BC}\|^2 = 36 + 4 + 0 = 40$

$\triangle ABC$ is isosceles, but not right

SURVIVAL HINT: *In identifying quadrics, let each variable, one at a time, equal zero and identify the resulting second degree conic in the coordinate plane. Two or more conics of the same type give the quadric the "oid" name and remaining conic describes the type. For example, if two coordinate planes have parabolic traces, and the third an ellipse, the surface is called an elliptic paraboloid.*

29. Plane; intercepts are (3, 0, 0), (0, 6, 0), and (0, 0, 2)

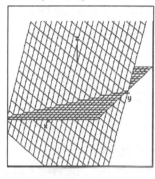

34. Parabolic cylinder

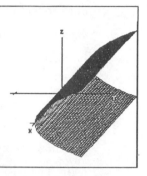

38. Cylinder cross-sections are logarithmic curves

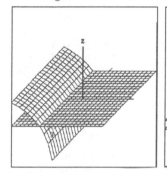

40. Hyperbolic cylinder

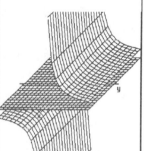

44. Hyperboloid of two sheets

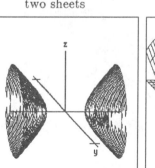

46. Hyperbolic paraboloid

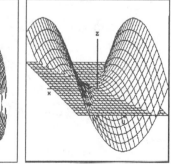

49. The center is the midpoint of **AB**; namely

$M(-\frac{1}{2}, \frac{5}{2}, 0)$; the diameter is

$$\|\mathbf{AB}\| = \sqrt{(-3)^2 + 1^2 + 6^2}$$

$$= \sqrt{46}$$

$r^2 = \frac{46}{4} = \frac{23}{2}$; the equation of the sphere is

$(x + \frac{1}{2})^2 + (y - \frac{5}{2})^2 + z^2 = \frac{23}{2}$ or

$(2x + 1)^2 + (2y - 5)^2 + 4z^2 = 46$

10.3 The Dot Product, Page 694–696

SURVIVAL HINT: *The motivation for the definition of the dot product comes from a desire to find the angle between two vectors. If we had done the theorem for the angle between two vectors (theorem 10.3) before defining the dot product, cos θ would equal an expression whose numerator was what we have called the **dot product**.*

3. $\mathbf{PQ} = (-1 - 1)\mathbf{i} + [1 - (-1)]\mathbf{j} + (4 - 3)\mathbf{k}$

$= -2\mathbf{i} + 2\mathbf{j} + \mathbf{k}$

$\|\mathbf{PQ}\| = \sqrt{(-2)^2 + (2)^2 + (1)^2}$

$= 3$

8. $\mathbf{v} \cdot \mathbf{w} = 2(0) + (-6)(-3) + 0(7)$

$= 18$

18. $\|2(\mathbf{i} - \mathbf{j} + \mathbf{k}) - 3(2\mathbf{i} + \mathbf{j} - \mathbf{k})\|^2$

$= \|-4\mathbf{i} - 5\mathbf{j} + 5\mathbf{k}\|^2$

$= 16 + 25 + 25 = 66$

20. $\|\mathbf{v}\|\mathbf{w} = \sqrt{1+4+4}(2\mathbf{i} + 4\mathbf{j} - \mathbf{k})$

$= 6\mathbf{i} + 12\mathbf{j} - 3\mathbf{k}$

23. Two vectors are parallel if they have proportional components; that is if

$$\langle a_1,\ b_1,\ c_1 \rangle = s\langle a_2,\ b_2,\ c_2 \rangle$$

for some number s.

$\mathbf{v} = 2\langle 2,\ -3,\ 5 \rangle = 2\mathbf{u}$, so $\mathbf{v}$ is parallel to $\mathbf{u}$.

29. $(\|\mathbf{v}\|\ \mathbf{w}) \cdot (\|\mathbf{w}\|\ \mathbf{v})$

$= [(\sqrt{9+4+1})(\mathbf{i}+\mathbf{j}-\mathbf{k})] \cdot [\sqrt{1+1+1}(3\mathbf{i}-2\mathbf{j}+\mathbf{k})]$

$= \sqrt{14}\sqrt{30}(3 - 2 - 1)$

$= 0$

33. $\cos\theta = \dfrac{\mathbf{v}\cdot\mathbf{w}}{\|\mathbf{v}\|\|\mathbf{w}\|}$

$= \dfrac{-2}{\sqrt{5}\sqrt{5}}$

$= -\dfrac{2}{5}$

$\theta \approx 114°$

35. The scalar projection:

$$\left|\frac{\mathbf{v}\cdot\mathbf{w}}{\|\mathbf{w}\|}\right| = \frac{2}{2} = 1$$

The vector projection:

$$\left(\frac{\mathbf{v}\cdot\mathbf{w}}{\mathbf{w}\cdot\mathbf{w}}\right)\mathbf{w} = \frac{2}{4}\mathbf{w}$$

$$= \tfrac{1}{2}(2)\mathbf{k}$$

$$= \mathbf{k}$$

SURVIVAL HINT: *Remember, the scalar projection is a **number**, whereas the vector projecting is a **vector**.*

45. Two vectors are orthogonal, if they have a dot product of 0. This means the two given vectors, call them $\mathbf{u}$ and $\mathbf{v}$, must have a dot product of 0:

$$\mathbf{u}\cdot\mathbf{v} = 6 - 2a - 2a = 0 \text{ or } a = \tfrac{3}{2}$$

54. Consider a Cartesian coordinate system with the end of the log at the origin and units in feet. The position vector along Fred's rope is

$$\mathbf{L}_f = x_f\mathbf{i} - \mathbf{j} + 2\mathbf{k}$$
$$\|\mathbf{L}_f\|^2 = x_f^2 + 1 + 4$$
$$= 64$$

Solve this later equation for x_f to find $x_f = \sqrt{59}$. The position vector along Sam's rope is

$$\mathbf{L}_S = x_s\mathbf{i} + \mathbf{j} + \mathbf{k}$$

$$\|\mathbf{L}_s\|^2 = x_s^2 + 1 + 1$$

$$= 64$$

Solving, we find $x_s = \sqrt{62}$. Thus, the resultant force on the log is

$$F_x = 30\left(\frac{\mathbf{L}_f}{\|\mathbf{L}_f\|}\right) + 20\left(\frac{\mathbf{L}_s}{\|\mathbf{L}_s\|}\right)$$

$$= \tfrac{30}{8}(\sqrt{59}\,\mathbf{i} + \mathbf{j} + 2\mathbf{k}) + \tfrac{20}{8}(\sqrt{62}\,\mathbf{i} - \mathbf{j} + \mathbf{k})$$

$$\approx 58.49\mathbf{i} + 1.25\mathbf{j} + 10\mathbf{k}$$

The force has magnitude $\|\mathbf{F}\| \approx 49.53$ lbs

and points in the direction of the unit vector $\langle 0.979, 0.025, 0.202 \rangle$.

56. **a.** The force vector is

$$\mathbf{F} = 50[(\cos \tfrac{\pi}{3})\mathbf{i} + (\sin \tfrac{\pi}{3})\mathbf{j}]$$

and the "drag" vector is $\mathbf{D} = 20\mathbf{i}$.

Work is

$$W = 50[(\cos \tfrac{\pi}{3})\mathbf{i} + (\sin \tfrac{\pi}{3})\mathbf{j}] \cdot 20\mathbf{i}$$

$$= 500 \text{ ft} \cdot \text{lb}$$

b. The horizontal vector is

$$\mathbf{F} = 50[(\cos \tfrac{\pi}{4})\mathbf{i} + (\sin \tfrac{\pi}{4})\mathbf{j}] \text{ and the}$$

"drag" vector is $\mathbf{D} = 20\mathbf{i}$. Work is

$$W = 50[(\cos \tfrac{\pi}{4})\mathbf{i} + (\sin \tfrac{\pi}{4})\mathbf{j}] \cdot 20\mathbf{i}$$

$$= 500\sqrt{2} \text{ ft} \cdot \text{lb}$$

61. Let θ be the angle between the vectors, and h the height of the triangle measured from the endpoint of $\mathbf{v}$ to the line determined by the vector $\mathbf{b}$.

$$A = \tfrac{1}{2}bh$$

$$= \tfrac{1}{2}\| \mathbf{w} \| \| \mathbf{v} \| \cos \theta$$

$$= \tfrac{1}{2} \mathbf{v} \cdot \mathbf{w}$$

Since $25\sqrt{3} = \tfrac{1}{2}\mathbf{v} \cdot \mathbf{w}$ we see $\mathbf{v} \cdot \mathbf{w} = 50\sqrt{3}$

66. **a.** $(\mathbf{v} + \mathbf{w}) \cdot (\mathbf{v} + \mathbf{w})$

$$= \mathbf{v} \cdot \mathbf{v} + \mathbf{v} \cdot \mathbf{w} + \mathbf{w} \cdot \mathbf{v} + \mathbf{w} \cdot \mathbf{w}$$

$$= \| \mathbf{v} \|^2 + 2\mathbf{v} \cdot \mathbf{w} + \| \mathbf{w} \|^2$$

b. $\| \mathbf{v} + \mathbf{w} \|^2 = (\mathbf{v} + \mathbf{w}) \cdot (\mathbf{v} + \mathbf{w})$

$$= \| \mathbf{v} \|^2 + \| \mathbf{w} \|^2 + 2\| \mathbf{v} \| \| \mathbf{w} \| \cos \theta$$

$$\leq \| \mathbf{v} \|^2 + \| \mathbf{w} \|^2 + 2\| \mathbf{v} \| \| \mathbf{w} \|$$

$$= (\| \mathbf{v} \| + \| \mathbf{w} \|)^2$$

Thus, $\| \mathbf{v} + \mathbf{w} \| \leq \| \mathbf{v} \| + \| \mathbf{w} \|$

SURVIVAL HINT: *The **triangle inequality** is a result you will run across again if you continue your mathematical studies.*

10.4 The Cross Product, Page 703–705

SURVIVAL HINT: *Remember that the dot product of two vectors is a **real number**, and the cross product of two vectors is **vector**. You will also want to remember that the dot product is a vector normal to the plane determined by the two give vectors, and is equal in magnitude to the area of the parallelogram determined by them.*

3. $\mathbf{v} \times \mathbf{w} = \begin{vmatrix} \mathbf{i} & \mathbf{j} & \mathbf{k} \\ 3 & 0 & 2 \\ 2 & 1 & 0 \end{vmatrix} = -2\mathbf{i} + 4\mathbf{j} + 3\mathbf{k}$

SURVIVAL HINT: *If you need to review determinants, see Section 2.7 of The Mathematics Handbook, however the most common method for finding cross product is to use a calculator or computer. Individual vectors are input using a format similar to:*

$$\text{Cross}([3, 0, 2], [2, 1, 0])$$

Check with you Owner's Manual.

10. $\mathbf{v} \times \mathbf{w} = \begin{vmatrix} \mathbf{i} & \mathbf{j} & \mathbf{k} \\ \cos \theta & \sin \theta & 0 \\ -\sin \theta & \cos \theta & 0 \end{vmatrix}$

$$= (\cos^2\theta + \sin^2\theta) \, \mathbf{k} = \mathbf{k}$$

15. $\sin \theta = \dfrac{\|\mathbf{v} \times \mathbf{w}\|}{\|\mathbf{v}\| \, \|\mathbf{w}\|}$

$= \dfrac{3\sqrt{6}}{\sqrt{14}\,\sqrt{77}}$

$= \dfrac{3\sqrt{33}}{77}$

18. $\mathbf{v} \times \mathbf{w} = \begin{vmatrix} \mathbf{i} & \mathbf{j} & \mathbf{k} \\ 0 & 1 & -3 \\ -1 & 1 & 1 \end{vmatrix}$

$= 4\mathbf{i} + 3\mathbf{j} + \mathbf{k}$

The unit normal is

$\dfrac{4\mathbf{i} + 3\mathbf{j} + \mathbf{k}}{\sqrt{4^2 + 3^2 + 1^2}} = \dfrac{4}{\sqrt{26}}\mathbf{i} + \dfrac{3}{\sqrt{26}}\mathbf{j} + \dfrac{1}{\sqrt{26}}\mathbf{k}$

23. $\mathbf{v} \times \mathbf{w} = \begin{vmatrix} \mathbf{i} & \mathbf{j} & \mathbf{k} \\ 4 & -1 & 1 \\ 2 & 3 & -1 \end{vmatrix}$

$= -2\mathbf{i} + 6\mathbf{j} + 14\mathbf{k}$

$A = \| -2\mathbf{i} + 6\mathbf{j} + 14\mathbf{k} \|$

$= \sqrt{4 + 36 + 196}$

$= 2\sqrt{59}$

27. $\mathbf{PQ} \times \mathbf{PR} = \begin{vmatrix} \mathbf{i} & \mathbf{j} & \mathbf{k} \\ 1 & 1 & -2 \\ 2 & -1 & -1 \end{vmatrix}$

$= -3\mathbf{i} - 3\mathbf{j} - 3\mathbf{k}$

$A = \tfrac{1}{2}\| -3\mathbf{i} - 3\mathbf{j} - 3\mathbf{k} \|$

$= \tfrac{3}{2}\sqrt{1 + 1 + 1}$

$= \tfrac{3}{2}\sqrt{3}$

35. $\begin{vmatrix} 2 & 1 & -1 \\ 3 & 0 & 1 \\ 0 & 1 & 1 \end{vmatrix} = -8;\ V = 8$

41. $\mathbf{u} = \mathbf{i} + \mathbf{j},\ \mathbf{v} = 2\mathbf{i} - \mathbf{j} + \mathbf{k},\ \mathbf{w} = \mathbf{i} + \mathbf{j} + t\mathbf{k}$;

$\mathbf{n}$ is normal to the plane of $\mathbf{u}$ and $\mathbf{v}$ if

$\mathbf{n} = \mathbf{u} \times \mathbf{v}$

$= \begin{vmatrix} \mathbf{i} & \mathbf{j} & \mathbf{k} \\ 1 & 1 & 0 \\ 2 & -1 & 1 \end{vmatrix}$

$= \mathbf{i} - \mathbf{j} - 3\mathbf{k}$

$\mathbf{n}$ must be orthogonal to every vector in the plane, so $\mathbf{n} \cdot \mathbf{w} = 0$, so $1 - 1 - 3t = 0$ or $t = 0$.

42. Let $\mathbf{v} = 2\mathbf{i} - \mathbf{j} + \mathbf{k}$;

$\mathbf{u} = \mathbf{PQ} = -2\mathbf{i} + 4\mathbf{j}$;

$\mathbf{w} = \mathbf{PR} = 4\mathbf{j} - 6\mathbf{k}$;

$\mathbf{n}$ is normal to the plane of $\mathbf{u}$ and $\mathbf{w}$ if

$\mathbf{n} = \mathbf{u} \times \mathbf{w}$

$= \begin{vmatrix} \mathbf{i} & \mathbf{j} & \mathbf{k} \\ -2 & 4 & 0 \\ 0 & 4 & -6 \end{vmatrix}$

$= -24\mathbf{i} - 12\mathbf{j} - 8\mathbf{k}$

Now,

$$\cos \theta = \frac{\mathbf{n} \cdot \mathbf{v}}{\|\mathbf{n}\| \|\mathbf{v}\|}$$

$$= \frac{-48 + 12 - 8}{\sqrt{784}\sqrt{6}}$$

$$= \frac{-11}{7\sqrt{6}}$$

so that $\theta \approx 130°$. The acute angle is $50°$, so the angle between the vector and the plane is $90° - 50° = 40°$.

48. The force is $\mathbf{F} = -40\mathbf{j}$ and

$$\mathbf{PC} = \left(\sqrt{5}\right)\mathbf{i} + 2\mathbf{j}$$

Thus, the torque is

$$\mathbf{T} = \mathbf{PC} \times \mathbf{F}$$

$$= \begin{vmatrix} \mathbf{i} & \mathbf{j} & \mathbf{k} \\ \sqrt{5} & 2 & 0 \\ 0 & -40 & 0 \end{vmatrix}$$

$$= -40\sqrt{5}\,\mathbf{k}$$

The maximum torque occurs when the seesaw is horizontal and $\mathbf{PC} = 3\mathbf{i}$:

$$3\mathbf{i} \times (-40\mathbf{j}) = -120\mathbf{k}$$

10.5 Lines and Planes in Space, Page 715–716

SURVIVAL HINT: *You should be able to represent a line in either parametric or symmetric form, and a plane is either normal or standard form.*

5. $-3(x-4) + 2(y+1) - 2(z+1) = 0$

$$-3x + 12 + 2y + 2 - 2z - 2 = 0$$

$$3x - 2y + 2z - 12 = 0$$

8. $\frac{x-1}{3} = \frac{y}{4}$, $z = -1$ and

$$x = 1 + 3t, \; y = 4t, \; z = -1$$

13. $\frac{x}{11} = \frac{y-4}{-6} = \frac{z+3}{10}$

$$x = 11t, \; y = 4 - 6t, \; z = -3 + 10t$$

17. $x = 4 + 4t, \; y = -3 + 3t, \; z = -2 + t$

$x = 0$; $t = -1$, for point $(0, -6, -3)$;

$y = 0$; $t = 1$, for point $(8, 0, -1)$;

$z = 0$; $t = 2$, for point $(12, 3, 0)$

24. A vector parallel to the first line is is $\mathbf{v}_1 = -4\mathbf{i} + \mathbf{j} + 5\mathbf{k}$. A vector parallel to the second line is $\mathbf{v}_2 = 3\mathbf{i} - \mathbf{j} - 2\mathbf{k}$. Since these lines do not have proportional direction numbers, the lines are not parallel or coincident. If they intersect, we must have:

for x: $2 - 4t_1 = 3t_2$ or $4t_1 + 3t_2 = 2$

for y: $1 + t_1 = -2 - t_2$ or $t_1 + t_2 = -3$

for z: $\frac{1}{2} + 5t_1 = 4 - 2t_2$

This system has no solution, so the lines do not intersect. Thus, they must be skew.

27. $\|\mathbf{v}\| = \sqrt{2^2 + (-3)^2 + (-5)^2} = \sqrt{38}$

$a_1 = 2, \; a_2 = -3, \; u_3 = -5$

$\cos \alpha = \frac{2}{\sqrt{38}}, \; \alpha \approx 1.24$ or $71°$;

$\cos \beta = \frac{-3}{\sqrt{38}}, \; \beta \approx 2.08$ or $119°$;

$\cos \gamma = \frac{-5}{\sqrt{38}}, \; \gamma \approx 2.52$ or $144°$

36. $-(x - 1) - 2(y - 1) + 3(z + 1) = 0$

$$x + 2y - 3z - 6 = 0$$

41. By inspection, the normal vector is

$\mathbf{N} = 2\mathbf{i} + 4\mathbf{j} - 3\mathbf{k}$; since

$\|\mathbf{N}\| = \sqrt{2^2 + 4^2 + (-3)^2} = \sqrt{29}$, the unit

vectors are $\pm \dfrac{1}{\sqrt{29}}(2\mathbf{i} + 4\mathbf{j} - 3\mathbf{k})$

43. $\mathbf{PQ} = 2\mathbf{i} + \mathbf{j} - 2\mathbf{k}$; $\mathbf{v} \cdot \mathbf{PQ} = 6 - 4 - 2 = 0$,

so $\mathbf{v}$ and $\mathbf{PQ}$ are orthogonal.

52. Parametric equations for the given line are

$x = 1 + 2t$, $y = -1 - t$, $z = 3t$. This line

intersection the plane when

$$3(1 + 2t) + 2(-1 - t) - 3t = 5$$
$$6t + 3 - 2t - 2 - 3t = 5$$
$$t = 4$$

Thus, the given point is $P(9, -5, 12)$.

57. $\mathbf{N}_1 = 3\mathbf{i} + \mathbf{j} - \mathbf{k}$, $\mathbf{N}_2 = \mathbf{i} - 6\mathbf{j} - 2\mathbf{k}$

$$\mathbf{N}_1 \times \mathbf{N}_2 = \begin{vmatrix} \mathbf{i} & \mathbf{j} & \mathbf{k} \\ 3 & 1 & -1 \\ 1 & -6 & -2 \end{vmatrix}$$

$$= -8\mathbf{i} + 5\mathbf{j} - 19\mathbf{k}$$

Now to find a point; if $x = 0$, then $y - z = 5$

and $-6y - 2z = 10$. Solving simultaneously,

we find the point $(0, 0, -5)$. The line of

intersection is:

$$\frac{x}{8} = \frac{y}{-5} = \frac{z + 5}{19}$$

10.6 Vector Methods for Measuring Distance in $\mathbb{R}^3$, Page 720-721

SURVIVAL HINT: *This section presents several formulas involving distance in $\mathbb{R}^3$. Be sure to ask your instructor if you need to have any (or all) of these formulas committed to memory.*

3. $d = \dfrac{|48 - 15 - 2|}{\sqrt{12^2 + 5^2}}$

$= \dfrac{31}{13}$

9. $d = \dfrac{|1 - 1 - 2 - 4|}{\sqrt{1^2 + 1^2 + 2^2}}$

$= 1$

15. The equation of the plane normal to the given

vector is $3x + y + 5z - (-9 + 5 + 5) = 0$, so

$d = \dfrac{|-3 + 2 + 5 - 1|}{\sqrt{9 + 1 + 25}}$

$= \dfrac{3}{\sqrt{35}}$

19. The given line is parallel to $\mathbf{v} = \mathbf{i} + \frac{1}{2}\mathbf{j} - \mathbf{k}$

and contains $Q(0, 0, 0)$. Thus

$\mathbf{PQ} = -\mathbf{i} + 2\mathbf{j} - 2\mathbf{k}$ and

$$\mathbf{PQ} \times \mathbf{v} = \begin{vmatrix} \mathbf{i} & \mathbf{j} & \mathbf{k} \\ -1 & 2 & -2 \\ 1 & \frac{1}{2} & -1 \end{vmatrix}$$

$$= -\mathbf{i} - 3\mathbf{j} - \frac{5}{2}\mathbf{k}$$

$$d = \frac{\|\mathbf{PQ} \times \mathbf{v}\|}{\|\mathbf{v}\|}$$

$$= \frac{\sqrt{(-1)^2 + (-3)^2 + (-\frac{5}{2})^2}}{\sqrt{1 + \frac{1}{4} + 1}}$$

$$= \frac{\sqrt{65}}{3}$$

26. $\|P_0P\|^2 = (x + 1)^2 + (y - 2)^2 + (z - 4)^2$

$$d^2 = \frac{|2x - 5y + 3z - 7|^2}{4 + 25 + 9}$$

Thus, $\|P_0P\| = d$ when

$(x + 1)^2 + (y - 2)^2 + (z - 4)^2$

$$= \frac{1}{38}(2x - 5y + 3z - 7)^2$$

28. The first line is parallel to $\mathbf{v}_1 = 3\mathbf{i} - 2\mathbf{j} + \mathbf{k}$ and contains the point $P(-1, 2, 1)$, while the second is parallel to $\mathbf{v}_2 = 5\mathbf{i} + \mathbf{j} + 3\mathbf{k}$ and contains $P_2(2, -1, 0)$. Then

$\mathbf{P}_1\mathbf{P}_2 = 3\mathbf{i} - 3\mathbf{j} - \mathbf{k}$;

$\mathbf{N} = \mathbf{v}_1 \times \mathbf{v}_2$

$$= \begin{vmatrix} \mathbf{i} & \mathbf{j} & \mathbf{k} \\ 3 & -2 & 1 \\ 5 & 1 & 3 \end{vmatrix}$$

$$= -7\mathbf{i} - 4\mathbf{j} + 13\mathbf{k}$$

$$d = \frac{|\mathbf{P}_1\mathbf{P}_2 \cdot \mathbf{N}|}{\|\mathbf{N}\|}$$

$$= \frac{|21 - 12 + 13|}{\sqrt{49 + 16 + 169}}$$

$$= \frac{22}{\sqrt{234}}$$

CHAPTER 10 REVIEW

Proficiency Examination, Pages 721-722

SURVIVAL HINT: *To help you review the concepts of this chapter, **hand write** the answers to each of these questions onto your own paper.*

1. A vector is a directed line segment and a scalar is a real number.

2. If $\mathbf{v} = \langle a_1, a_2, a_3 \rangle$, then $s\mathbf{v} = \langle sa_1, sa_2, sa_3 \rangle$; Geometrically, $a\mathbf{v}$ is a $a\|\mathbf{v}\|$ units long and points along $\mathbf{v}$ if $a > 0$ or in the opposite direction if $a < 0$.

3. If two vectors are arranged to that their initial points coincide, then the sum of the vectors is the diagonal of the parallelogram formed by the two vectors.

4.   a. $\mathbf{u} + \mathbf{v} = \mathbf{v} + \mathbf{u}$

    b. $(\mathbf{u} + \mathbf{v}) + \mathbf{w} = \mathbf{u} + (\mathbf{v} + \mathbf{w})$

    c. $\mathbf{u} + \mathbf{0} = \mathbf{u}$

    d. $\mathbf{u} + (-\mathbf{u}) = \mathbf{0}$

    e. $\|\mathbf{v}\| = (\mathbf{v} \cdot \mathbf{v})^{1/2}$

    f. $\mathbf{v} \cdot \mathbf{w} = \mathbf{w} \cdot \mathbf{v}$

    g. $c(\mathbf{v} \cdot \mathbf{w}) = (c\mathbf{v}) \cdot \mathbf{w} = \mathbf{u} \cdot (c\mathbf{w})$

    h. $\mathbf{u} \cdot (\mathbf{v} + \mathbf{w}) = \mathbf{u} \cdot \mathbf{v} + \mathbf{u} \cdot \mathbf{w}$

    i. $\mathbf{v} \times \mathbf{0} = \mathbf{0} \times \mathbf{v} = \mathbf{0}$

    j. $\mathbf{v} \times \mathbf{w} = -(\mathbf{w} \times \mathbf{v})$

    k. $\mathbf{u} \times (\mathbf{v} + \mathbf{w}) = (\mathbf{u} \times \mathbf{v}) + (\mathbf{u} \times \mathbf{w})$ or $(\mathbf{u} + \mathbf{v}) \times \mathbf{w} = (\mathbf{u} \times \mathbf{w}) + (\mathbf{v} \times \mathbf{w})$

5. If $\mathbf{u} = s\mathbf{v}$, then $\mathbf{u} \times \mathbf{v} = \mathbf{0}$.

6. $\|\mathbf{u}\| = \|a\mathbf{i} + b\mathbf{j} + c\mathbf{k}\| = \sqrt{a^2 + b^2 + c^2}$

7. $\|\mathbf{u} + \mathbf{v}\| \leq \|\mathbf{u}\| + \|\mathbf{v}\|$

8. $\mathbf{i}, \mathbf{j}, \mathbf{k}$

9. $(x - a)^2 + (y - b)^2 + (z - c)^2 = r^2$

10. Draw a planar curve. Define a direction (generatrix). Move a line along the curve parallel to the generatrix. The resulting surface is a cylinder.

11. The distance $\left| P_1 P_2 \right|$ between $P_1(x_1, y_1, z_1)$ and $P_2(x_2, y_2, z_2)$ is

$$\left| P_1 P_2 \right| = \sqrt{(x_2 - x_1)^2 + (y_2 - y_1)^2 + (z_2 - z_1)^2}$$

12. $\mathbf{u} = \dfrac{\mathbf{v}}{\|\mathbf{v}\|}$

13. $\|\mathbf{v} \times \mathbf{w}\|^2 = \|\mathbf{v}\|^2 \|\mathbf{w}\|^2 - (\mathbf{v} \cdot \mathbf{w})^2$

14. The dot product of vectors
$\mathbf{v} = a_1\mathbf{i} + a_2\mathbf{j} + a_3\mathbf{k}$ and $\mathbf{w} = b_1\mathbf{i} + b_2\mathbf{j} + b_3\mathbf{k}$
is the scalar denoted by $\mathbf{v} \cdot \mathbf{w}$ and given by

$$\mathbf{v} \cdot \mathbf{w} = a_1 b_1 + a_2 b_2 + a_3 b_3$$

Alternately, $\mathbf{u} \cdot \mathbf{v} = \|\mathbf{u}\| \|\mathbf{v}\| \cos \theta$ where θ is the angle between the vectors $\mathbf{u}$ and $\mathbf{v}$.

15. If θ is the angle between the nonzero vectors $\mathbf{v}$ and $\mathbf{w}$, then

$$\cos \theta = \frac{\mathbf{v} \cdot \mathbf{w}}{\|\mathbf{v}\| \|\mathbf{w}\|}$$

16. $\mathbf{u}$ and $\mathbf{v}$ are orthogonal vectors if the lines determined by those vectors are perpendicular. Algebraically, $\mathbf{u} \cdot \mathbf{v} = 0$

17. The vector projection of $\mathbf{AB}$ onto $\mathbf{AC}$ is the vector from $\mathbf{A}$ to a point D on $\mathbf{AC}$ so $\overline{BD}$ is perpendicular to the line formed by $\mathbf{AC}$. The formula for the vector projection of $\mathbf{v}$ in the direction of $\mathbf{w}$ is (a vector): $\left(\frac{\mathbf{v} \cdot \mathbf{w}}{\mathbf{w} \cdot \mathbf{w}} \right)\mathbf{w}$

18. The scalar projection of $\mathbf{AB}$ onto $\mathbf{AC}$ is the length of the vector projection. The formula for the scalar projection of $\mathbf{v}$ onto $\mathbf{w}$ is (a number): $\left| \frac{\mathbf{v} \cdot \mathbf{w}}{\|\mathbf{w}\|} \right|$

19. An object moving with displacement $\mathbf{R}$ against a constant force $\mathbf{F}$ does work $W = \mathbf{F} \cdot \mathbf{R}$

20. If $\mathbf{v} = a_1\mathbf{i} + a_2\mathbf{j} + a_3\mathbf{k}$ and $\mathbf{w} = b_1\mathbf{i} + b_2\mathbf{j} + b_3\mathbf{k}$, the cross product, written $\mathbf{v} \times \mathbf{w}$, is the vector
$$\mathbf{v} \times \mathbf{w} = (a_2 b_3 - a_3 b_2)\mathbf{i} + (a_3 b_1 - a_1 b_3)\mathbf{j} + (a_1 b_2 - a_2 b_1)\mathbf{k}$$
These terms can be obtained by using a determinant

$$\mathbf{v} \times \mathbf{w} = \begin{vmatrix} \mathbf{i} & \mathbf{j} & \mathbf{k} \\ a_1 & a_2 & a_3 \\ b_1 & b_2 & b_3 \end{vmatrix}$$

21. Place your right hand along the positive x-axis and wrap your fingers around the positive y-axis. Then your thumb points in the direction of the positive z-axis.

22. a. If $\mathbf{v}$ and $\mathbf{w}$ are nonzero vectors in $\mathbb{R}^3$, that are not multiples of one another, then $\mathbf{v} \times \mathbf{w}$ is orthogonal to both $\mathbf{v}$ and $\mathbf{w}$.

b. If $\mathbf{v}$ and $\mathbf{w}$ are nonzero vectors in $\mathbb{R}^3$ with

θ the angle between $\mathbf{v}$ and $\mathbf{w}$ $(0 \leq \theta \leq \pi)$,

then $\|\mathbf{v} \times \mathbf{w}\| = \|\mathbf{v}\| \|\mathbf{w}\| \sin \theta$

23. If $\mathbf{u} = a_1\mathbf{i} + a_2\mathbf{j} + a_3\mathbf{k}$, $\mathbf{v} = b_1\mathbf{i} + b_2\mathbf{j} + b_3\mathbf{k}$, and $\mathbf{w} = c_1\mathbf{i} + c_2\mathbf{j} + c_3\mathbf{k}$, then the triple scalar product can be found by evaluating the determinant

$$(\mathbf{u} \times \mathbf{v}) \cdot \mathbf{w} = \begin{vmatrix} a_1 & a_2 & a_3 \\ b_1 & b_2 & b_3 \\ c_1 & c_2 & c_3 \end{vmatrix}$$

24. The volume of a parallelepiped formed by $\mathbf{u}$, $\mathbf{v}$, and $\mathbf{w}$ is the absolute value of the triple scalar product, $|(\mathbf{u} \times \mathbf{v}) \cdot \mathbf{w}|$.

25. Suppose the line passing through the point (x_0, y_0, z_0) and parallel to $\mathbf{v} = A\mathbf{i} + B\mathbf{j} + C\mathbf{k}$.

    a. $x = x_0 + tA$, $y = y_0 + tB$, $z = z_0 + tC$

    b. $\dfrac{x - x_0}{A} = \dfrac{y - y_0}{B} = \dfrac{z - z_0}{C}$

26. If $\mathbf{v} = a_1\mathbf{i} + a_2\mathbf{j} + a_3\mathbf{k}$ is a nonzero vector, then the direction cosines of $\mathbf{v}$ are

    $\cos \alpha = \dfrac{a_1}{\|\mathbf{v}\|}$; $\cos \beta = \dfrac{a_2}{\|\mathbf{v}\|}$; $\cos \gamma = \dfrac{a_3}{\|\mathbf{v}\|}$

27. The plane $Ax + By + Cz + D = 0$ has normal vector $\mathbf{N} = A\mathbf{i} + B\mathbf{j} + C\mathbf{k}$

28. The plane continuing the point $P_0(x_0, y_0, z_0)$ with normal vector $\mathbf{N} = A\mathbf{i} + B\mathbf{j} + C\mathbf{k}$ has *point-normal* form

    $A(x - x_0) + B(y - y_0) + C(z - z_0) = 0$

29. The standard form of plane with normal

vector $\mathbf{N} = A\mathbf{i} + B\mathbf{j} + C\mathbf{z}$ is

$Ax + By + Cz + D = 0$

30. The distance from the point (x_0, y_0, z_0) to the plane $Ax + By + Cz + D = 0$ is given by

$$d = \left| \frac{Ax_0 + By_0 + Cz_0 + D}{\sqrt{A^2 + B^2 + C^2}} \right|$$

31. The shortest distance from the point P to the line L is given by the formula

$$d = \frac{\|\mathbf{v} \times \mathbf{QP}\|}{\|\mathbf{v}\|}$$

where $\mathbf{v}$ is a vector aligned with L and Q is any point on L.

33. a. $\mathbf{u} \times \mathbf{v} = \begin{vmatrix} \mathbf{i} & \mathbf{j} & \mathbf{k} \\ 2 & -3 & 1 \\ 1 & 1 & -2 \end{vmatrix} = 5\mathbf{i} + 5\mathbf{j} + 5\mathbf{k}$

    $(\mathbf{u} \times \mathbf{v}) \cdot \mathbf{w} = (5\mathbf{i} + 5\mathbf{j} + 5\mathbf{k}) \cdot (3\mathbf{i} + 5\mathbf{k})$

    $\qquad\qquad\qquad = 40$

    b. Not possible to take the cross product of a scalar and a vector.

    c. $\begin{vmatrix} \mathbf{i} & \mathbf{j} & \mathbf{k} \\ 2 & -3 & 1 \\ 1 & 1 & -2 \end{vmatrix} \times (3\mathbf{i} + 5\mathbf{j})$

    $= (5\mathbf{i} + 5\mathbf{j} + 5\mathbf{k}) \times (3\mathbf{i} + 5\mathbf{j})$

    $= \begin{vmatrix} \mathbf{i} & \mathbf{j} & \mathbf{k} \\ 5 & 5 & 5 \\ 3 & 0 & 5 \end{vmatrix}$

    $= 25\mathbf{i} - 10\mathbf{j} - 15\mathbf{k}$

    d. Not possible to take the dot product of a scalar and a vector.

36. The normals to the given planes are

$N_1 = 2i + 3j + k$ and $N_2 = j - 3k$

A vector parallel to the required line is

$$N_1 \times N_2 = \begin{vmatrix} i & j & k \\ 2 & 3 & 1 \\ 0 & 1 & -3 \end{vmatrix}$$

$$= \langle -10, 6, 2 \rangle$$

A point on the line of intersection is $P_0(-\frac{13}{2}, 5, 0)$ found by setting $z = 0$. Thus, the line has parametric form

$$x = -\frac{13}{2} - 10t, \quad y = 5 + 6t, \quad z = 2t$$

39. a. The direction numbers are not scalar multiples, so they are not parallel. If $z = 3$, $t = \frac{3}{2}$, $x = 0 \neq -2$. They are skew.

b. The direction numbers are not scalar multiples, so they are not parallel. To determine if they intersect we need to solve a system of equations.

1st line:

$$x = 7 + 5t_1, \quad y = 6 + 4t_1, \quad z = 8 + 5t_1$$

2nd line:

$$x = 8 + 6t_2, \quad y = 6 + 4t_2, \quad z = 9 + 6t_2$$

Solving these equations simultaneously, we find $t_1 = t_2 = -1$. Both equations contain the point $(2, 2, 3)$.

42. The first line contains $P_1(0, 0, -1)$ and is parallel to $v_1 = \langle 1, 2, 3 \rangle$, and the second contains $P_2(1, 2, 0)$ and is parallel to $v_2 = \langle -1, 1, 1 \rangle$. A normal to both line is

$$N = v_1 \times v_2$$

$$= \begin{vmatrix} i & j & k \\ 1 & 2 & 3 \\ -1 & 1 & 1 \end{vmatrix}$$

$$= -i - 4j + 3k$$

Then the distance between the lines is the scalar projection of $P_1 P_2$ on N:

$P_1 P_2 = i + 2j + k$, so

$$d = \left| \frac{N \cdot P_1 P_2}{\|N\|} \right|$$

$$= \frac{|\langle -1, -4, 3 \rangle \cdot \langle 1, 2, 1 \rangle|}{\sqrt{(-1)^2 + (-4)^2 + 3^2}}$$

$$= \frac{6}{\sqrt{26}}$$

45. The work performed on the sled is the horizontal component of the force times the displacement. In vector terms:

$$W = F \cdot PQ = \left\langle \frac{3\sqrt{3}}{2}, \frac{3}{2} \right\rangle \cdot \langle 50, 0 \rangle$$

$$= 75\sqrt{3} \approx 130 \text{ ft} \cdot \text{lbs}$$

CHAPTER 11

Vector-Valued Functions

SURVIVAL HINT: *With this chapter, you begin a new calculus topic, one involving vectors. You might wish to review vectors in the plane and space as presented in Chapter 10; in particular, remember that cross product is not commutative. Generally speaking the operations on vector-valued functions are exactly what you would expect them to be. They are the same as the scalar functions applied to the component functions. The ideas presented in this section are essential to the ideas presented in Chapter 14.*

11.1 Introduction to Vector Functions, Pages 734–736

3. The sine and cosine functions are defined for all values of t, but the tangent is not defined for odd multiples of $\frac{\pi}{2}$: $t \neq \frac{(2n+1)\pi}{2}$, n an integer

9. a parabola in the xy-plane

10. a hyperbola (vertical asymptote at $x = 1$) in the xy-plane

12. an ellipse in the xy-plane

15. a circular helix

23. $x = 2 \sin t$, $y = 2 \sin t$, $z = \sqrt{8} \cos t$.

$$x^2 + y^2 + z^2 = 4\sin^2 t + 4\sin^2 t + 8\cos^2 t$$

$$= 8(\sin^2 t + \cos^2 t)$$

$$= 8$$

Which is a sphere with center at the origin and a radius of $2\sqrt{2}$.

25. Parametrize the parabola $y = x^2$ by letting t be the variable which is squared, namely $x = t$; then $y = t^2$:

$$\mathbf{F}(t) = t\mathbf{i} + t^2\mathbf{j} + 2\mathbf{k}$$

30. Normals to the planes are:

$$\mathbf{N}_1 = 2\mathbf{i} + \mathbf{j} + 3\mathbf{k}; \ \mathbf{N}_2 = \mathbf{i} - \mathbf{j} - \mathbf{k}$$

Thus, a vector parallel to the line of intersection is

$$\mathbf{v} = \mathbf{N}_1 \times \mathbf{N}_2 = \begin{vmatrix} \mathbf{i} & \mathbf{j} & \mathbf{k} \\ 2 & 1 & 3 \\ 1 & -1 & -1 \end{vmatrix} = 2\mathbf{i} + 5\mathbf{j} - 3\mathbf{k}$$

For a point on the line of intersection, let $z = 0$, so that $x = 7/3$, $y = 4/3$:

$$x = \tfrac{7}{3} + 2t;$$

$$y = \tfrac{4}{3} + 5t;$$

$$z = -3t; \text{ thus,}$$

$$\mathbf{F}(t) = (\tfrac{7}{3} + 2t)\mathbf{i} + (\tfrac{4}{3} + 5t)\mathbf{j} - 3t\mathbf{k}$$

34. $\mathbf{F}(t) \cdot \mathbf{H}(t) = (2t\mathbf{i} - 5\mathbf{j} + t^2\mathbf{k}) \cdot (\sin t \, \mathbf{i} + e^t\mathbf{j})$

$$= 2t \sin t - 5e^t$$

37. $\mathbf{F}(t) \times \mathbf{H}(t) = \begin{vmatrix} \mathbf{i} & \mathbf{j} & \mathbf{k} \\ 2t & -5 & t^2 \\ \sin t & e^t & 0 \end{vmatrix}$

$$= -t^2e^t\mathbf{i} + t^2\sin t\mathbf{j} + (2te^t + 5\sin t)\mathbf{k}$$

41. This is a triple scalar product:

$$\mathbf{G}(t) \cdot [\mathbf{H}(t) \times \mathbf{F}(t)] = \begin{vmatrix} 1-t & 0 & \frac{1}{t} \\ \sin t & e^t & 0 \\ 2t & -5 & t^2 \end{vmatrix}$$

$$= t^2e^t - t^3e^t - 2e^t - \frac{5}{t}\sin t$$

46. $\lim\limits_{t \to 1}\left[\dfrac{t^3-1}{t-1}\mathbf{i} + \dfrac{t^2-3t+2}{t^2+t-2}\mathbf{j} + (t^2+1)e^{t-1}\mathbf{k}\right]$

$$= \lim_{t \to 1}\left[(t^2+t+1)\mathbf{i} + \frac{(t-2)(t-1)}{(t+2)(t-1)}\mathbf{j} + (t^2+1)e^{t-1}\mathbf{k}\right]$$

$$= 3\mathbf{i} - \frac{1}{3}\mathbf{j} + 2\mathbf{k}$$

53. The suspicious points are those for which the denominator is zero: $t^2 + t = 0$ or $t = 0, -1$. continuous for $t \neq 0, t \neq -1$

60. $\Delta(\mathbf{F} \times \mathbf{G})(t) = \mathbf{F}(t+\Delta t) \times \mathbf{G}(t+\Delta t) - \mathbf{F}(t) \times \mathbf{G}(t)$

$$= \mathbf{F}(t+\Delta t) \times \mathbf{G}(t+\Delta t) - \mathbf{F}(t+\Delta t) \times \mathbf{G}(t)$$

$$+ \mathbf{F}(t+\Delta t) \times \mathbf{G}(t) - \mathbf{F}(t) \times \mathbf{G}(t)$$

$$= \mathbf{F}(t+\Delta t) \times [\mathbf{G}(t+\Delta t) - \mathbf{G}(t)]$$

$$+ [\mathbf{F}(t+\Delta t) - \mathbf{F}(t)] \times \mathbf{G}(t)$$

$$= \mathbf{F}(t+\Delta t) \times \Delta\mathbf{G}(t) + \Delta\mathbf{F}(t) \times \mathbf{G}(t)$$

11.2 Differentiation and Integration of Vector Functions, Page 746-747

SURVIVAL HINT: *The rules for the derivatives of the product (scalar, dot, or cross) of vector functions are easy to remember because they all follow the same pattern as that of two real-valued functions: the product rule. Once again, we remind you to be careful with the cross product, as it is not commutative.*

3. $\mathbf{F}'(s) = \frac{1}{s}(s\mathbf{i} + 5\mathbf{j} - e^s\mathbf{k}) + (\ln s)(\mathbf{i} - e^s\mathbf{k})$

$$= (1 + \ln s)\mathbf{i} + 5s^{-1}\mathbf{j} - e^s(\ln s + s^{-1})\mathbf{k}$$

6. $\mathbf{F}'(s) = -4s\mathbf{i} + (\cos s - s \sin s)\mathbf{j} - \mathbf{k}$

$\mathbf{F}''(s) = -4\mathbf{i} + (-2\sin s - s \cos s)\mathbf{j}$

12. $f(x) = \|\mathbf{i} + (x^2 - e^x)\mathbf{j} - 2\mathbf{k}\|$

$$= \sqrt{5 + (x^2 - e^x)^2}$$

$$f'(x) = \frac{(x^2 - e^x)(2x - e^x)}{\sqrt{5 + (x^2 - e^x)^2}}$$

15. $\mathbf{V}(t) = -\sin t\mathbf{i} + \cos t\mathbf{j} + 3\mathbf{k};$

$$\mathbf{V}(\tfrac{\pi}{4}) = -\frac{\sqrt{2}}{2}\mathbf{i} + \frac{\sqrt{2}}{2}\mathbf{j} + 3\mathbf{k}$$

$\mathbf{A}(t) = -\cos t\mathbf{i} - \sin t\mathbf{j};$

$$\mathbf{A}(\tfrac{\pi}{4}) = -\frac{\sqrt{2}}{2}\mathbf{i} - \frac{\sqrt{2}}{2}\mathbf{j}$$

$$\text{speed} = \left\|\mathbf{V}(\tfrac{\pi}{4})\right\| = \sqrt{\tfrac{2}{4} + \tfrac{2}{4} + 9} = \sqrt{10}$$

Direction of motion is that of the unit vector

$$\frac{\mathbf{V}}{\|\mathbf{V}\|} = -\frac{1}{2\sqrt{5}}\mathbf{i} + \frac{1}{2\sqrt{5}}\mathbf{j} + \frac{3}{\sqrt{10}}\mathbf{k}$$

23. $\mathbf{F}'(t) = \cos t\mathbf{i} - \sin t\mathbf{j} + a\mathbf{k};$

$$\mathbf{F}'(\tfrac{\pi}{2}) = -\mathbf{j} + a\mathbf{k}$$

$$\mathbf{F}'(\pi) = -\mathbf{i} + a\mathbf{k}$$

28. $\displaystyle\int (3e^{-t}\mathbf{i} + te^{-t}\mathbf{j} + e^{-t}\sin t\,\mathbf{k})\,dt$

$$= -3e^{-t}\mathbf{i} - (te^{-t} + e^{-t})\mathbf{j}$$

$$- \tfrac{1}{2}e^{-t}(\cos t + \sin t)\mathbf{k} + \mathbf{C}$$

32. $\mathbf{R}(t) = \displaystyle\int \mathbf{V}(t)\,dt = \int \langle t, -t^{1/3}, e^t\rangle\,dt$

$$= \langle \tfrac{1}{2}t^2, -\tfrac{3}{4}t^{4/3}, e^t\rangle + C$$

$$\mathbf{R}(0) = \langle 0, 0, 1\rangle + \langle c_1, c_2, c_3\rangle = \langle 1, -2, 1\rangle,$$

so $C = \langle 1, -2, 0\rangle$

$$\mathbf{R}(t) = (\tfrac{1}{2}t^2 + 1)\mathbf{i} + (-\tfrac{3}{4}t^{4/3} - 2)\mathbf{j} + e^t\mathbf{k}$$

35. $\mathbf{V}(t) = \displaystyle\int \langle \cos t, 0, -t\sin t\rangle\,dt$

$$= \langle \sin t, 0, t\cos t - \sin t\rangle + C_1$$

$$\mathbf{V}(0) = \langle 0, 0, 0\rangle + C_1 = \langle 2, 0, 3\rangle;\ C_1 = \langle 2, 0, 3\rangle$$

$$\mathbf{V}(t) = (2 + \sin t)\mathbf{i} + (3 + t\cos t - \sin t)\mathbf{k}$$

$$\mathbf{R}(t) = \int \langle \sin t + 2, 0, 3 + t\cos t + \sin t\rangle\,dt$$

$$= \langle 2t - \cos t, 0, 3t + t\sin t\rangle + C_2$$

$$\mathbf{R}(0) = \langle -1, 0, 0\rangle + C_2 = \langle 1, -2, 1\rangle$$

$$C_2 = \langle 2, -2, 1\rangle$$

$$\mathbf{R}(t) = \langle 2 + 2t - \cos t, -2, 1 + 3t + t\sin t\rangle$$

44. Let $f(t) = t\|\mathbf{v}\| + t^2\|\mathbf{w}\|$ where $\|\mathbf{v}\|$ and $\|\mathbf{w}\|$

are constants; $\dfrac{d}{dt}f(t) = \|\mathbf{v}\| + 2t\|\mathbf{w}\|$

$$\frac{d^2}{dt^2}f(t) = 2\|\mathbf{w}\| = 2\sqrt{1 + 4 + 9} = 2\sqrt{14}$$

47. $(\mathbf{F}\cdot\mathbf{G})'(t) = [(3 + t^2)\sin(2 - t) - t^{-1}e^{2t}]'$

$$= -(3 + t^2)\cos(2 - t)$$

$$+ 2t\sin(2 - t) - 2t^{-1}e^{2t} + t^{-2}e^{2t}$$

Also,

$$\mathbf{F}'(t) = 2t\mathbf{i} + 3\sin 3t\mathbf{j} - t^{-2}\mathbf{k};$$

$$\mathbf{G}'(t) = -\cos(2 - t)\mathbf{i} - 2e^{2t}\mathbf{k}$$

and

$$(\mathbf{F}'\cdot\mathbf{G})(t) + (\mathbf{F}\cdot\mathbf{G}')(t)$$

$$= [2t\mathbf{i} + 3\sin 3t\mathbf{j} - t^{-2}\mathbf{k}][\sin(2 - t)\mathbf{i} - e^{2t}\mathbf{k}]$$

$$+ [(3 + t^2)\mathbf{i} - \cos 3t\mathbf{j}$$

$$+ t^{-1}\mathbf{k}]\cdot[-\cos(2 - t)\mathbf{i} - 2e^{2t}\mathbf{k}]$$

$$= 2t\sin(2 - t) + t^{-2}e^{2t}$$

$$- (3 + t^2)\cos(2 - t) - 2t^{-1}e^{2t}$$

Therefore, $(\mathbf{F}\cdot\mathbf{G})'(t) = (\mathbf{F}'\cdot\mathbf{G})(t) + (\mathbf{F}\cdot\mathbf{G}')(t)$

50. Two vectors are parallel if they have proportional direction numbers, so vector functions are parallel if one is a scalar multiple of the other. In particular,

$$\mathbf{F}'(t) = k(e^{kt}\mathbf{i} - e^{-kt}\mathbf{j})$$

$$\mathbf{F}''(t) = k^2(e^{kt}\mathbf{i} + e^{-kt}\mathbf{j}) = k^2\mathbf{F}(t)$$

Thus, $\mathbf{F}''(t)$ is parallel to $\mathbf{F}(t)$.

11.3 Modeling Ballistics and Planetary Motion,
  Page 754–757

SURVIVAL HINT: *This section is basically the same material covered in Section 3.4, except that the path of the projectile has been broken into its horizontal* and vertical components. This allows us to write a vector function, which gives the position, velocity, and acceleration at any time, t. A review of some of the ideas of Section 3.4 might be helpful.

1. The appropriate formulas are given on page 750.

$$T_f = \frac{2}{g} v_0 \sin \alpha = \frac{2}{32}(128)\sin 35° \approx 4.6 \text{ sec}$$

$$R = \frac{v_0^2}{g} \sin 2\alpha = \frac{128^2}{32} \sin 2(35°) \approx 481 \text{ ft}$$

10. $r = \| \mathbf{R}(t) \| = \sqrt{(\cos t)^2 + (\sin t)^2} = 1$

$$\frac{dr}{dt} = \frac{d^2 r}{dt^2} = 0$$

$$\theta = \tan^{-1}\left(\frac{\cos t}{\sin t}\right)$$

$$= -t + \frac{\pi}{2};$$

$$\frac{d\theta}{dt} = -1$$

$$\frac{d^2\theta}{dt^2} = 0$$

$$\mathbf{V}(t) = (0)\mathbf{u}_r + (1)(-1)\mathbf{u}_\theta$$

$$= -\mathbf{u}_\theta$$

$$\mathbf{A}(t) = [0 - (1)(-1)^2]\mathbf{u}_r + [1(0)+2(0)(-1)]\mathbf{u}_\theta$$

$$= -\mathbf{u}_r$$

12. $r = e^{t-1}$

$$\frac{dr}{dt} = e^{t-1}$$

$$= \frac{d^2 r}{dt^2}$$

$$\frac{d\theta}{dt} = -1$$

$$\frac{d^2\theta}{dt^2} = 0$$

$$\mathbf{V} = \frac{dr}{dt}\mathbf{u}_r + r\frac{d\theta}{dt}\mathbf{u}_\theta = e^{t-1}\mathbf{u}_r + e^{t-1}(-1)\mathbf{u}_\theta$$

$$\mathbf{A} = \left[\frac{d^2 r}{dt^2} - r\left(\frac{d\theta}{dt}\right)^2\right]\mathbf{u}_r + \left[r\frac{d^2\theta}{dt^2} + 2\frac{dr}{dt}\frac{d\theta}{dt}\right]\mathbf{u}_\theta$$

$$= e^{t-1}[(1-1)\mathbf{u}_r + (-2)\mathbf{u}_\theta]$$

$$= -2e^{t-1}\mathbf{u}_\theta$$

15. $\alpha = 45°$, so we can use the formula for maximum range: $R_m = v_0^2/g$.

$$2{,}000 = \frac{v_0^2}{9.8}$$

$$v_0 = 140 \text{ m/sec}$$

19. The maximum height is reached when $y'(t) = 0$. We can use this equation to find the time at which this occurs, then use that time in $y(t)$ to find the height.

$$y(t) = -16t^2 + (V_0 \sin \alpha)t + s_0$$

$$= -16t^2 + 45t + 4$$

$$y'(t) = -32t + 45$$

$$y'(t) = 0 \text{ when } t = \frac{45}{32} \approx 1.41 \text{ sec}$$

$$y(\tfrac{45}{32}) = -16(\tfrac{45}{32})^2 + 45(\tfrac{45}{32}) + 4$$

$$\approx 35.64 \text{ ft}$$

The ball will land when $y = 0$. We can use $y(t) = 0$ to find the time of flight, and then use that time to find $x(t)$.

$$-16t^2 + 45t + 4 = 0 \text{ when } t \approx 2.8987 \text{ sec}$$

$$x(t) = (v_0 \cos \alpha)t = \frac{\sqrt{3}}{2}(90)t$$

$$= 45\sqrt{3}\ t\quad x(2.8987)$$

$$\approx 225.93 \text{ ft}$$

To find the distance to the fence we will find t for $y(t) = 5$, then use that time in $x(t)$.

$$-16t^2 + 45t + 4 = 5 \text{ when } t \approx 2.79 \text{ sec.}$$

$$x(2.79) = 45\sqrt{3}(2.79)$$

$$\approx 217 \text{ ft}$$

22. Solve $-\frac{1}{2}(32)t^2 + 50(\frac{\sqrt{2}}{2})t + 6.5 = 6$

The positive solution is $t \approx 2.22376$

$$s = (50 \cos 45°)t$$

$$\approx 78.62 \text{ ft}$$

Jerry is 78.62 ft from Steve when he catches the pass. Since Jerry runs at 32 ft/sec the *most* he can be is 71.168 ft from the line of scrimmage when he catches the pass. There-fore, Steve must be

$$78.62 - 71.168 \approx 7.452 \text{ ft (or less)}$$

behind the line of scrimmage when he releases the ball. Therefore, Steve fades back about 7.452 ft before releasing the ball.

24. The ball reaches the the maximum height when $t = v_0 \sin \alpha/32$. Solving

$$-16\left(\frac{v_0 \sin \alpha}{32}\right)^2 + (v_0 \sin \alpha)\left(\frac{v_0 \sin \alpha}{32}\right) + 7 = 12$$

We find $v_0 \sin \alpha = 17.89$. The time for the ball is to reach the basket is found by solving

$$(v_0 \cos \alpha)t = 20$$

$$t = \frac{20}{v_0 \cos \alpha}$$

Since the ball is 10 ft above the floor at this time, we have

$$-16\left(\frac{20}{v_0 \cos \alpha}\right)^2 + (v_0 \sin \alpha)\left(\frac{20}{v_0 \cos \alpha}\right) = 3$$

$$v_0 \cos \alpha \approx 21.91$$

Since

$$\sin^2\alpha + \cos^2\alpha = \left(\frac{17.89}{v_0}\right)^2 + \left(\frac{21.91}{v_0}\right)^2 = 1$$

we have

$$v_0 \approx \sqrt{17.89^2 + 21.91^2}$$

$$\approx 28.29 \text{ ft/s}$$

33. Let s and h be the horizontal and vertical distances, respectively, from the helicopter to the bunker. Then,

$$h = s \tan 20° \text{ and } 10,000 - h$$

$$= s \tan 15°$$

so that

$$s = \frac{10,000}{\tan 15° + \tan 20°}$$

$$\approx 15,824.8 \text{ ft}$$

and the height of the bunker above the level ground is

$$h_1 = s \tan 15°$$

$$\approx 15,824.8 \tan 15°$$

$$\approx 4,240.2 \text{ ft}$$

Since the canister is "dropped" (no initial vertical velocity), it will take t_1 seconds to reach the level of the bunker, where

$$-16t_1{}^2 + 10,000 = 4,240.2$$

$$t_1 \approx 18.97$$

The time is about 19 seconds; the horizontal distance (in feet) traveled by the canister is

$$s_1 = 200\, t_1$$

$$\approx 3,794$$

Thus, the helicopter should travel

$$s - s_1 \approx 15,824.8 - 3,794$$

$$\approx 12,030.8 \text{ ft}$$

before the canister is released. At the rate of 200 ft/s, this takes

$$t \approx \frac{12,030.8}{200}$$

$$\approx 60.1$$

The Spy should wait one minute before releasing the canister.

34. The initial velocity of the rock is

$$\mathbf{V}_0 = 25\left(\frac{\sqrt{3}}{2}\mathbf{i} + \tfrac{1}{2}\mathbf{j}\right) + 15\mathbf{i}$$

and the initial position is

$$\mathbf{S}_0 = -10\mathbf{i} + 33\mathbf{j}$$

$$\mathbf{A} = -32\mathbf{j}$$

$$\mathbf{V} = (-32t)\mathbf{j} + \mathbf{V}_0$$

$$= -32t\mathbf{j} + \left(\frac{25\sqrt{3}}{2} + 15\right)\mathbf{i} + \frac{25}{2}\mathbf{j};$$

$$= \left(\frac{25\sqrt{3}}{2} + 15\right)\mathbf{i} + \left(\frac{25}{2} - 32t\right)\mathbf{j}$$

$$\mathbf{S} = \left[\left(\frac{25\sqrt{3}}{2} + 15\right)t\right]\mathbf{i} + \left[-16t^2 + \frac{25t}{2}\right]\mathbf{j} + \mathbf{S}_0$$

The rock hits the water when

$$-16t^2 + \frac{25t}{2} + 33 = 0$$

$$t = \frac{25 \pm \sqrt{9,073}}{64}$$

If we disregard the negative value, we find $t \approx 1.88$ sec. The distance from the base of the cliff is

$$x = \left(\frac{25\sqrt{3}}{2} + 15\right)\left(\frac{25 + \sqrt{9,073}}{64}\right) - 10 \approx 58.9 \text{ ft}$$

37. The first shot travels

$$\frac{(700)^2}{32}\sin 2(25°) \approx 11,730 \text{ ft}$$

This is 60 ft too far, and in the 30 second reloading period the target travels

$$30(10) = 300 \text{ ft}$$

Thus, when the second shot is fired, it is s_1 ft from the gun, where

$$s_1 = 11{,}730 - 60 + 300$$

$$= 11{,}970 \text{ ft}$$

If the second shell is fired at angle α, it will be in the air $\frac{2}{32}(700)\sin\alpha$ seconds, so

$$\frac{(700)^2}{32}\sin 2\alpha = 11{,}970 + 10\left[\frac{2}{32}(700)\sin\alpha\right]$$

$$\alpha \approx 26.3°$$

11.4 Unit Tangent and Normal Vectors; Curvature, Page 767-769

3. $\mathbf{R}(t) = e^t\cos t\,\mathbf{i} + e^t\sin t\,\mathbf{j}$

$\mathbf{R}'(t) = e^t(-\sin t + \cos t)\mathbf{i}$
$\qquad + e^t(\cos t + \sin t)\mathbf{j}$

$\|\mathbf{R}'(t)\| = \sqrt{2}\,e^t$

$\mathbf{T}(t) = \dfrac{\sqrt{2}}{2}[(\cos t - \sin t)\mathbf{i} + (\cos t + \sin t)\mathbf{j}]$

$\mathbf{N}(t) = -\dfrac{\sqrt{2}}{2}[(\sin t + \cos t)\mathbf{i} + (\sin t - \cos t)\mathbf{j}]$

SURVIVAL HINT: *The arc length formula is easily recalled if you think of it as the sum (definite integral) of lines in* $\mathbb{R}^3$ *(space diagonals);*

$$\sqrt{(\Delta x)^2 + (\Delta y)^2 + (\Delta z)^2}$$

where the delta change is found by using the derivative.

11. $\mathbf{R}'(t) = 3\mathbf{i} - (3\sin t)\mathbf{j} + (3\cos t)\mathbf{k}$

$\dfrac{ds}{dt} = \|\mathbf{R}'(t)\| = \sqrt{3^2 + 9\sin^2 t + 9\cos^2 t}$

$\qquad = 3\sqrt{2}$

$s = \displaystyle\int_0^{\pi/2} 3\sqrt{2}\,dt = \dfrac{3\sqrt{2}\pi}{2}$

20. $y' = 1 - x^{-2};\ y'' = 2x^{-3};$

at $x = 1$, $y' = 0$ and $y'' = 2$

$\kappa = \dfrac{|y''|}{[1+(y')^2]^{3/2}}$

$\quad = \dfrac{2}{[1+0]^{3/2}}$

$\quad = 2$

24. $y' = -\sin x;\ y'' = -\cos x;$

at $x = \dfrac{\pi}{4}$, $y' = -\dfrac{\sqrt{2}}{2}$ and $y'' = -\dfrac{\sqrt{2}}{2}$

$\kappa = \dfrac{|y''|}{[1+(y')^2]^{3/2}}$

$\quad = \dfrac{\sqrt{2}/2}{[1+1/2]^{3/2}}$

$\quad = \dfrac{2\sqrt{3}}{9}$

29. $\dfrac{d\mathbf{R}}{dt} = \dfrac{\cos t}{\sin t}\mathbf{i} - \dfrac{\sin t}{\cos t}\mathbf{j}$

$\qquad = \cot t\,\mathbf{i} - \tan t\,\mathbf{j}$

$\left\|\dfrac{d\mathbf{R}}{dt}\right\| = \sqrt{\cot^2 t + \tan^2 t}$; at $t = \dfrac{\pi}{3}$, the unit

tangent vector is

$\mathbf{T} = \dfrac{\dfrac{1}{\sqrt{3}}\mathbf{i} - \sqrt{3}\,\mathbf{j}}{\sqrt{\dfrac{10}{3}}}$

$\qquad = \dfrac{1}{\sqrt{10}}(\mathbf{i} - 3\mathbf{j})$

The unit normal vector is $\mathbf{N} = -\dfrac{1}{\sqrt{10}}(3\mathbf{i} + \mathbf{j})$

SURVIVAL HINT: *There are many different formulas for curvature dependent. The one you will use is dependent on the form of the given information (see page 767). You should ask your instructor if you are required to know (memorize) any of these formulas.*

31. **a.** $\mathbf{T} = \dfrac{\mathbf{R}'(t)}{\|\mathbf{R}'(t)\|}$

$\qquad = \dfrac{(\cos t)\mathbf{i} + (-\sin t)\mathbf{j} + \mathbf{k}}{\sqrt{\cos^2 t + \sin^2 t + 1}}$

$\qquad = \dfrac{\sqrt{2}}{2}[(\cos t)\mathbf{i} + (-\sin t)\mathbf{j} + \mathbf{k}]$

$\qquad \mathbf{T}(\pi) = \dfrac{\sqrt{2}}{2}(-\mathbf{i} + \mathbf{k})$

b. $\mathbf{R}'(t) = (\cos t)\mathbf{i} - (\sin t)\mathbf{j} + \mathbf{k}$

$\qquad \mathbf{R}'(\pi) = -\mathbf{i} + \mathbf{k}$

$\qquad \mathbf{R}''(t) = (-\sin t)\mathbf{i} - (\cos t)\mathbf{j}$

$\mathbf{R}''(\pi) = \mathbf{j}$

$\kappa = \dfrac{\|\mathbf{R}' \times \mathbf{R}''\|}{\|\mathbf{R}'\|^3}$

$\quad = \dfrac{\|(-\mathbf{i} + \mathbf{k}) \times \mathbf{j}\|}{(\sqrt{2})^3}$

$\quad = \dfrac{\sqrt{2}}{2\sqrt{2}}$

$\quad = \dfrac{1}{2}$

c. $s = \displaystyle\int_0^\pi \|\mathbf{R}'\|\,dt$

$\quad = \displaystyle\int_0^\pi \sqrt{2}\,dt$

$\quad = \sqrt{2}\pi$

33. $9x^2 + 4y^2 = 36$

$\qquad \dfrac{x^2}{4} + \dfrac{y^2}{9} = 1$

Parametrize this curve by letting $x = 2\cos t$, $y = 3\sin t$.

$\qquad x' = -2\sin t,\ y' = 3\cos t$

$\qquad x'' = -2\cos t,\ y'' = -3\sin t$

$\kappa = \dfrac{|x'y'' - y'x''|}{[(x')^2 + (y')^2]^{3/2}}$

$\quad = \dfrac{|(-2\sin t)(-3\sin t) - (3\cos t)(-2\cos t)|}{[(-2\sin t)^2 + (3\cos t)^2]^{3/2}}$

$\quad = \dfrac{6}{(4\sin^2 t + 9\cos^2 t)^{3/2}} = 6(4 + 5\cos^2 t)^{-3/2}$

$$\frac{d\kappa}{dt} = -\frac{6(3)}{2}(4 + 5\cos^2 t)^{-5/2}(-10\cos t \sin t)$$

$$\frac{d\kappa}{dt} = 0 \text{ if } t = 0, \frac{\pi}{2}, \pi, \frac{3\pi}{2}, 2\pi$$

At $t = 0$ and $t = \pi$, $\kappa = \dfrac{6}{(4+5)^{3/2}} = \dfrac{2}{9}$

(a minimum)

At $t = \frac{\pi}{2}$ and $t = \frac{3\pi}{2}$, $\kappa = \dfrac{6}{4^{3/2}} = \dfrac{3}{4}$

(a maximum)

The points at which a maximum occurs are $P(0, 3)$, and $Q(0, -3)$.

35. $y' = 6x^5 - 6x$; $y' = 0$ when $x = 0, 1, -1$

Since $y'' = 30x^4 - 6$, we have

$$\rho = \frac{1}{\kappa}$$

$$= \frac{[1 + (y')^2]^{3/2}}{|y''|}$$

$$= \frac{[1 + (6x^5 - 6x)^2]^{3/2}}{|30x^4 - 6|}$$

$\rho(0) = \frac{1}{6}$; $\rho(1) = \rho(-1) = \frac{1}{24}$

40. $\mathbf{R}(t) = (t - \cos t)\mathbf{i} + \sin t\,\mathbf{j} + 3\mathbf{k}$

$\mathbf{R}'(t) = (1 + \sin t)\mathbf{i} + \cos t\,\mathbf{j};$

$\mathbf{R}''(t) = (\cos t)\mathbf{i} - (\sin t)\mathbf{j}$

$$\mathbf{R}' \times \mathbf{R}'' = \begin{vmatrix} \mathbf{i} & \mathbf{j} & \mathbf{k} \\ 1 + \sin t & \cos t & 0 \\ \cos t & -\sin t & 0 \end{vmatrix}$$

$$= (-\sin t - \sin^2 t - \cos^2 t)\mathbf{k}$$

$$= -(1 + \sin t)\mathbf{k}$$

$$\|\mathbf{R}' \times \mathbf{R}''\| = 1 + \sin t$$

$$\|\mathbf{v}\| = \sqrt{2 + 2\sin t}$$

$$\kappa = \frac{1 + \sin t}{2^{3/2}(1 + \sin t)^{3/2}}$$

$$= \frac{1}{2\sqrt{2 + 2\sin t}}$$

41. $y = x^2$; $y' = 2x$; $y'' = 2$;

$$\kappa = \frac{2}{(1 + 4x^2)^{3/2}}$$

46. $r = 1 + \cos\theta$; $r' = -\sin\theta$; $r'' = -\cos\theta$

$$\kappa = \frac{\left|(1+\cos\theta)^2 + 2\sin^2\theta - (1+\cos\theta)(-\cos\theta)\right|}{(1 + 2\cos\theta + \cos^2\theta + \sin^2\theta)^{3/2}}$$

$$= \frac{1 + 2\cos\theta + \cos^2\theta + 2\sin^2\theta + \cos\theta + \cos^2\theta}{2^{3/2}(1 + \cos\theta)^{3/2}}$$

$$= \frac{1 + 3\cos\theta + 2(\cos^2\theta + \sin^2\theta)}{2^{3/2}(1 + \cos\theta)^{3/2}}$$

$$= \frac{3}{2^{3/2}\sqrt{1 + \cos\theta}}$$

52. a. $\mathbf{R}' = \|\mathbf{R}'\|\mathbf{T}$

$$\mathbf{R}'' = \|\mathbf{R}'\|'\mathbf{T} + \|\mathbf{R}'\|\mathbf{T}'$$

$$= \|\mathbf{R}'\|'\mathbf{T} + \|\mathbf{R}'\|\left(\frac{d\mathbf{T}}{ds}\frac{ds}{dt}\right)$$

$$= \|\mathbf{R}'\|'\mathbf{T} + \|\mathbf{R}'\|^2\kappa\mathbf{N}$$

since $\frac{ds}{dt} = \| \mathbf{R}' \|$ and $\frac{d\mathbf{T}}{ds} = \left\| \frac{d\mathbf{T}}{ds} \right\| \mathbf{N} = \kappa \mathbf{N}$

b. $\mathbf{R}' \times \mathbf{R}'' = \mathbf{R}' \times (\| \mathbf{R}' \| \mathbf{T} + \| \mathbf{R}' \|^2 \kappa \mathbf{N})$

$\qquad = \| \mathbf{R}' \| (\mathbf{R}' \times \mathbf{T}) + \| \mathbf{R}' \|^2 \kappa (\mathbf{R}' \times \mathbf{N})$

$\qquad = 0 + \| \mathbf{R}' \|^2 \kappa (\| \mathbf{R}' \| \mathbf{T} \times \mathbf{N})$

$\qquad = \| \mathbf{R}' \|^3 \kappa (\mathbf{T} \times \mathbf{N})$

since $\mathbf{R}' = \| \mathbf{R}' \| \mathbf{T}$.

c. $\dfrac{\| \mathbf{R}' \times \mathbf{R}'' \|}{\| \mathbf{R}' \|^3} = \dfrac{\left\| \| \mathbf{R}' \|^3 \kappa (\mathbf{T} \times \mathbf{N}) \right\|}{\| \mathbf{R}' \|^3}$

$\qquad = \kappa \| \mathbf{T} \times \mathbf{N} \|$

$\qquad = \kappa$

since $\mathbf{T}$ and $\mathbf{N}$ are unit vectors.

57. a. $\mathbf{R}(t)$ is given; compute $\kappa = \dfrac{\| \mathbf{R}' \times \mathbf{R}'' \|}{\| \mathbf{R}' \|^3}$ and $\rho = 1/\kappa$. Obtain $\mathbf{T}$ and $\mathbf{N}$. The center of the osculating circle is along $\mathbf{N}$ at a distance ρ from the point of contact on the curve.

b. $x(t) = 32t;\ y(t) = 16t^2 - 4;$

$\mathbf{R} = 32t\mathbf{i} + (16t^2 - 4)\mathbf{j};$

$\mathbf{R}'(t) = 32\mathbf{i} + 32t\mathbf{j};\ \mathbf{R}''(t) = 32\mathbf{j}.$

At $t = 1$, the point is $P(32, 12)$:

$\mathbf{R}' \times \mathbf{R}'' = \begin{vmatrix} \mathbf{i} & \mathbf{j} & \mathbf{k} \\ 32 & 32 & 0 \\ 0 & 32 & 0 \end{vmatrix}$

$\qquad = 32^2 \mathbf{k}$

$\| \mathbf{R}' \| = 32\sqrt{2}$

$\kappa = \dfrac{\| \mathbf{R}' \times \mathbf{R}'' \|}{\| \mathbf{R}' \|^3}$

$\quad = \dfrac{32^2}{(32)^3 (2)\sqrt{2}}$

$\quad = \dfrac{1}{64\sqrt{2}}$

$\rho = 32\sqrt{2}$

$\mathbf{T} = \dfrac{\mathbf{i} + t\mathbf{j}}{\sqrt{1 + t^2}}$

$\mathbf{T}(1) = \dfrac{\mathbf{i} + \mathbf{j}}{\sqrt{2}}$

The principal unit normal at $t = 1$ is

$\mathbf{N}(1) = \dfrac{-\mathbf{i} + \mathbf{j}}{\sqrt{2}}$

Let $C(a, b)$ be the center of the osculating circle. Then,

$$\mathbf{PC} = \rho \mathbf{N}$$

$\langle a - 32, b - 12 \rangle = 32\sqrt{2} \left[\dfrac{1}{\sqrt{2}} \langle -1, 1 \rangle \right]$

$a - 32 = -32$, or $a = 0$ and

$b - 12 = 32$, or $b = 44$

Thus, the equation of the osculating circle is

$$x^2 + (y - 44)^2 = (32\sqrt{2})^2$$

11.5 Tangential and Normal Components of Acceleration, Page 775-777

SURVIVAL HINT: *Most of these problems involve finding several different derivative; and the sums and products of several components. It is essential that your work be well organized and each step be properly labeled.*

2. $\mathbf{R}(t) = t\mathbf{i} + e^t\mathbf{j}$

$\mathbf{V}(t) = \mathbf{R}'(t) = \mathbf{i} + e^t\mathbf{j}$

$\mathbf{A}(t) = \mathbf{V}'(t) = e^t\mathbf{j}$

$\dfrac{ds}{dt} = \|\mathbf{V}(t)\| = \sqrt{1 + e^{2t}}$

$A_T = \dfrac{d^2s}{dt^2} = \dfrac{e^{2t}}{\sqrt{1 + e^{2t}}};$

$A_N = \sqrt{\|\mathbf{A}\|^2 - A_T^2}$

$\qquad = \sqrt{e^{2t} - \dfrac{e^{4t}}{1 + e^{2t}}} = \dfrac{e^t}{\sqrt{1 + e^{2t}}}$

7. $\mathbf{R}(t) = (\sin t)\mathbf{i} + (\cos t)\mathbf{j} + (\sin t)\mathbf{k}$

$\mathbf{V}(t) = \mathbf{R}'(t) = (\cos t)\mathbf{i} - (\sin t)\mathbf{j} + (\cos t)\mathbf{k}$

$\mathbf{A}(t) = \mathbf{V}'(t) = (-\sin t)\mathbf{i} - (\cos t)\mathbf{j} - (\sin t)\mathbf{k}$

$\dfrac{ds}{dt} = \|\mathbf{V}(t)\| = \sqrt{1 + \cos^2 t}$

$A_T = \dfrac{d^2s}{dt^2} = -\dfrac{\sin t \cos t}{\sqrt{1 + \cos^2 t}}$

$A_N = \sqrt{\|\mathbf{A}\|^2 - A_T^2}$

$\qquad = \sqrt{1 + \sin^2 t - \dfrac{\sin^2 t \cos^2 t}{1 + \cos^2 t}}$

$\qquad = \sqrt{\dfrac{2}{1 + \cos^2 t}}$

9. $\|\mathbf{V}_0\| = \sqrt{10}$

$\|\mathbf{A}_0\| = \sqrt{29}$

$\mathbf{T}_0 = \dfrac{1}{\sqrt{10}}\langle 1, -3 \rangle$

$\mathbf{N}_0 = \dfrac{1}{\sqrt{10}}\langle 3, 1 \rangle$

$A_T = \dfrac{\langle 1, -3 \rangle \cdot \langle 2, 5 \rangle}{\sqrt{10}}$

$\qquad = \dfrac{-13}{\sqrt{10}}$

$A_N = \sqrt{\|\mathbf{A}_0\|^2 - A_T^2}$

$\qquad = \sqrt{29 - \dfrac{169}{10}}$

$\qquad = \dfrac{11}{\sqrt{10}}$

12. $\|\mathbf{V}_0\| = \sqrt{30}$

$\|\mathbf{A}_0\| = \sqrt{50}$

$\mathbf{T}_0 = \dfrac{1}{\sqrt{30}}\langle 5, -1, 2 \rangle$

$A_T = \dfrac{\langle 5, -1, 2 \rangle \cdot \langle 1, 0, -7 \rangle}{\sqrt{30}}$

$\qquad = \dfrac{-9}{\sqrt{30}}$

$A_N = \sqrt{\|\mathbf{A}_0\|^2 - A_T^2}$

$\qquad = \sqrt{50 - \left(\dfrac{-9}{\sqrt{30}}\right)^2}$

$$= \sqrt{\frac{1{,}419}{30}}$$

$$A_N \mathbf{N}_0 = \mathbf{A}_0 - A_T \mathbf{T}_0$$

$$\mathbf{N}_0 = \sqrt{\frac{30}{1{,}419}} \left\{ \langle 1,\, 0,\, -7 \rangle \right.$$

$$\left. - \left(-\frac{9}{\sqrt{30}} \right)\left(\frac{1}{\sqrt{30}} \right)\langle 5,\, -1,\, 2 \rangle \right\}$$

$$= \frac{1}{\sqrt{42{,}570}} \langle 75,\, -9,\, -192 \rangle$$

14. $\|\mathbf{V}\| = \sqrt{t^2 + t + 1}$

$$A_T = \|\mathbf{V}\|'$$

$$= \frac{2t + 1}{2\sqrt{t^2 + t + 1}};$$

at $t = 3$, $A_T = \dfrac{7}{2\sqrt{13}}$

18. $\mathbf{R}'(t) = \langle 4t - 5,\, 5,\, 8t \rangle$

$$\text{speed} = \frac{ds}{dt}$$

$$= \|\mathbf{R}'(t)\|$$

$$= \sqrt{(4t - 5)^2 + 5^2 + (8t)^2}$$

$$= \sqrt{80t^2 - 40t + 50}$$

$$\frac{d^2 s}{dt^2} = \frac{80t - 20}{\sqrt{80t^2 - 40t + 50}}$$

$$= 0 \text{ when } t = \tfrac{1}{4}$$

The minimum speed is

$$\|\mathbf{R}'(\tfrac{1}{4})\| = \sqrt{80(\tfrac{1}{4})^2 - 40(\tfrac{1}{4}) + 50}$$

$$= 3\sqrt{5}$$

20. a. $\mathbf{R}(t) = (r \cos \omega t)\mathbf{i} + (r \sin \omega t)\mathbf{j}$

$$\mathbf{V}(t) = \mathbf{R}'(t)$$

$$= r\omega(-\sin \omega t \mathbf{i} + \cos \omega t \mathbf{j})$$

$$\mathbf{A}(t) = \mathbf{V}'(t)$$

$$= -r\omega(\cos \omega t \mathbf{i} + \sin \omega t \mathbf{j})$$

$$\frac{ds}{dt} = \|\mathbf{V}(t)\|$$

$$= r\omega$$

$$A_T = \frac{d^2 s}{dt^2} = 0$$

$$A_N = \sqrt{\|\mathbf{A}\|^2 - A_T{}^2}$$

$$= r\omega$$

b. $\dfrac{dx}{dt} = -r\omega \sin \omega t$

$$\frac{dy}{dt} = r\omega \cos \omega t$$

$$\frac{d^2 x}{dt^2} = -r\omega^2 \cos \omega t$$

$$\frac{d^2 y}{dt^2} = -r\omega^2 \sin \omega t$$

$$\kappa = \frac{r^2 \omega^3}{(r^2 \omega^2)^{3/2}}$$

$$= \frac{1}{r}$$

23. Since the pail moves in a vertical plane with

angular velocity ω rev/s, we have

$$\mathbf{R}(t) = \langle 3\cos 2\pi\omega t,\ 3\sin 2\pi\omega t\rangle$$

and

$$\mathbf{V}(t) = \langle -6\pi\omega\sin 2\pi\omega t,\ 6\pi\omega\cos 2\pi\omega t\rangle$$

$$\mathbf{A}(t) = \langle -12\pi^2\omega^2\cos 2\pi\omega t,\ -12\pi^2\omega^2\sin 2\pi\omega t\rangle$$

$$\frac{ds}{dt} = \|\mathbf{V}(t)\|$$

$$= 6\pi\omega$$

$$\|\mathbf{A}(t)\| = 12\pi^2\omega^2$$

$$A_T = \|\mathbf{V}\|' = 0$$

$$A_N = \sqrt{\|\mathbf{A}\|^2 - A_T{}^2}$$

$$= 12\pi^2\omega^2$$

The force due to the motion of the pail with mass 2/32 slugs is

$$F_n = mA_N$$

$$= \tfrac{2}{32}(12\pi^2\omega^2)$$

$$\approx 7.4\ \omega^2\ \text{lbs}$$

The force on the bottom of the pail is greatest at the lowest point of the swing where it equals

$$7.4\omega^2 + 2$$

The force is $7.4\omega^2 - 2$ lbs at the top of the swing, and to keep the water from spilling, we

must have

$$7.4\omega^2 - 2 = 0$$

$$\omega = 0.52\ \text{rev/s}\ (31.2\ \text{rev/min})$$

24. $\qquad 900x^2 + 400y^2 = 1$

$$x = \tfrac{1}{30}\cos t,\ y = \tfrac{1}{20}\sin t;$$

$$x' = -\tfrac{1}{30}\sin t,\ y' = \tfrac{1}{20}\cos t$$

$$x'' = -\tfrac{1}{30}\cos t,\ y'' = -\tfrac{1}{20}\sin t$$

$$\kappa = \frac{|x'y'' - y'x''|}{[(x')^2 + (y')^2]^{3/2}}$$

$$= \frac{\left|\left(\frac{-1}{30}\sin t\right)\left(\frac{-1}{20}\sin t\right) - \left(\frac{1}{20}\cos t\right)\left(\frac{-1}{30}\cos t\right)\right|}{\left[\left(\frac{-1}{30}\sin t\right)^2 + \left(\frac{1}{20}\cos t\right)^2\right]}$$

$$= \frac{\frac{1}{600}}{\left[\frac{1}{900}\sin^2 t + \frac{1}{400}\cos^2 t\right]^{3/2}}$$

The car's mass is $m = 2{,}700/32$ slugs, and is

$$\frac{ds}{dt} = 45\left(\frac{5{,}280}{3{,}600}\right)$$

$$= 66\ \text{ft/s}$$

Thus, the normal force required to keep the car from skidding at time t is

$$F_N = mA_N$$

$$= m\left(\frac{ds}{dt}\right)^2\kappa(t)$$

$$= \frac{2{,}700}{32}(66)^2\frac{1}{\rho(t)}$$

$$= \frac{367{,}537.5}{\rho(t)}$$

F_N is measured in pounds when $\rho(t)$ is measure in feet. At $(1/30, 0)$, were $t = 0$, we have

$$\kappa(0) = \frac{1}{600}\left(\frac{1}{400}\right)^{-3/2}$$

$$\approx 13.33$$

and

$$\rho(0) = \frac{1}{\kappa(0)}$$

$$\approx 0.075(5{,}280)$$

$$\approx 396 \text{ ft},$$

so

$$F_N = \frac{367{,}537.5}{396}$$

$$\approx 928 \text{ lbs}$$

At $(0, \frac{1}{20})$, we have $t = \frac{\pi}{2}$ and

$$\kappa\left(\frac{\pi}{2}\right) = \frac{1}{600}\left(\frac{1}{900}\right)^{-3/2}$$

$$= 45$$

Thus,

$$\rho\left(\frac{\pi}{2}\right) = \frac{1}{\kappa(\pi/2)}$$

$$\approx 0.022(5{,}280)$$

$$\approx 177.3 \text{ ft}$$

$$F_N = \frac{367{,}537.5}{177.3}$$

$$\approx 2{,}073 \text{ lbs}$$

25. **a.** Since the car moves in a circle, its tangential acceleration is 0. The force required to keep the car moving in a circle has magnitude

$$m\kappa\left(\frac{ds}{dt}\right)^2 = \frac{m}{\rho}\left(\frac{ds}{dt}\right)^2$$

where $m = W/g$ is the car's mass and $\rho = 1/\kappa$. We want this force to be balanced by the frictional force keeping the car on the road, so

$$\frac{m}{\rho}\left(\frac{ds}{dt}\right)^2 = \mu W = \mu(mg)$$

The m's cancel (so weight does not matter), and for $\mu = 0.47$, $\rho = 150$, and $g = 32$, the maximum safe speed is

$$\frac{ds}{dt} = \sqrt{\mu g \rho}$$

$$= \sqrt{(0.47)(32)(150)}$$

$$= 47 \text{ ft/s} \quad \text{(about 32 mi/h)}$$

b. With a roadway banked at angle θ, the horizontal force pulling the car toward the center of the circle has magnitude

$$\|\mathbf{F}_k\| = \|\mathbf{F}_N\|\sin\theta + \|\mathbf{F}_s\|\cos\theta$$

$$= \|\mathbf{F}_N\|\sin\theta + \mu\|\mathbf{F}_N\|\cos\theta$$

where $\mathbf{F}_N$ is the normal force and $\mathbf{F}_s$ is the friction force, which is directed downward along the bank. We also have

$$mg = \|\mathbf{F}_N\| \cos\theta - \|\mathbf{F}_s\| \sin\theta$$

$$= \|\mathbf{F}_N\| \cos\theta - \mu\|\mathbf{F}_N\| \sin\theta$$

so that

$$\|\mathbf{F}_N\| = \frac{mg}{(\cos\theta - \mu\sin\theta)}$$

and

$$\|\mathbf{F}_k\| = (\sin\theta + \mu\cos\theta)\|\mathbf{F}_N\|$$

$$= \frac{mg(\sin\theta + \mu\cos\theta)}{\cos\theta - \mu\sin\theta}$$

To find the optimal banking speed we set this expression for $\|\mathbf{F}_k\|$ equal to

$$\frac{m}{\rho}\left(\frac{ds}{dt}\right)^2 = \frac{mg(\sin\theta + \mu\cos\theta)}{\cos\theta - \mu\sin\theta}$$

$$\frac{ds}{dt} = \sqrt{\frac{\rho g(\sin\theta + \mu\cos\theta)}{\cos\theta - \mu\sin\theta}}$$

For $\mu = 0.47$, $\rho = 150$, $g = 32$, and $\theta = 17°$, we have

$$\frac{ds}{dt} = \sqrt{\frac{150(32)(\sin 17° + 0.47\cos 17°)}{\cos 17° - 0.47\sin 17°}}$$

$$= 65.94 \text{ ft/s} \quad (\text{about } 45 \text{ mi/h})$$

c. For the optimal safe speed to be 50 mi/h (73.33 ft/s), we want θ to satisfy

$$(73.33)^2 = \frac{150(32)(\sin\theta + 0.47\cos\theta)}{\cos\theta - 0.47\sin\theta}$$

$$\theta \approx 23.1°$$

29. $\mathbf{R}(t) = t\mathbf{i} + 2t\mathbf{j} + t^2\mathbf{k}$

$$\mathbf{R}'(t) = \mathbf{i} + 2\mathbf{j} + 2t\mathbf{k}$$

$$\mathbf{V}'(t) = \mathbf{R}''(t)$$

$$= 2\mathbf{k}$$

$$\|\mathbf{R}'(t)\| = \sqrt{1 + 4 + 4t^2}$$

$$= \sqrt{5 + 4t^2}$$

$$\mathbf{R}' \cdot \mathbf{R}'' = 4t$$

$$\mathbf{R}' \times \mathbf{R}'' = \begin{vmatrix} \mathbf{i} & \mathbf{j} & \mathbf{k} \\ 1 & 2 & 2t \\ 0 & 0 & 2 \end{vmatrix}$$

$$= 4\mathbf{i} - 2\mathbf{j}$$

$$\|\mathbf{R}' \times \mathbf{R}''\| = \sqrt{16 + 4}$$

$$= 2\sqrt{5}$$

$$A_T = \frac{\mathbf{R}' \cdot \mathbf{R}''}{\|\mathbf{R}'\|}$$

$$= \frac{4t}{\sqrt{5 + 4t^2}}$$

$$A_N = \frac{\|\mathbf{R}' \times \mathbf{R}''\|}{\|\mathbf{R}'\|}$$

$$= \frac{2\sqrt{5}}{\sqrt{5 + 4t^2}}$$

36. $\mathbf{R}(x) = x\mathbf{i} + f(x)\mathbf{j}$

$$\mathbf{R}' = \mathbf{i} + f'(x)\mathbf{j}$$

$$\|\mathbf{R}'\| = \sqrt{1 + [f'(x)]^2}$$

$$R'' = f''(x)\mathbf{j}$$

$$R' \cdot R'' = f'(x)f''(x)$$

$$R' \times R'' = \begin{bmatrix} \mathbf{i} & \mathbf{j} & \mathbf{k} \\ 1 & f'(x) & 0 \\ 0 & f''(x) & 0 \end{bmatrix} = f''(x)\mathbf{k}$$

$$A_T = \frac{R' \cdot R''}{\|R'\|}$$

$$= \frac{f'(x)f''(x)}{\sqrt{1 + [f'(x)]^2}}$$

$$A_N = \frac{\|R' \times R''\|}{\|R'\|}$$

$$= \frac{|f''(x)|}{\sqrt{1 + [f'(x)]^2}}$$

CHAPTER 11 REVIEW

Proficiency Examination, Page 777

SURVIVAL HINT: *To help you review the concepts of this chapter, **hand write** the answers to each of these questions onto your own paper.*

1. A vector-valued function (or, simply, a vector function) **F** with domain D assigns a unique vector $\mathbf{F}(t)$ to each scalar t in the set D. The set of all vectors **v** of the form $\mathbf{v} = \mathbf{F}(t)$ for t in D is the range of **F**.

2. $\mathbf{F}(t) = f_1(t)\mathbf{i} + f_2(t)\mathbf{j}$ in $\mathbb{R}^2$ (plane) or

$\mathbf{F}(t) = f_1(t)\mathbf{i} + f_2(t)\mathbf{j} + f_3(t)\mathbf{k}$ in $\mathbb{R}^3$ (space) where f_1, f_2, and f_3 are real-valued (scalar-valued) functions of the real number t defined on the domain set D. In this context f_1, f_2, and f_3 are called the components of **F**.

3. The graph of $\mathbf{F}(t) = f_1(t)\mathbf{i} + f_2(t)\mathbf{j} + f_3(t)\mathbf{k}$ in $\mathbb{R}^3$ (space) is the graph of the parametric equations $x = f_1(t)$, $y = f_2(x)$, $z = f_3(x)$.

4. The limit of a vector function consists of the vector sum of the limits of its individual components.

5. $\mathbf{F}'(t) = f_1{}'(t)\mathbf{i} + f_2{}'(t)\mathbf{j} + f_3{}'(t)\mathbf{k}$

6. $\displaystyle\int \mathbf{F}(t)\ dt$

$= \displaystyle\int f_1(t)\ dt\,\mathbf{i} + \int f_2(t)\ dt\,\mathbf{j} + \int f_3(t)\ dt\,\mathbf{k}$

7. A smooth curve is a trajectory $\mathbf{R}(t)$ with no corners. The first derivative $\mathbf{R}'(t)$ is continuous.

8. a. Linearity rule

$(a\mathbf{F} + b\mathbf{G})'(t) = a\mathbf{F}'(t) + b\mathbf{G}'(t)$

for constants a, b

b. Scalar multiple

$(h\mathbf{F})'(t) = h'(t)\mathbf{F}(t) + h(t)\mathbf{F}'(t)$

c. Dot product rule

$(\mathbf{F} \cdot \mathbf{G})'(t) = (\mathbf{F}' \cdot \mathbf{G})(t) + (\mathbf{F} \cdot \mathbf{G}')(t)$

d. Cross product rule

$(\mathbf{F} \times \mathbf{G})'(t) = (\mathbf{F}' \times \mathbf{G})(t) + (\mathbf{F} \times \mathbf{G}')(t)$

e Chain rule

$$[\mathbf{F}(h(t))]' = h'(t)\mathbf{F}'(h(t))$$

9. If the nonzero vector function $\mathbf{F}(t)$ is differentiable and has constant length, then $\mathbf{F}(t)$ is orthogonal to the derivative vector $\mathbf{F}'(t)$.

10. $\mathbf{R}(t) = x(t)\mathbf{i} + y(t)\mathbf{j} + z(t)\mathbf{k}$ is the position;

$$\mathbf{V}(t) = \frac{d\mathbf{R}(t)}{dt} = \mathbf{R}'(t) \text{ is the velocity;}$$

$$\mathbf{A}(t) = \frac{d\mathbf{V}(t)}{dt} = \frac{d^2\mathbf{R}(t)}{dt^2} \text{ is the acceleration}$$

11. The speed is $\|\mathbf{V}(t)\|$.

12. Consider a projectile that travels in a vacuum in a coordinate plane, with the x-axis along level ground. If the projectile is fired from a height of s_0 with initial speed v_0 and angle of elevation α, then at time t ($t \geq 0$) it will be at the point $(x(t), y(t))$, where

$$x(t) = (v_0\cos \alpha)t, \ y(t) = -\tfrac{1}{2}gt^2 + (v_0\sin \alpha)t + s_0$$

13. A projectile fired from ground level has time of flight T_f and range R given by the equations

$$T_f = \tfrac{2}{g}v_0\sin \alpha \text{ and } R = \frac{v_0{}^2}{g}\sin 2\alpha$$

The maximal range is $R_m = \frac{v_0{}^2}{g}$, and it occurs when $\alpha = \frac{\pi}{4}$.

14. 1. The planets move about the sun in elliptical orbits, with the sun at one focus.

    2. The radius vector joining a planet to the sun sweeps over equal areas in equal intervals of time.

    3. The square of the time of one complete revolution of a planet about its orbit is proportional to the cube of the orbit's semimajor axis.

15. $\mathbf{u}_r = (\cos \theta)\mathbf{i} + (\sin \theta)\mathbf{j}$ and
    $\mathbf{u}_\theta = (-\sin \theta)\mathbf{i} + (\cos \theta)\mathbf{j}$

16. If $\mathbf{R}(t)$ is a vector function that defines a smooth graph ($\mathbf{R}'(t) \neq 0$), then at each point a unit tangent is

$$\mathbf{T}(t) = \frac{\mathbf{R}'(t)}{\|\mathbf{R}'(t)\|}$$

and the principal unit normal vector is

$$\mathbf{N}(t) = \frac{\mathbf{T}'(t)}{\|\mathbf{T}'(t)\|}$$

17. Suppose the position of a moving object is $\mathbf{R}(t)$, where $\mathbf{R}'(t)$ is continuous on the interval $[a, b]$. Then the object has speed

$$\|\mathbf{V}(t)\| = \|\mathbf{R}'(t)\| = \frac{ds}{dt} \qquad \text{for } a \leq t \leq b$$

18. If C is a smooth curve defined by $\mathbf{R}(t) = x(t)\mathbf{i} + y(t)\mathbf{j} + z(t)\mathbf{k}$ on an interval $[a, b]$, then the arc length of C is given by

$$s = \int_a^b \|\mathbf{R}'(t)\| \, dt = \int_a^b \sqrt{[x'(t)]^2 + [y'(t)]^2 + [z'(t)]^2} \, dt$$

19. The curvature of a graph is an indication of

how quickly the graph changes direction.

$$\kappa = \left\| \frac{d\mathbf{T}}{ds} \right\|$$

where $\mathbf{T}$ is a unit vector.

20. If $\mathbf{V} = \mathbf{R}'$, $\mathbf{A} = \mathbf{R}''$, then $\kappa = \dfrac{\| \mathbf{V} \times \mathbf{A} \|}{\| \mathbf{V} \|^3}$

21. $\mathbf{T} = \dfrac{d\mathbf{R}}{ds}$ and $\mathbf{N} = \dfrac{1}{\kappa}\left(\dfrac{d\mathbf{T}}{ds} \right)$

22. The radius of curvature is the reciprocal of curvature $\rho = 1/\kappa$.

23. The acceleration $\mathbf{A}$ of a moving object can be written as $\mathbf{A} = A_T\mathbf{T} + A_N\mathbf{N}$, where $A_T = \dfrac{d^2s}{dt^2}$ is the tangential component; and

$A_N = \kappa \left(\dfrac{ds}{dt} \right)^2$ is the normal component.

24. This is a helix with radius of 3, climbing in a counter-clockwise direction.

$$s = \int_0^{2\pi} \|\mathbf{R}'\| \, dt$$

$\mathbf{R} = (3 \cos t)\mathbf{i} + (3 \sin t)\mathbf{j} + t\mathbf{k},$

$\mathbf{R}' = (-3 \sin t)\mathbf{i} + (3 \cos t)\mathbf{j} + \mathbf{k},$

$\|\mathbf{R}'\| = \sqrt{9 \sin^2 t + 9 \cos^2 t + 1} = \sqrt{10}$

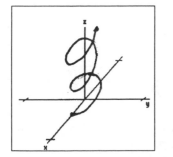

$$s = \int_0^{2\pi} \sqrt{10} \, dt = 2\pi\sqrt{10}$$

27. $\mathbf{F}'' = e^t\mathbf{i} - t^2\mathbf{j} + 3\mathbf{k},$

$\mathbf{F}' = e^t\mathbf{i} - \dfrac{t^3}{3}\mathbf{j} + 3t\mathbf{k} + \mathbf{C}$, but $\mathbf{F}'(0) = 3\mathbf{k}$ so

$\mathbf{F}' = (e^t - 1)\mathbf{i} - \dfrac{t^3}{3}\mathbf{j} + (3t + 3)\mathbf{k}$

$\mathbf{F} = (e^t - t)\mathbf{i} - \dfrac{t^4}{12}\mathbf{j} + \left(\dfrac{3t^2}{2} + 3t\right)\mathbf{k} + \mathbf{C}$, but

$\mathbf{F}(0) = \mathbf{i} - 2\mathbf{j}$ so

$\mathbf{F} = (e^t - t)\mathbf{i} - \left(\dfrac{t^4}{12} + 2\right)\mathbf{j} + \left(\dfrac{3t^2}{2} + 3t\right)\mathbf{k}$

30. **a.** $\mathbf{R} = [(v_0\cos \alpha)t]\mathbf{i}$
$+ [(v_0\sin \alpha)t - \tfrac{1}{2}gt^2 + s_0]\mathbf{j};$

In our case:

$\mathbf{R}(t) = (25\sqrt{3}\ t)\mathbf{i} + (25t - 16t^2)\mathbf{j}$

$\mathbf{R}'(t) = (25\sqrt{3})\mathbf{i} + (25 - 32t)\mathbf{j}$

The maximum height is reached when the $\mathbf{j}$ component of $\mathbf{R}'$ is 0; that is, when

$$25 - 32t = 0$$

$$t = \frac{25}{32}$$

$$y_{max} = 25\left(\tfrac{25}{32}\right) - 16\left(\tfrac{25}{32}\right)^2$$

$$\approx 9.77 \text{ ft}$$

b. $T_f = \tfrac{2}{g} v_0 \sin \alpha$

$= \tfrac{1}{16}(50)(\tfrac{1}{2})$

$$= \tfrac{25}{16} \text{ sec}$$

$$\text{Range} \ = \frac{v_0^{\,2}}{g} \sin 2\alpha$$

$$= \frac{50^2}{32} \sin 60°$$

$$= \frac{625\sqrt{3}}{16}$$

$$\approx 67.7 \text{ ft}$$

Cumulative Review for Chapters 7-11, Pages 787-787

SURVIVAL HINT: *This is the second of three cumulative reviews included in the text. This one (Chapters 7-11) can be very valuable to refresh some of the skills and concepts that you may have not used for a while. It is also a valuable tool in preparing for midterm or final examinations. If you do not have the time to actually do all of these problems, try looking at each one to see if you recall the concept involved and how to proceed with the solution. If you are confident about your ability to solve the problem, do not spend the time. If you feel a little uncertain about the problem, refer back to the appropriate section, review the concepts, look in your old homework for a similar problem, and then see if you can work it. Be more concerned about understanding the concept than about obtaining a correct answer. Do not spend a lot of your time looking for algebraic or arithmetic errors, but rather focus on important ideas.*

1.   Step 1. Simplify

      Step 2. Use basic formulas

      Step 3. Substitute

      Step 4. Classify

      Step 5. Try again.

      See Table 7.2, Pages 499-500.

2. Check the following tests for convergence:

    1. Divergence test

    2. Limit comparison test

    3. Ratio test

    4. Root test

    5. Integral test

    6. Direct comparison test

    7. Zero-infinity test

    See Table 8.1, Pages 579-580.

3. The graph of

$$Ax^2 + Bxy + Cy^2 + Dx + Ey + F = 0$$

is a quadric surface. Find and sketch the traces of the surface with the coordinate planes to get a clue to the shape of the overall surface. **See Table 10.1, Page 683.**

4. A vector is a directed line segment. A vector function is a function whose range is a set of vectors for each point in its domain. Vector calculus involves differentiation and integration of vector functions.

6. $\displaystyle\int x \ln \sqrt[3]{x}\ dx = \tfrac{1}{3} \int x \ln x \ \boxed{\text{Formula 502}}$

$$= \frac{x^2}{6} \ln x - \frac{x^2}{12} + C$$

9. $\displaystyle\int x\sqrt{16 - x}\ dx \ \boxed{x = 16 - u;\ dx = -\,du}$

$$= \int (16 - u)\sqrt{u}(-du)$$

$$= -\int (16u^{1/2} - u^{3/2})\, du$$

$$= -16\left(\tfrac{2}{3}\right)u^{3/2} + \tfrac{2}{5}u^{5/2} + C$$

$$= -\frac{32(16-x)^{3/2}}{3} + \frac{2(16-x)^{5/2}}{5} + C$$

12. $\displaystyle \int \frac{dx}{x^2(x^2+5)}$ $\boxed{\text{use partial fractions}}$

$$= \frac{1}{5}\int \left[\frac{1}{x^2} - \frac{1}{x^2+5}\right] dx$$

$$= \frac{1}{5}\left[-\frac{1}{x} - \frac{\sqrt{5}}{5}\tan^{-1}\left(\frac{x}{\sqrt{5}}\right)\right] + C$$

15. A vector normal to the plane is parallel to the line, so $\mathbf{N} = 2\mathbf{i} - 3\mathbf{j} + \mathbf{k}$,

$$\frac{x+1}{2} = \frac{y-2}{-3} = \frac{z-5}{1}$$

18. $\displaystyle \sum_{k=1}^{\infty} \frac{1}{k\cdot 4^k}$ converges by the ratio test

$$\lim_{k\to\infty} \frac{k\,4^k}{(k+1)4^{k+1}} = \frac{1}{4} < 1$$

21. $\displaystyle \sum_{k=1}^{\infty} \frac{k!}{2^k\cdot k}$ diverges by the ratio test

$$\lim_{k\to\infty} \frac{(k+1)!\,2^k\, k}{(k+1)2^{k+1}k!} = \lim_{k\to\infty} \frac{(k+1)k}{2(k+1)}$$

$$= \infty > 1$$

24. **a.** $\displaystyle S = \sum_{k=1}^{\infty} \frac{2^{k-1}}{5^{k+3}}$

$$= \frac{1}{5^4}\sum_{k=1}^{\infty} \frac{2^{k-1}}{5^{k-1}}$$

$$= \frac{1}{625}\left(\frac{1}{1-\tfrac{2}{5}}\right)$$

$$= \frac{1}{375}$$

b. $\displaystyle S = \sum_{k=1}^{\infty} \frac{1}{(3k-1)(3k+2)}$

$$S_n = \frac{1}{3}\sum_{k=1}^{n}\left[\frac{1}{3k-1} - \frac{1}{3k+2}\right]$$

$$= \frac{1}{3}\left[\left(\frac{1}{2} - \frac{1}{5}\right) + \left(\frac{1}{5} - \frac{1}{8}\right) + \cdots\right]$$

$$= \frac{1}{3}\left[\frac{1}{2} - \frac{1}{3n+2}\right]$$

$$S = \lim_{n\to+\infty} S_n = \frac{1}{6}$$

27. $\mathbf{F}(t) = 2t\mathbf{i} + e^{-3t}\mathbf{j} + t^4\mathbf{k}$

$$\mathbf{F}'(t) = 2\mathbf{i} - 3e^{-3t}\mathbf{j} + 4t^3\mathbf{k}$$

$$\mathbf{F}''(t) = 9e^{-3t}\mathbf{j} + 12t^2\mathbf{k}$$

30. $\displaystyle S = \sum_{k=1}^{\infty} \frac{(-1)^{k+1}}{\sqrt{k}}$ converges by the Leibniz's

alternating series test. The series alternates,

$$\lim_{k\to+\infty} \frac{1}{\sqrt{k}} = 0 \text{ and } \frac{1}{\sqrt{k+1}} < \frac{1}{\sqrt{k}}$$

$$\left|S_n - S\right| \le 0.00005$$

$$\frac{1}{\sqrt{n+1}} < 0.00005$$

$$\sqrt{n+1} > (0.00005)^{-1}$$

$$n+1 > 4(10^8)$$

$$n > 4(10^8) - 1$$

$$n > 399{,}999{,}999$$

33. $\frac{dy}{dx} + 2y = x^2$; the integrating factor is

$$I = e^{\int 2\,dx} = e^{2x}$$

$$y = \frac{1}{e^{2x}}\left[\int x^2 e^{2x}\,dx + C\right]$$

$$= \frac{1}{e^{2x}}\left[\frac{e^{2x}}{4}(2x^2 - 2x + 1) + C\right]$$

If $x = 0$, then $y = 2$, so

$$y = \frac{x^2}{2} - \frac{x}{2} + \frac{1}{4} + \frac{7}{4}e^{-2x}$$

36. $x = t^2 - 2t - 1,\ y = t^4 - 4t^2 + 2$

$$\frac{dx}{dt} = 2t - 2;\ \frac{dy}{dt} = 4t^3 - 8t$$

$$\mathbf{R}'(t) = \langle 2t - 2,\ 4t^3 - 8t\rangle$$

At $t = 1$, the point is $P(-2, -1)$, and the tangent line is parallel to the vector

$$\mathbf{R}'(1) = \langle 0,\ -4\rangle.$$

Thus, the tangent line is vertical with equation $x = -2$.

39. $\mathbf{V} = v_0\cos\alpha\,\mathbf{i} + (-gt + v_0\sin\alpha)\mathbf{j}$

$$\mathbf{R} = (v_0\cos\alpha)t\,\mathbf{i} + [-\frac{gt^2}{2} + (v_0\sin\alpha)t + s_0]\mathbf{j}$$

$$v_0 = 8,\ g = 32,\ s_0 = 120,\ \alpha = -\frac{\pi}{6}$$

$$-\frac{1}{2}gt^2 + (v_0\sin\alpha)t + s_0 = y(t)$$

$$-16t^2 - 4t + 120 = 0$$

$$4t^2 + t - 30 = 0$$

$$t = \frac{-1 \pm \sqrt{1 + 480}}{8}$$

$t \approx 2.6165$ sec (disregard negative value);

$x = 4\sqrt{3}(2.6165) \approx 18.13$ ft

CHAPTER 12

Partial Differentiation

12.1 Functions of Several Variables, Pages 797-799

3. $f(x, y, z) = x^2 y e^{2x} + (x + y - z)^2$

   a. $f(0, 0, 0) = 0$

   b. $f(1, -1, 1) = 1^2(-1)e^2 + (1 - 1 - 1)^2$

$$= -e^2 + 1$$

   c. $f(-1, 1, -1)$

$$= (-1)^2(1)e^{-2} + (-1 + 1 + 1)^2$$

$$= e^{-2} + 1$$

   d. $f(x, x, x) = x^2 x e^{2x} + (x + x - x)^2$

$$= x^3 e^{2x} + x^2$$

$$\frac{d}{dx} f(x, x, x) = 2x^3 e^{2x} + 3x^2 e^{2x} + 2x$$

   e. $f(1, y, 1) = 1^2 y e^2 + (1 + y - 1)^2$

$$= e^2 y + y^2$$

$$\frac{d}{dy} f(1, y, 1) = e^2 + 2y$$

   f. $f(1, 1, z^2) = 1^2 1 e^2 + (1 + 1 - z^2)^2$

$$= e^2 + (2 - z^2)^2$$

$$\frac{d}{dz} f(1, 1, z^2) = -4z(2 - z^2)$$

$$= 4z(z^2 - 2)$$

SURVIVAL HINT: *To find the domain of a function (in $\mathbb{R}^2$ or $\mathbb{R}^3$) look for values of the variable(s) that cause division by 0 or negative under a square root. Other possibilities are possible, and would be found by looking for values of the variable that cause the expression to be undefined.*

8. The domain includes values for which the expression under the radical is not negative, namely $x - y \geq 0$. For the range we note that $f(x, y)$ is equal to a square root which is never negative, so $f \geq 0$.

9. This is similar to Problem 8, except that division be zero must also be excluded, so the domain is $x - y > 0$ and the range is $f > 0$.

15. If $y = 2$, there is a division by zero, so the domain is all (x, y) values for which $y \neq 2$. Also since $e^u > 0$ for all values of u, we see that the range is $f > 0$.

19. Equations of the form $x^2 - y^2 = C$ (for C positive) we recognize this as the equation of a hyperbola. Choose some particular values to obtain the following graph:

27. If $C = 0$, $x + y - z = 0$, which we recognize as a plane. Draw the trace in each of the coordinate planes: if $z = 0$, then the trace in the xy-plane is $x + y = 0$; if $x = 0$, then the trace in the yz-plane is $y - z = 0$; and if $y = 0$, then the trace in the xz-plane is $x - z = 0$. A compute-generated graph is shown below:

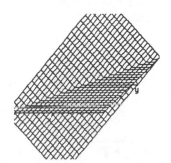

34. Recognize this as a paraboloid. For a trace in the xz-plane, let $y = $ a constant; say $y = 2$, then $z = x^2 + 1$ which is a parabola. For a trace in the yz-plane, let $x = $ a constant; say $x = 1$, then $z = \frac{1}{4}y^2 + 1$, which is a parabola. For a trace in the xy-plane, let $z = $ a constant; say $z = 1$, then

$$\frac{x^2}{1} + \frac{y^2}{4} = 1$$

which is an ellipse. Draw some representatives of these level curves to help with the graph (which was done using computer software):

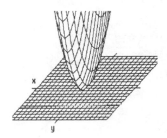

35. Recognize this a hyperbolic paraboloid; traces in the xz- and yz-planes are parabolas; trace in the xy-planes ia a hyperbola. Draw some level curves or use some software to help with this graph:

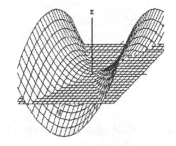

36. Recognize this as an elliptic cone; traces in the xz- and yz-planes are pairs of lines, and the trace in the xy-plane is the origin if $z = 0$ and is an ellipse if $z \neq 0$.

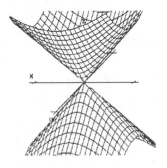

50. Let $z = 2x^2 + y^2$; if z is a constant (greater than zero), the graph is an ellipse in a plane parallel to the xy-plane. If x is a constant, then the trace in the xz-plane is a parabola. And finally, if y is a constant, then the trace in the yz-plane is a parabola. Draw these trace curves to obtain the following graph:

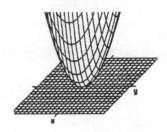

59.

$$Q(2K, 2L) = C2^r K^r 2^{1-r} L^{1-r}$$

$$= 2(CK^r L^{1-r})$$

This means that the function exactly doubles.

$$Q(3K, 3L) = C3^r K^r 3^{1-r} L^{1-r}$$

$$= 3(CK^r L^{1-r})$$

This means that the function exactly triples.

62. The price per unit is p and the quantity sold

is $Q = \dfrac{r^2}{2,000p} + \dfrac{s^2}{100} - s$

The total revenue is:

$$R = Qp = \frac{r^2}{2,000} + \frac{s^2 p}{100} - sp$$

SURVIVAL HINT: *The C trace y-f(x) in $\mathbb{R}^2$ is a point on a line. The C level curve for $z = f(x, y)$ in $\mathbb{R}^3$ is a curve or line in a plane, which is a slice of $\mathbb{R}^3$. If you can imagine a C level surface for $w = f(x, y, z)$ in $\mathbb{R}^4$ you would see a surface in $\mathbb{R}^3$. Since we are trapped in a three-dimensional world we cannot visualize $\mathbb{R}^4$, but the mathematics in not restricted to three variables.*

12.2 Limits and Continuity, Pages 805-807

SURVIVAL HINT: *It might be a good idea to review the concepts and definitions of limit and continuity as presented in Chapter 2, since the concepts and definitions for functions of several variables are a direct extension from $\mathbb{R}^2$ to $\mathbb{R}^3$. If you covered the δ-ε definition of limit and the three-part definition of continuity, then the multivariable definitions are the obvious extensions.*

3. $\displaystyle\lim_{(x,\ y)\to(-1,\ 0)} (xy^2 + x^3 y + 5)$

$$= (-1)0^2 + (-1)^3 0 + 5$$

$$= 5$$

6. $\displaystyle\lim_{(x,y)\to(3,\ 4)} \frac{x - y}{\sqrt{x^2 + y^2}} = \frac{3 - 4}{\sqrt{3^2 + 4^2}}$

$$= -\frac{1}{5}$$

12. $\displaystyle\lim_{(x,y)\to(1,2)} \frac{(x^2 - 1)(y^2 - 4)}{(x - 1)(y - 2)}$

$$= \lim_{(x,y)\to(1,2)} (x + 1)(y + 2)$$

$$= 8$$

15. $\displaystyle\lim_{(x,y)\to(0,0)} \frac{\sin(x + y)}{x + y} = \lim_{t\to 0} \frac{\sin t}{t}$

$$= 1$$

18. $\displaystyle\lim_{(x,y)\to(a,\ a)} \frac{x^4 - y^4}{x^2 - y^2}$

$$= \lim_{(x,y)\to(a,a)} (x^2 + y^2)$$

$$= 2a^2$$

23. $\lim\limits_{(x,y)\to(0,0)} \dfrac{x+y}{x-y}$

$\lim\limits_{(x,y)\to(0,0)} \dfrac{x+y}{x-y}$ along the line $x = 0$ is

$$\lim\limits_{y\to0} \dfrac{y}{(-y)} = \lim\limits_{y\to0} (-1)$$

$$= -1$$

$\lim\limits_{(x,y)\to(0,0)} \dfrac{x+y}{x-y}$ along the line $y = 0$ is

$$\lim\limits_{x\to0} \dfrac{x}{x} = \lim\limits_{x\to0} (1)$$

$$= 1$$

Limit does not exist.

30. $f(x, y) = \dfrac{x^4 y^4}{(x^2 + y^4)^3}$

Along the line $y = 0$, we have

$$\lim\limits_{x\to0} \dfrac{0}{(x^2 + 0)^3} = 0$$

and along the parabola $y = \sqrt{x}$:

$$\lim\limits_{x\to0} \dfrac{x^4 x^2}{(x^2 + x^2)^3} = \dfrac{1}{2}$$

Since these limits are not the same, the limit does not exist.

35. Along the line $y = kx$,

$$\lim\limits_{x\to0} \dfrac{k^3 x^4}{x^2 + k^6 x^6} = \lim\limits_{x\to0} \dfrac{k^3 x^2}{1 + k^6 x^4}$$

$$= 0$$

while along the path $x = y^3$,

$$\lim\limits_{x\to0} \dfrac{y^6}{y^6 + y^6} = \dfrac{1}{2}$$

Since these path limits are not the same, $f(x, y)$ has no limiting value as $(x, y) \to (0, 0)$. Thus, f is not continuous at $(0, 0)$.

39. $\lim\limits_{(x,y)\to(0,0)} \dfrac{3x^3 - 3y^3}{x^2 - y^2}$

$$= \lim\limits_{(x,y)\to(0,0)} \dfrac{3(x-y)(x^2 + xy + y^2)}{(x+y)(x-y)}$$

$$= \lim\limits_{(x,y)\to(0,0)} \dfrac{3(x^2 + xy + y^2)}{x+y}$$

Along the line $y = 0$:

$$\lim\limits_{(x,y)\to(0,0)} \dfrac{3x^3 - 3y^3}{x^2 - y^2} = \lim\limits_{(x,y)\to(0,0)} \dfrac{3x^3}{x^2}$$

$$= 0$$

Since f is to be continuous at $(0, 0)$, we must have $B = 0$.

42. $\left|2x^2 + 3y^2 - 0\right| \le 3\left|x^2 + y^2\right| < 3\sqrt{x^2 + y^2}$

for $|x| < 1$, $|y| < 1$ for a point (x, y) is near $(0, 0)$. Thus, if $\sqrt{x^2 + y^2} < \delta$, we have

$\left|(2x^2 + 3y^2) - 0\right| < 3\sqrt{x^2 + y^2} < 3\delta$ and

$\left|(2x^2 + 3y^2) - 0\right| < \epsilon$ if $\delta = \dfrac{\epsilon}{3}$.

12.3 Partial Derivatives, Pages 815–817

SURVIVAL HINT: *When you hold one variable fixed and find the derivative with respect to the other, you are reducing the surface in $\mathbb{R}^3$ to a line in $\mathbb{R}^2$. The first and second derivatives give the slope and concavity as you move along the curve determined by the trace through a given point. The mixed partial indicates how the slope would change if you moved to another trace. The analogy of moving in various directions from a point on a hillside is useful.*

4. $f(x, y) = (x + xy + y)^3$

For f_x hold y constant and differentiate with

respect to x:

$$f_x = 3(x + xy + y)^2(1 + y)$$

For f_y hold x constant and differentiate with respect to y:

$$f_y = 3(x + xy + y)^2(x + 1);$$

For f_{xx} use f_x and again hold y constant:

$$f_{xx} = 3(1 + y)(2)(x + xy + y)(1 + y)$$
$$= 6(1 + y)^2(x + xy + y)$$

For f_{yx} use f_y and hold y constant:

$$f_{yx} = 3[(x + xy + y)^2$$
$$+ (1 + x)(2)(x + xy + y)(1 + y)]$$
$$= 3(x + xy + y)(3xy + 3x + 3y + 2)$$

9. **SURVIVAL HINT:** *Contrast parts a and b, note the in part a, the function* sin x^2 *is multiplied by the function* cos y, *whereas in part b, the function is sine of the product* x^2cos y.

a. $f(x, y) = (\sin x^2)\cos y$

Treat y as a constant (not a product rule because cos y is not considered a variable):

$$f_x = (2x \cos x^2)(\cos y);$$

Now, treat x as a constant:

$$f_y = -(\sin x^2)(\sin y)$$

b. $f(x, y) = \sin(x^2\cos y)$

Treat y as a constant:

$$f_x = \cos(x^2\cos y)(2x \cos y)$$

Treat x as a constant:

$$f_y = \cos(x^2\cos y)(-x^2 \sin y)$$

13. $f(x, y) = x^2 e^{x+y}\cos y$

$$f_x = (\cos y)(x^2 e^{x+y} + 2xe^{x+y})$$
$$= xe^{x+y}(x + 2)\cos y$$
$$f_y = -x^2 e^{x+y}\sin y + x^2 e^{x+y} \cos y$$
$$= x^2 e^{x+y}(\cos y - \sin y)$$

20. $f(x, y, z) = \dfrac{xy + yz}{xz}$

$$= \frac{y}{z} + \frac{y}{x}$$

$$f_x = -x^{-2}y;$$
$$f_y = x^{-1} + z^{-1};$$
$$f_z = -yz^{-2}$$

26. $3x^2 - y^2 + 2yzz_x - 3z^2 z_x = 0$,

$$z_x = \frac{y^2 - 3x^2}{2yz - 3z^2};$$

$$-2xy + 2yzz_y + z^2 - 3z^2 z_y = 0$$

$$z_y = \frac{2xy - z^2}{2yz - 3z^2}$$

31. The level curve at $P(1, 1, 3)$ is

$$x^2 + xy^2 + y^3 = 3$$

$$2x + x(2y)\frac{dy}{dx} + y^2 + 3y^2\frac{dy}{dx} = 0$$

$$(2xy + 3y^2)\frac{dy}{dx} = -(2x + y^2)$$

$$\frac{dy}{dx} = -\frac{2x + y^2}{2xy + 3y^2}$$

At P,

$$\frac{dy}{dx}\bigg|_{(1,1)} = -\frac{2 + 1}{2 + 3}$$

$$= -\frac{3}{5}$$

34. $f_x = \dfrac{2x}{x^2+y^2};$

$$f_{xx} = \frac{2(x^2+y^2)-4x^2}{(x^2+y^2)^2}$$

$$= \frac{2(y^2-x^2)}{(x^2+y^2)^2}$$

Similarly, $f_{yy} = \dfrac{2(x^2-y^2)}{(y^2+x^2)^2};$

Thus, $f_{xx} + f_{yy} = 0.$

38. a. y is held constant;

$$f_x = y^{-1} - yx^{-2};$$

$$f_x(1,-1) = -1+1 = 0$$

b. x is held constant;

$$f_y = -xy^{-2} + x^{-1}$$

$$f_y(1,-1) = -1+1 = 0$$

46. $Q = 120K^{2/3}L^{2/5}$

a. $\dfrac{\partial Q}{\partial K} = 80K^{-1/3}L^{2/5}$

$\dfrac{\partial Q}{\partial L} = 48K^{2/3}L^{-3/5}$

b. $\dfrac{\partial^2 Q}{\partial K^2} = -\dfrac{80}{3}K^{-4/3}L^{2/5} < 0$

$\dfrac{\partial Q}{\partial L^2} = -\dfrac{144}{5}K^{2/3}L^{-8/5} < 0$

Interpretation: Marginal productivity of capital and labor are both decreasing functions. This is called the *law of eventually diminishing marginal productivity.*

48. a. $z_x = \dfrac{1}{ce^t}(\cos\frac{x}{c} - \sin\frac{x}{c})$

$$z_{xx} = -\frac{1}{c^2 e^t}(\sin\frac{x}{c} + \cos\frac{x}{c})$$

$$z_t = -e^{-t}(\sin\frac{x}{c} + \cos\frac{x}{c})$$

$z_t = c^2 z_{xx}$, so the given function satisfies the heat equation.

b. $z_x = 3\sin 3ct\cos 3x;$

$$z_{xx} = -9\sin 3ct\sin 3x$$

$$z_t = 3c\cos 3ct\sin 3x$$

$$z_{tt} = -9c^2\sin 3ct\sin 3x$$

$z_{tt} = c^2 z_{xx}$, so the given function satisfies the wave equation.

c. $z_x = -5\sin 5ct\sin 5x$

$$z_{xx} = -25\sin 5ct\cos 5x$$

$$z_t = 5c\cos 5ct\cos 5x$$

$$z_{tt} = -25c^2\sin 5ct\cos 5x$$

$z_{tt} = c^2 z_{xx}$, so the given function satisfies the wave equation.

12.4 Tangent Planes, Approximations, and Differentiability, Pages 825-827

SURVIVAL HINT: *The equation of a tangent plane can be remembered as an extension of the point-slope formula for a line in $\mathbb{R}^2$: $y - y_0 = m(x - x_0)$. For the plane in $\mathbb{R}^3$:*

$$z - z_0 = m(x - x_0) + n(y - y_0)$$

where m and n are the slopes in the x and y directions, found with the partial derivatives.

1. $z = (x^2 + y^2)^{1/2}$; the equation of a tangent

plane is given by the formula:

$$z - z_0 = f_x(x_0, y_0)(x - x_0) + f_y(x_0, y_0)(y - y_0)$$

For this problem, we let $z = f(x, y)$ so that

$$f_x = \tfrac{1}{2}(x^2 + y^2)^{-1/2}(2x)$$

$$= \frac{x}{\sqrt{x^2 + y^2}}$$

$$f_y = \frac{y}{\sqrt{x^2 + y^2}}$$

At $P_0(3, 1, \sqrt{10})$

$$f_x(3, 1) = \frac{3}{\sqrt{3^2 + 1^2}}$$

$$= \frac{3}{\sqrt{10}}$$

$$f_y(3, 1) = \frac{1}{\sqrt{3^2 + 1^2}}$$

$$= \frac{1}{\sqrt{10}}$$

The tangent plane is:

$$z - \sqrt{10} = \frac{3}{\sqrt{10}}(x - 3) + \frac{1}{\sqrt{10}}(y - 1)$$

$$3x + y - \sqrt{10}z = 0$$

6. $z = \ln\left| x + y^2 \right|$

$$z_x = \frac{1}{x + y^2};$$

$$z_y = \frac{2y}{x + y^2};$$

at P_0, $z_x = 1$, $z_y = -4$

$$z - 0 = 1(x + 3) - 4(y + 2)$$

$$x - 4y - z - 5 = 0$$

SURVIVAL HINT: *The total differential can be remembered as an $\mathbb{R}^3$ extension of the concepts of the differential in $\mathbb{R}^2$; $dy = f'(x)\,dx$. This says the change along the tangent line is the rate of change, $f'(x)$, multiplied by the change in the x-direction, Δx, or in the limiting case, dx. In $\mathbb{R}^3$ the change in z along the tangent plane, dz or df, is the rate of change in the x direction, $\partial z / \partial x$, multiplied by the change in the x-direction, dx, plus the same computation for change of z in the y-direction:*

$$df = \frac{\partial x}{\partial x}\,dx + \frac{\partial z}{\partial y}\,dy$$

8. The total differential is given by the formula:

$$df = f_x\,dx + f_y\,dy$$

$$f(x, y) = 8x^3y^2 - x^4y^5$$

$$df = (24x^2y^2 - 4x^3y^5)\,dx$$

$$+ (16x^3y - 5x^4y^4)\,dy$$

23. $f(x, y) = 3x^4 + 2y^4$;

$x_0 = 1$, $y_0 = 2$, $\Delta x = 0.01$, $\Delta y = 0.03$

$f_x = 12x^3$; $f_y = 8y^3$

$f(1.01, 2.03)$

$\approx f(1, 2) + f_x(1, 2)\Delta x + f_y(1, 2)\Delta y$

$\approx 35 + 12(0.01) + 64(0.03)$

$= 37.04$

By calculator,

$f(1.01, 2.03) \approx 37.08544565$

26. $f(x, y) = \sin xy$

$x_0 = \sqrt{\frac{\pi}{2}}, \; y_0 = \sqrt{\frac{\pi}{2}},$

$\Delta x = 0.01, \; \Delta y = -0.01$

$f_x = y \cos xy; \; f_y = x \cos xy$

$f(\sqrt{\frac{\pi}{2}} + 0.01, \sqrt{\frac{\pi}{2}} - 0.01)$

$\approx f\left(\sqrt{\frac{\pi}{2}}, \sqrt{\frac{\pi}{2}}\right) + f_x\left(\sqrt{\frac{\pi}{2}}, \sqrt{\frac{\pi}{2}}\right)\Delta x$

$\qquad + f_y\left(\sqrt{\frac{\pi}{2}}, \sqrt{\frac{\pi}{2}}\right)\Delta y$

$= 1 + 0(0.01) + 0(-0.01)$

$= 1$

By calculator,

$f(\sqrt{\frac{\pi}{2}} + 0.01, \sqrt{\frac{\pi}{2}} - 0.01) \approx 0.9999999995$

31. a. Since x and y are very small, we can take

$\Delta x = x$ and $\Delta y = y$. Then

$f(x, y) \approx f(0, 0) + xf_x(0, 0) + yf_y(0, 0)$

b. $f(x, y) = \frac{1}{1 + x - y}; \; f(0, 0) = 1$

$f_x = \frac{-1}{(1 + x - y)^2}; \; f_x(0, 0) = -1$

$f_y = \frac{1}{(1 + x - y)^2}; \; f_y(0, 0) = 1$

c. $f(x, y) = \frac{1}{(x + 1)^2 + (y + 1)^2}$

$f_x = -\frac{2(x + 1)}{[(x + 1)^2 + (y + 1)^2]^2}$

$f_y = -\frac{2(y + 1)}{[(x + 1)^2 + (y + 1)^2]^2}$

$f(0, 0) = \frac{1}{2}; \; f_x(0, 0) = -\frac{1}{2}; \; f_y(0, 0) = -\frac{1}{2}$

$f(x, y) \approx f(0, 0) + xf_x(0, 0) + yf_y(0, 0)$

$\qquad = \frac{1}{2} - \frac{1}{2}x - \frac{1}{2}y$

$\qquad = \frac{1}{2}(1 - x - y)$

33. Let x, y, and z be the length, width, and height of the box, respectively. The total cost is

$C = 2xy + 1.50(xy + 2xz + 2yz)$

$\quad = 3.5xy + 3xz + 3yz$

$C_x = 3.5y + 3z,$

$C_y = 3.5x + 3z,$

$C_z = 3x + 3y$

$\Delta C = (3.5y + 3z)\Delta x + (3.5x + 3z)\Delta y + (3x + 3y)\Delta z$

Since $x = 2$, $y = 4$, $z = 3$ and $|\Delta x| \le 0.02$,

$|\Delta y| \le 0.02$, and $|\Delta z| \le 0.02$, we have

$|\Delta C| \le |3.5(4) + 3(3)|(0.02)$

$\qquad + |3.5(2) + 3(3)|(0.02) + |3(2) + 3(4)|(0.02)$

$\qquad = 1.14$

Thus, the maximum possible error will cost $1.14.

39. Cal is an abbreviation for the unit of measurement called a *calorie.*

$$F(x, y) = \frac{1.786xy}{1.798x + y}$$

$$F_x = \frac{(1.798x + y)(1.786y) - (1.786xy)(1.798)}{(1.798x + y)^2}$$

$$F_y = \frac{(1.798x + y)(1.786x) - 1.786xy(1)}{(1.798x + y)^2}$$

$x = 5$, $y = 4$, $dx = 0.1$, $dy = 0.04$

$F_x(5, 4) \approx 0.1693$

$F_y(5, 4) \approx 0.4758$

$$\Delta F \approx F_x \, dx + F_y \, dy$$

$$\approx (0.1693)(0.1) + (0.4758)(0.04)$$

$$\approx 0.0360 \text{ cal}$$

45. Actually a football does not have the shape of an ellipsoid, but when modeling in mathematics, it is common to assume that the object of concern (a football) approximates the shape of an object whose shape or properties of a known equation.

$$V = \frac{4}{3}\pi abc$$

$$V_a = \frac{4}{3}\pi(bc)$$

$$V_b = \frac{4}{3}\pi(ac)$$

$$V_c = \frac{4}{3}\pi(ab)$$

For $a = 3$, $b = 6$, $c = 3$, $da = db = dc = \frac{1}{8}$

$$\Delta V \approx dV = V_a \, da + V_b \, db + V_c \, dc$$

$$= \frac{4}{3}\pi[6(3) + (3)(3) + (3)(6)]\left(\frac{1}{8}\right)$$

$$\approx 23.56$$

The volume of the shell is about 23.56 in.[3]

48. $A = hb = ab \sin \frac{\pi}{6} = \frac{1}{2}ab$;

$da/a = 0.04$

$db/b = -0.03$

$dA = \frac{1}{2}b \, da + \frac{1}{2}a \, db$

$$\frac{dA}{A} = \frac{b \, da}{ba} + \frac{a \, db}{ab}$$

$$= \frac{da}{a} + \frac{db}{b}$$

$$= 0.04 - 0.03$$

$$= 0.01$$

Thus, A increases by about 1%.

12.5 Chain Rules, Pages 832-834

5. $F(x, y) = (x^2 - y)^{3/2} + x^2 y - 2$

$F_x = \frac{3}{2}(x^2 - y)^{1/2}(2x) + 2xy$

$F_y = \frac{3}{2}(x^2 - y)^{1/2}(-1) + x^2$

$\frac{dy}{dx} = \frac{-F_x}{F_y}$

$$= \frac{-[3x(x^2 - y)^{1/2} + 2xy]}{-\frac{3}{2}(x^2 - y)^{1/2} + x^2}$$

SURVIVAL HINT: *Check to see if the given parameters restrict the domain of $f(x, y)$. In Problem 11, both x and y must be positive, so $f(x, y)$ has only first octant values.*

10. a. $f(t) = 2(-3t^2)(1 + t^3) + (1 + t^3)^2$

$$= -6t^2 - 6t^5 + 1 + 2t^3 + t^6$$

$$f'(t) = -12t - 30t^4 + 6t^2 + 6t^5$$

b. $f'(t) = \frac{\partial}{\partial x}(2xy + y^2)\frac{d}{dt}(-3t^2)$

$$+ \frac{\partial}{\partial y}(2xy + y^2)\frac{d}{dt}(1 + t^3)$$

$$= (2y)(-6t) + (2x + 2y)(3t^2)$$

$$= -12ty + 6xt^2 + 6yt^2$$

$$= -12t(1 + t^3) + 6(-3t^2)t^2$$

$$+ 6(1 + t^3)t^2$$

$$= -12t - 30t^4 + 6t^2 + 6t^5$$

14. a. $F(u, v) = u + v + (u - v)^2$

$$\frac{\partial F}{\partial u} = 1 + 2(u - v)$$

$$\frac{\partial F}{\partial v} = 1 - 2(u - v)$$

b. $\frac{\partial F}{\partial u} = \frac{\partial F}{\partial x}\frac{\partial x}{\partial u} + \frac{\partial F}{\partial y}\frac{\partial y}{\partial u}$

$$= (1)(1) + (2y)(1)$$

$$= 1 + 2(u - v)$$

$$\frac{\partial F}{\partial v} = \frac{\partial F}{\partial x}\frac{\partial x}{\partial v} + \frac{\partial F}{\partial y}\frac{\partial y}{\partial v}$$

$$= (1)(1) + (2y)(-1)$$

$$= 1 - 2(u - v)$$

20. $\frac{\partial t}{\partial x} = \frac{\partial t}{\partial u}\frac{\partial u}{\partial x} + \frac{\partial t}{\partial v}\frac{\partial v}{\partial x}$

$$\frac{\partial t}{\partial y} = \frac{\partial t}{\partial u}\frac{\partial u}{\partial y} + \frac{\partial t}{\partial v}\frac{\partial v}{\partial y}$$

$$\frac{\partial t}{\partial z} = \frac{\partial t}{\partial v}\frac{\partial v}{\partial z}$$

$$\frac{\partial t}{\partial w} = \frac{\partial t}{\partial u}\frac{\partial u}{\partial w} + \frac{\partial t}{\partial v}\frac{\partial v}{\partial w}$$

24. $\frac{dw}{dt} = \frac{\partial w}{\partial x}\frac{dx}{dt} + \frac{\partial w}{\partial y}\frac{dy}{dt} + \frac{\partial w}{\partial z}\frac{dz}{dt}$

$$= (ze^{xy^2})(y^2)\cos t + (ze^{xy^2})2xy(-\sin t)$$

$$+ e^{xy^2}(2 \sec^2 2t)$$

$$= e^{xy^2}[y^2 z \cos t - 2xyz \sin t + 2 \sec^2 2t]$$

28. a. $x^3 + y^2 + z^2 = 5$

$$3x^2 + 2zz_x = 0; \ z_x = \frac{-3x^2}{2z}$$

Similarly, $z_y = \frac{-y}{z}$

$$\frac{\partial^2 z}{\partial x \partial y} = \frac{\partial}{\partial x}\left(\frac{\partial z}{\partial y}\right)$$

$$= \frac{\partial}{\partial x}\left(-\frac{y}{z}\right)$$

$$= -y\left(\frac{-1}{z^2}z_x\right)$$

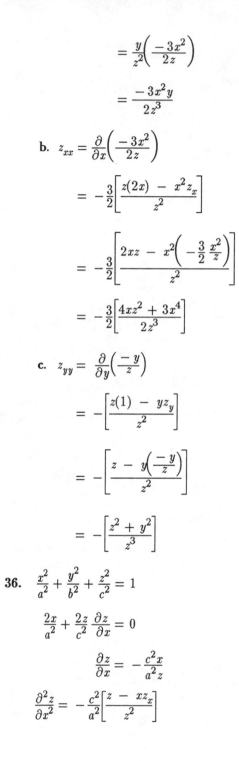

$$= \frac{y}{z^2}\left(\frac{-3x^2}{2z}\right)$$

$$= \frac{-3x^2 y}{2z^3}$$

b. $z_{xx} = \dfrac{\partial}{\partial x}\left(\dfrac{-3x^2}{2z}\right)$

$$= -\frac{3}{2}\left[\frac{z(2x) - x^2 z_x}{z^2}\right]$$

$$= -\frac{3}{2}\left[\frac{2xz - x^2\left(-\frac{3}{2}\frac{x^2}{z}\right)}{z^2}\right]$$

$$= -\frac{3}{2}\left[\frac{4xz^2 + 3x^4}{2z^3}\right]$$

c. $z_{yy} = \dfrac{\partial}{\partial y}\left(\dfrac{-y}{z}\right)$

$$= -\left[\frac{z(1) - yz_y}{z^2}\right]$$

$$= -\left[\frac{z - y\left(\frac{-y}{z}\right)}{z^2}\right]$$

$$= -\left[\frac{z^2 + y^2}{z^3}\right]$$

36. $\dfrac{x^2}{a^2} + \dfrac{y^2}{b^2} + \dfrac{z^2}{c^2} = 1$

$$\frac{2x}{a^2} + \frac{2z}{c^2}\frac{\partial z}{\partial x} = 0$$

$$\frac{\partial z}{\partial x} = -\frac{c^2 x}{a^2 z}$$

$$\frac{\partial^2 z}{\partial x^2} = -\frac{c^2}{a^2}\left[\frac{z - xz_x}{z^2}\right]$$

$$= -\frac{c^2}{a^2}\left[\frac{1}{z} - \frac{x}{z^2}\left(-\frac{c^2}{a^2}\right)\frac{x}{z}\right]$$

$$= -\frac{c^2}{a^2}\left[\frac{a^2 z^2 + c^2 x^2}{a^2 z^3}\right]$$

Similarly, $z_y = -\dfrac{c^2 y}{b^2 z}$

$$\frac{\partial^2 z}{\partial x \partial y} = \frac{\partial}{\partial x}\left(\frac{\partial z}{\partial y}\right)$$

$$= \frac{\partial}{\partial x}\left(\frac{-c^2 y}{b^2 z}\right)$$

$$= \frac{-c^2}{b^2}\left(\frac{-y}{z^2}z_x\right)$$

$$= \frac{-c^2}{b^2}\left(\frac{-y}{z^2}\right)\left(\frac{-c^2 x}{a^2 z}\right)$$

$$= \frac{-c^4 xy}{a^2 b^2 z^3}$$

38. $f(x, y) = 10xy^{1/2}; \; x = 30, \; y = 36, \; dx = 1$

$$10xy^{1/2} = C$$

$$(\tfrac{1}{2})xy^{-1/2}dy + y^{1/2}dx = 0$$

$$dy = \frac{-\sqrt{y}\,dx\,(2)\sqrt{y}}{x}$$

$$= -\frac{2y\,dx}{x}$$

$$= -\frac{2(36)(1)}{30}$$

$$= -2.4$$

The manufacturer should decrease the level of

unskilled labor by about 2.4 hours.

Alternatively, we can work with approximations

$$\Delta f \approx df = (10y^{1/2})\,dx + (5xy^{-1/2})dy$$

For f to stay constant when $x = 30$, $y = 36$, $dx = 1$, we want $\Delta f = 0$. Thus, dx must satisfy

$$10(36)^{1/2}(1) + 5(30)(36)^{-1/2}\,dy = 0$$

$$dy \approx \frac{-10(36)}{5(30)} = -2.4$$

44. $\frac{1}{R} = \frac{1}{R_1} + \frac{1}{R_2} + \frac{1}{R_3}$

$$-\frac{1}{R^2}\frac{\partial R}{\partial R_1} = -\frac{1}{R_1{}^2}; \frac{\partial R}{\partial R_1} = \left(\frac{R}{R_1}\right)^2$$

Similarly,

$$\frac{\partial R}{\partial R_2} = \left(\frac{R}{R_2}\right)^2; \frac{\partial R}{\partial R_3} = \left(\frac{R}{R_3}\right)^2$$

$$\frac{dR}{dt} = \left(\frac{R}{R_1}\right)^2\frac{dR_1}{dt} + \left(\frac{R}{R_2}\right)^2\frac{dR_2}{dt} + \left(\frac{R}{R_3}\right)^2\frac{dR_3}{dt}$$

When $R_1 = 100$, $R_2 = 200$, $R_3 = 300$

$$\frac{1}{R} = \frac{1}{100} + \frac{1}{200} + \frac{1}{300}, \text{ so } R \approx 54.545$$

With $\frac{dR_1}{dt} = -1.5$, $\frac{dR_2}{dt} = 2$, $\frac{dR_3}{dt} = -1.5$,

$$\frac{dR}{dt} \approx \left(\frac{54.545}{100}\right)^2(-1.5) + \left(\frac{54.545}{200}\right)^2(2)$$

$$+ \left(\frac{54.545}{300}\right)^2(-1.5)$$

≈ -0.3471

The joint resistance is decreasing at the approximate rate of 0.3471 ohms/second.

48. Let $w = uv$, so $z = u + f(w)$

$$\frac{\partial z}{\partial u} = 1 + \frac{df}{dw}\cdot\frac{\partial w}{\partial u} = 1 + [f'(w)](v)$$

$$\frac{\partial z}{\partial v} = \frac{df}{dw}\cdot\frac{\partial w}{\partial v} = [f'(w)](u)$$

$$u\frac{\partial z}{\partial u} - v\frac{\partial z}{\partial v} = u[1 + f'(w)v] - v[f'(w)u] = u$$

12.6 Directional Derivatives and the Gradient, Pages 846-848

7. $\nabla f = \cos(x + 2y)(\mathbf{i} + 2\mathbf{j})$

10. $\nabla f = \frac{(xy - 1)(1) - (z + x)(y)}{(z + x)^2}\mathbf{i}$

$$+ \frac{x}{x + z}\mathbf{j} - \frac{xy - 1}{(z + x)^2}\mathbf{k}$$

$$= \frac{1 - xy}{(z + x)^2}\mathbf{i} + \frac{x}{x + z}\mathbf{j} - \frac{xy - 1}{(z + x)^2}\mathbf{k}$$

16. $\mathbf{u} = \frac{3}{\sqrt{10}}\mathbf{i} - \frac{1}{\sqrt{10}}\mathbf{j};$

$$\nabla f = \cos xy(y\mathbf{i} + x\mathbf{j})$$

$$\nabla f(\sqrt{\pi}, \sqrt{\pi}) = -\sqrt{\pi}(\mathbf{i} + \mathbf{j})$$

$$D_{\mathbf{u}}f = \frac{\sqrt{\pi}(-3 + 1)}{\sqrt{10}}$$

$$= \frac{-2\sqrt{\pi}}{\sqrt{10}}$$

SURVIVAL HINT: *Using the hillside analogy: If you are standing on the hillside $z = f(x, y)$ at the point P, and walk in the compass direction indicated by the* *unit vector **u**, the directional derivative will tell you the instantaneous rate of change in x.*

18. $N = \nabla f = 4x^3\mathbf{i} + 4y^3\mathbf{j} + 4z^3\mathbf{k}$

$N(1, -1, -1) = 4\mathbf{i} - 4\mathbf{j} - 4\mathbf{k}$

$N_u = \pm\dfrac{N}{4\sqrt{3}} = \pm\dfrac{\sqrt{3}}{3}(\mathbf{i} - \mathbf{j} - \mathbf{k})$

The tangent plane is:

$(x - 1) - (y + 1) - (z + 1) = 0$

$$x - y - z - 3 = 0$$

27. $\nabla f = 3x^2\mathbf{i} + 3y^2\mathbf{j}$

a. $\nabla f(3, -3) = 27(\mathbf{i} + \mathbf{j}); \ \|\nabla f\| = 27\sqrt{2}$

b. $\nabla f(-3, 3) = 27(\mathbf{i} + \mathbf{j}); \ \|\nabla f\| = 27\sqrt{2}$

37. Let $f(x, y) = \dfrac{x^2}{a^2} + \dfrac{y^2}{b^2} - 1$ so $f(x, y) = 0$

$\nabla f = \dfrac{2x}{a^2}\mathbf{i} + \dfrac{2y}{b^2}\mathbf{j} = 2a^{-2}b^{-2}(b^2 x\mathbf{i} + a^2 y\mathbf{j})$

$\mathbf{u} = \pm\dfrac{b^2 x_0\mathbf{i} + a y_0\mathbf{j}}{\sqrt{b^4 x_0^2 + a^4 y_0^2}}$

39. $\mathbf{u} = \cos\dfrac{\pi}{6}\mathbf{i} + \sin\dfrac{\pi}{6}\mathbf{j} = \dfrac{1}{2}(\sqrt{3}\,\mathbf{i} + \mathbf{j})$

$\nabla f = \nabla(x^2 + y^2) = 2(x\mathbf{i} + y\mathbf{j})$

$\nabla f(1, 1) = 2(\mathbf{i} + \mathbf{j}); \ D_u f = \sqrt{3} + 1$

42. **a.** $\nabla f = \nabla(2x^2 - y^2 + 3z^2 - 8x - 4y + 201)$

$= (4x - 8)\mathbf{i} + (-2y - 4)\mathbf{j} + (6z)\mathbf{k}$

$\nabla f(2, -\tfrac{3}{2}, \tfrac{1}{2}) = -\mathbf{j} + 3\mathbf{k}$

b. $P_0O = -2\mathbf{i} + \tfrac{3}{2}\mathbf{j} - \tfrac{1}{2}\mathbf{k}$

$\cos\theta = \dfrac{P_0O \cdot \nabla f_0}{\|P_0O\|\,\|\nabla f_0\|}$

$= \dfrac{-\tfrac{3}{2} - \tfrac{3}{2}}{\sqrt{4 + \tfrac{9}{4} + \tfrac{1}{4}}\,\sqrt{1 + 9}}$

$= -\dfrac{3}{\sqrt{65}}$

49. To find the directional derivative of f in the direction of u we need f_x and f_y, which we can find with a system of equations.

$$\begin{cases} (f_x\mathbf{i} + f_y\mathbf{j}) \cdot \left(\dfrac{3\mathbf{i} - 4\mathbf{j}}{5}\right) = 8 \\ (f_x\mathbf{i} + f_y\mathbf{j}) \cdot \left(\dfrac{12\mathbf{i} + 5\mathbf{j}}{13}\right) = 1 \end{cases}$$

$$\begin{cases} 3f_x - 4f_y = 40 \\ 12f_x + 5f_y = 13 \end{cases}$$

Solving simultaneously: $f_x = 4$, $f_y = -7$

Now for $V = 3\mathbf{i} - 5\mathbf{j}$:

$(f_x\mathbf{i} + f_y\mathbf{j}) \cdot \left(\dfrac{3\mathbf{i} - 5\mathbf{j}}{\sqrt{34}}\right) = (4\mathbf{i} - 7\mathbf{j}) \cdot \left(\dfrac{3\mathbf{i} - 5\mathbf{j}}{\sqrt{34}}\right)$

$= \dfrac{12 + 35}{\sqrt{34}}$

≈ 8.06

55. First, note that $T(x, y)$ is minimized when $x = 6$ and $y = 1$; that is, at the point $(6, 1)$. If we let the path he follows be expressed in vector form as

$$\mathbf{R}(t) = x(t)\mathbf{i} + y(t)\mathbf{j},$$

then $\mathbf{R}'(t) = x'(t)\mathbf{i} + y'(t)\mathbf{j}$. Since he always moves in the direction of maximum temperature decrease, we must have

$$\mathbf{R}'(t) = -\nabla T$$

so that

$$\frac{dx}{dt} = -6(x - 6) \text{ and } \frac{dy}{dt} = -3(y - 1)$$

or

$$\frac{dx}{dt} + 6x = 36 \quad \text{and} \quad \frac{dy}{dt} + 3y = 3$$

Solving these first order differential equations, we obtain

$$x(t) = 6 + C_1 e^{-6t}$$

$$y(t) = 1 + C_2 e^{-3t}$$

Since $x = 1$ and $y = 5$ when $t = 0$, it follows that $C_1 = -5$ and $C_2 = 4$, so

$$x(t) = 6 - 5e^{-6t}$$

$$y(t) = 1 + 4e^{-3t}$$

We can write

$$e^{-6t} = \frac{6 - x}{5} \text{ and } e^{-3t} = \frac{y - 1}{4}$$

so that

$$\left(\frac{y - 1}{4}\right)^2 = \frac{6 - x}{5}$$

$$x = 6 - \tfrac{5}{16}(y - 1)^2$$

Thus, the spy walks along the parabola

$$x = 6 - \tfrac{5}{16}(y - 1)^2$$

from (1, 5) to (6, 1). The distance (arc

length) that he travels is given by the integral

$$L = \int_1^5 \sqrt{1 + \left(\frac{dx}{dy}\right)^2} \, dy$$

$$= \int_1^5 \sqrt{1 + \left[-\frac{10}{16}(y - 1)\right]^2} \, dy$$

$$= \tfrac{4}{5}\left(\sqrt{1 + \tfrac{25}{64}(y - 1)^2} \left[\tfrac{5}{8}(y - 1)\right]\right.$$

$$\left. + \ln\left|\sqrt{1 + \tfrac{25}{64}(y - 1)^2} + \tfrac{5}{8}(y - 1)\right|\right)\Big|_1^5$$

$$\approx 6.7 \text{ ft}$$

He reaches the hole in about 1 min 40 sec — plenty of time for a cup of tea.

12.7 Extrema of Functions of Two Variables, Pages 858-861

SURVIVAL HINT: *Note that, as in Section 4.1, the critical points are only **candidates** for extrema. If you are walking in the x-direction along a level trial on a hillside, $\partial f/\partial x = 0$ but $\partial f/\partial y$ may go upslope to your right and downslope to your left. The point is not an extreme. If you are at a saddle point, **both** partials are zero and the candidate is still not an extreme. The candidate must be tested with the determinant.*

8. $f(x, y) = \dfrac{9x}{x^2 + y^2 + 1}$

$$f_x = \frac{9(x^2 + y^2 + 1 - 2x^2)}{(x^2 + y^2 + 1)^2} = \frac{9(y^2 + 1 - x^2)}{(x^2 + y^2 + 1)^2}$$

$$f_y = -\frac{9x(2y)}{(x^2 + y^2 + 1)^2} = \frac{-18xy}{(x^2 + y^2 + 1)^2}$$

$f_x = f_y = 0$ only when $x = \pm 1$, $y = 0$

$$f_{xx} = \frac{18x^3 - 54xy^2 - 54x}{(x^2 + y^2 + 1)^3}$$

$$f_{xy} = \frac{54x^2y - 18y^3 - 18y}{(x^2 + y^2 + 1)^3}$$

$$f_{yy} = \frac{54xy^2 - 18x^3 - 18x}{(x^2 + y^2 + 1)^3}$$

x	y	f_{xx}	f_{xy}	f_{yy}	D	Classify
1	0	$-\frac{9}{2}$	0	$-\frac{9}{2}$	$+$	rel max
-1	0	$\frac{9}{2}$	0	$\frac{9}{2}$	$+$	rel min

12. $f(x, y) = e^{-(x^2+y^2)}$

$f_x = -2xe^{-(x^2+y^2)}$; $f_y = -2ye^{-(x^2+y^2)}$

$f_x = f_y = 0$ only when $x = y = 0$

$f_{xx} = (4x^2 - 2)e^{-(x^2+y^2)}$

$f_{xy} = 4xye^{-(x^2+y^2)}$

$f_{yy} = (4y^2 - 2)e^{-(x^2+y^2)}$

x	y	f_{xx}	f_{xy}	f_{yy}	D	Classify
0	0	-2	0	-2	$+$	rel max

18. $f(x, y) = 2x^3 + y^3 + 3x^2 - 3y - 12x - 4$

$f_x = 6x^2 + 6x - 12 = 6(x + 2)(x - 1)$

$f_y = 3y^2 - 3 = 3(y - 1)(y + 1)$

$f_x = f_y = 0$ when $x = 1, -2$ and $y = \pm 1$

Critical points are $(1, 1)$, $(1, -1)$, $(-2, 1)$,

$(-2, -1)$.

$f_{xx} = 12x + 6$; $f_{xy} = 0$; $f_{yy} = 6y$

x	y	f_{xx}	f_{xy}	f_{yy}	D	Classify
-2	-1	-18	0	-6	$+$	rel max
-2	1	-18	0	6	$-$	saddle point
1	-1	18	0	-6	$-$	saddle point
1	1	18	0	6	$+$	rel min

22. $f(x, y) = 3xy^2 - 2x^2y + 36xy$

$f_x = 3y^2 - 4xy + 36y$; $f_y = 6xy - 2x^2 + 36x$

$f_x = f_y = 0$ when

$$\begin{cases} y(3y - 4x + 36) = 0 \\ x(6y - 2x + 36) = 0 \end{cases}$$

If $x = 0$, then $y = 0$ or -12;

if $y = 0$, then $x = 0$ or 18.

If $x \neq 0$, $y \neq 0$, then

$$\begin{cases} 4x - 3y = 36 \\ 2x - 6y = 36 \end{cases}$$

which implies $x = 6$, $y = -4$.

The critical points are $(0, 0)$, $(0, -12)$,

$(18, 0)$, $(6, -4)$.

$f_{xx} = -4y$; $f_{xy} = 6y - 4x + 36$; $f_{yy} = 6x$

x	y	f_{xx}	f_{xy}	f_{yy}	D	Classify
0	0	0	36	0	$-$	saddle point
0	-12	48	-36	0	$-$	saddle point
18	0	0	-36	108	$-$	saddle point
6	-4	16	-12	36	$+$	rel min

SURVIVAL HINT: *In $\mathbb{R}^2$ the extreme value theorem requires a continuous function on a closed interval. Note that the $\mathbb{R}^3$ extension of the extreme value theorem requires that f be continuous on a closed and bounded set S. In $\mathbb{R}^2$ the curve may have corners, cups, or vertical tangents, as long as it is continuous. Likewise in $\mathbb{R}^3$ the surface may have creases, pointed peaks, and vertical tangents if it is continuous. It is sometimes difficult to verify the continuity of a surface. Most of your examples will be sums or products of continuous functions, which are continuous.*

27. $f(x, y) = 2\sin x + 5\cos y$

$f_x = 2\cos x; f_y = -5\sin y;$

$f_x = f_y = 0$ has no solution

On $x = t$, $y = 0$ for $0 \le t \le 2$;

$F_1(t) = f(t, 0)$

$\qquad = 2\sin t + 5$

$F_1{}'(t) = 2\cos t$

$\qquad 2\cos t = 0$ when $t = \frac{\pi}{2}$

Point $(\frac{\pi}{2}, 0)$

On $x = 2$, $y = t$ for $0 \le t \le 5$;

$F_2(t) = f(2, t)$

$\qquad = 2\sin 2 + 5\cos t$

$F_2{}'(t) = -5\sin t$

$\qquad -5\sin t = 0$ when $t = 0, \pi$

Points $(2, 0)$, $(2, \pi)$

On $y = 5$, $x = t$ for $0 \le t \le 2$;

$F_3(t) = f(t, 5)$

$\qquad = 2\sin t + 5\cos 5$

$F_3{}'(t) = 2\cos t$

$\qquad 2\cos t = 0$ when $t = \frac{\pi}{2}$

Point $(\frac{\pi}{2}, 5)$

On $x = 0$, $y = t$ for $0 \le t \le 5$;

$F_4(t) = f(0, t)$

$\qquad = 5\cos t$

$F_4{}'(t) = -5\sin t$

$\qquad -5\sin t = 0$ when $t = 0, \pi$

Points $(0, 0)$, $(0, \pi)$

There are no interior critical points; four boundary critical points $(\frac{\pi}{2}, 0)$, $(2, \pi)$, $(\frac{\pi}{2}, 5)$, $(0, \pi)$; and four boundary endpoints $(0, 0)$, $(2, 0)$, $(2, 5)$, $(0, 5)$.

x	y	$f(x, y)$	
$\pi/2$	0	7	max
2	π	-3.18	
$\pi/2$	5	3.42	
0	π	-5	min
0	0	5	
2	0	6.82	
2	5	3.24	
0	5	1.42	

The largest value of f on S is 7 and the smallest is -5.

SURVIVAL HINT: *When doing a least squares regression, it is essential that you carefully organize and label your data.*

33. $m = \dfrac{n \sum\limits_{k=1}^{n} x_k y_k - \left(\sum\limits_{k=1}^{n} x_k\right)\left(\sum\limits_{k=1}^{n} y_k\right)}{n \sum\limits_{k=1}^{n} x_k^{2} - \left(\sum\limits_{k=1}^{n} x_k\right)^{2}}$ and

$b = \dfrac{\sum\limits_{k=1}^{n} x_k^{2} \sum\limits_{k=1}^{n} y_k - \left(\sum\limits_{k=1}^{n} x_k\right)\left(\sum\limits_{k=1}^{n} x_k y_k\right)}{n \sum\limits_{k=1}^{n} x_k^{2} - \left(\sum\limits_{k=1}^{n} x_k\right)^{2}}$

Organize the data:

x	y	x^2	xy
3	5.72	9	17.16
4	5.31	16	21.24
6.2	5.12	38.44	31.744
7.52	5.32	56.55	40.0064
8.03	5.67	64.48	45.5301
Sum: 28.75	27.14	184.471	155.6805

$m = \dfrac{5(155.68) - (28.75)(27.14)}{5(184.47) - (28.75)^2}$

≈ -0.02

$b = \dfrac{184.47(27.14) - (28.75)(155.68)}{95.79}$

≈ 5.54

$y = -0.02x + 5.54$

35. Minimize $S = x^2 + y^2 + z^2$ subject to $y^2 = 4 + xz$. We have,

$S(x, z) = x^2 + (4 + xz) + z^2$

$S_x = 2x + z$

$S_z = x + 2z$

and $S_x = S_z = 0$

when

$z = -2x = -\frac{1}{2}x$

$x = 0,\ z = 0,\ y = \pm 2.$

The closest points are $(0, 2, 0)$ and $(0, -2, 0)$.

40. $P(x, y) = x(100 - x) + y(100 - y) - x^2 - xy - y^2$

$= -2x^2 - 2y^2 + 100x + 100y - xy$

$P_x = -4x + 100 - y = 0$

$P_y = -4y + 100 - x = 0$

Solving these equations simultaneously, we find $x = 20,\ y = 20$. Since

$P_{xx} = -4;\ P_{xy} = -1;\ P_{yy} = -4$

We see that $D = P_{xx}P_{yy} - P_{xy}^{\,2} > 0$ and

$P_{xx} < 0$ at $(20, 20)$, so the profit is maximized when $x = 20,\ y = 20$.

45. The profit for each bottle of California water is $x - 2$, and for each bottle of New York water is $y - 2$. The profit is

$P(x, y) = (x - 2)(40 - 50x + 40y)$

$\qquad + (y - 2)(20 + 60x - 70y)$

$$= -50x^2 + 100xy - 70y^2 + 20x + 80y - 120$$

$$P_x = -100x + 100y + 20$$

$$P_y = 100x - 140y + 80$$

Solving simultaneously, $x = 2.7$, $y = 2.5$

$$P_{xx} = -100; \ P_{xy} = 100; \ P_{yy} = -140;$$

Then $D > 0$, $P_{xx} < 0$, so the profit is maximized at (2.7, 2.5). The owner should charge $2.70 for California water and $2.50 for New York water.

47. Domestic profit $= x(60 - 0.2x + 0.05y) - 10x$

$$= x(50 - 0.2x + 0.05y)$$

Foreign profit $= y(50 - 0.1y + 0.05x) - 10y$

$$= y(40 - 0.1y + 0.05x)$$

$P(x, y) = x(50 - 0.2x + 0.05y)$

$$+ \ y(40 - 0.1y + 0.05x)$$

$$= -0.2x^2 + 0.1xy - 0.1y^2 + 50x + 40y$$

$$P_x = -0.4x + 0.1y + 50 = 0$$

$$P_y = 0.1x - 0.2y + 40 = 0$$

Solving simultaneously, $x = 200$, $y = 300$

$$P_{xx} = -0.4; \ P_{xy} = 0.1; \ P_{yy} = -0.2;$$

$D > 0$ and $D_{xx} < 0$, so (200, 300) is a maximum. That is, 200 machines should be supplied to the domestic market and 300 to the foreign market.

12.8 Lagrange Multipliers, Pages 868-870

SURVIVAL HINT: *The method of Lagrange multipliers requires the solution of a system of equations. There is no single set of steps to follow in solving a system of equations. Substitution, addition, matrices, or some cleverness are usually required. Often one equation can be solved for λ, and that value substituted into the other equations involving λ. Solve the resulting equation with the constraint equation to find x and y. These values can then be used to evaluate λ.*

3. $f(x, y) = 16 - x^2 - y^2; \ g(x, y) = x + 2y - 6$

$$f_x = -2x, \ f_y = -2y, \ g_x = 1, \ g_y = 2$$

Solve the system

$$\begin{cases} -2x = \lambda \\ -2y = 2\lambda \\ x + 2y = 6 \end{cases}$$

to find $x = \frac{6}{5}$, $y = \frac{12}{5}$

$f(\frac{6}{5}, \frac{12}{5}) = \frac{44}{5}$ is the constrained maximum.

9. $f(x, y) = \cos x + \cos y; \ g(x, y) = y - x - \frac{\pi}{4}$

$$f_x = -\sin x, \ f_y = -\sin y, \ g_x = -1, \ g_y = 1$$

Solve the system

$$\begin{cases} -\sin x = -\lambda \\ -\sin y = \lambda \\ y = x + \frac{\pi}{4} \end{cases}$$

to find $x = \frac{(8n - 1)\pi}{8}$, $y = \frac{(8n + 1)\pi}{8}$

If $n = 1$, $f(\frac{7\pi}{8}, \frac{9\pi}{8}) \approx -1.8478$;

If $n = 2$, $f(\frac{15\pi}{8}, \frac{17\pi}{8}) \approx 1.8478$;

The constrained maximum is approximately 1.8478 for $f(-\frac{\pi}{8} + n\pi, \frac{\pi}{8} + n\pi)$ with n even

15. $f(x, y, z) = 2x^2 + 4y^2 + z^2$

$g(x, y, z) = 4x - 8y + 2z - 10$

$f_x = 4x, f_y = 8y, f_z = 2z,$

$g_x = 4, g_y = -8, g_z = 2$

Solve the system

$$\begin{cases} 4x = 4\lambda \\ 8y = -8\lambda \\ 2z = 2\lambda \\ 4x - 8y + 2z = 10 \end{cases}$$

to find $\lambda = x = -y = z$ and then

$x = \frac{5}{7}, y = -\frac{5}{7}, z = \frac{5}{7}$

$f(\frac{5}{7}, -\frac{5}{7}, \frac{5}{7}) = \frac{25}{7}$ is the constrained minimum. By using negative values for any two variables in the constraint equation, the third variable can be made arbitrarily large, thus f can be made arbitrarily large and does not have a maximum.

20. Minimize the square of the distance

$f(x, y) = x^2 + y^2$ subject to $g(x, y) = 0$ where

$g(x, y) = 5x^2 - 6xy + 5y^2 - 4$

$f_x = 2x, f_y = 2y, g_x = 10x - 6y,$

$g_y = -6x + 10y$

Solve the system

$$\begin{cases} 2x = \lambda(10x - 6y) \\ 2y = \lambda(-6x + 10y) \\ 5x^2 - 6xy + 5y^2 = 4 \end{cases}$$

to find $x = \pm y$. The solutions are $(1, 1)$,

$(-1, -1), (\frac{1}{2}, -\frac{1}{2}), (-\frac{1}{2}, \frac{1}{2})$ and

$f(\frac{1}{2}, -\frac{1}{2}) = f(-\frac{1}{2}, \frac{1}{2}) = \frac{1}{2}$; $d = \frac{\sqrt{2}}{2}$ is the

constrained minimum distance.

$f(1, 1) = f(-1, -1) = 2;$

$d = \sqrt{2}$ is the constrained maximum distance.

26. Let x (along the river) and y be the sides of the rectangle. Then minimize

$f(x, y) = x + 2y$

$g(x, y) = xy - 3,200$

$f_x = 1, f_y = 2, g_x = y, g_y = x$

Solve the system

$$\begin{cases} 1 = \lambda y \\ 2 = \lambda x \\ xy = 3,200 \end{cases}$$

to find $x = 80, y = 40$

The least amount of fencing will be used when there is 80 yd along the river and 40 yd on the sides.

28. Let x and y be the radius and height of the cylinder. We wish to minimize

$f(x, y) = 2\pi x^2 + 2\pi xy$; subject to $g(x, y) =$

$\pi x^2 y - 6.89\pi = 0$

$f_x = 4\pi x + 2\pi y, \; f_y = 2\pi x,$

$g_x = 2\pi xy, \; g_y = \pi x^2$

Solve the system

$$\begin{cases} 4\pi x + 2\pi y = 2\lambda\pi xy \\ 2\pi x = \lambda\pi x^2 \\ x^2 y\pi = 6.89\pi \end{cases}$$

to obtain $y = 2x$, and then find $x \approx 1.51$, $y \approx 3.02$. A real can of Pepsi has a radius of about 1.125 in. (as compared to 1.51) and a height of 4.5 in. (as compared with 3.02). Such a waste!

30. Let x, y, and z be the length, width, and height of one-eight of the rectangular box, respectively. We wish to maximize

$f(x, y, z) = xyz$ subject to $g(x, y, z) = 0$ where

$g(x, y, z) = x^2 + \dfrac{y^2}{4} + \dfrac{z^2}{9} - 1$

$f_x = yz, \; f_y = xz, \; f_z = xy,$

$g_x = 2x, \; g_y = \dfrac{y}{2}, \; g_z = \dfrac{2z}{9}$

Solve the system

$$\begin{cases} yz = 2\lambda x \\ xz = \dfrac{\lambda y}{2} \\ xy = \dfrac{2\lambda z}{9} \\ x^2 + \dfrac{y^2}{4} + \dfrac{z^2}{9} = 1 \end{cases}$$

to find $x = \dfrac{1}{\sqrt{3}}, \; y = \dfrac{2}{\sqrt{3}}, \; z = \dfrac{3}{\sqrt{3}}$

The maximum volume is $f(\dfrac{1}{\sqrt{3}}, \dfrac{2}{\sqrt{3}}, \dfrac{3}{\sqrt{3}})$

$= \dfrac{2}{\sqrt{3}}$ cubic units.

33. Let s be the length of the living space. The height of the equilateral triangular face is

$h = \dfrac{\sqrt{3}}{2} x$

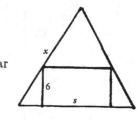

so by similar triangles,

$$\dfrac{\dfrac{\sqrt{3}}{2} x - 6}{\dfrac{\sqrt{3}}{2} x} = \dfrac{\dfrac{s}{2}}{\dfrac{x}{2}}$$

$$s = x - 4\sqrt{3}$$

The volume of the livable space is

$V = 6(x - 4\sqrt{3})y = 6xy - 24\sqrt{3}\,y$

and the surface area of the building is

$S = 2\left[\dfrac{1}{2}\left(\dfrac{\sqrt{3}}{2} x^2\right)\right] + 2xy = \dfrac{\sqrt{3}}{2} x^2 + 2xy$

The problem is to maximize

$V = 6(x - 4\sqrt{3})y$ subject to

$S = \dfrac{\sqrt{3}}{2} x^2 + 2xy = 500$

We have, $V_x = 6y, \; V_y = 6x - 24\sqrt{3},$

$S_x = \sqrt{3}\,x + 2y, \; S_y = 2x,$ so we must solve the system

$$\begin{cases} 6y = \lambda(\sqrt{3}\,x + 2y) \\ 6x - 24\sqrt{3} = \lambda(2x) \\ \dfrac{\sqrt{3}}{2} x^2 + 2xy = 500 \end{cases}$$

We find that $\lambda = \dfrac{6y}{\sqrt{3}\,x + 2y} = \dfrac{6x - 24\sqrt{3}}{2x}$

so that $y = \dfrac{x^2}{8} - \dfrac{\sqrt{3}}{2}x$, and then

$\dfrac{\sqrt{3}}{2}x^2 + 2x\left(\dfrac{x^2}{8} - \dfrac{\sqrt{3}}{2}x\right) = 500$

$x \approx 13.87$ and $y \approx 12.04$

41. $f(x,\,y,\,z) = x^2 + y^2 + z^2$;

$g(x,\,y,\,z) = x + y - 4$

$h(x,\,y,\,z) = y + z - 6$

$f_x = 2x,\ f_y = 2y,\ f_z = 2z$

$g_x = 1,\ g_y = 1,\ g_z = 0$

$h_x = 0,\ h_y = 1,\ h_z = 1$

Solve the system

$\begin{cases} 2x = \lambda \\[4pt] 2y = \lambda + \mu \\[4pt] 2z = \mu \\[4pt] x + y = 4 \\[4pt] y + z = 6 \end{cases}$

to find $x = 2/3,\ y = 10/3,\ z = 8/3$

The minimum is $f(\frac{2}{3},\,\frac{10}{3},\,\frac{8}{3}) = \frac{56}{3}$

45. PROFIT = REVENUE − COST

$P(x,\,y) = \left(\dfrac{320y}{y + 2} + \dfrac{160x}{x + 4}\right)150$

$\qquad - \left(\dfrac{320y}{y + 2} + \dfrac{160x}{x + 4}\right)50 - 1{,}000(x + y)$

a. $g(x,\,y) = x + y - 8$

$P_x = \dfrac{100(160)(4)}{(x + 4)^2} - 1{,}000$

$P_y = \dfrac{100(320)(2)}{(y + 2)^2} - 1{,}000$

$g_x = 1,\ g_y = 1$

Since $P_x = P_y = \lambda$,

$\dfrac{100(160)(4)}{(x + 4)^2} - 1{,}000$

$= \dfrac{100(320)(2)}{(y + 2)^2} - 1{,}000$

or $x + 4 = \pm\,(y + 2)$

Reject the negative solution as leading to negative spending. Substituting $y = x + 2$ in the constraint equation $x + y = 8$ leads to $x = 3$ thousand dollars for development and $y = 5$ thousand dollars for promotion.

b. $\lambda = P_y = -\dfrac{64{,}000}{49} - 1{,}000 \approx 306.122$

(for each \$1,000). Since the change in this promotion/development is \$100, the corresponding increase in profit is \$30.61. Remember that the Lagrange multiplier is the change in maximum profit for a unit (one thousand dollar) change in the constraint. The actual increase in profit is \$29.69.

c. To maximize the profit when unlimited funds are available maximize $P(x, y)$ without constraints. To do this, find the critical points by setting $P_x = 0$ and $P_y = 0$, that is

P_x: $\dfrac{64}{(x + 4)^2} - 1 = 0$

$$(x + 4)^2 = 64$$

$$x = 4$$

and

P_y: $\dfrac{64}{(y + 2)^2} - 1 = 0$

$$(y + 2)^2 = 64$$

$$y = 6$$

Thus, \$4,000 should be spent on development and \$6,000 should be spent on promotion to maximize profit.

d. If there were a restriction on the amount spent on development and promotion, then constraints would be

$g(x, y) = x + y = k$

for some positive constant k. The corresponding Lagrange equations would be

$$\frac{64}{(x + 4)^2} - 1 = \lambda; \frac{64}{(y + 2)^2} - 1 = \lambda;$$

and $x + y = k$. To obtain the answer in part **a** eliminate λ. Beginning with the

Lagrange equations from part **a**, set $\lambda = 0$ to obtain

$64/(x + 4)^2 - 1 = 0$ or $x = 4$, and

$64/(y + 2)^2 - 1 = 0$ or $y = 6$, just

as we found in part c.

CHAPTER 12 REVIEW

SURVIVAL HINT: *To help you review the concepts of this chapter, **hand write** the answers to each of these questions onto your own paper.*

1. A function of two variables is a rule that assigns to each ordered pair (x, y) in a set D a unique number $f(x, y)$.

2. The set D in the answer to Problem 1 is called the domain of the function, and the corresponding values of $f(x, y)$ constitute the range of f.

3. When the plane $z = C$ intersects the surface $z = f(x, y)$, the result is the space curve with the equation $f(x, y) = C$. Such an intersection is called the trace of the graph of f in the plane $z = C$. The set of points (x, y) in the xy-plane that satisfy $f(x, y) = C$ is called the level curve of f at C, and an entire family of level curves (or contour curves) is generated as C varies over the range of f.

4. The notation

$$\lim_{(x, y) \to (x_0, y_0)} f(x, y) = L$$

means that the functional values $f(x, y)$ can be made arbitrarily close to L by choosing a point (x, y) sufficiently close (but not equal) to the point (x_0, y_0). In other words, given some $\epsilon > 0$, we wish to find a $\delta > 0$ so that for any point (x, y) in the punctured disk of radius δ centered at (x_0, y_0), the functional value $f(x, y)$ lies between $L + \epsilon$ and $L - \epsilon$.

5. Suppose

$$\lim_{(x, y)\to(x_0, y_0)} f(x, y) = L$$

and

$$\lim_{(x, y)\to(x_0, y_0)} g(x, y) = M$$

Then, for a constant a,

a. $$\lim_{(x, y)\to(x_0, y_0)} [af](x, y) = aL$$

b. $$\lim_{(x, y)\to(x_0, y_0)} [f + g](x, y)$$

$$= \left[\lim_{(x, y)\to(x_0, y_0)} f(x, y) \right]$$

$$+ \left[\lim_{(x, y)\to(x_0, y_0)} g(x, y) \right]$$

$$= L + M$$

c. $$\lim_{(x, y)\to(x_0, y_0)} [fg](x, y)$$

$$= \left[\lim_{(x, y)\to(x_0, y_0)} f(x, y) \right]$$

$$\times \left[\lim_{(x, y)\to(x_0, y_0)} g(x, y) \right]$$

$$= LM$$

d. $$\lim_{(x, y)\to(x_0, y_0)} \left[\frac{f}{g}\right](x, y)$$

$$= \frac{\lim_{(x, y)\to(x_0, y_0)} f(x, y)}{\lim_{(x, y)\to(x_0, y_0)} g(x, y)} = \frac{L}{M} \quad (M \neq 0)$$

6. The function $f(x, y)$ is continuous at the point (x_0, y_0) if and only if

1. $f(x_0, y_0)$ is defined;

2. $$\lim_{(x,y)\to(x_0,y_0)} f(x, y) \text{ exists;}$$

3. $$\lim_{(x, y)\to(x_0, y_0)} f(x, y) = f(x_0, y_0).$$

Also, f is continuous on a set S in its domain if it is continuous at each point in S.

7. If $z = f(x, y)$, then the (first) partial derivatives of f with respect to x and y are the functions f_x and f_y, respectively, defined by

$$f_x(x, y) = \lim_{\Delta x \to 0} \frac{f(x + \Delta x, y) - f(x, y)}{\Delta x}$$

$$f_y(x, y) = \lim_{\Delta y \to 0} \frac{f(x, y + \Delta y) - f(x, y)}{\Delta y}$$

provided the limits exist.

8. The line tangent at the $P_0(x_0, y_0, z_0)$ to the trace of $z = f(x, y)$ in the plane $y = y_0$ has slope $f_x(x_0, y_0)$. Likewise, the line tangent at P_0 to the trace of $z = f(x, y)$ in the plane $x = x_0$ has slope $f_y(x_0, y_0)$.

9. $z = f(x, y);\ \dfrac{\partial^2 f}{\partial x^2},\ \dfrac{\partial^2 f}{\partial y^2},\ \dfrac{\partial^2 f}{\partial x \partial y},\ \dfrac{\partial^2 f}{\partial y \partial x}$

10. Let $z = f(x, y)$; $\Delta z = \dfrac{\partial f}{\partial x}\Delta x + \dfrac{\partial f}{\partial y}\Delta y$

    where $\Delta x = dx$ and $\Delta y = dy$.

11. Suppose $f(x, y)$ is defined at each point in a circular disk that is centered at (x_0, y_0) and contains the point $(x_0 + \Delta x, y_0 + \Delta y)$. Then f is said to be differentiable at (x_0, y_0) if, the increment of f can be expressed as

    $\Delta f = f_x(x_0, y_0)\Delta x + f_y(x_0, y_0)\Delta y + \epsilon_1\Delta x + \epsilon_2\Delta y$

    where $\epsilon_1 \to 0$ and $\epsilon_2 \to 0$ as both $\Delta x \to 0$ and $\Delta y \to 0$ (and $\epsilon_1 = \epsilon_2 = 0$ when $\Delta x = \Delta y = 0$). Also, $f(x, y)$ is said to be differentiable on the region R of the plane if f is differentiable at each point in R.

12. If $f(x, y)$ and its partial derivatives f_x and f_y are defined in an open region R containing the point $P(x_0, y_0)$ and f_x and f_y are continuous at P, then

    $\Delta f = f(x_0+\Delta x, y_0 +\Delta y) - f(x_0, y_0)$

    $\approx f_x(x_0, y_0)\Delta x + f_y(x_0, y_0)\Delta y$

    so that

    $f(x_0 + \Delta x, y_0 + \Delta y)$

    $\approx f(x_0, y_0) + f_x(x_0, y_0)\Delta x + f_y(x_0, y_0)\Delta y$

13. If $z = f(x, y)$ and Δx and Δy are increments of x and y, respectively, and if we let $dx = \Delta x$ and $dy = \Delta y$ be differentials for x and y,

respectively, then the total differential of $f(x, y)$ is

$$df = \frac{\partial f}{\partial x}\,dx + \frac{\partial f}{\partial y}\,dy = f_x(x, y)\,dx + f_y(x, y)\,dy$$

14. Let $f(x, y)$ be a differentiable function of x and y, and let $x = x(t)$ and $y = y(t)$ be differentiable functions of t. Then $z = f(x, y)$ is a differentiable function of t, and

    $$\frac{dz}{dt} = \frac{\partial z}{\partial x}\frac{dx}{dt} + \frac{\partial z}{\partial y}\frac{dy}{dt}$$

15. Suppose $z = f(x, y)$ is differentiable at (x, y) and that the partial derivatives of $x = x(u, v)$ and $y = y(u, v)$ exist at (u, v). Then the composite function $z = f[x(u, v), y(u, v)]$ is differentiable at (u, v) with

    $$\frac{\partial z}{\partial u} = \frac{\partial z}{\partial x}\frac{\partial x}{\partial u} + \frac{\partial z}{\partial y}\frac{\partial y}{\partial u} \text{ and } \frac{\partial z}{\partial v} = \frac{\partial z}{\partial x}\frac{\partial x}{\partial v} + \frac{\partial z}{\partial y}\frac{\partial y}{\partial v}$$

16. Let f be a function of two variables, and let $\mathbf{u} = u_1\mathbf{i} + u_2\mathbf{j}$ be a unit vector. The directional derivative of f at $P_0(x_0, y_0)$ in the direction of $\mathbf{u}$ is given by

    $D_u f(x_0, y_0)$

    $$= \lim_{h\to 0} \frac{f(x_0 + hu_1, y_0 + hu_2) - f(x_0, y_0)}{h}$$

    provided the limit exists.

17. Let f be a differentiable function at (x, y) and let $f(x, y)$ have partial derivatives $f_x(x, y)$ and $f_y(x, y)$. Then the gradient of f, denoted by ∇f, is a vector given by

$$\nabla f(x,\, y) = f_x(x,\, y)\mathbf{i} + f_y(x,\, y)\mathbf{j}$$

18. Let f and g be differentiable functions. Then

    a. $\nabla c = \mathbf{0}$ for any constant c

    b. $\nabla(af + bg) = a\nabla f + b\nabla g$

    c. $\nabla(fg) = f\nabla g + g\nabla f$

    d. $\nabla\!\left(\dfrac{f}{g}\right) = \dfrac{g\nabla f - f\nabla g}{g^2}$ $g \neq 0$

    e. $\nabla(f^n) = nf^{(n-1)}\nabla f$

19. If f is a differentiable function of x and y, then the directional derivative at the point $P_0(x_0,\, y_0)$ in the direction of the unit vector $\mathbf{u}$ is
    $$D_{\mathbf{u}}f(x,\, y) = \nabla f \cdot \mathbf{u}$$

20. Suppose f is differentiable and let ∇f_0 denote the gradient at P_0. Then if $\nabla f_0 \neq \mathbf{0}$:

    (1) The largest value of the directional derivative of $D_{\mathbf{u}}f$ is $\|\nabla f_0\|$ and occurs when the unit vector $\mathbf{u}$ points in the direction of ∇f_0.

    (2) The smallest value of $D_{\mathbf{u}}f$ is $-\|\nabla f_0\|$ and occurs when $\mathbf{u}$ points in the direction of $-\nabla f_0$.

21. Suppose the function f is differentiable at the point P_0 and that the gradient at P_0 satisfies $\nabla f_0 \neq \mathbf{0}$. Then ∇f_0 is orthogonal to the level surface $f(x,\, y,\, z) = K$ at P_0.

22. Suppose the surface S has a nonzero normal vector $\mathbf{N}$ at the point P_0. Then the line through P_0 parallel to $\mathbf{N}$ is called the normal line to S at P_0, and the plane through P_0 with normal vector $\mathbf{N}$ is the tangent plane to S at P_0.

23. The function $f(x,\, y)$ is said to have an absolute maximum at $(x_0,\, y_0)$ if $f(x_0,\, y_0) \geq f(x,\, y)$ for all $(x,\, y)$ in the domain D of f. Similarly, f has an absolute minimum at $(x_0,\, y_0)$ if $f(x_0,\, y_0) \leq f(x,\, y)$ for all $(x,\, y)$ in D. Collectively, absolute maxima and minima are called absolute extrema.

24. Let f be a function defined at $(x_0,\, y_0)$. Then $f(x_0,\, y_0)$ is a relative maximum if $f(x,\, y) \leq f(x_0,\, y_0)$ for all $(x,\, y)$ in an open disk containing $(x_0,\, y_0)$. $f(x_0,\, y_0)$ is a relative minimum if $f(x,\, y) \geq f(x_0,\, y_0)$ for all $(x,\, y)$ in an open disk containing $(x_0,\, y_0)$. Collectively, relative maxima and minima are called relative extrema.

25. A critical point of a function f defined on an open set S is a point $(x_0,\, y_0)$ in S where either one of the following is true:

    (1) $f_x(x_0,\, y_0) = f_y(x_0,\, y_0) = 0$.

    (2) $f_x(x_0,\, y_0)$ or $f_y(x_0,\, y_0)$ does not exist (one or both).

26. Let $f(x,\, y)$ have a critical point at $P_0(x_0,\, y_0)$ and assume that f has continuous partial derivatives in a disk centered at $(x_0,\, y_0)$. Let

$$D = f_{xx}(x_0, y_0)f_{yy}(x_0, y_0) - [f_{xy}(x_0, y_0)]^2$$

Then, a relative maximum occurs at P_0 if

$$D > 0 \text{ and } f_{xx}(x_0, y_0) < 0$$

A relative minimum occurs at P_0 if

$$D > 0 \text{ and } f_{xx}(x_0, y_0) > 0$$

A saddle point occurs at P_0 if $D < 0$.

If $D = 0$, then the test is inconclusive.

27. A function of two variables $f(x, y)$ assumes an absolute extremum on any closed, bounded set S in the plane where it is continuous. Moreover, all absolute extrema must occur either on the boundary of S or at a critical point in the interior of S.

28. Given a set of data points (x_k, y_k), a line $y = mx + b$, called a regression line, is obtained by minimizing the sum of squares of distances $y_k - (mx_k + b)$.

29. Assume that f and g have continuous first partial derivatives and that f has an extremum at $P_0(x_0, y_0)$ on the smooth constraint curve $g(x, y) = c$. If $\nabla g(x_0, y_0) \neq \mathbf{0}$, there is a number λ such that $\nabla f(x_0, y_0) = \lambda \nabla g(x_0, y_0)$.

30. Suppose f and g satisfy the hypotheses of Lagrange's theorem, and suppose that $f(x)$ has an extremum (minimum and/or a maximum) subject to the constraint $g(x, y) = c$. Then to

find the extreme values, proceed as follows:

1. Simultaneously solve the following three equations:

    $$f_x(x, y) = \lambda g_x(x, y)$$
    $$f_y(x, y) = \lambda g_y(x, y)$$
    $$g(x, y) = c$$

2. Evaluate f at all points found in Step 1. The largest of these values is the maximum value of f and the smallest of these values is the minimum value of f.

33. $f(x, y, z) = xy + yz + xz$ at $(1, 2, -1)$

    a. $\nabla f = (y + z)\mathbf{i} + (x + z)\mathbf{j} + (y + x)\mathbf{k}$

    $\nabla f_0 = \mathbf{i} + 3\mathbf{k}$ at $P_0(1, 2, -1)$

    b. $\mathbf{u} = \dfrac{P_0 Q}{\|P_0 Q\|}$

    $= \dfrac{-2\mathbf{i} - \mathbf{j}}{\sqrt{5}}$

    $D_u(f) = \nabla f \cdot \mathbf{u}$

    $= \dfrac{-2}{\sqrt{5}}$

    $= \dfrac{-2\sqrt{5}}{5}$

    c. The directional derivative has its greatest value in the direction of the gradient, $\mathbf{u} = \dfrac{\mathbf{i} + 3\mathbf{k}}{\sqrt{10}}$. The magnitude is

    $\|\nabla f\| = \sqrt{10}.$

36. $f(x, y, z) = x^2y + y^2z + z^2x$

$f_x = 2xy + z^2$

$f_y = x^2 + 2yz$

$f_z = y^2 + 2zx$

$f_x + f_y + f_z = 2xy + z^2 + x^2 + 2yz + y^2 + 2zx$

$$= (x + y + z)^2$$

39. $f(x, y) = x^2 + 2y^2 + 2x + 3$ subject to

$g(x, y) = x^2 + y^2 - 4$

$2x + 2 = 2x\lambda$, $4y = 2y\lambda$, and $x^2 + y^2 = 4$

From the second equation: $\lambda = 2$ or $y = 0$.

If $\lambda = 2$, $2x + 2 = 4x$, $x = 1$, and from the constraint equation $y = \pm\sqrt{3}$. If $y = 0$ the constraint equation gives $x = \pm 2$. The set of candidates: $(1, \sqrt{3})$, $(1, -\sqrt{3})$, $(2, 0)$, $(-2, 0)$.

$f(1, \sqrt{3}) = 12$; $f(1, -\sqrt{3}) = 12$;

$f(2, 0) = 11$; $f(-2, 0) = 3$.

$f(x, y)$ has a maximum of 12 at $(1, \pm\sqrt{3})$ and a minimum of 3 at $(-2, 0)$.

CHAPTER 13

Multiple Integration

13.1 Double Integration Over Rectangular Regions, Pages 887-889

SURVIVAL HINT: *Be careful to use the x boundaries with dx and y boundaries with dy, for whatever iteration you choose.*

$$\int_{x_1}^{x_2} \int_{y_1}^{y_2} f(x,\ y)\ dy\ dx \quad \text{or} \quad \int_{y_1}^{y_2} \int_{x_1}^{x_2} f(x,\ y)\ dx\ dy$$

3. $\displaystyle \int_1^{e^2} \int_1^2 \left[\frac{1}{x} + \frac{1}{y}\right] dy\ dx = \int_1^{e^2} \left[\ln\ y + \frac{y}{x}\right]\Big|_1^2 dx$

$$= \int_1^{e^2} (\ln\ 2 + x^{-1})\ dx$$

$$= (e^2 - 1)(\ln\ 2) + 2$$

SURVIVAL HINT: *Problems 7-12 are concerned with the idea of evaluating a double integral by relating it to a volume.*

7. $\displaystyle \int_R \int 4\ dA = 4\ \underbrace{(2)(4)}_{\text{area of base}} \overset{\text{height}}{} = 32$

12. $\displaystyle \int_R \int \frac{y}{4}\ dA = \underbrace{\frac{1}{2}(8)(2)}_{\text{area of triangle}} \overset{\text{height}}{(2)} = 16$

14. $\displaystyle \int_R \int (x + 2y)\ dA = \int_2^3 \int_{-1}^1 (x + 2y)\ dy\ dx$

$$= \int_2^3 (xy + y^2)\Big|_{-1}^1 dx$$

$$= \int_2^3 2x\ dx = x^2\Big|_2^3$$

$$= 5$$

17. $\displaystyle \int_R \int \frac{2xy\ dA}{x^2 + 1} = \int_0^1 \int_1^3 \frac{2xy}{x^2 + 1}\ dy\ dx$

$$= 4\int_0^1 \frac{2x}{x^2 + 1}\ dx$$

$$= 4\ln\ 2$$

21. $\displaystyle \int_R \int (2x + 3y)\ dA = \int_0^1 \int_0^2 (2x + 3y)\ dy\ dx$

$$= \int_0^1 (4x + 6)\ dx$$

$$= 8$$

24. $\displaystyle \int_0^b \int_0^c axy\ dy\ dx = \frac{ac^2}{2} \int_0^b x\ dx$

$$= \frac{ab^2c^2}{4}$$

33. A double integral $\displaystyle\int_R\int f(x, y)\, dA$ is often evaluated as an iterated integral

$$\int\left[\int f(x, y)\, dy\right] dx$$ in which y-integration is

performed first with x held constant, and then x-integration is performed. Likewise, the

iterated integral $\displaystyle\int\left[\int f(x, y)\, dx\right] dy$ involves

x-integration, then y-integration. Fubini's theorem says that the two iterated integrals are equal:

$$\int\left[\int f(x, y)\, dy\right] dx = \int\left[\int f(x, y)\, dx\right] dy$$

$$= \int_R\int f(x, y)\, dA$$

38. $\displaystyle\int_0^2\int_0^1 x(1 - x^2)^{1/2} e^{3y}\, dx\, dy = \frac{1}{3}\int_0^2 e^{3y}\, dy$

$$= \frac{e^6}{9} - \frac{1}{9}$$

42. $z = f(x, y)$ is a paraboloid opening downward with vertex at $z = 4$ and intercepts of $(\pm 2, 0, 0)$ and $(0, \pm 2, 0)$. The integral represents the volume above the unit square in the first octant. The minimum value for $z = f(1, 1) = 2$. Since $z \geq 2$ over the given region R, the value of the integral will be

greater than the volume of the "box" with unit base and height 2.

46. $\displaystyle\int_R\int \frac{\partial}{\partial y}\left[\frac{\partial f(x, y)}{\partial x}\right] dA = \int_{x_1}^{x_2}\int_{y_1}^{y_2} \frac{\partial}{\partial y}\left[\frac{\partial f(x, y)}{\partial x}\right] dy\, dx$

$$= \int_{x_1}^{x_2} \frac{\partial}{\partial x} f(x, y)\Big|_{y=y_1}^{y=y_2} dx$$

$$= \int_{x_1}^{x_2}\left[\frac{\partial f(x, y_2)}{\partial x} - \frac{\partial f(x, y_1)}{\partial x}\right] dx$$

$$= f(x, y_2) - f(x, y_1)\Big|_{x=x_1}^{x=x_2}$$

$$= f(x_2, y_2) - f(x_1, y_2) - f(x_2, y_1) + f(x_1, y_1)$$

13.2 Double Integration Over Nonrectangular Regions, Pages 895-897

SURVIVAL HINT: *Draw a sketch of the region of integration and decide on vertical or horizontal strips. For vertical strips you must have numerical values for the x limits and either numerical or $y = g(x)$ expressions for the y-limits:*

$$\int_{x_1}^{x_2}\int_{y_1 = g_1(x)}^{y_2 = g_2(x)} f(x, y)\, dy\, dx$$

For horizontal strips, you must have numerical values for the y limits and either numerical or $x = h(y)$ for the x-limits:

$$\int_{y_1}^{y_2}\int_{x_1 = h_1(x)}^{x_2 = h_2(x)} f(x, y)\, dx\, dy$$

3. Use vertical strips:

$$\int_0^4 \int_0^{4-x} xy \; dy \; dx \;=\; \int_0^4 \frac{x}{2}(4-x)^2 \; dx$$

$$=\frac{32}{3}$$

7. Use horizontal strips:

$$\int_0^{2\sqrt{2}} \int_{y^2/4}^{\sqrt{12-y^2}} dx \; dy \;=\; \int_0^{2\sqrt{2}} \left(\sqrt{12-y^2} - \frac{y^2}{4}\right) dy$$

$$=\left(\frac{y}{2}\sqrt{12-y^2} + 6\sin^{-1}\frac{y}{2\sqrt{3}} - \frac{y^3}{12}\right)\Bigg|_0^{2\sqrt{2}}$$

(Formula #231)

$$= 6\tan^{-1}\sqrt{2} + \frac{2\sqrt{2}}{3}$$

$$\approx \; 6.6747$$

SURVIVAL HINT: *Your might want to find out from your instructor if you should refer to your procedure as Type I and Type II, or if you should simply use the words vertical strips or horizontal strips, respectively.*

13. Use vertical strips:

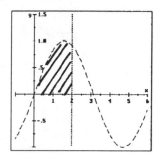

$$\int_0^2 \int_0^{\sin x} y\cos x \; dy \; dx \;=\; \frac{1}{2}\int_0^2 \sin^2 x \cos x \; dx$$

$$= \frac{1}{6}\sin^3 2$$

$$\approx 0.1253$$

19. Use vertical strips:

$$\int_0^1 \int_{x^3}^{\sqrt{x}} 48\,xy \; dy \; dx \;=\; 24\int_0^1 (x^2 - x^7)\;dx$$

$$= 5$$

24. Use horizontal strips:

$$\int_0^1 \int_{y-1}^{-y+1} (2x+1)\;dx\;dy \;=\; 2\int_0^1 (-y+1)\;dy$$

$$= 1$$

31.

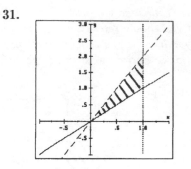

a. vertical strips

$$\int_0^1 \int_x^{2x} e^{y-x} \, dy \, dx = \int_0^1 (e^x - 1) \, dx$$

$$= e - 2$$

b. horizontal strips

$$\int_0^1 \int_{y/2}^{y} e^{y-x} \, dx \, dy + \int_1^2 \int_{y/2}^{1} e^{y-x} \, dx \, dy$$

$$= -\int_0^1 (1 - e^{y/2}) \, dy - \int_1^2 (e^{y-1} - e^{y/2}) \, dy$$

$$= e - 2$$

35.

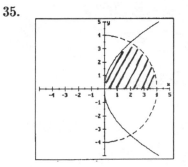

a. horizontal strips

$$\int_0^{2\sqrt{3}} \int_{y^2/6}^{\sqrt{16-y^2}} dx \, dy$$

$$= \int_0^{2\sqrt{3}} \left(\sqrt{16 - y^2} - \frac{y^2}{6} \right) dy$$

$$= \left[8 \sin^{-1} \frac{y}{4} + \frac{y}{2} \sqrt{16 - y^2} - \frac{y^3}{18} \right] \Bigg|_0^{2\sqrt{3}}$$

$$= \frac{8\pi}{3} + \frac{2\sqrt{3}}{3}$$

$$\approx 9.5323$$

b. vertical strips

$$\int_0^2 \int_0^{\sqrt{6x}} dy \, dx + \int_2^4 \int_0^{\sqrt{16-x^2}} dy \, dx$$

$$= \int_0^2 \sqrt{6x} \, dx + \int_2^4 \sqrt{16 - x^2} \, dx$$

$$= \frac{8\sqrt{3}}{3} + \left(-2\sqrt{3} + \frac{8\pi}{3} \right)$$

$$\approx 9.5323$$

38.

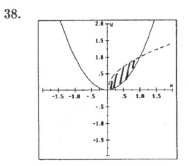

$$\int_0^1 \int_{y^2}^{\sqrt{y}} f(x, y) \ dx \ dy$$

41.

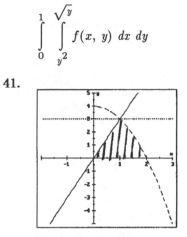

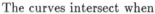

The curves intersect when

$$\frac{y}{3} = \sqrt{4 - y}$$

$$y^2 + 9y - 36 = 0$$

$$(y - 3)(y + 12) = 0$$

$$y = 3, \ -12$$

Intersection: $(1, 3)$

$$\int_0^1 \int_0^{3x} f(x, y) \ dy \ dx \ + \ \int_1^2 \int_0^{4-x^2} f(x, y) \ dy \ dx$$

51. The projection of the ellipsoid on the xy-plane is the ellipse

$$\frac{x^2}{a^2} + \frac{y^2}{b^2} = 1$$

Using symmetry of the ellipse, we have

$$V = 4 \int_0^a \int_0^{(b/a)\sqrt{a^2 - x^2}} c\sqrt{1 - \frac{x^2}{a^2} - \frac{y^2}{b^2}} \ dy \ dx$$

54.

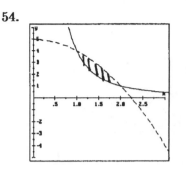

We find the intersection points:

$$\frac{4}{x^2} = 5 - x^2$$

$$x^4 - 5x^2 + 4 = 0$$

$$(x^2 - 4)(x^2 - 1) = 0$$

$$x = \pm 1, \ \pm 2$$

Intersections: $(1, 4), \ (2, 1)$

Using horizontal strips:

$$\int_1^4 \int_{2/\sqrt{y}}^{\sqrt{5-y}} dx \ dy$$

Using vertical strips:

$$\int_1^2 \int_{4/x^2}^{5-x^2} dy \ dx \ = \ \int_1^2 \left(5 - x^2 - \frac{4}{x^2} \right) dx$$

$$= \frac{2}{3}$$

61.

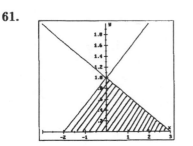

The lines intersect at $(-2, 0)$, $(3, 0)$, and $(0, 1)$.

$$\int_0^1 \int_{2y-2}^{3-3y} (x^2 - xy - 1)\, dx\, dy$$

$$= \int_0^1 \frac{5}{6}(-17y^3 + 48y^2 - 39y + 8)\, dy$$

$$= \frac{5}{24}$$

13.3 Double Integrals in Polar Coordinates, Pages 903–906

SURVIVAL HINT: *Since polar equations are often periodic [e.g. $f(0) = f(2\pi)$], it is sometimes a good idea to make use of any symmetry in the graph. Find the area of the smallest piece and multiply by the number of such pieces.*

2.
$$\int_0^\pi \int_0^{1+\sin\theta} dr\, d\theta$$

$$= \int_0^\pi (1 + \sin\theta)\, d\theta$$

$$= \pi + 2$$

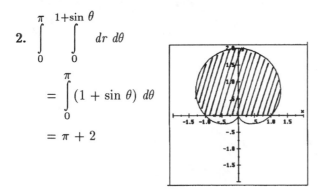

6.
$$\int_0^{\pi/2} \int_1^3 r^2 \cos^2\theta\, dr\, d\theta$$

$$= \frac{26}{3} \int_0^{\pi/2} \cos^2\theta\, d\theta$$

$$= \frac{13\pi}{6}$$

$$\approx 6.8068$$

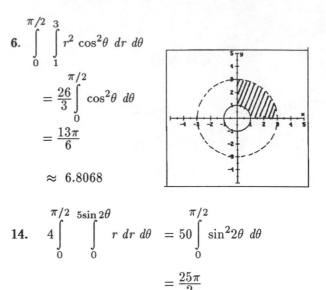

14.
$$4 \int_0^{\pi/2} \int_0^{5\sin 2\theta} r\, dr\, d\theta = 50 \int_0^{\pi/2} \sin^2 2\theta\, d\theta$$

$$= \frac{25\pi}{2}$$

19. Use symmetry about the polar axis and the equation of the quarter circle.

$$2[\tfrac{1}{4}\pi(1)^2] + 2 \int_{\pi/2}^{\pi} \int_0^{1+\cos\theta} r\, dr\, d\theta$$

$$= \frac{\pi}{2} + 2 \int_{\pi/2}^{\pi} \left(\frac{1}{2}\cos^2\theta + \cos\theta + \frac{1}{2} \right) d\theta$$

$$= \frac{\pi}{2} + \frac{3\pi - 8}{4}$$

$$= \frac{5\pi}{4} - 2$$

$$\approx 1.9270$$

23. The bottom half of the loop is scanned out as θ varies from $2\pi/3$ to π. Thus, the area is

$$A = 2 \int_{2\pi/3}^{\pi} \int_0^{1+2\cos\theta} r\, dr\, d\theta$$

$$= \pi - \frac{3\sqrt{3}}{2}$$

$$\approx 0.5435$$

SURVIVAL HINT: *One of the most common errors when converting from Cartesian to polar integration is forgetting the factor of "r." That is,*

$$dy\ dx = dA = r\ dr\ d\theta$$

30. $4 \int_0^{\pi/2} \int_0^{a} r \ln(a^2 + r^2)\ dr\ d\theta$

$$= 4 \int_0^{\pi/2} [-a^2 \ln \tfrac{1}{2} + a^2 \ln a - \tfrac{a^2}{2}]\ d\theta$$

$$= 2\pi(a^2 \ln 2 + a^2 \ln a - \tfrac{a^2}{2})$$

$$= \pi a^2(\ln 4 + 2 \ln a - 1)$$

33. $\int_D \int e^{x^2+y^2}\ dA = 4 \int_0^{\pi/2} \int_0^{3} re^{r^2}\ dr\ d\theta$

$$= 4 \int_0^{\pi/2} \tfrac{1}{2}(e^9 - 1)$$

$$= \pi(e^9 - 1)$$

$$\approx 25{,}453$$

39.

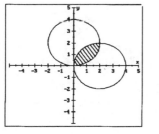

The curves intersect at $\theta = \pi/4$.

$\int_0^{\pi/4} \int_0^{4\sin\theta} r^3 \sin\theta \cos\theta\ dr\ d\theta$

$+ \int_{\pi/4}^{\pi/2} \int_0^{4\cos\theta} r^3 \sin\theta \cos\theta\ dr\ d\theta$

$$= 4^3 \left[\int_0^{\pi/4} \sin^5\theta \cos\theta\ d\theta + \int_{\pi/4}^{\pi/2} \cos^5\theta \sin\theta\ d\theta \right]$$

$$= \frac{4}{3} + \frac{4}{3}$$

$$= \frac{8}{3}$$

44. The sphere and paraboloid intersect where

$$3z + z^2 = 4;\ z = 1$$

Thus, the curve of intersection projects onto the curve $x^2 + y^2 = 3$ in the xy-plane.

$$V = \int_D \int \left[\sqrt{4 - x^2 - y^2} - \tfrac{1}{3}(x^2 + y^2) \right] dA$$

$$= \int_0^{2\pi} \int_0^{\sqrt{3}} [\sqrt{1\ \ r^2} - \tfrac{1}{3}r^2]\ r\ dr\ d\theta$$

$$= \frac{19\pi}{6}$$

$$\approx 9.9484$$

49. $\displaystyle\lim_{n\to\infty} \int_0^{\pi/2} \int_0^{n} r(r^2 + 1)^{-3/2}\ dr\ d\theta$

$$= \lim_{n \to \infty} \int_0^{\pi/2} \frac{\sqrt{n^2 + 1} - 1}{\sqrt{n^2 + 1}} \, d\theta$$

$$= \frac{\pi}{2}$$

57. $\quad I_1^2 = \int_0^\infty e^{-x^2} \, dx \cdot \int_0^\infty e^{-y^2} \, dy$

$$= \int_0^\infty \int_0^\infty e^{-(x^2 + y^2)} \, dx \, dy$$

$$= \int_0^{\pi/2} \int_0^\infty r e^{-r^2} \, dr \, d\theta$$

$$= \frac{\pi}{4}$$

Thus, $I_1 = \dfrac{\sqrt{\pi}}{2}$ and by symmetry,

$$I = \int_{-\infty}^\infty e^{-x^2} \, dx$$

$$= 2 \int_0^\infty e^{-x^2} \, dx$$

$$= 2 I_1$$

$$= \sqrt{\pi}$$

1. $\quad z = f(x, y) = 2 - \frac{1}{2}x - \frac{1}{4}y$

$$f_x = -\frac{1}{2}; \ f_y = -\frac{1}{4}$$

$$\sqrt{f_x^2 + f_y^2 + 1} = \sqrt{\frac{1}{4} + \frac{1}{16} + 1}$$

$$= \frac{\sqrt{21}}{4}$$

$$S = \int_0^4 \int_0^{-2x+8} \frac{\sqrt{21}}{4} \, dy \, dx$$

$$= \frac{\sqrt{21}}{4} \int_0^4 (-2x + 8) \, dx$$

$$= \frac{16\sqrt{21}}{4}$$

$$= 4\sqrt{21}$$

$$\approx 18.3303$$

6. $\quad z = f(x, y) = 2x + 2y$

$$f_x = 2; \ f_y = 2$$

$$\sqrt{f_x^2 + f_y^2 + 1} = \sqrt{4 + 4 + 1}$$

$$= 3$$

$$S = \int_0^1 \int_0^1 3 \, dy \, dx$$

$$= 3$$

13.4 Surface Area, Pages 912-914

SURVIVAL HINT: *Do not try to evaluate any but the simplest of the radical expressions "in your head." You will make fewer errors if you take the time to write down the values f_x, f_y, square them, add 1, and then take the root.*

SURVIVAL HINT: *In any expression where you find a factor $x^2 + y^2$ you should consider changing to polar coordinates.*

12. $\quad z = f(x, y) = \sqrt{25 - x^2 - y^2}$

$$f_x = \frac{-x}{\sqrt{25 - x^2 - y^2}}$$

$$f_y = \frac{-y}{\sqrt{25 - x^2 - y^2}}$$

$$\sqrt{f_x^2 + f_y^2 + 1} = \sqrt{\frac{x^2 + y^2 + 25 - x^2 - y^2}{25 - x^2 - y^2}}$$

$$= 5\sqrt{\frac{1}{25 - r^2}}$$

$$S = \int_0^{2\pi} \int_0^4 \frac{5r\; dr\; d\theta}{\sqrt{25 - r^2}}$$

$$= \int_0^{2\pi} 10\; d\theta$$

$$= 20\pi$$

$$\approx 62.8319$$

16. The intersection of the two surfaces (which is also the projection onto the z-plane) is found by eliminating the z: $x^2 + y^2 = 4$

$$z = f(x, y) = \sqrt{8 - x^2 - y^2};$$

$$f_x = \frac{-x}{\sqrt{8 - x^2 - y^2}}$$

$$f_y = \frac{-y}{\sqrt{8 - x^2 - y^2}}$$

$$\sqrt{f_x^2 + f_y^2 + 1} = \sqrt{\frac{x^2 + y^2 + 8 - x^2 - y^2}{8 - x^2 - y^2}}$$

$$= \frac{\sqrt{8}}{\sqrt{8 - r^2}}$$

The projected region is found by intersecting the two surfaces to obtain $x^2 + y^2 = 4$. Since half the surface lies above the xy-plane, we have

$$S = 2\int_0^{2\pi} \int_0^2 \frac{2\sqrt{2}r}{\sqrt{8 - r^2}}\; dr\; d\theta$$

$$= 8\int_0^{\pi/2} (8 - 4\sqrt{2})\; d\theta$$

$$= 16\pi(2 - \sqrt{2})$$

$$\approx 29.4448$$

23. $z = f(x, y) = \frac{1}{C}(D - Ax - By)$

$$f_x = -\frac{A}{C};\; f_y = -\frac{B}{C}$$

$$\sqrt{f_x^2 + f_y^2 + 1} = \sqrt{\frac{A^2}{C^2} + \frac{B^2}{C^2} + 1}$$

$$= \frac{\sqrt{A^2 + B^2 + C^2}}{C}$$

$$S = \int_0^{D/A} \int_0^{-\frac{A}{B}x + \frac{D}{B}} \frac{\sqrt{A^2 + B^2 + C^2}}{C}\; dy\; dx$$

$$= \frac{\sqrt{A^2 + B^2 + C^2}}{C} \int_0^{D/A} \left(-\frac{A}{B}x + \frac{D}{B}\right) dx$$

$$= \frac{D^2}{2ABC} \sqrt{A^2 + B^2 + C^2}$$

26. $z = f(x, y) = \sqrt{9 - x^2}$

$$f_x = \frac{-x}{\sqrt{9 - x^2}}$$

$$f_y = 0$$

$$\sqrt{f_x^2 + f_y^2 + 1} = \sqrt{\frac{x^2}{9 - x^2} + 0 + 1}$$

$$= \frac{3}{\sqrt{9 - x^2}}$$

The projected region on the xy-plane is the disk $x^2 + y^2 \leq 9$. Since half the surface lies above the xy-plane and one-fourth of that lies above the first quadrant, we have

$$S = 8 \int_0^3 \int_0^{\sqrt{9 - x^2}} \frac{3}{\sqrt{9 - x^2}} \, dy \, dx$$

$$= 8 \int_0^3 3 \, dx$$

$$= 72$$

Note: It is tempting to use polar coordinates on this problem, but that approach leads to much harder integrations.

31. Solve $z = e^{-x} \sin y$ for x:

$$x = \ln(\sin y) - \ln z$$

$$x_y = \frac{\cos y}{\sin y}$$

$$= \cot y$$

$$x_z = \frac{-1}{z}$$

$$\sqrt{x_y^2 + x_z^2 + 1} = \sqrt{\cot^2 y + \frac{1}{z^2} + 1}$$

$$= \sqrt{\csc^2 y + z^{-2}}$$

$$S = \int_0^1 \int_0^y \sqrt{\csc^2 y + z^{-2}} \, dz \, dy$$

36. $z = f(x, y) = x^2 + 3xy + y^2;$

$$f_x = 2x + 3y$$

$$f_y = 2y + 3x$$

$$\sqrt{f_x^2 + f_y^2 + 1} = \sqrt{(2x + 3y)^2 + (2y + 3x)^2 + 1}$$

$$S = \int_0^4 \int_0^x \sqrt{(2x + 3y)^2 + (2y + 3x)^2 + 1} \, dy \, dx$$

40. $R_u \times R_v = \begin{vmatrix} \mathbf{i} & \mathbf{j} & \mathbf{k} \\ 2 \sin v & 2 \cos v & 2u \sin 2v \\ 2u \cos v & -2u \sin v & 2u^2 \cos 2v \end{vmatrix}$

$$= (4u^2 \cos v \cos 2v + 4u^2 \sin v \sin 2v)\mathbf{i}$$

$$+ (4u^2 \cos v \sin 2v - 4u^2 \sin v \cos 2v)\mathbf{j}$$

$$- 4u\mathbf{k}$$

$$\|R_u \times R_v\| = 4|u|\sqrt{u^2 + 1}$$

43.

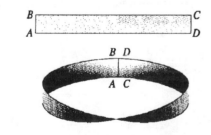

$\mathbf{R}(x,\,y,\,z) = \langle \cos v + u \cos \frac{v}{2} \cos v,$

$\qquad \sin v + u \cos \frac{v}{2} \sin v, \; u \sin \frac{v}{2} \rangle$

$\mathbf{R}_u = \langle \cos v \cos \frac{v}{2}, \; \sin v \cos \frac{v}{2}, \; \sin \frac{v}{2} \rangle$

$\mathbf{R}_v = \langle -u \sin v \cos \frac{v}{2} - \frac{u}{2} \cos v \sin \frac{v}{2} - \sin v,$

$\qquad u \cos v \cos \frac{v}{2} - \frac{u}{2} \sin v \sin \frac{v}{2} + \cos v,$

$\qquad \frac{u}{2} \cos \frac{v}{2} \rangle$

The fundamental cross product is

$\mathbf{R}_u \times \mathbf{R}_v = \frac{1}{2}\left(-\frac{u}{2}\sin 2v + u \sin v - 2 \cos v \sin \frac{v}{2}\right)\mathbf{i}$

$\qquad + \frac{1}{2}\left(-u\sin^2 v - u \cos v - 2 \sin v \sin \frac{v}{2}\right)\mathbf{j}$

$\qquad + \frac{1}{2}\left(2u \cos^2 \frac{v}{2} + 2 \cos \frac{v}{2}\right)\mathbf{k}$

13.5 Triple Integrals, Pages 921-924

SURVIVAL HINT: *It takes considerable skill and practice to determine which of the six possible permutations of dV will be "easiest" for a given problem. The most common situation is two functions of the form $z = f(x,\,y)$; in which case you would use $dz\,dA$, where the region A is determined by the intersection of the two functions. For other iterations, be certain that the limits for the first integration are either constants or functions of the remaining two variables, the limits of the second integration are constants or functions of the remaining variable, and the limits for the final integration are constants.*

2. $\displaystyle\int_0^4 \int_0^{\sqrt{x}} \int_0^{4-x} dz\,dy\,dx; \quad \int_0^2 \int_{y^2}^4 \int_0^{4-x} dz\,dx\,dy$

$\displaystyle\int_0^4 \int_0^{4-x} \int_0^{\sqrt{x}} dy\,dz\,dx \; ; \quad \int_0^4 \int_0^{4-z} \int_0^{\sqrt{x}} dy\,dx\,dz$

$\displaystyle\int_0^4 \int_0^{\sqrt{4-z}} \int_{y^2}^4 dx\,dy\,dz; \quad \int_0^2 \int_0^{4-y^2} \int_{y^2}^4 dx\,dz\,dy$

3. $\displaystyle\int_1^4 \int_{-2}^3 \int_2^5 dx\,dy\,dz = \int_1^4 \int_{-2}^3 (5-2)\,dy\,dz$

$\displaystyle\qquad\qquad\qquad = \int_1^4 3(3+2)\,dz$

$\displaystyle\qquad\qquad\qquad = (3)(5)(4-1)$

$\displaystyle\qquad\qquad\qquad = 45$

8. $\displaystyle\int_0^1 \int_{\sqrt{x}}^{\sqrt{1+x}} \int_0^{xy} y^{-1}z\,dz\,dy\,dx$

$\displaystyle\qquad = \frac{1}{2}\int_0^1 \int_{\sqrt{x}}^{\sqrt{x+1}} x^2 y\,dy\,dx$

$\displaystyle\qquad = \frac{1}{4}\int_0^1 x^2(1 + x - x)\,dx$

$\displaystyle\qquad = \frac{1}{12}$

13. $\displaystyle\int_1^4 \int_{-1}^{2z} \int_0^{\sqrt{3}\,x} \frac{x-y}{x^2+y^2}\,dy\,dx\,dz$

$\displaystyle = \int_1^4 \int_{-1}^{2z} \left[\frac{\pi}{3} - \ln 2\right] dx\,dz$

$\displaystyle = \int_1^4 \left[\frac{2\pi z}{3} - (2\ln 2)z + \frac{\pi}{3} - \ln 2\right] dz$

$= 6\pi - 18\ln 2$

≈ 6.3729

17. $\displaystyle\int_0^1 \int_0^{1-x} \int_0^{1-x-y} xyz\,dz\,dy\,dx$

$\displaystyle = \frac{1}{2}\int_0^1 \int_0^{1-x} xy(1-x-y)^2\,dy\,dx$

$\displaystyle = \frac{1}{24}\int_0^1 x(x-1)^4\,dx$

$\displaystyle = \frac{1}{720}$

22. $\displaystyle\int_0^3 \int_0^{\sqrt{9-z^2}} \int_0^{\sqrt{9-y^2-z^2}} yz\,dx\,dy\,dz$

$\displaystyle = \int_0^3 \int_0^{\sqrt{9-z^2}} yz(9-y^2-z^2)^{1/2}\,dy\,dx$

$\displaystyle = \int_0^3 \frac{z(9-z^2)^{3/2}}{3}\,dz$

$\displaystyle = \frac{81}{5}$

25. $\displaystyle 8\int_1^2 \int_2^A \int_3^B dz\,dy\,dx$ where

$$A = 2 + \sqrt{1-(x-1)^2}$$

and

$$B = 3 + \sqrt{1-(x-1)^2-(y-2)^2}$$

$\displaystyle = 8\int_1^2 \int_2^A \sqrt{1-(x-1)^2-(y-2)^2}\,dy\,dx$

$\displaystyle = 8\int_1^2 \frac{\pi}{4}(2x-x^2)\,dx$

$\displaystyle = \frac{4\pi}{3}$

This result is easily verified with the formula for a sphere.

29. The intersection of the two surfaces gives the region of integration in the xy-plane:

$$6 - x^2 - y^2 = 2x^2 + y^2$$

$$3x^2 + 2y^2 = 6$$

$\displaystyle V = 4\int_0^{\sqrt{2}} \int_0^{\sqrt{(6-3x^2)/2}} \int_{2x^2+y^2}^{6-x^2-y^2} dz\,dy\,dx$

$\displaystyle = 4\int_0^{\sqrt{2}} \int_0^{\sqrt{(6-3x^2)/2}} [6-x^2-y^2-(2x^2+y^2)]\,dy\,dx$

$$= 4 \int_0^{\sqrt{2}} [6y - 3x^2 y - \frac{2y^3}{3}] \Big|_0^{\sqrt{(6-3x^2)/2}} \, dx$$

$$= \int_0^{\sqrt{2}} [-16 \cdot 2^{-3/2}(x^2 - 2)\sqrt{6 - 3x^2} \, dx$$

$$= 3\sqrt{6}\,\pi$$

$$\approx 23.0859$$

34. $\displaystyle \int_0^1 \int_{x+1}^2 \int_0^x f(x, y, z) \, dy \, dz \, dx$

40. Set up coordinates so the xy-plane is the horizontal cutting plane of the wedge and the z-axis of symmetry of the cylinder. The slant plane forming the wedge has the equation $z = (\tan \theta)y$. Thus, the volume of the wedge is

$$V = 2 \int_0^R \int_0^{\sqrt{R^2 - x^2}} \int_0^{(\tan \theta)y} dz \, dy \, dx$$

$$= 2 \int_0^R \int_0^{\sqrt{R^2 - x^2}} y \tan \theta \, dy \, dx$$

$$= 2 \int_0^R \frac{(r^2 - x^2)\tan \theta}{2} \, dx$$

$$= \frac{2}{3} r^3 \tan \theta$$

53. $\displaystyle \int_0^4 \int_0^{4-x} \int_0^{4-x-y} \int_0^{4-x-y-z} e^{x-2y+z+w} \, dw \, dz \, dy \, dx$

$$= \int_0^4 \int_0^{4-x} \int_0^{4-x-y} e^{4-3y} - e^{x-2y+z} \, dz \, dy \, dx$$

$$= \int_0^4 \int_0^{4-x} [e^{x-2y} - e^{4-3y}(x + y - 3)] \, dy \, dx$$

$$= \int_0^4 \left[\frac{e^4(8 - 3x)}{9} - \frac{e^{3x-8}}{18} + \frac{e^x}{2} \right] dx$$

$$= \frac{74e^{12} - 27e^8 + 1}{54e^8}$$

$$\approx 74.3197$$

13.6 Mass, Moments, and Probability Density Functions, Pages 931-935

SURVIVAL HINT: *When finding the center of mass for a lamina, you probably thought of the moment about a particular axis as a rotational force. The moment about the y-axis is the same as all of the mass at the centroid: $M_y = m\overline{x}$. The algebraic extension of this concept to volumes is exactly the same. The moment about the yz-plane is the same as all of the mass at the centroid: $M_{yz} = m\overline{x}$. However, the geometric visualization of "rotation" is impossible. A lamina can be rotated about a line by moving in $\mathbb{R}^3$. To "rotate" our volume about a plane we have to move into $\mathbb{R}^4$. Fortunately, the algebra is not restricted by our $\mathbb{R}^3$ world.*

5. Use $\overline{x} = \dfrac{M_y}{m}$; $\overline{y} = \dfrac{M_x}{m}$.

$$m = \int_0^3 \int_0^4 5 \, dy \, dx = 60$$

$$M_x = \int_0^3 \int_0^4 5 \, y \, dy \, dx$$

$$= \frac{5}{2} \int_0^3 16 \, dx$$

$$= 120$$

$$M_y = \int_0^3 \int_0^4 5 \, x \, dy \, dx$$

$$= 20 \int_0^3 x \, dx$$

$$= 90$$

$$(\overline{x}, \overline{y}) = \left(\frac{90}{60}, \frac{120}{60}\right) = \left(\frac{3}{2}, 2\right)$$

8.
$$m = 4 \int_0^{1/2} \int_0^{\sin(\pi x/2)} dy \, dx$$

$$= 4 \int_0^{1/2} \sin \frac{\pi x}{2} \, dx$$

$$= \frac{8}{\pi}\left(1 - \frac{\sqrt{2}}{2}\right)$$

$$\approx 0.7459$$

$$M_x = 4 \int_0^{1/2} \int_0^{\sin(\pi x/2)} y \, dy \, dx$$

$$= 2 \int_0^{1/2} \sin^2 \frac{\pi x}{2} \, dx$$

$$= \frac{1}{2} - \frac{1}{\pi}$$

$$\approx 0.1817$$

$$M_y = 4 \int_0^{1/2} \int_0^{\sin(\pi x/2)} x \, dy \, dx$$

$$= 4 \int_0^{1/2} x \sin \frac{\pi x}{2} \, dx$$

$$= 4\left[-\frac{\sqrt{2}}{2\pi} + \frac{2\sqrt{2}}{\pi^2}\right]$$

$$\approx 0.246$$

$$(\overline{x}, \overline{y}) \approx (0.3298, 0.2436)$$

13.
$$m = 2 \int_0^3 \int_0^{\sqrt{9 - x^2}} (x^2 + y^2) \, dy \, dx$$

$$= 2 \int_0^{\pi/2} \int_0^3 r^2 \, r \, dr \, d\theta$$

$$= 2 \int_0^{\pi/2} \frac{81}{4} \, dr$$

$$= \frac{81\pi}{4}$$

$\overline{x} = 0$ (by symmetry)

$$M_x = 2 \int_0^3 \int_0^{\sqrt{9-x^2}} y(x^2 + y^2) \, dy \, dx$$

$$= 2 \int_0^3 [\tfrac{1}{2}x^2(9 - x^2) + \tfrac{1}{4}(81 - 18x^2 + x^4)] \, dx$$

$$= \frac{486}{5}$$

$$\overline{y} = \frac{486(4)}{5(81\pi)}$$

$$= \frac{24}{5\pi}$$

$$(\overline{x}, \overline{y}) = (0, \tfrac{24}{5\pi})$$

18.
$$m = \int_0^2 \int_0^{e^{-x}} y \, dy \, dx$$

$$= \frac{1}{2} \int_0^2 e^{-2x} \, dx$$

$$= \frac{1}{4}(1 - e^{-4})$$

$$M_x = \int_0^2 \int_0^{e^{-x}} y^2 \, dy \, dx$$

$$= \frac{1}{3} \int_0^2 e^{-3x} \, dx$$

$$= \frac{1}{9}(1 - e^{-6})$$

$$M_y = \int_0^2 \int_0^{e^{-x}} xy \, dy \, dx$$

$$= \frac{1}{2} \int_0^2 xe^{-2x} \, dx$$

$$= \frac{1}{8}(1 - 5e^{-4})$$

$$(\overline{x}, \overline{y}) = \left(\frac{1 - 5e^{-4}}{2(1 - e^{-4})}, \frac{4(1 - e^{-6})}{9(1 - e^{-4})} \right)$$

$$\approx (0.4627, 0.4516)$$

22. $\rho = x^2 + y^2 + z^2 = r^2 + z^2;$

$\overline{y} = 0$ (by symmetry)

$$m = \int_{-\pi/2}^{\pi/2} \int_0^3 \int_0^{r^2} r(r^2 + z^2) \, dz \, dr \, d\theta$$

$$= \int_{-\pi/2}^{\pi/2} \int_0^3 \frac{r^5(r^2 + 3)}{3} \, dr \, d\theta$$

$$= \frac{3,159}{8} \int_{-\pi/2}^{\pi/2} d\theta$$

$$= \frac{3,159\pi}{8}$$

$$M_{xy} = \int_{-\pi/2}^{\pi/2} \int_0^3 \int_0^{r^2} rz(r^2 + z^2) \, dz \, dr \, d\theta$$

$$= \int_{-\pi/2}^{\pi/2} \int_0^3 \frac{r^7(r^2 + 2)}{4} \, dr \, d\theta$$

$$= \int_{-\pi/2}^{\pi/2} \frac{150,903}{80} \, d\theta$$

$$= \frac{150{,}903\pi}{80}$$

$$M_{yz} = \int_{-\pi/2}^{\pi/2} \int_0^3 \int_0^{r^2} r(r\cos\theta)(r^2 + z^2)\, dz\, dr\, d\theta$$

$$= \int_{-\pi/2}^{\pi/2} \int_0^3 \frac{1}{3} r^6 (r^2 + 3)\cos\theta\, dr\, d\theta$$

$$= \int_{-\pi/2}^{\pi/2} \frac{7{,}290}{7}\cos\theta\, d\theta$$

$$= \frac{14{,}580}{7}$$

$$(\overline{x}, \overline{y}, \overline{z}) = \left(\frac{14{,}580(8)}{7(3{,}159\pi)},\ 0,\ \frac{150{,}903\pi(4)}{40(3{,}159\pi)} \right)$$

$$\approx (1.6790,\ 0,\ 4.7770)$$

26. $\quad m = \displaystyle\int_0^{\pi/2} \int_0^{\sqrt{2\sin 2\theta}} r\, dr\, d\theta$

$$= \int_0^{\pi/2} \sin 2\theta\, d\theta$$

$$= 1$$

$$M_y = \int_0^{\pi/2} \int_0^{\sqrt{2\sin 2\theta}} (r\cos\theta)\, r\, dr\, d\theta$$

$$= \int_0^{\pi/2} \frac{2\sqrt{2}}{3}\cos\theta(\sin 2\theta)^{3/2}\, d\theta$$

$$\approx 0.5554$$

(numerical computer approximation)

$$\overline{x} \approx 0.5554$$

$$\overline{y} \approx 0.5554 \text{ (by symmetry)}$$

$$(\overline{x}, \overline{y}) = (0.5554, 0.5554)$$

33. If $\delta = 1$ then $m = A = \pi ab$. Using symmetry:

$$I_x = 4\int_0^a \int_0^{\frac{b}{a}\sqrt{a^2 - x^2}} y^2\, dy\, dx$$

$$= \frac{4}{3}\int_0^a \left(\frac{b}{a}\sqrt{a^2 - x^2} \right)^3 dx$$

$$= \frac{4b^3}{3a^3}\int_0^a (a^2 - x^2)^{3/2}\, dx \quad \text{(Formula \#245)}$$

$$= \frac{b^3}{3a^3}\left(\frac{3a^4\pi}{4} \right)$$

$$= \frac{ab^3\pi}{4}$$

Substituting $m = \pi ab$: $\quad I_x = \dfrac{mb^2}{4}$

38. $P(X + Y \le 3) = \dfrac{1}{6}\displaystyle\int_0^3 \int_0^{3-x} e^{-x/2} e^{-y/3}\, dy\, dx$

$$= \frac{1}{2}\int_0^3 (e^{-x/2} - e^{-x/6-1})\, dx$$

$$= -3e^{-1} + 2e^{-3/2} + 1$$

$$\approx 0.3426$$

The probability is roughly 34%.

$$= \frac{3}{2}$$

40. $P(X+Y<30) = \frac{1}{300}\int_0^{30}\int_0^{30-x} e^{-x/30}e^{-y/10}\, dy\, dx$

$$= -\frac{1}{30}\int_0^{30} e^{-x/30}\left(e^{(x-30)/10} - 1\right) dx$$

$$= -\frac{1}{30}\int_0^{30}\left(e^{x/15-3} - e^{-x/30}\right) dx$$

$$= -\frac{1}{2}\left(\frac{3}{e} - \frac{1}{e^3} - 2\right)$$

$$\approx 0.4731$$

44. $V = \int_0^1 \int_0^{1-x} \int_0^{1-x-y} dz\, dy\, dx$

$$= \int_0^1 \int_0^{1-x} (1 - x - y)\, dy\, dx$$

$$= \int_0^1 \left[(1-x)^2 - \frac{1}{2}(1-x)^2\right] dx$$

$$= \frac{1}{6}$$

$$\mathrm{AV} = \frac{1}{V}\int_0^1 \int_0^{1-x} \int_0^{1-x-y} (x+2y+3z)\, dz\, dy\, dx$$

$$= 3\int_0^1 \int_0^{1-x} (x^2 - 4x - y^2 - 2y + 3)\, dy\, dx$$

$$= \int_0^1 (-2x^3 + 9x^2 - 12x + 5)\, dx$$

52. Set up a coordinate system with the centroid of each figure at the origin so that each moment of inertia is in relation to the x-axis.

a. For the rectangle,

$$I_1 = \int_{-1/3}^{1/3} \int_{-1}^{1} y^2\, dy\, dx \approx 0.4444$$

b. For the concave shape,

$$I_2 = 4\int_0^{0.9} \int_0^{y^2+0.1} y^2\, dx\, dy \approx 0.5696$$

c. For the convex shape,

$$I_3 = 4\int_0^{2^{-1/3}} \int_0^{2^{-2/3}-y^2} y^2\, dx\, dy \approx 0.1680$$

Thus, according to the stated criterion, the concave shape is the stiffest.

54. a. Note that $(h - z)/p$ is the cosine of the angle the force vector makes with the z-axis, so it will project this vector onto the z-axis.

b. Just sum up above ΔF.

c. $F = \dfrac{GmM}{p^2} = 5Gm$

d. Numerical integration gives $F = 4.39741\,Gm$ vs $5.0\,Gm$

e. Changing h to 200 makes $F = 0.008$ and the integral 0.0079982. The center of mass approximation is quite accurate for a large separation (both from a numerical and a geometric point of view).

13.7 Cylindrical and Spherical Coordinates, Pages 241-244

SURVIVAL HINT: *The best way to convert from one coordinate system to another is to understand the derivations and "visualize" the graph. Lacking that skill, you will find it necessary to memorize the transformation equations. The reasons we did not give solutions for Problems 1-30 because there is not much more that using these formulas and checking your result with the answers in the back of the book.*

31. $\displaystyle \int_0^\pi \int_0^2 \int_0^{\sqrt{4-r^2}} r \sin \theta \, dz \, dr \, d\theta$

$\displaystyle = \int_0^\pi \int_0^2 (\sin \theta)\sqrt{4-r^2} \, r \, dr \, d\theta$

$\displaystyle = \frac{8}{3} \int_0^\pi \sin \theta \, d\theta$

$\displaystyle = \frac{16}{3}$

34. $\displaystyle \int_0^{\pi/2} \int_0^{\pi/4} \int_0^{\cos \phi} \rho^2 \sin \phi \, d\rho \, d\theta \, d\phi$

$\displaystyle = \frac{1}{3} \int_0^{\pi/2} \int_0^{\pi/4} \cos^3\phi \sin \phi \, d\theta \, d\phi$

$\displaystyle = \frac{\pi}{12} \int_0^{\pi/2} \cos^3\phi \sin \phi \, d\phi$

$\displaystyle = \frac{\pi}{48}$

38. $\displaystyle \int_0^{\pi/3} \int_0^{\cos \theta} \int_0^{\phi} \rho^2\sin \theta \, d\rho \, d\phi \, d\theta$

$\displaystyle = \int_0^{\pi/3} \int_0^{\cos \theta} \frac{1}{3}\phi^3 \sin \theta \, d\phi \, d\theta$

$\displaystyle = \int_0^{\pi/3} \frac{1}{12} \sin \theta \cos^4\theta \, d\theta$

$\displaystyle = \frac{31}{1,920}$

SURVIVAL HINT: *Cylindrical coordinates are dz with polar coordinates for the dA. Do not forget the "r." That is,*

$$dz \, dy \, dx = dV = dz \, r \, dr \, d\theta$$

On the other hand, do not forget that when you find

$$x^2 + y^2 + z^2$$

in a function you should consider changing to spherical coordinates.

42. $\displaystyle \iiint_S z(x^2 + y^2)^{-1/2} \, dx \, dy \, dz$

$\displaystyle = \int_0^{2\pi} \int_0^2 \int_{r^2/2}^2 z(r^2)^{-1/2}r \, dz \, dr \, d\theta$

$\displaystyle = \frac{1}{2} \int_0^{2\pi} \int_0^2 \left(4 - \frac{r^4}{4}\right) dr \, d\theta$

$\displaystyle = \frac{16}{5} \int_0^{2\pi} d\theta$

$$= \frac{32\pi}{5}$$

44. $\quad m = \int\limits_0^{2\pi} \int\limits_0^1 \int\limits_r^1 r\ dz\ dr\ d\theta$

$$= \int\limits_0^{2\pi} \int\limits_0^1 (r - r^2)\ dr\ d\theta$$

$$= \frac{\pi}{3}$$

$\overline{x} = \overline{y} = 0$ by symmetry.

$$M_{xy} = \int\limits_0^{2\pi} \int\limits_0^1 \int\limits_r^1 rz\ dz\ dr\ d\theta$$

$$= \frac{1}{2} \int\limits_0^{2\pi} \int\limits_0^1 r(1 - r^2)\ dr\ d\theta$$

$$= \frac{\pi}{4}$$

$\overline{z} = \left(\frac{\pi}{4}\right)\left(\frac{3}{\pi}\right) = \frac{3}{4}$; centroid is $(0, 0, \frac{3}{4})$.

48. The sphere has volume $V = \frac{4}{3}\pi(3)^3 = 36\pi$.

The average value of θ over the sphere is:

$$A V_\theta = \frac{1}{V} \int\limits_0^{2\pi} \int\limits_0^\pi \int\limits_0^3 \theta \rho^2 \sin\phi\ d\rho\ d\phi\ d\theta$$

$$= \frac{1}{V} \int\limits_0^{2\pi} \int\limits_0^\pi 9\theta \sin\phi\ d\phi\ d\theta$$

$$= \frac{1}{V} \int\limits_0^{2\pi} 18\theta\ d\theta$$

$$= \frac{36\pi^2}{36\pi}$$

$$= \pi$$

The average value of ϕ is

$$A V_\theta = \frac{1}{V} \int\limits_0^{2\pi} \int\limits_0^\pi \int\limits_0^3 \phi \rho^2 \sin\phi\ d\rho\ d\phi\ d\theta$$

$$= \frac{1}{V} \int\limits_0^{2\pi} \int\limits_0^\pi 9\phi \sin\phi\ d\phi\ d\theta$$

$$= \frac{1}{V} \int\limits_0^{2\pi} 9[\sin\phi - \phi\cos\phi]\Big|_0^\pi\ d\theta$$

$$= \frac{1}{V} \int\limits_0^{2\pi} 9\pi\ d\theta$$

$$= \frac{18\pi^2}{36\pi}$$

$$= \frac{1}{2}\pi$$

52. $\quad \int\int\limits_S\int z^2\ dx\ dy\ dz$

$$= 4 \int\limits_0^{\pi/2} \int\limits_0^{\pi/2} \int\limits_0^1 \rho^4 \cos^2\phi \sin\phi\ d\rho\ d\theta\ d\phi$$

$$= \frac{4}{5} \int\limits_0^{\pi/2} \int\limits_0^{\pi/2} \sin\phi \cos^2\phi\ d\theta\ d\phi$$

$$= \frac{2\pi}{5} \int\limits_0^{\pi/2} \sin\phi \cos^2\phi\ d\phi$$

$$= \frac{2\pi}{15}$$

$$\approx 0.4189$$

57. $V = 2 \displaystyle\int_0^{\pi/2} \int_0^{2\sin\theta} \int_0^{4-r^2} r \, dz \, dr \, d\theta$

$$= \int_0^{\pi/2} \int_0^{2\sin\theta} 2r(4 - r^2) \, dr \, d\theta$$

$$= \int_0^{\pi/2} 8 \sin^2\theta \cos^2\theta + 8 \sin^2\theta \, d\theta$$

$$= \frac{5\pi}{2}$$

$$\approx 7.8540$$

61. **a.** Force $= \dfrac{GmM}{R^2} = \dfrac{Gm\delta(4\pi a^3)}{3R^2}$

b. With $R = 4$ and $a = 3$, we obtain

Force $= \dfrac{Gm\delta(9\pi)}{4}$

c. With a rectangular mass m, we got a poor approximation using the center of mass when the separating distance was small. The approximation improves as the distance increases. With the sphere we always get perfect agreement. Apparently the symmetry of the sphere play the key role. Either a computer with symbolic integration capability or determined work by hand will show that

for the sphere the center of mass method gives the exact result.

63. $I = I_x + I_y + I_z$

$$= \iiint\limits_S (y^2 + z^2) \, dV + \iiint\limits_S (x^2 + z^2) \, dV$$

$$+ \iiint\limits_S (x^2 + y^2) \, dV$$

$$= \iiint\limits_S (2x^2 + 2y^2 + 2z^2) \, dV$$

$$= 2 \int_0^\pi \int_0^{2\pi} \int_0^1 \rho^2 \, \rho^2 \sin\phi \, d\rho \, d\theta \, d\phi$$

$$= 2 \int_0^{2\pi} \int_0^\pi \int_0^1 \rho^4 \sin\phi \, d\rho \, d\phi \, d\theta$$

$$= \frac{2}{5} \int_0^{2\pi} \int_0^\pi \sin\phi \, d\phi \, d\theta$$

$$= \frac{4}{5} \int_0^{2\pi} d\theta$$

$$= \frac{8\pi}{5}$$

13.8 Jacobians: Change of Variables, Pages 948-950

1. $x = u + v, \; y = uv$

$$\frac{\partial(x, y)}{\partial(u, v)} = \begin{vmatrix} \dfrac{\partial x}{\partial u} & \dfrac{\partial x}{\partial v} \\ \dfrac{\partial y}{\partial u} & \dfrac{\partial y}{\partial v} \end{vmatrix}$$

$$= \begin{vmatrix} 1 & 1 \\ v & u \end{vmatrix}$$

$$= u - v$$

7. $x = e^{u+v}, \, y = e^{u-v}$

$$\frac{\partial(x, y)}{\partial(u, v)} = \begin{vmatrix} \dfrac{\partial x}{\partial u} & \dfrac{\partial x}{\partial v} \\ \dfrac{\partial y}{\partial u} & \dfrac{\partial y}{\partial v} \end{vmatrix}$$

$$= \begin{vmatrix} e^{u+v} & e^{u+v} \\ e^{u-v} & -e^{u-v} \end{vmatrix}$$

$$= -2e^{u+v}e^{u-v}$$

$$= -2e^{2u}$$

11. $x = u \cos v, \, y = u \sin v, \, z = we^{uv}$

$$\frac{\partial(x, y, z)}{\partial(u, v, w)} = \begin{vmatrix} \cos v & -u \sin v & 0 \\ \sin v & u \cos v & 0 \\ vwe^{uv} & uwe^{uv} & e^{uv} \end{vmatrix}$$

$$= ue^{uv}$$

15. The boundary lines of the figure are $y = 0$, $y = 4$, $y = 2x$, and $y = 2x - 10$. Thus, the transformed boundaries are $v = 0$ and

$y = 4$: $u = x^2 - 16$, $v = 8x$ so $u = \left(\dfrac{v}{8}\right)^2 - 16$

$y = 2x$: $u = -3x^2$, $v = 4x^2$ so $v = -\dfrac{4}{3}u$

$y = 2x - 10$: $u = -3x^2 + 40x - 100$,

$v = 4x^2 - 20x$, so (in parametric form)

$u = -3t^2 + 40t - 100, \, v = 4t^2 - 20t$.

The vertices of the figure are transformed as follows:

A(5, 0) $\rightarrow$ (25, 0); B(7, 4) $\rightarrow$ (33, 56);

C(2, 4) $\rightarrow$ (-12, 16); O(0, 0) $\rightarrow$ (0, 0)

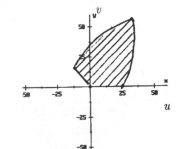

18. $x = u^2 - v^2, \, y = 2uv$

$$\frac{\partial(x, y)}{\partial(u, v)} = \begin{vmatrix} \dfrac{\partial x}{\partial u} & \dfrac{\partial x}{\partial v} \\ \dfrac{\partial y}{\partial u} & \dfrac{\partial y}{\partial v} \end{vmatrix}$$

$$= \begin{vmatrix} 2u & -2v \\ 2v & 2u \end{vmatrix}$$

$$= 4(u^2 + v^2)$$

$$dx \, dy = 4(u^2 + v^2) \, du \, dv$$

21. $u = x - y, \, v = x + y$, so $x = \dfrac{u + v}{2}$,

$y = \dfrac{v - u}{2}$. The boundary lines $x = 0$, $y = 0$, $x + y = 1$ become $-v = u$, $v = u$, $v = 1$, respectively. The Jacobian of the transformation is

$$\frac{\partial(x,\ y)}{\partial(u,\ v)} = \begin{vmatrix} \dfrac{\partial x}{\partial u} & \dfrac{\partial x}{\partial v} \\ \dfrac{\partial y}{\partial u} & \dfrac{\partial y}{\partial v} \end{vmatrix}$$

$$= \begin{vmatrix} \dfrac{1}{2} & \dfrac{1}{2} \\ -\dfrac{1}{2} & \dfrac{1}{2} \end{vmatrix}$$

$$= \frac{1}{2}$$

$$dy\ dx = \tfrac{1}{2}\ du\ dv$$

$$\int\!\!\int_D \left(\frac{x-y}{x+y}\right)^5 dy\ dx = \int_0^1 \int_{-v}^{v} \frac{u^5}{v^5}\frac{1}{2}\ du\ dv$$

$$= \frac{1}{12}\int_0^1 (v-v)\ du$$

$$= 0$$

31. $\displaystyle\int\!\!\int_S (2x+y)\tan^{-1}(x-2y)\ dy\ dx$

$$= \int_0^1\int_0^1 (5u)\tan^{-1}(5v)\ 5\ dv\ du$$

$$= \int_0^1 -\frac{5}{2}\Big[\ln 26 + 10\tan^{-1}\tfrac{1}{5} - 5\pi\Big]u\ du$$

$$= -\frac{5}{4}\Big[\ln 26 + 10\tan^{-1}\tfrac{1}{5} - 5\pi\Big]$$

$$\approx 13.0949$$

35. By looking at the function we see a suitable transformation can be obtained when
$a = b = s = 1$ and $r = -1$.

$u = x + y,\ v = -x + y;$ so $y = \tfrac{1}{2}(u+v),$
$x = \tfrac{1}{2}(u-v)$

$$\frac{\partial(x,\ y)}{\partial(u,\ v)} = \begin{vmatrix} \dfrac{\partial x}{\partial u} & \dfrac{\partial x}{\partial v} \\ \dfrac{\partial y}{\partial u} & \dfrac{\partial y}{\partial v} \end{vmatrix}$$

$$= \begin{vmatrix} \dfrac{1}{2} & -\dfrac{1}{2} \\ \dfrac{1}{2} & \dfrac{1}{2} \end{vmatrix}$$

$$= \frac{1}{2}$$

$A(0,\ 0) \to (0,\ 0),\quad B(1,\ 1) \to (2,\ 0),$
$C(-1,\ 1) \to (0,\ 2),\quad D(0,\ 2) \to (2,\ 2).$
$dy\ dx = \tfrac{1}{2}\ du\ dv$

$$\int\!\!\int_R \left(\frac{x+y}{2}\right)^2 e^{(y-x)/2}\ dy\ dx$$

$$= \int_0^2\int_0^2 (\tfrac{u}{2})^2 e^{v/2}(\tfrac{1}{2})\ dv\ du$$

$$= \frac{1}{4}(e-1)\int_0^2 u^2\ du$$

$$= \frac{2}{3}(e-1)$$

$$\approx 1.1455$$

38. a. $x = u\cos\theta - v\sin\theta,\ y = u\sin\theta + v\cos\theta$

$$\frac{\partial(x,\ y)}{\partial(u,\ v)} = \begin{vmatrix} \dfrac{\partial x}{\partial u} & \dfrac{\partial x}{\partial v} \\ \dfrac{\partial y}{\partial u} & \dfrac{\partial y}{\partial v} \end{vmatrix}$$

$$= \begin{vmatrix} \cos\theta & -\sin\theta \\ \sin\theta & \cos\theta \end{vmatrix}$$

$$= 1$$

$$dy\ dx = du\ dv$$

b. A rotation of $\theta = \frac{\pi}{4}$ eliminates the uv-term, so use the transformation

$$x = \frac{\sqrt{2}}{2}(u - v),\ y = \frac{\sqrt{2}}{2}(u + v)$$

Then $x^2 + xy + y^2$

$$= \left[\frac{\sqrt{2}}{2}(u - v)\right]^2 + \left[\frac{\sqrt{2}}{2}(u - v)\right]\left[\frac{\sqrt{2}}{2}(u + v)\right]$$

$$+ \left[\frac{\sqrt{2}}{2}(u + v)\right]^2$$

$$= \tfrac{1}{2}(3u^2 + v^2)$$

$$= 3$$

$$\int_E \int y\ dy\ dx = 4 \int_0^{\sqrt{2}} \int_0^{\sqrt{6-3u^2}} \frac{\sqrt{2}}{2}(u + v)(1)\ dv\ du$$

$$= 2\sqrt{2} \int_0^{\sqrt{2}} [u\sqrt{6 - 3u^2} - \tfrac{3}{2}u^2 + 3]\ du$$

$$= \tfrac{8}{3}(3 + \sqrt{3})$$

$$\approx 12.6188$$

41. $x = r\cos\theta,\ y = r\sin\theta,\ z = z$

$$\frac{\partial(x,\ y,\ z)}{\partial(r,\ \theta,\ z)} = \begin{vmatrix} \cos\theta & -r\sin\theta & 0 \\ \sin\theta & r\cos\theta & 0 \\ 0 & 0 & 1 \end{vmatrix}$$

$$= r$$

So $dx\ dy\ dz$ becomes $r\ dr\ d\theta\ dz$.

CHAPTER 13 REVIEW

Proficiency Examination, Pages 950-951

SURVIVAL HINT: *To help you review the concepts of this chapter,* **hand write** *the answers to each of these questions onto your own paper.*

1. If f is defined on a closed, bounded region R in the xy-plane, then the double integral of f over R is defined by

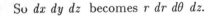

$$\int_R \int f(x,\ y)\ dA = \lim_{\|P\| \to 0} \sum_{k=1}^{N} f(\overset{*}{x}_k,\ \overset{*}{y}_k)\Delta A_k$$

provided this limit exists. If the limit exists, we say that f is integrable over R.

2. If $f(x,\ y)$ is continuous over the rectangle R: $a \le x \le b$, $c \le y \le d$, then the double integral

$$\int_R \int f(x,\ y)\ dA$$

may be evaluated by either iterated integral; that is,

$$\int_R \int f(x,\ y)\ dA\ =\ \int_c^d \int_a^b f(x,\ y)\ dx\ dy$$

$$=\ \int_a^b \int_c^d f(x,\ y)\ dy\ dx$$

3. A type I region contains points $(x,\ y)$ such that for each fixed x between constants a and b, y varies from $g_1(x)$ to $g_2(x)$, where g_1 and g_2 are continuous functions. Think of a vertical strip.

$$\int_D \int f(x,\ y)\ dA\ =\ \int_a^b \int_{g_1(x)}^{g_2(x)} f(x,\ y)\ dy\ dx$$

whenever both integrals exist.

4. A type II region contains points $(x,\ y)$ such that for each fixed y between constants c and d, x varies from $h_1(y)$ to $h_2(y)$, where h_1 and h_2 are continuous functions. Think of a horizontal strip.

$$\int_D \int f(x,\ y)\ dA\ =\ \int_c^d \int_{h_1(y)}^{h_2(y)} f(x,\ y)\ dx\ dy$$

whenever both integrals exist.

5. The area of the region D in the xy-plane is given by $A = \int_D \int dA$

6. If f is continuous and $f(x,\ y) \geq 0$ on the region D, the volume of the solid under the surface $z = f(x,\ y)$ above the region D is given by $V = \int_D \int f(x,\ y)\ dA$

7. **a.** Linearity rule: for constants a and b,

$$\int_D \int [af(x,\ y) + bg(x,\ y)]\ dA$$

$$=\ a\int_D \int f(x,\ y)\ dA + b\int_D \int g(x,\ y)\ dA$$

b. Dominance rule: If $f(x,\ y) \geq g(x,\ y)$ throughout a region D, then

$$\int_D \int f(x,\ y)\ dA\ \geq\ \int_D \int g(x,\ y)\ dA$$

c. Subdivision rule: If the region of integration D can be subdivided into two subregions D_1 and D_2, then

$$\int_D \int f(x,\ y)\ dA$$

$$=\ \int_{D_1} \int f(x,\ y)\ dA\ +\ \int_{D_2} \int f(x,\ y)\ dA$$

8. If f is continuous in the polar region D such that for each fixed θ between α and β, r varies between $h_1(\theta)$ and $h_2(\theta)$, then

$$\int_D \int f(r,\ \theta)\ dA = \int_\alpha^\beta \int_{h_1(\theta)}^{h_2(\theta)} f(r,\ \theta)\ r\ dr\ d\theta$$

9. Let Q denote the first quadrant of the Cartesian plane, and let C_n denote the quarter circular region described by $r \leq n$, $0 \leq \theta \leq \frac{\pi}{2}$. Then the improper integral

$$\int_Q \int f(x,\ y)\ dA$$

is defined in polar coordinates as

$$\lim_{n \to \infty} \int_{C_n} \int f(r\cos\theta, \, r\sin\theta) r \, dr \, d\theta$$

$$= \lim_{n \to \infty} \int_0^{\pi/2} \int_0^n f(r\cos\theta, r\sin\theta) r \, dr \, d\theta$$

If the limit in this definition exists and is equal to L, we say that the improper integral converges to L. Otherwise, we say that the improper integral diverges.

10. Assume that the function $f(x, y)$ has continuous partial derivatives f_x and f_y in a region R of the xy-plane. Then the portion of the surface $z = f(x, y)$ that lies over R has surface area

$$S = \int_R \int \sqrt{[f_x(x, y)]^2 + [f_y(x, y)]^2 + 1} \, dA$$

11. Let D be a region in the xy-plane on which x, y, z and their partial derivatives with respect to u and v are continuous. Also, let S be a surface defined by a vector function

$$\mathbf{R}(u, v) = x(u, v)\mathbf{i} + y(u, v)\mathbf{j} + z(u, v)\mathbf{k}$$

Then the surface area is defined by

$$S = \int_D \int \| \mathbf{R}_u(u, v) \times \mathbf{R}_v(u, v) \| \, du \, dv$$

12. If $f(x, y, z)$ is continuous over a rectangular solid R: $a \le x \le b$, $c \le y \le d$, $r \le z \le s$, then the triple integral may be

evaluated by the iterated integral

$$\int_R \int \int f(x, y, z) \, dV = \int_r^s \int_c^d \int_a^b f(x, y, z) \, dx \, dy \, dz$$

The iterated integration can be performed in any order (with appropriate adjustments) to the limits of integration: $dx \, dy \, dz$, $dx \, dz \, dy$, $dz \, dx \, dy$, $dy \, dx \, dz$, $dy \, dz \, dx$, $dz \, dy \, dx$.

13. If V is the volume of the solid region S, then

$$V = \int_S \int \int dV$$

14. If δ is a continuous density function on the lamina corresponding to a plane region R, then the mass m of the lamina is given by

$$m = \int_R \int \delta(x, y) \, dA$$

15. If δ is a continuous density function on a lamina corresponding to a plane region R, then the moments of mass with respect to the x-axes is

$$M_x = \int_R \int y \, \delta(x, y) \, dA$$

16. If m is the mass of the lamina, the center of mass is $(\overline{x}, \overline{y})$, where

$$\overline{x} = \frac{M_y}{m} \qquad \text{and} \qquad \overline{y} = \frac{M_x}{m}$$

If the density δ is constant, the point $(\overline{x}, \overline{y})$ is called the centroid of the region.

17. The moments of inertia of a lamina of variable density δ about the x- and y-axes,

respectively, are

$$I_x = \int\int_R y^2 \delta(x, y) \, dA$$

and $I_y = \int\int_R x^2 \delta(x, y) \, dA$

18. A joint probability density function for the random variables X and Y is a continuous, nonnegative function $f(x, y)$ such that

$$P[(X, Y) \text{ in } R] = \int\int_R f(x, y) \, dy \, dx$$

where $P[(X, Y) \text{ in } R]$ denotes the probability that (X, Y) is in the region R in the xy-plane.

19. Rectangular to cylindrical:

$$r = \sqrt{x^2 + y^2}; \tan\theta = \frac{y}{x}; z = z$$

Rectangular to spherical:

$$\rho = \sqrt{x^2 + y^2 + z^2}; \tan\theta = \frac{y}{x}$$

$$\phi = \cos^{-1}\left(\frac{z}{\sqrt{x^2 + y^2 + z^2}}\right)$$

Cylindrical to rectangular:

$$x = r\cos\theta; y = r\sin\theta; z = z$$

Cylindrical to spherical:

$$\rho = \sqrt{r^2 + z^2}; \theta = \theta; \phi = \cos^{-1}\left(\frac{z}{\sqrt{r^2 + z^2}}\right)$$

Spherical to rectangular:

$$x = \rho\sin\phi\cos\theta; y = \rho\sin\phi\sin\theta; z = \rho\cos\phi$$

Spherical to cylindrical:

$$r = \rho\sin\phi; \theta = \theta; z = \rho\cos\phi$$

20. Let f be a continuous function on the bounded, solid region S. Then the triple integral of f over S is given by:

a. $$\int\int\int_S f(r, \theta, z) \, r \, dz \, dr \, d\theta$$

in cylindrical coordinates

b. $$\int\int\int_S f(\rho, \theta, \phi) \, \rho^2 \sin\phi \, d\rho \, d\theta \, d\phi$$

in spherical coordinates

21. $$\left|\frac{\partial(x, y)}{\partial(u, v)}\right| = \begin{vmatrix} \frac{\partial x}{\partial u} & \frac{\partial x}{\partial v} \\ \frac{\partial y}{\partial u} & \frac{\partial y}{\partial v} \end{vmatrix} = \frac{\partial x}{\partial u}\frac{\partial y}{\partial v} - \frac{\partial y}{\partial u}\frac{\partial x}{\partial v}$$

22. Let f be a continuous function on a region D, and let T be a one-to-one transformation that maps the region D^* in the uv-plane onto a region D in the xy-plane under the change of variable $x = g(u, v)$, $y = h(u, v)$ where g and h are continuously differentiable on D^*. Then

$$\int\int_D f(x, y) \, dy \, dx$$

$$= \int\int_{D^*} f[g(u, v), h(u, v)] \, |J(u, v)| \, du \, dv$$

24. $$\int_{-1}^{1}\int_0^z\int_y^{y-z} (x + y - z) \, dx \, dy \, dz$$

$$= \int\limits_{-1}^{1} \int\limits_{0}^{z} \left(\frac{(y-z)^2}{2} + (y-z)y - (y-z)z \right.$$

$$\left. - \frac{y^2}{2} - y^2 + yz \right) dy \, dz$$

$$= \int\limits_{-1}^{1} \int\limits_{0}^{z} \left(-2yz + \frac{3z^2}{2} \right) dy \, dz = 0$$

27. The appliance fails during the first year if both components fail in that time; that is, if (X, Y) lies in the square $0 \le x \le 1$, $0 \le y \le 1$. The probability of this occurring is

$$P = \int\limits_{0}^{1} \int\limits_{0}^{1} \frac{1}{4} e^{-x/2} e^{-y/2} \, dy \, dx$$

$$= \int\limits_{0}^{1} \frac{1}{4} e^{-x/2} [-2e^{-y/2}] \Big|_{0}^{1} \, dx$$

$$= \left(\frac{1 - e^{-1/2}}{2} \right) \int\limits_{0}^{1} e^{-x/2} \, dx$$

$$= (1 - e^{-1/2})^2$$

$$\approx 0.1548$$

Thus, the probability of product failure is about 15%.

30. Let $u = x + y$ and $v = x - 2y$, so that $x = \frac{1}{3}(2u + v)$, $y = \frac{1}{3}(u - v)$.

$$\frac{\partial(x,y)}{\partial(u,v)} = \begin{vmatrix} \frac{2}{3} & \frac{1}{3} \\ \frac{1}{3} & -\frac{1}{3} \end{vmatrix}$$

$$= -\frac{1}{3}$$

The region R is bounded by the lines $y = 0$, $y = 2 - x$, $y = x$ which transform into the lines $u = v$, $u = 2$, and $u = -2v$.

$$\int\limits_{R} \int (x + y) e^{x - 2y} \, dy \, dx$$

$$= \int\limits_{0}^{2} \int\limits_{-u/2}^{u} u e^{v} \left| -\frac{1}{3} \right| dv \, du$$

$$= \frac{1}{3} \int\limits_{0}^{2} \left(u e^{u} - u e^{-u/2} \right) du$$

$$= \frac{1}{3}(e^2 + \frac{8}{e} - 3)$$

$$\approx 2.4440$$

CHAPTER 14

Vector Analysis

14.1 Properties of a Vector Field: Divergence and Curl, Pages 965-966

Answers to Problems 3-8 may vary.

4. The particular graph depends, of course, on the particular choice for x and y:

(x, y)	Vector
$(1, 1)$	$-\mathbf{i} + \mathbf{j}$
$(-1, 2)$	$\mathbf{i} + 2\mathbf{j}$
$(-2, -1)$	$2\mathbf{i} - \mathbf{j}$
$(1, -1)$	$-\mathbf{i} - \mathbf{j}$

We graph each of these vectors:

SURVIVAL HINT: *Remember that div F is always a scalar function and curl F is always a vector function.*

9. $\operatorname{div} \mathbf{F} = \nabla \cdot \mathbf{F}$

$$= \left(\frac{\partial}{\partial x}\mathbf{i} + \frac{\partial}{\partial y}\mathbf{j} + \frac{\partial}{\partial z}\mathbf{k} \right) \cdot (x^2\mathbf{i} + xy\mathbf{j} + z^3\mathbf{k})$$

$$= 2x + x + 3z^2 = 3x + 3z^2$$

$$\operatorname{curl} \mathbf{F} = \nabla \times \mathbf{F} = \begin{vmatrix} \mathbf{i} & \mathbf{j} & \mathbf{k} \\ \frac{\partial}{\partial x} & \frac{\partial}{\partial y} & \frac{\partial}{\partial z} \\ x^2 & xy & z^3 \end{vmatrix}$$

$$= 0\mathbf{i} - 0\mathbf{j} + (y - 0)\mathbf{k}$$

$$= y\mathbf{k}$$

14. $\operatorname{div} \mathbf{F} = \nabla \cdot \mathbf{F}$

$$= \left(\frac{\partial}{\partial x}\mathbf{i} + \frac{\partial}{\partial y}\mathbf{j} + \frac{\partial}{\partial z}\mathbf{k} \right) \cdot (xz\mathbf{i} + y^2z\mathbf{j} + xz\mathbf{k})$$

$$= z + 2yz + x$$

$$\operatorname{curl} \mathbf{F} = \nabla \times \mathbf{F} = \begin{vmatrix} \mathbf{i} & \mathbf{j} & \mathbf{k} \\ \frac{\partial}{\partial x} & \frac{\partial}{\partial y} & \frac{\partial}{\partial z} \\ xz & y^2z & xz \end{vmatrix}$$

$$= -y^2\mathbf{i} - (z - x)\mathbf{j}$$

At $(1, -1, 2)$,

$$\operatorname{div} \mathbf{F} = 2 - 4 + 1$$

$$= -1$$

$$\operatorname{curl} \mathbf{F} = -\mathbf{i} - \mathbf{j}$$

18. $\operatorname{div} \mathbf{F} = \nabla \cdot \mathbf{F}$

$$= \left(\frac{\partial}{\partial x}\mathbf{i} + \frac{\partial}{\partial y}\mathbf{j} + \frac{\partial}{\partial z}\mathbf{k} \right)$$

$$\cdot (e^{-x}\sin y)\mathbf{i} + (e^{-x}\cos y)\mathbf{j} + \mathbf{k}$$

$$= -e^{-x}\sin y - e^{-x}\sin y = -2e^{-x}\sin y$$

curl $\mathbf{F} = \nabla \times \mathbf{F}$

$$= \begin{vmatrix} \mathbf{i} & \mathbf{j} & \mathbf{k} \\ \frac{\partial}{\partial x} & \frac{\partial}{\partial y} & \frac{\partial}{\partial z} \\ e^{-x}\sin y & e^{-x}\cos y & 1 \end{vmatrix}$$

$= 0\mathbf{i} - 0\mathbf{j} - 2e^{-x}\cos y\ \mathbf{k}$

At $(1, 3, -2)$, div $\mathbf{F} = -2e^{-1}\sin 3$

curl $\mathbf{F} = (-2e^{-1}\cos 3)\mathbf{k}$

24. div $\mathbf{F} = \nabla \cdot \mathbf{F}$

$$= \left(\frac{\partial}{\partial x}\mathbf{i} + \frac{\partial}{\partial y}\mathbf{j}\right) \cdot (x^2\mathbf{i} - y^2\mathbf{j})$$

$= 2x - 2y$

curl $\mathbf{F} = \nabla \times \mathbf{F} = \begin{vmatrix} \mathbf{i} & \mathbf{j} & \mathbf{k} \\ \frac{\partial}{\partial x} & \frac{\partial}{\partial y} & \frac{\partial}{\partial z} \\ x^2 & -y^2 & 0 \end{vmatrix} = 0$

29. div $\mathbf{F} = \nabla \cdot \mathbf{F}$

$$= \left(\frac{\partial}{\partial x}\mathbf{i} + \frac{\partial}{\partial y}\mathbf{j} + \frac{\partial}{\partial z}\mathbf{k}\right) \cdot (xy\mathbf{i} + yz\mathbf{j} + xz\mathbf{k})$$

$= x + y + z$

curl $\mathbf{F} = \begin{vmatrix} \mathbf{i} & \mathbf{j} & \mathbf{k} \\ \frac{\partial}{\partial x} & \frac{\partial}{\partial y} & \frac{\partial}{\partial z} \\ xy & yz & xz \end{vmatrix}$

$\quad = -y\mathbf{i} - z\mathbf{j} - x\mathbf{k}$

35. $u_x = -e^{-x}(\cos y - \sin y)$

$u_{xx} = e^{-x}(\cos y - \sin y)$

$u_y = e^{-x}(-\sin y - \cos y)$

$u_{yy} = e^{-x}(-\cos y + \sin y)$

$u_{xx} + u_{yy} = 0;\ u$ is harmonic

39. $\mathbf{F} \times \mathbf{G} = \begin{vmatrix} \mathbf{i} & \mathbf{j} & \mathbf{k} \\ 2 & 2x & 3y \\ x & -y & z \end{vmatrix}$

$= (2xz + 3y^2)\mathbf{i} + (3xy - 2z)\mathbf{j} + (-2y - 2x^2)\mathbf{k}$

curl$(\mathbf{F} \times \mathbf{G}) = \begin{vmatrix} \mathbf{i} & \mathbf{j} & \mathbf{k} \\ \frac{\partial}{\partial x} & \frac{\partial}{\partial y} & \frac{\partial}{\partial z} \\ 2xz+3y^2 & 3xy-2z & -2y-2x^2 \end{vmatrix}$

$= (-2 + 2)\mathbf{i} - (-2x - 4x)\mathbf{j} + (3y - 6y)\mathbf{k}$

$= 6x\mathbf{j} - 3y\mathbf{k}$

46. $r = \sqrt{x^2 + y^2 + z^2};\ \frac{\partial r}{\partial x} = \frac{x}{r},\ \frac{\partial r}{\partial y} = \frac{y}{r},\ \frac{\partial r}{\partial z} = \frac{z}{r}$

curl $\mathbf{F} = \begin{vmatrix} \mathbf{i} & \mathbf{j} & \mathbf{k} \\ \frac{\partial}{\partial x} & \frac{\partial}{\partial y} & \frac{\partial}{\partial z} \\ f(r)x & f(r)y & f(r)z \end{vmatrix}$

$= \left[\frac{\partial(zf(r))}{\partial y} - \frac{\partial(yf(r))}{\partial z}\right]\mathbf{i}$

$\quad - \left[\frac{\partial(zf(r))}{\partial x} - \frac{\partial(xf(r))}{\partial z}\right]\mathbf{j}$

$\quad + \left[\frac{\partial(yf(r))}{\partial x} - \frac{\partial(xf(r))}{\partial y}\right]\mathbf{k}$

$= \left[zf'(r)\frac{\partial r}{\partial y} - yf'(r)\frac{\partial r}{\partial z}\right]\mathbf{i}$

$\quad - \left[zf'(r)\frac{\partial r}{\partial x} - xf'(r)\frac{\partial r}{\partial z}\right]\mathbf{j}$

$$+ \left[yf'(r) \frac{\partial r}{\partial x} - xf'(r) \frac{\partial r}{\partial y} \right] \mathbf{k}$$

$$= f'(r) \left\{ \left[z\left(\frac{y}{r}\right) - y\left(\frac{z}{r}\right) \right] \mathbf{i} - \left[z\left(\frac{x}{r}\right) - x\left(\frac{z}{r}\right) \right] \mathbf{j} \right.$$

$$\left. + \left[y\left(\frac{x}{r}\right) - x\left(\frac{y}{r}\right) \right] \mathbf{k} \right\}$$

$$= \mathbf{0}$$

53. Let $\mathbf{F} = f_1 \mathbf{i} + f_2 \mathbf{j} + f_3 \mathbf{k}$ and

$\mathbf{G} = g_1 \mathbf{i} + g_2 \mathbf{j} + g_3 \mathbf{k}$

$$\mathbf{F} \times \mathbf{G} = \begin{vmatrix} \mathbf{i} & \mathbf{j} & \mathbf{k} \\ f_1 & f_2 & f_3 \\ g_1 & g_2 & g_3 \end{vmatrix}$$

$$= (f_2 g_3 - f_3 g_2)\mathbf{i} + (f_3 g_1 - f_1 g_3)\mathbf{j}$$

$$+ (f_1 g_2 - f_2 g_1)\mathbf{k}$$

$$\operatorname{div}(\mathbf{F} \times \mathbf{G}) = (f_2 g_3 - f_3 g_2)_x + (f_3 g_1 - f_1 g_3)_y$$

$$+ (f_1 g_2 - f_2 g_1)_z$$

I. $(\operatorname{div} \mathbf{F})(\operatorname{div} \mathbf{G})$

$$= [(f_1)_x + (f_2)_y + (f_3)_z][(g_1)_x + (g_2)_y + (g_3)_z]$$

$$\neq \operatorname{div}(\mathbf{F} \times \mathbf{G})$$

II. $(\operatorname{curl} \mathbf{F}) \cdot \mathbf{G} - \mathbf{F} \cdot (\operatorname{curl} \mathbf{G})$

$$= \langle (f_3)_y - (f_2)_z, (f_1)_z - (f_3)_x,$$

$$(f_2)_x - (f_1)_y \rangle \cdot \langle g_1, g_2, g_3 \rangle$$

$$- \langle f_1, f_2, f_3 \rangle \cdot \langle (g_3)_y - (g_2)_z,$$

$$(g_1)_z - (g_3)_x, (g_2)_x - (g_1)_y \rangle$$

$$= g_1[(f_3)_y - (f_2)_z] + g_2[(f_1)_z - (f_3)_x]$$

$$g_3[(f_2)_x - (f_1)_y] - f_1[(g_3)_y - (g_2)_z]$$

$$- f_2[(g_1)_z - (g_3)_x] - f_3[(g_2)_x - (g_1)_y]$$

$$= (f_2 g_3 - f_3 g_2)_x + (f_3 g_1 - f_1 g_3)_y$$

$$+ (f_1 g_2 - f_2 g_1)_z$$

$$= \operatorname{div}(\mathbf{F} \times \mathbf{G})$$

III. $\mathbf{F}(\operatorname{div} \mathbf{G}) + (\operatorname{div} \mathbf{F})\mathbf{G}$ is a vector, so it

can't possibility equal $\operatorname{div}(\mathbf{F} \times \mathbf{G})$.

IV. $(\operatorname{curl} \mathbf{F}) \cdot \mathbf{G} + \mathbf{F} \cdot (\operatorname{curl} G)$

$$= \left[g_3{}^2 \left(\frac{f_2}{g_3}\right)_x + g_2{}^2 \left(\frac{f_3}{g_2}\right)_x \right]$$

$$+ \left[g_3{}^2 \left(\frac{f_1}{g_3}\right)_y + g_1{}^2 \left(\frac{f_3}{g_1}\right)_y \right]$$

$$+ \left[g_2{}^2 \left(\frac{f_1}{g_2}\right)_z + g_1{}^2 \left(\frac{f_2}{g_1}\right)_z \right]$$

$$\neq \operatorname{div}(\mathbf{F} \times \mathbf{G})$$

14.2 Line Integrals, Pages 974-976

3. Let $x = t, \ y = 4t^2$ on $0 \leq t \leq 1$

$$(- y\ dx + x\ dy) = - 4t^2 dt + t(8t)dt$$

$$= 4t^2 dt$$

$$\int_C (- y\ dx + x\ dy) = 4 \int_1^0 t^2\ dt$$

$$= -\frac{4}{3}$$

SURVIVAL HINT: *If C is not a smooth curve (continuous and differentiable) then the line integral needs to be computed for each smooth segment.*

7. C needs to be considered as two regions:

let $x = t$ then $y = - 2t$ on $- 1 \leq t \leq 0$

and $y = 2t$ on $0 \leq t \leq 1$

On $[- 1, 0]$:

$$[(x + y)^2 dx - (x - y)^2 dy]$$

$$= (- t)^2 dt - (3t)^2(- 2dt)$$

$$= 19t^2 dt$$

On $[0, 1]$:

$$[(x + y)^2 dx - (x - y)^2 dy]$$

$$= (3t)^2 dt - (- t)^2(2dt)$$

$$= 7t^2 dt$$

$$\int_C [(x + y)^2 dx - (x - y)^2 dy]$$

$$= \int_{-1}^0 19t^2 dt + \int_0^1 7t^2 dt$$

$$= \frac{19}{3} + \frac{7}{3} = \frac{26}{3}$$

10.   **a.**   Let $x = t$ and $y = t^2$ on $0 \leq t \leq 2$

$$x^2 y\ dx + (x^2 - y^2)\ dy$$

$$= t^2(t^2\ dt) + (t^2 - t^4)(2t\ dt)$$

$$= (t^4 + 2t^3 - 2t^5)\ dt$$

$$\int_C [x^2 y\ dx + (x^2 - y^2)\ dy]$$

$$= \int_0^2 (t^4 + 2t^3 - 2t^5)\ dt$$

$$= -\frac{104}{15}$$

b.   Let $x = t$ and $y = 2t$ on $0 \leq t \leq 2$

$$x^2 y\ dx + (x^2 - y^2)\ dy$$

$$= t^2(2t)\ dt + (t^2 - 4t^2)(2\ dt)$$

$$= (2t^3 - 6t^2)\ dt$$

$$\int_C [x^2 y\ dx + (x^2 - y^2)\ dy]$$

$$= \int_0^2 (2t^3 - 6t^2)\ dt$$

$$= - 8$$

12.   We must use two regions:

On $[- 1, 0]$: $x = t$, $y = 1$

$(-xy^2\ dx + x^2\ dy) = -t\ dt$

On $[0, \frac{\pi}{2}]$: $x = \sin\theta$ and $y = \cos\theta$

$(-xy^2\ dx + x^2\ dy)$

$\quad = -\sin\theta\cos^2\theta(\cos\theta\ d\theta) + \sin^2\theta(-\sin\theta\ d\theta)$

$\quad = (-\sin\theta\cos^3\theta - \sin^3\theta)\ d\theta$

$\displaystyle\int_C (-xy^2\ dx + x^2\ dy)$

$\displaystyle = \int_{-1}^{0} (-t)\ dt + \int_{0}^{\pi/2} (-\sin\theta\cos^3\theta - \sin^3\theta)\ d\theta$

$= \frac{1}{2} + (-\frac{11}{12})$

$= -\frac{5}{12}$

19. We need two regions:

On $(0, 0)$ to $(0, 1)$:

$\mathbf{R} = t\mathbf{j}$, for $0 \le t \le 1$

$d\mathbf{R} = (dt)\mathbf{j}$

$\mathbf{F} \cdot d\mathbf{R} = 0\ dt$

On $(0, 1)$ to $(2, 1)$:

$\mathbf{R} = t\mathbf{i} + \mathbf{j}$, for $0 \le t \le 2$

$d\mathbf{R} = (dt)\mathbf{i}$

$\mathbf{F} \cdot d\mathbf{R} = (5t + 1)\ dt$

$\displaystyle\int_C \mathbf{F} \cdot d\mathbf{R} = \int_0^1 0\ dx + \int_0^2 (5t + 1)\,dt$

$\qquad = 12$

21. a. $\displaystyle\int_C (x\ dx + y\ dy + z\ dz)$

$\displaystyle = \int_0^{\pi/2} [\cos t(-\sin t) + \sin t(\cos t) + t]\ dt$

$= \dfrac{\pi^2}{8}$

b. C: $x = 1 - t$, $y = t$, $z = \frac{\pi}{2}t$, $0 \le t \le 1$

$\displaystyle\int_C (x\ dx + y\ dy + z\ dz)$

$\displaystyle = \int_0^1 [(1 - t)(-1) + t + (\frac{\pi}{2}t)(\frac{\pi}{2})]\ dt$

$= \dfrac{\pi^2}{8}$

28. C: $\quad x^2 + 4y^2 - 8y + 3 = 0$

$\dfrac{x^2}{13} + \dfrac{4(y-2)^2}{13} = 1$

Let $x = \sqrt{13}\cos t$, $y = \dfrac{\sqrt{13}}{2}\sin t + 2$,

$z = 0$; $0 \le t \le 2\pi$

$\mathbf{F} = (\sqrt{13}\cos t)\mathbf{i}$

$\quad + (\sqrt{13}\cos t)\left(\dfrac{\sqrt{13}}{2}\sin t + 2\right)\mathbf{j} + 0\mathbf{k};$

$$\mathbf{R} = (\sqrt{13}\cos t)\mathbf{i} + \left(\frac{\sqrt{13}}{2}\sin t + 2\right)\mathbf{j} + 0\mathbf{k};$$

$$d\mathbf{R} = \left[-\sqrt{13}\sin t\,\mathbf{i} + \frac{\sqrt{13}}{2}\cos t\mathbf{j} + 0\mathbf{k}\right]dt$$

$$\int_C \mathbf{F}\cdot d\mathbf{R} = \int_0^{2\pi}\left[-13\cos t\sin t\right.$$
$$\left. + \frac{13}{2}\cos^2 t\left(\frac{\sqrt{13}}{2}\sin t + 2\right)\right]dt = 13\pi$$

35. For $0 \le t \le 2\pi$, $x = \cos t$, $y = \sin t$;

$$dx = -\sin t\,dt;\ dy = \cos t\,dt$$

$$\frac{x\,dy - y\,dx}{x^2 + y^2} = \frac{\cos^2 t + \sin^2 t}{\cos^2 t + \sin^2 t}\,dt = 1\,dt$$

$$\int_C \frac{x\,dy - y\,dx}{x^2 + y^2} = \int_0^{2\pi}1\,dt = 2\pi$$

37. C_1: $y = 0$, $\mathbf{R} = x\mathbf{i}$; $d\mathbf{R} = \mathbf{i}\,dx$

C_2: $x = 2$, $\mathbf{R} = 2\mathbf{i} + y\mathbf{j}$; $d\mathbf{R} = \mathbf{j}\,dy$

C_3: $y = 2$, $\mathbf{R} = x\mathbf{i} + 2\mathbf{j}$; $d\mathbf{R} = \mathbf{i}\,dx$

C_4: $x = 0$, $\mathbf{R} = y\mathbf{j}$; $d\mathbf{R} = \mathbf{j}\,dy$

$$W = \int_C \mathbf{F}\cdot d\mathbf{R}$$

$$= \int_0^2 x^2\,dx + 4\int_0^2 y\,dy + \int_2^0 (-4 + x^2)\,dx + 0$$

$$= \frac{8}{3} + 8 - \left(\frac{8}{3} - 8\right)$$

$$= 16$$

40. $W = \displaystyle\int_C \mathbf{F}\cdot d\mathbf{R}$

$$= \int_0^1 [(t^2)^2 - (t^3)^2 + 2(t^2)(t^3)(2t) - t^2(3t^2)]\,dt$$

$$= \int_0^1 (t^4 - t^6 + 4t^6 - 3t^4)\,dt$$

$$= \frac{1}{35}$$

46. $\mathbf{R} = 5{,}000(\cos t\mathbf{i} + \sin t\mathbf{j})$;

$$d\mathbf{R} = 5{,}000(-\sin t\mathbf{i} + \cos t\mathbf{j})\,dt$$

$$\mathbf{F} = 5{,}000(5{,}000\cos t\mathbf{i}, 5{,}000\sin t\mathbf{j})$$

$$W = \int_C \mathbf{F}\cdot d\mathbf{R}$$

$$= \int_0^{2\pi} (5{,}000)^3(-\cos t\sin t + \sin t\cos t)\,dt$$

$$= 0$$

14.3 Independence of Path, Pages 981-984

SURVIVAL HINT: *The fundamental theorem of calculus provides a simple method for the evaluation of a definite integral. Likewise, the fundamental theorem on line integrals provides a simple method for the evaluation of a line integral. Just as the hypotheses of the fundamental theorem of calculus requires a continuous f', the hypothesis of the fundamental theorem on line integrals requires a conservative vector field. If the hypothesis is met, we have independence of path, and the value of the line integral is the different in the scalar potentials at the ending and beginning points. So the essence of a problem becomes verifying* *that* **F** *is conservative, and finding* f.

4. $\mathbf{F} = y^2\mathbf{i} + 2xy\mathbf{j}; \dfrac{\partial f}{\partial x} = y^2$

$f(x, y) = xy^2 + c(y)$, so

$$\frac{\partial f}{\partial y} = 2xy + c'(y) = 2xy$$

$c'(y) = 0$, so $c(y) = K$. If we pick $K = 0$, then

$f(x, y) = xy^2$. The field is conservative.

9. $\mathbf{F} = (e^{2x}\sin y)\mathbf{i} + (e^{2x}\cos y)\mathbf{j}$

$\dfrac{\partial}{\partial y}(e^{2x}\sin y) = e^{2x}\cos y; \dfrac{\partial}{\partial x}(e^{2x}\cos y) = 2e^{2x}\cos y$

These are not the same, so by the cross-partials test, the field is not conservative.

11. $\displaystyle\int_C (3x + 2y)\,dx - (2x + 3y)\,dy$

$\dfrac{\partial}{\partial y}(3x + 2y) = 2; \dfrac{\partial}{\partial x}(-2x - 3y) = -2;$

These are not the same, so by the cross-partials test, the field is not conservative.

a. $x = \cos t, y = \sin t; 0 \le t \le \pi$

$$\int_0^\pi [(3\cos t + 2\sin t)(-\sin t)$$

$$- (2\cos t + 3\sin t)(\cos t)]\,dt$$

$$= \int_0^\pi (-6\cos t \sin t - 2)\,dt$$

$$= -2\pi$$

b. $C_1: x = 1 - t, y = t; 0 \le t \le 1$

$C_2: x = -t, y = 1 - t; 0 \le t \le 1$

$$\int_0^1 [3(1 - t) + 2t](-dt) - \int_0^1 [2(1 - t) + 3t]\,dt$$

$$+ \int_0^1 [-3t + 2(1 - t)](-dt)$$

$$- \int_0^1 [2(-t) + 3(1 - t)](-dt)$$

$$= -4$$

c. The circular part is the same as in part **a**, and the line segment is

$C_3: x = t - 1, y = 0, 0 \le t \le 2$

$$\int_C \mathbf{F}\cdot d\mathbf{R} = -2\pi + \int_0^2 3(t - 1)\,dt$$

$$= -2\pi + 0$$

$$= -2\pi$$

13. $\displaystyle\int_C 2xy\,dx + x^2\,dy$

$\dfrac{\partial u}{\partial y} = 2x; \dfrac{\partial v}{\partial x} = 2x; u_y = v_x$, so the line integral is path independent.

a. The integral is 0 because the path is closed.

b. $C: x = t, y = 2t^2; 0 \le t \le 2$

$$\int_0^2 8t^3\,dt = 32$$

c. C_1: $x = -t$, $y = t^2$; $0 \leq t \leq 2$

C_2: $x = t$, $y = t + 6$; $-2 \leq t \leq 2$

$$\int_0^2 [2t(t^2) + t^2(2t)]\, dt + \int_{-2}^2 [2t(t + 6) + t^2]\, dt$$

$$= 32$$

SURVIVAL HINT: *Note the answers to parts **b** and **c** bust be the same since the line integral is path independent.*

14. $\frac{\partial u}{\partial y} = 2$; $\frac{\partial v}{\partial x} = 2$; $\mathbf{F}$ is conservative.

$$f(x, y) = \frac{x^2}{2} + 2xy + c(y)$$

$$\frac{\partial f}{\partial y} = 2x + c'(y) = 2x + y;$$

$$c'(y) = y, \text{ so } c(y) = \frac{y^2}{2}$$

$$f(x, y) = \frac{x^2}{2} + 2xy + \frac{y^2}{2};$$

$$\int_A^B \mathbf{F} \cdot d\mathbf{R} = f(1, 1) - f(0, 0)$$

$$= 3 - 0$$

$$= 3$$

20. $\frac{\partial u}{\partial y} = 12xy$; $\frac{\partial v}{\partial x} = 12xy$; $\mathbf{F}$ is conservative.

$$\frac{\partial f}{\partial x} = 3x^2 + 6xy^2; f(x, y) = x^3 + 3x^2y^2 + c(y)$$

$$\frac{\partial f}{\partial y} = 6x^2y + c'(y)$$

$$= 6x^2y + 4y^2$$

$c'(y) = 4y^2$, so $c(y) = \frac{4}{3}y^3$

$f(x, y) = x^3 + 3x^2y^2 + \frac{4}{3}y^3$

$$W = \int_A^B \mathbf{F}\, d\mathbf{R}$$

$$= f(0, 1) - f(1, 0)$$

$$= \frac{4}{3} - 1$$

$$= \frac{1}{3}$$

21. $\frac{\partial u}{\partial y} = 2y$; $\frac{\partial v}{\partial x} = 2y$; $\mathbf{F}$ is conservative

$$\frac{\partial f}{\partial x} = 3x^2 + 2x + y^2;$$

$$f(x, y) = x^3 + x^2 + xy^2 + c(y)$$

$$\frac{\partial f}{\partial y} = 2xy + c'(y) = 2xy + y^3$$

$$c'(y) = y^3, \text{ so } c(x) = \frac{1}{4}y^4$$

$$f(x, y) = x^3 + x^2 + y^2x + \frac{y^4}{4}$$

$$\int_C (3x^2 + 2x + y^2)\, dx + (2xy + y^3)\, dy$$

$$= \int_A^B \mathbf{F}\, d\mathbf{R}$$

$$= f(1, 1) - f(0, 0)$$

$$= \frac{13}{4} - 0$$

$$= \frac{13}{4}$$

26. $\frac{\partial u}{\partial y} = -e^x \sin y; \frac{\partial v}{\partial x} = -e^x \sin y$

F is conservative.

$\frac{\partial f}{\partial x} = e^x \cos y; f(x, y) = e^x \cos y + c(y)$

$\frac{\partial f}{\partial y} = -e^x \sin y + c'(y) = -e^x \sin y$

$c'(y) = 0$, so $c(y) = 0$

$f(x, y) = e^x \cos y$

When $t = 0$, $(x, y) = (1, 0)$

when $t = \pi/2$, $(x, y) = (0, 1)$

$\int_C (e^x \cos y)dx + (-e^x \sin y)dy$

$\quad = f(0, 1) - f(1, 0)$

$\quad = \cos 1 - e$

$\quad \approx -2.1780$

32. We want $\mathbf{G} = \langle g(x)(x^2 + y^2 + x), g(x)(xy)\rangle$ to

be conservative, so

$\frac{\partial}{\partial y}[g(x)(x^2 + y^2 + x)] = \frac{\partial}{\partial x}[g(x)(xy)]$

$\quad g(x)(2y) = g'(x)(xy) + g(x)y$

$\quad \frac{g'(x)}{g(x)} = \frac{1}{x}$

$\quad \ln g(x) = \ln x + C_1$

$$g(x) = Cx$$

for any constant $C \neq 0$.

37. The bucket moves in the circle C

described by

$\mathbf{R}(t) = (3 \cos t)\mathbf{i} + (3 \sin t)\mathbf{j}; 0 \leq t \leq 2\pi$

The bucket and water have mass $m = \frac{30}{32}$ and

moves with speed $v = 2\pi(3) = 6\pi$ ft/s.

The magnitude of the force **F** is

$$\|\mathbf{F}\| = \frac{mv^2}{r} = \frac{30}{32}\left(\frac{1}{3}\right)(6\pi)^2 = \frac{45}{4}\pi^2$$

and since **F** always points toward the

center of the circle, we have

$$\mathbf{F} = \frac{45}{4}\pi^2(-\cos t\,\mathbf{i} - \sin t\,\mathbf{j})$$

Thus, the work performed is

$W = \int_C \mathbf{F} \cdot d\mathbf{R}$

$\quad = \int_0^{2\pi} \frac{45}{4}\pi^2[(-\cos t)(-\sin t)$

$\qquad\qquad + (-\sin t)(\cos t)]\ dt = 0$

Alternatively, note that **F** is conservative,

so $\int_C \mathbf{F} \cdot d\mathbf{R} = 0$ around the closed curve C.

38. To the Spy's surprise, he finds that the

Death Force is a conservative field:

$$\frac{\partial}{\partial y}(ye^{xy} + 2xy^3) = (xy + 1)e^{xy} + 6xy^2$$

$$= \frac{\partial}{\partial x}(xe^{xy} + 3x^2y^2 + \cos y)$$

It does not matter what path he takes, the work will be the same! Since he wants to get out of the room as quickly as possible, he walks in a straight line from $(0, 0)$ to $(10, 10)$ and leaves.

39. a. Since $\frac{\partial}{\partial y}(-a) = 0 = \frac{\partial}{\partial x}(-b)$, the wind force $\mathbf{F}$ is conservative, so the work integral $W = \int_C \mathbf{F} \cdot d\mathbf{R}$ is independent of the path C. The line segment C_1 between $A(0, 0)$ and $B(2, 1)$ can be parametrized as $C_1 : x = 2t, y = t; 0 \leq t \leq 1$.

$$W = \int_C \mathbf{F} \cdot d\mathbf{R}$$

$$= \int_0^1 [-a(2) - b(1)]\, dt$$

$$= -(2a + b)$$

b. The force $\mathbf{F}_1 = \langle -a, -ae^{-y} \rangle$ is also conservative since

$$\frac{\partial}{\partial y}(-a) = 0 = \frac{\partial}{\partial x}(-ae^{-y})$$

The work, computed along the line segment C_1 given in part **a** is

$$W_1 = \int_{C_1} \mathbf{F}_1 \cdot d\mathbf{R}$$

$$= \int_0^1 [-a(2) - ae^{-t}(1)]\, dt$$

$$= a(e^{-1} - 3)$$

c. The force $\mathbf{F}_2 = \langle -a, -ae^{-y+x/9} \rangle$ is not conservative since

$$\frac{\partial}{\partial y}(-a) = 0$$

but

$$\frac{\partial}{\partial x}(-ae^{-y+x/9}) = \frac{-a}{9}e^{-y+x/9}$$

The work performed varies with the path chosen. For instance, let C_1 be the linear path used in parts **a** and **b** and let C_2 be the path along the x-axis from $(0, 0)$ to $(2, 0)$, then along $x = 2$ form $(2, 0)$ to $(2, 1)$. Then

$$W_2 = \int_{C_1} \mathbf{F}_2 \cdot d\mathbf{R}$$

$$= \int_0^1 -a(2) - ae^{-t+2/9}\, dt$$

$$= \frac{a}{7}(9e^{-7/9} - 23)$$

and

$$W_3 = \int_{C_2} \mathbf{F}_2 \cdot d\mathbf{R}$$

$$= \int_0^1 - a(2)\ dt + \int_0^1 - ae^{-t+2/9}\ dt$$

$$= -ae^{-7/9}(2e^{7/9} + e - 1)$$

44. We prove that $\mathbf{F}$ is conservative by showing that $\int_C \mathbf{F} \cdot d\mathbf{R}$ is path independent. Let C_1 and C_2 be any two curves in D with the same endpoints P and Q. Denote the path along C_2 from Q to P by $-C_2$. Then $C = C_1 \cup (-C_2)$ is a closed path (from P to Q along C_1, then back to P along $-C_2$) and

$$\int_C \mathbf{F} \cdot d\mathbf{R} = \int_{C_1} \mathbf{F} \cdot d\mathbf{R} + \int_{-C_2} \mathbf{F} \cdot d\mathbf{R} = 0$$

$$= \int_{C_1} \mathbf{F} \cdot d\mathbf{R} - \int_{C_2} \mathbf{F} \cdot d\mathbf{R}$$

Thus, $\int_{C_1} \mathbf{F} \cdot d\mathbf{R} = \int_{C_2} \mathbf{F} \cdot d\mathbf{R}$ which shows that $\int_C \mathbf{F} \cdot d\mathbf{R}$ is path independent, and $\mathbf{F}$ must be conservative.

14.4 Green's Theorem, Page 993-995

SURVIVAL HINT: *When using Green's theorem to find area, take the time to write out the values of dx and dy before substituting (except in the simplest of problems), and do not forget the factor of $\frac{1}{2}$.*

1.
$$\int_C (y^2\ dx + x^2\ dy) = \int_0^1 \int_0^1 (2x - 2y)\ dy\ dx$$

$$= \int_0^1 (2x - 1)\ dx = 0$$

Alternatively, on C:

$C_1: y = 0$; $C_2: x = 1$; $C_3: y = 1$; $C_4: x = 0$

$$\int_0^1 0\ dx + \int_0^1 dy + \int_1^0 dx + \int_1^0 0\ dy = 0$$

4.
$$\int_C (y^2\ dx + 3xy^2\ dy) = \int\int_D (3y^2 - 2y)\ dA$$

$$= \int_0^1 \int_y^{2-y} (3y^2 - 2y)\ dx\ dy$$

$$= \int_0^1 (6y^2 - 6y^3 - 4y + 4y^2)\ dy$$

$$= -\frac{1}{6}$$

Alternatively, on C:

$C_1: x = y = 1 - t;\ 0 \le t \le 1$

$C_2:\ x = 2t,\ y = 0;\ 0 \le t \le 1$

$C_3:\ x = 2 - t,\ y = t;\ 0 \le t \le 1$

$$\int_0^1 [(1 - t)^2(- dt) + 3(1 - t)(1 - t)^2(- dt)]$$

$$+ \int_0^1 0\ dt + \int_0^1 t^2(- dt) + 3(2 - t)t^2\ dt$$

$$= -\frac{13}{12} + \frac{11}{12} + 0 = -\frac{1}{6}$$

7. $\displaystyle\int_C (2y\,dx - x\,dy) = \int\int_D (-1-2)\,dA$

$$= -3\left[\tfrac{1}{2}\pi(2)^2\right]$$

$$= -6\pi$$

13. $\displaystyle W = \int_C \mathbf{F}\cdot d\mathbf{R}$

$$= \int_C [(3y-4x)\mathbf{i} + (4x-y)\mathbf{j}]\cdot[\mathbf{i}\ dx + \mathbf{j}\ dy]$$

$$= \int\int_D (4-3)\,dA$$

$$= 2(1)\pi$$

$$= 2\pi$$

since the semimajor and semiminor axes of the ellipse are 2 and 1, respectively.

17. C_1: $x = t,\ y = 0;\ 0 \le t \le 4$

C_2: $x = 4 - t,\ y = t;\ 0 \le t \le 3$

C_3: $x = 1\ -\ t,\ y = 3;\ 0 \le t \le 1$

C_4: $x = 0,\ y = 3\ -\ t;\ 0 \le t \le 3$

$$A = \tfrac{1}{2}\int_C (-y\,dx + x\,dy)$$

$$= \tfrac{1}{2}\int_0^4 0\ dt + \tfrac{1}{2}\int_0^3 [-t(-1) + (4\ -\ t)]\ dt$$

$$+ \tfrac{1}{2}\int_0^1 (-3)(-1)\ dt + \tfrac{1}{2}\int_0^3 0\ dt = \tfrac{15}{2}$$

Check: $A = \tfrac{1}{2}(b_1 + b_2)h = \tfrac{1}{2}(1 + 4)(3) = \tfrac{15}{2}$

21. $\displaystyle I = \int_C (5 - xy - y^2)\,dx - (2xy - x^2)\,dy$

$$= \int\int_D (-2y + 2x + x + 2y)\ dA$$

$$= 3\int\int_D x\ dA = 3M_y;\ M_y$$

$$= \tfrac{1}{3}I$$

The square has area $A = 1$, so

$$\bar{x} = \frac{M_y}{A}$$

$$= \frac{\tfrac{1}{3}I}{1}$$

This implies $I = 3\bar{x}$.

22. $\displaystyle W = \int_C \mathbf{F}\cdot d\mathbf{R}$

$$= \int_C [0\ dx + (x + 2y^2)\ dy]$$

$$= \int\int_D 1\ dA$$

$$= A$$

$$= \pi$$

since the circular disk D has area $\pi(1)^2 = \pi$.

24. C_1: $x = t,\ y = (\tan\theta_1)t;\ 0 \le t \le g(\theta_1)\cos\theta_1$

C_2: $x = g(t)\cos t,\ y = g(t)\sin t,\ \theta_1 \le t \le \theta_2$

C_3: $x = t,\ y = (\tan\theta_2)t;\ 0 \le t \le g(\theta_2)\cos\theta_2$

$$A = \frac{1}{2}\int_C (-y\,dx + x\,dy)$$

$$= \frac{1}{2}\int_0^{g(\theta_1)\cos\theta_1} [-(\tan\theta_1)\,t + t(\tan\theta_1)]\,dt$$

$$+ \frac{1}{2}\int_{\theta_1}^{\theta_2} [-g(t)\sin t(g'(t)\cos t + g(t)(-\sin t))$$

$$+ g(t)\cos t(g'(t)\sin t + g(t)\cos t)]\,dt$$

$$- \frac{1}{2}\int_0^{g(\theta_2)\cos\theta_2} [-(\tan\theta_2)t + t(\tan\theta_2)]\,dt$$

$$= 0 + \frac{1}{2}\int_{\theta_1}^{\theta_2} g^2(t)(\sin^2 t + \cos^2 t)\,dt + 0$$

$$= \frac{1}{2}\int_{\theta_1}^{\theta_2} g^2(t)\,dt$$

27.

Let C_1 be a circle centered at the origin with radius R so small that all of C_1 is contained within the given curve C.

Assume C_1 is oriented clockwise, and let D be the region between C_1 and C. Then,

according to Green's theorem for doubly-connected regions,

$$\int_C \frac{x\,dx + y\,dy}{x^2 + y^2} + \int_{C_1} \frac{x\,dx + y\,dy}{x^2 + y^2}$$

$$= \int\int_D \left[\frac{\partial}{\partial x}\left(\frac{y}{x^2 + y^2}\right) - \frac{\partial}{\partial y}\left(\frac{x}{x^2 + y^2}\right)\right] dA$$

$$= \int\int_D \left[\frac{-2xy}{(x^2 + y^2)^2} - \frac{-2xy}{(x^2 + y^2)^2}\right] dA$$

$$= 0$$

To evaluate the line integral about C_1, use the parametrization

C_1: $x = \sin\theta$, $y = \cos\theta$; $0 \leq \theta \leq 2\pi$

(Remember, C_1 is oriented clockwise.) Thus,

$$\int_C \frac{x\,dx + y\,dy}{x^2 + y^2} = -\int_{C_1} \frac{x\,dx + y\,dy}{x^2 + y^2}$$

$$= -\int_0^{2\pi} \frac{(\sin\theta)(\cos\theta) + (\cos\theta)(-\sin\theta)}{\sin^2\theta + \cos^2\theta}\,d\theta$$

$$= 0$$

30. Since $\mathbf{N} = \dfrac{dy}{ds}\mathbf{i} - \dfrac{dx}{ds}\mathbf{j}$ is a unit normal to the curve.

$$\int_C \frac{\partial z}{\partial n}\,ds = \int_C (\nabla z \cdot \mathbf{N})\,ds$$

$$= \int_C z_x\,dy - z_y\,dx$$

$$= \int_C [4x\,dy - 6y\,dx]$$

$$= \int\int_{\text{circle}} [4 - (-6)] \, dy \, dx$$

$$= 10(\text{area of circle } x^2 + y^2 = 16)$$

$$= 10(\pi 4^2)$$

$$= 160\pi$$

36. a. $\displaystyle\int_C f \frac{\partial g}{\partial n} \, ds = \int_C f \nabla g \cdot \mathbf{N} \, ds$

$$= \int_C f(g_x\mathbf{i} + g_y\mathbf{j}) \cdot (dy \, \mathbf{i} - dx \, \mathbf{j})$$

$$= \int_C [fg_x \, dy - fg_y \, dx]$$

$$= \int\int_D \left[\frac{\partial}{\partial x}(fg_x) + \frac{\partial}{\partial y}(fg_y) \right] dA$$

$$= \int\int_D [f_x g_x + fg_{xx} + f_y g_y + fg_{yy}] \, dA$$

$$= \int\int_D [f(g_{xx} + g_{yy}) + f_x g_x + f_y g_y)] \, dA$$

$$= \int\int_D [f\nabla^2 g + \nabla f \cdot \nabla g] \, dA$$

b. $\displaystyle\int_C \left(f \frac{\partial g}{\partial n} - g \frac{\partial f}{\partial n} \right) ds$

$$= \int_C (f\nabla g \cdot \mathbf{N} - g\nabla f \cdot \mathbf{N}) \, ds$$

$$= \int_C [f(g_x\mathbf{i} + g_y\mathbf{j}) - g(f_x\mathbf{i} + f_y\mathbf{j})] \cdot (dy\mathbf{i} - dx\mathbf{j})$$

$$= \int_C [(fg_x - gf_x) \, dy + (fg_y - gf_y)(-dx)]$$

$$= \int\int_D \left[\frac{\partial}{\partial x}(fg_x - gf_x) + \frac{\partial}{\partial y}(fg_y - gf_y) \right] dA$$

$$= \int\int_D [fg_{xx} + g_x f_x - gf_{xx} - f_x g_x + fg_{yy}$$
$$+ f_y g_y - gf_{yy} - g_y f_y] \, dA$$

$$= \int\int_D [f(g_{xx} + g_{yy}) - g(f_{xx} + f_{yy})] \, dA$$

$$= \int\int_D [f\nabla^2 g - g\nabla^2 f] \, dA$$

14.5 Surface Integrals, pages 1001–1002

SURVIVAL HINT: *If you think of a surface integral as a double integral over a curved service, rather than a flat region of a plane, then the radical is the "slope" factor to transform R into S. Since there are several steps in finding the value of the radical, taking the time to carefully write them out will save time in the long run, as you have fewer error.*

4. $z = \sqrt{4 - x^2 - y^2}$;

$$z_x{}^2 + z_y{}^2 + 1 = \left(\frac{-x}{z}\right)^2 + \left(\frac{-y}{z}\right)^2 + 1 = \frac{4}{z^2}$$

$$dS = \sqrt{z_x{}^2 + z_y{}^2 + 1} \, dA_{xy} = \frac{2}{z} \, dA_{xy}$$

R is the circular disk $x^2 + y^2 \le 4$.

$$\int\int_S (5 - 2x)\,dS$$

$$= \int\int_R (5 - 2x)\left(\tfrac{2}{z}\right)\,dA_{xy}$$

$$= \int_0^{2\pi}\int_0^2 (5 - 2r\cos\theta)\,\frac{2}{\sqrt{4-r^2}}\,r\,dr\,d\theta$$

$$= 4\int_0^{2\pi} (5 - \pi\cos\theta)\,d\theta$$

$$= 40\pi$$

8. $z = 4 - x - y;\ z_x = -1,\ z_y = -1$

$$dS = \sqrt{(-1)^2 + (-1)^2 + 1}\,dA_{xy}$$

$$= \sqrt{3}\,dy\,dx$$

$$\int\int_S xy\,dS = \int_0^4\int_0^4 xy(\sqrt{3}\,dy\,dx)$$

$$= \frac{\sqrt{3}}{4}(4^2)(4^2)$$

$$= 64\sqrt{3}$$

12. $z = 4 - x;\ z_x = -1,\ z_y = 0$

$$dS = \sqrt{(-1)^2 + 0^2 + 1}\,dA_{xy}$$

$$= \sqrt{2}\,dA_{xy}$$

$$\int\int_S (x^2 + y^2)\,dS$$

$$= \int_0^2\int_0^2 (x^2 + y^2)\,\sqrt{2}\,dy\,dx$$

$$= \sqrt{2}\int_0^2 \left(2x^2 + \tfrac{8}{3}\right)\,dx$$

$$= \frac{32\sqrt{2}}{3}$$

16. $z = x^2 + y^2 = r^2;\ z_x = 2x,\ z_y = 2y;$

$$dS = \sqrt{(2x)^2 + (2y)^2 + 1}\,dA_{xy}$$

$$= \sqrt{4r^2 + 1}\,dA_{r\theta}$$

The projected region R is the disk $x^2 + y^2 \le 4$.

$$\int\int_S (4 - z)\,dS$$

$$= \int_0^{2\pi}\int_0^2 (4 - r^2)r\sqrt{1 + 4r^2}\,dr\,d\theta$$

$$= \int_0^{2\pi}\left[\frac{289\sqrt{17}}{120} - \frac{41}{120}\right]$$

$$= \pi\left[\frac{289\sqrt{17}}{60} - \frac{41}{60}\right]$$

$$\approx 60.2441$$

20. $z = 1 - x - y;\ z_x = -1,\ z_y = -1$

$$dS = \sqrt{(-1)^2 + (-1)^2 + 1}\,dA_{xy}$$

$$= \sqrt{3}\,dy\,dx$$

projected region R is $x + y \le 1$; $x \ge 0$, $y \ge 0$

$$\int_0^1 \int_0^{1-x} 2x\sqrt{3}\ dy\ dx = \int_0^1 -2\sqrt{3}\ x(x-1)\ dx$$

$$= \frac{\sqrt{3}}{3}$$

24. $\mathbf{F} = x\mathbf{i} + y\mathbf{j} + 2z\mathbf{k}$

Front: $x = 1$; $\mathbf{N} = \mathbf{i}$; $\mathbf{F} \cdot \mathbf{N} = x$; $dS = dy\ dz$

$$\iint_S 1\ dA = 1$$

Back: $x = 0$; $\mathbf{N} = -\mathbf{i}$; $\mathbf{F} \cdot \mathbf{N} = -x$; $dS = dy\ dz$

$$\iint_S 0\ dA = 0$$

Top: $z = 1$; $\mathbf{N} = \mathbf{k}$; $\mathbf{F} \cdot \mathbf{N} = 2z$; $dS = dx\ dy$

$$\iint_S 2\ dA = 2$$

Bottom: $z = 0$; $\mathbf{N} = -k$; $\mathbf{F} \cdot \mathbf{N} = -2z$; $dS = dx\ dy$

$$\iint_S 0\ dA = 0$$

Right: $y = 1$; $\mathbf{N} = \mathbf{j}$; $\mathbf{F} \cdot \mathbf{N} = y$; $dS = dx\ dz$

$$\iint_S dA = 1$$

Left: $y = 0$; $\mathbf{N} = -\mathbf{j}$; $\mathbf{F} \cdot \mathbf{N} = -y$; $dS = dx\ dz$

$$\iint_S 0\ dA = 1$$

$$\iint_S \mathbf{F} \cdot \mathbf{N}\ dS = 1 + 2 + 1 = 4$$

26. $z = \sqrt{5 - x^2 - y^2}$; $z_x = \frac{-x}{z}$; $z_y = \frac{-y}{z}$

$$dS = \sqrt{\frac{x^2}{z^2} + \frac{y^2}{z^2} + 1}\ dA_{xy}$$

$$= \frac{\sqrt{5}}{z}\ dA_{xy};$$

$$f(x, y, z) = x^2 + y^2 + z^2 = 5$$

$$\nabla f = 2(x\mathbf{i} + y\mathbf{j} + z\mathbf{k});$$

$$\mathbf{N} = \frac{\nabla f}{\|\nabla f\|}$$

$$= \frac{1}{\sqrt{5}}(x\mathbf{i} + y\mathbf{j} + z\mathbf{k});$$

$$\mathbf{F} \cdot \mathbf{N} = \frac{1}{\sqrt{5}}(2x^2 - 3y^2);\ z = 1\ \text{intersects}$$

$x^2 + y^2 + z^2 = 5$ at $x^2 + y^2 = 4$ so the

projected region R is the disk $x^2 + y^2 \le 4$.

$$\iint_S \mathbf{F} \cdot \mathbf{N}\ dS = \iint_R \frac{1}{\sqrt{5}}(2x^2 - 3y^2)\left(\frac{\sqrt{5}}{z}\ dy\ dx\right)$$

$$= \int_0^{2\pi} \int_0^2 \frac{2r^2\cos^2\theta - 3r^2\sin^2\theta}{\sqrt{5 - r^2}}\ r\ dr\ d\theta$$

$$= \int_0^{2\pi} \frac{-2(5\sqrt{5} - 7)}{3}(5\sin^2\theta - 2)\ d\theta$$

$$= \frac{2\pi}{3}[7 - 5\sqrt{5}]$$

$$\approx -8.75528$$

29. $\mathbf{R} = u^2\mathbf{i} + v\mathbf{j} + u\mathbf{k}$; $\mathbf{R}_u = 2u\mathbf{i} + \mathbf{k}$; $\mathbf{R}_v = \mathbf{j}$

$$\mathbf{R}_u \times \mathbf{R}_v = \begin{vmatrix} \mathbf{i} & \mathbf{j} & \mathbf{k} \\ 2u & 0 & 1 \\ 0 & 1 & 0 \end{vmatrix}$$

$$= -\mathbf{i} + 2u\mathbf{k}$$

$$\|\mathbf{R}_u \times \mathbf{R}_v\| = \sqrt{1 + 4u^2};$$

$$\int\int_S (x - y^2 + z)\, dS, \text{ where}$$

$$= \int_0^1 \int_0^1 (u^2 - v^2 + u)\sqrt{1 + 4u^2}\, dv\, du$$

$$= \int_0^1 (u^2 - \tfrac{1}{3} + u)\sqrt{1 + 4u^2}\, du$$

$$= -\frac{19\ln(\sqrt{5} + 2)}{192} + \frac{17\sqrt{5}}{32} - \frac{1}{12}$$

$$\approx 0.9617$$

33. $z = 4 - x - 2y;\ z_x = -1,\ z_y = -2$

$$dS = \sqrt{(-1)^2 + (-2)^2 + 1}\, dA_{xy} = \sqrt{6}\, dy\, dx$$

The projected region R is $x + 2y \le 4;\ x \ge 0,\ y \ge 0$

$$m = \int\int_R x(\sqrt{6}\, dy\, dx)$$

$$= \sqrt{6}\int_0^4 \int_0^{(4-x)/2} x\, dy\, dx$$

$$= \sqrt{6}\int_0^4 \frac{x(4 - x)}{2}\, dx$$

$$= \frac{16\sqrt{6}}{3}$$

$$\approx 13.0639$$

41. $z = \sqrt{a^2 - x^2 - y^2};\ z_x = \frac{-x}{z},\ z_y = \frac{-y}{z}$

$$dS = \sqrt{\left(\tfrac{x}{z}\right)^2 + \left(\tfrac{y}{z}\right)^2 + 1}\, dA_{xy}$$

$$= \frac{ar\, dr\, d\theta}{\sqrt{a^2 - r^2}}$$

$$m = 2\int_0^{2\pi} \int_0^a a(a^2 - r^2)^{-1/2}\, r\, dr\, d\theta = 4\pi a^2$$

$$I_z = 2a\int_0^{2\pi} \int_0^a r^3(a^2 - r^2)^{-1/2}\, dr\, d\theta$$

$$= \frac{16a^4}{3}\int_0^{\pi/2} d\theta$$

$$= \frac{8\pi a^4}{3}$$

$$= \tfrac{2}{3}ma^2$$

14.6 Stokes' Theorem, Pages 1009-1011

SURVIVAL HINT: *Green's theorem relates a double integral over a flat region of a plane to a line integral over the boundary of the region. Stokes' theorem relates a double integral over a curved surface in $\mathbb{R}^3$ to the line integral over its boundary.*

As with any theorem, Stokes' theorem has a hypotheses that must be verified before the conclusion can be applied. In each case, verify that the orientation of C is compatible with the orientation on S.

1. Evaluating the line integral $\displaystyle\int_C \mathbf{F} \cdot d\mathbf{R}$

where C is the curve $x = 3\cos\theta,\ y = 3\sin\theta,$

$z = 0;\ 0 \le \theta \le 2\pi.$

$$\int_C \mathbf{F} \cdot d\mathbf{R} = \int_C (z\ dx + 2x\ dy + 3y\ dz)$$

$$= \int_0^{2\pi} 0 + 2\int_0^{2\pi} 9\cos^2\theta\ d\theta + 3\int_0^{2\pi} 0$$

$$= 18\pi$$

Evaluating the integral $\displaystyle\int\int_S \text{curl } \mathbf{F} \cdot \mathbf{N}\ dS$

$$\text{curl } \mathbf{F} = \begin{vmatrix} \mathbf{i} & \mathbf{j} & \mathbf{k} \\ \dfrac{\partial}{\partial x} & \dfrac{\partial}{\partial y} & \dfrac{\partial}{\partial z} \\ z & 2x & 3y \end{vmatrix}$$

$$= 3\mathbf{i} + \mathbf{j} + 2\mathbf{k}$$

$f(x,\ y,\ z) = x^2 + y^2 + z^2 = 9;\ \nabla f = \langle 2x,\ 2y,\ 2z\rangle$

$\mathbf{N} = \dfrac{1}{3}\langle x,\ y,\ z\rangle;\ z = \sqrt{9 - x^2 - y^2}$

$$dS = \sqrt{\left(\dfrac{-x}{z}\right)^2 + \left(\dfrac{-y}{z}\right)^2 + 1}\ dA_{xy}$$

$$= \dfrac{3}{\sqrt{9 - r^2}}\ r\ dr\ d\theta$$

The projected region D is the disk $x^2 + y^2 \le 9$.

$$\int\int_S \text{curl } \mathbf{F} \cdot \mathbf{N}\ dS = \int\int_D \dfrac{1}{3}(3x + y + 2z)\ dS$$

$$= \dfrac{1}{3}\int_0^{2\pi}\int_0^3 (3r\cos\theta + r\sin\theta + 2\sqrt{9 - r^2})\dfrac{3r\ dr}{\sqrt{9 - r^2}}\ d\theta$$

$$= \int_0^{2\pi}\int_0^3 \dfrac{3r^2\cos\theta\ dr\ d\theta}{\sqrt{9 - r^2}} + \int_0^{2\pi}\int_0^3 \dfrac{r^2\sin\theta\ dr\ d\theta}{\sqrt{9 - r^2}}$$

$$+ \int_0^{2\pi}\int_0^3 2r\ dr\ d\theta$$

$$= 0 + 0 + 18\pi$$

$$= 18\pi$$

7. $\mathbf{F} = z\mathbf{i} + x\mathbf{j} + y\mathbf{k}$

$$\text{curl } \mathbf{F} = \begin{vmatrix} \mathbf{i} & \mathbf{j} & \mathbf{k} \\ \dfrac{\partial}{\partial x} & \dfrac{\partial}{\partial y} & \dfrac{\partial}{\partial z} \\ z & x & y \end{vmatrix}$$

$$= \mathbf{i} + \mathbf{j} + \mathbf{k}$$

The triangle is the portion of the plane
$2x + y + 3z = 6$ in the first octant, and since
the orientation is clockwise, the normal is

$$\mathbf{N} = \dfrac{-2\mathbf{i} - \mathbf{j} - 3\mathbf{k}}{\sqrt{14}},\ \text{so curl } \mathbf{F} \cdot \mathbf{N} = \dfrac{-6}{\sqrt{14}}$$

Since $z = \dfrac{1}{3}(6 - 2x - y)$, we have $z_x = -\dfrac{2}{3}$,

$z_y = -\dfrac{1}{3}$, and

$$dS = \sqrt{\left(-\dfrac{2}{3}\right)^2 + \left(-\dfrac{1}{3}\right)^2 + 1}\ dA_{xy}$$

$$= \dfrac{\sqrt{14}}{3}\ dy\ dx$$

The projected region D is $2x + y \le 6$ for
$x \ge 0,\ y \ge 0$. By Stokes' theorem

$$\int_C \mathbf{F} \cdot d\mathbf{R} = \int\int_S \text{curl } \mathbf{F} \cdot \mathbf{N}\ dS$$

$$= \int_0^3 \int_0^{6-2x} \left(-\frac{6}{\sqrt{14}} \right) \left(\frac{\sqrt{14}}{3} \right) \, dy \, dx$$

$$= \int_0^3 -2(6 - 2x) \, dx$$

$$= -18$$

10. $\mathbf{F} = y\mathbf{i} + z\mathbf{j} + y\mathbf{k};$

$$\text{curl } \mathbf{F} = \begin{vmatrix} \mathbf{i} & \mathbf{j} & \mathbf{k} \\ \frac{\partial}{\partial x} & \frac{\partial}{\partial y} & \frac{\partial}{\partial z} \\ y & z & y \end{vmatrix} = -\mathbf{k}$$

Take S to be the boundary plane $x + y + z = 0$.
Then the outer normal is $\mathbf{N} = \frac{1}{\sqrt{3}}(\mathbf{i} + \mathbf{j} + \mathbf{k})$
and curl $\mathbf{F} \cdot \mathbf{N} = \frac{-1}{\sqrt{3}}$. Since $z = -x - y$, we
have $z_x = -1$, $z_y = -1$, and $dS = \sqrt{3} \, dA_{xy}$.
The intersection of $x^2 + y^2 + z^2 = 4$ and
$x + y + z = 0$ is $x^2 + y^2 + (-x - y)^2 = 4$,
so the projected region D is the ellipse (with
interior) $x^2 + xy + y^2 \le 2$. By Stokes'
theorem,

$$\int_C \mathbf{F} \cdot d\mathbf{R} = \int\int_S \text{curl } \mathbf{F} \cdot \mathbf{N} \, dS$$

$$= \int\int_D \frac{-1}{\sqrt{3}}(\sqrt{3}) \, \mathrm{d}A_{xy}$$

$$= -\int\int_D dA_{xy}$$

$$= -(\text{area of } D)$$

$$= -\pi(2)\left(\frac{2}{\sqrt{3}} \right)$$

$$= \frac{-4\pi}{\sqrt{3}}$$

Alternate: The principal axes of the ellipse
are $y = x$ and $y = -x$. With $y = x$, we have
$x^2 + x^2 + x^2 = 2$, so $x = \sqrt{2/3}$ and with
$y = -x$, $x^2 - x^2 + x^2 = 2$ and $x = \sqrt{2}$.
Thus, the semimajor axis has length

$$a = \sqrt{(\sqrt{2})^2 + (\sqrt{2})^2} = 2$$

and the semiminor axis has length

$$b = \sqrt{\left(\sqrt{\frac{2}{3}} \right)^2 + \left(\sqrt{\frac{2}{3}} \right)^2} = \frac{2}{\sqrt{3}}$$

so the ellipse has area

$$\pi ab = \pi(2)\left(\frac{2}{\sqrt{3}} \right) = \frac{4\pi}{\sqrt{3}}$$

15. The boundary curve C is a square in the xy-
plane $(z = 0)$:

C_1: $x = t$, $y = 0$ for $0 \le t \le 1$

C_2: $x = 1$, $y = t$ for $0 \le t \le 1$

C_3: $x = 1 - t$, $y = 1$ for $0 \le t \le 1$

C_4: $x = 0$, $y = 1 - t$ for $0 \le t \le 1$

$$\int\int_S \text{curl } \mathbf{F} \cdot \mathbf{N} \, dS = \int_C xy \, dx - z \, dy$$

$$= \int_0^1 0 \, dt + \int_0^1 0 \, dt + \int_0^1 (1 - t)(-1) \, dt$$

$$+ \int_0^1 0 \, dt$$

$$= -\tfrac{1}{2}$$

17. The paraboloid and the plane intersect where

$x^2 + y^2 = y$ or $r = \sin\theta$ (in polar form).

Thus, the curve C can be parametrized as:

$$x = (\sin\theta)\cos\theta = \tfrac{1}{2}\sin 2\theta$$

$$y = z = (\sin\theta)\sin\theta = \tfrac{1}{2}(1 - \cos 2\theta),\ 0 \le \theta \le \pi$$

$$\iint_S \text{curl } \mathbf{F} \cdot \mathbf{N}\ dS = \int_C xy\ dx + x^2\ dy + z^2\ dz$$

$$= \int_0^\pi [\tfrac{1}{4}\sin 2\theta(1 - \cos 2\theta)(\cos 2\theta)$$

$$+ \tfrac{1}{4}\sin^2 2\theta(\sin 2\theta) + \tfrac{1}{4}(1 - \cos 2\theta)^2(\sin 2\theta)]\ d\theta$$

$$= \int_0^\pi [1 - \cos 2\theta + \sin^2 2\theta]\tfrac{1}{4}\sin 2\theta\ d\theta\ = 0$$

Here is an interesting alternate solution:

$\mathbf{F} = xy\mathbf{i} + x^2\mathbf{j} + z^2\mathbf{k}$; the intersection projects

onto the xz-plane as $x^2 = z - y^2 = z - z^2$

$$\int_C (xy\ dx + x^2\ dy + z^2\ dz)$$

$$= \int_0^1 \left[\sqrt{z - z^2}\ \frac{z(1 - 2z)}{2\sqrt{z - z^2}} + (z - z^2) + z^2\right] dz$$

$$+ \int_1^0 \left[-\sqrt{z - z^2}\left(\frac{z(1 - 2z)}{2\sqrt{z - z^2}}\right) + (z - z^2) + z^2\right] dz$$

$$= 0$$

20. Choose S_1 to be the elliptical cylinder

$\dfrac{x^2}{4} + y^2 = 1$. Then C is the intersection of S_1

with the plane $z = 1$. A normal to the plane

is $\mathbf{N} = \mathbf{k}$ and since the plane is parallel to the

xy-plane, we have $dS = dA_{xy}$ and the

projected region D is the elliptic disk

$\dfrac{x^2}{4} + y^2 \le 1$.

$$\mathbf{F} = (1 + y)z\mathbf{i} + (1 + z)x\mathbf{j} + (1 + x)y\mathbf{k}$$

$$\text{curl } \mathbf{F} = \begin{vmatrix} \mathbf{i} & \mathbf{j} & \mathbf{k} \\ \dfrac{\partial}{\partial x} & \dfrac{\partial}{\partial y} & \dfrac{\partial}{\partial z} \\ (1+y)z & (1+z)x & (1+x)y \end{vmatrix}$$

$$= \mathbf{i} + \mathbf{j} + \mathbf{k}$$

$\text{curl } \mathbf{F} \cdot \mathbf{N}\ dS = (1)\ dS = dA_{xy}$, so

$$\int_C \mathbf{F} \cdot d\mathbf{R} = \iint_D \text{curl } \mathbf{F} \cdot \mathbf{N}\ dS$$

$$= \iint_D 1\ dA_{xy}$$

$$= (\text{area of the ellipse})$$

$$= \pi(2)(1)$$

$$= 2\pi$$

24. $\mathbf{V} = y\mathbf{i} + \ln(x^2 + y^2)\mathbf{j} + (x + y)\mathbf{k}$

$$\text{curl } \mathbf{V} = \begin{vmatrix} \mathbf{i} & \mathbf{j} & \mathbf{k} \\ \dfrac{\partial}{\partial x} & \dfrac{\partial}{\partial y} & \dfrac{\partial}{\partial z} \\ y & \ln(x^2 + y^2) & x + y \end{vmatrix}$$

$$= \mathbf{i} - \mathbf{j} + \left[\frac{2x}{x^2 + y^2} - 1\right]\mathbf{k}$$

Take S to be the plane $z = 0$, so $\mathbf{N} = \mathbf{k}$,

$\text{curl } \mathbf{V} \cdot \mathbf{N} = \dfrac{2x}{x^2 + y^2} - 1$, and $dS = dA_{xy}$.

The projected region D is the triangle

$x + y \leq 1$, $x \geq 0$, $y \geq 0$. By Stokes' theorem

$$\int_C \mathbf{V} \cdot d\mathbf{R} = \int\int_S \text{curl } \mathbf{F} \cdot \mathbf{N} \, dS$$

$$= \int\int_D \left(\frac{2x}{x^2 + y^2} - 1 \right) dA_{xy}$$

$$= \int_0^1 \int_0^{1-x} \left(\frac{2x}{x^2 + y^2} - 1 \right) dy \, dx$$

$$= \int_0^1 \left[-2 \tan^{-1}\left(\frac{x - 1}{x} \right) + x - 1 \right] dx$$

$$= \tfrac{1}{2}(\pi - 1)$$

26. $\mathbf{V} = y^2 \mathbf{i} + \tan^{-1} z \mathbf{j} + (x^2 + 1)\mathbf{k}$

$$\text{curl } \mathbf{V} = \begin{vmatrix} \mathbf{i} & \mathbf{j} & \mathbf{k} \\ \frac{\partial}{\partial x} & \frac{\partial}{\partial y} & \frac{\partial}{\partial z} \\ y^2 & \tan^{-1} z & x^2 + 1 \end{vmatrix}$$

$$= \left(\frac{-1}{1 + z^2} \right) \mathbf{i} - (2x)\mathbf{j} + (-2y)\mathbf{k}$$

Take S to be the plane $z = y$, so

$$\mathbf{N} = \frac{1}{\sqrt{2}}(-\mathbf{j} + \mathbf{k}),$$

$$\text{curl } \mathbf{V} \cdot \mathbf{N} = \frac{2}{\sqrt{2}}(x - y),$$

and $dS = \sqrt{2} \, dA_{xy}$.

The projected region D is the disk

$$x^2 + y^2 \leq 2x$$

or $r \leq 2 \cos \theta$ (in polar form) for $-\frac{\pi}{2} \leq \theta \leq \frac{\pi}{2}$

By Stokes' theorem

$$\int_C \mathbf{V} \cdot d\mathbf{R} = \int\int_S \text{curl } \mathbf{F} \cdot \mathbf{N} \, dS$$

$$= \int\int_D \frac{2}{\sqrt{2}} (x - y)\sqrt{2} \, dA_{xy}$$

$$= 2 \int_{-\pi/2}^{\pi/2} \int_0^{2\cos\theta} (r\cos\theta - r\sin\theta) \, r \, dr \, d\theta$$

$$= \pi$$

31. $\text{curl } \mathbf{F} = \begin{vmatrix} \mathbf{i} & \mathbf{j} & \mathbf{k} \\ \frac{\partial}{\partial x} & \frac{\partial}{\partial y} & \frac{\partial}{\partial z} \\ \frac{y}{z} & \frac{x}{z} & -\frac{xy}{z^2} \end{vmatrix}$

$$= \left(-\frac{x}{z^2} + \frac{x}{z^2} \right)\mathbf{i} - \left(-\frac{y}{z^2} + \frac{y}{z^2} \right)\mathbf{j} + \left(\frac{1}{z} - \frac{1}{z} \right)\mathbf{k}$$

$$= \mathbf{0}$$

$\mathbf{F}$ is conservative from Theorem 14.8.

$$\frac{\partial f}{\partial x} = \frac{y}{z}; \; f = \frac{xy}{z} + c(y, z)$$

$$\frac{\partial f}{\partial y} = \frac{x}{z} + \frac{\partial c}{\partial y} = \frac{x}{z}$$

$$\frac{\partial c}{\partial y} = 0, \; c = c_1(z); \; f = \frac{xy}{z} + c_1(z)$$

$$\frac{\partial f}{\partial z} = -\frac{xy}{z^2} + c_1'(z) = -\frac{xy}{z^2}; \; c_1' = 0, \; c_1 = 0$$

$$f(x, y, z) = \frac{xy}{z}$$

40. $\text{curl}(f \nabla g + g \nabla f)$

$$= \begin{vmatrix} \mathbf{i} & \mathbf{j} & \mathbf{k} \\ \frac{\partial}{\partial x} & \frac{\partial}{\partial y} & \frac{\partial}{\partial z} \\ fg_x + gf_x & fg_y + gf_y & fg_z + gf_z \end{vmatrix}$$

$= \mathbf{0}$

By Stokes' theorem

$$\int_C \left(f \nabla g + g \nabla f \right) \cdot d\mathbf{R}$$

$$= \int\int_S \text{curl}(f \nabla g + g \nabla f) \cdot \mathbf{N} \ dS$$

$$= \mathbf{0}$$

14.7 Divergence Theorem, Pages 1017-1019

SURVIVAL HINT: *Green's theorem, which found a relationship between a double integral over a region in a plane and the line integral of its boundary, is extended to the divergence theorem. This gives the relationship between the triple integral over a portion of space, D, and the surface integral over the boundary, S, of that region in* $\mathbb{R}^3$.

1. Evaluating the surface integral $\int\int_S \mathbf{F} \cdot \mathbf{N} \ dS$

   For the top portion:

   $\mathbf{F} = xz\mathbf{i} + y^2\mathbf{j} + 2z\mathbf{k}$; $z = \sqrt{4 - x^2 - y^2}$

   $z_x = -\frac{x}{z}, \ z_y = -\frac{y}{z}; \ dS = \frac{2}{z} dA_{xy}$

   (upward normal): $\mathbf{N} = \frac{x}{2}\mathbf{i} + \frac{y}{2}\mathbf{j} + \frac{z}{2}\mathbf{k}$

   $$\int\int_{S_T} \mathbf{F} \cdot \mathbf{N} \ dS = \int\int_R \left(x^2 + \frac{y^3}{z} + 2z \right) dA_{xy}$$

   $$= \int\int_R \left(x^2 + \frac{y^3}{\sqrt{4 - x^2 - y^2}} + 2\sqrt{4 - x^2 - y^2} \right) dy \ dx$$

$$= \int_0^{2\pi}\int_0^2 \left(r^3 \cos^2\theta + \frac{r^4\sin^3\theta}{\sqrt{4 - r^2}} + 2r\sqrt{4 - r^2} \right) dr \ d\theta$$

$$= \int_0^{2\pi} \left(4\cos^2\theta + 3\pi \sin^3\theta + \frac{16}{3} \right) d\theta$$

$$= \frac{44\pi}{3}$$

For the bottom portion:

$\mathbf{F} = xz\mathbf{i} + y^2\mathbf{j} + 2z\mathbf{k}$; $z = -\sqrt{4 - x^2 - y^2}$

$z_x = \frac{x}{\sqrt{4 - x^2 - y^2}};$

$z_y = \frac{y}{\sqrt{4 - x^2 - y^2}}$

$dS = -\frac{2}{z} dA_{xy}$

(downward normal): $\mathbf{N} = \frac{x}{2}\mathbf{i} + \frac{y}{2}\mathbf{j} + \frac{z}{2}\mathbf{k}$

$$\int\int_{S_B} \mathbf{F} \cdot \mathbf{N} \ dS$$

$$= \int\int_R \left(-x^2 + \frac{y^3}{\sqrt{4 - x^2 - y^2}} + 2\sqrt{4 - x^2 - y^2} \right) dA_{xy}$$

$$= \int_0^{2\pi}\int_0^2 \left[-r^3\cos^2\theta + \frac{r^4\sin^3\theta}{\sqrt{4 - r^2}} + 2r\sqrt{4 - r^2} \right] dr \ d\theta$$

$$= \frac{20\pi}{3}$$

Thus $\int\int_S \mathbf{F} \cdot \mathbf{N} \ dS = \frac{44\pi}{3} + \frac{20\pi}{3} = \frac{64\pi}{3}$

Evaluating the integral $\int\int\int_D \text{div} \ \mathbf{F} \ dV$

$$= \int\int\int_D (z + 2y + 2) \ dV$$

$$= \int_0^\pi\int_0^{2\pi}\int_0^2 \left(\rho\cos\phi + 2\rho\sin\phi\sin\theta + 2 \right)\rho^2\sin\phi \ d\rho \ d\theta \ d\phi$$

$$= \int_0^\pi \int_0^{2\pi} \left(4\,\sin\phi\cos\phi + 8\sin^2\phi\sin\theta + \frac{16}{3}\sin\phi\right) d\theta\, d\phi$$

$$= \int_0^\pi \left(8\pi\,\sin\phi\,\cos\phi + \frac{32\pi}{3}\sin\phi\right) d\phi = \frac{64\pi}{3}$$

6. Let S_C denote the closed surface consisting of the sides of the cylinder S, its top S_1, and bottom S_2. Then $\mathbf{F} = xyz\mathbf{j}$; div $\mathbf{F} = xz$;

$$\iint_{S_C} \mathbf{F}\cdot\mathbf{N}\, dS = \iiint_D \text{div } \mathbf{F}\, dV$$

$$\iiint_D xz\, dV = \int_0^{2\pi}\int_0^3\int_0^5 z(r\cos\theta)\, r\, dz\, dr\, d\theta$$

$$= \frac{25}{2}\int_0^{2\pi}\int_0^3 r^2\cos\theta\, dr\, d\theta$$

$$= \frac{9(25)}{2}\int_0^{2\pi} \cos\theta\, d\theta$$

$$= 0$$

On S_1, $\mathbf{N} = \mathbf{k}$, so $\mathbf{F}\cdot\mathbf{N} = 0$ and $\iint_{S_1} \mathbf{F}\cdot\mathbf{N}\, dS$

$= 0$. Similarly, on S_2, $\mathbf{N} = -\mathbf{k}$ and

$$\iint_{S_2} \mathbf{F}\cdot\mathbf{N}\, dS = 0. \text{ Thus,}$$

$$\iint_S \mathbf{F}\cdot\mathbf{N}\, dS$$

$$= \iint_{S_C} \mathbf{F}\cdot\mathbf{N}\, dS - \iint_{S_1} \mathbf{F}\cdot\mathbf{N}\, dS - \iint_{S_2} \mathbf{F}\cdot\mathbf{N}\, dS$$

$$= 0 - 0 - 0$$

$= 0$

11. Let S_C denote the closed surface consisting of the paraboloid S and the top disk S_d. Then $\mathbf{F} = x\mathbf{i} + y\mathbf{j} + z\mathbf{k}$; div $\mathbf{F} = 1 + 1 + 1 = 3$,

$$\iint_{S_C} \mathbf{F}\cdot\mathbf{N}\, dS = \iiint_D \text{div } \mathbf{F}\, dV$$

$$= \int_0^{2\pi}\int_0^3\int_{r^2}^9 3\, r\, dz\, dr\, d\theta$$

$$= 3\int_0^{2\pi}\int_0^3 (9 - r^2)\, r\, dr\, d\theta$$

$$= 6\pi\int_0^3 (9r - r^3)\, dr$$

$$= \frac{243\pi}{2}$$

For the disk $x^2 + y^2 \le 9$, $z = 9$ and $\mathbf{N} = \mathbf{k}$, so

$\mathbf{F}\cdot\mathbf{N} = z = 9$; $dS = dA_{xy}$ and

$$\iint_{S_d} \mathbf{F}\cdot\mathbf{N}\, dS = \iint_{S_d} 9\, dA_{xy}$$

$$= 9(\text{area of disk})$$

$$= 9\pi(3)^2$$

$$= 81\pi$$

Thus,

$$\iint_S \mathbf{F}\cdot\mathbf{N}\, dS = \iint_{S_C} \mathbf{F}\cdot\mathbf{N}\, dS - \iint_{S_d} \mathbf{F}\cdot\mathbf{N}\, dS$$

$$= \frac{243\pi}{2} - 81\pi$$

$$= \frac{81\pi}{2}$$

15. $\operatorname{div} \mathbf{F} = 1 + 1 + 2z = 2(z+1)$

$$\iint_S \mathbf{F} \cdot \mathbf{N}\, dS = \iiint_D \operatorname{div} \mathbf{F}\, dV$$

$$= 2\int_0^{2\pi}\int_0^2\int_0^1 (z+1)\, dz\, r\, dr\, d\theta$$

$$= 3\int_0^{2\pi}\int_0^2 r\, dr\, d\theta$$

$$= 6\int_0^{2\pi} d\theta$$

$$= 6(2\pi)$$

$$= 12\pi$$

20. a. $\mathbf{F} = x\mathbf{i} + y\mathbf{j} + z\mathbf{k};\ \operatorname{div} \mathbf{F} = 3$

$$V(D) = \iiint_D dV$$

$$= \frac{1}{3}\iiint_D \operatorname{div} \mathbf{F}\, dV$$

$$= \frac{1}{3}\iint_S \mathbf{F} \cdot \mathbf{N}\, dS$$

$$= \frac{1}{3}\iint_S (x\mathbf{i} + y\mathbf{j} + z\mathbf{k}) \cdot \mathbf{N}\, dS$$

b. $f = x^2 + y^2 + z^2 - R^2;$

$$\mathbf{N} = \frac{1}{R}(x\mathbf{i} + y\mathbf{j} + z\mathbf{k});$$

$$\mathbf{F} \cdot \mathbf{N} = \frac{1}{R}(x^2 + y^2 + z^2);\ dS = \frac{R}{z}\, dA_{xy}$$

$$\mathbf{F} \cdot \mathbf{N}\, dS = \frac{x^2 + y^2 + z^2}{z}\, dA_{xy}$$

$$= \frac{R^2}{\sqrt{R^2 - r^2}}\, dA_{xy}$$

From part **a**,

$$V = \frac{1}{3}\iint_S \mathbf{F} \cdot \mathbf{N}\, dS$$

$$= \frac{1}{3}\iint_S \frac{R^2\, r\, dr\, d\theta}{\sqrt{R^2 - r^2}}$$

$$= \frac{1}{3}\int_0^{2\pi}\int_0^R \frac{R^2\, r\, dr\, d\theta}{\sqrt{R^2 - r^2}}$$

$$= \frac{R^3}{3}\int_0^{2\pi} d\theta$$

$$= \frac{2}{3}\pi R^3$$

30. a. Since $\nabla \times \mathbf{E} = -\frac{\partial \mathbf{B}}{\partial t}$, we have

$$\operatorname{curl}(\operatorname{curl} \mathbf{E}) = \nabla \times (\nabla \times \mathbf{E}) = \nabla \times \left(-\frac{\partial \mathbf{B}}{\partial t}\right)$$

$$= -\frac{\partial}{\partial t}(\nabla \times \mathbf{B})$$

$$= -\frac{\partial}{\partial t}(\nabla \times (\mu \mathbf{H}))$$

$$= -\mu \frac{\partial}{\partial t}(\operatorname{curl} \mathbf{H})$$

b. Let $\mathbf{F} = \langle f, g, h \rangle$. Then

$$\operatorname{curl} \mathbf{F} = \langle h_y - g_z, f_z - h_x, g_x - f_y \rangle$$

$$\operatorname{curl}(\operatorname{curl} \mathbf{F}) = \begin{vmatrix} \mathbf{i} & \mathbf{j} & \mathbf{k} \\ \frac{\partial}{\partial x} & \frac{\partial}{\partial y} & \frac{\partial}{\partial z} \\ h_y - g_z & f_z - h_x & g_x - f_y \end{vmatrix}$$

$$= \langle g_{xy} - f_{yy} - f_{zz} + h_{xz},$$
$$h_{yz} - g_{zz} - g_{xx} + f_{yx},$$
$$f_{zx} - h_{xx} - h_{yy} + g_{zy}\rangle$$
$$= \langle f_{xx} + g_{yx} + h_{zx}, f_{xy} + g_{yy} + h_{zy},$$
$$f_{xz} + g_{yz} + h_{zz}\rangle - \langle f_{xx} + f_{yy} + f_{zz},$$
$$g_{xx} + g_{yy} + g_{zz}, h_{xx} + h_{yy} + h_{zz}\rangle$$
$$= \nabla(\nabla \cdot \mathbf{F}) - (\nabla \cdot \nabla)\mathbf{F}$$
$$= \nabla(\text{div } \mathbf{F}) - (\nabla \cdot \nabla)\mathbf{F}$$

c. In particular, when $\mathbf{F} = \mathbf{E}$,

$$\nabla(\text{div } \mathbf{E}) - (\nabla \cdot \nabla)\mathbf{E} = \text{curl}(\text{curl } \mathbf{E})$$

$$= -\mu \frac{\partial}{\partial t}(\text{curl } \mathbf{H}) \quad \textit{From part } \boldsymbol{a}.$$

$$= -\mu \frac{\partial}{\partial t}(\sigma \mathbf{E} + \epsilon \frac{\partial \mathbf{E}}{\partial t})$$
$$\textit{Given formula for curl } \mathbf{H}.$$

d. If $Q = 0$, then $Q = \text{div } \mathbf{E} = 0$

$$0 - (\nabla \cdot \nabla)\mathbf{E} = -\mu \frac{\partial}{\partial t}(\sigma \mathbf{E} + \epsilon \frac{\partial \mathbf{E}}{\partial t})$$

This is equivalent to Maxwell's equation.

CHAPTER 14 REVIEW

Proficiency Examination, Pages 1021-1022

SURVIVAL HINT: *To help you review the concepts of this chapter, **hand write** the answers to each of these questions onto your own paper.*

1. A vector field is a collection S of points in space together with a rule that assigns to each point (x, y, z) in S exactly one vector $\mathbf{V}(x, y, z)$.

2. The divergence of a vector field
$$\mathbf{V}(x, y, z) = u(x, y, z)\mathbf{i} + v(x, y, z)\mathbf{j} + w(x, y, z)\mathbf{k}$$

is denoted by div $\mathbf{V}$ and is defined by

$$\text{div } \mathbf{V} = \frac{\partial u}{\partial x}(x, y, z) + \frac{\partial v}{\partial y}(x, y, z) + \frac{\partial w}{\partial z}(x, y, z)$$

3. The curl of a vector field
$$\mathbf{V}(x, y, z) = u(x,y,z)\mathbf{i} + v(x,y,z)\mathbf{j} + w(x,y,z)\mathbf{k}$$
is denoted by curl $\mathbf{V}$ and is defined by

$$\text{curl } \mathbf{V} = \left(\frac{\partial w}{\partial y} - \frac{\partial v}{\partial z}\right)\mathbf{i} + \left(\frac{\partial u}{\partial z} - \frac{\partial w}{\partial x}\right)\mathbf{j} + \left(\frac{\partial v}{\partial x} - \frac{\partial u}{\partial y}\right)\mathbf{k}$$

4. The del operator is defined by

$$\nabla = \frac{\partial}{\partial x}\mathbf{i} + \frac{\partial}{\partial y}\mathbf{j} + \frac{\partial}{\partial z}\mathbf{k}$$

5. The Laplacian of f is

$$\nabla^2 f = \nabla \cdot \nabla f = \frac{\partial^2 f}{\partial x^2} + \frac{\partial^2 f}{\partial y^2} + \frac{\partial^2 f}{\partial z^2}$$
$$= f_{xx} + f_{yy} + f_{zz}$$

The equation $\nabla^2 f = 0$ is called Laplace's equation.

6. A line integral involves taking a limit of a Riemann sum formed by parametrizing with respect to a curve in space. An "ordinary" Riemann integral is formed by parametrizing with respect to the x-axis.

7. Let $\mathbf{F}(x, y, z) = u(x, y, z)\mathbf{i} + v(x, y, z)\mathbf{j} + w(x, y, z)\mathbf{k}$ be a vector field, and let C be the curve with parametric representation

$$\mathbf{R}(t) = x(t)\mathbf{i} + y(t)\mathbf{j} + z(t)\mathbf{k} \quad \text{for } a \leq t \leq b$$

Using $d\mathbf{R} = dx\,\mathbf{i} + dy\,\mathbf{j} + dz\,\mathbf{k}$, we denote the line integral of $\mathbf{F}$ over C by $\int_C \mathbf{F} \cdot d\mathbf{R}$ and define it by

$$\int_C \mathbf{F} \cdot d\mathbf{R} = \int_C u\ dx + v\ dy + w\ dz$$

$$= \int_a^b u[x(t),\ y(t),\ z(t)]\ \frac{dx}{dt} + v[x(t),\ y(t),\ z(t)]\ \frac{dy}{dt}$$

$$+\ w[x(t),\ y(t),\ z(t)]\ \frac{dz}{dt}dt$$

8. Let $\mathbf{F}$ be a continuous force field over a domain D. Then the **work** W done by $\mathbf{F}$ as an object moves along a smooth curve C in D is given by the line integral

$$W = \int_C \mathbf{F} \cdot d\mathbf{R}$$

9. Let f be continuous on a smooth curve C. If C is defined by

$\mathbf{R}(t) = x(t)\mathbf{i} + y(t)\mathbf{j} + y(t)\mathbf{k}$, where $a \leq t \leq b$,

then $\int_C f(x,y,z)\ ds$

$$= \int_a^b f[x(t),\ y(t),z(t)]\ \sqrt{[x'(t)]^2+[y'(t)]^2+[z'(t)]^2}\ dt$$

10. Let $\mathbf{F}$ be a conservative vector field on the region D and let f be a scalar potential function for $\mathbf{F}$; that is, $\nabla f = \mathbf{F}$. Then, if C is any piecewise smooth curve lying entirely within D, with initial point P and terminal point Q, we have

$$\int_C \mathbf{F} \cdot d\mathbf{R} = f(Q) - f(P)$$

Thus, the line integral $\int_C \mathbf{F} \cdot d\mathbf{R}$ is independent of path in D.

11. A vector field $\mathbf{F}$ is said to be conservative in a region D if it can be represented in D as the gradient of a continuously differentiable function f, which is then called a scalar potential of $\mathbf{F}$. That is, $\mathbf{F} = \nabla f$ for (x, y) in D.

12. If $\mathbf{F}$ is a conservative vector field and $\mathbf{F} = \nabla f$, then f is a scalar potential for $\mathbf{F}$.

13. A Jordan curve is a closed curve with no self intersections.

14. Let D be a simply connected region with a positively oriented piecewise-smooth boundary C. Then if the vector field

$$\mathbf{F}(x,\ y) = M(x,\ y)\mathbf{i} + N(x,\ y)\mathbf{j}$$

is continuously differentiable on D, we have

$$\int_C (M\ dx + N\ dy) = \int\int_D \left(\frac{\partial N}{\partial x} - \frac{\partial M}{\partial y} \right) dA$$

15. $A = \dfrac{1}{2}\displaystyle\int_C (-y\ dx + x\ dy)$

16. The normal derivative of f is denoted by $\partial f/\partial n$ and is the directional derivative of f in the direction of the normal $\mathbf{N}$ pointing to the exterior of the domain of f.

$$\frac{\partial f}{\partial n} = \nabla f \cdot \mathbf{N}$$

where $\mathbf{N}$ is an outer unit normal.

17. Let S be a surface defined by $z = f(x,\ y)$ and R_{xy} its projection on the xy-plane. If f, f_x,

and f_y are continuous in R_{xy} and g is continuous on S, then the surface integral of g over S is

$$\int\int_S g(x,y,z)\,dS$$

$$= \int\int_{R_{xy}} g(x,y,f(x,y))\sqrt{[f_x(x,y)]^2+[f_y(x,y)]^2+1}\;dA_{xy}$$

18. If a surface S is defined parametrically by the vector function

$$\mathbf{R}(u,\,v) = x(u,\,v)\mathbf{i} + y(u,\,v)\mathbf{j} + z(u,\,v)\mathbf{k}$$

and $f(x,\,y,\,z)$ is continuous on D, the surface integral of f over D is given by

$$\int\int_S f(x,\,y,\,z)\,dS = \int\int_D f(\mathbf{R})\,\|\,\mathbf{R}_u \times \mathbf{R}_v\,\|\,du\,dv$$

19. The flux integral of a vector field $\mathbf{F}$ across a surface S is given by

$$\int\int_S \mathbf{F}\cdot\mathbf{N}\,dS$$

20. Let S be an oriented surface with unit normal vector $\mathbf{N}$, and assume that S is bounded by a closed, piecewise smooth curve C whose orientation is compatible with that of S. If $\mathbf{F}$ is a vector field that is continuously differentiable on S, then

$$\int_C \mathbf{F}\cdot d\mathbf{R} = \int\int_S (\text{curl }\mathbf{F}\cdot\mathbf{N})\;dS$$

21. If $\mathbf{F}$ and curl $\mathbf{F}$ are continuous in a simply connected region D, then $\mathbf{F}$ is conservative in D if and only if curl $\mathbf{F} = \mathbf{0}$

22. Let D be a region in space bounded by a smooth, orientable closed surface S. If $\mathbf{F}$ is a continuous vector field whose components have continuous partial derivatives in D, then

$$\int\int_S \mathbf{F}\cdot\mathbf{N}\;dS = \int\int\int_D \text{div }\mathbf{F}\;dV$$

where $\mathbf{N}$ is an outward unit normal to the surface S.

24. $\mathbf{F} = x^2 y\mathbf{i} - e^{yz}\mathbf{j} + \frac{x}{2}\mathbf{k}$

$\text{div }\mathbf{F} = 2xy - ze^{yz}$

$$\text{curl }\mathbf{F} = \begin{vmatrix} \mathbf{i} & \mathbf{j} & \mathbf{k} \\ \frac{\partial}{\partial x} & \frac{\partial}{\partial y} & \frac{\partial}{\partial z} \\ x^2 y & -e^{yz} & \frac{x}{2} \end{vmatrix}$$

$$= ye^{yz}\mathbf{i} - \tfrac{1}{2}\mathbf{j} - x^2\mathbf{k}$$

27. By the divergence theorem

$$\int\int_S \mathbf{F}\cdot\mathbf{N}\;dS = \int\int\int_D \text{div }\mathbf{F}\;dV$$

$\mathbf{F} = x^2\mathbf{i} + (y+z)\mathbf{j} - 2z\mathbf{k};$

$\text{div }\mathbf{F} = 2x + 1 - 2 = 2x - 1$

$$\int\int\int_D \text{div }\mathbf{F}\;dV = \int\int\int_D (2x-1)\;dV$$

$$= \int_0^1 \int_0^1 \int_0^1 (2x - 1)\, dz\, dy\, dx$$

$$= \int_0^1 (2x - 1)\, dx$$

$$= 0$$

30. Since $\mathbf{F}$ is conservative with scalar potential

$\phi = \dfrac{m\omega^2}{2}(x^2 + y^2 + z^2)$, we have

$$W = \int_C \mathbf{F} \cdot d\mathbf{R} = \phi(-3, 0, 2) - \phi(3, 0, 2)$$

$$= \frac{m\omega^2}{2}\left[(-3)^2 + 0^2 + 2^2\right] - \frac{m\omega^2}{2}[3^2 + 0^2 + 2^2]$$

$$= 0$$

This result should have been anticipated as z is constant and $\mathbf{R}$ is symmetric about the y-axis.

CHAPTER 15

Introduction to Differential Equations

15.1 First-Order Differential Equations, Pages 1038-1041

SURVIVAL HINT: *In this chapter you will encounter solutions to differential equations such as*

$$y = e^{\ln|\cos x|^{-1}} + C$$

The simplification steps (which are not usually shown) are:

$$y = e^{\ln|\cos x|^{-1}} + C$$

$$y = e^{\ln|\cos x|^{-1}} e^C$$

$$y = e^C(|\cos x|^{-1}) \quad since \ e^{\ln M} = M$$

$$y = B\sec x \quad since \ e^C \ is \ a \ constant, \ B$$

Do you see how the constant changed from C to B? You will frequently need to carry out these steps.

1.
$$xy \, dx = (x - 5) \, dy$$

$$\int \frac{x}{x - 5} \, dx = \int y^{-1} \, dy$$

$$\int \left(1 + \frac{5}{x - 5}\right) dx = \int y^{-1} \, dy$$

$$x + 5\ln|x - 5| = \ln|y| + C_1$$

$$\ln|y| = x + \ln|x - 5|^5 + C$$

$$y = e^{x + \ln|x - 5|^5} + C$$

SURVIVAL HINT: *In this problem we left the answer as a function of x. However, many differential equation problems have a form which is not easily solvable for y. For this reason, it is often acceptable to leave your answer in a form*

which is not technically simplified. For this problem, it would probably be acceptable to leave your answer as

$$\ln|y| = x + \ln|x - 5|^5 + C$$

SURVIVAL HINT: *The letters D.E. is often used as an abbreviation for* **differential equation.**

6.
$$xy \frac{dy}{dx} = x^2 + y^2 + x^2 y^2 + 1$$

$$xy \frac{dy}{dx} = (x^2 + 1)(y^2 + 1)$$

$$\int \frac{y \, dy}{y^2 + 1} = \int \frac{(x^2 + 1)}{x} \, dx$$

$$\tfrac{1}{2}\ln(y^2 + 1) = \tfrac{1}{2}x^2 + \ln|x| + C_1$$

$$\ln(y^2 + 1) = x^2 + 2\ln|x| + C$$

8. $p(x) = \frac{1}{x}, \ q(x) = \frac{\sin x}{x},$

$$I(x) = e^{\int (1/x) \, dx} = x$$

$$y = \frac{1}{x}\left[\int x \cdot \frac{\sin x}{x} \, dx + C\right]$$

$$= \frac{1}{x}(-\cos x) + Cx^{-1}$$

$$= \frac{-\cos x}{x} + Cx^{-1}$$

Particular value: $0 = \dfrac{-\cos(-2)}{-2} + \dfrac{C}{-2};$

$$C = \cos 2;$$

Particular solution: $y = \frac{1}{x}(\cos 2 - \cos x)$

13. Show the equation is homogeneous.

$$\frac{dy}{dx} = \frac{-(3x - y)}{x + 3y} \cdot \frac{1/x}{1/x} = \frac{-(3 - \frac{y}{x})}{1 + 3(\frac{y}{x})}$$

Let $f(v) = \frac{-3 + v}{1 + 3v}$ where $v = \frac{y}{x}$

$$\frac{dv}{\frac{-3 + v}{1 + 3v} - v} = \frac{dx}{x}$$

$$\int \frac{1 + 3v}{-3v^2 - 3} \, dv = \int \frac{dx}{x}$$

$$-\frac{1}{2}\ln(v^2 + 1) - \frac{1}{3}\tan^{-1}v = \ln|x| + C$$

$$-\frac{1}{2}\ln\left(\frac{y^2}{x^2} + 1\right) - \ln|x| - \frac{1}{3}\tan^{-1}\frac{y}{x} = C$$

$$-\ln\sqrt{x^2 + y^2} - \frac{1}{3}\tan^{-1}\frac{y}{x} = C$$

18. Show the equation is homogeneous.

$$x \, dy - (y + \sqrt{xy}) \, dx = 0$$

$$\frac{dy}{dx} = \frac{y + \sqrt{xy}}{x} = \frac{y}{x} + \sqrt{\frac{y}{x}}$$

Let $f(v) = v + \sqrt{v}$ where $v = \frac{y}{x}$

$$\frac{dv}{v + \sqrt{v} - v} = \frac{dx}{x}$$

$$\int v^{-1/2} \, dv = \int x^{-1} \, dx$$

$$2v^{1/2} = \ln|x| + C$$

$$2\left(\frac{y}{x}\right)^{1/2} = \ln|x| + C$$

$$\sqrt{y} = \frac{1}{2}\sqrt{x}\ln|x| + C$$

19. $M(x, y) = 3x^2y + \tan y \qquad \frac{\partial M}{\partial y} = 3x^2 + \sec^2 y$

$N(x, y) = x^3 + x\sec^2 y \qquad \frac{\partial N}{\partial x} = 3x^2 + \sec^2 y$

Since $\frac{\partial M}{\partial y} = \frac{\partial N}{\partial x}$, the D.E. is exact.

$$f(x, y) = \int (3x^2y + \tan y) \, dx$$

$$= x^3y + x\tan y + u(y)$$

$$\frac{\partial f}{\partial y} = x^3 + x\sec^2 y + u'(y)$$

Compare this with $N(x, y)$ to see $u'(y) = 0$, so $u(y) = C_1$. Thus,

$$x^3y + x\tan y = C$$

23. $M(x, y) = 2x\cos 2y - 3y(1 - 2x)$

$N(x, y) = -2x^2\sin 2y - 3(2 + x - x^2)$

$\frac{\partial M}{\partial y} = -4x\sin 2y - 3(1 - 2x)$

$\frac{\partial N}{\partial x} = -4x\sin 2y - 3(1 - 2x)$

Since $\frac{\partial M}{\partial y} = \frac{\partial N}{\partial x}$, the D.E. is exact.

$$f(x, y) = \int (2x\cos 2y - 3y(1 - 2x) \, dx$$

$$= x^2\cos 2y - 3xy + 3x^2y + u(y)$$

$$\frac{\partial f}{\partial y} = -2x^2\sin 2y - 3x + 3x^2 + u'(y)$$

Compare with $N(x, y)$ to see $u'(y) = -6$

Integrate to find $u(y) = -6y + C_1$. Thus,

$$x^2\cos 2y - 3xy + 3x^2y - 6y = C$$

25. **a.** $\dfrac{dy}{dx} - y = x$ is a first-order D.E.

$$I(x) = e^{\int - dx} = e^{-x}$$

$$y = e^x \left[\int xe^{-x}\, dx + C \right]$$

$$= e^x[-xe^{-x} - e^{-x} + C]$$

$$= -x - 1 + Ce^x$$

At $(1, 2)$: $2 = -1 -1 + Ce$; $C = 4e^{-1}$

Particular solution: $y = -x - 1 + 4e^{x-1}$

b. Isoclines are lines of the form $x + y = C$

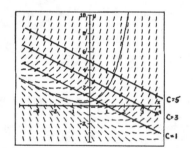

c.

n	x_n	y_n	$f(x_n, y_n)$	$y_{n+1} = y_n + 0.2f(x_n, y_n)$
0	1	2	3	2.60
1	1.2	2.60	3.80	3.36
2	1.4	3.36	4.76	4.31
3	1.6	4.31	5.91	5.49
4	1.8	5.49	7.29	6.95
5	2.0	6.95	8.95	8.74

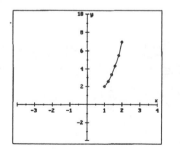

28. $\dfrac{dy}{dx} = 2x(x^2 - y) = f(x, y)$; $h = 0.2$

n	x_n	y_n	$f(x_n, y_n)$	$y_{n+1} = y_n + 0.2f(x_n, y_n)$
0	0	4	0	4.0000
1	0.2	4.00	-1.584	3.6832
2	0.4	3.68	-2.819	3.1195
3	0.6	3.12	-3.311	2.4572
4	0.8	2.46	-2.908	1.8757
5	1.0	1.88	-1.751	1.5254

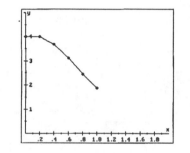

32. $M = x^2 + y^2$; $N = 3xy$; $f(x, y) = x^n$

We want

$$\frac{\partial}{\partial y}[x^n(x^2 + y^2)] = \frac{\partial}{\partial x}[x^n(3xy)]$$

$$2x^n y = 3(n + 1)x^n y$$

$$2 = 3n + 3$$

$$n = -\tfrac{1}{3}$$

Thus, the equation is

$$x^{-1/3}(x^2 + y^2)\, dx + x^{-1/3}(3xy)\, dy = 0$$

$$\frac{\partial f}{\partial x} = x^{-1/3}(x^2 + y^2);\ f = \tfrac{3}{8}x^{8/3} + \tfrac{3}{2}x^{2/3}y^2 + u(y)$$

$$\frac{\partial f}{\partial y} = 3x^{2/3}y + u'(y) = x^{-1/3}(3xy)$$

$$u'(y) = 0;\ u = C_1$$

Solution: $\tfrac{3}{8}x^{8/3} + \tfrac{3}{2}x^{2/3}y^2 = C$

35. $M(x, y) = \frac{2x}{y} - \frac{y^2}{x^2}$ $\qquad \frac{\partial M}{\partial y} = -\frac{2x}{y^2} - \frac{2y}{x^2}$

$N(x, y) = \frac{2y}{x} - \frac{x^2}{y^2} + 3$ $\qquad \frac{\partial N}{\partial x} = -\frac{2y}{x^2} - \frac{2x}{y^2}$

Since $\frac{\partial M}{\partial y} = \frac{\partial N}{\partial x}$, the D.E. is exact.

$f(x, y) = \int \left(\frac{2x}{y} - \frac{y^2}{x^2} \right) dx = \frac{x^2}{y} + \frac{y^2}{x} + u(y)$

$\frac{\partial f}{\partial y} = -\frac{x^2}{y^2} + \frac{2y}{x} + u'(y)$

Compare with $N(x, y)$, we see $u'(y) = 3$ so that $u(y) = 3y + C_1$. Thus,

$\frac{x^2}{y} + \frac{y^2}{x} + 3y = C$

36. $(x^2 - xy - x + y) \, dx - (xy - y^2) \, dy = 0$ is separable (if $x \neq y$).

$[x(x - y) - (x - y)] \, dx - y(x - y) \, dy = 0$

$\int (x - 1) \, dx = \int y \, dy$

$\frac{(x - 1)^2}{2} + C_1 = \frac{y^2}{2}$

$y^2 = (x - 1)^2 + C$

38. This is a first-order linear D.E.

$x^2 \frac{dy}{dx} + 2xy = \sin x$

$\frac{dy}{dx} + \frac{2}{x} y = \frac{\sin x}{x^2}$

$p(x) = \frac{2}{x}$, $q(x) = \frac{\sin x}{x^2}$; integrating factor is

$I(x) = e^{\int (2/x) \, dx} = e^{2 \ln|x|} = x^2$

$y = \frac{1}{x^2} \left[\int x^2 \cdot \frac{\sin x}{x^2} \, dx + C \right]$

$= \frac{1}{x^2} [-\cos x + C]$

$= -\frac{\cos x}{x^2} + \frac{C}{x^2}$

40. The given D.E. is homogeneous.

$\frac{dy}{dx} = \frac{y}{x} + x \cos \frac{y}{x}$; let $u = \frac{y}{x}$, so $y = ux$ and

$\frac{dy}{dx} = u + x \frac{du}{dx}$ which implies (by inspection)

that $\frac{du}{dx} = \cos u$, which is now separable.

$\int \frac{du}{\cos u} = \int dx$

$\ln|\sec u + \tan u| = x + C_1$

$\sec u + \tan u = Be^x$

$\sec \frac{y}{x} + \tan \frac{y}{x} = Be^x$

45. The given D.E. is homogeneous.

$\left(x \sin^2 \frac{y}{x} - y \right) dx + x \, dy = 0$

$\frac{dy}{dx} = \frac{y}{x} - \sin^2 \frac{y}{x}$

Let $f(v) = v - \sin^2 v$ where $v = \frac{y}{x}$

$\frac{dv}{v - \sin^2 v - v} = \frac{dx}{x}$

$-\int \frac{dv}{\sin^2 v} = \int \frac{dx}{x}$

$\cot v = \ln|x| + C$

$\cot \frac{y}{x} = \ln|x| + C$

If $x = \frac{4}{\pi}$ when $y = 1$, we have

$\cot \frac{\pi}{4} = \ln(\frac{4}{\pi}) + C$ so that $C = 1 - \ln \frac{4}{\pi}$

$\cot \frac{y}{x} = \ln|x| + 1 - \ln \frac{4}{\pi}$

$\cot \frac{y}{x} = \ln \left| \frac{\pi x}{4} \right| + 1$

48. The D.E. is first order linear.

$\frac{dy}{dx} = 1 + 3y \tan x$

$\frac{dy}{dx} - 3(\tan x) \, y = 1$

$p(x) = -3 \tan x, \; q(x) = 1,$

$I(x) = e^{\int -3\tan x \, dx} = \cos^3 x$

$$y = \frac{1}{\cos^3 x}\left[\int \cos^3 x \; dx + C\right]$$

$$= \frac{1}{\cos^3 x}\left[\tfrac{1}{3}\cos^2 x \sin x + \tfrac{2}{3}\sin x + C\right]$$

When $x = 0$, $y = 2$, so $C = 2$. Thus,

$$y = \sec^3 x\left[\tfrac{1}{3}\cos^2 x \sin x + \tfrac{2}{3}\sin x + 2\right]$$

49. $M(x, y) = \sin(x^2 + y) + 2x^2\cos(x^2 + y)$

$N(x, y) = x \cos(x^2 + y)$

$\dfrac{\partial M}{\partial y} = \cos(x^2 + y) - 2x^2\sin(x^2 + y)$

$\dfrac{\partial N}{\partial x} = \cos(x^2 + y) - 2x^2\sin(x^2 + y)$

Since $\dfrac{\partial M}{\partial y} = \dfrac{\partial N}{\partial x}$, the D.E. is exact.

$$f(x, y) = \int x\cos(x^2 + y) \; dy$$

$$= x\sin(x^2 + y) + u(x)$$

$\dfrac{\partial f}{\partial x} = \sin(x^2 + y) + 2x^2\cos(x^2 + y) + u'(x)$

Compare with $M(x, y)$ we see $u'(x) = 0$ so

$u(x) = C$. Also, since $x = y = 0$, $C = 0$.

Thus,

$$x\sin(x^2 + y) = 0$$

50. $y\dfrac{dy}{dx} = e^{x+2y}\sin x$ is separable.

$$\int ye^{-2y}dy = \int e^x\sin x \; dx$$

$-\tfrac{1}{2}ye^{-2y} - \tfrac{1}{4}e^{-2y} = -\tfrac{1}{2}e^x\cos x + \tfrac{1}{2}e^x\sin x + C$

$x = 0$ when $y = 0$ so $-\tfrac{1}{4} = -\tfrac{1}{2} + C$ or $C = \tfrac{1}{4}$

$2ye^{-2y} + e^{-2y} - 2e^x\cos x + 2e^x\sin x + 1 = 0$

$(2y + 1)e^{-2y} + 2(\sin x - \cos x)e^x + 1 = 0$

59. "A skydiver's velocity can never exceed $\sqrt{32/0.002}$," sneers the red Purity, "so I'd say she's going about 125 ft/s when she hits the 1,000 ft mark."

The Spy prefers a more analytical approach (because of his mathematical background, no doubt). He notes that the skydiver's velocity satisfies

$$m\frac{dv}{dt} = mg - 0.01v^2$$

where $m = \dfrac{160}{32} = 5$ (slugs) is her mass.

Solving,

$$\frac{dv}{dt} = 32 - \frac{0.01}{5}v^2 = 32 - 0.002v^2$$

the Spy obtains

$$\int \frac{dv}{32 - 0.002v^2} = \int dt$$

$$\frac{5}{8}\sqrt{10}\,\ln\left|\frac{400 + \sqrt{10}\,v}{400 - \sqrt{10}\,v}\right| = t + C_1$$

Since $v = 0$ when $t = 0$,

$$\frac{400 + \sqrt{10}\,v}{400 - \sqrt{10}\,v} = \exp\frac{8t}{5\sqrt{10}}$$

$$\approx e^{0.506t}$$

$$v = 40\sqrt{10}\left[\frac{e^{0.506t} - 1}{e^{0.506t} + 1}\right]$$

Let $s(t)$ be the distance the skydiver has fallen

at time t (seconds). Then,

$$\frac{ds}{dt} = 40\sqrt{10}\left[\frac{e^{0.506t} - 1}{e^{0.506t} + 1}\right]$$

$$s \approx 500\ln(e^{0.506t} + 1) - 126.5t + C_2$$

Since $s(0) = 0$, it follows that $C_2 = -500\ln 2$, so the skydiver has fallen 1,000 ft when

$$1,000 = 500\ln(e^{0.506t} + 1) - 126.5t - 500\ln 2$$

Solving, the Spy finds that $t \approx 10.6267$ s, and the skydiver's velocity at that time is

$$v(10.627) \approx 125.33 \text{ ft/s}$$

The red Purity's estimate was a good one.

15.2 Second-Order Homogeneous Linear Differential Equations, Pages 1050-1052

2. $y'' + y' - 2y = 0$

$$r^2 + r - 2 = 0$$

$$(r + 2)(r - 1) = 0$$

$$r = -2, 1$$

Particular solutions: $y_1 = e^{-2x}$, $y_2 = e^x$

General solution: $y = C_1 e^{-2x} + C_2 e^x$

4. $y'' + 4y = 0$

$$r^2 + 4 = 0$$

$$r = \pm 2i$$

$$\alpha = 0, \beta = 2$$

General solution: $y = C_1\cos 2x + C_2\sin 2x$

6. $y'' + 8y' + 16y = 0$

$$r^2 + 8r + 16 = 0$$

$$(r + 4)(r + 4) = 0$$

$$r = -4 \text{ (mult 2)}$$

General solution: $y = C_1 e^{-4x} + C_2 x e^{-4x}$

13. $7y'' + 3y' + 5y = 0$

$$7r^2 + 3r + 5 = 0$$

$$r = \frac{-3 \pm \sqrt{9 - 4(7)(5)}}{2(7)}$$

$$= -\frac{3}{14} \pm \frac{\sqrt{131}}{14}i$$

$$\alpha = -\frac{3}{14}, \beta = \frac{\sqrt{131}}{14}$$

General solution:

$$y = e^{(-3/14)x}\left[C_1\cos\left(\frac{\sqrt{131}}{14}x\right) + C_2\sin\left(\frac{\sqrt{131}}{14}x\right)\right]$$

18. $y^{(4)} + 10y'' + 9y = 0$

$$r^4 + 10r^2 + 9 = 0$$

$$(r^2 + 1)(r^2 + 9) = 0$$

$$r = \pm i, \pm 3i$$

$$y = C_1\cos x + C_2\sin x + C_3\cos 3x + C_4\sin 3x$$

19. $y''' + 2y'' - 5y' - 6y = 0$

$$r^3 + 2r^2 - 5r - 6 = 0$$

$$(r + 1)(r - 2)(r + 3) = 0$$

$$r = 2, \, -3, \, -1$$

$$y = C_1 e^{2x} + C_2 e^{-3x} + C_3 e^{-x}$$

22. $y'' + 6y' + 9y = 0$

$$r^2 + 6r + 9 = 0$$

$$(r + 3)^2 = 0$$

$$r = -3 \quad \text{(mult. 2)}$$

$$y = C_1 e^{-3x} + C_2 x e^{-3x}$$

$y(0) = 4$, so $4 = C_1(1) + 0$; $C_1 = 4$

$$y' = -3C_1 e^{-3x} + C_2(-3xe^{-3x} + e^{-3x})$$

$y'(0) = -3$, so

$$-3 = -3(4)(1) + C_2(0 + 1); \quad C_2 = 9$$

$$y = 4e^{-3x} + 9xe^{-3x} = e^{-3x}(4 + 9x)$$

27. $W(e^{-2x}, e^{3x}) = \begin{vmatrix} e^{-2x} & e^{3x} \\ -2e^{-2x} & 3e^{3x} \end{vmatrix}$

$$= 3e^x + 2e^x = 5e^x \neq 0$$

34. $2y'' - y' - 6y = 0$; $y_1 = e^{2x}$

$$y_2 = ve^{2x}; \quad y_2' = v'e^{2x} + 2ve^{2x}$$

$$y_2'' = v''e^{2x} + 4v'e^{2x} + 4ve^{2x}$$

$$2(v'' + 4v' + 4v)e^{2x} - (v' + 2v)e^{2x} - 6ve^{2x} = 0;$$

$$2v'' + 7v' = 0$$

$$\frac{v''}{v'} = -\frac{7}{2}$$

$$\ln|v'| = -\frac{7}{2}x$$

$$v' = e^{-7x/2}$$

$$v = -\frac{2}{7}e^{-7x/2}$$

$$y_2 = \left(-\frac{2}{7}e^{-7x/2}\right)e^{2x} = -\frac{2}{7}e^{-3x/2}$$

$$W(e^{2x}, -\frac{2}{7}e^{-3x/2}) = \begin{vmatrix} e^{2x} & -\frac{2}{7}e^{-3x/2} \\ 2e^{2x} & \frac{3}{7}e^{-3x/2} \end{vmatrix}$$

$$= \frac{3}{7}e^{x/2} + \frac{4}{7}e^{x/2}$$

$$= e^{x/2} \neq 0$$

General solution: $y = C_1 e^{2x} + C_2 e^{-3x/2}$

38. $(1-x)^2 y'' - (1-x)y' - y = 0$; $y_1 = 1 - x$

$$y_2 = vy_1 = v(1 - x); \quad y_2' = v'(1 - x) - v$$

$$y_2'' = v''(1 - x) - 2v'$$

$$(1 - x)^2[v''(1 - x) - 2v']$$

$$- (1 - x)[v'(1 - x) - v] - v(1 - x) = 0$$

$$(1 - x)^3 v'' - 3(1 - x)^2 v' = 0$$

$$\frac{v''}{v'} = \frac{3}{1 - x}$$

$$\ln|v'| = -3\ln|1 - x|$$

$$v' = (1 - x)^{-3}$$

$$v = \frac{1}{2}(1 - x)^{-2}$$

$$y_2 = vy_1 = \frac{1}{2}(1 - x)^{-1}$$

$$W(1 - x, \frac{1}{2}(1 - x)^{-1})$$

$$= \begin{vmatrix} 1 - x & \frac{1}{2}(1 - x)^{-1} \\ -1 & \frac{1}{2}(1 - x)^{-2} \end{vmatrix}$$

$$= (1 - x)^{-1} \neq 0$$

General solution:

$$y = C_1(1 - x) + C_2(1 - x)^{-1}$$

39. The spring constant is

$$k = \frac{16 \text{ lb}}{(8/12) \text{ ft}} = 24 \text{ lb/ft}$$

and the mass is

$$m = \frac{16 \text{ lb}}{32 \text{ ft/sec}^2} = \tfrac{1}{2} \text{slug}$$

The governing equation has the form

$$\tfrac{1}{2} y'' + cy' + 24y = 0$$

With $y_0 = \tfrac{1}{2}$, $y_0' = v_0 = -8$, $c = 0$

(negative because velocity is upward)

$$y'' + 48y = 0$$

$$r^2 + 48 = 0$$

$$r = \pm 4\sqrt{3}\, i$$

General solution:

$$y = C_1 \cos(4\sqrt{3}\, t) + C_2 \sin(4\sqrt{3}\, t)$$

$$y' = v(t) = -4\sqrt{3}\, C_1 \sin(4\sqrt{3}\, t)$$

$$+ 4\sqrt{3}\, C_2 \cos(4\sqrt{3}\, t)$$

Now, $y(0) = \tfrac{1}{2}$, so $\tfrac{1}{2} = C_1 \cdot 1 + C_2 \cdot 0$

$$\text{or } C_1 = \tfrac{1}{2}$$

$y'(0) = -8$, so $-8 = 4\sqrt{3}\, C_2 \cdot 1$ or $C_2 = \dfrac{-2}{\sqrt{3}}$

Solution: $y = \tfrac{1}{2} \cos(4\sqrt{3}\, t) - \dfrac{2}{\sqrt{3}} \sin(4\sqrt{3}\, t)$

46. $y''' - 6y'' + 12y' - 8y = 0$

The characteristic equation is:

$$r^3 - 6r^2 + 12r - 8 = 0$$

$$(r - 2)^3 = 0$$

$$r = 2 \quad (\text{mult. } 3)$$

$y = C_1 e^{2x} + C_2 x e^{2x} + C_3 x^2 e^{2x}$, so y_1, y_2, and y_3 are particular solutions. To show they are linearly independent, consider

$W(y_1,\, y_2,\, y_3)$

$$= \begin{vmatrix} e^{2x} & xe^{2x} & x^2 e^{2x} \\ 2e^{2x} & e^{2x}(1+2x) & 2xe^{2x}(1+x) \\ 4e^{2x} & 4e^{2x}(1+x) & 2e^{2x}(1+4x+2x^2) \end{vmatrix}$$

$$= 2e^{6x} \neq 0$$

48. a. $mL\theta'' + kL\theta' + mg\theta = 0$

The characteristic equation is:

$$r^2 + \left(\frac{k}{m}\right)r + \left(\frac{g}{L}\right) = 0$$

If $\left(\frac{k}{m}\right)^2 > 4\left(\frac{g}{L}\right)$, then

$$r_1 = \frac{-k}{2m} + \frac{1}{2}\sqrt{\left(\frac{k}{m}\right)^2 - 4\left(\frac{g}{L}\right)}$$

$$r_2 = \frac{-k}{2m} - \frac{1}{2}\sqrt{\left(\frac{k}{m}\right)^2 - 4\left(\frac{g}{L}\right)}$$

are both negative and

$$\theta(t) = C_1 e^{r_1 t} + C_2 e^{r_2 t}$$

so $\displaystyle\lim_{t \to +\infty} \theta(t) = 0.$

If $\left(\frac{k}{m}\right)^2 = 4\left(\frac{g}{L}\right)$, then $r_1 = r_2 = \frac{-k}{2m}$ and

$$\theta(t) = C_1 e^{-kt/2m} + C_2 t e^{-kt/2m}$$

so again, $\lim\limits_{t \to +\infty} \theta(t) = 0$

b. If $k^2 < \frac{4gm^2}{L}$, the roots are complex.

Let $B = g - \frac{Lk^2}{4m^2}$. Then

$$\frac{1}{2}\sqrt{4\left(\frac{g}{L}\right) - \left(\frac{k}{m}\right)^2} = \sqrt{\frac{B}{L}} \text{ and}$$

$$\theta(t) = e^{-kt/2m}\left[C_1\cos\left(\sqrt{\frac{B}{L}}\,t\right) + C_2\sin\left(\sqrt{\frac{B}{L}}\,t\right)\right]$$

$$= e^{-kt/2m}\cos\left(\sqrt{\frac{B}{L}}\,t + C\right)$$

where $C = \tan^{-1}(-C_2/C_1)$, found by using a trigonometric identity.

c. The period of the oscillation in part **b** is

$$\frac{2\pi}{\sqrt{\frac{B}{L}}} = \frac{4\pi m}{\sqrt{\frac{4gm^2}{L} - k^2}}$$

and the time difference between successive vertical positions is about half this period, namely,

$$T = 2\pi m\sqrt{\frac{L}{4gm^2 - k^2 L}}$$

53. a. $m(t)s''(t) + m'(t)v_0 + m(t)g = 0$

The weight of the rocket at time t is $(w - rt)$ and its mass is

$$\frac{w - rt}{g} = m(t)$$

Thus,

$$s''(t) = -\frac{m'(t)}{m(t)}v_0 - g$$

$$= -\frac{[-\frac{r}{g}]}{[\frac{w - rt}{g}]}v_0 - g$$

$$= \frac{rv_0}{w - rt} - g$$

Integrating, we obtain

$$s'(t) = -v_0\ln|w - rt| - gt + C_1$$

and since $s'(0) = 0$, we have

$$s'(0) = -v_0\ln(w - 0) - g(0) + C_1,$$

so $C_1 = v_0\ln w$

Thus,

$$s'(t) = -v_0\ln(w - rt) - gt + v_0\ln w$$

$$= -v_0\ln\left(\frac{w - rt}{w}\right) - gt$$

b. Integrating a second time, we find

$$s(t) = -v_0\left[t\ln\left(\frac{w - rt}{w}\right) - t - \frac{w}{r}\ln(w - rt)\right]$$
$$- \frac{gt^2}{2} + C_2$$

Since $s(0) = 0$,

$$0 = -v_0[0 - 0 - \frac{w}{r}\ln w] - 0 + C_2$$

so $C_2 = -\frac{v_0}{r}w\ln w$

Thus,

$$s(t) = -v_0\left[t\ln\left(\frac{w - rt}{w}\right) - t - \frac{w}{r}\ln(w - rt)\right]$$
$$- \frac{gt^2}{2} - \frac{v_0}{r}w\ln w$$

$$= \frac{v_0(w - rt)}{r}\ln\left(\frac{w - rt}{w}\right) - \tfrac{1}{2}gt^2 + v_0 t$$

c. The fuel is consumed when $rt = w_f$; that is, when $t = w_f/r$.

d. At the time when $t = w_f/r$, the height is

$$s\left(\frac{w_f}{r}\right) = \frac{v_0\left[w - r\left(\frac{w_f}{r}\right)\right]}{r}\ln\left[\frac{w - r\left(\frac{w_f}{r}\right)}{w}\right]$$

$$- \tfrac{1}{2}g\left(\frac{w_f}{r}\right)^2 + v_0\left(\frac{w_f}{r}\right)$$

$$= \frac{v_0(w - w_f)}{r}\ln\left(\frac{w - w_f}{w}\right)$$

$$- \tfrac{1}{2}\frac{g w_f^2}{r^2} + \frac{v_0 w_f}{r}$$

15.3 Second-Order Nonhomogeneous Linear Differential Equations, Pages 1060–1061

3. $y'' + 2y' + 2y = 0$

$$r^2 + 2r + 2 = 0$$

$$r = -1 \pm i$$

$y_h = e^{-x}(C_1 \cos x + C_2 \sin x); \quad F(x) = e^{-x}$

$\overline{y}_p = Ae^{-x}$

6. $2y'' - y' - 6y = 0$

$$2r^2 - r - 6 = 0$$

$$r = 2, -\tfrac{3}{2}$$

$y_h = C_1 e^{2x} + C_2 e^{-3/(2x)}; \quad F(x) = x^2 e^{2x}$

$\overline{y}_p = (A + Bx + Cx^2)xe^{2x}$

10.

$$r^2 + 6r + 9 = 0$$

$$(r + 3)^2 = 0$$

$$r = -3 \quad \text{(mult. 2)}$$

$y_h = (C_1 + C_2 x)e^{-3x}$

$F(x) = 2x^2 e^{4x};$

$\overline{y}_p = (A_2 x^2 + A_1 x + A_0)e^{4x}$

17. $y'' + y' = 0$

Characteristic equation: $r^2 + r = 0$

$$r(r + 1) = 0$$

$$r = 0, -1$$

$$y_h = C_1 + C_2 e^{-x}$$

$F(x) = -3x^2 + 7$

$\overline{y}_p = A_2 x^3 + A_1 x^2 + A_0 x$

$\overline{y}_p' = 3A_2 x^2 + 2A_1 x + A_0$

$\overline{y}_p'' = 6A_2 x + 2A_1$

Substitute into the given D.E.:

$$(6A_2 x + 2A_1) + (3A_2 x^2 + 2A_1 x + A_0)$$

$$- = -3x^2 + 7$$

This gives rise to the system of equations

$$\begin{cases} 3A_2 = -3 \\ 2A_1 + 6A_2 = 0 \quad \text{which has solution:} \\ A_0 + 2A_1 = 7 \quad A_0 = 1, \; A_1 = 3, \; A_2 = -1 \end{cases}$$

Thus,

$$\overline{y}_p = -x^3 + 3x^2 + x$$

Solution: $y = C_1 + C_2 e^{-x} - x^3 + 3x^2 + x$

21. $y'' + 2y' + 2y = 0$

Characteristic equation: $\quad r^2 + 2r + 2 = 0$

$$r = -1 \pm i$$

$$y_h = e^{-x}[C_1\cos x + C_2 \sin x]$$

$F(x) = \cos x$

$\overline{y}_p = A\cos x + B\sin x$

$\overline{y}_p{}' = -A\sin x + B\cos x$

$\overline{y}_p{}'' = -A\cos x - B\sin x$

Substitute into the given D.E.:

$$[-A\cos x - B\sin x] + 2[-A\sin x + B\cos x]$$

$$+ 2[A\cos x + B\sin x] = \cos x$$

This gives rise to the system of equations

$$\begin{cases} A + 2B = 1 \\ -2A + B = 0 \end{cases} \quad \text{which has solution:}$$

$$A = \tfrac{1}{5}, \ B = \tfrac{2}{5}$$

Solution:

$$y = e^{-x}(C_1\cos x + C_2 \sin x) + \tfrac{1}{5}\cos x + \tfrac{2}{5}\sin x$$

25. $y'' - y' = 0$

Characteristic equation: $\quad r^2 - r = 0$

$$r(r - 1) = 0$$

$$r = 0, 1$$

$$y_h = C_1 + C_2 e^x$$

$F(x) = x^3 - x + 5$

$\overline{y}_p = A_3 x^3 + A_2 x^2 + A_1 x + A_0$; since we have

$r = 0$ (mult. 1), we multiply by x:

$\overline{y}_p = A_3 x^4 + A_2 x^3 + A_1 x^2 + A_0 x$

$\overline{y}_p{}' = 4A_3 x^3 + 3A_2 x^2 + 2A_1 x + A_0$

$\overline{y}_p{}'' = 12A_3 x^2 + 6A_2 x + 2A_1$

Substitute into the given D.E.:

$$[12A_3 x^2 + 6A_2 x + 2A_1] - [4A_3 x^3 + 3A_2 x^2$$

$$+ 2A_1 x + A_0] = x^3 - x + 5$$

This gives rise to the system of equations

$$\begin{cases} -4A_3 = 1 \\ 12A_3 - 3A_2 = 0 \\ 6A_2 - 2A_1 = -1 \\ 2A_1 - A_0 = 5 \end{cases} \quad \text{which has solution:}$$

$$A_0 = -10, \ A_1 = -\tfrac{5}{2},$$

$$A_2 = -1, \ A_3 = -\tfrac{1}{4}$$

Solution:

$$y = C_1 + C_2 e^x - (\tfrac{1}{4}x^4 + x^3 + \tfrac{5}{2}x^2 + 10x)$$

30. $y'' + 8y' + 16y = 0$

Characteristic equation: $\quad r^2 + 8r + 16 = 0$

$$(r + 4)^2 = 0$$

$$r = -4 \text{ (mult. 2)}$$

$$y_1 = e^{-4x}, \ y_2 = xe^{-4x}$$

$F(x) = xe^{-2x}$; Let $D = y_1 y_2{}' - y_2 y_1{}' = e^{-8x}$

$$\overline{y}_p = uy_1 + vy_2$$

$$u' = \frac{-y_2 F(x)}{D} = \frac{-xe^{-4x}(xe^{-2x})}{e^{-8x}} = -x^2 e^{2x}$$

$$u = \int -x^2 e^{2x}\, dx = -\tfrac{1}{4}(2x^2 - 2x + 1)e^{2x}$$

$$v' = \frac{e^{-4x}F(x)}{D} = \frac{e^{-4x}(xe^{-2x})}{D} = xe^{2x}$$

$$v = \int xe^{2x}\, dx = -\tfrac{1}{4}(-2x + 1)e^{2x}$$

$$\overline{y}_p = uy_1 + vy_2$$

$$= [-\tfrac{1}{4}(2x^2 - 2x + 1)e^{2x}]e^{-4x}$$

$$+ [-\tfrac{1}{4}(-2x + 1)e^{2x}]xe^{-4x}$$

$$= \tfrac{1}{4}(x - 1)e^{-2x}$$

Solution:

$$y = C_1 e^{-4x} + C_2 xe^{-4x} + \tfrac{1}{4}(x - 1)e^{-2x}$$

33. $y'' + 4y = 0$

Characteristic equation: $r^2 + 4 = 0$

$$r = \pm 2i$$

$$y_1 = \cos 2x, \ y_2 = \sin 2x$$

$F(x) = \sec 2x \tan 2x$

Look for a particular solution of the form

$$\overline{y}_p = uy_1 + vy_2 = u\cos 2x + v\sin 2x$$

$$u' = \frac{(-\sin 2x)(\sec 2x \tan 2x)}{2} = -\tfrac{1}{2}\tan^2 2x$$

$$u = \int -\tfrac{1}{2}\tan^2 2x\, dx = \tfrac{x}{2} - \tfrac{1}{4}\tan 2x$$

$$v' = \frac{\cos 2x(\sec 2x \tan 2x)}{2} = \tfrac{1}{2}\tan 2x$$

$$v = \int \tfrac{1}{2}\tan 2x\, dx = -\tfrac{1}{4}\ln|\cos 2x|$$

Solution:

$$y = C_1\cos 2x + C_2\sin 2x + \tfrac{1}{2}x\cos 2x$$
$$- \tfrac{1}{4}\sin 2x(\ln|\cos 2x|)$$

36. $y'' - 4y' + 4y = 0$

Characteristic equation: $\quad r^2 - 4r + 4 = 0$

$$r = 2 \ (\text{mult. } 2)$$

$$y_1 = e^{2x}, \ y_2 = xe^{2x}$$

$$F(x) = \frac{e^{2x}}{1 + x}$$

Look for a particular solution of the form

$$\overline{y}_p = ue^{2x} + vxe^{2x}$$

$$u' = \frac{-xe^{2x}\left(\dfrac{e^{2x}}{1 + x}\right)}{e^{2x}(2x + 1)e^{2x} - xe^{2x}(2e^{2x})} = -\frac{x}{x + 1}$$

$$u = \int \frac{-x}{x + 1}\, dx = -x + \ln|x + 1|$$

$$v' = \frac{e^{2x}\left(\dfrac{e^{2x}}{1 + x}\right)}{e^{4x}} = \frac{1}{x + 1}$$

$$v = \int (x + 1)^{-1} dx = \ln|x + 1|$$

Solution:

$$y = C_1 e^{2x} + C_2 xe^{2x} + (1 + x)e^{4x}\ln|x + 1| - xe^{4x}$$

41. $y'' + 9y = 0$

Characteristic equation: $\quad r^2 + 9 = 0$

$$r = \pm 3i$$

$$y_h = C_1\cos 3x + C_2\sin 3x$$

$F(x) = 4e^{3x}$

$$\overline{y}_p = Ae^{3x}; \ \overline{y}_p{}' = 3Ae^{3x}; \ \overline{y}_p{}'' = 9Ae^{3x}$$

Substitute into the given D.E.:

$9Ae^{3x} + 9Ae^{3x} = 4e^{3x}$, or $A = \frac{2}{9}$

General solution:

$y = C_1\cos 3x + C_2\sin 3x + \frac{2}{9}e^{3x}$

$y(0) = C_1 \cdot 1 + C_2 \cdot 0 + \frac{2}{9} = 0$ or $C_1 = -\frac{2}{9}$

$y' = \frac{2}{3}\sin 3x + 3C_2\cos 3x + \frac{2}{3}e^{3x}$

$y'(1) = 0 + 3C_2 \cdot 1 + \frac{2}{3} = 2$ or $C_2 = \frac{4}{9}$

Solution: $y = -\frac{2}{9}\cos 3x + \frac{4}{9}\sin 3x + \frac{2}{9}e^{3x}$

44. $y'' + y' = 0$

Characteristic equation: $r^2 + r = 0$

$r = 0, -1$

$y_h = C_1 + C_2e^{-x}$

$F(x) = 2\sin x$

$\overline{y}_p = A_1\sin x + A_2\cos x$

$\overline{y}_p{}' = A_1\cos x - A_2\sin x$

$\overline{y}_p{}'' = -A_1\sin x - A_2\cos x$

Substitute into the given D.E.:

$(-A_1\sin x - A_2\cos x) + (A_1\cos x - A_2\sin x)$

$= 2\sin x$

This gives rise to the system of equations

$\begin{cases} -A_1 - A_2 = 2 \\ -A_2 + A_1 = 0 \end{cases}$ which has solution: $A_1 = -1, A_2 = -1$

$\overline{y}_p = -\sin x - \cos x$

General solution:

$y = C_1 + C_2e^{-x} - \cos x - \sin x$

$y(0) = C_1 + C_2 \cdot 1 - 0 - 1 = 0$

$y' = -C_2e^{-x} - \cos x + \sin x$

$y'(0) = -C_2 - 1 + 0 = -4$

Solve:

$\begin{cases} C_1 + C_2 = 1 \\ -C_2 = -3 \end{cases}$ which has solution:

$C_1 = -2, C_2 = 3$

Solution: $y = -2 + 3e^{-x} - \sin x - \cos x$

47. $F(x) = \begin{cases} 2x & \text{for } 0 \le x \le 1 \\ 2 & \text{for } 1 < x < 3 \\ -2x + 8 & \text{for } 3 \le x \le 4 \end{cases}$

Characteristic equation: $r^2 + 5r + 6 = 0$

$r = -2, -3$

$y_h = C_1e^{-2x} + C_2e^{-3x}$

If $0 \le x \le 1$,

$\overline{y}_1 = A_1x + A_2$

$\overline{y}_1{}' = A_1$

$\overline{y}_1{}'' = 0$

Substitute into the given D.E. equation:

$0 + 5A_1 + 6(A_1x + A_2) = 2x$

This gives rise to the system of equations:

$\begin{cases} 6A_1 = 2 \\ 5A_1 + 6A_2 = 0 \end{cases}$ which has solution: $A_1 = \frac{1}{3}, A_2 = -\frac{5}{18}$

$\overline{y}_1 = \frac{1}{3}x - \frac{5}{18}$

If $1 < x < 3$, $\overline{y}_2 = C$; $6C = 2$; $C = \frac{1}{3}$, so

$y_2 = \frac{1}{3}$

If $3 \le x \le 4$,

$\overline{y}_3 = B_1x + B_2$

$\overline{y}_3{}' = B_1$

$\overline{y}_3{}'' = 0$

Substitute into the given D.E.:

$0 + 5B_1 + 6(B_1x + B_2) = -2x + 8$

This gives rise to the system of equations:

$\begin{cases} 6B_1 = -2 \\ 5B_1 + 6B_2 = 8 \end{cases}$ which has solution:

$$B_1 = -\tfrac{1}{3}, \; B_2 = \tfrac{29}{18}$$

$$\overline{y}_3 = -\tfrac{1}{3}x + \tfrac{29}{18}$$

General solution:

$$y = C_1 e^{-2x} + C_2 e^{-3x} + G(x)$$

where

$$G(x) = \begin{cases} \tfrac{1}{3}x - \tfrac{5}{18} & \text{for } 0 \le x \le 1 \\ \tfrac{1}{3} & \text{for } 1 < x < 3 \\ -\tfrac{1}{3}x + \tfrac{29}{18} & \text{for } 3x \le x \le 4 \end{cases}$$

48.

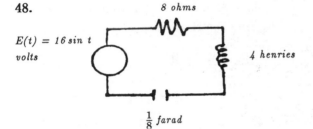

$E(t) = 16\sin t$ volts

8 ohms

4 henries

$\tfrac{1}{8}$ farad

$$I(0) = 0; \; I'(0) = 0$$

The governing equation is:

$$L\frac{dI}{dt} + RI + \frac{Q}{C} = E$$

$$L\frac{d^2 I}{dt^2} + R\frac{dI}{dt} + \frac{I}{C} = \frac{dE}{dt} \qquad \text{since } I = \frac{dQ}{dt}$$

$$4\frac{d^2 I}{dt^2} + 8\frac{dI}{dt} + \frac{I}{1/8} = 16\cos t$$

$$4I'' + 8I' + 8I = 16\cos t$$

Characteristic equation: $\quad 4r^2 + 8r + 8 = 0$

$$r = -1 \pm i$$

$$I_h(t) = e^{-t}[C_1\cos t + C_2\sin t]$$

$$\overline{y}_p = A_1\cos t + A_2\sin t$$

$$\overline{y}_p{}' = -A_1\sin t + A_2\cos t$$

$$\overline{y}_p{}'' = -A_1\cos t - A_2\sin t$$

Substitute into the given D.E.:

$$4(-A_1\cos t - A_2\sin t) + 8(-A_1\sin t$$
$$+ A_2\cos t) + 8(A_1\cos t + A_2\sin t)$$
$$= 16\cos t$$

This gives rise to the system of equations

$$\begin{cases} 4A_1 + 8A_2 = 16 \\ -8A_1 + 4A_2 = 0 \end{cases}$$

which has solution:

$$A_1 = \tfrac{4}{5}, \; A_2 = \tfrac{8}{5}$$

General solution:

$$I(t) = e^{-t}[C_1\cos t + C_2\sin t] + \tfrac{4}{5}\cos t + \tfrac{8}{5}\sin t$$

$$I(0) = 1\cdot[C_1\cdot 1 + 0] + \tfrac{4}{5}\cdot 1 + 0 = 0,$$

$$\text{so } C_1 = -\tfrac{4}{5}$$

$$I'(t) = -e^{-t}[C_1\cos t + C_2\sin t]$$
$$+ e^{-t}[-C_1\sin t + C_2\cos t]$$
$$- \tfrac{4}{5}\sin t + \tfrac{8}{5}\cos t$$

$$I'(0) = -1\cdot[C_1 + 0] + 1\cdot[0 + C_2]$$
$$- 0 + \tfrac{8}{5}\cdot 1 = 0$$

This gives rise to the system of equations

$$\begin{cases} -C_1 + C_2 = -\tfrac{8}{5} \\ C_1 = -\tfrac{4}{5} \end{cases}$$

which has solution:

$$C_1 = -\tfrac{4}{5}, \; C_2 = -\tfrac{12}{5}$$

Solution:

$$I(t) = e^{-t}\left[-\tfrac{4}{5}\cos t - \tfrac{12}{5}\sin t\right] + \tfrac{4}{5}\cos t + \tfrac{8}{5}\sin t$$

CHAPTER 15 REVIEW
Proficiency Examination, Page 1062

SURVIVAL HINT: *To help you review the concepts of this chapter,* **hand write** *the answers to each of these questions onto your own paper.*

1. A *separable differential equation* is one that can be written in the form

    $$\frac{dy}{dx} = \frac{g(x)}{f(y)}$$

    and then be solved by separating the variables and integrating each side.

2. A differential equation of the form

    $$M(x, y) \, dx + N(x, y) \, dy = 0$$

    said to be *homogeneous differential equation* if it can be written in the form

    $$\frac{dy}{dx} = f\!\left(\frac{y}{x}\right)$$

    In other words, dy/dx is isolated on one side of the equation and the other side can be expressed as a function of y/x.

3. A first order linear differential equation is one of the form

    $$\frac{dy}{dx} + p(x)y = q(x)$$

Its general solution is given by

$$y = \frac{1}{I(x)}\left[\int I(x) \; q(x) \; dx + C\right]$$

where $I(x)$ is the *integrating factor*

$$I(x) = e^{\int p(x)dx}$$

4. An *exact differential equation* is one that can be written in the general form

    $$M(x, y) \, dx + N(x, y) \, dy = 0$$

    where M and N are functions of x and y that satisfy the cross-derivative test

    $$\frac{\partial N}{\partial x} = \frac{\partial M}{\partial y}$$

5. Euler's method is a procedure for approximating a solution of the initial value problem

    $$\frac{dy}{dx} = f(x, y), \; y(x_0) = y_0$$

    It depends on the fact that the portion of the solution curve near (x_n, y_n) is close to the line

    $$y = y_n + f(x_n, y_n)(x - x_n)$$

6. The functions $y_1, y_2, \ldots y_n$ are said to be *linearly independent* if the equation

    $$C_1 y_1 + C_2 y_2 + \ldots + C_n y_n = 0$$

    for constants $C_1, C_2, \ldots$ has only the trivial solution $C_1 = C_2 = \ldots = C_n = 0$. Otherwise the y_k's are *linearly dependent*.

7. The *Wronskian* $W(y_1, y_2, \ldots, y_n)$ of n functions $y_1, y_2, \ldots, y_n$ having $n - 1$

derivatives on an interval I is defined to be the determinant function $W(y_1, y_2, \ldots, y_n)$

$$= \begin{vmatrix} y_1 & y_2 & \cdots & y_n \\ y_1' & y_2' & \cdots & y_n' \\ \vdots & \vdots & & \vdots \\ y_1^{(n-1)} & y_2^{(n-1)} & \cdots & y_n^{(n-1)} \end{vmatrix}$$

The functions $y_1, \cdots y_n$ are linearly independent if and only if $W \neq 0$

8. **a.** The *characteristic equation* of $y'' + ay' + by = 0$ is the equation $r^2 + ar + b = 0$.

   b. If r_1 and r_2 are the roots of the characteristic equation $r^2 + br + c = 0$, then the general solution of the homogeneous linear equation $y'' + by' + cy = 0$ can be expressed in one of these forms:

   $b^2 - 4c > 0$: The general solution is
   $$y = C_1 e^{r_1 x} + C_2 e^{r_2 x}$$

   $b^2 - 4c = 0$: The general solution is
   $$y = C_1 e^{-bx/2} + C_2 x e^{-bx/2}$$
   $$= (C_1 + C_2 x) e^{-bx/2}$$

   $b^2 - 4c < 0$: The general solution is
   $$y = e^{-bx/2} [C_1 \cos (\frac{\sqrt{4c - b^2}}{2} x)$$
   $$+ C_2 \sin (\frac{\sqrt{4c - b^2}}{2} x)]$$

9. Let y_p be a particular solution of the nonhomogeneous second-order linear equation $y'' + ay' + by = F(x)$. Let y_h be the general solution of the related homogeneous equation
   $$y'' + ay' + by = 0.$$

   Then the general solution of
   $$y'' + ay' + by = F(x),$$

   is given by the sum $y = y_h + y_p$.

10. To solve $y'' + ay' + by = F(x)$ when $F(x)$ is one of the following forms:

    (1) $F(x) = P_n(x)$, a polynomial of degree n

    (2) $F(x) = P_n(x) e^{kx}$

    (3) $F(x) = e^{kx}[P_n(x) \cos \alpha x + Q_n(x) \sin \alpha x]$, where $Q_n(x)$ is another polynomial of degree n

    Outline of the procedure:

    1. The solution is of the form $y = y_h + y_p$, where y_h is the general solution and y_p is a particular solution.

    2. Find y_h by solving the homogeneous equation $y'' + ay' + by = 0$

    3. Find y_p by picking an appropriate trial solution $\overline{y}_p$:

       a. Form: $P_n(x) = c_n x^n + \ldots + c_1 x + c_0$

       Corresponding trial expression:

       $$A_n x^n + \ldots + A_1 x + A_0$$

b. Form: $P_n(x)e^{kx}$

Corresponding trial expression:

$$[A_n x^n + A_{n-1}x^{n-1} + \ldots + A_0]e^{kx}$$

c. Form: $e^{kx}[P_n(x)\cos\alpha x + Q_n(x)\sin\alpha x]$

Corresponding trial expression:

$$e^{kx}[(A_n x^n + \ldots + A_0)\cos\alpha x$$
$$+ (B_n x^n + \ldots + B_0)\sin\alpha x]$$

4. If no term in the trial expression $\overline{y}_p$ appears in the general homogeneous solution y_h, the particular solution can be found by substituting $\overline{y}_p$ into the equation $y'' + ay' + by = F(x)$ and solving for the undetermined coefficients.

5. If any term in the trial expression $\overline{y}_p$ appears in y_h, multiply $\overline{y}_p$ by x^k, where k is the smallest integer such that no term in $x^k\overline{y}_p$ is in y_k. Then proceed as in Step 4, using $x^k\overline{y}_p$ as the trial solution.

11. To find the general solution of

$$y'' + P(x)y' + Q(x)y = F(x)$$

1. Find the general solution,

$$y_h = C_1 y_1 + C_2 y_2$$

to the related homogeneous equation

$$y'' + Py' + Qy = 0.$$

2. Set $y_p = uy_1 + vy_2$ and substitute into the formulas:

$$u' = \frac{-y_2 F(x)}{y_1 y_2' - y_2 y_1'}, \qquad v' = \frac{y_1 F(x)}{y_1 y_2' - y_2 y_1'}$$

3. Integrate u' and v' to find u and v.

4. A particular solution is $y_p = uy_1 + vy_2$, and the general solution is $y = y_h + y_p$.

12.

$$\frac{dy}{dx} = \sqrt{\frac{1 - y^2}{1 + x^2}}$$

$$\int \frac{dy}{\sqrt{1 - y^2}} = \int \frac{dy}{\sqrt{1 + x^2}}$$

$$\sin^{-1}y = \sinh^{-1}x + C$$

15. $xy\, dy = (x^2 - y^2)\, dx$

$$\frac{dy}{dx} = \frac{x^2 - y^2}{xy}$$

$$= \frac{x}{y} - \frac{y}{x}$$

Let $f(v) = v^{-1} - v$ where $v = \frac{y}{x}$.

$$\int \frac{dv}{\frac{1}{v} - v - v} = \int \frac{dx}{x}$$

$$\int \frac{v\, dv}{1 - 2v^2} = \int \frac{dx}{x}$$

$$-\frac{1}{4}\ln|1 - 2v^2| = \ln|x| + C_1$$

$$1 - 2v^2 = Cx^{-4}$$

$$1 - 2\left(\frac{y}{x}\right)^2 = Cx^{-4}$$

$$x^2(x^2 - 2y^2) = C$$

18. $M(x, y) = 3x^2 e^{-y} + y^{-2} + 2xy^{-3}$

$N(x, y) = -x^3 e^{-y} - 2xy^{-3} - 3x^2 y^{-4}$

$\dfrac{\partial M}{\partial y} = -3x^2 e^{-y} - 2y^{-3} - 6xy^{-4}$

$\dfrac{\partial N}{\partial x} = -3x^2 e^{-y} - 2y^{-3} - 6xy^{-4}$

Since $\dfrac{\partial M}{\partial y} = \dfrac{\partial N}{\partial x}$, the D.E. is exact.

$$f(x, y) = \int (3x^2 e^{-y} - y^{-2} + 2xy^{-3})\, dx$$

$$= x^3 e^{-y} - xy^{-2} + x^2 y^{-3} + u(y)$$

$\dfrac{\partial f}{\partial y} = -x^3 e^{-y} + 2xy^{-3} - 3x^2 y^{-4} + u'(y)$

Compare with $N(x, y)$ we see

$u'(y) = 0$, so $u(y) = C$. Thus,

$$x^3 e^{-y} - xy^{-2} + x^2 y^{-3} = C$$

Cumulative Review for Chapters 12-15, Pages 1069-1070

SURVIVAL HINT: *The Cumulative Review for Chapters 12-15 can be very valuable to refresh some of the skills and concepts that you may not have been using for a while. It can also serve as a valuable tool in preparing for a final examination. If you do not have the time to actually do all of the problems, try looking at each one to see if you can recall the concept involved and how to proceed with the solution. If you are confident about your ability to solve the problem, do not spend the time. If you feel a little uncertain about the problem, refer back to the appropriate section, review the concepts, look in your old homework for a similar problem, and then see if*

you can answer the question. Be more concerned about understanding the concept than about getting exactly the correct answer. Do not spend a lot of your time looking for algebra and arithmetic errors.

1. Calculus is the study of dynamic processes (rather than the static). It is the study of infinitesimals, the behavior of functions at or near a point. The are three fundamental ideas of calculus; the notion of a limit, derivatives (the limit of difference quotients), and integrals (the sum of infinitesimal quantities). Calculus is also the study of transformations of reference frames (coordinate systems), and motion with respect to reference frames (vector analysis).

2. The notation $\lim\limits_{x \to c} f(x) = L$ is read "the limit of $f(x)$ as x approaches c is L" and means that the functional values $f(x)$ can be made arbitrarily close to L by choosing x sufficiently close to c. See Chapter 6 of the *Mathematics Handbook* for a summary of all the limit ideas in this book. The derivative of f at x is given by

$$f'(x) = \lim_{\Delta x \to 0} \frac{f(x + \Delta x) - f(x)}{\Delta x}$$

provided this limit exists. See Chapter 7 of the *Mathematics Handbook* for a summary of the derivative ideas in this book. If f is defined on the closed interval $[a, b]$ we say f is integrable on $[a, b]$ if

$$I = \lim_{\|P\| \to 0} \sum_{k=1}^{n} f(\overset{*}{x}_k) \Delta x_k$$

exists. This limit, if it exists, is called the definite integral of f from a to b. The definite integral is denoted by

$$I = \int_a^b f(x)\, dx$$

See Chapter 8 of the *Mathematics Handbook* for a summary of the integral ideas in this book.

3. Multivariable calculus involves limits, derivatives, and integrals of functions of more than one variable.

4. *Form of Equation*   *Method*

First-order differential equations
___

$\dfrac{dy}{dx} = \dfrac{g(x)}{f(y)}$ Separate the variables.

$\dfrac{dy}{dx} = f\left(\dfrac{y}{x}\right)$ Homogeneous — use a change of variable $v = y/x$.

$\dfrac{dy}{dx} + p(x)y = q(x)$ Use an integrating factor

$M(x,\, y)\, dx + N(x,\, y)\, dy = 0$

     Exact if $\dfrac{\partial M}{\partial y} = \dfrac{\partial N}{\partial x}$; use partial integration to find $f(x,\, y)$ so $df = M\, dx + N\, dy$

Second-order differential equations
___

$y'' + ay' + by = 0$ Homogeneous; use characterization theorem

$y'' + ay' + by = F(x)$ Nonhomogeneous; $y = y_h + y_p$ use method of undetermined coefficients or variation of parameters to find a particular solution y_p.

6. $f(x,\, y) = x^2 e^{y/x}$

$f_x = e^{y/x}(2x - y);\ f_y = xe^{y/x};$

$f_{xy} = e^{y/x}(1 - y/x)$

9. $f(x,\, y) = e^{x+y}$

$f_x = e^x e^y;\ f_y = e^x e^y;$

$f_{xy} = e^x e^y$

12. $\displaystyle\int_0^1 \int_x^{2x} e^{y-x}\, dy\, dx = \int_0^1 (e^x - 1)\, dx$

$$= e - 2$$

15. $\displaystyle\int_0^{15\pi} \int_0^{\pi} \int_0^{\sin \phi} \rho^3 \sin \phi\, d\rho\, d\theta\, d\phi$

$$= \frac{1}{4}\int_0^{15\pi} \int_0^{\pi} \sin^5 \phi\, d\theta\, d\phi$$

$$= \frac{\pi}{4} \int_0^{15\pi} \sin^5\phi \ d\phi$$

$$= \frac{4\pi}{15}$$

18. $\iint\limits_R \sin(x+y) \ dA$

$$= \int_0^{\pi/2} \int_0^{\pi/4} \sin(x+y) \ dy \ dx$$

$$= -\int_0^{\pi/2} [\cos(x+\tfrac{\pi}{4}) - \cos x] \ dx$$

$$= 1$$

21. $\int_C (5 \ xy \ dx + 10 \ yz \ dy + z \ dz)$

$$= \int_0^1 [5(t^2)(t)(2t) + 10(t)(2t^3) + (2t^3)(6t^2)] \ dt$$

$$= \int_0^1 (30t^4 + 12t^5) \ dt$$

$$= 8$$

24. $\dfrac{dy}{dx} + \left(\dfrac{1}{2x}\right)y = \sqrt{x} \ e^x$

$$p(x) = \frac{1}{2x}, \ q(x) = \sqrt{x} \ e^x,$$

$$I(x) = e^{\int (1/2x) \, dx} = e^{\ln|x|^{1/2}} = \sqrt{x}$$

$$y = \frac{1}{\sqrt{x}}\left[\int \sqrt{x}(\sqrt{x} \ e^x) \ dx + C\right]$$

$$= \frac{1}{\sqrt{x}}\left[e^x(x-1) + C\right]$$

$$= \sqrt{x} \ e^x - \frac{e^x}{\sqrt{x}} + \frac{C}{\sqrt{x}}$$

27. $y'' + y' - 2y = x^3 + x^2 - 2x + 5$

Characteristic equation: $\qquad r^2 + r - 2 = 0$

$$r = -2, 1$$

$$y_h = C_1 e^{-2x} + C_2 e^x$$

$$\overline{y}_p = A_3 x^3 + A_2 x^2 + A_1 x + A_0$$

$$\overline{y}_p{}' = 3A_3 x^2 + 2A_2 x + A_1$$

$$\overline{y}_p{}'' = 6A_3 x + 2A_2$$

Substitute into the given D.E. equation:

$$(6A_3 x + 2A_2) + (3A_3 x^2 + 2A_2 x + A_1)$$

$$- 2(A_3 x^3 + A_2 x^2 + A_1 x + A_0)$$

$$= x^3 + x^2 - 2x + 5$$

This gives rise to the system of equations

$$\begin{cases} -2A_3 = 1 \\ 3A_3 - 2A_2 = 1 \\ 6A_3 + 2A_2 - 2A_1 = -2 \\ 2A_2 + A_1 - 2A_0 = 5 \end{cases}$$

which has solution:

$$A_0 = -\tfrac{37}{8}, \ A_1 = -\tfrac{7}{4}, \ A_2 = -\tfrac{5}{4}, \ A_3 = -\tfrac{1}{2}$$

Solution:

$$y = C_1 e^{-2x} + C_2 e^x - \tfrac{1}{4}(2x^3 + 5x^2 + 7x + 18.5)$$

30. $xy' - 2y = x^2$; $y' - \frac{2}{x}y = x$

$p(x) = -\frac{2}{x},\ q(x) = x,$

$I(x) = e^{\int -2/x\,dx} = x^{-2}$

$y = x^2\left[\int x^{-2}x\,dx + C\right]$

$\quad = x^2(\ln|x| + C)$

If $x = 1$, then $y = 5$, so $C = 5$.

Solution: $y = x^2\ln|x| + 5x^2$

33. Maximize

$P(x,\ y) = \left[\dfrac{250y}{y+2} + \dfrac{100x}{x+5}\right](350)$

$- \left[\left(\dfrac{250y}{y+2} + \dfrac{100x}{x+5}\right)(150) + 1{,}000x + 1{,}000y\right]$

a. $P_x = \dfrac{100{,}000}{(x+5)^2} - 1{,}000$

$\quad P_y = \dfrac{100{,}000}{(y+2)^2} - 1{,}000$

$\quad P_x = P_y$ when $y - x = 3$

b. Maximize $P(x,\ y)$ subject to $x + y = 11$

$\dfrac{100{,}000}{(x+5)^2} - 1{,}000 = (1)\lambda$

$\dfrac{100{,}000}{(y+2)^2} - 1{,}000 = (1)\lambda$

Solving, we obtain $y + 2 = x + 5$, so

$y = x + 3$ and $x + (x + 3) = 11$. Thus,

$x = 4$ and $y = 11 - 4 = 7$.

36. $V = \displaystyle\int_0^{2\pi}\int_0^1\int_0^{1+r^2} r\,dz\,dr\,d\theta$

$= \displaystyle\int_0^{2\pi}\int_0^1 r(1 + r^2)\,dr\,d\theta$

$= \displaystyle\int_0^{2\pi} \frac{3}{4}\,d\theta$

$= \dfrac{3\pi}{2}$

39. $\mathbf{F} = \langle x - 2y,\ y - 2x\rangle$

$u(x,\ y) = x - 2y; \dfrac{\partial u}{\partial y} = -2;$

$v(x,\ y) = y - 2x; \dfrac{\partial v}{\partial x} = -2,$

so $\mathbf{F}$ is conservative.

$f_x = x - 2y; f = \dfrac{x^2}{2} - 2xy + a(y)$

$f_y = -2x + a'(y) = -2x + y; a(y) = \dfrac{y^2}{2} + C$

$f(x,\ y) = \dfrac{x^2}{2} + \dfrac{y^2}{2} - 2xy + C$

$W = \displaystyle\int_C \mathbf{F}\cdot d\mathbf{R} = f(0,\ 1) - f(1,\ 0)$

$\quad = \dfrac{1}{2} - \dfrac{1}{2} = 0$

APPENDIX A

Introduction to the Theory of Limits

1. For any chosen value of ϵ we want the distance between $f(x)$ and L to be less than ϵ. In absolute value notation this is

$$\left| f(x) - L \right| < \epsilon$$

For our function and limit we need

$$\left| (2x - 5) - (-3) \right| < \epsilon$$
$$\left| 2x - 2 \right| < \epsilon$$
$$2 \left| x - 1 \right| < \epsilon$$

So the distance between x and 1 needs to be less than $\frac{\epsilon}{2}$. Therefore, let $\delta = \frac{\epsilon}{2}$.

3. $\lim\limits_{x \to 1} (3x + 1) = 4 \neq 5$; the interval on the y-axis in the neighborhood corresponding to $x = 1$ can be arbitrarily restrictive.

$$0 < \left| x - 1 \right| < \delta$$

must apply and the given statement is false. The actual limit is 4.

7. $\left| f(x) - L \right| = \left| (x + 3) - 5 \right| = \left| x - 2 \right| < \delta$

Choose $\delta = \epsilon$.

8. $\left| f(t) - L \right| = \left| (3t - 1) - 0 \right| < \left| 3t - 1 \right|$

The statement is false. Choose $\epsilon = 0.3$ and it is not possible to find a delta.

13. In order for $f(x)$ to be continuous at $x = 0$, $\lim\limits_{x \to 0} f(x)$ must equal $f(0)$. To show that $\lim\limits_{x \to 0} \sin \frac{1}{x} = 0$ we need to show that for any $\epsilon > 0$ there exists a $\delta > 0$ such that

$$\left| f(x) - L \right| < \epsilon \text{ when } \left| x - 0 \right| < \delta.$$

Arbitrarily letting $\epsilon = .5$ we need to find a δ-interval about 0 such that $\left| \sin \frac{1}{x} \right| < .5$.

However any interval about 0 contains a point $x = \frac{2}{\pi n}$ (with n odd) where $\sin \frac{1}{x}$

$= \sin \frac{\pi n}{2} = \pm 1$. Therefore, there does not exist a δ-interval about 0 such that

$\left| \sin \frac{1}{x} \right| < 0.5$, and $f(x)$ must be discontinuous at $x = 0$.

16. By hypotheses, $\lim\limits_{x \to c} f(x) = L_1$ which means there exists an $\epsilon_1 > 0$ such that

$$\left| f(x) - L_1 \right| < \epsilon_1 \text{ with } 0 < \left| x - c \right| < \delta.$$

Similarly $\lim\limits_{x \to c} g(x) = L_2$ which means there exists an $\epsilon_2 > 0$ such that $\left| g(x) - L_2 \right| < \epsilon_2$

with $0 < |x - c| < \delta$. Let $\frac{\epsilon}{2} = \max(a\epsilon_1, b\epsilon_2)$.

Then,

$$\left| a[f(x) - L_1] + b[g(x) - L_2] \right| < \frac{\epsilon}{2} + \frac{\epsilon}{2} = \epsilon$$

This says that for any $\epsilon > 0$ there exists a

$\delta > 0$ such that $\lim\limits_{x \to c}[af(x) + bg(x)]$

$= a \lim\limits_{x \to c} f(x) + b \lim\limits_{x \to c} g(x)$ whenever

$0 < |x - c| < \delta$.

22. a. $\left| f(x) \right| < \frac{3|L|}{2}$,

$$\left| f(x) - L \right| \le \left| f(x) \right| + |L| < |L| + \frac{3|L|}{2} = \frac{5|L|}{2}$$

Now, if L is replaced by $-L$,

$$\left| f(x) - (-L) \right| = \left| f(x) + L \right| < \frac{5|-L|}{2} = \frac{5|L|}{2}$$

b. $\left| [f(x)]^2 - L^2 \right| = \left| f(x) + L \right| \left| f(x) - L \right|$

$$\le \left[\left| f(x) \right| + |L| \right] \left| f(x) - L \right| < \frac{5|L|}{2}\epsilon_2;$$

$$\left| f(x) - L \right| < \epsilon_2 \text{ for } 0 < |x - c| < \delta_2$$

because $\lim\limits_{x \to c} f(x) = L$, by hypotheses.

c. Let $\epsilon = \frac{5|L|}{2}\epsilon_2$, then $\left| [f(x)]^2 - L^2 \right| < \epsilon$

for $0 < |x - c| < \delta$ where $\delta = \min(\delta_1, \delta_2)$

26. Since (as it turns out) the slope at $x = 3$ is 26; picking $K = 26$ or larger works.

CONGRATULATIONS!!! YOU ARE A SURVIVOR.....